# Beyond Smart Cities

José A. Ondiviela

# Beyond Smart Cities

Creating the Most Attractive Cities for
Talented Citizens

Springer

José A. Ondiviela (iD)
Universidad Francisco de Vitoria
Madrid, Spain

ISBN 978-3-030-83373-2        ISBN 978-3-030-83371-8   (eBook)
https://doi.org/10.1007/978-3-030-83371-8

This Springer imprint is published by the registered company Springer Nature Switzerland AG
The registered company address is: Gewerbestrasse 11, 6330 Cham, Switzerland

# Disclosure

Personal thoughts and opinions expressed in this book are the author's alone and do not represent any official statement from companies or institutions the author may work for or collaborate with.

# Preface

Our cities live in unprecedented times. Cities are, in essence, a place and time where humans meet or encounter, where every social activity happens. Cities are, accordingly, the epicenter of human activity, the central engine of social interaction, economic growth, and innovation. In the current context of social stability (both in economy – no major crisis – and peace – no war threats), cities are the factories where creativity and human development is produced, and that turns them into international hubs of talent flow. Welcome to the era of cities.

Without a clear leader in the 4th Industrial Revolution, cities are fiercely competing to attract talent. Western cities need additional human capital. Eastern and emerging countries' cities are working on building up their own (from their young people) and retaining it to serve as the base pillar for their future prosperity. The current pandemic has accelerated this race for talent. The city that recovers the fastest will enjoy a significant competitive edge over others in this global competition.

We live, undoubtedly, in the best moment in human history. Technology enables us to modify our physical environment and enjoy a longer and more comfortable life. Investing in technology and innovation (SmartCities) is an essential and mandatory condition to draw that talent in, yet it is not sufficient by itself. Choosing a city to live in is a complex but human decision, like making a major purchase, getting married, or signing a main contract or commitment. So, the question is: what makes a city attractive to talent?

This book's main objective is to understand what could be done and what is needed to make a city attractive for those talented citizens. There are many partial studies about happiness, employment, safety, lost traffic hours, expat treatment, social services, economy, and cost of living, but none has attempted to give talented citizens a comprehensive vision of this new era of cities.

In this book, it is postulated that, as with every human decision, there is a compromise between two parties: the emotional component, which we will call *City Magnetism*, and the rational component, which we will call *City Profitability*. Citizens will first select those cities they like, based on the emotional input and perceived image they get from them, then evaluate the rational components (services, cost of living) to finally make the right decision.

We are studying the world's top 140 most attractive cities according to international research institutions in our custom model made up of more than hundred main indicators. The objective is twofold: to help talented citizens evaluate the main world cities to find which ones will best help them reach their full potential, and to help mayors and city directors create the conditions that make their city as attractive as possible. This implies to find a balanced point between improving the services quality and quantity delivered to locals, with investments on external image and future innovation.

In addition to the described talent attraction contest, mayors are now forced to accelerate decisions and mid-term plans, prioritize the recovery funds, and make the right decisions in short time. Technology (data-driven cities, fueled by data, run on artificial intelligence) is again the best ally to help them achieve the digital transformation they are seeking. Balancing a social and economic sustainability with an environmental one means an intensive knowledge of own citizens, businesses, spaces, and physical environments, so data analytics and artificial intelligence can guide well-informed decisions.

Enjoy reading and use the smartphone app to find the best cities matching your emotional and rational preferences.

Madrid, Spain                                                               José A. Ondiviela

# Acknowledgment

To my family, Conchi, Patricia, and Toño, who has allowed me to steal a massive amount of time from them to write this. I hope its impact compensates them for these 2 years of work.

To my company, Microsoft, which kept me up to date on the latest technology, and also taught me how much human values, ethical principles, and environmental sustainability can be matched with technology innovation.

To my beloved cities, magical places for human social development and solid foundations for mankind's future dreams.

# Contents

# About the Author

**José A. Ondiviela** is the Microsoft Western Europe public sector government industry executive for cities and regions. He joined Microsoft in 1995 and has a wealth of experience in field sales, sales strategy, partners management, operations, and marketing.

Frequent speaker at international events, such as SmartCityExpo, Mobile World Forum, TEDTalk, and EU events, he is also UNESCO-NetExplo SmartCities SME.

MS in telecommunications engineering from UPM Madrid, MS in human sciences from UFV Madrid, MS in enterprise and institutional communication management from UAB Barcelona, and MS in financial business from INSEAD (online), Prof. Ondiviela also holds a PhD from UFV, Madrid, for the thesis "Beyond SmartCities: How to create an Attractive City for Talented Citizens." He is also associate fellow researcher and director of WW Observatory for Attractive Cities at UFV (Universidad Francisco Vitoria, Madrid, Spain) in association with Fira Barcelona (SmartCityExpo).

Passionate about cities, Prof. Ondiviela combines his job at Microsoft, providing the most innovative technological solutions, with writing articles and delivering lecturers and seminars about future of cities and the challenges they are facing at the beginning of 4th Industrial Revolution and now, in addition, with the main objective of achieving the fastest post-pandemic recovery.

Mail: joseondiviela@outlook.com
Social: https://www.linkedin.com/in/jondiviela/
ORCID: 0000-0001-6732-8754

# Chapter 1
# Introduction

## 1.1 Motivation for this Research

I travel often due to my job, and that allows me to visit many countries and observe why people move and what motivates them to go to a particular city.

I love cities. I think they are the most important physical creation mankind has ever constructed. If we were to show an alien the most brilliant man-made realizations, we would definitely include quite a few cities. At the same time, I also see anti-human cities: chaotic, amorphous, meaningless agglomerations that are even an impediment to human development, because rather than stimulate, they block and nullify it.

I am an engineer, but also a humanist. Through my job, I've seen countless proposals on improving cities' efficiency with technology being the driver of their development. All of them explain the benefits, savings and advantages for city managers (the customers), but none mention what they bring to the table for citizens, for people.

I have some urbanist friends. They usually give me the same, pure technological approach made at designers' offices, with thousands of architects creating buildings with CAD computer tools, not paying the slightest attention to who is actually going to live/work inside those geometric boxes.

We talk a lot about SmartCities – but are we helping citizens to become SmartCitizens? My experience with buildings designed by famous architects is poor. They are wonderful on the outside, on the design plane or even in a photo, but uncomfortable and almost uninhabitable inside. Perhaps the problem is that nobody talked to those buildings' end users and asked about their preferences. The same thing happens to me when it comes to city management technology projects. They imply a significant improvement in efficiency and large savings, but few are based on, or take into account citizens' uses, customs or priorities.

J. A. Ondiviela, *Beyond Smart Cities*, https://doi.org/10.1007/978-3-030-83371-8_1

This is why I decided to try and to connect a good use of technology with human development within the place where great collective human innovations are cooked; where the social animal that we are, finally manages to be, social: the city.

Cities are currently the epicenter of human activity. In the context of global stability (economic, military/peace), cities lead innovation and human development. We are living, indisputably, in the best moment in the history of mankind. Technology allows us to increasingly dominate our world/environment and enjoy a longer and more comfortable life. However, we must not idolize it; technology helps us, but its foundation and development is -we must remember- only human, so it won't respond to all of our needs, and it is of course useless to answer our fundamental, existential or transcendental questions.

Cities are the administration closest to citizens. From an efficiency standpoint, this is great when it comes to the provision of public services. Yet, cities also require a constant adaptation to citizens' needs: to connect with them using their language, communication mechanisms and habits. The city must be a partner that helps, that facilitates human activity, and this implies a great challenge.

There are big issues that impact citizens and that the city is to resolve. In its position of *nearest administration* to citizens, it has the capacity for execution and for the effective provision of services. Unfortunately, cities do not have enough resources or sufficient budget to respond to all challenges. Here is where technology provides an enormous benefit: it fundamentally reduces problems, makes them more manageable and allows scarce economic and human resources to be more effectively used.

When I talk to politicians and especially to city mayors, I honestly feel some compassion for them. The challenges they will face in the upcoming years are so complex, and will imply so significant societal impacts, that regardless of what they do, they will be harshly judged as they are the first visible administrative face to slap, incapable of solving all challenges – yet please, keep trying!

Cities have embarked on a journey to attract and retain talent. This is fundamental if they expect to play a role in the 4th Industrial Revolution. The question is, will they do so? The alternative is languishing from an aging social structure and disappear. Yes, this possibility is intimidating, but we just have to look at archeology to understand that cities can also die. An aging population, Industry 4.0 and the predominant role of the *creative class*, digital privacy, global sustainability are huge issues, where the city's decisions will be critical, and where its capacity for success depends greatly on the civilization to which it pertains, its geographic location and its sphere of influence. There are many other highly important issues such as urban mobility, physical security, social services, participation and city co-creation, decarbonization, culture, urban planning. With these, the city can play a much more active role, deploying technology and obtaining visible and tangible results that impact city prosperity in the short-medium term.

So, a City is a very complex dynamic model. If you are good at math, you can visualize a city as a NP-complete problem: as you add more variables linearly, the complexity or time to resolve situations increases exponentially (Garey & Johnson, 1979). Some experts like Dan Doctoroff (NYC former deputy mayor, then Toronto's

Sidewalk Labs CEO) says that, *"cities are always going to be immensely complex human organisms to manage, likening the challenge to trying to solve a 50-sided Rubik's cube"* (Thornhill, 2019). Understanding what can be done and setting priorities which attempt to anticipate consequences is really tough. Our city managers need help, mainly in the form of massive amounts of data about the city, Artificial Intelligence algorithms and analytic tools with which to glean insights from them and an almost constant interaction with citizens to make best- and better-informed decisions.

My friend Pablo decided to move from Madrid to Singapore two years ago. At his farewell party, I asked him why he chose Singapore, and he described his list of motivations: good job, high salary, low taxes, safe city, excellent urban mobility, good on-the-job training, and excellent conditions for a single, 25-year-old digital nomad with no current dependents to care for. He also explained the downsides: the government regime, some local customs, weather, distance...but he considered this as a few-years investment for his professional career to improve his skills, understanding the rampant Asia-Pacific market, then return with a brilliant CV and money to buy a house.

A colleague of mine, Juan, told me last month about his decision to leave the company and return to his birthplace, where his wife is highly valued as a master craftswoman: she creates and designs local folk culture dresses. He preferred to prioritize his wife's career, work for a local mid-size company and make half his previous salary, but in a city in which it is much cheaper to live in than Madrid, and where he will enjoy a wonderful life with his wife and daughter. So, getting a good job is not always the main motivation behind moving cities.

Around 50,000 qualified professionals left Spain during the 2010–2014 crisis. (Fita, 2013) Spanish engineers left for Germany and Northern Europe; nurses went to the UK,..all emigrated to find a better job, with the capacity to return home with just a two-hour flight. Some left looking back, others not. Assuming each worker was a public university graduate, with an associated publicly funded training cost of 5,000€/year × 4year average, imagine the mega lost for Spain, not only in terms of brains, but for investment (1billion euros). Fortunately for Spain, many are already returning.

These situations made me reflect on the great competition for talent that is arising early on in this 4th Industrial Revolution and the role of cities in that global contest. As a result, I decided to dedicate this research to understanding what makes and is needed for a city to be considered attractive by these talented citizens.

There are many insights which partially answer this question: research studies about employment, safety, happiness, expat treatment, the economy, cost of living...however, none gives talented citizens an integrated vision on this new world of cities.

## 1.2  Objectives

Main research Objective:

The objective of a research in the field of Humanities is always knowledge from which practical consequences can be derived. Therefore, the main objective here is to answer how, within a 4th Industrial Revolution framework, the city is competing to become more attractive for talent, and furthermore to define which elements enhance attractiveness, and what options exist for cities to do so. The practical consequences are twofold:

1. Help citizens choose the best city in the world for them to realize their full potential, realize their goals as a citizen and as a person, and make the greatest possible contribution to society.
2. Advise mayors and city managers on how to create the most attractive city possible in order to retain and attract talented citizens, and furthermore build a more prosperous, innovative, fair and human city. Help them design, prioritize and implement a:

   • Long-term Transformational Plan
   • Short/Mid-term Improvement/Integrated Plan

## 1.3  Research Material vs Formal Objects

The material object is the city. The city as a destination, as a meeting place, as a platform for human development. And also, as an entity that struggles to have a relevant global role in the XXI century. Thanks to technology, change is the new ruling constant, and this change occurs at a speed that we had never experienced before. Decisions, therefore, must be made quickly, to match the speed of change as much as its consequences. The margin for error is consequently smaller and the need for technology to assist us is even more crucial. Inaction is not an option. Inaction implies missing the train of the new economy and innovation: you are left behind.

The research formal object is the perspective that we will use (*quod*). It is City Attractiveness. It is what made Pablo, Juan and many others decide to migrate to another city. It is about studying the reasons for that decision and learning from it in order to improve a city's current status. It is about attractive cities in the sense that they are magnetic, dazzling, cost-effective, convenient and abundant in conclusive decision-making elements. The idea is to pin down those elements which make a city more or less attractive and analyze their impact. Then, we will look at creating a model (a basic reduction, simplification and conceptualization of a very complex reality) and compare the main world cities against it.

## 1.4 Research Discipline

The scope of the research is multidisciplinary. Since talent moves where innovation is being driven, it is clear that in order to attract talent, leadership on the development of new technologies and their implementation is necessary. It is about, from a humanistic perspective, valuing technology as an enabler, evaluating its impact on the city not only from a performance or economic points of view, but from an ethical and social one, always based on extreme respect for human dignity. Talented citizens are attracted to places of technological innovation, but they are human after all, and therefore, there are other aspects they consider in whether a city is attractive or not, such as inclusiveness, equality, ethics, human values, identity, creativity, etc.

So why is this study written from the arena of Humanism? Along the text, we will discover how Humanism, Urbanism and Technology and their many disciplines intertwine to provide the key components that constitute an attractive city. All these lines of thought and scientific development will contribute to creating a more human city, citizen-centered, with man as the fundamental objective to serve and develop to his full potential. The city sets the mechanisms and conditions so that the man's social facet can unfold. A man without a city is an asocial, dehumanized being. For this reason, everything described in this work, although it includes very diverse disciplines and advanced technological components, is centered by and for humans.

We are aware that this integrative approach is not going to appeal to any specialist and that each one will want to deepen their own discipline more in detail, but we must recognize that the greatness of a culture, and specifically, a city's culture, is based on the diversity from different contributions, on the richness made up of human facets, all of them contributing to its growth and prosperity. For this reason, we will be combining philosophical, sociological, ethical and aesthetic chapters, with other socio-economic, urban, social, geopolitical combined with current technologies and trends in innovation.

Therefore, the view to use is a birds-eye perspective, like a drone flying over the thin bridge that links current technology and Western humanism.

Starting with the idea of technology as the main enabler, the fundamental concept to be described in this research is how it could help transform our cities to prepare them to tackle (or at least better face) the main XXI century challenges that lie ahead of them.

## 1.5 Main Hypothesis

Main City Challenges which can be addressed with technology are:

- Impact of Industry 4.0. The Rise of a *Creative Class*.
- An Aging Population. How to maintain a welfare society without increasing costs, taxes.
- Power Shift to Data. Controlling the World. Sensoring. Internet of Things (IoT).

- Citizen at the Center: Communicating/Listening to citizens (Social Networks, Online). Soft-Power (opinions, trends). City Co-Creation.
- Urban Mobility = Cities' bloodstream. Traffic, Intelligent transportation.
- Safety. Threats (Terrorism, Natural Disasters). Resiliency.
- Citizens Trust (CyberSecurity, Privacy, Compliance, Transparency). EU GDPR (European Union General Data Protection Regulation).
- Environmental Sustainability (Energy Efficiency, Water Care, $CO_2$ Emissions reduction-Carbon Neutral). Waste Management. Circular Economy.
- Necessary Financing. Avoid Taxes Fraud. Cashless Cities.

Disruptive new technologies show up onto these scenes. They can help or possibly complicate things further. To name just some of the most impactful: 5G high-speed networks, autonomous cars, higher-capacity batteries helping to electrify/decarbonize, sensorized homes, omnipresent Artificial Intelligence to understand huge amounts of data and extract valuable insights, Cloud computing providing all needed massive computing power and storage, 3D-printing of any physical thing.

### 1.5.1 Seven Main Postulates

1. Cities are taking the key role as Centers for Human Development. There is a hidden, bloodless, but fierce competition to attract the *creative class* people, those who will rule the Innovation led by 4th Industrial Revolution. Technology is again the vital aspect of the SmartCities conversation, but Cities that focus and design technology *around* their population will be better prepared for the inevitable future.
2. City Prosperity Recipe = 3T's (Technology, Talent, Tolerance)
3. 4th Industrial Revolution is about Artificial Intelligence/Robotics. Artificial Intelligence (AI) is made of: Massive Data (from IoT world, social networks) + Computing Power (from large Cloud Datacenters) + Algorithms (made by Talent, again, to understand, predict, analyze, visualize, speak, obtain insights, react in real-time…). No single city leads this revolution, but no one wants to be left behind, so competition for talented citizens is even more crucial.
4. SmartCities approach uses technology to transform/improve Cities and makes them more attractive for talented citizens.
5. City Attractiveness = City Magnetism x City Profitability (yield)
6. City Magnetism = Conditions that make you like/love the City. Mostly permanent, slowly evolving concept/not easy to quickly change/evolve conditions that impact people emotionally. To significantly change them, you must invest in a City Transformation Plan of 10+ years.
7. City Profitability (Yield) = Conditions that make you value the City performance. It's a balance between give's and gets. It's relatively easy and quick to impact. The problem is how to prioritize and integrate all performance

components into a comprehensive strategy. You should invest on a City Improvement/Quick Transformation Plan of 2+ years. This is the main rational component. City Profitability (Yield) is made up of services that you receive from the City compared to the Cost associated with Living in that City = CITIZENSHIP CONTRACT.

## 1.6 Research Methodology

There are some basic, well-known sources of inspiration, coming from some books like Schwab, K. talking about the 4th Industrial revolution, and Prof. Florida and his famous *Creative Class* concept, linked to the 4th Industrial Revolution paradigm. Urbanists like Jane Jacobs explain why cities that don't work for and listen to citizens are heading towards a chasm; Jan Gehl, the best modern urbanist, highlighting Copenhagen as a model to follow; and a few others like Rem Koolhaas explaining just how inhuman a city can become (Generic City) (Koolhaas, 1997). Better inspiration for ideating the City came from philosophers: Aristotle, Plato, Julián Marias, Ortega y Gasset, and Wittgenstein, who was influenced by the city and circumstances which he lived (Vienna, end of XIX century). Main concepts about Ethics, Aesthetics, Anthropology and Arts have been critical to understanding why these city challenges are so relevant.

All the other hundreds of references come from the Internet, and most are dated from less than five years ago, so the explained concepts and issues are hyper-current and realistic.

There is a ton of information about SmartCities coming from the 50 main technology companies trying to sell their solutions. But most of this info is technical, laden with architectural descriptions, and uses case studies without mentioning nature or root causes of the problems, or the benefits for citizens and not just for the IT (Information Technologies) Department (the customer who directly pays for those solutions).

The working model will be based on the Bibliography, attended International Congresses, and other related sources of information (mainly the Internet).

We built a model for the top 140 most attractive cities worldwide. The idea is not to create another ranking. Cities hate rankings, except for the one at the top. The attractiveness concept is quite personal, and the most attractive city for one individual may not be so attractive for another, depending on their different value scales to measure the city performance indicators, different aesthetic or personal preferences (proximity to mountains or the ocean or both, spoken languages, religion...), and personal status (family dependencies: children or elderly people at their charge...). The model allows for comparisons between cities within the same geo-cluster and produces a City Attractiveness snapshot to determine which areas to prioritize for improvement. It also provides a list of cities that best fit each citizen's values and preferences.

## 1.6.1  Cities Sample Size and Selection Criteria

Main Most Attractive 140 World Cities.

- Selection Criteria: Top at Quality of Living (Mercer, 2018) and Cities in Motion (IESE, 2018) reports and scoring over 50 (no personal risk or severe living restrictions) in the Global Liveability Index (The Economist, 2018)
- Like any good/useful set of indicators, all info included from external studies/ rankings must comply with some basic principles: It must be benchmark-able, replicable, with the data acquisition costs near zero, facts/data-based (no surveys, rumors, opinions, subjective topics), relevant, fair, manageable, so we can compare apples to apples (cities on the same playing field), and dynamic, as the city changes and a new indicator could show up and better describe one particular topic.
- This study was conducted by early 2020, so most sources are dated from 2019. New yearly indicators and updated versions will be published.

## 1.6.2  City Magnetism Model

- 67 Indicators (self-made from open sources or selected from Universities, international bodies, key actors in already published studies/analyses)
- Each selected SmartCity (140) status analysis from the city website, Published SmartCity plan.

## 1.6.3  City Profitability (Yield) Model

- 33 Indicators (self-made from open sources or selected from Universities, international bodies, key actors already published studies/analyses)
- So, the total number of evaluated indicators is 100, but many of them include a large number of sub indicators, raising the total number of city dimensions analyzed to around 500.

## 1.6.4  Research. Surveys Run to Check Model Accuracy

- Survey of 4,500 attendees in (NordicEdge, 2018) event, Stavanger (Norway) September 2018. Largest SmartCities event in the Nordic countries.
- Survey of 21,334 attendees in (SmartCity Expo, 2018) & WW Congress, Barcelona November 2018, largest SmartCities event worldwide. Dataset will be used

to create a reference city ranking based on Magnetism and Performance, and test the model.

### 1.6.5 Model Reliability

- Medium on City Magnetism. High on City Profitability.
- Again, plan is not to create another Cities ranking. A personal tool (App) is provided, so the main topics will be weighted based on individual citizen input. Results will vary from citizen to citizen preferences or different life status (age, family dependents).
- Model obtained from the two surveys conducted with: 95% Confidence, <5% Error

### 1.6.6 Proposal's Innovative Characteristics

This publication is the first discussion on City Attractiveness components (Magnetism, Profitability), and the concept of Citizenship Contract. These topics have not yet been described in academic literature or elsewhere. It also contains the conclusions from the first-time survey of all SmartCityExpo participants, who were asked to rank their preferences about which they consider the most attractive City.

## References

Fita, J. (2013). El talento emigra de España. *La Vanguardia.* https://www.lavanguardia.com/vida/20130505/54371747713/el-talento-emigra-de-espana.html. Accessed 20 Mar 2018.

Garey, M., & Johnson, D. (1979). *Computers and intractability; A guide to the theory of NP-completeness.* W. H. Freemand and Company.

Global Liveability Report. (2018). *The Economist.* https://store.eiu.com/article.aspx?productid=455217630 and https://www.eiu.com/public/topical_report.aspx?campaignid=liveability2018. Accessed 12 Mar 2018.

IESE. (2018). *Cities in Motion Index 2018.* https://media.iese.edu/research/pdfs/ST-0471-E.pdf. Accessed 12 Mar 2018.

Koolhaas, R. (1997). *Acerca de la ciudad.* (2014) Barcelona: GG, from *The Generic City.* num. 791 (pp. 8–12). Domus.

MERCER. (2018). *Quality of Living Mercer Index 2018.* https://mobilityexchange.mercer.com/Insights/quality-of-living-rankings. Accessed 12 Mar 2018.

NordicEdge. (2018). *Stavanger.* https://www.nordicedge.org/. Accessed 12 Mar 2018.

SmartCity Expo. (2018). *Barcelona.* http://www.smartcityexpo.com/en/home. Accessed 12 Mar 2018.

Thornhill, J. (2019) Smart cities still need a human touch. *Financial Times,* p. 2 https://www.ft.com/content/67c52480-b51f-11e9-8cb2-799a3a8cf37b. Accessed 31 Aug 2019.

# Chapter 2
# Cities in the XXI Century. Main Challenges Technology Tackles

## 2.1 Introduction. The Era of Cities

In 2019, we celebrated the centennial anniversary of the end of WWI, which ended with the Treaty of Versailles, and marked the end of the old empires. The end of WWII with the Yalta and Potsdam conferences created a world made of countries, and the birth of the United Nations as an international organization. Now, at the beginning of the XXI century, we are spectators of a new era: The Age of Cities.

*The 19th century was a century of empires. The 20th century was a century of nation-states. The 21st century will be a century of cities,* said Wellington E. Webb, former Mayor of Denver, US, at a meeting in Colorado, 2000.

### 2.1.1 Urbanization Process

For the first time in history, today more than half of us live in cities—a total of four billion people. The global population was split evenly between urban and rural by 2007 (Glaeser, 2011), and today, the urban population represents 55% of the total (75% in Europe). By 2030, the city population will double to 6.5 billion people (the equivalent to adding three Brazils and one new China), or 70% of total world population. (Rhodan, 2013)

This trend is creating the concept of MegaCities (or cities with over 20 million inhabitants). According to the (UN, 2018), by 2030, we will have 43 megacities across the globe, rising from just two in 1950. The fastest-growing urban agglomerations are cities with less than one million inhabitants, most located in Asia and Africa. By 2028, there will be close to 500 cities with more than one million people (OECD, 2018). For every eight people alive today, one lives in a MegaCity, three in a large city, and four (half of total) in cities with less than 500,000 inhabitants. We are collectively building the equivalent of another NYC every month, and the pace

J. A. Ondiviela, *Beyond Smart Cities*, https://doi.org/10.1007/978-3-030-83371-8_2

**Fig. 2.1**  Correlation between Urban population Share and GDP/Capita. (Bolt et al., 2020)

will continue for the next 40 years, when we are going to build as many cities as in all our past human history (Gates & Gates, 2019).

Since the beginning of civilization, man has gathered in cities to obtain the benefits and synergies of living together. As cities have become more attractive and more competitive in the various industrial revolutions, they have attracted more citizens from the rural environment. A city's performance and its prosperity depend not only on having any population, but of possessing a talented one, one that generates wealth by developing the latest innovations and technological advances. By becoming the engine of the economy and for human development, it is easy to understand the correlation between Urban Population and GDP/Capita as shown in Fig. 2.1

Cities are nerve centers of economic growth, social interaction and innovation. Today, 1.5 billion people are living in the 600 largest urban agglomerations, which are responsible for nearly 60% of the gross world product (GWP). Today, we observe that 80% of total world wealth is generated in cities (World Bank, 2013). Cities consume 75% of the world's natural resources, use 80% of global energy, and produce 75% of global carbon emissions. (UN Environment Program, 2018). In 2014, 41% of total U.S. energy was consumed in residential and commercial buildings alone (US Energy Information Administration, 2018).

Urbanization is happening very quickly and by means that we did not anticipate a few years ago. It was thought that by digitalizing the cities and our daily lives, we would observe a dispersion of the population in its territory, at least slowing down the process of urbanization, with people not needing as much direct human contact. On the contrary, as we digitalize, we are experiencing the acceleration of urbanization. What happened?

First, we need to consider that half the human population lives in China and Asia. With the rise of the middle class in Asia, its purchasing power has increased. This is producing a social transformation, pushing people to move to cities. We can also see this effect from the increase in Asian tourism. The classic or Industrial Urbanization, related to production and factories, and led by China with its five special development zones, has meant an increase of the urban population by about 600 million. However, here is another contemporary urbanization phenomenon which is not linked to industrialization: it is that of Africa. Africa's population is of approximately one billion today, and on route to reach two billion by 2030 and no less than three billion by 2040. This African urbanization is occurring at the same rate as China's, but is not driven by industrialization or employment or work; rather, by Information Technology. This mainly mobile technology is revolutionizing African society, with citizens equipped with smartphones and African telcos growing wildly. We could say that Africans are urbanizing and growing their cities to get mobile coverage... In a meeting, Bill and Melinda Gates explained that the key to foster development in Africa is to provide women with smartphones, with which they can access the world of culture. If we take into account that the average age of the Cameroonian population is less than 18 years-old and we compare it with the European one, (around 44 years-old) then we will immediately realize that African citizens are called to populate the rest of the world, with the Chinese to manufacture the necessary technology (already 70% of smartphones and 90% of computers are manufactured there). But this African urbanization is very poorly planned and currently implies that 65% of Sub-Saharan houses are slums. Africa's main problem is this bad planning and reality that the main power's agenda (mainly the U.S., Europe) doesn't include a plan for Africa. We already know the disastrous consequences of poor planning based on examples like Mexico City or Cairo: poorly urbanized territories or suburbs can become incubators for extremism. Out of these types of suburbs arose the Arab Spring, or, looking no further than Europe, the terrorists from the attack in Brussels came from the worst suburb in the city.

This said, the value of urbanization is indisputable. Greater urban density leads to greater prosperity and wealth. It is obvious that converting 1 m$^2$ of land into 1 m$^2$ of urbanized city space increases property value, but the city must bring the necessary services and utilities to these urbanized spaces – and this implies a cost. If we compare the municipal budget of an European city (around 1000€/cap/year) and compare it with the one in Nairobi, (only 6€/cap/year) then it becomes obvious what kind of urbanization is possible in one place or another. If the value created from urbanizing is greater than its cost, this topic turns into a mere question of speed. Furthermore, the immense societal value in bringing people together, or more specifically, talent, is the generation of wealth that results from their close interaction.

From the beginning of the urbanization of our planet, it is clear that humans find synergies, savings, advantages and opportunities by living together, and that space where they live together is called a city. The value of city property changes and is increased by two factors: one, real estate value, which depends exclusively on a property's location within the city, and second, the value of agglomeration, a value determined by the proximity of the factors of production, available talent and cultural and scientific development. A new indicator is added to the traditional production factors (land, capital and labor): information. Information transforms cities into huge knowledge hubs, with massive data generation and consumption, mirroring the traditional industrial urbanization. Thus, the city will play a fundamental role in the post-Industrial era, or in the so-called 4th Industrial Revolution. This is driven by the new economy, which is not only fueled by industrial development, but by the information economy; by the digital revolution that involves the connection of billions of things to the network (Internet of Things or IoT); by the Green Economy as the only solution to curb climate change and render its consequences only serious and non-lethal; and by a new form of production called Artificial Intelligence and Robotics, which will take advantage of Cloud Computing's (Cloud) technical capability (massive computing, data storage and data analytics power), so that talent (and not capital or land) can generate new business models.

Urbanization is inherently good from the point of view of sustainability: apart from the synergies that human beings achieve by living in community in a city, from an environmental point of view, a person who lives in a city causes less of an environmental footprint than a person in the countryside. City inhabitants use their cars less frequently because they have an efficient public transportation and they consume scarce resources such as housing, health services, water and energy more efficiently than their rural counterparts.

In this context, the city is life's natural space, it is our nest, and citizens increasingly see the state or nation as a more distant reference, preferring to pay taxes to the city as they perceive a more direct return based on the services they get.

Talent, as part of human capital, can be found throughout the world, but though one's DNA may predispose them for greatness, talent requires development: it's solidified and developed at universities and is socially constructed in the city. We can say that talent is urban: it flocks to the city and develops there. The greater the city, the more talent it attracts, and the greater its capacity to generate culture and innovation.

It is said that to maintain an opera house you need a population of more than five million. We see some people returning to rural areas. Yet, there's only a few rich people who are returning to enjoy the nature, and their livelihood is not from agriculture; furthermore, they always have the means to go into the city whenever they need to. As the former mayor of Bogotá, Enrique Peñalosa once said. "*A developed and advanced city is one in which the poor have a car and the rich go by bicycle*".

Urban planning was formerly very bureaucratic and complicated, now it is multidisciplinary in technologies and professions. You have to think about citizens from the very beginning. How could anyone have thought that the enormous internal distances in Brasilia were good for economic development? Quite the opposite.

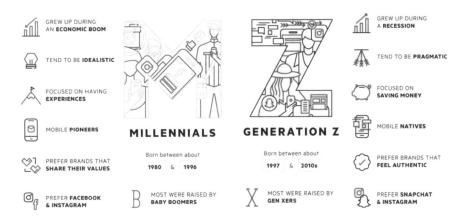

**Fig. 2.2** Meet Generation Z: The newest member to the workplace. Visualcapitalist. (Desjardins, 2019)

Population density is a good indicator of development, as is population size. Average salary is correlated to city size and this relationship is not affected by the technological revolution. Mid-sized cities models work well provided they have adequate population density, excellent access to Information Technologies and cooperate with other similar or larger ones. Anna Wellenstein, Director, The World Bank explained this concept at the SmartSuisse meeting in Basel (Switzerland), 2018, pointing that hyper dense city centers like London, New York or Hong Kong achieve more than 120.000 up to 151.000 jobs/km$^2$.

But urbanization process is also challenging. Rapid urbanization is adding pressure on cities' aging infrastructure: transportation, safety, communications, environmental (water, energy), and housing, health and social services. Citizen's trust of emergency and safety forces has decreased due to cases of improper use of force and jihadist terrorism. Cybercrime is soaring, taking advantage of the massive use of social networks, easy access to massive impact technologies and low associated costs. The healthcare burden has been on the rise around the world in the face of rampant public debt, stalled budgets, an ever-aging population, and an increase in life expectancy.

Although the definition of *millennial* is not clear, assuming it gathers those born from 1980 to 1996, it describes a group of 1.7 billion people that can decide the ideal city in which to develop their potential. They are citizens of the world. The revolution in the falling cost of transportation makes the easy movement of people possible. We are referring to talented citizens, with language skills, citizens that every city desire to attract and retain, with the aim of thriving and generating wealth. Find at Fig. 2.2 a comparison between millennials and their evolution: Generation Z. While we consider their differences a curiosity, the key fact here is the unprecedented amount of people eager to explore the world, creating, on the one hand, a movement of talented citizens to the best city to develop their full potential, and on the other, a fierce competition between main cities to attract those talented citizens. An incredible people demand vs supply adjustment at a global level. Their main characteristics are mobility capacity, native use of technology, languages, lack of strong family or country roots, desire to grow (money, power or even notoriety), and lack of cultural barriers. All these factors pave the way for a continuous flow of talent all over the world (Desjardins, 2019). More than 80 percent of millennials believe that SmartCity technologies are positively impacting our lives. The number of millennials is currently estimated at 1.7 billion, so it's a strong force asking for better places in which to live. *"Every ounce of logic says technology should have whipped geography by now, flattening the world,"* in Thomas Friedman's words, by allowing people to live anywhere and still stay engaged and connected to the global digital economy. But location matters, and the decision about where to live is not only determined by technological access. Millennials prefer specific cities which offer compelling, attractive reasons for which to live there (Maney, 2015).

While there is not an exact consensus on the categorization, we can describe generations as the following:

- Generation Z: Born 1997–2012
- Generation Y or Millennials: Born 1980–1996
- Generation X: Born 1965–1980
- Baby Boomers: Born 1946–1964
- Silent Generation: Born 1925–1939
- Lost generation: Born before 1925.

A good description of these segments can be found at SocialMarketing (WJOS CHROER, 2018). Watch out for the next generation, Alpha, as the first generation whose members were all born in the XXI Century. Those born after 2010 have always been fully connected, are fast-data demanding, respectful of diversity, are the best-educated generation ever and will become the biggest taxes payers for the retirement of previous generations ... (Perano, 2019)

### 2.1.2 Cities' Transformation

After listening to the latest breaking news on his smartphone, a citizen gets a notice from an augmented reality application that the building in front of him is a former palace, now refurbished as the City Hall. He decides to apply for a census certificate because his university asks him for it, and he enters the building. To his surprise, he must handwrite some forms and papers, identify himself with his ID card or passport, and wait several days for the Napoleonic-era-dated approval bureaucratic process to be finished so he can obtain the requested certificate by paper, mailed to his home.

This is still the current situation in many of our cities. You can perceive the contrast when our digital citizens use technology through some still-existing ways to connect and receive city services. But things are changing very quickly with new technologies as disruptive enablers.

Our cities are facing XXI$^{st}$ Century Challenges,
  Responding with XX$^{th}$ Century tools,
   Managed by XIX$^{th}$ Century bureaucratic Processes,
  Based on XVIII$^{th}$ Century Institutions.

We wrote this flashy summary to illustrate the modernization challenge. Historical reasons, reluctancy to change, traditional immobilism are all stalling the process, but technology is helping to gain lost time and update city services in a reasonable amount of time. Yet, Ancient Greek reminds us, *"The only thing that is constant is change,"* said by Heraclitus of Ephesus (c. 535 BC – 475 BC)

So, because we are human, we are reluctant to change. But change is becoming the accelerated name of the game in the digital era.

Citizens around the world are moving to city centers at historical rates. This fast change paired with innovative technology solutions providing very critical problem resolution and basically impacting even the most remote cities, demonstrate that we are living in times of digital transformation. It's impacting the way we live, work, relate, trade, meet and interact with the rest of humanity. Local leaders are extending the traditional boundaries of local government management to make their cities smarter, healthier, safer, more sustainable, more economically competitive, and more efficient for their citizens. They are looking to adopt technology to make a positive and inclusive transformation. It's time to elevate the conversation on connected cities and citizens working together. When we think about connected societies, we probably think about a broad range of services related to citizen's lives including energy, water, transportation, buildings, education, healthcare and social services, housing, culture, urban planning and public safety. There is a need for city infrastructure and services to evolve and become more integrated and connected.

Cities around the world share a number of challenges. Traffic congestion is increasing in most metropolitan areas. In the developed economies, physical infrastructure needs to be updated. In the emerging world, a massive new physical infrastructure needs to be built. Citizens everywhere have growing concerns about public safety and cybersecurity. The growth of healthcare costs seems to be accelerating with an aging population. In education, we need to provide, both our young people and adults looking to change careers, with the job skills necessary to compete in the XXI century. Finally, controlling our energy consumption and our resulting emissions to ensure sustainability in a context of finite resources.

These challenges are not new. We have been wrestling with many of these issues for a long time. We've experienced some of them for hundreds of years: traffic, clean water and air, crime, reliable power, education and employment, and the list goes on and on. Cities need to be strong enough to survive, adapt, and thrive despite the challenges they are experiencing. What is different now is that we currently have the technology to address most of these challenges in new ways.

One key aspect of this future connected society that is growing quickly today is urban mobility; transportation of both people and goods, as retail options are soaring online, challenging the ways those goods are reaching their destinations. This is a tough problem for the city of Amsterdam, where the narrow, water-channel side streets are collapsed daily by couriers delivering goods purchased online.

As civilizations have evolved, so have our means of transportation. First by foot, then by horse and now by an array of large and small, public and private vehicles. But the increase in new mobility options like *sharing* (cars or bicycles or scooters), Cars-as-a-Service options, autonomous cars and other are completely changing the scene. Cars are integrating more technology to become *smarter*, taking advantage of the latest connectivity technologies like 5G, allowing them to seamlessly interact with a smart city infrastructure and with other vehicles and users (new V2X – vehicle-to-other paradigm). This also implies that the necessity of owning one or more cars per family will decrease. So, cities' infrastructure will need improvements to accommodate the smart car of tomorrow, reducing the space for cars and regaining pedestrian areas, making cities more walkable. Mobility options will be available in real time, reporting incidences and providing alternative routes, making traffic flow more fluid, safer and easier than ever before. City transportation services will take advantage of predictive models to anticipate probable complications and reduce their impact.

A city that harnesses its capability, capacity and human capital to focus squarely on improving infrastructure is actually cementing a lasting impact for decades to come, not only in terms of the well-being of its citizens, but also for the economic potential and competitiveness of the city to attract talented citizens.

In addition to technology, collaboration enables this connected society. This entails city leaders, citizens, academics and utility providers all working together to enable our neighbors and enrich our communities.

By leading this change in a thoughtful manner, cities are creating environments that are more sustainable, prosperous and inclusive for all. Through different initiatives, cities are working to eliminate the digital divide for elderly people and people with disabilities.

By creating welcoming environments that attract new businesses and talented citizens from other places, and also build up and retain existing ones, cities will thrive in global influence, reputation and attractiveness. This openness to external talent from other cultures is underpinned by tolerance. All this work is done for and by people.

### 2.1.3  People Matter for Thriving

*People come to cities for the sake of life, and they stay for the sake of the good life.* (Aristot. Pol. 1)

When Aristotle refers to the *good life*, he does not mean enjoying a life full of leisure and pleasure. Aristotle speaks of the good life as that which is enjoyed by the *good citizen*, the one who takes advantage of living in the polis because he has the skills and the rationality to lead a *good life*, contributing to the existence of the polis. The polis offers the conditions for citizens to develop and exercise this *good life*.

Cities will increasingly need to compete to attract the people they need to thrive. Migration from rural to urban areas is slowing, but city-to-city migration continues. Talented, single individuals with no family dependencies are moving to new cities in large quantities and even whole family moves are usual. The modern digital era gives citizens the power of choice over where they want to live. In the past, they used to follow job opportunities; now those job offerings come to them. Employability is a key factor in choosing a city, but it's not the only one and it's no longer the most relevant. Honestly, we consider it arrogant that a large technology and e-commerce company's negotiation over where to place its second headquarters in the U.S. was held like an auction. Skilled employees won't go just anywhere to work and live, so companies like that tech firm should find a very attractive city for citizens and then settle down there, not in the one that offers the best tax and logistics conditions for the company. Otherwise, their capacity to attract the best workers will be diminished by the lack of city attractiveness. Manufacturing jobs tied to a factory location now account for less than one in ten jobs across developed regions; many retail and service-sector jobs, the largest and fastest-growing job categories, tend to follow people, not the other way around. A rising number of digital jobs can be performed at a distance (teleworking), and older-knowledge workers may choose more flexible work arrangements in their jobs as they approach retirement. Digital platforms enable people to be matched to jobs wherever they are.

The cities that retain their talented citizens and attract others from abroad will thrive; those that fail to keep their citizens and make themselves appealing to new workers and families will not, lagging behind as places for only elderly people to live, losing young talent, with low competitiveness and dynamism. In the past, cities' economic strategy hinged on appealing to businesses; increasingly, it needs to focus on what the city can offer citizens and the services it will provide. If it does, people will come, then businesses will follow.

There is much for city leaders to do to successfully compete for these increasingly empowered citizens, not least of which includes creating stable, innovative employment, which requires mayors to broaden their focus from urban planning to genuine economic development and talent competitiveness, connecting them to citizens and making them participants in the city development.

It may, of course, be that people's expectations are rising beyond what governments are able to deliver within budget constraints. But it may also reflect the fact that urban management today is not designed to focus first and foremost on citizens. If it were, money might be invested more wisely, and results would improve.

## *2.1.4  Realizing the* SmartCity *Vision*

So, cities are investing in technology to work out many problems, improve the quality of services and become more attractive to talent. The considerable rewards of smart cities will only be realized if they put citizens front and center of strategy and execution, and that means understanding them: who they are, how they spend their days, how they move within the city, what they love or hate, their values, how they interact with city services. . . then, design policies and services accordingly. Citizen-centered governance is, in many ways, no different from the way that corporations focus on user experience when delivering their services, always listening to customer feedback. A working mother of three who lives in a residential neighborhood will have very different needs to the 73-year-old widow who lives in a nursing home. They will interact with city services very differently. Change the word citizen for customer and think about some of the evidence-based marketing strategies. It's important to note that the city needs to act responsibly and very respectfully, otherwise citizen's trust is lost (in the next elections).

The more detailed the city's understanding of its citizens, the better for practical policy. Different citizen activities involve multiple touchpoints with different public services. Do they commute via public transport, or do they walk? What is their cost in money and time? How many times does a citizen visit the health center or hospital, and for what reason? What jobs do people perform, and are they formal or informal? Such data is a gold mine for providing targeted and effective public services.

We have seen in all the Industrial Revolutions how technology has always been the driving force of economies worldwide, but what about for cities? Cities have to develop efficient operational models to provide infrastructure and physical and digital services to their citizens. However, most services and infrastructure are built upon a mixture of investments that can span decades. The adoption of new technologies has been historically slow, frequently with investments that are far out of proportion with other important community needs, always considered a priority. Information Technologies started to play a relevant role in municipalities in the tax department. It took decades for these new technologies to manage the core of citizen contact through Citizen Relationship Management Solutions (mainly call centers). Now, it's impossible to manage a modern city with its complexity of systems, items, things, matter, people, buildings, spaces, generated data (structured in data bases or unstructured like WhatsApp or Facebook messages) without Information Technologies as the real brain of the city.

Elected leaders are increasingly being asked about technology in the community such as residential broadband, how to welcome autonomous cars, and how to embrace remote home care technologies, to mention a few examples. Citizens expect rapid development and adoption of technology in their daily lives and in their businesses. They don't want to see lines drawn between enterprise and public services, just the opposite: they demand better quality systems serving them from the public domain than from the commercial sector. For residents and visitors, the expectation is for the city to meet ever-escalating demands. How do cities innovate and leverage technology to not only provide the services citizens need but also to build a model that supports the rapid growth required to attract and sustain highly successful inhabitants: talented citizens?

Urbanization is therefore crucial for achieving sustainable economic growth. At the same time, this development is creating major challenges related to natural resources, environmental impact and livability of cities. These challenges are not only dedicated to serving (or retaining) current citizens, but to attract new ones coming into the city with the expectations of better living conditions.

### 2.1.5 City as a Catalyst for Creativity: Wittgenstein's Vienna

Cities are positive or negative catalysts of human creativity, and therefore, of economic and social development. They are the breeding ground where art can be created and expressed, science developed, and society can advance in equality and ethical values. On the other hand, it can also be the furnace where all this is destroyed with war, hatred and inequality. Let's study the best example of how a city can empower its citizens by taking them to the category of geniuses: Wittgenstein's Vienna (Janik & Toulmin, 1973a). This city, at the end of the XIX century, together with the Athens of Aristotle, represent the two culminating moments of our human culture: the two moments where a single city could collectively foster development in all the arts and human sciences, and therefore, bring forth the geniuses who pioneered the study of Ethics, Aesthetics and Human Sciences.

The Vienna of the late XIX and early XX centuries (end of century or fin-de-siècle) brought together an enormous, almost irreplicable concentration of talent, creativity and human development, comparable only to Aristotle's Athens. More than one hundred of the best creators in Philosophy, Writing, Theater, Music, Painting, Architecture, Applied Sciences, Engineering, Mathematics, Physics, Mechanics, Medicine lived and met every day in Vienna, many of them still today great references in their disciplines (Janik & Toulmin, 1973b). They met, grouped together, discussed the current issues of the time, and most importantly, about humanity. They discussed the essence of man and the meaning of existence, reality, the ability of language and science to explain it, and the most relevant, what cannot be expressed in words, what is transcendent, what is essentially human. All were philosophers in their own way, and from their respective area of knowledge, all led advances about the conception of man and his existence. Many developed disruptive ideas, which marked a new way of living, a new humanity after the death of this life. Aesthetically, a Kantian base was breathed, of essential knowledge, on which the search for new forms of expression, of knowledge and artistic development was erected, in a city of dreams (Janik & Toulmin, 1973c) on the edge of a historical precipice: the destruction of the world as it had been conceived, by the barbarism of war and deranged authoritarianism. Vienna was a Gaia Big Mother cooking a ratatouille of geniuses in a pan about to burn. Fresh and tasty vegetables of different colors and disciplines mixing, bringing flavors and intensities to each other, under the fire of an Empire on the verge of collapse, with the threat of nationalist dismemberment, war and the totalitarian social currents engendered at that time: the Nazi anti-Semitic fascist totalitarianisms on one hand, and the Marxist proletariat dictatorships on the other.

And that process kept going, in a small Vienna frying pan, with little space and little available housing, so burning that it made it unbearable for many, who opted for suicide, but so intense and rich in creativity that it made a dense, excellent, chef-worthy result, something unique and sublime, brutal and overwhelmingly human. All seasoned with the spices and salt provided by the hallucinatory waltz, the *Sachertorte* with cream, and the peppered touch of *grüner veltliner* (wine) to escape from the reality of a decadent empire displaced by liberalism, opening minds and a relaxing of the moral conscience.

A Vienna above all human, critical, moral, ethical, creative, but also deranged social concoction of hypersensitive people, with an enormous capacity to move from press manipulation, with its front pages signed by the best writers, to the back ones, announcing prostitution, in a spectrum of avant-garde creativity to the transcendent on one extreme, and the most dirty and self-destructive side of humanity on the other. A dizzying aesthetic collage of contrasts, a *Kakania* (Janik & Toulmin, 1973d) (as Musil calls it), with its real, imperial K's, of greatness, and its likeliness to excrement, a fecal hole, baseness. A city with plenty of aesthetic contrasts: the new architecture of the *Wiener Werkstätte*, with open lines, concepts and spaces and revaluing natural materials, inspiring the subsequent *Bauhaus*, developed by the great LeCorbusier or Mies van de Rohe; the new expressionist painting from the *Secession*, with the Academy rules breaking and the arrival of the sensation of what is not seen directly, which later the great French expressionists developed; new writers and critics of the current social swarming movements by the *Young Vienna* group; the new medicine that tried to understand the human mind with Freud and his school of psychoanalysis; the *Vienna Circle*, where philosophers as remarkable as Wittgenstein, influenced by Nietzsche, Schopenhauer, Brentano, Husserl, Kafka, discovered that the value of humanity is beyond what language can express, that the meaning of life is beyond the obvious, more profound than reality, and what is important is not said, but done, shown. There is a scientific revolution where the material accompanies the Hertz and Mach's immaterial waves, the Newtonian positivisms are overcome by Einstein's relativity; from the crammed, cold, dirty houses, to the heat of the cafés, the friends and lovers, the castles and mansions with their parties and pageantry; from imperial splendor to revolution, destruction and annihilation, to the *last days of humanity* (Janik & Toulmin, 1973e)as it was then conceived; from a matrix of cultural creation to the nightmare of degenerating into a *world destruction testing field* (Janik & Toulmin, 1973f); from the human greatness of avant-garde creation, to despair, and suicide; from ethical and disciplined rigor, to seek a mental order in psychoanalysis; from Wittgenstein's *Tractatus* (Wittgensteisn, 1921) transcendence to the abyss of the most sordid prostitution; from the covered woman made an object of a mercantile contract (Janik & Toulmin, 1973g), that goes away from home tasks and procreation, to a new valuation and fight for her rights, from the Klimt's spider woman devouring the man, to lead, forever since then, the way of world humanization around gender equality. And these contrasts coexisted with Kraus' sharp pen in the local press, criticizing society and even language itself, in case someone was not yet aware of the moment in which he was living. Did we miss anything? Of course, under the cloudy sky, over the

Danube, the ever-present background music and exceptionally and majestically, in the new Opera, with the new Wagner compositions, conducted by Bruno Walter's genius hand. Can there be anything more comprehensive, intense and beautiful? And by the time all sense of reality was gone, they had two options: give it all up or go to the psychoanalyst.

If someone invents the D-leap (inter-dimensional) machine, I already know the space-time moment that I want to travel to: this 1905 Vienna, to a gathering in the Wittgenstein castle, listening to Ludwig talking about how you cannot say anything but only show it with facts, his sister on the piano playing Wagner, with Boltzmann explaining Thermodynamics, Frege and his mathematical analysis, Hertz with his waves, Loos talking about his new building, Klimt portraying the scene bringing golden tones to the dark night, and Kraus writing everything in the next magazine. As guests, Lou Andreas-Salomé talking about psychoanalysis with Freud, in poet Rilke's arms, or both...

Vienna is the symbol and beacon of humanity at that time. That Vienna makes us think about cities' leadership in the different transformations that have taken place in our world. After the imminent war to this Vienna, we observed the disappearance of the traditional Empires. Then, after the Second World War, we saw how the world was consolidated into countries, grouped in the United Nations. Today, in an environment of economic stability and peace, we see again the role of cities' leadership in the creation of wealth and technological. The most cutting-edge cities in this revolution of the information society and Artificial Intelligence are, as it happened in Vienna, those that manage to gather talent and generate the conditions for this to happen (social environment, investment/patronage, openness to new trends, access to culture with leading universities and an extreme sensitivity to ethical and human values).

A city is a space-time point where humans encounter/meet. If a decent number of talented citizens are gathered and provided a good education, and that talent is fostered from power and investment (patronage at that time), then the city will attract even more talent. There is an acceleration in this process as a positive feedback loop, where some enrich others and complement them, and therefore, the total capacity for wealth creation soars exponentially, as at this end of the XIX century Vienna, attracting both local talent, and that of all the Balkans, Germany, and even England.

We learned from Dr. Joan Clos (ex-director for UN-Habitat, ex-Spanish minister and ex-mayor of Barcelona) that when choosing, talent always moves to the largest possible city, and that city density is closely linked to its capacity for development and generation of wealth. It is not a matter of extension or quantity, but of *collision* (in a mile-radius circle around the city center, also named as *almond*) by the highest density of talents. There they live, they dream, they have coffee together, they share, even lovers, they meet at the university or, as it was then, at the Secession or in Wittgenstein's castle, more than 100 of the most qualified human talents who lived at that time. Unfortunately, the war stopped it all and destroyed everything.

What made this unique and magical combination of talents possible? On the one hand, the German-Austrian intellectual leadership, with a leading university in

Vienna. On the other hand, an innovative bourgeoisie with the ability to take advantage of the latest technologies and innovations and leverage them to do business. Not only that, a culturally advanced society paved success not only for business, but for patronizing cultural activities with the obtained money.

To get social recognition, you had to be innovative and successful in business and use your wealth to develop more culture, more innovation. This became a virtuous circle of cultural and scientific progress and development. This required political and economic stability in general. Nobody discussed power to the Emperor, considered as almost divine. There was not much expected of him beyond taking a hands-off approach and providing stability *laisser-faire*, but in the case of Emperor Franz Joseph I of Austria we find another great patron, who reconstructs and enlarges the city, transforming it. It refuses the advancements of the telephone, the car, the typewriter or the electric lighting (Janik & Toulmin, 1973h)...it could not be perfect and for all these advances the private investment from the Viennese bourgeoisie was exceeded.

This situation reinforces the value of the middle class. As already anticipated by Plato in the *Republic IV* (Plato Rep.IV) the middle class is fundamental for the development of a city, because it does not compete for power or for survival, rather, it builds the city and causes it to thrive. This bourgeois middle class was the engine of Vienna. The key was striking a fortune through business to invest in patronage, which in turn attracted more talent and pushed even more business and cultural activity . . . unstoppable? No, we are humans, and we also invented that which is self-destructive: separation and war.

In Ortega y Gasset's logic, *"I am me and my circumstance,"* the city resembles the *circumstance* where the ego moves around in the pan where human activity is cooked in, next to one other. This ability to stay together, to relate, to have $1+1+1=111$ since social aggregation and collective thinking boosts creativity, is possible by urban mobility and means of transport. This is the reason why urban mobility is citizens' most appreciated public service. Because, in essence, as Julián Marías once said, a city is a *"sum of collective past and present experiences"*, (Marías et al., 1983) that make up the city's past identity and present dynamism. That was Vienna, with a great difference in the quality of its citizens, who were constantly speaking in terms of Kant and Schopenhauer, who were well-versed in language, Ethics, and Logic, with Philosophy at the center of all conversations. As Wittgenstein explains in his *Tractatus*, what is important is not what is said, but what is shown: the facts, your actions. We think that in these meetings in the cafés and halls of Vienna, the most important thing was not the wine, but with whom it was drunk.

Two reflections arise from that Vienna's climate: one on the effect of anxiety, of urgency, of living on the edge of the abyss of human cultural production; the other on the power of the press and media.

It seems that we push ourselves to give our best when in circumstances of need and risk, and to comfortably relax when we do not have that stimulus. In that Vienna, there was capacity for investment and patronage, good life and good conditions for human development, but it also had to be earned with effort and talent, with intense study, all in this cramped, substandard housing society, with women very much displaced to the kitchen or to the brothel, and with frivolous political power, weak and threatened by the insurrections, nationalisms and the shadow of imminent war and social revolutions. It is clear to me that this context also stimulated Viennese artists.

Another reflection that comes to me was with regards to the power of the press and its ability to connect, relate to, attract new voices and different and stimulating movements, to communicate and influence people and to keep the whole community at the forefront of knowledge and innovation, favoring collective progress. The Karl Kraus and the work of more than 50 other prominent writers and journalists made this possible in Vienna. The power of daily communication (written, in this case) is evident in Vienna's accelerated development as it's time's global cultural center. Something that today seems obvious to us, but at that time was very revolutionary, because over the usual key knowledge from books, the speed of daily impact was added. The speed of communication's diffusion and connection began, something that we permanently experience today.

This exceptional situation reaffirms the value of the city as an enhancing and cohesive element of human development. The city as an enabling space for the potential of talented citizens, a magnet for those who seek values and a platform for those who seek to make their fortune.

But it also suggests the concept of contributing (and not only in the form of taxes) to the city. We live expecting the city to provide us with public services and offer us perfect conditions for prosperity. But...what do we do for the city? Can we, as President Kennedy urged his country, do something for our city? Of course, we can contribute with our time, our opinion, our work, our use of resources, spaces and possibilities offered by the city. By doing this, we can create a more prosperous, advanced and attractive city for talent, for the benefit of all.

It was said that new technologies were going to encourage cold, dispersed, wide cities, with distant people. Quite the opposite. New technologies connect, but the wealth of a city is still associated with its density, the closeness and contact of its inhabitants, and social life. One lesson that we can obtain from this Vienna is the value of social gatherings, of the group of friends and experts talking about a common topic, of the sharing of experiences and enriching all with knowledge. Social networks connect us and multiply our ability to meet people. They create an environment in which to learn and share, but the city continues to provide the space and conditions to broaden our life and our wisdom thanks to our colleagues. Another way to build a city is to use it, occupy it, take advantage of its spaces in order to meet with others. Cultural development is supported on these bases: family, university, the city; new technologies contribute the necessary speed and proximity, but with the objective of connecting us no matter where we live, or where we meet.

To me, this suggests the following question: what could I do to make my city look more like that Vienna, (referring to its good side, noting that the tragedies it endured are well over?) Of course: by entering into the artistic and cultural circles, of people and spaces, where the city's artistic and human development is cooked, at university, where talent is formed, and in paying attention to the family, where I find calmness and love. And if my city is governed by *ineptocracy*, despises talent, it is blind to the future, and it is not rich in these spaces and proposals of environmental development, then obviously I should reconsider my *citizenship contract* and look for another city, another place where I could develop my human potential. The Vienna of *then* is gone, but it's a matter of finding the *Vienna* that exists today, at this moment.[1]

The current main challenges for Cities where technology plays a significant role as solution enabler are described in the next subchapters.

## 2.2    Impact of the Industry 4.0 Revolution. A Quantum Leap

Each industrial revolution has been associated with a key invention or disruptive technology, its inventor or inventors and a flagship city/area where all of these factors merged.

In the first one, we can recall the steam engine, with its inventor Watson, and London/England as the leading city/area. The impact on cities came with the emergence of factories, attracting a massive number of workers from rural areas, creating suburbs of workers around traditional urban centers. The impact on society was tremendous, with the birth of the class struggle, and movements as well-known as Marxism, Socialism and Communism. This massive shift from rural to urban areas is still present today. It constitutes one of the main factors in the descent of the birth rate and, therefore, of the current aging of the population.

In the second one, the main innovation was electricity; above all, the electrification of the territories, the ability to transport energy over long distances. As the main inventor, we want to highlight Nicola Tesla. A Serbian immigrant, he moved to NYC where he installed his famous laboratory. The impact on the cities meant their electrification. The availability of home appliance machines made it possible to live in buildings and not just in houses with enough space to wash and do other manual tasks. The use of electricity as a heat source provided a good alternative to burning coal and reducing the horrible pollution existing in industrial zones. At the same time, one of the cities' owners appeared: cars.

The Third Industrial Revolution came hand in hand with computers. we have several favorite inventors for this revolution, like Alan Turing (who computed mainly algorithms), Tim Bernes-Lee (creator of the World Wide Web or current Internet), John von Neumann (architect of Digital Computers), Bill Gates (creator of Microsoft, Windows, Office) or Steve Jobs (genius of Apple, Macs, iPhones). And as a place of explosion and development, it is obvious that we must think about the

---

[1] Note to reader: Please find at Appendix I a detailed description of the 104 great thinkers that took place in Vienna at the same time, permanently or occasionally, but with enormous influence on thought and work onwards. Find highlighted in colors the most influential groups such as *Wiener Werkstätte* in Architecture, Vienna Circle in Philosophy and Sciences, *Secession* in Painting, decoration and art, *Young Vienna* in Literature and in pink, the circle of Lou Andreas-Salomé lovers.

cities of Silicon Valley (San Francisco) and Seattle (US). This Revolution brought the automation of many city functions, the mechanization of administrative tasks such as the issuance of taxes, the installation of automatisms for traffic control and the opportunity to show off the city to the world through the www. This made our cities *informational cities* (Castells, 1995).

The Fourth Industrial Revolution could well be considered as an evolution of the third, if not for its tremendous impact on society. The incredible improvement in computing capacity and in the acquisition and handling of enormous amounts of data enable the effective development of Artificial Intelligence and one of its most important applications: Robotics. This impact is very well described in a related book (Schwab, 2016).

### 2.2.1  Cities' Prosperity Recipe: 3T's: Technology + Talent + Tolerance

Professor Florida describes in his book (Florida, 2007a) the equation behind world-wide leading cities' success. All these cities: London, New York, Amsterdam, Paris, Berlin have developed a profound social transformation due to the past industrial revolutions. In all of them, technology has been the main driver: a surge of new, disruptive technology transforming the way we work, manufacture, trade, and develop the human activity that attracts talent. Talented citizens are attracted by this new technology and the possibilities and advances it entails because they see a new way to develop their potential and creativity. From research to the development of new products and their marketing, talented citizens can use their creativity and skills to achieve a breakthrough in society. In addition, this new technology entails the creation of highly-qualified and well-paid jobs, making the attractiveness of a given city reach its peak. With new, rampant technology in place and talented people developing it, we only have to allow them to meet in a common space: a city. The way to make this happen is exercising tolerance, opening the door to anyone who demonstrates talent and a willingness to contribute to the development of the city while respecting local laws and customs. Thus, we can say that the recipe for the prosperity of the most advanced cities has been determined by the rule of the 3 T's: Technology, Talent and Tolerance. Technology as the main trigger of each industrial revolution and as the main enabler. Then, talented citizens approaching that technology in a prominent city/area, and finally, the tolerant civic conditions necessary allowing for this human development.

## 2.2.2  Artificial Intelligence (AI) = Massive DATA + CLOUD Power + TALENT

Now, we are at the beginning of the Fourth Industrial Revolution. In this one, there is not a single city/area winner, or at least, not a main one. It seems clear that the epicenter of economic growth derived from new technologies moves eastward, owing to the strong thrust of the four Asian Tigers, plus China, fueled by a strong investment in AI and new advanced communications: 5G.

The most relevant countries in the world have recently announced massive AI Country Plans like France's 1.5-billion-euro plan, the UK's 1 billion pound one, the EU's 20 billion one, and China's $150 billion plan in less than 15 years. The competition to lead this race is clear.

Data is the new oil; AI is the new engine of the Fourth Industrial Revolution, or in other words, Cities are fueled by data, run on AI.

Artificial Intelligence (AI) is the ability of a machine to mimic intelligent human behavior: from data collection, analysis, learning, reasoning and problem solving, and much more. Through AI, machines can analyze data, texts, videos and images, understand speech, interact naturally and make predictions using data such as when a machine needs maintenance or what type of product the customer wants to buy next time. In fact, machines simulate the way we perceive, react, process information and think.

From the first moment when a scientist or a philosopher (roles interspersed up to the Modern Age) speculated with the assumption that the process of human thinking could be mechanized, to this day, many algorithms and projects were carried out. AI is not new: we can study early Middle-Age thinkers like Ramon Llull, Gottfried Leibniz, Thomas Hobbes and René Descartes. The term *AI* itself was first mentioned by John McCarthy in 1956 at the famous Dartmouth Conference, and is considered the birth of modern AI. Scientists have been talking about Artificial Intelligence (AI) for decades, but in many applications, including cities, AI is already having an impact. Some smart systems are already optimizing themselves and the benefits are real for improving the quality of services, reducing risks and predicting undesired situations.

But if there were already algorithms, programming languages and certain tools, what has happened for the AI explosion to occur? We had and we have talent, but the *means* were missing. Today, we have the two components that we lacked in the equation: first, a huge amount of data on any element to use for modelling -data that come from sensors, things connected to the Internet (Internet of Things or IoT), human production as social networks, etc. Second, we have a great computing capacity, unimaginable a few years ago, derived from the use of large public data centers (Cloud).

For this reason, now is the time when these algorithms have an exhaustive amount of data and a capacity to process it in almost real time, which facilitate creation of new technologies that simulate the human way of thinking (neural networks, deep learning), to perceive the reality and to function like our senses (cognitive algorithms). Thus, we can complete the equation and deploy the full potential of this new technology (AI), impacting with such a capacity for change and disruption in our society that it does not seem to be just an evolution of the use of computers (the 3rd Revolution), but an entirely new revolution. Massive Computing Power from Cloud Systems, plus low-cost Analytics for the huge amount of data available from sensors and social networks is making this revolution happen.

A special category within Artificial Intelligence is machine learning. Machine learning is a data science methodology which allows computers to learn from existing data as they are obtained, without being permanently adapted by human intervention, simply by applying a previously programmed model, rules of inference or neural models, with the end goal of, foreseeing future behaviors, results, and trends.

The main impact is that all non-creative jobs could potentially be done by machines/robots. All those agricultural, working *old-style* manual mechanical jobs, and even service professions (like cooks, waiters, taxi drivers, etc.) can see their days coming to an end. Most jobs manage tasks that are more or less subject to automation. Everything repetitive can easily be delivered by a machine: 24 hours a day, tireless, complaint-free, worker union-less, and for a fraction of the cost.

According to urban theorist (and Citylab cofounder) Richard Florida, a rising *creative class* of workers is fashioning an economy in which *the creative ethics is increasingly dominant* (Florida, 2007b). Prof. Florida describes that only the *Creative Class* (just 30% of total labor force) remains untouched. By chance, 8 out of 10 of the most demanded jobs today didn't exist back in 2000, and it's said that 80% of jobs for the next 20 years are still unknown today.

All of us are more or less creative by genetics, as creativity is part of the essence of the human being. What is not creative is most of our jobs, so let's change them, inventing new creativity-intense jobs for humans, delivering a value that AI can't, or can't easily provide.

Let me dream for a while of a new revival of culture due to the increasing appreciation of human work, the arts, and the essential principles of human beings as creative: beauty, goodness, truth. In fact, everything that makes us more human and different from robots.

Previous human destiny was labor. The future of humanity now points to an overhead mission with creative value. But we need to unlock the full capacity of every human as a creative mind.

In any future scenario, the labor market will be severely impacted, with many jobs disappearing without a replacement, mainly among aging workers, due to the lack of skills and qualifications in the new needed technologies. Then, most governments will take into account the UBI (Universal Basic Income), with the obvious controversy associated with it. The UBI will give a salary to those jobless people because there is a machine that simply makes it cheaper, and probably with better accuracy. On the one hand, some will find in UBI the easy way out to the problems of unemployment, while on the other, some will consider it a trigger for the creation of a *lazy* class, that simply lives off the other more creative workers. The social debate is definitely present.

Many other effects of Artificial Intelligence and Robotics on our skills, wages and jobs can be found in these two books. First, from (Brynjolfsson & McAfee, 2012) explains why the current median income and working population are stalling or declining. The reason is not the popularly accepted *technological stagnation*. Just the opposite; we are starting a new digital revolution with many positive implications like productivity growth, costs reduction, and overall economic growth. Traditionally, employees that were able to handle computers had greater employability and wages. But workers whose skills have been designed to handle computers in an automated way now have less to offer the job market and see their wages and future prospects recede. Only if they improve their skills to perform more advanced tasks, or better said, more *creative* tasks like those of data scientists, designers. . . then their market appreciation will rise.

In the second, (Rifkin, 1996) describes the beginning of the fourth Industrial Revolution as a new era in history. It is marked by a steady decline in jobs and a society divided into two radically opposed classes: one that controls the economy based on technological use, and uses that technology with great efficiency and productivity, and another made of workers with no future and no hope of finding it in a completely automated world, where all non-creative work is delivered by an automaton. This will lead to the creation of a different future world and the disappearance of our civilization as we know it today. A new society with a great revaluation of the human spirit. This reality points to my dream of a Cultural Renaissance because of the rebirth of human values and appreciation of human creativity, making the arts and creative-intense work gain higher value, wages and recognition.

## 2.3   Citizen at the Center. A Copernican Shift

Modern SmartCities are investing in technology to improve the quality of their services for citizens and their ability for attracting and retaining talent.

Yet, they are not connected to their citizens. They try to connect, with moderate success. The problem is that everyday affairs require concentration and that leads to a certain despotism. We can't compare it to a new edition of XVIII century illustrated despotism, *Everything for the citizen, but without the citizen.* The fact is that for most citizens, there is a missing connection and conversation about the city's future with the managers and politicians except for once every four years; to gather their trust in the form of a vote.

Therefore, one of the most important and urgent challenges of modern cities is to reconnect to their citizens and make them part of their city, contributing not only with taxes. It is a return to the ancient Greek city-state model. In Athens, a citizen, on average, participated up to four times along his life in the direct management of the city. There were roles drawn, juries were made up of 501 citizens, etc. That participation meant a lot for the time, especially considering that life expectancy was barely 40 years.

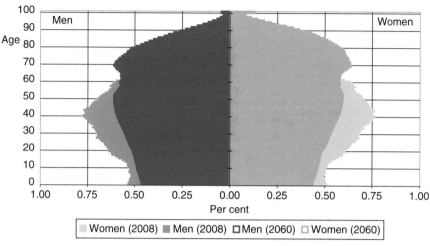

Source: Eurostat, EUROPOP2008 convergence scenario

**Fig. 2.3** Demographics evolution Europop2008. (Source Eurostat, 2009)

Most of the investment in SmartCities is focused on obtaining data to improve the control of the city, develop predictive analyses, anticipate potential problems, be more resilient and improve management. Data is at the center of innovation. It is therefore necessary to make a Copernican shift and reposition the citizen to the center of all activity in the city, with data as an instrument at their service, providing the necessary knowledge to improve city performance. Once again, data and technology should be the enablers serving the citizen.

There are three main aspects of this citizen-centered city: An aging population (a massive problem, rapidly approaching); Creation of new links to connect with citizens; Gaining citizens to trust technology, while preserving their virtual identity and privacy.

## 2.3.1   An Aging Population. The Incoming Tsunami

By 2050, 80% of elderly people in developed countries will live in urban areas (OECD, 2018). Many challenges must be faced to provide for everyone's legitimate right to a long, happy and healthy life. Chronic and infectious diseases and microbial resistance due to the abuse of antibiotics are increasing. Pandemics' spread to other areas is underpinned by global mobility. Demographic data on aging are increasing the demand for social and health services. Health services are usually offered by national or regional entities, but social services remain on the shoulders of cities. Unfortunately, cities are not prepared for this tsunami, neither financially nor infrastructurally, nor in terms of service provision. The current demographic curve in the advanced countries is shaped like a *baobab*, (see Fig. 2.3), with a large proportion of people in its central zone, threatening by a massive incorporation of elderly people into the retiree area, with a high demand for services and no contribution to Social Security to finance it. This situation will undoubtedly mean an exponential increase in service costs, which will lead to the collapse of the current system.

The direct effects of an aging population should be addressed: the number of people in the EU (Eurostat, 2017) over 65 will have increased by 70% by 2050, and the population over 60 is growing 3.5 times faster than the overall population. It is expected that the proportion of the population aged 65 or older will increase from 17.4% in 2010 to 30% by 2060 in Europe. The share of those aged 80 or over (the *oldest-elderly*) is growing faster than any other segment of the population, and is projected to triple by 2060. The old-age dependency ratio (the part of the population aged 65 years or over in relation to that 20 to 64 years old) is projected to more than double, from 28% in 2010 to 59% by 2060. The implication is that by 2060, there will be about one person of working age (labor force) for every dependent person (those under 19 or over 65) in the EU-27. Japan leads global life expectancy of living 26 more years from the age of 60 (UNData, 2019), which points to a total expectation of 86 years (data from 2012 with an upward trend). It is followed very closely by most modern countries at 85 and 84 years. If you reach retirement age at 65, this means that, on average, our population expects around 20 years of receiving a pension, social and health services and many others, without contributing to the maintenance of the system. This trend also contributes to increasing the total cost of the benefits guaranteed for retirees.

According to the United Nations (UN, 2017), the number of elderly people globally is expected to reach nearly 2.1 billion by 2050. Not only are older people increasing in number, but they take an increasing share of total population in every country. This has implications for most sectors of society. These new age distributions will lead to fewer workers sustaining each elderly person. This trend will continue for the next 60 years because of decreasing fertility rates. In rural environments, all hands are welcome, and fertility is higher than in urban areas, where raising children is harder and more expensive. The number of potential workers per elderly person has declined at approximately the same rate between 2000 and 2020 as it did between 1960 and 2000.

The number of face-to-face doctor visits per year in advanced countries exceeds 10 and rapidly points to 15 (already 17 in South Korea) (STATISTA, 2018). This trend is unaffordable and unpayable. Most of these visits are made, obviously, by the elderly. With technological investments, mainly towards remote care and for devices to monitor patients at home, Nordic countries are reducing this to four visits or less (Sweden at 2.8).

There are only two ways to contain the cost of social and health services: simply cutting them, assuming the impact on the modern welfare society and the political cost; or ration their use, using technology to get people to use the services strictly when truly essential. Going to the doctor to renew a chronic prescription or simply to socialize for a while and go back home is unsustainable. Some governments are considering setting up a basic minimal fee per visit, to prevent this behavior. There are much cheaper ways to achieve those objectives. Our services continue to collapse every flu season. Technology can help us stay healthy without having to physically go to the doctor. First things first: prevent problems and maintain healthy habits with the advice of a personal monitoring system. Then, use remote care to deal with minor illnesses, so to prevent visiting the doctor if health indicators are under control and basic prescriptions are working. Finally, use remote specialized care for serious but chronic diseases, such as dementia, Alzheimer's, Parkinson's, ...

Keep people at home for treatment unless really necessary to do otherwise.

A citizen with any disease at a hospital is considered a patient, and the responsibility falls upon the healthcare system. The same person with the same non-urgent disease at home is a citizen with some dependencies, or who needs some care. Then, the responsible authority is mainly the city. This will imply an exponentially demanded service which cities are not prepared for. Anyway, it's widely proven that the best way to support a person with a chronic disease is by keeping them at home. It's cheaper for the system, and better for the citizen's health. Another alternative for elderly people is staying in a nursing home.

With the aging of the population, are we all going to end up in a nursing home? Home care should increasingly become the best option to keep the costs of care for the elderly under control. Keeping the elderly at home with remote assistance is more beneficial for seniors and their families than keeping them in a nursing home.

As 90% of elderly people prefer to live at home, that means they link their happiness with living at home, surrounded by family, neighbors and friends while maintaining access to community centers where they can connect with other seniors.

Some of the benefits:

- When the elderly can no longer live in their own homes, they can be taken in by family members and get external assistance from caregivers while family members are at work. Many Nordic families build extra rooms at home to keep their loved ones closer.
- A person's home is more familiar, therefore if they stay in their homes as long as possible, they remain happy.
- At home, elderly people maintain some of their independence and confidence even though they may need assistance with certain things. They know where things are, routines are easier to maintain, everything is friendlier. Homes can be adapted to become age-friendly.
- It will always be more dignified to live (especially the last years of your life) at home than in a nursing home or hospital.
- Technology can provide resources at home to assist the elderly. Advanced remote monitoring devices plus modern communications and Artificial Intelligence solutions can provide excellent service while fully respecting privacy.
- Different, new technologies help avoid undesired loneliness by connecting people (Collier, 2019).

Elderly people will have different requirements, depending on their mental and physical condition. The idea is to always provide the most positive attitude, balancing:

- Socialization instead of isolation. Avoid loneliness.
- Focus on health more than illness. Enjoy life, every day.
- Activity over inaction. Activity is always better (heart rate, blood pressure, glucose, cholesterol levels are very dependent on activity)
- Better to work on prevention than providing treatment.
- Freedom of choice instead of coercion. Always respect human dignity.
- Monitoring to prevent problems or to quickly react to alerts vs a *Big Brother* reality of continuous surveillance. The right to privacy right is a must. Avoid cameras when possible.

We can identify four key scenarios where technology can provide a clear, direct benefit in making the welfare society in which we live more affordable, by the time the tsunami of people in their 50–60s reach retirement age and so begin the massive demand for benefits.

1. Better budgeting and anticipation of the amount of services necessary to be provided. Currently, most social grants are provided without having analyzed exhaustive data on potential beneficiaries. Goodwill is used. . . If last year a grant was requested by X people, this year it's increased by 10% and launched. This means that many grants are not really requested for and are often taken by those ready to pounce on an opportunity, not those who really need them. With the new, massive data technology system called Business Intelligence Data Analysis, we can know exactly who we need to target, and we can analyze multiple sources of data that identify potential beneficiaries, one by one. So, instead of publishing a grant application on the web, we can proactively go to each potential recipient's home and offer it. What's more, we'll obtain a better idea of the impact of a grant in a few months.
2. Publish the grant and offer a simple, reliable, and fraud-proof method so that citizens can easily apply for it. This scenario is the best in practice today. Citizen Relations Management (CRM) systems allow you to register each application and handle the entire approval process. These systems are multichannel and allow for all types of communication (including face-to-face). For each application, a case is opened, which culminates in an approval or a rejection, after the verification of data, authentication of the citizen, etc. The main barriers come from a lack of citizen knowledge about a grant's availability and the basic computer skills necessary to apply.
3. Deliver the service. This social service delivery varies from country to country. From the Nordic model where civil servants are directly delivering it to citizens' homes (this is very exceptional as only the richest countries on the planet can afford this large group of permanent workers' cost, making the share of civil servants over total labor force rise by 31% or more), to other models where external companies deliver, or NGOs in the poorest countries. Quality of service provided varies accordingly, from well-trained specialized caregivers to low-paid, almost unqualified *visitors*. Here, technology is critical to manage that community of caregivers, tasks, appointments, schedules...Another CRM where caregivers' agendas are managed is needed. This way, the caregiver's

efficiency is maximized while the cost of the overall service is kept under control. Today, the main used technology is SMS and WhatsApp messages.

4. Technology at home. It's clear that best place to live for elderly people is at home, but they need remote aid. Most advanced cities and systems have started to insert some technology at home in the form of devices and sensors. The purpose is to know more about the current situation there and get alerts about specific conditions. That way, with better quality information, decisions are better made, services more targeted and always-scarce caregivers service more efficient. Alerts can save lives, obviously. But filling an elderly person's home with sensors hasn't proven to be a great decision. Two main, negative consequences arise: one about data, another about caregiver's service. More sensors don't mean better knowledge. A massive amount of non-integrated information is meaningless. The input from the sensors must be processed with specific tools to provide meaningful information. Here, Artificial Intelligence algorithms are critical. It's not a question of getting more data, but recognizing activities, because the neurologist is prescribing activities (taking pills, doing exercise, sleeping well,...) and those activities determine the improvement in the desired quality of life. So, the way to analyze the improvement on happiness and quality of life is not just by asking the monitored person, but to observe that the prescribed, good, healthy activities being done. Second is about caregivers' service. We can make their duty more complicated and assume that they can and should maintain or operate devices or sensors. Equipment at home must be simple, a one-time, easy to install process, and integrated. Caregivers should only notice that those systems are in place and working, nothing else. Otherwise, they will be the first to reject these new technologies because of the distraction they cause to their main duties. Finally, these technologies must be non-intrusive (avoiding cameras), respectful (can be switched off at any time), and ethical, always considering that in the end, they are managing humans, and human dignity should always go first and ahead. That way, the value provided by technology will be superior: alerting about any urgent circumstance while creating a home behavioral model (with deep neural networks) to report performed activities, so caregivers can better adapt their service based on real medical knowledge, not only citizens' answers.

## Society's Challenges

This aging population, however, is not the only common city challenge impacting public care services. Other challenges at the center of most political agendas include:

Funding. The ratio of retired-to-working people is getting bigger, leading to fewer taxes to pay for services. Public debt is already outrageous and can't be the solution anymore.

Technology also improves medical science and healthcare tools (new drugs, visualization tools, less intrusive operations, better diagnoses, preventive care...).

Social inclusion, or the desire that no one is excluded from accessing public services, due to age, sex, disability, race, ethnic or religious profile.

Expectations of high-quality healthcare, and access to medical advances are not only ever-rising, but considered a vital right, whether that be financed and provided for by the state or the private sector.

Loneliness (and specifically undesired loneliness) is an increasing problem for elderly people in modern societies. Their children go out every day to work or move to another city to work, study or follow other opportunities. Mobile communications and online services are also eliminating the social contact. Most people over 70 are living alone, which increases their risks of many problems and exacerbates their dependency.

Digital inclusion (avoid the digital gap); the shift towards online services by the public sector is creating the risk of leaving a significant share of people behind, especially among the elderly, the disabled, the poor and the low-technical skilled communities.

Access to quality housing; a bedrock for maintaining good health is also to enjoy decent-quality homes.

Migration, with many people moving from the developing world to escape conflict or persecution, or just in pursuit of better life opportunities means the demands on public services and housing are inevitably increasing.

One could fill a book only with the enormous amount of statistics on these concepts. This is not the purpose of this document; however, some points of reference may be necessary: The UN Enable program published that 650 million people, approximately 10% of the world population, live with a disability, and more updated reports point to one billion.(Ecosoc, 2008) The United Nations Population Fund reported that in 2017, 65 million people had been forcibly displaced (UNFPA, 2018) from their homes around the world. The International Labor Organization World Social Protection Report indicates that four billion, more than half of the people in the world, are left without social protection (ILO, 2017). In the UK alone, according to AgeUK, 3.6 million elderly people live alone, and 1.9 million say they often feel ignored or invisible (AgeUK, 2018).

Elderly people are at greater risk of cognitive deterioration, frailty and multiple chronic health conditions with implications for their independence, their quality of life (and that of their families), but also for the general sustainability of social assistance systems. The challenge now is to develop safe, intelligent and respectful digital solutions for integrated care which guarantee a truly personalized provision of health and social assistance, while consolidating advances in the efficiency of service delivery, and guaranteeing the trust of users and public officials on access, privacy and data exchange

## 2.3.2  Connecting/Listening to Citizens. City Co-creation

*Cities have the capability of providing something for everybody, only because, and only when, they are created by everybody.* (Jacobs, 1961)

Citizens' new language is digital and flows through social networks and instant messaging tools. So should cities use those means to communicate with them. More and more, citizens are digital humans, technology-savvy people, and they expect their cities to react and provide the same quality online services (or even better) than those they might get from private sector companies. On the other side of the digital divide, those isolated from or non-familiar with technology are struggling to operate in an online world.

Many cities are investing on capturing data, but not on connecting with citizens. Many city electronic services are provided from a website, and this website is organized by the different areas or city departments responsible for each service or task delivery. This might be an easy-to-understand model for civil servants, who know very well who does what and what department can serve us at any time. Yet, citizens' problems are not organized using that schema. Citizens experience life facts and needs associated to those services. So, it seems obvious that city services should be designed, organized and presented to match those realities of life. Citizens want their cities to *step into their shoes* and tell them what to do, who to talk to when they want to move into a new house, or get married, or when they have given birth to a new citizen. Imagine a civil servant knocking on a citizen's door with a bouquet of flowers in hand. Suppose that the couple living in that house very recently had a baby. They open the door to the identified city civil servant, who immediately says, *Congratulations on the new citizen you have brought to our city. We knew from the hospital. Please, accept this modest bunch of flowers and allow me to help you. Because of your situation (you had a baby), you are entitled to receive some city services. Then, she opens a portfolio and suggests: May I offer you registration, a vaccination schedule, kindergarten options? What about booking for a school in advance? Just let me know and sign these forms.* This could be a great example of a Zero Administrative model. A proactive way to provide services based on previous information management or predictive data analysis. Science-fiction? Not at all; in fact, it's a reality at (Hollands-Kroon, 2016) (a city in the Netherlands). This 50,000-population coastal city in the North Holland province of the Netherlands is the result of a recent merge of several smaller cities to improve efficiency. The first decision was not to build another city hall, but to reuse old buildings and work in a very innovative way: all civil servants telework from home, or in virtual teams, and service is delivered as close as possible to the citizens.

The six main largest cities in Finland work together in an innovation consortium called (6Aika, 2019). The objective of the 6Aika group is to develop more intelligent services for the citizens in order to create new economic models, businesses and jobs in Finland. Espoo, the second largest city in Finland with 275,000 inhabitants, is one of most proactive members in 6Aika. Espoo uses the latest Artificial Intelligence technologies for design thinking to proactively predict and anticipate the services citizens will demand. Espoo manages around half-a-billion rows of data through its *datalake* and applies Bayesian methods to make a prediction and provide proactive guidance for citizens. In other words, *Based on all the data we already have about your past experience with city services and your current personal information, we predict that your most probable next service demand will be X. Accordingly, we proactively provide you guidance and quick access to that service.* The city's main goal is to maximize the quality of public services while improving efficiency and cost savings. They started by understanding their families' child-welfare status and found 280 indicators to model it.

Citizens are relying heavily on social networks for real-time news, information sharing, and social interaction, so they have great expectations of their government's adoption of these same technologies to connect with them.

Here, most of applicable communication methodologies are the same as those used by commercial retailers to engage with their customers, creating a community of loyal customers. Four main approaches can be used here: Social Listening, Social Intelligence, Social Engagement and Social Citizen Relationship Management.

Social listening. Technology helps to listen to what everybody, and especially your citizens are saying across the main social media networks like Twitter, Facebook, YouTube, WordPress, and around 4000 existing news publications and other digital sources. It's important to determine the main patterns and key words, key influencers, and also alert specific city managers when something especially relevant is trending. Sometimes, you don't know beforehand what you are looking for. Technology can inform you on the main topics of conversation, semantically associate them to your *hot* topics and adapt the search to find what's relevant. Citizens may have been talking about something critical for you in a way, language, code or slang that is not obvious at first glance. Knowing the key influencers in your city could be important to connecting to your community. These people can help city managers to resonate main messages or to stop fake news or other undesired mis-understandings, controlling the message. When a mayor wants to reach the entire population, especially young people, the power of this connection and its viral effect could be of tremendous help. To reach influencers, there are popularity indexes like *Klout*.

Social Intelligence. The main technology here is Sentiment Analysis. Using Artificial Intelligence algorithms, the tools understand citizens' feelings about a particular topic. The information analyzed includes multilanguage, emoticons, symbols, phrases, specific language nuances and terminology. Imagine how relevant it could be to know citizens' reactions to any breaking news about the city or spontaneous opinions about the city's main projects or activities, not to mention the overall city and mayor popularity. Sentiment Analysis helps cities to prioritize resources, track performance and connect with their communities. Automated triage tools detect any type of intentions. With this information at hand, the city can react and proactively propose those services or give guidance. If demand seems to be high, the capacity to deliver can be extended or increased in advance. Finally, you can obtain a *Buzz Analysis* to watch a dashboard with insights and rich analytics about location, volume, share of voice, content and sentiment analysis.

**Social Engagement** You can participate as well! Apart from listening and analyzing the voice of your citizens out there, social networks help you to interact, using the city's own accounts, or the mayor's, or other main city leaders'. But here you have to proceed with caution: use rich multimedia tools to provide a trustworthy image and a message signaling to easily connect. A suggestion is to hire a community manager or social media manager to make a great impact in this area. Social conversations can serve as the trigger for the execution of internal tasks to provide what's needed or to react to a good suggestion with a new kind of service, or simply to respond to a question. You can start communication and use all the networks' power to share what you want to highlight or announce. This interactivity can build end-to-end complete interactions, from a citizen initial post to a complete answer from the city.

The small Spanish municipality of Jun (Granada, Spain) has served as a model for MIT on the effective use of Twitter to permanently communicate with citizens and civil servants (Ventas, 2015).

Social Citizen Relationship Management. You can use social networks as another main channel of your integrated citizen services' platform. You can perform social marketing activities, identifying segments of the population with specific needs, monitor social movements or track social trends. You can try to control your city's reputation, nurture influencers, measure city actions' effectiveness and strengthen your citizen engagement, creating the sense of *belonging*. You can't imagine how surprised a citizen would be, if after complaining online about a particular city service or condition, they receive a proactively given response from the city. Comments like, *wow, they are listening, and they respond*, are excellent in gaining citizens' trust. You can also set up notifications to help you quickly alert first-response emergency teams.

Most times, citizens are reluctant to accept new applications for their smartphones, as they are very worried about privacy, security and identity misuse. Recent massive data leakages, security breaches, and abuses from companies like Facebook are not helping the case. It's even harder to trust city services when confidence of the whole network security has been lost. Connecting to citizens is not just a question of proposing a new app, it's a question of providing significant value to citizens by using their own communication flows, or creating a nice, new way to engage with them, making them feel proud of their city (using the idea of *belonging* to awake their participation and cooperation to collectively build a better city).

The service provided must be as personalized as possible. The more we know our citizens, the more personalized that service provision should be. In the recent EU eGov Services Analysis,(EU, 2015) three main challenges remain for the EU countries' government services to match citizen expectations: Mobile-Friendly (only one in four public services meets this); Open & Transparent (only 41% of websites are transparent about their service process, estimated duration and response times; only 35% of websites inform visitors about their ability to participate in policy making processes); Personalized & Simplified (only 45% of online forms are pre-filled with already-known personal data, and in only 4% of cases, services are proactively offered to citizens).

Cities are using creative ways to engage with citizens and make them participate in city activities. Gamified creative proposals to reward civic behaviors with

*CityPoints* like in the award-winner (World Summit Award App) (WSA, 2017) application from (Cascais, 2018) (Portugal) are a good example. Those points can later be used for discounts on services and mainly on private purchases due to PPP (Public-Private-Partnership) agreements like discounts for the movies or restaurants. That way, participation is encouraged and rewarded. There are many other examples, like Istanbul offering free transportation tickets in exchange for recycling items, or Rotterdam rewarding workers in cash, applied to their salary, according to the kilometers they ride by bike to work. Copenhagen is providing creative grants for citizens who contribute to the collective task of becoming carbon neutral by 2025. Gamification on recycling is a clear trend. City of Santander (Spain) *CityBrain* Active App to interact with citizens and generate ideas for crowdsourcing is another clear example (Santander, 2019). Madrid holds a nice initiative *"Madrid te abraza"* or *"Madrid Hugs You"* as a new city icon to try to connect and engage with citizens, highlighting its sense of hospitality, capacity of receiving people, and easily integrating expats (Madrid, 2019).

In Seoul, citizens gather in squares to talk. In Vancouver, they do it in gardens and civic centers. In Madrid and Seville and many other cities, a significant percentage of the municipal budget is allocated towards collective decisions (participatory budgets). While these initiatives are not yet as popular as they should be, and many times we can observe the *same ten people attending to the same meetings* phenomenon, it's clear that this is a growing trend, empowering citizens.

One of most recent, innovative Artificial-Intelligence (AI) based tools to interact with citizens is the bot (or chatbot). Very popular at main commercial brands websites, a bot in a city is like a virtual civil servant or a virtual robot which responds to queries or chats from citizens or visitors. Fueled from a knowledge database made of questions and answers, and an AI engine that's trained and enhances its accuracy with every interaction, a bot is a virtual assistant designed to operate 24/7, providing information or advanced services on the city's behalf. Interaction is made by natural language. Many cities are providing services with this new technology, like Copenhagen, North Charleston (U.S.), Kansas City, LA, Boston, Birmingham (UK), Vienna among many others.

A final reflection on connecting to citizens: in the same vein as US President John F. Kennedy once said, *"Do not think what your country can do for you, but what you can do for your country,"* (Kennedy, 1961) we should question ourselves about what we can do for our city, beyond just demanding services. True, we pay taxes, but it's not only about money; we can contribute with our time, dedication, giving, philanthropy, or just by reporting things that must be fixed, or providing our opinion about what's working well or not. Cities are putting in place eDemocracy solutions and offering participative budget assignments. eDemocracy solutions are fine for getting a pulse on citizens' opinions, but it cannot replace voting as the full population reach is not guaranteed yet. Even with the best electronic identification systems to certify the identity of the user, we cannot guarantee impersonation won't occur (like the granddaughter who votes on behalf of the grandmother or just stands right behind her, telling her *what to do* to exercise the vote). Anyway, the modern tools to gain the pulse on citizens' opinion must be used and considered. Its capacity to improve community participation and engagement, take real-time pulse, interact with city officials (even directly with the mayor), explain city projects, influence city decision making, and raise awareness is unquestionable. Another reflection is about who's the best to connect to for city cocreation. Mid-class citizens here are hyper-relevant: first, because societies with larger middle classes are proven to be wealthier and the most developed; second, because mid-class citizens are eager to improve and contribute to city development and cocreation. (Plato Rep.IV) wrote that a city needs the mid-class because that group doesn't fight for power or against poverty, but rather to create a more prosperous city. In our times, this is still very true: the richest don't take care about city, but about their properties, the poorest just fight to survive, and mid-class citizens want to create a better city, so they will thrive as well. They want to enjoy the best conditions to grow, and the city sets the conditions for that to happen.

### 2.3.3   Citizens' Trust (CyberSecurity, Privacy, Compliance). GDPR

Yet, if we want citizens to trust our cities' managing and handling their identity, data and services, we must ensure a proper use of them, with the maximum security and respect for privacy, while observing the strictest compliance laws (the most important in Europe – GDPR).

A McKinsey Cybersecurity report describes the main threat of digital technologies: data breaches (Poppensieker & Riemenschnitter, 2018). Since 2011, major cyberattacks have successfully obtained access to all kind of data, identities and intellectual property. Names like Dragonfly, WannaCry ransomware, NotPetya ransomware, Meltdown and Spectre to mention some; also, the recent Facebook data exposure scandal are creating the feeling that our virtual world and the overall www is an unsecure place. Only 16% of the main world companies say they are well prepared to deal with cyber risk. According to Gemalto's, 2017 Breach Level Index report (Gemalto, 2017), approximately four million data records were compromised every hour during the first half of 2017, a growth of 164% compared to the previous year. Identity theft was the most frequent type of data breach. Cybercrime alone costs the global economy over $445 billion, and growing, every year (Reuters, 2014a). Data privacy issues have impacted (and are causing full project to fail) many city projects like first eVoting in Barcelona by 2010 or Quayside, a conceptual Google's smart neighborhood in Toronto (Summers, 2018).

A modern protection strategy in a data-sensitive entity, such as a city, must use the available tools to build the right defenses and fend off attacks, but it must assume that hackers have already entered and looked for where the loophole is, and what information they have accessed. It is clear that a virtual war is happening worldwide, where some try to seize information and/or control over others. A large entity can receive hundreds of thousands of attacks every day. Although there may be surprises due to breaches in the security of current systems, we can assure that the good ones are always winning the battle, although we must always be prepared for an unexpected problem or human error (misuse of passwords...). Risk is present and growing. If we consider that by 2020, 46% of all Internet-through interactions will be machine-to-machine, without any human operators, security must be unbreakable. The main technology companies are cooperating with government agencies to monitor network security. Main, large datacenter providers offer extreme security to all entities. This is especially relevant for those that can't afford the needed systems and personnel to protect by themselves.

In terms of privacy, most governments are taking citizens' sensitive data with the expected care. Legislation varies from country to country, but it is worth mentioning the GDPR. (EU-GDPR, 2018) or General Data Protection Regulation is a mandatory European law since last May 2018, which protects any European citizen data privacy managed by any company or government organization. Citizens have the right to know which data any entity has on them, and they can order to delete, forget, or transfer to other entity. Owning data without express consent or transferring or dealing it without permission may lead to fines worth a maximum of two options, 20 million euros, or 4% of annual turnover. That way, the cost of not observing the law is bigger than investing in a methodology to keep citizens' privacy protected. We can say that Europeans enjoy the most protective privacy system in the world. Many non-European companies and governments are endorsing that rule.

"*Privacy is a human right*" (IndiaNewEngland, 2018), a statement recently said by Microsoft's President, Satya Nadella. One of the most common controversial discussion topics here is facial recognition. It's clear that this advanced AI technology has an immense potential to solve society's problems like finding missing children, diagnosing diseases or identifying bad guys in crowded spaces, but legislation and regulation must be put into place to avoid undesired dystopias like George Orwell's *1984* from happening. In this article (Nickelsburg, 2018), Microsoft's president Brad Smith explains that governments could follow anyone anywhere by 2024, in a scary, real implementation of a *Big Brother* concept, the same as shown in *1984*. So, many civil organizations are raising their serious concerns about this possibility. It's clear that regulations and an ethical code are more than needed at a global level. A new revision of the UN Human Rights declaration? Microsoft's leader is also pointing to another serious topic: facial recognition and other AI-Ethics issues are developed by the technology companies as part as their continuous race to innovate, compete and release the most advanced products to market. This may collide with citizens' consent and privacy. So, another Ethics-code at the development phase should be agreed upon between all market actors, including fairness, respect for privacy, testing by other parties...to avoid the legitimate commercial interests to prevail over citizens' privacy or force companies to decide whether to stay competitive with intrusive solutions or simply lose market share. This must become another global decision, as ethics and commercial scruples also vary very much country to country.

Privacy (physical or virtual) is a right, and an exercise of our human dignity. We must trust in well-used technology, for it frees Man from the bondage of the environment. Technology allows us to avoid natural evil, control the elements and overcome diseases, allowing us to enjoy more time of creation, its beauty and other humans, taking advantage of that extra time for the good of humanity. It is *us* and not technology, who use it in an improper and tortuous way, who can use it for the manipulation of information, the theft of virtual identity, the control of the world from the web, transhumanism, etc. By its intention, technology is good, and allows us to live in the most developed and perfect moment of humanity's entire existence: today.

## 2.4 DATA: XXI Century Gold

Data is in century what oil was in last one (The Economist, 2017a). If data is the fuel, then AI (Artificial Intelligence) is the engine of fourth Industrial Revolution. Data means knowledge, knowledge means power. For a city, data means the capacity to generate services and value to citizens, control the environment, anticipate risks, quickly respond to natural or human-provoked disasters, create a better place for living, a more competitive, attractive city, and a more efficient one, saving time and resources for citizens; also, saving lives because of creation of better environmental conditions and reducing crime and traffic accidents. Data is gold, it's needed, mandatory, but it's not the end objective, it's the enabler to create modern services and make well-informed decisions in a city. In the use of data, cities must think as women, in the way Chad Eastham explains in his book *"Guys are waffles, Girls are spaghetti"* (Eastham, 2009) meaning cities should operate in a more interconnected way (same as women's brains) and less split into isolated data silos (as men's brains do).

### 2.4.1   Power Shift to DATA. Internet of Things (IoT)

Intelligent (smart) cities use Information Technologies to create a better place for living, for developing new businesses, for the environment, for attracting investors, and for raising high standards for Education, Healthcare, Safety, Justice, Democracy and Wealth. With Cloud datacenters' power and scalability, data management system costs are decreasing, while capacity is exponentially lifting off. In parallel, we are spectators of a data-explosion phenomenon, with huge volumes of data created daily by myriads of devices, sensors, smartphones, gadgets. . .things? According to IDC (Kanellos, 2016), our datasphere (the global amount of data stored into digital systems) will reach 180 Zettabytes (Zb) by 2025. A Zettabyte is an incredible amount of data, far more than what our brains can understand, exactly $10^{21}$ bytes. If just one byte is a combination of eight 0s or 1s and can represent one of the letters of this document, try to think about how massive that number is. This will happen at an accelerated ratio, growing from 4.4 Zb by 2013 to 44 Zb by 2020.

Today, growth is mainly due to massive generation of multimedia data from smartphones (72% of all that newly generated data is multimedia). Another approach to understanding that acceleration could be the fact that we are generating more information in one year than in all past human history. Future massive acceleration will mainly come from information generated by sensors (in cars and in another large number of items) and transmitted by a next-generation, high-speed network: 5G. This new world is called the Internet of Things, (IoT) as we are connecting everything which can be controlled or monitored to Internet, generating data. In a Cisco report (Columbus, 2016), mentioning Gartner as the data estimation source, it's stated that one million new devices go online (adding over the IoT) every hour by 2020.

We are spectators of our cities being sensorized. Millions of sensors are installed in our cities to capture more and more data about everything measurable out there. The IoT sector was born in 2008–2009, and is growing into a trillion-dollar industry in this next decade.

Looking to the future, Cisco IBSG predicted there will are 50 billion devices connected to the Internet by 2020.

So, cities can be ruled based on data, and make better informed decisions, as Barcelona's mayor Mr. Trias once said, *"I want to rule my city based on data, facts, not rumors, isolated opinions, partial surveys or wishful thinking."* To do this, new Predictive Analytics tools facilitate their anticipating issues, becoming more resilient and delivering a better service, saving money, time and lives. Because of this relevance of data in city governance, all cities are seriously considering hiring Data Scientists.

IoT will help make life in our cities more comfortable, safe and sustainable. In the safety area, cities are among the largest users of IoT-enabled cameras. They use other IoT devices to track environmental conditions such as temperature, humidity, air pollution, gases and fog density, or to manage traffic status or make parking an easy task. There are many available parking apps for your smartphone to save you time by finding a free spot near your destination. Another very popular use is street lighting. Replacing old bulbs or yellow sodium-vapor lamps by modern LEDs improves quality of light, while reducing energy consumption to a fraction of what it usually is. If light poles are equipped with IoT technology, then you can take control and improve savings even more. With sensor technologies' capabilities, the light can dim down at night if nobody is around or no movement is detected, then flash on when needed. Likewise, you can remotely control them to provide extra illumination to a particular area if needed, to better manage an emergency or special event. Savings are so clear that these projects are obvious examples of energy-savings performance contracts, (ESPCs) or projects which pay themselves.

Since we are connecting cars and those cars are smarter, so much that they are becoming autonomous, the impact on urban mobility will be enormous. Connected cars, streets and roads are among the largest next generation of IoT users. When we are driving, we watch and process many different images, places, road works, cars, traffic signals, weather conditions, road conditions, pedestrians, bicycles, other vehicles, emergency vehicles, etc. This massive amount of information must be processed into an autonomous car in real-time to make precise decisions in a tiny fraction of a second. Furthermore, the autonomous car will interact and share information with the city (road, traffic system, traffic management) and other users/cars. All of this should flow through the IoT network. Here are two examples: In the first, *the road* will inform the car about the presence of a patch of ice a short distance ahead, or an ambulance approaching in the same direction. In the second, the car can report unexpected, slow traffic or congestion or the beginning of a rainshower. These connected cars/roads will make life easier and safer.

Artificial Intelligence (AI) needs a massive amount of data to take into account all potential aspects of a particular topic in order to model it, or simply to have sufficient experience (data from same observations) to understand patterns and behaviors. IoT is the main source for that needed data.

Modern C-ITS (Cooperative Intelligent Transport Systems) integrates IoT information from cars, roads, and traffic systems, and makes it possible to change traffic lights to green for an ambulance driving fast, while slowing and placing apart all existing traffic: all managed by intelligent-enough or autonomous cars.

All citizens hate red traffic lights, and with the speed at which our society moves, they look like an irksome waste of time. With AI (McCaney, 2018), the traffic lights and autonomous cars are interconnected, informing each other about their proximity and speed. This will make it possible for the stops and delays to be the minimum and strictly necessary to avoid accidents, maximize the use of space, prioritize their use for emergencies, etc. So, each intersection will manage itself and be synchronized with the overall system. Predictions point to wait times at intersections reduced by 40% and overall traffic time improvement by 25% (Ebi, 2018).

Cities started to gather data from all city-related items sometime in the 80s, but that info very much depended on the owner's department and was managed in an isolated way: on-premises, in siloed solutions. When the Internet came in the 90s, cities were enabled to use webpages and portals to present data from the entire city in an integrated way through a unified view. But the backoffice data wasn't really integrated. Websites were just a presentation layer over those multiple scattered systems. Then, in the 2010s, large external (public) datacenters started to offer massive computing and data storage rental services at affordable prices to cities, which made possible the dream of knowing potentially everything about everything connected to Internet. Cities are starting to proactively publish data of general interest (opendata) and embrace the Internet of Things (IoT) revolution. Most deploy a large number of sensors to *sensorize and control the city*. The first models were sending all information received to the Cloud. A second generation did some aggregation of data first, then sent it out. The latest generation of sensors and devices are intelligent enough to do some kind of data processing directly, which is referred as *the edge*, so they have some intelligence and sometimes some Artificial Intelligence to provide very advanced capacities to the overall system. This intelligent edge connects items to items without the need to pass through a central brain at the Cloud, so they can work very independently and quickly react to special circumstances. Cloud intelligence will process complex tasks or supervise the full service. In other words, rather than having an autonomous car send data to the Cloud and then wait for a response, the car and the traffic pole can communicate to each other directly. The next step will be to replace the red traffic light (saving energy on lights) by an intelligent pole that is connected to and allowing the car to pass or not according to the context, so the chance to stop traffic (wasting energy on the pause) will be very little, and the traffic flow will improve. Who needs traffic lights if cars are *talking to each other*, alerting each other about their presence, speed and intentions?

Artificial Intelligence will change our lives, that's clear.

With all this data, we need to create a model to watch it all and extract the slice of information needed at every moment for different purposes. That model is commonly named as a *Digital Twin*. A digital twin is a digital model or *avatar* of a physical thing, maybe a building, a factory, a house, a company, or a whole city. The concept relies on gathering all available data for that particular thing, applying data analytics tools and AI algorithms to better understand how that thing operates in order to increase its performance, predictability and profitability. For a city, a key first step is to choose a way to place everything in the right place, as all services and city management decisions are always geoposition-dependent. So, first we need a mapping system to re-position things. Then, we need a way to visualize those things, using images and 3D-drawing to create a virtual city layout like a 3D-canvas. Once we have this virtual representation of everything, we need to define what kind of data we want to use to describe every item. It's not a question of available data, but the type that is informative or relevant for our final management purposes. There are some standardization initiatives to create semantic models for city items or processes. That way we can define what's relevant to be measured and compare city to city on the same areas. For example, to compare waste management efficiency between different cities, we have to use the same data (number of dumpsters, collection frequency, waste weight, recycling share, etc). Some models include the CityGML (dm, 2006), (ISO TC211, 2019), NGSI-LD as base for and (FIWARE, 2019) data models, to mention the most relevant. With these models ready, all we need is the data. Data will be permanently collected from the IoT world (from sensors, drones or other IoT devices). This raw data will be preprocessed on origin (edge) or later in the Cloud, with advanced analytics and Artificial Intelligence (AI) algorithms or an advanced version of them like machine-learning or deep-neural systems to gain real-time insights. These insights deliver very valuable knowledge about any city item or the city as a whole. We can analyze the performance, profitability of any item, but also we can interact with it depending on the conditions (i.e.: we can modify the patterns for red traffic lights according to the circumstances). It's very important to note that the main benefits of this approach are coming from integration of different items and cooperative tasks. Due to the information from sensors in one area, one can decide to increase the service frequency in another, or reduce risks by updating the items in yet another. Finally, if we add the most critical information: all we know about our citizens (regarding taxes, properties, vehicles, water, energy consumption…personal health information…or even, bank cards transactions…and their posts on social networks) we can create full, integrated city services. For example, alerted about a fire by our sensors in a drugstore, we can immediately send the emergency services, prioritize traffic routes, analyze the wind direction and alert citizens who live around to not to open the windows in the next hours to avoid potential toxic smoke, etc. And we can deliver this service instantaneously and automatically, without any human decision in between, again, due to Artificial Intelligence systems in place.

So, the IoT world is clearly a revolution in the overall city management and operations. Some additional examples of challenges which IoT is clearly helping to tackle could be:

*More than **500,000 people die prematurely** every year due to poor air quality in Europe.* (Libelium IoT Applications Report (Libelium, 2019))

There are 2.1 billion people who do not have **access to clean and safe drinking water** at home. Water demand is expected to increase 33% by 2050, and there is a long list of huge water-related challenges (UN Peace, 2019).

Natural disasters such as storms or extreme drought occurring between 2005 and 2015 caused world-wide **losses of $26.5 billion,** as well as biological disasters, such as pests and infestations, causing crop losses of $9.5 billion (FAO, 2019).

In San Francisco, a report concluded that a smart parking solution could **reduce 43% of time wasted looking for parking,** 30% of miles traveled with a vehicle searching for a parking spot, and 8% of the overall traffic volume and 40% of greenhouse gas emissions (parkingnetwork, 2018).

## 2.4.2   A Reflection About Omnipresent Data and Sensors

Massive sensorizing is creating the misunderstanding that Information Technologies departments can capture whatever data they want, as if simply by installing millions of sensors everywhere, and they have enough power to process that huge amount of data. The real question is: how much of that obtained raw data is transformed into insight, knowledge to provide a better service or better-informed decisions? Should we better first think about which applications and analysis we want to perform, and then get the needed data? Currently, most cities are not minimally extracting the value from all the data they already have. Should we start from here? Information about our citizens, their interactions, payments, opinions, grants, reports is already there, ready to provide pure-gold conclusions for better governance.

It's not about installing a plethora of sensors across the city, but obtaining relevant information which could produce insights, with some rules in mind:

- Data acquisition costs near zero.
- Prioritize data sources and types.
- Avoid exponential costs. (Avoid those sensors that imply using a phone ID, or an IP address, for example)
- Keep installing, and especially keep maintenance costs under control (i.e. Think twice about installing battery-powered sensors under asphalt...)
- Get ready to cope with ambiguity, as there is no standard defined for everything.

- Be careful with sensitive data. Stay GDPR/other-applicable-regulations compliant.

While a sensor to measure water quality seems vital, putting a sensor on each and every light pole is not worth the cost. We can easily identify many other more priority/useful locations/functions for that sensor.

### 2.4.3   Connectivity. The 5G Revolution

There are more mobile phones than humans in the world, and almost all of them are smartphones that allow you to connect to the Internet. At the most basic level of data transmission, we have telecommunications' infrastructures. Traditionally, these were wired infrastructures, with copper cables, then fiber, but increasingly we have enjoyed wireless infrastructures whose capacity is increasing exponentially (name, year of launch, main new standard, maximum speed of data transmission ): 1G (1979, AMPS, 2.4 kbps), 2G (1990, GSM, 64 kbps), 2.5G (2003, GPRS/EDGE, 384 kbps), 3G (2000, UMTS, 2Mbps), 4G (2010, LTE, 100 Mbps), WiMax, WiFi, satellites, and now 5G (2015, OWA/OTP, 20 Gbps). By looking at these numbers, it is easy to calculate the accelerated capacity ratio from 30, to 50 to 200 times every 10, then 5 years. All this requires constant improvement and renewal of the tele-communications network and the infrastructures through which these data are transmitted. This phenomenal growth in capacity must be accompanied by a global network that connects all the information from where it is initially stored (servers connected to the World Wide Web) along with the users that require it at every moment. Wireless technologies cover short distances. For long distances, fiber-optic cables are used. These elements have also been improving exponentially in recent years. As an example, one of the latest, most advanced submarine cables installed: MAREA.

MAREA (Krishna, 2017) has been called the *mother of all cables*. Financed by Microsoft and Facebook, this 4100-mile cable can transmit up to 160 Tbps, which makes it the largest capacity on Earth. Connecting Virginia Beach (U.S.) with Sopelana (near Bilbao in Spain), MAREA aims to improve communications between the U.S. and Southern Europe as a gateway to a growing demand from Iberia and even further South, from Africa, alleviating the traditional mass traffic between the U.S. and the British Isles, and helping provide a reliable, high-speed connection for online and Cloud systems (Cloud, or large datacenters). MAREA's main innovation is the use of eight pairs of fiber instead of the traditional two in these types of cables. We understand that for many people these figures seem great, but most times, one does not really perceive its dimensions. By doing some calculations, we can estimate that this cable can transmit the entire National Library of Spain (about 20 million books or all books ever written in Spanish throughout its history) three times every second.

For short distances, connecting the elements of a city, the new 5G technology represents a revolution in capacity and connectivity. It is about extreme speed across short spaces. Very little of the instant-information transmission activity is going to require cables like MAREA. If we think of an autonomous car, it will fundamentally interact with the infrastructure of the city: traffic lights, traffic management systems and other relevant, local data. In these short distances is where 5G will develop its full potential.

If we compare it with the current 4G, this new technology allows for transmission speeds of up to 20 Gbps (100–1000× that of 4G) (multiplied by 1000× the number of concurrent devices), latency or time between communications <1ms (/30 to /70 that of 4G), which is really needed to be able to connect the exorbitant growth of IoT devices. These improvements will pave the way for many, new smart city applications, including, but not limited to, smart buildings/homes, excellent traffic improvements, city resiliency and ability to quickly respond to alerts or natural disasters and autonomous vehicles. To achieve these parameters, you need many more antennas (10–100×), which although smaller and more discreet. The *Small Cells* (pizza box size) with a range of 200 meters will not be enough to avoid controversies regarding aesthetic concerns, the not-demonstrated impact of radiation on health, etc. In addition, by increasing both its number and its cost, the decision to have massive deployments based on profitability will be more questioned than ever. The telcos are still trying to make their return on investment, and make a profit after their previous 4G investments and fees they paid governments for their licenses. In addition, most of them drag a huge debt. The increase in cost due to the higher density required in 5G antennas will make the implementation decision obvious in business centers and commercial centers in the city, but unprofitable outside, relegating rural areas to inferior, cheaper, or more outdated technologies. 5G will not reach these areas, or will not do so for a long time, increasing the technological gap, and therefore diminishing the possibilities of development and attracting talent from those rural areas and small cities. Access to broadband is being considered as important as human rights. Not enough bandwidth means no chance to grow/thrive, no opportunity in the new post-industrial knowledge era. We remember listening in the last presidential election's campaign to some U.S. rural areas claiming for the inclusion of *good-enough bandwidth* as a Constitutional right. Linked to this, city connectivity is considered as one of key city attractiveness attributes.

5G means not only better speed and connectivity, but it also brings many advanced features to improve the way devices communicate, use the network, prioritize, and operate. A big step for implementing IoT.

### 2.4.4  Teleworking on Duty. Place Civil Servants Closer to Citizens

New technologies can also empower civil servants, helping them to deliver a better service while improving efficiency, satisfaction on duty and proactivity. The new technologies' availability together with the continuous renewal in city workers, (replacing retiring servants with digital-native, educated young people who are willing to build careers in civil service) are creating the conditions to seriously think about teleworking as a valid public service working option. From my estimations, 75% of civil servants could telework (25% already serve from outside the office, 25% should stay on traditional duty because of the profession's nature and requirements). After pandemic, more than 50% will keep working remotely, in a flexible and distributed way (hybrid model). With new technologies like smartphones, portable computers, and applications and data fully accessible from anywhere, anytime from the Cloud, civil servants could easily get connected and telework, with the aim of fulfilling their duty closer to citizens, all while improving efficiency and work-life balance.

In the already mentioned city of Hollands Kroon (The Netherlands) example, designing a new way of working for civil servants, with all of them organized into virtual teams, working from home or wherever, has demonstrated the expected increases in efficiency and servant/citizen satisfaction. The municipality employees' morale is up, labor absences and costs are down (saving on space and electricity, not to mention transportation costs and emissions). At the same time, employees have access to all the information they need from the Cloud, under a fully digitized service, being able to analyze the data when needed and improving decision making. *"We are well aware that society is changing, so we are focused on strengthening accountability and self-reliance of both our employees and our citizens,"* said Jaap Nawijn, Hollands Kroon's mayor. We already looked at this example from the citizens service point of view. From the civil servant point, it is a clear example of how a proactive administration anticipates and offers the services which respond to the citizens life facts. Pandemic has demonstrated that this is applicable to all cities/regions services.

In the same way, a city official could proactively go to visit groups of companies which need some permits or could access new grants, or meet with citizens who need social services and offer them certain services.

Transforming the employees of the city into Fourth Industrial Revolution workers requires a cultural change, as well as an investment in technology. Most public workers are vocational and want to explore what new technologies can help improve the quality of their service. Therefore, they are willing to face the challenge. In a survey conducted in 2017 by Thornton Review, it was found that although 90% of city employees sought to improve their productivity, only 55% believed that they had the necessary skills and resources (*The* Thornton Review 2017). The benefits of a digitally equipped workforce are enormous. These investments improve the ability of city employees to do their jobs and increase public satisfaction. They allow workers to offer better services with the same personnel. Equally important, the opportunity to break new ground with modern technological tools also makes it easier to attract and retain talent.

When we have talked about the idea of teleworking with public administration directors, we have always encountered the same objections: efficiency will be hard to measure, we will lose in coordination, public service laws do not allow for it, etc. With the negative public image government officials have in many countries, where citizens very unfairly think they have a great absenteeism, work little and we should not hire more...imagine if we sent them home to work without overbearing over them... Once again, pandemic (confinement) forced them to do so from one day to next, and technology responded and facilitated an always-on continuum service. We firmly believe that in the private sector, technology has already demonstrated that teleworking is excellent and can be executed efficiently, and with all the controls necessary, and that in the public sector we should learn more from Dutch pragmatism and simplicity applied in Hollands-Kroon.

## 2.4.5 New DataCenters. Cloud Computing

Managing huge amounts of data and obtaining insights and knowledge from them while controlling a very complex ecosystem of people, processes and items in a city requires an equally massive amount of computing power, storage and analytics tools. So, cities have two options: the traditional self-operated datacenter, investing large amounts of money in machines, tools and the people to manage them; or trusting huge, external datacenters managed by the largest specialized computing (Cloud computing) companies in the world: Microsoft, Amazon, Google to mention the top ones. The main advantages favoring Cloud Computing are:

- The total cost of ownership falls to a fraction of the previous on-premises system (it depends on the case, but reductions up to 90% have been observed)
- In the Cloud computing model, the user pays for what they use, (pay-per-use) and does not need to make upfront investments for that which won't be permanently used. A typical example is the payroll application for a large government agency or city. This application may require a large processing capacity during the last three days of each month, while the rest of the days is only handling the few ins and outs, promotions, changes, with a minimum-needed capacity. Why pay for maximum capacity permanently (with a real machine in the office) if it is used only a fraction of the time? With Cloud computing, you pay exactly for the services you have in-use at any time.
- There are new, intensive applications such as massive-information analytics, AI algorithms, or live streaming city council sessions that would require a huge investment in resources for a limited time of use. Why buy a supercomputer that could cost several millions if it's only going to be used for a few minutes? Cloud computing allows us to provision in an elastic and scalable way, with as much

capacity as needed and paying only for the time used. For example, broadcasting a live soccer game to 80,000 simultaneous users without network problems requires a couple hundred servers and a very large bandwidth capacity. This is unaffordable for a municipality, but this same task from Cloud could cost a few thousand dollars, making it affordable.

- Systems depreciate and become obsolete quickly. Using Cloud computing, this is not your problem, since you only pay for services/benefits. You are not the systems owner, which means it is not your burden to bear.
- Maintaining your own datacenter means paying for a room, space, refrigeration, personnel, managing applications and software and hardware updates, backups, preventive maintenance, etc...all tasks that do not have to do directly with the public service we are offering. Using Cloud computing, all these tasks are carried out by the Cloud provider, and city specialists can devote themselves to thinking and developing new services, applications or improving existing ones, that really matter for the city.
- With the new, advanced and constant threats in cybersecurity, a city does not have the tools or the qualified personnel to keep citizens' information safe without overinvesting. Cloud providers know how to handle this challenge (their reputation and business depend on it).
- Moving from fixed costs to variable ones has unquestionable advantages.
- In security and reliability, Cloud systems offer the needed redundancy, resilience, multisystem based, or even multilocation structure. They are the safest information systems on earth, with the best experts and tools operating them.
- Cloud systems are much more efficient and environmentally friendly (green), so the carbon footprint produced by the city decreases. We can talk about efficiencies in terms of PUE (Power Usage Effectiveness) (42U, 2019): 1.05, i.e., 1.05 Watts used from the datacenter input power to feed processors with 1 Watt to execute real tasks. So, Cloud datacenters are extremely efficient in refrigeration, backup, resilience and general operations.
- Governments demand greater compliance with regulations such as GDPR, privacy, security, etc. Meeting their own demands can be very costly for a public institution. Cloud systems along with a methodology in the operations and use of data make it possible to comply with these regulations at an acceptable cost.

On the other hand, a small number of cities still presents objections regarding issues like data sovereignty (concern over the location of the data outside of institution walls), data commercialization (using that same data for commercial purposes; some Cloud providers are mainly dedicated to selling ads or retail goods), powerlessness over data control (losing control of data could allow foreign hands to handle citizen information). The main Cloud providers are investing hugely on Datacenters inside the borders of its regulated territory, like a country or EU, complying with the strictest regulations, hiring local people for operations, signing contracts with clear, no-data movements out of country, and providing accurate information as to where data is at any time. In addition, they protect from commercial use of the data, and do not allow for external exchanges unless a judge requires it.

## 2.5   Urban Mobility: Cities' Bloodstream

*"Urban mobility is one of the toughest challenges that cities face today as existing mobility systems are close to breakdown."* Arthur D. Little Report (Van Audenhove et al., 2018) Urban mobility is considered the most important public service provided by the city. We conducted a survey among those attending the most important worldwide event on SmartCities, (the SmartCityExpo & WW Congress in Barcelona in November 2018) and urban mobility turned out to be the most relevant service for these city technology experts (See Table 2.1).

This preference is not coincidental. If we reflect on the role of the city, facilitating citizens' ability to meet, connect, and interrelate, public transport is the means that makes everything possible. Thus, urban mobility connects people, families, businesses, experiences, economies and processes, and it gives you a good idea of what the city is like (Fig. 2.4).

If we think again of the image of Vienna as a ratatouille of geniuses, urban mobility would be personified as the chef, who puts each ingredient in contact with the others.

Citizens need to meet, and a city's center, or downtown, takes a prominent role in that capacity for meeting. Going back to the importance and the direct relationship between density and prosperity, cities should therefore make it easier for citizens to access the city downtown by the fastest and most efficient way.

Citizens are welcome, not their cars…In our Information Era, everything happens at an accelerated speed. It is true that the car took more than 50 years to become popular, but in our era, modern transport systems are very quickly adopted. Three years ago, we were able to attend the launch of the first autonomous bus at the

**Table 2.1**  Most valued City Services. SmartCityExpo, 2018 Survey

| CITY SERVICES – SCALE OF VALUES | RK |
|---|---|
| URBAN MOBILITY/TRANSPORTATION | 1 |
| SOCIAL SERVICES/HEALTH | 2 |
| ENV. SUSTAINABILITY | 3 |
| SAFETY (PHYSICAL/VIRTUAL) | 4 |
| EDUCATION | 5 |
| EMPLOYABILITY | 6 |
| URBAN PLANNING | 7 |
| GOVERNANCE | 8 |
| CONNECTED CITY | 9 |
| CULTURAL SERVICES/TOURISM | 10 |

Source: Author. Nov 2018
Survey conducted at SmartCity Expo 2018 (Barcelona). 21.300 attendees (Confidence: 95%, Error Margin: 2,4%)

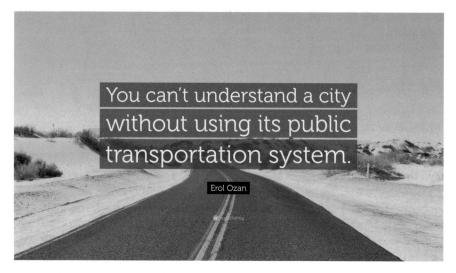

You can't understand a city without using its public transportation system.

Erol Ozan

**Fig. 2.4**  Photo from Quotefancy (2019)

SmartCityExpo, and it is already in operation (as a pilot) in several cities such as Barcelona and Stavanger (Norway). This past year, we saw the first autonomous taxi, and it will not take long to have a massive presence in our streets.

There is, therefore, a massive change in the use and expectations that our citizens have about transportation systems. This change is fueled by the revolution in electric transport, triggered by environmental, economic and health issues. The new technologies in batteries' efficiency are making the dream of an efficient electric transport which is faster, cheaper and more sustainable than the traditional internal combustion systems. Private transport is moving in the same direction. Although I seriously question this, it is reported that the amount of cars will more than double by 2050 to 2.5 billion, so if you think the roads are now at the limit of their capacity, consider the situation will only get worse. Urban development and traffic congestion are now global problems.

According to the (INRIX, 2019) Global Traffic Scorecard traffic congestion costs the economy of the United States $87 billion in 2018, and citizens lost 97 hours/year on average stuck in a traffic jam.[2] In Dublin, the location with the slowest city-center traffic speed, a human can walk at roughly half the cars' speed (5.9 mph compared to 3.1 mph).

A very illustrative indicator of transportation efficiency is the Transportation Mass Efficiency Ratio, which is calculated by dividing the effective weight that is moving compared to the total weight that needs to be moved. The most efficient thing is walking, where to move a human body of about 75 kg, one really moves 75 kg, which gives an efficiency of 1 (100%). If we go by bicycle, we move our

---

[2]Note. INRIX Scorecard Hours Lost in Congestion: The total number of hours lost per year in congestion during peak commute periods (6–9 am, 4–7pm on 240 working days per year).

weight plus that of the bicycle, say 75/(75 + 5), or 75/80, or 94%. If we drive alone by car, we have 75/1275 or 6%. Think of the worst case where we go alone in an empty train wagon that weighs 30 tons or a full train or an airplane or a boat... (75/30075 or only 0.2%). These figures relate to the energy, space needed, regulations, and time spent to move that mass.

Another excellent analysis is calculating the cost for a citizen and for society associated with each method of transport. The city of (Calgary, 2019) has made those calculations on cost/km by different options. Because of the benefits for healthcare and associated medical care savings, walking has a negative cost, biking has an overall zero cost (including the cost of the bicycle but compensated by the health savings), then Public transportation with a positive 67 $ct/km, and finally, driving your private car with almost double that number.

Main urban mobility challenges where technology is the transformation enabler:

• Reducing pollution.

This is the main reason to eliminate traffic from the city center. The harmful effects of pollution on health are more than demonstrated (Kampa & Castanas, 2008). Many cities have a pollution alert protocol in place when minimum limits are exceeded. As an example, let's look at the Valkenburgerstraat Street in Amsterdam: one of the filthiest and unhealthiest streets in Europe. Breathing there is the equivalent of smoking six cigarettes a day, as a result of a narrow street at the exit of a heavy traffic tunnel with long red lights making cars stop there for a long time ( VALKENBURGERSTRAAT, 2018).

Solutions are not unique. There are creative proposals such as installing panels that act as air filters, planting more trees, or waiting for the weather to change and receive rain or wind to clean the atmosphere. But obviously, the clearest and most obvious solution is to replace the internal combustion engines by electric ones, both in public and private transport. Electric transport begins with the electrification of all vehicles (public ones such as buses, taxis, and private vehicles such as cars and even bicycles, motorcycles and e-scooters). It also means providing the necessary recharging points (in public spaces such as taxi stops) (Norway and Holland are leading this) or in homes, so the city will be cleaner, less noisy and the transport cheaper.

In terms of energy, it is well known that the problem is not in producing it (we have a wonderful sun that provides almost all renewable energies), but in its storage (here, technology is doing its job by developing batteries capable of storing energy at a cost comparable to using the energy stored in an oil barrel). Cities see that their future is cleaner, quieter and less expensive when it is electric. New technologies in autonomous cars can only scale when the vehicle is electric. In addition, governments have established different regulatory environments that prioritize electricity and entrepreneurs who innovate in this area. The most advanced cities already hold a plan to have all public transportation made electric (California, 2029, for example). The (C40, 2017) organization made a public announcement in Paris (France) that by October 2017, the top 12 relevant city mayors (from London, Paris, Los Angeles, Copenhagen, Barcelona, Quito, Vancouver, Mexico City,

Milan, Seattle, Auckland & Cape Town) would commit to a list of targets to make their cities greener and healthier by signing the "C40 Fossil-Fuel-Free Streets Declaration". This declaration mainly states that all buses must be electric (or zero-emission) by 2025, and a main city area would become zero-emission by 2030. The belief that electric vehicles will not work well in cold environments has been proven false with the example of Norway. Norway is well known for its rapid adoption of plug-in EVs (VEP). The Norwegian government was very ambitious and has put in place policies that promote and incentivize these vehicles.

Thus, its market share reached 50% in 2018 (Shepard, 2019). And they are continuing to do so, with the firm determination to achieve a complete transformation from conventional fossil fuel vehicles into electric ones by 2025. Very soon, the VEP and battery EV (BEV) will be available for all vehicle segments. As vehicles have a higher utilization because their use is shared, (and especially those vehicles used in commercial functions where staying immobile means losing business) the need for fast charging is more important. Current technology using plug-in chargers provides a load rate of 6 miles/minute, 17 if we use ultrafast (and more expensive) chargers. If we compare this with the charge rate of fossil energy (gasoline, diesel) of about 250 miles/minute, then we can observe a large gap. This problem is being creatively resolved by taking advantage of idle downtime. Again, Norway leads this innovation with Oslo by implementing a wireless, fast-charging solution for taxis while waiting for passengers. It is not a definitive solution, but provides a charge of 4 extra miles/minute, helping to give more life to this public service. Another smart solution is the use of fast, replaceable standard batteries (such as F1 pitstops). These types of improvements are becoming popular in cities with clear decarbonization efforts such as the C40 mentioned above. London has a plan to renew its curious taxis fleet by early 2020s. Some U.S. cities such as NYC, LA, Seattle and San Francisco have committed to change 100% of the urban transport to battery-powered by 2025. This is not only due to the emissions reduction, but also because the total cost of ownership in the twelve-year lifespan of a bus reduces by about $200,000 a vehicle. In NYC alone, with about 6000 buses, this equates to an annual savings of $74 million.

- Infrastructures' capacity is reaching its limits.

We have been able to analyze it with the extensive (INRIX, 2019) report. The solution to the problem is not to build more capacity. In many cities, the costs and annoyances, including direct citizen protests on the almost permanent construction works on the streets, make it unviable to continue building traffic capacity. The solution must come from a more efficient use of the existing infrastructures capacity and the reduction of private traffic use. Only a notable increase in the population in a particular area (or its new urbanization) justifies the construction of more streets, roads and capacity for traffic.

- Zero traffic deaths. Vision Zero Initiative

Deaths from traffic accidents represent a leading cause of death in modern countries. Most countries and cities are adopting the Vision Zero initiative (Tingvall

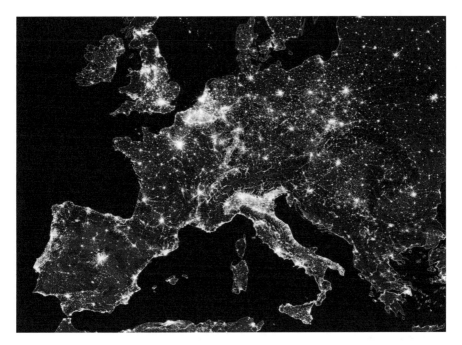

**Fig. 2.5**   Megaregions of Europe. (Mapsland, 2019)

& Haworth, 1999). Vision Zero is a project originating in 1997 in the Swedish Parliament that aims to achieve a traffic system without any death or serious injury, and establishes the ethical principle, *"life and health can never be exchanged for other benefits within the Society,"* (such as urban mobility). Improving the traffic network (like any other resource) follows the conventional cost/benefit rules. This ethical principle puts the achievement of avoiding fatalities over any economic question. It can never be ethically acceptable to have people killed or seriously injured while they move using the transportation system.

- The real *human* size of a city is determined by the efficiency of urban transportation. If we use as limit the maximum commuting time that a citizen takes to reach his city downtown, let's say for working or shopping (taking the case of one of worst traffic cities: Los Angeles, with an average of 90 minutes) then we have that our city reaches a radius of 100 miles or 160 km or a surface of 8 mHa, and growing. . .growing not only due to urbanization development, but because of the improvement in public transportation, which makes cities merge into metropolises. City corridors, sometimes international, are established. Cities merge with their regions. Paris is the same as Ille-de-France, Madrid surpasses the current Madrid Region, Brussels-Antwerp-Amsterdam-Rotterdam merge, London reaches half of England's area (see Fig. 2.5). And this must be taken into account, since from the psychological and human point of view, and well over political borders (established a century ago, or more?), all this reachable space is, in fact, the same city.

- In a context of political, economic and military stability, our vision of the world by 2050 could be summarized into a set of eight cultural blocks (civilizations), 50 megacities (cities larger than 20 million people) and around 1500 major metropolises. Advanced, high-speed trains and improvements on road transportation are creating these cities grouping on corridors, or areas of intense trading and relationship. As an example of this, you can study the *South European Diagonal* concept developed by (Fundación Metropoli, 2019), a highly reputable urban-planning strategic think tank. This European Diagonal as a mega-region of the South of Europe, is creatively connecting the very high, economic-potential Mediterranean area from Lisbon to Venice, with Milan, Marseille, Barcelona, Madrid and Lisbon as main cities and Seville, Porto, Valencia, Bilbao, Zaragoza, Toulouse, Bordeaux, Montpellier, Lyon, Turin, Genoa, Venice as mid-sized contributors. This diagonal, plus the Northwest European *pentagon* (Paris, London, Hamburg, München, Milano) constitutes the core planning area of Europe and the two main mega-regions. New *creative* transportation solutions: air, orthogonal buses, TEB (Transit Elevated Buses), drones (not only for moving goods, but also humans), tele-cabins will help to leverage space where it simply doesn't exist.
- Intelligent transportation. Advanced Traffic Control (ATC) and traffic analytics.

In addition to the already mentioned world of data and IoT, C-ITS (Cooperative Intelligent Transport Systems) which made possible the direct communication to, and between vehicles to improve the overall traffic patterns, the Advanced Traffic Control provides an integrated city, region, and country way to manage traffic flow. These technologies help improve road safety, significantly reduce levels of traffic congestion, speed up rapid response for emergency services and reduce greenhouse gas (GHG) emissions. The development of intelligent intersections, which make it possible to streamline the flow of vehicles, prioritize public transportation and synchronize communications with connected vehicles which solves one of the most important challenges in the city: maximizing efficiency in the use of public space designated for transportation. In addition, these technologies can solve the traditional problems arising from the different government structures and jurisdictions: city, province, region, and country level, which create silos of management and lack of coordination. In this way, the dream of a universal intermodal transportation system seems closer, with all the integrated possibilities (cars, buses, trains, ferries, bicycles, etc.) interconnected to provide an end-to-end service, even integrating with medium and long-distance transportation. These systems have a different implementation stages depending on the city. Basically, all cities start with the collection of data from existing traffic, level, quality, routes, schedules, capacities, etc, from cameras, sensors, smartphones, GPS from vehicles, etc. This provides a first vehicle detection and data collection. This data is analyzed so that administrators can develop improvement strategies in the network operation (such as optimizing the traffic lights' timing, adding or decreasing capacity in one direction or another, optimize routing, etc.). Prior knowledge, historical patterns and predictive analysis are fundamental tools in this decision making. The most advanced cities are starting to use Cloud-based Artificial Intelligence systems to analyze these situations in real time, allowing for direct communication with the intelligent vehicles and infrastructures, and optimizing the overall mobility ecosystem in an adaptative traffic model.

- Autonomous vehicles. Legislation. Ethics. MIT Survey

A final challenge in urban mobility is the rise of autonomous vehicles. Its advantages are unquestionable in terms of comfort. Although there has been much debate about their security and the maturity of the technology that supports them, it is clear that their massive adoption is very imminent, and their security is far superior to that of human ability. This makes us think of a future where authorities will prefer automata to humans as drivers, with the objective of Vision Zero that we covered earlier. Its advanced communication capacity within traffic infrastructure, improved by the new 5G networks, will make them indispensable for optimized traffic control. Being able to synchronize the speeds of several vehicles so they do not collide at the next intersection is something that surpasses us as humans and that today could only be reached by professional drivers with great reflexes and overall context information (just the opposite of a relaxed trip). If technology is ready, what prevents this disruptive proposal from massively reaching the market? The price does not stop falling as it becomes more popular. The main problem is the lack of legislation. It is a matter of responsibilities. Our legislative and judicial system assigns responsibility for any unnatural event to a human or group of humans. But in the case of an accident with an autonomous car, who is responsible for it? Its owner, the manufacturer, the algorithms designers/programmers...? At the moment, the manufacturers clearly indicate that the steering wheel should not be released and thus assign the responsibility to the driver. This is irony: why buy an autonomous car if it cannot be used entirely autonomously? Technology is ahead of legislation and requires an effort in this regard. A major problem is that this legislative effort should have some international consensus, as car manufacturers are international and so are many roads. By putting our lives in the hands of technology in an autonomous car, ethical issues arise. Imagine that the autonomous car is in a critical situation: there has been a mechanical failure and it has no brakes or can't stop fast enough to avoid running over someone in its path. The decision on the prioritization of which people to kill over others is a severe ethical problem, which has long been debated for humans, and which now arises for an autonomous car.

Formulated for the first time in the late 1960s, the "Trolley/Tram Problem" (Cassani, 2015) is a famous philosophical dilemma. A tram car without control advances at full speed. On its direct path there are five people who can't avoid it. You can activate a lane-change lever and move it to a different path where there is only one innocent person. Should you activate the lever to save five lives by killing one? Should you let fate continue its course? Who are you to decide over life and death?

This decision, is it a matter of quantity? Should other considerations be taken into account such as who these people are, age, sex, status, etc?

In 2014, researchers from the MIT Media Lab proposed a kind of survey in the form of an experiment called "Moral Machine" (MIT, 2019). It asked people about their moral decisions in different variations of the *trolley problem*. There was a lot of speculation on the different moral scales according to different cultures. The experiment lasted four years and got a massive response, with some 40 million responses from 233 countries, the largest ever on moral issues. The user was exposed to the "Moral Machine" on nine different situations where the autonomous car's computer would have to decide: prioritize humans vs pets, passengers vs pedestrians, number of lives (more lives or less) women vs men, seniors vs young people (Hao, 2018), healthy vs sick, high vs low social status, criminals vs innocent people. Finally, the basic question: is it necessary to decide or not, to let fate continue on its way or take control and decide, action or inaction? Dr. Edmond Awad (MIT Media Lab) concluded (Bush, 2018): "We found that there are three elements that people seem to approve of the most. They are:

- Sparing the lives of humans over the lives of other animals
- Sparing the lives of many people over a few
- Preserving the lives of the young, rather than older people"

While the first two seem clear to everybody, there are variations about the third, and many alternatives on the other questions like passengers vs pedestrians, gender, etc. If we look at the results for the test comparing different ages (elderly vs young) we find that Western countries (Europe, US, Australia) give more emphasis on saving the young while Oriental cultures save the elder. The researchers speculated on the reason for this clear distinction. Is it about individualistic cultures over collectivist ones, or is it a question of Eastern respect towards the elderly, or the development potential that is given to young people in the West, or the value of a young person in a low birth rate place like the West vs one of highest, like in East? Do we more deeply respect experience or potential, life already lived or life to live ...?

The poorest countries with the weakest legal systems tolerate more the passer-by who jaywalks, than the pedestrians who cross the zebra crossing legally. Economic inequality also influences the morality applied to people with high or low social status. Individualist cultures, such as Western countries and the U.S. gave more relevance to the number of lives saved than others. This was recognized as the value of the individual and the person as a concept and the collective as a power. In the East, culture is collectivist, but each individual puts himself ahead of others, especially in China.

If we compare saving pedestrians vs passegers, we can see how Chinese consumers would more easily enter/buy a car that protects themselves (and the passengers) over pedestrians. Highly respectful Japanese people place innocent pedestrians front and ahead. The U.S. doesn't provide a clear answer for this question as a consequence of its deep social imbalance, with individualism as a signal of success on one hand, and giving, altruism and philanthropy on the other.

So, should we adjust each autonomous car for each country/city, or according to the legislation (nonexistent until now)? Or personally, having each buyer indicate their ethics, and accordingly, being responsible for the decision consequences?

Car manufacturers are trying to produce specific cars for each market preference, but this level of personalization goes beyond any market benefit. This leads to other questions: If I have defined the ethics that apply, I should also be responsible for the legal consequences. If ethics is defined by a country (or is universally accepted), then, the car owner cannot be held responsible for the applied ethical decisions. If, as clearly shown, the ethical considerations have different valuation according to location and user's culture, should the manufacturers make a car adjusted differently for each country/city? What happens if the car moves to another country or is sold internationally? It should auto-load the new configuration when you move to another place. With the difference in laws on the death penalty in different states in the U.S., will there be different criteria, and will cars have different behaviors when crossing the state border?

If I hire an autonomous taxi, should the taxi respond to a legally established ethical scale, or change according to my values as user? Can I change the configuration if I do not agree with the existing one, accepting the responsibility?

The MIT test also points out the similarities between nearby countries and three clusters: East, West and South. We would say that it is a question of civilizations/cultures. Western civilization is present in America, Europe and Australia, so it is not a matter of geographical orientation. The main determinant of each civilization/culture scale of values is the religion on which it is based. Thus, we would have about eight different models, applicable to different areas and describing a different scale of ethical values.

This debate on the question of "Moral Machine" shows that legislation on the ethics of Artificial Intelligence is more than necessary. The question of ethics in Artificial Intelligence is bigger than a country's legislation. It should be agreed upon at the UN or obtain a similar broad agreement and involve the manufacturers themselves. Some leading companies like Microsoft are starting to seriously think about an AI Ethics (Microsoft, 2019a) code.

As soon as technology improves, we are closing the gap to building the first self-conscious machine. In that case, would the car's *opinion* count? The car will obviously try to protect itself...

Strategies. At a recent session at the largest SmartCities WW Event (SmartCity Expo & WW Congress, Barcelona), the Fig. 2.6 infographic was released describing the three main Urban Mobility strategies cities are taking, depending on density, status, available budget, and political leadership.

1. For large super-populated and polluted areas, SHARING is the key word. This is the easiest and cheapest way to reduce the number of cars. Cities like Cairo, Mexico City, Mumbai, Delhi apply this strategy.
2. For vast areas from high-income developed cities, a private car is still a must-have, so let's make it ELECTRIC (or EV, for Electric Vehicle). Wide-extended

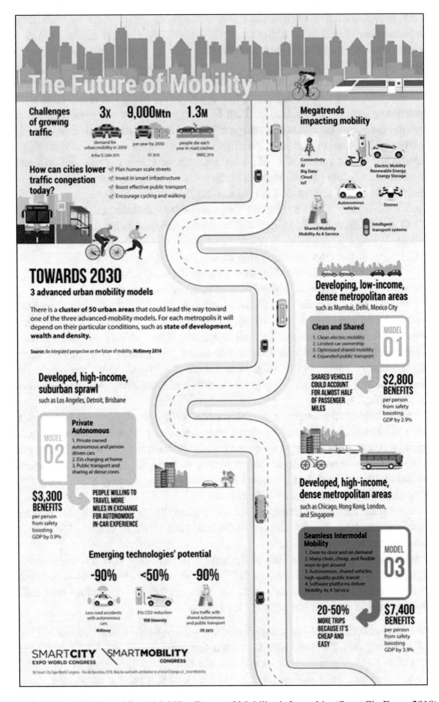

**Fig. 2.6** SmartCityExpo / SmartMobility Future of Mobility infographic. (SmartCityExpo, 2018)

American cities like L.A., and Detroit where public transportation is poor, and citizens are highly car-dependent follow this approach.
3. For dense, concentrated and developed cities, there is no space left for cars, so MULTIMODAL, efficient and clean transportation is the main driver. Intensive use of public transportation and sharing (Mobility-as-a-Service). Hong-Kong, Singapore, and most European cities are here. Space is limited and car use is on decline.

So, different strategies are put into place to achieve similar objectives. These strategies vary according to the most suitable and affordable means to be used in each case. A city that does not easily fit in any of these groups will take on a mixed strategy of the main three just described.

There are also strategies according to their application urgency. In that way, we consider three strategies: short-term (eliminate external private traffic in the city downtown); in the medium term, develop a strategy of MaaS (Mobility-as-a-Service) that encourages the use of public transport, end-to-end mobility and vehicle sharing; in the long term, we have the chance to change the shape of the city because we will not need so many vehicles: the dream of turning a city built for cars into a city built for humans.

## 2.5.1 Short-term. Avoid Private Traffic Downtown

The main and immediate objective for cities in relation to urban mobility is to reduce (or avoid as much as possible) private, non-resident traffic in the city center. The reasons are clear: pollution, lack of space, loss of time and productivity, noise, etc. Cities that create new opportunities and alternatives for pedestrians and cyclists have a greater reduction in their use of energy, a reduction in greenhouse gas emissions, and improvement in air quality and health and mental well-being. The war on the car (Sabatini, 2018) for some time in European cities is clear, where the question of space is fundamental. Areas have been defined where the use of the car is penalized, or even prohibited. These limitations start with the most polluting vehicles. The cities of Madrid, Brussels and Paris forced the European Union to set the agenda for the end of diesel, when it is more than questionable if the excessive production of NOx is worse than the $CO$-$CO_2$ produced by gasoline engines. In any case, the electric car is favored, which seems good for the city and the planet in general. The future has some clear ACES (Autonomous, Connected, Electric and Shared) cars or vehicles.

Yet, authorities cannot simply place a few signs to get rid of traffic. Citizens do not go downtown with their polluting cars for pleasure, but because they have to, and they do not have the purchasing power to change to a wonderful and expensive autonomous car immediately. The process must have its rhythm. And here, once again, Information Technology is key. First, analyze, then provide or build alternatives, then set policies and impact.

- Analyze the traffic and commuting patterns.

By using sensors, cameras and IoT devices, we can determine the quantity and quality of traffic approaching the city center every day. We have all this information about the number of cars, paths, commuting patterns, waiting time, time spent on the road, on arrival to destination, occupancy, kind of vehicle (car, motorcycle, van, small or large truck, bus), estimated pollution contribution, where bottlenecks occur, etc. Powerful Analytics are finally converting this massive data into insights. If we can determine that every day, between 7:30 and 8:00, several thousand cars leave a certain area and go downtown, arrive before 08:45 and return to that area between 19:00 and 20:30h, then we can certainly think about offering or encouraging alternatives to the car (or the highly polluting car) for that group of citizens. We want them to go to the center, of course, (remember that density means prosperity) but NOT in their cars. Weather conditions, seasonality life facts, city official's holidays, special events, and all other historical data is also very powerful information to consider. As an example, the city of Antwerp (Belgium) is analyzing these patterns with the objective of reducing as many as 20.000 cars downtown during rush hours every day.

- Provide alternatives.

Following the example, in Antwerp (Belgium), the "Slim naar Antwerpen" (Antwerp, 2019) tool offer these alternatives, combining different means (car, train, tram, bus, shared bikes, foot) to citizens. Rotterdam is offering 0.50€/per km ridden if one bikes-to-work downtown. This incentive is under consideration in Paris and other cities (Reuters, 2014b). A clear alternative is to offer parking solutions in the most convenient places, secure, cheap or free, connected to efficient public transportation, so citizens can approach the city, leave the car there, and get into the inner one-mile radius area by public transportation, riding bicycles or e-scooters, or other creative solutions. Some studies point to an average of 30% of current traffic being from those just looking for parking (with exceptional peaks like Freiberg (Germany), with 74% moving cars trying to do so) (Reinventing Parking, 2019). So, parking lots are very relevant resources, and city governments are setting strong rules against parking spaces in new buildings...ok to the new buildings, but cars must be placed under them...Parking lots are precious assets, adding as much as 67% to the cost of building a new shopping center in Los Angeles (The Economist, 2017b). Then, we can see the rise of multiple intelligent applications to help drivers find a parking spot. These new apps are so smart that they can lead the driver to the exact location of a free spot and automatically charge them for the time used, avoiding complex transactions and delays. EasyPark or ParkHelp are among the most popular apps.

Cities are investing as well in the car-sharing concept, bicycle renting, and e-Scooter renting, doing so directly or indirectly by allowing private companies to use public space to park these vehicles, incentivizing by reducing or avoiding taxes, providing free parking spaces, facilitating charging stations' deployment, and many other incentives. Car sharing (or temporal use of vehicles) or its evolution as Car-as-a-Service concept is a clear, disruptive motion. Car sharing is in its early stages, but it will become the standard for medium-distance mobility in the coming years. All main cities have a bike rental system, and this is not just a touristic benefit, it's a very commonly used service. As an example, NYC offers around 12,000 bikes from its system (Citibike, 2019). Favoring cyclists is a must, so cities are looking to the masters here: the Dutch and the Danish. In many Dutch cities, the bicycle is so popular that building enough parking for them has risen as a problem. In Copenhagen, even traffic lights have been adapted to favor cyclists over cars, reducing commuting time by 17% and 57% of the $CO_2$ emissions (Orbismesh, 2019), something critical for this city in its journey to become Carbon Neutral by 2025.

- Ban private non-residential traffic downtown.

Then, when traffic has been analyzed and alternative measures and proposals put in place so citizens can avoid using their private car to go to the city, it is when you can think about limiting or prohibiting the use of the private car to go downtown. Not before! Not before, unless the citizens' dissatisfaction and its political price is assumed. Some examples of these policies are in London, one of the pioneers in traffic-congestion charging, which has reduced up to 70,000 cars downtown daily by restricting some areas using traffic cameras, license plate recognition to fine users still entering them, and those who exceed the maximum allowed emissions (Young, 2017). Stockholm has decreased traffic by 20% by combining different technologies like cameras, sensors, data on traffic flows, etc (Cisco, 2014a). And these policies are also increasing the use of public parking open spaces as a source of funding. Barcelona is making more than $50million annually from parking solutions on streets, through sensors and related apps (Cisco, 2014b). An example of a strong controversy and citizen pushback because of outright banning without previously offering alternatives is the Madrid Central policy.Another consequence of this market shift towards electric cars is the need to build a powerful, electrified infrastructure and provide chargers in each and every public and private parking, which means a huge opportunity for power companies.

## 2.5.2  Mid-term. Mobility-as-a-Service. (MaaS)

As changes and revolutions in transport systems are consolidated, a need arises for integrated systems, multimodal services, point-to-point or end-to-end, where the user does not have to make complicated calculations to combine some systems with others: Mobility-as-a-Service. Users will pay for a mobility service, not for a vehicle ownership that just solves partially the problem, which entails many additional costs and that needs care, maintenance and space. The user needs to go from A to B by the cheapest, most efficient and most ecological way possible, combining the latest media and technologies, provided by specialized companies or provided and facilitated by the city.

- Car-as-a-Service.

Being the proud owner of a car begins to be similar to the role of the nostalgic antique collector. Why do we spend so much money, time and space on a machine that we only use 4–5% of our time? (The Economist, 2017b). In addition, buying a car is ruinous from the point of view of taxes (especially in Singapore) and depreciation (nothing depreciates as much as 27% when just leaving the car dealer). And the remaining 95% of the time the car is parked. . .anyone who knows a little about the transportation market can explain to us that vehicles should be in use as long as possible to be profitable. This also happens with airplanes, trains, and buses. Thus, its use is maximized, and its inevitable depreciation is compensated. For this 95% of time that our car remains parked, it occupies a place (parking space) that is very expensive, in the city center. We are always surprised to see couples living in a minuscule apartment whose size is almost comparable to the space occupied by their sports cars in the garage. True, the car is also a social status indicator, but it won't be for long.

For these reasons, car sales are falling and the models of property-less car use such as renting, or leasing are increasing. Everybody talks about the Car-as-a-Service model, or paying for a mobility service. Some manufacturers, car insurers and other automotive market players are making their business cases to launch Car-as-a-Service products on the market. In this model, you pay for the service or for the use of the car. It differs from using a taxi or an Uber because you are the driver, and you choose the car. Imagine a car brand for which a fixed monthly price gives us a number of car use credits. Every time we need a car, we ask for it, choosing its characteristics and the expected time/distance. The car manufacturer offers us its entire fleet and is responsible not only to produce them, but to keep them in optimal conditions, ready to be used. To go to work I need a small electric one or two-seater. I find it near my house, ready, and I pay for its use for one day using one credit. On the weekend, I need a van to go out with the family, so I will pay more credits. Or I go to a wedding with my partner, and I want a sports car, then I will pay more accordingly. I don't care about car maintenance, tires pressure, filling the tank, insurances, and most important, I don't need a parking spot anymore. . .if I already have one, I can reuse it for storage. . .Soon we will see luxury brands that offer this, then the most common ones, then brokers that will offer a many-model catalog from several manufacturers. The number of manufacturers and models will be reduced (today there are many models that share many pieces). If we continue thinking about the future and we add to this situation the autonomous car revolution, then we can conclude that we will not only not be the owners of cars, but we will not drive them either. Will the authorities take the decision to forbid humans to drive with the intention to get more fluid traffic and the Zero fatalities vision? Definitely. Those who still want to drive must go to protected areas such as racing circuits or pay a premium for doing it off-road.

MaaS (Mobility-as-a-Service) is not a concept that emerged in the last few years and is not even exclusive to the automobile sector. The first formal regulation of MaaS dates from the mid-XVII century in London. Long before Uber and others were even imagined, and more than 200 years before the internal combustion engine was invented, London citizens shared carriages. What has changed is that instead of raising a hand or handkerchief to a passing driver, we use a mobile application to request the service and make the payment electronically instead of using cash. With shared autonomous vehicles, we could dream of a city where all transport is public, sometimes by drones, and citizens only pay for the service or trip. The city delivers again its mission to connect citizens by the best possible way.

- Fleet Management. Public Transportation Optimization.

To offer an efficient transport system at the lowest cost to the citizen and with the minimum environmental impact, cities need to renew their fleet of vehicles (buses, trams, waste collection trucks, inspection vehicles, police cars, etc.) with electric ones. In addition, they should optimize their maintenance, parts, materials, supplies, cleaning. For this, modern predictive systems based on IoT and AI are used. (Example Barcelona-TMB with more than 1100 buses (Wonderware, 2017)). It is also necessary to control and optimize routes, make them more efficient, with less energy consumption, adapting them to the circumstances and user needs. The GPS, IoT, AI, telemetry and its interaction with the city allow for this. (for example, optimization of bus routes in Helsinki) (CGI, 2018)

- Door-to-door commuting.

As we studied earlier, from the human point of view, the size of a city is determined by the efficiency of its public transport: the city expands to the concept of metropolis or metropolitan area, and public transport is the key enabler. This growth is an economic, social and political challenge because the metropolitan area is much larger than the basic political entity of the original city. It is a sum of entities that must work together towards the development of the whole. When there are political differences between the small cities that make up the metropolitan area, inefficiencies, injustices and imbalances are constantly happening that citizens eventually endure. To move around this extended area, citizens need a complete integrated mobility service (MaaS) that takes them door-to-door, using the most appropriate means in each case: by foot, bicycle, train, metro, bus, etc. This coordination is not easy. It is necessary to know the status and situation of each element, its trajectory, capacity, external conditions like weather or seasonality, and cost and synchronize it with the others. To do this, the IoT world provides the necessary data from the sensorization. Previously, only the transport authorities' managers had this information. Now, all citizens have smartphone applications that, in real time, will take them through the extended city by the most optimal way (example like Waze, Moovit and others)

- Efficient systems. Area Smart Mobility Analytics

Obviously, with that huge amount of data, AI/Analytics can generate the insights needed to improve the system in general. The combination of intelligent sensors, remote monitoring, pattern analysis, machine learning and the production of intelligent models based on neural networks allow us to think about the dream of having a transport network which could dynamically adapt itself to demand, in real time and according to the circumstances. The smart autonomous vehicles' permanent interconnection with this infrastructure will strengthen this network, making it less unpredictable and more secure. As an example, take the integral management of the Porto area (Portugal) (ARMIS, 2018), the advanced analysis in Rio de Janeiro by Waze reduced traffic congestion by 27% according to analysis of the area data (WAZE, 2019), and it is helping citizens to choose the most convenient car pool at any time and location, and provide advice about *dark areas* or those with the highest crime rates.

- MaaS Payment.

Another system that is being implanted gradually in our large metropolitan areas is the integral payment for transportation. It is about making it easier for the citizen to use all the transport elements at their disposal in an extended area. Through the use of Information Technologies, a card, or an app is provided as is the case of the Hong Kong Octopus Card (HongKong, 2018), or London (TfL Oyster Card) (Tfl, 2018), or the use of any credit card in Milano (ATM). Once a month, and depending on the trips made, it is paid according to the most advantageous rates based on the citizen profile (young student, retired, etc.). These systems are so popular that they are being accepted as micropayment cards, as they are verified by an official entity. In Hong Kong, Octopus is the most used card for this purpose. Another example is Turku (Finland), which has a comprehensive regional transport system.

### 2.5.3  Long-term. Rebuild the City for Humans

Another main reason to transform the way we use transportation is the use of space. As less cars are needed, so is the space dedicated to then. So, we can start thinking about regaining spaces for humans. We can very easily understand this by looking at Fig. 2.7, where each image shows different ways and spaces needed to move the same amount of people. This opportunity to transform the city shape by reusing lost spaces allows for an entire city new urban planning and design, creating spaces for humans where before there were just cars. Cities like Madrid (placing the inner ring or M-30 into 36 km tunnels), or Seoul (making the whole city center walkable and avoiding pedestrians intersecting with traffic), or even NYC's Broadway (PPS, 2019), where half of this famous street has been regained for pedestrians, with terraces and places to meet, improving the city's capability to foster humans ability to meet, share, trade, learn...a more human city, undoubtedly.

Jan Gehl, in his book *"Cities for people"* makes a masterful description of a new way of organizing the urban planning of a city, locating the appropriate distances and the ideal spaces to encourage citizens to be comfortably talking, sharing, working (Gehl, 2010a). Cities are the catalyst for human activity (economic, social, artistic, industrial and human development). But we all know that catalysts can be positive (accelerate) or negative (retard). In the past, all human activity happened on the street

**Fig. 2.7**   Source: WeRideAustralia (2012)

(markets, agoras, important events, even executions ...). In the XX century, the car has seized the street, invaded our cities, pushing humans out from the streets. As we need less cars and use more efficient means of public transport, we have the opportunity to reconquer our streets. In the urban development of the XX century, low priority has been given to pedestrians or public space for people and high priority to traffic movement.

More space for traffic means more cars. Yet, there is no more space available. What if we try going the other direction of this equation: less space, less cars? This has already been successfully tested in some areas of leading cities. The new urban planners have to have several skills in disciplines such as architecture, sociology, data analysis technology, Artificial Intelligence, anthropology; they are no longer just designers working on a table. They face the challenge of rebuilding cities to encourage human development.

It has been demonstrated that when certain streets of the center are made only-pedestrian, the social and economic activity increases remarkably, the price of properties rises, leisure and recreation areas arise, quality of life soars, group activities are encouraged...they are humanized. *"We shape cities, and they shape us,"* says Mr. Gehl in his book. (Gehl, 2010b). Man at the center of city's activities: that's the main theme. Man as city's main attraction. (Gehl, 2010c). It is not just about making an attractive city from the aesthetic point of view (cities as an art gallery, colors, inspiring sensorial expressions) but also from the economic point of view (creating meeting/trading places). Let's think about Man. Man has a physical configuration and an attitude marked by his body. Our body has been made for walking: we have to make cities walkable; if not, we are fostering obesity and the many diseases that it entails. Our vision is frontal, and we see things poorly from above and below: we must position the city elements in that perspective. You have to think about the distances when designing the city: learn from the atrocities committed in Brasilia or LaDefense (Paris) (Gehl, 2010d) and handle distances (Gehl, 2010e) that allow human relationships (100 m for watching movement in a stadium, 35 m for seeing expression on faces in a theater, 5 m to hold a conversation, avoid noise, pollution, use urban furniture). You have to assess the facades, avoid the disruptive angles, the cold and inhuman cities. It is good to make a beautiful city, but it also needs to be one in which the Fourth Industrial Revolution can be boosted. Density is better as we already explained, but the right kind of density (Gehl, 2010f), a combination of buildings where we always allow small spaces to share areas with large ones. Build places for people to meet: pedestrian areas, democracy expression meetings (agoras), playgrounds, energy/creativity development areas, areas for sports/gymnastics, festivals, parades, fireworks, demonstrations, or simply places to sit and talk, chairs, benches (Gehl, 2010g) It's about setting priorities: first of all humans, why should I have to press a button at a traffic light to ask cars for permission to cross? (Gehl, 2010h), then bicycles, as the best tool for humans to move, Copenhagen already made that distinction. First humans, then spaces for humans, then spaces for buildings, not the other way around (Gehl, 2010i) *"Look at the cats in your city: if they seem to be happy, so will humans"* (Gehl, 2010j).

Seven images/experiences of my life remind me of these concepts:

- Teruel, Spain, small city of the interior, not Madrid, not the coast: the *deep Spain*, summer 1980, 11pm. Citizens had already finished their dinner and instead of watching television, they took their chairs out of their houses, on the street to talk to neighbors about life, the human and the divine, watching people and the stars go by.
- Atlanta (GE), U.S., downtown, summer 2010, 8pm. We arrived two days before a huge company event, nothing open, no cars, it looked like a ghost town with only skyscrapers and concrete. It seemed that something had happened that had exterminated the humans. Two days later, they opened the bars, restaurants, when 15,000 employees arrived.
- Copenhagen, winter 2015, 7°C, 8pm, longest pedestrian street in Europe, terraces with gas stoves burning, people sitting with blankets at the terrace on the street, having lively and interesting conversations, yet it was freezing...
- Lisbon, today, new area of the Expo98, very nice pavement of little, small cobblestones, impossible to walk on, impossible to carry a wheel suitcase, ladies: forget about heels.
- Amsterdam, today, the red-light district, fewer and fewer red areas and more and more restaurants: Due to global warming (and after spending some summer times in Spain), the Dutch have discovered how wonderful it is to go out to dinner with friends. Say welcome to the *Café Culture*. It was one of main factors for *fin-de-siècle* Vienna, as explained.
- Oslo, today, the Opera house mixing with the environment, roof with floor, integrated, walking to the roof from the street. Building like an iceberg floating on one side, merged with the streets on the other, wonderful. See Fig. 2.8.
- Los Angeles (CA), U.S., Tourism with the family, summer 2009, 12pm, my brother-in-law crosses a street, running to get a good perspective to shoot a family

**Fig. 2.8**   Oslo opera House. Photo by: By Rafał Konieczny – Own work, CC BY-SA 4.0

photo in front of a museum, then a patrol car stops and asks him why he runs, why he walks down the street, do you need us to drive you anywhere, any help? Kind policemen, but cities should be made for walking or running...

- Sao Paulo (Brasil), 2008 at a luxury hotel lobby, 10am, *where can I buy an amethyst (semiprecious stone abundant in Brazil)? No problem, you can take our bulletproof van to go to a jewelry located in a popular square in the city center. You can get out of the car 1 m from the jewelry store door and the driver will wait for you right there.*

So, spaces mark the life in cities, as they define the areas where humans will move and develop their activities.

There are great technologies specialized in visualizing the city (GIS), flat and in 3D, that help to redesign the city. There are technologies that based on high-precision laser (LIDAR) images (<2 cm accuracy) can obtain 360° images of the city. Over these images, advanced AI algorithms *visualize* the city and obtain the necessary information about distances and elements. On top of this information, you can overlay entire city *Digital Twins*: virtual city models, positioning on top all the other information that we already have, but now georeferenced. We can add the layers of IoT information, the data we already have from citizens, their expressions on social networks, etc. In that way, we can redesign the city, taking into accounting for exactly what we have, what we can do with the available distances and spaces, and most importantly, who lives there and what we want to achieve in the future. We can think about the future of our cities, how we would like them to be, and more importantly, we all can contribute as co-creators. Think about the urban upgrade, the city of 2030 (Beebe & Einsnor, 2019). The new concept of ideal city: the 15' city (Whittle, 2020); a city where you can reach in less than 15' commuting time, by means of public transportation or an individual electric micro-vehicle 95% of everything you need, including your job.

## 2.6   Environmental Sustainability

The re!magining Cities Foundation (Re!magining, 2019) points to three main components of Cities' Sustainability, namely the 3 P's:

People – Social; Planet – Environmental; Profit or Prosperity – Economic.

Only when all three Sustainability components are achieved, can we talk about a true, sustainable SmartCity, actively working towards improving citizens' quality of life. Some cities from the emerging world pay little attention to the environment because they face social challenges and economic shortages which prevent them from dedicating resources. So, fixing those basics is clearly the first task to work out.

Cities use 75% of the planet's natural resources, consume 80% of energy, produce 75% of global $CO_2$ emissions, and consequently generate more than 80% of global greenhouse gas emissions. At the COP21 Conference (Paris, 2015), cities took a relevant two-fold role: on the one hand, main megacities were pointed to as clearly responsible for global warming; on the other, with cities declaring their responsibility and assuming the responsibility for implementing the needed actions regardless the different position taken by their countries' politics (NYC or San Francisco vs U.S. President Trump)

There is a global alert on climate change, and a collective conscience is developing about the very serious impact that the abuse of the planet's resources will have on our lives and those of future generations. There is no longer talk about avoiding global warming, it is already accepted. Now, efforts are aimed at trying to keep it at a level with non-fatal consequences for life on our planet, and there are speculations on the maximum level of gas emissions that will not destroy it...but there is no certainty in these calculations...is it already too late? On the other hand, there are cities and countries that believe they have the right to continue polluting the common atmosphere, *because they arrived late to the table, and the most advanced countries cemented their development at the expense of contamination.* We must break this direct relationship between development and ruining our planet, find ways to use renewable energy and development mechanisms that do not have negative consequences for our common environment. There has been an increase in the mobilization of citizens over this terrible threat in recent years, and the green parties (very radical on this issue) have been incorporated into the governments of most countries and cities in Europe. From the United Nations, and specifically from UN Habitat, global initiatives on this problem have been promoted, but there are still not enough global and solid agreements.

Cities face the challenge of establishing policies and forceful measures on environmental sustainability, but this is neither easy nor cheap, and it consumes resources that could be devoted to the economic development of the city. Yet citizens, and especially the most enlightened and talented, demand a clean and sustainable city. If cities want to retain or attract them, they should be attractive in this regard. The health problems associated with pollution and the environment also push to this position. Nobody wants to live in a non-environment-friendly city. Using renewable energy and avoiding gas emissions is still more expensive than traditional systems based on fossil-pollutant energy, but the difference is shrinking and becoming acceptable and socially welcome. Our planet does not have an energy problem. We have a wonderful star nearby, the Sun, which originates diverse, inexhaustible sources of renewable energies (solar, wind, hydro, sea tides, marine currents, etc.). The problem is in storing that energy for the time it is needed. High-capacity, fast-charging battery technologies are evolving, although not as fast as others. It is estimated that by 2023, the cost of storing one unit of energy (kWxh) in a battery will be comparable to the one stored in an oil barrel. In that disruptive moment, oil producers will start to lower the price in order to compete. Those whose extraction price is high will have to stop producing, and only those with a cheap extraction cost will stay. However, the electrification of our cities, garages, cars seems inevitable. Decarbonization is underway. The question is whether it will arrive on time so that the caused planetary damage by global warming is not irremediable or even fatal.

Becoming environmentally sustainable is a must-do for cities and companies. It is about attracting citizens or clients (aren't they the same person?).

Cities want to be sustainable for various reasons: ecological, political, public health. Above all, to appeal to retain and attract talented citizens, citizens who can choose in which city to develop their life and personal and professional potential. It is also a question of prestige, but prestige is translated into a projected image, which also acts as a magnet for new generations of talents.

Companies launch internal social responsibility programs in which they invest to become carbon neutral or as sustainable as possible. They do it because they need to attract the best professionals as employees (such as cities) and also as advertising for their products' consumers. We all prefer products manufactured with renewable energy or with zero net carbon emission, unless the comparable price is very high, and, for the time being, it hasn't been found as a barrier. These tendencies, together with the social green movement, (in the good sense) push us in the direction of de-carbonification.

City de-carbonification is not cheap nor easy, but it also seems not optional if the city wants to compete in the world's premier league of attractive cities.

## 2.6.1  Resources Available

The research work done by (Global Footprint Network, 2019) analyzing the balance between natural consumed resources and Earth's renewed resources is remarkable. By 2016, we were collectively consuming 1.6 times more resources (fresh water, energy, food, materials, etc.) than what the Earth can renew in one year, so, we are overusing (or ruining) part of Earth reserves. (1.75 times by 2019). This situation can not last forever, since these reserves are finite, so if we don't stop the current rate of consumption, we will reach a time when all available resources on Earth will have been used. In Fig. 2.9, we can watch our own biological capacity by country. In other words, starting on January 1$^{st}$, and consuming them at current speed, which day of

**Fig. 2.9** Global Footprint resources analysis. Country overshoot days 2021. (Earth Overshoot Day, 2019)

the year our country's own reserves will last. It is interesting to note the high external resource-dependent countries like Qatar, UAE or the U.S., compared with other more self-sufficient ones like Vietnam, Jamaica or Colombia. Note that none are completely self-sufficient, meaning that Earth can't renew itself at our consumption speed, so natural reserves are declining every year.

Very clearly, a more efficient and intelligent use of existing resources is needed, especially of water and land, and to produce more food, while reducing overall consumption, and wasting less scarce materials. In 2019, the 29th of July marked the day of the world's having consumed the year's resources: "Earth Overshoot Day".

### 2.6.2   Climate Change. Decarbonizing. Carbon-Neutral Cities

The current concentration of $CO_2$ in the atmosphere (2019) is the highest it's been in the last three million years, with 415 ppm (particles per million) (Nugent, 2019).

The Intergovernmental Panel on Climate Change (UN-IPCC, 2019) estimates that a concentration of 430 ppm would lead to a global increase of 1.5°C. Rising up to

450 ppm would mean 2°C, and catastrophic consequences. In 2016, it was the hottest year recorded to date (as of 2019): an increase in 1.78 degrees F (0.99 °C) with respect to the XX century average (NASA, 2016). In Spain, if 2016 had the driest winter in 44 years and 2017 the wettest of the last 76, is it possible to not think something is happening to our planet? (EuropaPress, 2017)

Poor people always take the worst share of this living situation (UN SDG, 2019): 75% of the world's population lived in a low-lying coastal area in 2000, making them very vulnerable to rising sea levels, and 11% of those had no other choice due to scarce resources. There is a concentration of poor people in arid, semi-arid and dry areas which covers approximately 40% of the Earth's surface. Twenty-nine percent of the world population lives in these areas and faces an additional challenge due to climate change.

The 2015 Paris Climate Change Agreement (COP21) (EU, 2019a) was signed by 195 countries, and includes limiting global warming, adapting to it and protecting nature. To pay for all these necessary changes, 0.1% of global GDP would suffice (Conservation International, 2019).

A study in the United States, UK, France and Germany showed that road congestion costs the economy on average of 1% of GDP in wasted time and productivity loss. This not only slows down our economies, but also harms our health and the environment through the air quality worsening. Recent data show that polluted air produces almost 4.5 million premature deaths per year and impacts all other lives, especially children, with diseases such as asthma.

In the coming years, extreme natural disasters, like hurricanes, tornados, tropical cyclones, heavy Monsoon or *El Niño* conditions will undoubtedly increase.

The climate impact during the next decade is already unstoppable and inevitable, but the future impact (which can be catastrophic) depends on the decarbonization action that we must take during the next two decades. Facing this challenge also involves new opportunities for development, growth, innovation and investment in resilience by cities (McKinsey, 2019a).

Man needs to implement gigantic changes to avoid catastrophic climate change in the coming decades. Staying below a 2°C increase in global warming requires drastic changes in the way we consume natural resources, energy and many materials. This can only be possible if we deeply change the way we experience our mobility, our buildings and spaces, and the way we produce and consume food (Climate-KIC, 2019).

A philosophical reflection: we live in a positivist, scientific society. Technology will solve all of our problems. Climate change is not another problem, it is an *Armageddon* that must be stopped before it destroys us. And there is no fear of it. There is some concern but not a strong collective conscience to decarbonize everything we do. We think that technology will solve it, like everything. It is true that, without technology, we would be dead from cold or hunger, fragile animals at the bottom of our cavern, at the mercy of elements like inclement weather and vermin. I am an optimist, and I think we live TODAY in the best moment of human history, thanks to technology. The problem is that we have made it like a God, assuming that it is capable of giving us everything, including the answers to our existential questions. Serious error. We hope that someone will invent a wonderful machine powered by the sun's energy, which extracts $CO_2$ from the atmosphere and turns it into nice, cool rocks and clean, breathable oxygen. Problem solved, and we can continue playing to be mini Gods, owners of the Earth. This mistake is only human, and comes from attributing to technology a transcendent, almost divine dimension. Technology is human work, and we must never forget it. Nor must we demonize it, we must understand it and use it for the purpose it was developed, nothing more, nothing less. That supposed machine is chemically possible, but unfeasible. We do not sufficiently understand a process as complex as climate. The well-known phrase that a butterfly flutter can trigger a storm on the other side of the planet seems an aesthetically beautiful story. Scientists are not sure either that it is too late, nor that we can contain the rise in temperature to no more than 2°C, nor that this will be enough. Hands on deck! What is clear is that we have to get down to work already, as a collective massive taskforce. The great challenge is that all humanity, for the first time ever, must agree and decarbonize, in all our personal, individual and collective actions, assuming that it can seriously impact those economies that still heavily depend on fossil fuels for energy generation. Technology will be a faithful and decisive ally.

And another thought: It is ethically unacceptable that the rich countries that have mainly caused this situation due to a vertiginous and unsustainable development, will be the least affected by its consequences, while the poor will suffer terribly from natural disasters and their social impacts.

Evolution of $CO_2$ emissions from a city should set dates on this path:

NOW → NetZero (Carbon Neutral) → Net Negative → Zero Emissions Target

From positive net emissions, where the total amount of emitted $CO_2$ is not compensated by the amount of $CO_2$ that the city uses up (basically by trees and plant matter, which are the fundamental tool for fixing $CO_2$ from the air), we turn to a stage of NetZero or Carbon Neutral, where emissions are offset by green matter plus the so-called *carbon offsets*, or investments outside the city in activities that use up the remaining $CO_2$ (such as planting a forest in Tanzania, improving crops, avoiding emissions by compensations or alternatives, etc.), all of which must be regulated and certified by internationally recognized entities. Yet, this is not enough to stop climate change. In order to not exceed the target of the 2°C increase, it is necessary to capture more than what is emitted (NetNegative) (Burke, 2019) or even reach zero emissions (a scenario that will always be NetNegative because of a city's forest mass).

The first company to announce *Net Negative* plans has been Microsoft. It's the first serious movement from a leading company understanding that achieving a carbon neutral is not enough for stopping global warming: we must consider capturing the already-emitted $CO_2$ currently present in the atmosphere. The company plans to become Carbon Negative by 2030, and started investing $1 billion starting in 2020. This means to capture more $CO_2$ than emitted and remove, by 2050, all the $CO_2$ the company has emitted since its foundation in 1975 (Bass, 2020).

There are many voices that shout these facts, declaring the gravity of the situation and encouraging the formation of a city conscience and urging country managers to act. One of the most famous is the Swedish environmental activist Greta Thunberg, who at16 was able to make clear the consequences of inaction. In just six months, she gained more attention than the entire global climate change movement so far (Barclay & Bhalla, 2019).

Cities are leading the way on implementing active climate actions which create jobs in a new and dynamic sector, grow economies and create new companies, and save lives by combating its effect on health. As an example, after the political decision to become Carbon Neutral by 2025, Copenhagen ruled in 2012 that all vehicles purchased by the city would be electric (cars (Zach, 2015) and buses (Vestergaard Andersen, 2016)), and since then its growing fleet has been reducing pollution and saving money.

The European Commission is leading the environmental sustainability movement, promoting a sustainable industry and looking for profitable ways for the European economy to remain competitive and at the same time climate conscious. The roadmap for a low-carbon economy was established at the European Conference on Climate and Energy and set clear objectives for 2030 together with an objective to reduce greenhouse gases by 2050:

- By 2050, the EU should reduce greenhouse gas emissions to 80% below 1990 levels. This should be done only through domestic reductions (i.e.: not relying on international credits, or external *carbon offsets*).
- To achieve this, the main milestones are: 40% emissions' reduction by 2030 and 60% by 2040.
- All sectors of activity must contribute.
- A low-carbon transition is feasible and affordable.

To achieve this goal, the EU must continue to move towards a decarbonization of society.

The road of Carbon Neutral.

To obtain the precious *Carbon Neutral* certificate, companies and cities must follow a clear process:

1. Evaluate the starting point. What is my current carbon footprint? How many tons of $CO_2$ do we emit into the atmosphere as a result of our activity, operations, production? To do this, it is necessary to measure. Measure, with sensors (IoT) the consumption of fossil fuel energy being used, because that consumption generates $CO_2$.
2. Prioritize and implement decisions and processes that significantly reduce this carbon footprint. Contract renewable energy, replace fuel-engine vehicles with electric ones, adopt energy-saving computing solutions (automatic on and off systems, heating, intelligent buildings' management, etc.). This builds a roadmap of investments and achievements.
3. The remaining inevitable emissions (or non-avoidable in the determined timeframe) must be compensated with actions which capture the same amount

of $CO_2$ from atmosphere. For now, the only thing that absorbs and fixes $CO_2$ from the atmosphere is called *trees* (or plant mass). Ok, let's go counting trees...in the case of companies, we may not find many in our garden, but in the case of cities, this concept is very significant (parks, gardens, forests, etc.). There is an equivalence between living trees and their size and the amount of $CO_2$ they capture per year.

4. To finally achieve the goal of zero net emissions, we must compensate this final amount. It is about investing in activities that encourage the planting and use of plant material (use of compost or compostable materials from sustainable forests, planting forests, or reducing emissions elsewhere through these investments). These investments, Carbon offsets, are valid anywhere in the world because, let's remember, our atmosphere is unique and common to all of us. There are organizations that issue a valid certificate for removing these tons of $CO_2$ and fixing them in the ground that our money has paid for.

In the case of cities, we observe two speeds, or two different processes: the easy and the difficult one:

The easiest way is to achieve the status of Carbon Neutral only in city operations; that is, in the emissions produced by city vehicles, (cars, police cars, garbage trucks, fire trucks, ambulances, etc.) mayor and other officials' working trips, city lighting and other uses of electricity that comes from fossil fuels.

The complicated (or extended) way includes the energy used by all citizens (not companies). We must add each citizen's carbon footprint and thus, the total city footprint is greatly increased.

Copenhagen (Denmark) is the first world capital with a serious, clear target to become Carbon Neutral (in the extended version, including the citizens) by 2025 (Copenhagen, 2019), with a creative district heating system, leveraging all citizens' involvement (Mathiesen et al., 2019). This was a political decision which took more than 10 years and required agreement by different politicians. To make this happen, Copenhageners have to use bicycles or public transportation for 85% of their commuting. We really like this fact because it means a collective task, something to which all the citizens should contribute, all can feel proud of, reinforcing their sense of belonging, and making their city the most attractive in the world from a sustainability point of view.

Many other cities are following this leadership (see Table 2.2).

At the moment, we cannot imagine a city that wants to be attractive for talent and lead the Fourth Industrial Revolution without a clear plan to become Carbon Neutral in the next coming years.

To solve one third of the problem, we can allow nature to simply do its job. Natural solutions (Griscom et al., 2017) are among the easiest and cheapest ways to decarbonize (it seems obvious: more forests, plants mean more $CO_2$ captured and fixed in the ground). It is estimated that 37% of the needed decarbonization to achieve the 2°C target by 2030 may come from natural climate solutions like forest conservation, land management (wet, grass, agriculture). So, let's invest first in our

**Table 2.2** Main Climate action targets for main cities

|  | Denmark | 2025 |  |
| --- | --- | --- | --- |
|  | Copenhagen | **Carbon neutral target** | **Reduction in emissions x%** |
| Nottingham | UK | 2028 |  |
| Malmö, Glasgow, Bristol, Newcastle, Brighton, Zaragoza | SWE, UK, SPA | 2030 |  |
| Helsinki, Bonn | FIN, GE | 2035 |  |
| Manchester | UK | 2038 |  |
| Stockholm, Westminster, Reykjavík, Vienna | UK | 2040 |  |
| San Francisco, Honolulu | USA | 2045 |  |
| All other EU main Cities | EU | 2050 |  |
| New York, Miami, Adelaide, Melbourne, Seattle, Sydney, Washington DC, Kuala Lumpur, Tokyo, Boston, Seoul | USA, AUS, MAL, JPN, SKOR | 2050 |  |
| Phoenix | USA | 2060 |  |
| Amsterdam, Hamburg | NED, GE | 2050 | 95% |
| Minneapolis, Boulder, London, Portland, Rio de Janeiro, Toronto, Vancouver, Yokohama, Denver | USA, UK, BRA, CAN, JPN | 2050 | 80% |
| Sydney | AUS | 2030 | 70% |
| London | UK | 2025 | 60% |
| Singapore | Singapore | 2050 | 50% |
| San Francisco | USA | 2025 | 40% |
| Seoul | SKOR | 2030 | 40% |
| Mexico City | MEX | 2020 | 30% |
| Boston | USA | 2020 | 25% |

Cities websites. Data as of 2020. Author

green areas and allow photosynthesis to do its job, for free. (Nature4Climate, 2019) is a UN Initiative which tries to prioritize this.

We have the collective mission to feed more than nine billion people by 2050, while maintaining the planet's sustainability and people's health. The latest Smart Agriculture technologies using drones and sensors to understand and adapt crops' growth to weather conditions and maximize growth are revolutionizing the land yield, preserving wide forestall areas, avoiding wildfires and helping nature to make our world greener.

The objective is to maximize wood production, but not to burn it. New construction techniques will use wood instead of cement (which requires intensive carbon emissions) to build large buildings (where all that carbon will remain fixed). Organizations like (SilviaTerra, 2019) are showing the way to take care of forests.

Other tools that could be used to combat climate change are:

- Stop using coal/oil to produce energy. Use non-polluting, clean energies.
- End subsidies for fossil fuels. Do not use public money to maintain coal mining or similar.

- Reduce consumption: inform citizens on carbon footprint's association to meat, dairy, gasoline/diesel cars, energy efficiency in buildings, etc.
- Continue using existing nuclear power plants. They are dangerous, but the danger is already present, and in these moments of urgent action they produce a lot of clean energy. So, yes, we should dismantle them, but not so soon.
- Capture carbon. They are inventing chemical processes which can help to capture it in compounds such as gypsum, or calcium carbonate, or bury it.

In everything we do, in each product we buy and consume, we must think about whether or not it has the required carbon emission and try to opt for the cleaner alternative. The leading companies in the world know that consumers are going to demand this type of clean products and their employees also want to work in clean, environmentally respectful companies. For this reason, many companies detail in their annual reports the growing or complete use of renewable energies in their operations and in their products. Some detail a *Company Ethics* code related to sustainability. Many incorporate these green investments in their Corporate Social Responsibility (CSR) programs, and even encourage the development of initiatives in this sense through grants. As an example, Microsoft has a program to help develop applications that improve sustainability based on Artificial Intelligence. (AI for Earth) (Microsoft, 2019b)

According to a recent PwC report commissioned by Microsoft, Artificial Intelligence technology alone can help reduce global greenhouse gases emissions by 4% in 2030, while increasing the world GDP by an impressive 4.4% and creating 38 million new jobs in multiple sectors like water, energy, agriculture, and transport (PwC, 2019).

### 2.6.3   Efficient Energy & Water Use

Energy transition: the boom in renewable energy. Let's go electric!

It is expected that global emissions related to energy production will reach their peak by 2024 and then decrease by 20% until 2050, mainly due to the decrease in the use of coal in the electricity power sector, despite the expected growth in electricity demand. However, this trajectory is still far from the path to not overpass the 2°C increase limit.

Less carbon means more flexibility when it comes to producing electricity, and recognizing the importance of alternative sources such as sun, wind, etc. The key is, as mentioned, the performance of storage systems, batteries. As soon as we have good ones (with a larger capacity, minimal space, small weight and less required charging time), we can turn cars into electric vehicles and petrol stations into pit-stop battery replacing areas.

The intensive use of renewables is creating a massive number of new jobs and promoting the economy. Forbes estimates there will be $160 trillion in climate change costs by 2050. In spite of this, we can still see barriers to the solar power industry in the U.S., or the plans to open a large coil mine in Australia, very much contested (Ellsmoor, 2019). The U.S. is perceived as, *"a hotbed of climate change denial"*, (Milman & Harvey, 2019) accusing China of being the problem root cause. Hopefully, the main U.S. cities are acting the opposite way and taking action. In the other direction, we begin to see exciting news, like to the fact that the UK will run without carbon-based generation by 2025, already tested in a week without burning coal for electricity, something that has not happened since 1882 (Jolly, 2019).

One main power consumption area in the cities is street lightening. There are about 320 million light poles in our cities and only 1% are *smart* (they allow some communication and remote control – IoT). Intelligent lighting is one of the basic issues for any smart city. It is the most visible aspect of intelligent technology, which often paves the way for other utilities such as water to follow the example. The lamp post is used to add many other sensors and often cameras. The benefits of intelligent lighting are indisputable: it improves public safety, reduces light pollution, and saves electricity/money. The savings usually comes from saved energy (in the switch from bulbs or sodium vapor bulbs to LEDs). The Energy Savings Performance Contracts (ESPC) make these investments pay for themselves with the savings from unused consumption. They are very popular and a no-brainer for early Smartcity plans. Let's understand the process of how SmartLighting is getting integrated into the overall Smartcity energy plan. First, the simple bulb replacement by LEDs is saving up to 50% on energy. If we add additional intelligence, so we can dim lights on and off according to specific conditions, then savings can reach 80%. Finally, additional benefits arise because of integration with the overall city IoT platform.

Although electricity generation accounts for 25% of all greenhouse gas emissions, being the largest contributor to climate change, its solution and replacement by renewables must also be a boost for the economy. With clean electricity, we can not only generate the energy we need for lighting, but help reduce the other 75% of activities that also emit these harmful greenhouse effect gases. Just think about transportation, cooling and heating systems, factories, etc.

It seems clear that we must improve production, with an expected half of energy generated by renewables by 2030. It's also necessary to improve its storage, to have the energy available when we do not have the source available (no sun, no wind, etc.) (Gates, 2019) With global warming, some cities that to date had paid scant attention to having an efficient water management system, simply because it was never needed due to its abundance, see how constant leaks and old pipes are compromising the supply. Water gives us life; as a precondition for all forms of life and climate regulation, it is a vital resource that must be managed properly. Its quality, quantity, avoiding leaks, measuring its use by an integrated manner, are fundamental issues in a smart city. It is not only about the supply in homes and industries, but in the management of rivers, aquifers, wetlands and reservoirs/dams. Once again, the IoT sensors, permanent quality tests, early leak detection and consumption measurement are supported by the latest technologies. Even underground drones are available for the sewer's inspection with artificial vision. As an example of the water crisis, we can mention India. Droughts, floods, a water pipe system which is too old or inexistent, and an inefficient waste of water on agriculture has led a country with more water than needed to a crisis where 600 million inhabitants face critical problems due to water supply. Seventy percent of the country's water is contaminated which results in 200,000 deaths a year (Temple, 2019).

### 2.6.4  Circular Economy. Waste Management

Most current production systems operate in a linear fashion: extraction of raw materials, production of goods, disposal of waste. This is called the traditional, linear 'take-make-dispose' concept.

As we saw earlier when talking about the Earth's resources, we cannot continue with the current rate of Earth's exploitation. We must recycle.

If the rising demand and insufficient recycling of plastic continues its current trajectory, the global volume of plastic waste will increase from 260 million tons per year in 2016 to 460 million by 2030. If we continue at that speed, by 2050, there will be more plastic than fish in the sea... WEFORUM (Bruce-Lockhart, 2017) suggests three actions to tackle this on:

1. Rethink the use and design of packaging systems to avoid that 30% of what we produce ends up in the ground or in oceans, and that the inevitable part is the least harmful and most quickly biodegradable. So, redesign to use less plastic.
2. Make at least another 20% of plastic waste be reusable.
3. For the remaining 50% of plastic, recycling should be profitable.

In other words, apply the famous 3 R's (Reduce, Reuse, Recycle) to the plastic cycle.

The waste value chain in a city, and how waste is managed to maximize recycling and energy generation could be summarized in a linear process: Collection of matter-Processing (including Recycling and Composting)-Energy production (producing fuel or energy)-Disposal (final dumping or landfilling) (Sookyoung & Woods, 2016).

The linear consumption model is reaching its limits. The traditional take-make-dispose approach no longer works, and resource constraints and sustainability make us firmly believe that the future of our cities has to be circular.

A city with a circular economy is regenerative by design and is based on three principles: no waste, no materials obsolescence (recycling) and regeneration of Earth's natural systems.

We are generating, on average, 1.42 kg of solid waste/capita/day (2.2 kg in the OECD countries) (Kaza et al., 2018).

Twenty-three pioneer cities have signed the C40 Advancing Towards Zero Waste Declaration (C40, 2019). They commit to (1) reduce the city solid waste generation per capita by at least 15% by 2030 compared to 2015; (2) Reduce the amount of city solid waste disposed for landfill and incineration by at least 50% by 2030 compared to 2015.The decrease in the waste generation, reuse and intelligent design are aimed at making products' life cycle circular, stopping the plastic proliferation and offering advantages both to the environment and for economic development. According to the European Parliament, the gradual transition to a circular economy model could save EU companies some 600 billion euros, reduce total greenhouse gases' annual emissions from 2% to 4%, and reach a 65% city-waste recycling rate by 2035.

The circular economy is not just a new methodology to improve sustainability, it's a completely different way of developing business. Traditional and new companies that emerge taking advantage of this opportunity must innovate, taking into account the scarcity of resources and climate change, developing new products within the circular paradigm responding to the demands of consumers who want to buy these types of products and sustainable proposals. The opportunity is huge. It is valued by Accenture at $4.5 trillion by 2030 (Accenture, 2015).

This circular economy requires a company digital transformation, including its entire value chain, always maintaining the minimum consumption and maximum regeneration and reuse of materials. However, there is still a lack of awareness about the circular economy, its financing models, and how companies and cities can take advantage of it.

An important key is packaging. Some considerations:

- Replace the packages with others following a circular economy model. Work with suppliers to transition to this new packaging and manage their impact on the business.
- Develop an impactful communication plan directed at consumers about this new packaging.
- Generate new marketing strategies based on the circular economy.
- Make a transition plan to a circular economy that does not compromise the brand. On the contrary, take advantage of it to strengthen it.
- Design a new-materials, waste and polluting elements' management.

The example of entrepreneur Albina Ruiz turning waste mountains into an opportunity to generate new jobs, care for the environment, and improve quality of life in Peru in very famous "*Ciudad Saludable*" (Emprendesocial, 2011).

Very relevant to this concept is Barcelona's initiative called FabCity (Downing, 2019). FabCity points to a self-re-generation of everything the city consumes in 40 years. Started in 2014, the initiative has been endorsed in a manifesto by 34 cities (FabCity, 2019), with the aim of becoming a full circular economy by 2054. Then, the question is about distances. If we go back to the concept of an extended city, where a city from the human perspective includes everything reachable in less than 90 minutes using public transportation, then there must be enough space to generate all the city's needs. (see Sect. 2.5 about Urban Mobility). Does this sound like the Ancient Greek self-sufficient State-Cities?

Artificial Intelligence technology helps with waste recycling through advanced artificial vision-based infrared imaging (for plastic, wood, metals, paper or cardboard, glass and organic material selection and processing). An algorithm evaluates the type of material and informs the robot of its components in order to separate them, estimating the calorific waste value to be sent to the incinerator. Another solution observes waste items that are deposited into a dumpster through artificial vision. For packages with barcodes, the type of material (bottle, plastic packaging, etc.) is scanned and detected, then some *green* points are assigned to the citizen who has recycled them according to the type of material. These points will be later exchanged for benefits or discounts due to public-private agreements.

### 2.6.5  Building Management: A Pending Subject for SmartCities

Buildings account for 39% of U.S. $CO_2$ emissions and 70% of electricity consumption (EESI, 2019). In 2014, 31% of total global energy consumed and 33% of $CO_2$ emissions came from residential and commercial buildings (Ürge-Vorsatz, 2015).

From total city emissions, around 85% comes from buildings and cars (McKinsey, 2019b).

There is a significant confusion between Building Information Modelling and Building Information Management. While the first is harnessing the future design of cities and urban planning, (BIMForum, 2019) the second is critical in obtaining an efficient use of one of the most relevant assets for any city: public buildings where multiple services are delivered.

Building Information Management, otherwise known as a Building Automation System (BAS), is a computer-based system installed in buildings that controls and monitors the building's mechanical and electrical equipment such as ventilation, lighting, power systems, fire systems, and security systems. It is often confused with the term *Smart Buildings*, which mainly applies to new, advanced, fully-sensorized and monitored buildings. You can learn more about this by reading about the World's Greenest Office Building (Deloitte offices in Amsterdam, The Edge). It is a flagship of IoT and Data Management applied to buildings (Randall, 2015). More than talking about incredible, new buildings, we are going to focus on the existing huge amount of official buildings currently in cities. They are a great asset, but very expensive to maintain. Yet, technology can help with efficiency.

What's the problem?

Based on some research we conducted, a modern city has an average of one public building per 1000 inhabitants. Surprised? We were surprised too after asking this question to many cities. A city with just 100,000 inhabitants has 100–130 buildings, while a city with a population of one million has around 1000 buildings. This count excludes services not provided by the city itself, like certain schools, universities, hospitals, government offices. It only includes the city hall, districts, libraries, local police departments, firefighter stations, civic centers, social services, cultural centers, city theaters, city kindergartens. We can observe some challenging realities that are making even more relevant the need to control them, and make buildings more efficient while keeping their maintenance costs under control:

- Back to center. Movements from the past decade to place public services out of downtown are now being questioned. Long distances and required travel time are suggesting that reusing old buildings in downtown could be a better way to serve the community. They are easy to reach, well connected, and contribute to a more dynamic and vibrant city. So, cities are reconsidering the use of these available centrally-placed buildings.

- Digitalization of Public Administration requires less office space and paperwork, so many traditional city buildings are empty today. An empty building is just a cost, useless for the community (apart from the touristic value, if any). We estimate this *free space* accounts for 15% of these unused official buildings, and that is available. Many civic associations are easily getting a space to meet because of this excess. This also creates another, tougher problem: squatting.
- Cultural Heritage Buildings. Especially relevant for countries with many centuries of history, cultural heritage buildings are a massive touristic asset, but also a burden on maintenance costs. Many of them are still in use for city services. Look at any of Europe's capital cities' City Halls: you will find centuries-old, big, cold stone walls, low external natural lighting, wooden floors, high ceilings, old pipes, difficult facilities, inefficient heating system, low ventilation, almost impossible to refurbish (some are simply untouchable) —just the opposite of efficient building management. Look at (ICOMOS, 2019) (*International Council on Monuments and Sites*), an UNESCO department, to know more about the dimensions of this human patrimony. Many old European cities simply can't afford the maintenance cost and must ask for special grants from the central government.

How can technology help? A low-cost, easy-to-install, Cloud-based solution to preserve and make an efficient use of these buildings is required. Access control, and utilities' efficiency (mainly energy) are a must here. It's necessary to have IoT sensors to capture information and generate dashboards, providing the needed intelligence to make decisions on the best strategies to achieve maximum efficiency. Most of these buildings are empty during off-duty hours, weekends and holidays, so some intelligence adds important savings. There are many examples where by monitoring only the main 10% of existing buildings in a city, under an Energy Performance Contract (an energy specialist doing changes to improve performance and get paid based on savings), we can obtain a 25 to 31% savings on those priority buildings, or 15% on savings in total city energy consumption, in the first year!

The efficiencies from Cloud computing on gathering the information from IoT sensors in real time, processing it with advanced analytics, and providing accurate information to obtain savings are making a difference for these existing buildings. Plus, the solution is simple, not requiring special works or a long implementation process.

How many city buildings are waiting for energy efficiency solutions?

And savings on energy are the least of the cost savings one could obtain by applying a SmartBuildings strategy. For each $1 on energy savings, $10 can be saved on needed space, and $100 on productivity, with efficient modern workplace and smartbuilding combined technologies.

## 2.7 Resilient City. Safety. Threats (Terrorism, Security)

What is city resilience? Urban resilience can be defined as *"the capacity of individuals, communities, institutions, businesses and systems within a city to survive, adapt and thrive, no matter what kinds of chronic stresses and acute shocks they experience."* (Dawson, 2016)

City resilience is the capacity to adapt to a new emergency situation, with exceptional conditions; to resist and quickly recover from public service interruptions that have happened. Resilience to human violence such as terrorist attacks or street riots, pandemics and threats to public health, natural catastrophes and, finally, modern attacks and threats to cybersecurity, require coordinated and programmed preparation between the city and other national levels of government, businesses and citizens.

Human violence.

The nature and patterns of urban violence greatly vary according to the place and size of the city. All cities must address street crime as the fundamental basis of public safety, as well as organized crime, which includes extortion, drug trafficking and smuggling. These types of crime can sometimes be intertwined with homicides. In fact, the first objective in public security is to reduce homicides. A high homicide rate means a city with a corrupted social fabric, with no capacity for development or attractiveness for talent. Annual homicide rates of more than 10 per 100,000 residents are considered unacceptable and make the city unsafe for its inhabitants and visitors. In addition, these rates denote the triumph of evil and the weakness of the authorities to take charge, which leads to a spiral of increased violence.

- Terrorism, specifically terrorism in the name of religion, which affects a wide variety of cities.
- Other forms of disorder, such as insurgency in urban spaces.

Operational resilience.

In the daily operations of the city government, from administrative work to activities where advanced technology is used, city services are potentially vulnerable and could be stopped in the case of a specific circumstance, with the consequent physical or economic damage. This creates vulnerability in urban infrastructure, including utility networks such as electricity, gas, drinking water distribution networks or Internet connectivity.

Cybernetic Resilience

Ensure that the government can prepare, mitigate, control and recover from: attacks in cybersecurity, deliberate attacks in which attackers use digital technologies or take advantage of technological failures, access citizens' confidential data and their properties, identity phishing in front of citizens.

Natural disasters Resilience

Natural catastrophes, such as earthquakes and their consequences such as tsunamis, floods, wildfires, or rising sea level (Felbab-Brown, 2016).

With the Rockefeller Foundation's support, the (100 Resilient Cities, 2018) Association has given a very important push to this issue. Thanks to their efforts, many cities have seriously raised the concept of resilience, hired a CRO (Chief Resilience Officer) and developed thousands of projects and initiatives.

Technology plays a fundamental role in the immediate response: minimizing damage, managing the impact of natural disasters, improving quick communication and coordination, securing and protecting citizens' information, and also building a predictive system, a resilience plan and a situation analysis for rapid recovery.

The security concept entails, once again, an ethical dilemma: how far new Artificial Intelligence based systems can reach and penetrate our privacy in order to preserve our security? We have already talked about our data security, but in terms of physical security, the concern over video surveillance and face recognition arises.

In a context of threats of global terrorism, it seems obvious that we must secure the most crowded spaces, such as airports, train stations, sports stadiums, shows/spectacles areas, busy pedestrian streets, public transport, etc. For those of us who travel a lot, knowing that these places are video surveillance controlled gives peace of mind, although we pay the price of time spent in passing through the security check and knowing our face has been scanned and compared.

Facial recognition is commonly used in public spaces to identify criminals. There are thousands of cameras installed in Moscow, and after the terrorist attacks, many were also installed in Brussels (Genetec, 2015). In the United Kingdom, the police constantly compare their criminal databases with those photos taken by installed cameras. After the terrorist attacks, France deployed a complete facial recognition system at the entrance of the UEFA Euro Football Cup 2016 stadiums. The Zurich airport also uses cameras to identify faces. In Germany, the Hamburg police used facial recognition during the riots at the G20 Summit in 2017.

However, the Data Protection Commissioner of Hamburg and that of Germany considered biometric evaluation video material illegal, as there is still no legal basis for it. The problem lies in the use of this facial recognition for non-security-related purposes. San Francisco and Somerville, (MA) in the U.S. have recently banned the use of face recognition.

The arguments in favor of this decision state that this facial recognition technology can generate discrimination and abuse against privacy and equality. It points to accuracy problems and errors when processing images of women's faces and people of color. In addition, we can find the indiscriminate use of personal information. A legal study conducted at Georgetown University revealed that most American adults are already in a police facial recognition database, even if they didn't know it (O'Neill, 2019).

The pros are clear: safety improvement, crime reduction, quick resolution of traffic accident disputes, avoiding the human bias effect (or just tiredness) on emergencies decision making. The mentioned precision biases are questioned. It is explained by MIT that with adequate training, technology will have fewer errors than a human.

But the cons are strong:

Retail companies use Artificial Intelligence algorithms to analyze the dress preferences of those in front of the store window. That way, the retailer can deduce their *next logical purchase* and make a quick *special* offer. This brings memories of the absolute identity control scenario based on face and eyes recognition in the movie *"Minority Report"* (Spielberg, 2002), set in 2054. The character played by Tom Cruise had an eye transplant to avoid being identified. People were arrested before they even committed crimes...

Even the most accurate facial recognition software could be used to infringe upon civil liberties, as the MIT Technology Review (Hao, 2019) describes. The controversy arises from the ethical problem when the good pursued causes a discrimination or other evil (Kyburz, 2019). Amazon tried to sell its facial recognition system to the U.S. ICE service (Immigration and Customs Control Service) to track illegal immigrants in public places. Apart from looking like a *witch hunt*, the people detected could not receive any medical treatment in any public service, which would encourage hiding and foster human exploitation. According to this report (Joseph & Lipp, 2018), IBM used images from the NYC police department without informing citizens, in order to improve their facial recognition ethnicity-analysis technology.

Cynthia Wong, representative of the human rights organization Human Rights Watch, points out that if police surveillance is applied to public spaces, freedom of assembly and expression would be violated, because citizens would avoid participating in demonstrations so as not to be captured and categorized, analyzed and monitored depending on the demonstration's aim. She indicates that the latest algorithms will try to obtain conclusions (by comparing with existing patterns) about your identity, your beliefs, what you have done, and your potential future intentions (Minority Report again?) (Wong, 2018). The AI Now Institute (Whittaker et al., 2018) from New York University explains the impact of facial recognition on race, gender, and other personal information. There is also *affective recognition*, a facial recognition subcategory which could potentially analyze your personality, feelings, mental health status, or your likelihood to become an excellent worker. Imagine if this information were supplied to insurance providers, employers, trainers or others. There are Chinese experiments frequently discussed, which use Artificial Intelligence and facial recognition cameras in public spaces to predict whether an individual will adhere to the established rules or not, and to look for political activists. (Human Rights Watch, 2019) also reported last year that the Chinese use of software-assisted predictions based on data taken from surveillance cameras, as well as medical and bank records, has already led to suspects' arrests.

Security is a must-have, but if it needs face recognition, maybe the privacy price and risk it carries is still too high.

What is really mandatory is regulation, clear rules outlining the use of these technologies and balancing the new technologies' progress with human rights and respect for human dignity. This is a big problem for lawmakers and again, the need for a global consensus is coming back on the table (Lecher, 2019).

Some companies like Microsoft are seriously developing an Ethics for AI principles (Microsoft, 2019a), in an attempt to lead by example, and publicly committing to never placing commercial advantages over Ethical principles.

## 2.8  Financing. Avoid Tax Fraud. Cashless Cities

With a global public deficit around $4 trillion, governments need to find additional sources of financing. Increasing taxes or increasing tax burden is not the solution. The richest would leave the country, while on the other end, poverty would impact more people, not to mention the image/press impact and risk of losing voters. The clear solution is to fight fiscal fraud, improving tax systems' transparency and extract the maximum from the current system. Information technologies are key to this.

After the 2011 bailout decision (of $108 billion), Portugal had to implement all potential fraud combat initiatives to recover the economy and pay the bailout back. With a regular (on most products and services) tax of 23% (also known as the Value-Added Tax or VAT), they found no way to increase it. The only way was to make the most of it. The first action was to get unpaid VAT from small transactions, bars, restaurants, and so, have all payments taxed, even the smallest ones. To make this happen, they invented a weekly raffle among all VAT invoices issued, so you could get a coupon per each 10€ on invoice by including your TaxID (European Union, 2014). So, from April 17, 2014, onwards, the *Lucky Receipts* lottery began, modelling similar programs in Puerto Rico, Brazil and Slovakia. It allows Portuguese tax payers to win an Audi A4 car every week (an Audi A6 twice a year) just from the purchase of a cup of coffee (AT-Portugal, 2019). Citizens become civilian *tax inspectors*, reducing black-market activity, (estimated at some 25% of GDP) preventing tax evasion and unfair competition in a manner that pursues a more equitable tax system and swells the state's coffers.

Detractors argue there is a loss in productivity upon registering the nine-digit tax number for every customer who buys a newspaper, and a promotion of gambling through the use of luxury foreign cars as prizes (now changed to earning 35,000 € in Portuguese Treasure Bonds). But the benefits are clear:

- Fight tax evasion [reducing the *tax gap*]
- Increase tax revenues without increasing tax rates.
- Reduce unfair competition between non-compliant and compliant taxpayers.
- Reduce social costs through an increase in voluntary compliance.
- Citizen involvement on fighting tax evasion.

The results? About 8.5 million Portuguese have invoices issued in their names and participate in the Lucky Invoice Draw every week: an increase of 800 million euros per year on VAT, and only 9% VAT evasion. Consumption has increased 1.9%, in VAT Taxes to 4.3%. It seems the Tax Agency has discovered the beneficial effects of compulsive gambling. . .

And this is just the first step. The follow up is setting the requirement for companies with computerized accounting to produce the SAF-T audit file according to the OECD Model. This allows the Tax Agency to monitor the economy in real time, crossing invoice issuers with payers from the information contained in that XML file, preventing tax fraud and errors from large companies, and obtaining a predictive taxes model. Again, Information Technologies, and especially massive Cloud Computing Analytics make this possible.

Yet, these are just the first steps. In our opinion, the Tax Agency will intensively use Information Technologies to generate all the necessary invoices by itself. Simply connect, provide the information, and the Tax Agency will notify both parts, immediately taking its share of the business.

So how do we remove that remaining 9–10% VAT evasion? The answer is simple: eliminate cash.

Sponsored by some banks and credit companies like VISA, MasterCard, Citi, UBI, BancoPopolare, some cities have launched the *Cashless City* initiative. The Indian cities of Visakhapatnam (YO!VIZAG, 2017) and Chandigarh (Deep, 2019) claim to be the first on this journey. Bergamo-Lombardy (Guerrini, 2016) (Italy) also made a large initiative, increasing the use of electronic transactions 10 points.

No cash means all transactions must be electronic, allowing the cities and governments to track all expenses and associated taxes, meaning full tax transparency.

Fighting the untaxed, *black* economy and helping to tackle corruption seems obvious and positive (experts also believe that this will even prevent a banking crisis), but the smallest traders and poorest inhabitants will suffer. Transaction costs are fixed, so small transactions are costly, and the homeless don't have a bank account to receive your donations. Will we return to community work exchange and basic goods trading? Some cities see these social practices rising.

Large bank notes are questioned and could soon be removed from circulation. Payment for quantities larger than a few dollars must be done by credit card or transfer (as low as 70€ in Greece). Cash movements across countries are prosecuted, with little quantities allowed to be brought in by tourists. So, governments are on their way to getting rid of cash. But complete abolition of cash threatens our freedom and rights of citizens in so many areas (WashingtonPost, 2015). Central banks could apply negative interests to our deposits (they are starting to set this), so our money could evaporate, like whiskey's angels share. . . . This was already demonstrated recently by the example of a Swiss pension fund, which withdrew its money from the bank in a big way, and now stores it in cash and in vaults in order to escape the financial repression due to negative interest rates. Furthermore, central governments' hunger for citizens' money would be facilitated (remember Argentina's *corralito*).

Amsterdam could be the first main city to become completely cashless by 2030 (Weinswig, 2016), due mainly to mobile payments, while Sweden is predicted to be the first country due to the intensive use of Swish (Etienne, 2017) (a very popular payment App). Mobile payment is everywhere in Kenya, with M-Pesa. Launched by Vodafone and Safaricom, with M-Pesa, mobile phone users can transfer money and pay for products and services by sending PIN-secured text messages (no bank account needed).

Other initiatives are linking the concept to transportation cards. Transportation payment through an official card/app gives citizens the trust they need on micropayments, so these cards or mobile payments are widely used for many other consumer purposes (i.e.: Hong-Kong's Octopus **or Transport for London (TfL) Oyster Card)**

### 2.8.1  New Funding for Projects. Public Private Partnerships (PPP) and New Models for Maximum Investment

Some creative, new funding models:

- Public private partnerships (PPPs) establish public-private agreements where the private sector invests in a public project. This investment may have a mere social interest, and could try to connect to potential customers through the public project. The city should not promote a brand through ads or marketing, but if the project is of great importance, and if privacy and restricted access to citizens' information is verified, it can be justified. In general, all help is welcome if it is philanthropic. Adding a logo or a *sponsored by* label does not bother anyone and is a public acknowledgment that the company has paid for or contributed to the project. The other extreme would be to *sell* citizens' data in exchange for a private investment. This is a crime and carries a heavy fine according to GDPR. Therefore, we must be open to these collaborations without compromising compliance or ethical standards.
- Energy Savings Performance Contracts (ESPCs). These contracts allow cities to address street lighting improvement projects and others related to energy savings without having to provide up-front investments. These models are popular in the U.S. The new technology (basically the use of LEDs) means a significant cost reduction or energy savings. Because of that, the agreement lays out a constant price for a period of time which compensates the investment. After this period, the net cost reduction starts to impact the city's accounts. One day, these models will pay for electric vehicles as well.
- Investment recovery. These contracts assume that the investment has a ROI or Return on Investment in a given period of time. Cities work for the improvement of citizens' services, not for ROI, but in some cases, the savings or cost reductions justify these investments. The city doesn't have the capital needed upfront, so these contracts include an external player or financing company that is also committed in the ROI. That company gets compensation annually from the ROI or savings, and eventually recovers all the up-front capital, plus a margin compensating the risk.
- Social Impact Bonds (SIBs). Very popular in the UK, the social impact bonds are investments in which interest, or the success margin depends on the social impact made by the investment. It's not really a bond, as Return on Investment is contingent on the social outcome achievement. If the pursued social impact is not achieved, then neither the principal nor the interest is repaid. Most times, it is considered a social investment from private companies' Corporate Social Responsibility program, and return is not expected, so these are considered

philanthropic programs, but risky investments, as many times the social impact is not easy to quantify or measure. In any case, these programs are very common and help companies to improve their image as social contributors and give back to community.

- EU Grants (Structural, Horizon Europe, ERDFs, and many other). The EU wants to keep some leadership on the most advanced topics on technology. There are some specific programs to invest in cities as part of Horizon programs (EU, 2019b) and many more. Basically, the EU asks for multinational cities' (three or more) applications for grants. The grants cover 70% or more of the total project cost. Projects are mainly driven by universities, as some research is needed, but cities endorsing and showing some commitment to finally deploy the project are awarded. Topics vary depending on the main EU focus, but cover AI, Data Analytics, borders security, transportation, energy, etc. We strongly recommend all EU cities to hire a small team to proactively apply to these programs directly or to endorse an existing consortium of universities and other cities. There is a lot of funding, and the chance to get it depends on the quality of the application, but it may cover 50%-70% of costs if the application is well prepared. The result? Cities enjoy a wonderful, tailor-made project to help them design their Smartcities strategy.

## 2.9   City Main Challenges. Conclusions

- Mankind faces the most complex challenges of its history. Some seem controllable, others have effects that are still unknown, such as COVID-19 pandemic or global warming.
- To solve them, it will be necessary for all humans to work together (which has never happened before, on a planet divided into blocks and civilizations).
- Many of the massive migratory movements of today are no longer brought on by hardship, hunger or war, but by the attractiveness of living in the city that best helps develop each person's potential. The world's center of gravity moves incessantly Eastward. The human future in terms of number of inhabitants will come from Africa.
- In a context of peace and macroeconomic stability, cities no longer need their respective countries as centralized policy managers and can thus become centers/hubs of their own international development.
- In a context where machines are going to do all kind of non-creative work, jobs must evolve and take advantage of the human creativity that we all have. This allows me to be optimistic and dream of a rebirth (a new Renaissance) of arts and humanities and a special appreciation for human creation.
- Ethics becomes the inseparable companion of technological development, as new technologies have a tremendous impact on people's lives and must, therefore, adapt to basic ethical criteria and respect for human dignity. The ethics to regulate

Artificial Intelligence are already urgent and necessary, and needs a worldwide consensus.

- We cannot stop our planet's destruction from global warming if we do not all act in coordination. It will require the largest global coordination since WWII. It has already been assumed that there will be serious unavoidable damage. The objective of not exceeding a 2°C increase may not be enough to avoid fatal consequences.
- The city creates the conditions for the development of human relations, and therefore, economic and cultural prosperity.

# References

100Resilient Cities. (2018). https://www.100resilientcities.org/. Accessed 7 Aug 2018.

42U. (2019). What is PUE/DCiE? How to calculate, What to measure. 42U Solutions for the next Generation Data Center. https://www.42u.com/measurement/pue-dcie.htm. Accessed 9 Apr 2019.

6Aika. (2019). https://6aika.fi/en/frontpage/. Accessed 3 Jan 2019.

Accenture. (2015). The circular economy could unlock $4.5 trillion of economic growth. https://newsroom.accenture.com/news/the-circular-economy-could-unlock-4-5-trillion-of-economic-growth-finds-new-book-by-accenture.htm. Accessed 19 Mar 2019.

ageUK. (2018). Loneliness. https://www.ageuk.org.uk/information-advice/health-wellbeing/loneliness/. Accessed 8 Feb 2018.

Antwerp. (2019). https://www.slimnaarantwerpen.be/en/home. Accessed 3 Mar 2019.

Aristotle., *Politics Book I*, 1252b27-30, IV BC.

Armis. (2018). Intelligent transport systems. http://www.armis.pt/intelligent-transport-systems/. Accessed 10 Oct 2018.

AT-Portugal. (2019). e-Fatura. https://faturas.portaldasfinancas.gov.pt/. Accessed 2 May 2019

Barclay, E., & Bhalla, J. (2019). 12 excuses for climate inaction and how to refute them. VOX https://www.vox.com/energy-and-environment/2019/5/17/18626825/alexandria-ocasio-cortez-greta-thunberg-climate-change. Accessed 10 Oct 2019.

Bass, D. (2020). Microsoft to invest $1 billion in carbon-reduction technology. Software maker commits to becoming 'carbon negative' by 2030. Bloomberg. https://www.bloomberg.com/news/articles/2020-01-16/microsoft-to-invest-1-billion-in-carbon-reduction-technology. Accessed 27 Jan 2020.

Beebe, A., & Einsnor, D. (2019). A tale of two cities, 2030 edition. GreenBiz Article. https://www.greenbiz.com/article/tale-two-cities-2030-edition. Accessed 23 May 2019.

BIMFORUM. (2019). https://bimforum.org/. Accessed 10 Apr 2019.

Bolt, J., et al. (2020). Maddison project database, version 2020. Maddison style estimates of the evolution of the world economy. A new 2020 update. Urbanization. Our world in data. https://ourworldindata.org/urbanization. Accessed 6 Sept 2020.

Bruce-Lockhart, A. (2017). More plastic in the sea than fish? Not if we do these 3 things. WEFORUM. https://www.weforum.org/agenda/2017/01/more-plastic-in-sea-than-fish-3-strategies. Accessed 11 Apr 2019.

Brynjolfsson, E., & McAfee, A. (2012). *Race against the machine: How the digital revolution is accelerating innovation, driving productivity, and irreversibly transforming employment and the economy.* Theoklesia, LLC..

Burke, J. (2019). What does net zero mean? GreenBiz. https://www.greenbiz.com/article/what-does-net-zero-mean. Accessed 12 June 2019.

Bush, S. (2018) MIT surveys driver-less car ethics, and learns three things. ElectronicsWeekly.com https://www.electronicsweekly.com/news/research-news/mit-surveys-driver-less-car-ethics-learns-three-things-2018-10/. Accessed 12 Mar 2019.

C40. (2017). Mayors of 12 pioneering cities commit to create green and healthy streets. C40 Cities., https://www.c40.org/press_releases/mayors-of-12-pioneering-cities-commit-to-create-green-and-healthy-streets. Accessed 13 June 2018.

C40. (2019). Zero waste declaration. C40 https://www.c40.org/other/zero-waste-declaration. Accessed 18 Mar 2019.

Calgary. (2019). Travel cost calculator results. City of Calgary. https://www.calgary.ca/Transportation/TP/Pages/Travel-cost-calculator/Calculator-results.aspx. Accessed 22 Nov 2019.

Cascais. (2018). CITYPOINTS. https://www.cascais.pt/citypoints. Accessed 5 Dec 2018.

Cassani, L. (2015). Would you pull the trolley switch? Does it matter? The Atlantic. https://www.theatlantic.com/technology/archive/2015/10/trolley-problem-history-psychology-morality-driverless-cars/409732/. Accessed 27 Jan 2018.

Castells, M. (1995). La ciudad informacional (p. 67). Alianza Editorial.

CGI. (2018). Using smart data to improve Helsinki's bus system. https://www.cgi.com/en/case-study/using-smart-data-improve-helsinkis-bus-system. Accessed 14 June 2018.

Cisco. (2014a). IoE-driven congestion charging system enables Stockholm to reduce traffic and CO2 emissions. https://www.cisco.com/c/dam/m/en_us/ioe/public_sector/pdfs/jurisdictions/Stockholm_Jurisdiction_Profile_051914_REV.pdf. Accessed 24 Mar 2019.

Cisco. (2014b). IoE-driven smart city Barcelona initiative cuts water bills, boosts parking revenues, creates jobs & more. https://www.cisco.com/assets/global/ZA/tomorrow-starts-here/pdf/barcelona_jurisdiction_profile_za.pdf. Accessed 7 Mar 2018.

Citibike. (2019). https://www.citibikenyc.com/how-it-works. Accessed 17 Apr 2019.

Climate-KIC. (2019). Making an impact. https://www.climate-kic.org/who-we-are/making-an-impact/. Accessed 12 Jan 2019.

Collier C. (2019). Lonely people in big cities: How technology is both creating and solving the isolation crisis. SmartCitiesConnect. http://smartcitiesconnect.org/lonely-people-in-big-cities-how-technology-is-both-creating-and-solving-the-isolation-crisis. Accessed 2 May 2019.

Columbus, L. (2016). Gartner's top 10 predictions for IT organizations in 2017 and beyond. Forbes. https://www.forbes.com/sites/louiscolumbus/2016/10/19/gartners-top-10-predictions-for-it-organizations-in-2017-and-beyond/#758d541d59fd. Accessed 10 Oct 2018.

Conservation International. (2019). Climate change: 11 facts you need to know. https://www.conservation.org/stories/Pages/11-climate-change-facts-you-need-to-know.aspx. Accessed 13 Jan 2019.

Copenhagen. (2019). Carbon neutral capital. https://international.kk.dk/artikel/carbon-neutral-capital. Accessed 24 Jan 2019.

Dawson, B. (2016). Chief resilience officer, City of Sydney, Australia, Rockefeller Foundation. The power of three for smarter, more resilient cities. p. 6. EY. https://www.ey.com/Publication/vwLUAssets/EY-the-power-of-three-for-smarter-more-resilient-cities/$FILE/EY-the-power-of-three-for-smarter-more-resilient-cities.pdf. Accessed 22 May 2019.

Deep, A. (2019). Chandigarh all set to become India's first cashless city & here's how it will work. Chandigarh Metro, https://chandigarhmetro.com/cashless-city-chandigarh-india-first/. Accessed 28 May 2019.

Desjardins, J. (2019). Meet generation Z: The newest member to the workplace. Visual Capitalist. https://www.visualcapitalist.com/meet-generation-z-the-newest-member-to-the-workforce/. Accessed 1 Feb 2019.

Dm. (2006). CityGML: An open standard for 3d city models. https://www.directionsmag.com/article/2898. Accessed 22 Feb 2019.

Downing, S. (2019). Fab City, the global circular economy movement centered around local makers. GREENBIZ. https://www.greenbiz.com/article/fab-city-global-circular-economy-movement-centered-around-local-makers. Accessed 21 Oct 2019.

Earth Overshoot Day. (2019). Country Overshoot Days. https://www.overshootday.org/newsroom/country-overshoot-days/. Accessed 21 Aug 2019.

Eastham, C. (2009). *Guys are waffles, girls are spaghetti*. Thomas Nelson.

Ebi, K. (2018) Three new ways AI is helping cities to become smarter. SmartCitiesCouncil. https://na.smartcitiescouncil.com/article/three-new-ways-ai-helping-cities-become-smarter. Accessed 11 Aug 2018.

ECOSOC. (2008). Resolution 2008/21. p.1 https://www.un.org/en/ecosoc/docs/2008/resolution%202008-21.pdf. Accessed 28 Aug 2019

EESI. (2019). Buildings & built infrastructure. https://www.eesi.org/topics/built-infrastructure/description. Accessed 28 Mar 2019.

Ellsmoor, J. (2019). Renewable energy could save $160 trillion in climate change costs by 2050. Forbes. https://www.forbes.com/sites/jamesellsmoor/2019/04/14/renewable-energy-could-save-160-trillion-in-climate-change-costs-by-2050. Accessed 27 May 2019.

Emprendesocial. (2011). Albina Ruiz, una emprendedora social que encontró una oportunidad en la basura. https://emprendesocial.com/2011/11/21/albina-ruiz-emprendedora-social-encontro-oportunidad-en-la-basura-la-basura/. Accessed 10 Mar 2019.

Etienne. (2017). Swish, the secret Swedish FinTech payment company created by Nordic banks and used by 50% of Swedes is challenging Swedish unicorns. Medium. https://medium.com/@etiennebr/swish-the-secret-swedish-fintech-payment-company-created-by-nordic-banks-and-used-by-50-of-swedes-cfcf06f59d6f. Accessed 2 Apr 2019.

EU. (2015). Future-proofing eGovernment for the digital single market. https://publications.europa.eu/en/publication-detail/-/publication/465ec58b-e6ab-4043-9a72-5cccd2d5b270/language-en. Accessed 12 Oct 2018.

EU. (2019a). Paris agreement. https://ec.europa.eu/clima/policies/international/negotiations/paris_en. Accessed 20 Mar 2019.

EU (2019b). What is horizon 2020? https://ec.europa.eu/programmes/horizon2020/en/what-horizon-2020. Accessed 8 May 2019.

EU-GDPR. (2018). https://gdpr.eu/. Accessed 11 May 2018.

EuropaPress. (2017). El invierno 2016-2017, el más húmedo de los últimos 76 años. https://www.europapress.es/murcia/noticia-invierno-2016-2017-mas-humedo-ultimos-76-anos-20170321140121.html. Accessed 29 Jan 2019.

European Union. (2014). Improving VAT compliance. https://ec.europa.eu/taxation_customs/sites/taxation/files/resources/documents/taxation/gen_info/economic_analysis/tax_papers/taxation_paper_51.pdf. Accessed 7 May 2019.

EUROSTAT. (2009). Archive: Population projections. https://ec.europa.eu/eurostat/statistics-explained/index.php?title=Archive:Population_projections&oldid=59201. Accessed 8 Jan 2019.

EUROSTAT. (2017). People in the EU – statistics on an ageing society. https://ec.europa.eu/eurostat/statistics-explained/index.php/People_in_the_EU_-_statistics_on_an_ageing_society. Accessed 9 Apr 2018.

FABCITY. (2019). Manifesto, https://fab.city/uploads/Manifesto.pdf. Accessed 17 Oct 2019.

FAO. (2019). Libelium report inspired by FAO. http://www.libelium.com/libelium-summarizes-the-most-demanded-features-of-iot-technology-for-smart-agriculture-in-a-new-quick-report/. FAO: http://www.fao.org/home/en/ both Accessed 13 Mar 2019.

Felbab-Brown, V. (2016). Safe in the City: Urban spaces are the new frontier for international security. BROOKINGS, https://www.brookings.edu/blog/order-from-chaos/2016/02/18/safe-in-the-city-urban-spaces-are-the-new-frontier-for-international-security/. Accessed 3 Apr 2019.

FIWARE DATA MODELS. (2019). https://fiware-datamodels.readthedocs.io/en/latest/. Accessed 9 Feb 2019.

Florida, R. (2007a). *The flight of the creative class* (p. 37). Collings.

Florida, R. (2007b). *The flight of the creative class* (p. 26). Collings.

Fundación Metropoli. (2019). Territorial Diamonds. Fundación Metropoli. http://www.fmetropoli.org/en/cities-lab/territorial-diamonds/european-diagonal/. Accessed 30 Mar 2019.

Gates, B. (2019). A critical step to reduce climate change. Gates Notes. http://www.gatesnotes.com/
Energy/A-critical-step-to-reduce-climate-change. Accessed 20 May 2019.

Gates, B., & Gates, M. (2019). Our 2019 annual letter. Things we didn't see coming. Bill & Melinda
Gates Foundation. https://www.gatesnotes.com/media/AL2019/PDFs/2019AnnualLetter-EN.
pdf. Accessed 1 Apr 2019.

Gehl, J. (2010a). *Cities for people*. Island Press.

Gehl, J. (2010b). Cities for people. (p. Foreword IX). Island Press.

Gehl, J. (2010c). *Cities for people* (p. 25). Island Press.

Gehl, J. (2010d). *Cities for people* (p. 55). Island Press.

Gehl, J. (2010e). *Cities for people* (p. 33). Island Press.

Gehl, J. (2010f). *Cities for people* (p. 69). Island Press.

Gehl, J. (2010g). *Cities for people* (p. 154). Island Press.

Gehl, J. (2010h). *Cities for people* (p. 125). Island Press.

Gehl, J. (2010i). *Cities for people* (p. 193). Island Press.

Gehl, J. (2010j). *Cities for people* (p. 167). Island Press.

Gemalto. (2017). https://www.gemalto.com/press/pages/first-half-2017-breach-level-index-report-
identity-theft-and-poor-internal-security-practices-take-a-toll.aspx. Accessed 17 Nov 2018.

Genetec. (2015). Security Center is Brussels' latest move towards becoming a Smart City. https://
resources.genetec.com/security-center-unified-security-platform/security-center-is-brussels-lat
est-move-towards-becoming-a-smart-city. Accessed 29 Jan 2018.

Glaeser, E. (2011). *Triumph of the city* (p. 1). The Penguin Press.

Global Footprint Network. (2019). Measure what you treasure. https://www.footprintnetwork.org/.
Accessed 28 May 2019.

Griscom, B. W., et al. (2017). Natural climate solutions. *PNAS*, published Oct 2017, corrected Feb
2019. https://www.pnas.org/content/114/44/11645. Accessed 12 May 2019.

Guerrini, F. (2016). Cashless payments: How one city has made electronic transactions pay off.
ZDNet. https://www.zdnet.com/article/cashless-payments-how-one-city-has-made-electronic-
transactions-pay-off/. Accessed 27 May 2019.

Hao, K. (2018). Should a self-driving car kill the baby or the grandma? Depends on where you're
from. MIT Technology Review. https://www.technologyreview.com/s/612341/a-global-ethics-
study-aims-to-help-ai-solve-the-self-driving-trolley-problem/. Accessed 28 Dec 2018.

Hao, K. (2019). Making face recognition less biased doesn't make it less scary. MIT. https://www.
technologyreview.com/s/612846/making-face-recognition-less-biased-doesnt-make-it-less-
scary/. Accessed 19 June 2019.

Hollands-Kroon. (2016). Youtube. https://youtu.be/62f_ktSSMIs . Watch from 1:08 to 1:22.
Accessed 7 Jan 2019.

HongKong. (2018). Octopus – A must have accessory in Hong Kong. hongkong.net. https://www.
hongkong.net/transportation/octopus-card. Accessed 26 Oct 2018.

Human Rights Watch. (2019). https://www.hrw.org/. Accessed 2 Aug 2019.

ICOMOS. (2019). https://www.icomos.org/en/. Accessed 11 May 2019.

ILO. (2017). World Social Protection Report 2017. http://www.ilo.org/global/about-the-ilo/
newsroom/news/WCMS_601903/lang%2D%2Den/index.htm. Accessed 28 May 2019.

IndiaNewEngland. (2018). Privacy is human right: Satya Nadella. India New England News. http://
indianewengland.com/2018/11/privacy-is-human-right-satya-nadella/. Accessed 22 Jan 2019.

INRIX. (2019). Scorecard. http://inrix.com/scorecard/. Accessed 22 Mar 2019.

IPCC. (2019). Intergovernmental Panel on Climate Change (IPCC). United Nations. https://www.
ipcc.ch/. Accessed 3 Aug 2019.

ISO/TC211. (2019). https://www.isotc211.org/. Accessed 12 Feb 2019.

Jacobs, J. (1961). The death and life of great American cities, Random House, 2002 (first published
1961), republished Entrelíneas, 2013, p. 238.

Janik, A., & Toulmin, S. (1973a). S. *Wittgenstein's Vienna* Sevilla: ATHENAICA. 2017. Originally published 1973.

Janik, A., & Toulmin, S. (1973b). S. *Wittgenstein's Vienna* Sevilla: ATHENAICA. 2017. Originally published 1973. p. 39.

Janik, A., & Toulmin, S. (1973c). S. *Wittgenstein's Vienna* Sevilla: ATHENAICA. 2017. Originally published 1973. p. 50.

Janik, A., & Toulmin, S. (1973d). S. *Wittgenstein's Vienna* Sevilla: ATHENAICA. 2017. Originally published 1973. p. 73.

Janik, A., & Toulmin, S. (1973e). S. *Wittgenstein's Vienna* Sevilla: ATHENAICA. 2017. Originally published 1973. p. 45.

Janik, A., & Toulmin, S. (1973f). S. *Wittgenstein's Vienna* Sevilla: ATHENAICA. 2017. Originally published 1973. p. 113.

Janik, A., & Toulmin, S. (1973g). S. *Wittgenstein's Vienna* Sevilla: ATHENAICA. 2017. Originally published 1973. p. 87.

Janik, A., & Toulmin, S. (1973h). S. *Wittgenstein's Vienna* Sevilla: ATHENAICA. 2017. Originally published 1973. p. 80.

Jolly, J. (2019). Britain passes one week without coal power for first time since 1882. *The Guardian*. http://www.theguardian.com/environment/2019/may/08/britain-passes-1-week-without-coal-power-for-first-time-since-1882. Accessed 16 May 2019.

Joseph, G., & Lipp, K. (2018). IBM used NYPD surveillance footage to develop technology that lets police search by skin color. The Intercept. https://theintercept.com/2018/09/06/nypd-surveillance-camera-skin-tone-search/. Accessed 28 Aug 2019.

Kampa, M., & Castanas, E. (2008). Human health effects of air pollution. *Environmental Pollution, 151*(2), 362–367. https://doi.org/10.1016/j.envpol.2007.06.012

Kanellos, M. (2016). 152,000 smart devices every minute in 2025: IDC outlines the future of smart things. Forbes, https://www.forbes.com/sites/michaelkanellos/2016/03/03/152000-smart-devices-every-minute-in-2025-idc-outlines-the-future-of-smart-things/#469096cf4b63. Accessed 24 Feb 2018.

Kaza, S., et al. (2018). *What a waste 2.0: A global snapshot of solid waste management to 2050* (p. 47). World Bank.

Kennedy, J. F. (1961). President John F. Kennedy inaugural address 'ask not what your country can do for you' video. https://www.youtube.com/watch?v=P1PbQlVMp98. Accessed 19 Jan 2018.

Krishna, S. (2017). Microsoft and facebook's massive undersea data cable is complete. engadget. https://www.engadget.com/2017/09/25/marea-data-cable-is-finished/. Accessed 14 Jan 2018.

Kyburz, K. (2019). Should we ban public face recognition? TECH GARAGE. https://techgarage.blog/en/should-we-ban-public-face-recognition/. Accessed 18 Aug 2019.

Lecher, C. (2019). Congress faces 'hard questions' on facial recognition as activists push for ban. THE VERGE. https://www.theverge.com/2019/7/10/20688932/congress-facial-recognition-hearing-ban. Accessed 31 Aug 2019.

LIBELIUM. (2019). http://www.libelium.com/resources/white-papers/. Accessed 1 Apr 2019.

Madrid. (2019). MADRID TE ABRAZA. https://www.esmadrid.com/madrid-te-abraza. Accessed 3 May 2019.

Maney, K. (2015). Why millennials still move to cities Newsweek. Article. https://www.newsweek.com/2015/04/10/why-cities-hold-more-pull-millennials-cloud-317735.html. Accessed 15 May 2019.

Mapsland. (2019). https://www.mapsland.com/maps/europe/large-satellite-image-photo-of-europe-at-night.jpg. Accessed 25 Mar 2019.

Marías et al. (1983). *Ciudades* (p. 231). Editorial Prensa Española.

Mathiesen, B., et al. (2019). This is how Copenhagen plans to go carbon-neutral by 2025. WEFORUM. https://www.weforum.org/agenda/2019/05/the-copenhagen-effect-how-europe-can-become-heat-efficient/. Accessed 17 June 2019.

McCaney, K. (2018). 4 examples of how AI can make cities smarter. GovernmentCIO. https://www.governmentciomedia.com/4-examples-how-ai-can-make-cities-smarter.          Accessed 20 Sept 2018.

McKinsey. (2019a). Sustainability at a tipping point. https://www.mckinsey.com/business-functions/sustainability/our-insights/Sustainability-at-a-tipping-point. Accessed 17 Jan 2019.

McKinsey. (2019b). How a city paved the way to a new low-carbon economy. https://www.mckinsey.com/business-functions/sustainability/how-we-help-clients/impact-stories/how-a-city-paved-the-way-to-a-new-low-carbon-economy. Accessed 15 Apr 2019.

Microsoft. (2019a). Microsoft AI principles. https://www.microsoft.com/en-us/AI/our-approach-to-ai. Accessed 7 Aug 2019.

Microsoft. (2019b). AI for Earth. http://www.microsoft.com/en-us/ai/ai-for-earth. Accessed 2 Feb 2019.

Milman, O., & Harvey, F. (2019). US is hotbed of climate change denial, major global survey finds. http://www.theguardian.com/environment/2019/may/07/us-hotbed-climate-change-denial-international-poll. Accessed 22 Mar 2019.

MIT. (2019). Moral Machine. http://moralmachine.mit.edu/. Accessed 21 Mar 2019.

NASA. (2016). NOAA data show 2016 warmest year on record globally. https://climate.nasa.gov/news/2537/nasa-noaa-data-show-2016-warmest-year-on-record-globally/. Accessed 18 Jan 2019.

Nature4Climate. (2019). Natural climate solutions. https://nature4climate.org/. Accessed 19 Mar 2019.

Nickelsburg, M. (2018). Could '1984' become reality by 2024? Microsoft's Brad Smith calls for regulation of facial recognition. GeekWire. https://www.geekwire.com/2018/1984-become-reality-2024-microsofts-brad-smith-calls-regulation-facial-recognition/. Accessed 12 Jan 2019.

Nugent, C. (2019). Carbon dioxide concentration in the earth's atmosphere has hit levels unseen for 3 million years. TIME. http://time.com/5588794/carbon-dioxide-earth-climate-change/. Accessed 4 June 2019.

OECD. (2018). Governing cities. http://www.oecd.org/gov/cities.htm. Accessed 10 Jan 2018.

O'Neill, P. H. (2019). Face recognition surveillance banned by second American City. GIZMODO. https://gizmodo.com/face-recognition-surveillance-banned-by-second-american-1835945552. Accessed 11 July 2019.

Orbismesh. (2019). The anatomy of a SmartCity. https://www.orbismesh.com/the-anatomy-of-a-smart-city/. Accessed 4 Apr 2019.

Parkingnetwork. (2018). Benefits of smart parking: How smart parking reduces traffic. http://www.parking-net.com/parking-industry-blog/get-my-parking/how-smart-parking-reduces-traffic. Accessed 20 Apr 2019.

Perano, U. (2019). Meet generation alpha, the 9-year-olds shaping our future, AXIOS. https://www.axios.com/generation-alpha-millennial-children-63438b10-6817-483e-8472-38810df77880.html. Accessed 5 Aug 2019.

Plato., Republic, Book IV, 380 BC, 422a1to 425a.

Poppensieker, T., & Riemenschnitter, R. (2018). A new posture for cybersecurity in a networked world. McKinsey. https://www.mckinsey.com/business-functions/risk/our-insights/a-new-posture-for-cybersecurity-in-a-networked-world. Accessed 23 Oct 2018.

PPS. (2019). Broadway boulevard: Transforming Manhattan's most famous street. Project for Public Spaces. https://www.pps.org/article/broadway-boulevard-transforming-manhattans-most-famous-street-to-improve-mobility-increase-safety-and-enhance-economic-vitality. Accessed 12 May 2019.

PwC. (2019). How AI can enable a sustainable future. https://www.pwc.co.uk/services/sustainability-climate-change/insights/how-ai-future-can-enable-sustainable-future.html. Accessed 17 May 2019.

Quotefancy. (2019). You can't understand a city without using its public transportation system. Erol Ozan. https://quotefancy.com/quote/127686/Erol-Ozan-You-can-t-understand-a-city-without-using-its-public-transportation-system. Accessed 20 Mar 2019.

Randall, T. (2015). The smartest building in the world. Bloomberg. https://www.bloomberg.com/features/2015-the-edge-the-worlds-greenest-building/. Accessed 29 May 2019.

Re!magining. (2019). Cities foundation. https://www.re-cities.org/about. Accessed 12 Oct 2019

ReinventingParking. (2019). https://www.reinventingparking.org/2013/10/is-30-of-traffic-actually-searching-for.html. Accessed 17 Mar 2019.

Reuters. (2014a). Cyber crime costs global economy $445 billion a year: Report. Reuters Technology News. https://www.reuters.com/article/us-cybersecurity-mcafee-csis/cyber-crime-costs-global-economy-445-billion-a-year-report-idUSKBN0EK0SV20140609. Accessed 22 Apr 2018.

Reuters. (2014b). France experiments with paying people to cycle to work. https://www.reuters.com/article/us-france-bicycles-idUSKBN0ED1O120140602. Accessed 5 Mar 2019.

Rhodan, M. (2013). UN: Number of city-dwellers to double by 2050. TIME. http://world.time.com/2013/12/09/un-number-city-double/. Accessed July 2018.

Rifkin, J. (1996). *The end of work: Decline of the global labor force and the dawn of the post-market era.* : Warner Books.

Sabatini, J. (2018). The War on Cars Is Real, and It's Being Led by Cities. CARANDDRIVER. https://www.caranddriver.com/features/a25634960/the-war-on-cars/. Accessed 9 Jan 2019.

Santander. (2019). CITYBRAIN. https://www.santandercitybrain.com/. Accessed 5 Apr 2019.

Schwab, K. (2016). *The Fourth Industrial Revolution* (World Economic Forum). Penguin Random House.

Shepard, S. (2019). Oslo innovates to make 100% EV market possible. Guidehouse insights. https://www.navigantresearch.com/news-and-views/oslo-innovates-to-make-100-ev-market-possible. Accessed 23 May 2019.

Silviaterra. (2019). Measuring and valuing every acre. https://silviaterra.com/bark/index.html. Accessed 12 Apr 2019.

SMARTCITYEXPO. (2018). www.smartcityexpo.com. Accessed 20 Jan 2019.

Sookyoung Jung, C., & Woods, E. (2016). *Smart waste collection* (p. 3). Navigant Research.

Spielberg, S. (2002). *Minority report.*

STATISTA. (2018). Number of doctor visits per capita in selected countries as of 2018. STATISTA Reports. https://www.statista.com/statistics/236589/number-of-doctor-visits-per-capita-by-country/. Accessed 9 Jan 2018.

Summers, N. (2018). Google's smart city dream is turning into a privacy nightmare. engadget. https://www.engadget.com/2018-10-26-sidewalk-labs-ann-cavoukian-smart-city.html. Accessed 17 Jan 2019.

Temple, J. (2019). India's water crisis is already here. Climate change will compound it. MIT Technology Review. http://www.technologyreview.com/s/613344/indias-water-crisis-is-already-here-climate-change-will-compound-it/. Accessed 17 May 2019.

TfL. (2018). Oyster cards. Transport for London https://oyster.tfl.gov.uk/oyster/entry.do. Accessed 28 Oct 2018.

The Economist. (2017a). The world's most valuable resource is no longer oil, but data. https://www.economist.com/leaders/2017/05/06/the-worlds-most-valuable-resource-is-no-longer-oil-but-data. Accessed 30 June 2019.

The Economist. (2017b). The perilous politics of parking. https://www.economist.com/leaders/2017/04/06/the-perilous-politics-of-parking. Accessed 18 Mar 2019.

ThorntonReview. (2017). Public sector innovation and the culture factor, p. 6. https://www.cisco.com/c/dam/en-us/solutions/industries/docs/scc/digital-cities-value-at-stake.pdf.        Accessed 10 May 2019.

Tingvall, C., & Haworth, N. (1999). Vision Zero – An ethical approach to safety and mobility. Monash University, https://www.monash.edu/muarc/archive/our-publications/papers/visionzero. Accessed 23 May 2018.

UN. (2017). UN world population ageing report, p.1 https://www.un.org/en/development/desa/population/publications/pdf/ageing/WPA2017_Highlights.pdf. Accessed 17 May 2019.

UN. (2018). The weight of cities UN environment programme. http://www.unep.org/news-and-stories/story/weight-cities. Accessed 19 Dec 2018.

UN. (2019). Water. UN Peace, dignity and equality on a healthy planet. https://www.un.org/en/sections/issues-depth/water/. Accessed 23 Apr 2019

UN SDG. (2019). UN Sustainable Development goals https://www.un.org/ sustainabledevelopment/blog/2016/10/report-inequalities-exacerbate-climate-impacts-on-poor/ . Accessed 26 Jan 2019.

UNDATA. (2019). Life expectancy at age 60 (years). http://data.un.org/Data.aspx?q=life +expectancy&d=WHO&f=MEASURE_CODE%3AWHOSIS_000015. Accessed 8 Jan 2019.

UNFPA. (2018). 51st session of the Commission on Population and Development. p.2 https://www. un.org/en/development/desa/population/pdf/commission/2018/documents/openingstatements/ Opening_Statement_UNFPA.pdf. Accessed 28 Feb 2019.

United Nations. (2018). 2018 Revision of World Urbanization Prospects. https://www.un.org/ development/desa/publications/2018-revision-of-world-urbanization-prospects.html. Accessed 1 July 2018.

Ürge-Vorsatz, D. (2015) Energy end-use: Buildings. Chapter10, p.653. Germany: Fraunhofer Institute for Systems and Innovation Research. www.iiasa.ac.at/web/home/research/Flagship-Projects/Global-Energy-Assessment/GEA_CHapter10_buildings_lowres.pdf. Accessed 18 Apr 2019.

US Energy Information Administration. (2018). http://www.eia.gov/tools/faqs/faq.cfm?id=86& t=1. Accessed 1 July 2018.

Valkenburgerstraat. (2018). https://valkenburgerstraat.wordpress.com/. Accessed 22 Sept 2018.

Van Audenhove, F-J. et al. (2018). The Future of Mobility 3.0. Arthur DLittle. https://www.adlittle. com/en/insights/viewpoints/future-mobility-30. Accessed 12 Nov 2018.

Ventas, L. (2015). España: Jun, el pueblo que se convirtió en modelo para MIT por su uso revolucionario de Twitter BBC NEWS. https://www.bbc.com/mundo/noticias/2015/06/ 150625_tecnologia_pueblo_espana_jun_twitter_lv. Accessed 4 Feb 2018.

Vestergaard Andersen, A. (2016). City of Copenhagen to replace diesel-powered buses with electric buses. Green State. https://stateofgreen.com/en/partners/state-of-green/news/city-of-copenha gen-to-replace-buses-fuelled-by-diesel-with-electric-buses/. Accessed 20 Mar 2019.

WashingtonPost. (2015). https://washingtonsblog.com/2015/05/why-the-powers-that-be-are-push ing-a-cashless-society.html. Accessed 7 May 2019.

Waze. (2019). Waze Carpool in Rio de Janeiro, Brazil. https://www.waze.com/es/carpool/cities/ BR/Rio%20De%20Janeiro?city=Rio%20De%20Janeiro. Accessed 24 Apr 2019.

Weinswig, D. (2016). Europe Approaching Cashless Society, With High-Volume, Low-Value Transactions to Drive Mobile Payment Uptake, Says Fung Global Retail & Technology Report. https://www.deborahweinswig.com/news/press-releases/europe-approaching-cashless-society-with-high-volume-low-value-transactions-to-drive-mobile-payment-uptake-says-fung-global-retail-technology-report/. Accessed 19 Mar 2019.

WeRideAustralia. (2012). Camberra Transport Photo. https://www.weride.org.au/events/the-transport-photo-that-went-global/. Accessed 13 Mar 2019.

WJOSCHROER. (2018). Marketing. Research. Strategy. http://socialmarketing.org/archives/gen-erations-xy-z-and-the-others/ Accessed 22 August 2018

Whittaker, M., et al. (2018). AI Now Report 2018. AINOW. https://ainowinstitute.org/AI_Now_ 2018_Report.pdf. Accessed 26 Aug 2019.

Whittle, N. (2020). Welcome to the 15-minute city. Financial Times. https://www.ft.com/content/ c1a53744-90d5-4560-9e3f-17ce06aba69a. Accessed 7 May 2019.

Wittgensteisn, L. (1921). Tractatus Logico-Philosophicus. W. Ostwald's Annalen der Naturphilosophie.

Wonderware. (2017). Case Study TMB. https://www.wonderware.es/wp-content/uploads/2015/10/ Transports_Metropolitans_Barcelona_historia_exito_Wonderware.pdf. Accessed 28 Apr 2017.

Wong, C. (2018). We underestimate the threat of facial recognition technology at our peril. The Guardian. https://www.theguardian.com/commentisfree/2018/aug/17/we-underestimate-the-threat-of-facial-recognition-technology-at-our-peril. Accessed 11 Aug 2019.

World Bank. (2013). Harnessing urbanization to end poverty and boost prosperity in Africa. http:// documents.worldbank.org/curated/en/710431468191672231/Harnessing-urbanization-to-end-poverty-and-boost-prosperity-in-Africa-an-action-agenda-for-transformation. Accessed 1 July 2018.

WSA. (2017). City Points Cascais. https://www.worldsummitawards.org/winner/city-points-cascais/. Accessed 6 Mar 2018.

YO!VIZAG. (2017). Visakhapatnam to become the 'First Cashless City' in the world. https://www.yovizag.com/cashless-city-visakhapatnam/. Accessed 31 May 2019.

Young, J. (2017). How will the new congestion charge affect London drivers & businesses in 2017? The London Economic. https://www.thelondoneconomic.com/news/business/will-new-conges tion-charge-affect-london-drivers-businesses-2017/19/04/. Accessed 22 Aug 2018.

Zach. (2015). Electric bicycles, buses and cars in Copenhagen. EV Obsession. https://evobsession. com/electric-bikes-buses-cars-in-copenhagen-video/. Accessed 10 Mar 2019.

# Chapter 3
# SmartCities. Technology as Enabler

## 3.1 Introduction. Technology Can Help Cope with Challenges

Cities use technology to meet challenges. But, creating the best possible city is not only a matter of technology. Urban planning and development (the *brick & mortar* physical Smartcity) and a humanistic conception of that development are also necessary, always keeping in mind the impact and benefit for citizens.

We do not believe in extreme models such as Cyborg *Zero-Human* City vs *Solo Human* 100% Community City (as defined by Netexplo SmartCities research) (Cathelat, 2019a). The first is a dystopia with an entire-city, automatic cybernetic control, and the second describes a decision-making process as if it were the social conduct of an ancient tribe. We think it is about finding the perfect combination of using the latest technology with a humanistic, ethical basis, where everything is decided with the utmost respect for human dignity, but where the citizen constantly participates in decisions in which they are qualified. We consider a mistake to ask the citizen about technical or urban decisions, because that is what the city has its technical staff for. Neither for political issues nor strategy, because that is why an election is held, where representatives are elected based on a program describing all those strategies. All other issues (and there are many) can and should be asked or opened to active participation, not forgetting about spontaneous feedback, reporting or proposals.

Creating an ideal city from scratch is an ancient notion. The Greek philosophers were already playing with the idea, and the ancient empires developed the concept for their main capitals. The XIX century industrial capitalists tried it in Europe. Now, authoritarian governments such as China (Chengdu), Saudi Arabia (Neom), Morocco (Zenata), and Singapore are investing in new cities as beacons of innovation. Some democracies have also invested in new, ideal cities in their expansion plans such as Brazil for its capital, Brasilia, or South Korea with Songdo.

© The Author(s), under exclusive license to Springer Nature Switzerland AG 2021    103
J. A. Ondiviela, *Beyond Smart Cities*, https://doi.org/10.1007/978-3-030-83371-8_3

It is easier and faster to build that ideal from scratch in a new city or neighborhood, or even through expansion, than to transform an existing old one.

Cities are handling a complex reality in which technology simultaneously offers solutions to our main challenges, but at the same time, uncovers and highlights deep problems by virtually allowing the entire population to have access to communicate, express their opinion, denounce an inequality, know the possibilities and demand them. That's because of XXI century technology access democratization: citizens are becoming massively digital, so new technologies are inherent to whatever they do.

City leaders desperately need help in two main areas: Knowledge and Financing.

The world's major cities play an increasingly important role in the XXI century global power distribution. City-level government policy decisions impact major international problems, such as climate change, housing, transportation, security, social services and financial and commercial developments.

To be effective, a city's ecosystem cannot be limited to the political or physical city boundaries. Central/federal governments must be key partners for these ecosystems. Two important reasons for this are:

- Central/federal governments are increasingly awakening to the importance of cities, and the need to establish future city development plans. Significant amounts of state funding have been made available in Europe, (through the European Union and national governments) and in many other countries around the world to support these plans: constant dialogue is key to be well positioned to take advantage of these financing opportunities.
- The future cities' initiatives have regulatory implications that must be studied at national and international level (either the need to change existing regulations or create regulations for completely new ways of interacting with citizens. This is especially necessary to regulate the ethical use of new technologies such as video surveillance, virtual identity, autonomous systems and Artificial Intelligence).

Collaboration with other cities / regions is also key for several reasons:

- Be able to take advantage of lessons learned, knowledge and solutions in all cities, avoiding the *reinvention of the wheel*.
- Find the synergies to undertake large investments in technologies and solutions that, without the collaboration from a group of cities, would not have the size to be economically justifiable.
- Be able to compete for funding opportunities that require collaboration between multiple cities and partners (as is the case with European Union grants, HorizonEurope, and others)

While it is clear that city leaders recognize that smart technologies can help address the XXI century challenges and improve quality of life, economic opportunities and livability of their cities, they often have extreme difficulty in finding financing for smart city projects. Promoting solutions based only on laboratory pilots or research projects to commercial deployments is especially difficult for many cities.

**Fig. 3.1** Governance vs
Technology for SmartCities.
(Source: Author)

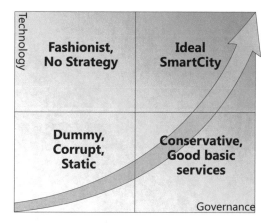

To better illustrate the impact of technology on the city management and its evolution, we have drafted the following chart in Fig. 3.1.

Fix the basics: In the lower left corner, we can find cities with poor governance and little or no use of technology. These cities barely know their citizens except to collect taxes. City government does not respond to the basic needs in infrastructure and services, either due to corruption or extreme poverty. Urban development is randomly done as a dummy houses' agglomeration. The city's future is very much in question, and citizens will basically try to find better opportunities far away as soon as they can.

Embrace Technology: In the lower right corner we can find cities with poor use of technology for many reasons: lack of professionals, planning, strategy, the mayor's leadership, fear of new technologies' challenges. Governance is right: things happen on time, within budget, and the city functions. But citizens are way ahead of the city in terms of embracing technology, and they demand the same level of quality services they get from private sector (retail, banks) now from public city services. Most cities have some development areas in this stage due to area managers' inaction, lack of funding or conformism/reluctance to change. Some cities are here because they don't perceive the need to invest in the latest technologies because they are already very attractive to talent due to some specific country conditions (some Swiss cities), but this is changing.

Populist, Press-driven technologists: In the top left corner, we can find fashionable, strategy-less cities. When we study a SmartCity plan and we find dozens of little, nice, press-oriented actions without a main clear strategy or list of priorities, then we understand that city is using the SmartCities motion to *sell action*, but real implementation is poor. Innovation is used in front of the press for electoral purposes or to hide some chronic main internal issues, like populist propaganda. Again, all cities have some areas/projects around this concept. We need to understand the need to go to the press to demonstrate small, quick wins in order to justify a mid/long-term strategy. That's ok, but if we can't find anything else but scattered, low-impact and

**Fig. 3.2** City of Bodegraven, (The Netherlands) LED light strips on the sidewalk synchronized with traffic signals. (Contreras, 2017)

high-visibility projects, then technology is just a shiny façade, not an impactful enabler.

Finally, the top right corner includes the balance between intensive use of the latest technology, and the need to have better governance, better-informed decisions, fully integrating citizens' opinions and contributions and creating an inclusive, resilient, sustainable and advanced city.

To provide an example from a city well-positioned in this magic quadrant, let us mention Helsinki. *"Smart is not just about technology. Technology is only a tool to achieve more human goals, such as strengthening democracy, increasing resident participation, boosting mobility, increasing trust, being more inclusive and helping the environment."* Anni Sinnemäki, Helsinki Deputy Major.

There are many smart solutions that do not necessarily involve the use of advanced information systems, such as special, walking-with-phone lanes in Chong-qing, Buenos Aires' traffic lights installed in the ground, and countless urban elements such as urban furniture, ambient marketing (using public spaces and transportation vehicles to advertise services or public proposals), city beacons (high-bandwidth connected totems that interact with citizens), projections on the bus stops' ground, or simply a red line illumination at cross walks, so that teenagers smartphone users with their heads down do not cross on red. (See Fig. 3.2)

For most cities, becoming a smart city is no longer an option, it is essential. Technology is taking a growing role in cities' evolution and growth.

Apart from all the challenges described before, new technologies are catalyzing many other global trends, such as the sharing revolution. The increasing use of digital platforms and mobile applications are catalyzing the development of the shared economy, and peer-to-peer business models are becoming more common. Urban shared mobility (bicycle sharing, public bicycle sharing, car sharing, scooters sharing and smart parking) is an area that has undergone a major transformation because of these models.

## 3.2   What's a SmartCity?

The *Smart City* concept is much too simple an expression to describe a very complex environment, a multidimensional reality where technology, urban and human city development are combined. How can cities intelligently respond to the challenges posed in Chap. 2, such as achieving the city decarbonization, eliminating pollution, violence or human and natural hazards, achieving a dynamic and efficient urban mobility system, offering social services demanded by an aging society, all while promoting the education, employability and welfare of their citizens?

### 3.2.1   Balancing Technological Innovation with Citizens' Quality of Life

How can we balance technological innovation with noble human aspirations in terms of quality of life? This concept is not only complex and multifaceted: it is an evolving system, which emphasizes different priorities as the city progresses. We will see later the different phases by which it develops.

In 2009, IBM was the first company to talk about *Smarter Cities*, understanding the fast-growing importance of cities in the global context, the scarce or very limited use of technology they had, (and therefore the great opportunity for modernization) and the citizens exponential demand for digital services. Its proposal was, *"A comprehensive approach to help cities function more efficiently, save money and resources, and improve the quality of life of citizens."*(IBM 100, 2018) Under a strong decline in its consulting business, IBM had a legion of consultants sitting with their *arms crossed* that it could use to *donate* projects to certain selected cities to achieve a strong position and experience in this new and huge market.

The rest of the large, technology consulting companies like KPMG, PwC, Deloitte, EY and CapGemini applauded and endorsed this bet and the *SmartCities* concept was popularized, especially in Europe. Only one important accelerator was needed: financing. Soon, the European Union understood that this line of innovation fit perfectly in its investment in innovation to maintain some leadership ahead of the U.S. and China, and assigned an important part of its EU FP7 research grants and structural programs, and subsequently Horizon2020 (EU Horizon2020, 2018) to this concept. Then, we began to see very innovative large projects led by major European cities such as Amsterdam, Barcelona, Helsinki, Manchester...

From that moment on, every relevant city wanted to address the issue and position itself as an innovative city: the competition to attract talent was intensifying with the evolution of Information Technologies. Thus, groups of cities, associations such as (Eurocities, 2018), (Major Cities of Europe, 2018) and others were organized to jointly access European funding. In addition, each country developed its events and meetings to discuss the issue and share experiences. The world's largest SmartCities event, the (SmartCity Expo, 2018) & WW Congress held in Barcelona every November, started in 2011, as a demonstration of the latest state-of-the-art technology applied to cities. It is a remarkable, unusual event, where demand and supply are in the same expo. Thus, technology companies showcase their latest innovations in front of city stands that also show their latest projects, in their eagerness to demonstrate their leadership in innovation and their attractiveness.

The SmartCity concept has different definitions depending on who proposes them.

In their research, Professor (Albino et al., 2015) and (Gil-García et al., 2015) mention no less than 20 definitions from different authors.

The most technological entities focus more on technology's role, while politicians and civic organizations highlight the improvement in citizens' quality of life.

As examples of definitions loaded towards the technology side, we mention: the (Smart Cities Council, 2018) (a group of leading companies advised by top universities, research laboratories and standardization bodies aiming to help or sell consultancy services to cities) definition of the term, *"a smart city uses Information and Communications Technology to enhance a city's livability, workability, and sustainability. A city in which digital technologies are integrated into all the functions of the city. We envision a world where digital technology and intelligent design have been harnessed to create smart, sustainable cities with high-quality living and high-quality jobs. A Smart City can be defined as multiple, integrated information and communication technology, as well as the Internet of Things, (IoT) solutions to manage the assets and operations of a city. The IoT is challenging the way people live and work, and how government and businesses interact. This new ecosystem forms the foundation for Smart Cities."*

What constitutes a SmartCity is not well defined. In the broadest sense, a Smart City is one that uses electronic means to provide services to its residents. The value of the data that comes mainly from the IoT world and that allows us to control the city from the physical point of view is emphasized. In these definitions, human issues and the role of citizens are presupposed, but not specified. With the arrival of Artificial Intelligence, you have the opportunity to turn all that huge mountain of data into knowledge, and bring technology closer to the citizen (who are very well equipped with a smartphone). But there is also the friction (Rosenbaum, 2018) of super-automating or dehumanizing the city management, regulating the Artificial Intelligence ethical limits, and establishing the trust boundaries between what a city official should continue to do and what an automated system can do instead.

On the opposite side, criticisms have arisen regarding the exaggerated value given to the SmartCity concept, used by many cities as part of its image and branding and the fascination for new technologies, forgetting about citizens. This article (Keeton,

2019) is very critical and even talks about *stupid* SmartCities. It explains that a truly intelligent city must leave room for spontaneity, participation and grassroots citizen initiatives. Instead of so much control, it should collect diversity and offer transparency by default in all activities. The city must only be a reflection of its citizens and their collective desires.

From the most human point of view, highlighting the quality-of-life improvement as the main objective, with technology as a means, we can find some definitions from politicians:

> *A smart city involves relevant use of new technologies to serve the daily needs of city residents, equitably share technological progress, accepted by residents who perceive an answer to their needs, after being informed, made aware and encouraged to express their needs and participate.* Miguel Gamiño (former CIO of San Francisco and CTO of New York City) (Alphonse, 2018)

> *When I think of technology and investing in a SmartCity, it's how a city adapts, using data to get on the front end of a problem, rather than on the back end. Technology is a means, not an end, to help the public.* (Walker, 2018) Rahm Emanuel, Mayor of Chicago.

> *The objective is to promote cities that will provide their citizens with essential infrastructure and decent quality of life, in a context of sustainable development and by applying smart solutions. This development must be inclusive.* Ministry of Urban Development of the (Government of India, 2019).

Obviously, the most commonly accepted definition is a balanced midpoint between the use of the latest state-of-art technology, and the benefit of fully-engaged and participative citizens.

Today, however, we are starting to see the turn from the *very-focused on sensors and data initial SmartCities*, to some new approaches that, taking advantage of technology, involve not only the city government, but also citizens, visitors and companies in a smart and connected ecosystem.

It is about improving the citizen experience by operating at the intersection of the 3Ds: Data, Digital and human-centered Design (Eggers & Skowron, 2018). Data is key and is the information base that operates with the rest of areas. As Barcelona mayor Xavier Trías said at SmartCityExpo, Barcelona, 2014, *"To rule the city I just need data, not opinions, rumors or partial surveys. Give me data and we will make decisions."* The objective is to allow a better decision-making process through the use of data by all interested parties: government, companies and citizens.

The focus of any Smart City should be its people, providing benefits such as:

- A better quality of life for citizens and visitors
- Security and physical and virtual resilience
- Economic competitiveness to attract industry and talent
- Environmental sustainability

Another balanced definition comes from the United Cities and Local Governments Association (UCLG, 2019a), *"A city can be defined as a SmartCity when it shows good performance in these three fields (Entrepreneurship and generation of economic activity, Knowledge and Talent, Digital Society and Economy), and when it has been built based on a Smart combination of elements (communications, infrastructure, economic development) and on purposeful and independent citizen activities (participation, education) that allow for sound management of the available resources through open governance.*"(UCLG, 2017)

Since 2005, the European Union (EU) has dedicated increasing investments to designing a smart, urban-growth strategy for its metropolitan city regions. The EU has developed a series of programs under the *Europe Digital Agenda.* (European Union, 2019) According to this digital agenda, the EU aims to achieve, "*A smart city is a place where traditional networks and services become more efficient with the use of digital and telecommunications technologies, for the benefit of its inhabitants and businesses. With this vision in mind, the European Union is investing in research and innovation in ICT and developing policies to improve the quality of life of citizens and make cities more sustainable in view of Europe's goals.*"

In addition to this balance between quality of life and use of latest technologies, we can't forget the permanent urban development (the physical evolution of the city), which is transforming the city shape and identity in the mid-long term.

A Smart City is defined as an integrated system that interacts with human and social capital using Information Technologies' solutions. Its objective is to efficiently achieve city sustainable development goals and quality of life, based on the cooperation between different social agents like citizens, City Managers, urbanists, technologists, universities and entrepreneurs. In this context, smart cities are becoming the solution for achieving a more sustainable urban development, while increasing citizens' quality of life through the use of new technologies. (Neirotti et al., 2014)

A good integration of these three components come from this BSI Group definition:

> *A city is smart when it displays effective integration of physical, digital and human systems in the built environment to deliver a sustainable, prosperous and inclusive future for its citizens.* (BSI, 2019)

Finally, let's go to check the standards bodies' definition. The current working definition from the ISO Board Smart City Advisory Group is:

> *A Smart City is one that...*
>
> *...dramatically increases the pace at which it improves its social, economic and environmental (sustainability) outcomes, responding to challenges such as climate change, rapid population growth, and political and economic instability...*
>
> *...by fundamentally improving how it engages society, how it applies collaborative leadership methods, how it works across disciplines and city systems, and how it uses data information and modern technologies...*
>
> *...in order to provide better services and quality of life to those in and involved with the city (residents, businesses, visitors), now and for the foreseeable future, without unfair disadvantage to others or degradation of the natural environment.* (Welch & Dadaglio, 2015)

In summary:

The SmartCity concept is very broad, and no one can say with exact precision what it refers to or not. But, everybody in the cities' arena is talking about it from many different angles. Although there is no standard definition and even the ISO Board approach is very ample in areas and topics to consolidate and integrate, we'll try to synthesize a common template. The SmartCities umbrella includes any kind of technology applied to cities to provide value in many different areas, always placing the citizen at the center as user, beneficiary, passive or active contributor, and always inspired by the UN SDG (Sustainable Development Goals) 2030 Agenda. Obviously, the SmartCities trend is here to stay, it's a work in progress, and every city has to set priorities according to its needs. So, the main, first tough decision is where to start from, how to set priorities and assign the scarce available resources to make the greatest advancement and improvement.

What our SmartCity may become is based on our hopes and our dreams, and relies on our execution capacity, leadership and available resources.

Ok, and what are those areas to consider so we can make a first assessment on where we are, what achievements we want to accomplish, and assign resources?

Again, there are abundant proposals from most technological providers, and thousands of available solutions to impact. Most are grouping those areas into some six to ten main ones, with some correlation between them.

There are dozens, but let us show just five examples:

One of most famous is Boyd Cohen's Smart City wheel, where this urban and climate strategist describes six main areas and 18 subareas for action around SmartCities. (Smart Economy, Government, Environmental, Mobility, Living, People) (Cohen, 2019)

The approach from the IoT World (Techtarget, 2019) extends this to 10 areas (Smart Manufacturing, Government, Mobility/WI-FI, Digital Citizens, Open Data, Health, Farming/Agriculture, Buildings, Grid/energy/Utilities and Transportation). Very technologically driven, the citizen is placed in only one area, *Smart/Digital Citizens*, and city areas are mixed in parallel with specific technologies like OpenData or Wi-Fi.

KPMG, in its 53-cities Benchmarking City Services (Beatty & Mitchell, 2017) Analysis simplifies these 12 basic functions to assess city services quality: Road access, Transit, Small and medium enterprise development, building permit and enforcement, Park access, Recreational facility access, Drinking water supply, Wastewater removal, Storm water drainage, Fire rescue, Garbage collection, Waste diversion and Recycled waste collection.

Deloitte (Eggers & Skowron, 2018) proposes six main areas (Smart Environment, Economy, Mobility, Security, Education, Living) surrounded by general objectives, necessary infrastructure and associated strategy. From the inner core focus on the three fundamental objectives (Economic Competitiveness, Sustainability and Quality of Life), the Information and Communications Technology infrastructures together with the analysis and security tools allow us to address the six development areas under the strategies of Collaboration, Transparency, Inclusion and Engagement. It is very complete, though it does not contemplate the transformation of physical urban infrastructure.

The Boston Consulting Group (Rubel, 2014) focuses on technology for six fundamental areas (Smart Social, Transport, Water&Waste, Energy, ICT Infrastructure and Buildings), placing the citizen in one of them: *Smart social.*

It seems clear that the SmartCity concept is multidimensional, trying to describe the *what to do* and the *how to achieve it* using the latest technologies.

## 3.2.2  From Objectives POV

Deloitte described the three fundamental SmartCity objectives as Economic Competitiveness, Sustainability and Quality of Life. This leads us to think about three main city models depending on the weight each city puts on each of them. That way, we can talk about a Business/Competitive City, an Eco/Sustainable City and a Human/Citizens/Livable City. These different weights are associated to political orientations and electoral promises. Typically, conservative/right wing are more focused on Business/Competitive while socialist/left wing are talking more about Eco/Sustainable. Human/Citizens/Livable City is in everybody's program, even from the Populists, but with different interpretations. Anyway, this varies from city to city, and sometimes is too linked to the mayor's willingness and leadership.

### Business/Competitive City

With the incessant globalization, cities face the challenge of continuously maintaining and improving their competitiveness. From this point of view, everything should be prioritized in the SmartCity plan to make the city more powerful and solid to develop the local economy and attract external investors. All other components will come later as a consequence. Therefore, the collective enrichment of the city/region, the development of growth factors and the ability to attract investment, are now the most important objectives for large urban agglomerations, competing for international status/recognition of the Smart city. A good example of this objective as a core one is taken by the UK Innovation research agency (Future City Catapult, 2018):

> The digital technologies deployed (at Smart City Demonstrators) help address environmental, economic and financial challenges. A successful outcome is market creation and investment for businesses and SMEs and the creation of an exciting and healthy environment for citizens to live, work and play.

There are here two main motions in this business-focused objective:

External focus (inbound)

The main objective is to attract multinationals and their investments in manufacturing, retail or operations plants and research. Especially relevant are technology companies (digital giants) and financial companies. We are seeing how Amsterdam, Dublin, Paris and mainly Frankfurt were competing (2019) to attract financial companies that are divesting in London due to the impending Brexit. It is necessary to adapt local universities to generate the requested talent. The priority objective of this SmartCity strategy is external, it is external marketing, *selling* the city's attractiveness in order to attract investments.

Local economic development objective (outbound)

This other direction of economic development is linked to the previous one. The idea here is to encourage the creation and development of local service companies to complement the installed multinationals, and in parallel, innovative new companies that are going to be projected internationally.

Therefore, all *smart* actions that offer the best quality of life for international companies' expatriate executives and retain young local talent by stimulating the generation of new, innovative companies from university clusters, should be prioritized.

**Eco/Sustainable City**
The term sustainability is often reduced to ecology, although with the global warming threat, strong initiatives have been developed such as the Paris Agreement and the C40 manifesto and many others that point to cities' decarbonization and increasing investments in electrification, energy efficiency and a circular economy. The new generations appreciate remarkably the concept of a *GreenCity*, so cities are increasingly committed to this goal and dedicating significant investments.

> *At Helsinki, the Sustainable Development Goals turn from the agenda into action especially at the city level.* (Helsinki, 2019a) Jan Vapaavuori, Mayor of Helsinki

**Human/Citizens/Livable City**
In this third approach, which is still a minority in the world, the citizens' quality of life and social interaction are the main priority. For all other kinds of projects, citizen are passive actors, like in a guinea-pig approach, in which city managers only want to analyze their reactions to the developed innovations. Business City obviously tries to promote citizen's wealth and Sustainable/Eco projects make city more livable, more ecologically pleasant. In this model, Citizen impact is not a consequence, but the main action point, through which sustainable and business goals are then achieved. Cities like Sao Paulo and Medellín are convinced that if they focus on the citizen, then the business objective will come.

> *If I look only for business, I miss out on the potential of the city. I miss out on the inclusive city and the sustainable city, connected, even in safety. The least important factor is the business aspect. The focus is on the citizen. When the goal is the citizen, the business environment gets built as a consequence.* (Cathelat, 2019b) João Octaviano de Machado Neto, Mobility & Transportation Secretary, Sao Paulo.

Medellín (Colombia) has evolved from being one of the most dangerous cities in the world under the social disaster caused by Escobar's drug cartel, to become one of the most innovative SmartCities in Latin America, with a priority focus on integration and equity in the access to social assistance by all segments of the population. It is based on building a strong identity around progress and innovation led by trusted leaders. Although these advances require technology, the technicians who implement them smile and get surprised at their highly humanistic content. Over dreaming of the enrichment of the city, being technologically attractive and purely ecological, Medellín has based its transformation on social cohesion and rebirth after the past social chaos.

**Citizen-Centric Functions**

Helsinki 2017–2021 City Strategy (Helsinki, 2019b) aims to make Helsinki *"the most functional city in the world."* Citizen-centric seems to be a secondary objective behind the Eco/Sustainable City (carbon-neutral target). But this concept of functionalism improves the quality of life from all angles. All city administrative processes' simplification and acceleration, digitalization projects, free Wi-Fi access in public spaces, advanced citizen services in a safe and clean city are contributing to economic growth and improving governance transparency. It is clear here that the Citizen City is not reluctant to endorse new technologies, but just the opposite, as citizens are more and more digital and technology is not an external tool anymore, but something familiar which they daily use. Generation Z are digital natives, so using the latest technologies is natural for them.

Finally, technology allows citizen to take a more active role in the city management and future development. They can become active actors on improving their quality of life. After some failed attempts to involve citizens in large-scale decisions, such as urban planning or heavy investments (citizens do not know in general about urban planning and for that, the city has its own qualified technicians), it seems obvious that citizen involvement should start from the neighborhood or district, so in an environment they live closer to and know better, and based on providing ideas and opinions about things they quite well know or suffer from or enjoy every day.

Citizens feel more empowered and listened to, and while taking responsibility for producing cooperation and collective knowledge, they also gain more self-respect as a community. In addition, the proud-of-belonging feeling is growing and the links with the city are reinforced. This is very relevant for those talented citizens who will feel themselves more comfortable in a certain city, so the chance to explore other attractive cities will decrease. There are many initiatives aimed at generating this collective, shared participation. City Apps, participatory budgets, feedback and reporting tools, chatbots are very common in the most advanced cities. The concept of small testing, then massive deployment is widely used through the concept of *citylabs*, also promoting local innovation and the creation of new companies. Helsinki is continuously testing this for wellbeing services through the (Forum Virum, 2019) in the district of Kalasatama, Jätkäsaari in Mobility, and more.

Citizens' active participation is also promoted with incentives to recycle, use bicycles (Rotterdam) or reduce their use of a car, civic behaviors (like the project we mentioned from City of Cascais (Portugal)).

This collaboration is even materialized in real, brick & mortar actions like co-building social houses in Chile. Pritzker-prize-awarded architect Alejandro Aravena developed a project in Iquique (ArchitectMagazine, 2019) to build social houses, or better said, to build *half* a house, allowing the citizens to complete it by themselves. This is reducing costs, allows the houses to be placed in a

**Fig. 3.3**  Quinta Monroy Aravena's half-a-house social housing concept. (Aravena, 2016)

better-connected space (not very far from the city center), creates the *I-did-it-myself* sentiment, and helps transform a slum into an integrated neighborhood. The project tries to overcome our cities' circle of poverty and inequity, while promoting self-development, not just another basic social expense. See Fig. 3.3.

So, a SmartCity model is a balance between these three, non-divergent, overlapping objectives: A Business/Competitive City, Eco/Sustainable City and Human/Citizens/Livable City (Cathelat, 2019c). We can say that it should be a linear combination of them, where the associated weights to each one are set by politics, starting and final destination, funding and external cooperation (Public-Private-Partnership or similar). On the other hand, a good SmartCity plan can't leave out any of them. Technology is omnipresent, as the great overall enabler.

## 3.3   Why SmartCities?

The motivations to invest in the SmartCity concept respond to a global trend and to each city's specific needs. In parallel, there are some internal motivations aimed at offering the best service to citizens and other external, within a global competition, positioning the city as an attractive place for talented citizens and investors. We have already studied the growing urbanization trend, and the increasingly important role of cities in global development. This positioning makes cities accelerate the use of all available technologies to improve their internal services and their external projection. Being more relevant in the international context, mayors also have greater responsibility and awareness. In many countries, the mayor of the country's capital seems to be only one step away from being a future prime minister.

Citizens increasingly see the central government as a group of politicians who only talk about macroeconomic issues, taxes and international issues, which are perceived as very distant from everyday reality. On the other hand, the city is perceived as closer, and local political actions have a clearer and more concrete effect on citizens' lives. In a context of military peace and economic stability, issues related to defense or macroeconomics are of little concern if they are compared to daily local conditions. In the same vein, citizens are increasingly digital, and the penetration of smartphones exceeds 100% of the population, which requires a local electronic administration that offers comparable quality services to those from the private sector. In addition, the technological evolution allows the provision of electronic services, massive data capturing from sensors, (IoT world) and the use of advanced Artificial Intelligence systems in a very cost-effective way. These costs mean a fraction of the associated cost of offering them face-to-face or by telephone, so that technological innovation enjoys all the advantages: improvement in current services and quality of life at lower costs and the provision of new, advanced services at acceptable and justifiable costs. We cannot talk about ROI (Return on Investment) as it is understood in the private sector, but we can quantify the return on service improvements, time savings for civil servants and citizens, and a return on institutional objectives' improvements or achievements.

From an internal point of view, making the city a more comfortable, safe, sustainable, connected and vibrant economy is the mission of all city politicians and managers. For that, technology is no longer a plus, but a must-have. It is unimaginable to enjoy the services and quality of life we already have today without the right technological basics. Just as it is unthinkable to look to the future (AI, 5G, autonomous cars) without discussing technology, therefore, the concept of SmartCity is the indispensable means of its implementation.

From an external point of view, within the unstoppable globalization process, our cities compete in a global context for becoming a reference in innovation, relevant in international decision making and a beacon for attracting talent.

### 3.3.1   The Competition for Talent

As we have already studied, cities are globally competing to retain and attract talent. Talent is the key to the city's economic development. Without talent or sufficient talent, the city is not innovative, it does not generate enough wealth or employment, it is not a leader in powerful new initiatives. Even worse, the talent attraction has a positive acceleration feedback: talent calls talent but also the opposite, the lack of attractiveness makes talent migrate, so the chances of being attractive are reduced. There is therefore a fierce competition to achieve this resource: talented citizens.

We talked in Chap. 2 about the 3T's as a recipe for cities' prosperity (Technology, Talent and Tolerance), as the magic equation to boost economic growth. Cities must rule with sufficient tolerance to allow immigrants to get access to the city in order to work and develop new ideas and business opportunities, attracting talented citizens and investors, and using technology as an enabler for this transformation. Technology is the key component of this trilogy. Other authors assume that a modern city is tolerant enough by default, and they exchange this T (Tolerance) by Trade, giving importance to international commerce relations or to city credibility in the business area. (Technology + Talent + Trade). Other authors add the term *climate change* as a fundamental factor in attracting new generations of talent: so, they get Talent + Technology + Climate Change as key axes of the future city.

In all this, it seems clear that there is a kind of Cold War, or hidden competition for talent among the most important cities in the world.

There are many more things I admire than detest from the American way of life. One of the things that I like best is its pragmaticism and lack of hypocrisy in matters that could be controversial, but that everyone previously knows and moves forward with. This is one of them. We can find direct offers to talented citizens to move to a certain U.S. city. They offer them all kinds of grants, even paying for their pending studies' loans if they commit to live and work with new companies in that city/state for a period of time. It seems reasonable to me to offer grants or scholarships to study in your own city/state, but it surprises me that rural, or not-as-attractive as main cities areas literally go to *catch/fish talents* where they have been nurtured (in cities with the best universities). Some examples: Kansas offering to pay off student loan debt if they move there and stay. Other cities also offering grants for building a house. (Berger, 2018) Another five U.S. cities with different grants if you move there. (White, 2017) If you plan to move and start a business, then 37 U.S. states offer you different grants and incentives. See the full guide. (Business Facilities, 2019)

This demand for talent is happening globally. In Portugal, they are calling all talented emigrants who decided to leave back with tax incentives. They offer tax breaks, help with relocation and more. (Elliot, 2019) A Finnish friend living in Spain is receiving a call every six months literally saying, *We need you back. Your country needs you. How can we help you make that decision?* Ireland has active policies on this as well.

We also talked about the 4th Industrial Revolution and the role of talent. This era of change is definitely marked by Artificial Intelligence and Robotics. Many decades ago, scientists already designed algorithms and systems based on Artificial Intelligence (AI). They were never released because of the lack of useful and massive data to build and debug the model and computing capacity to obtain results in a reasonable time, tending to real time. It is today when the massive data acquisition environments (IoT and other BigData) and the huge data processing power from Cloud DataCenters allow Artificial Intelligence to impact in all human spheres, not just the very technological ones such as manufacturing plants or retail businesses, but also those that connect with people, such as the services offered by a city. This makes people with skills to work in Artificial Intelligence highly demanded.

That way, companies look for roles with the 3 D's: Developers, Designers, Data Scientists. It is the human part of Artificial Intelligence. And even beyond, HR departments must seek disruptive roles in this new digital world, such as cognitive data managers, privacy auditors, product incubation managers, blockchain specialists, behavioral scientists, geospatial engineers, ethics advisors and emerging technology specialists. (Snyder, 2019)

For ATKearny, as reported in his famous *"Global Cities Index"*, talent or human capital is the key differentiator for competitive cities. And the talent is growing from inside, but also coming from outside in a global competition. (Mendoza & Dessibourg-Freer, 2019)

This competition for talent was also affecting the negotiations of the treaty between the U.S. and China. President Trump did not want young Chinese talent to be trained and obtain the know-how from American universities. (Bloomberg, 2019) We are clearly in a global war for talent. In other words, talent is considered a fundamental, strategic asset in the trade agreement. It is the element that can make a country lead the world's future, or be relegated to a secondary basic service-provider role.

Another factor that increases the value of talent is the decline in birth rates in the most advanced countries. This lack of young talent makes HR departments make special efforts to retain this profile of workers; a profile of young people from the Millennial Generation and Generation Z, which as we studied in the previous chapter, are not easy to motivate. New strategies are being developed in this task. (Allas et al., 2019) At the city level, the game is not only to attract companies and innovative businesses, but to create a vibrant, attractive city which will motivate this target group to move there.

In this situation of talent search, countries want to filter among potential citizens who apply for residence, work permit or a visa, to favor those who will generate wealth and development due to their skills and work compared to those who are simply looking for a better place to live and enjoy the social achievements and benefits. Designing this filter is a complex problem with ethical connotations. Finland and Australia have seriously considered the idea of setting an exam which could determine the question of talent. In general, companies' HR departments are the best filter. If a company is willing to hire a foreigner for a highly qualified position and has already found them, we should give that person all the necessary facilities. It is clear that the company specialists have made the filter and are willing to bet on that person. Another criterion is to own a company that is already making significant revenues in the country. It is assumed that if you have achieved that, it is because you have enough talent.

Keep an eye on your locals! Given the fierce competition for talent across cities, dissatisfied citizens will be tempted to leave for more attractive environments.

Look at my TED Talk session: Attractive SmartCities: Contest for Talent (Author, 2019)

## 3.3.2   An Increasingly-Connected World

With the constant improvements in efficiency in the means of transportation and the effects of globalization, the movement of the so-called *digital nomads* has been created. We can find workers from virtual service companies that are located in very remote locations scattered throughout the world. They are people with the talent, skills and the necessary languages to be able to develop their work in any place that offers a good enough connection to the Internet. As (Ratti, 2019), one of the most prestigious city designers, explains, digital nomads do not live in a fixed place, but instead live in different cities where they quickly integrate. Thus, they take advantage of the best from these cities at all times and when working or weather conditions change, or simply when they get bored, they move to another city. *"They meet other people at coworking or co-living spaces"*, said the MIT Senseable City Lab Director.

Cities are adapting to attract these digital nomads. While some cities were already cosmopolitan and well prepared to host the expatriates, others are actively developing policies and infrastructure (co-working or smartworking/co-living spaces) to attract foreign talents.

And we must remember that we are social animals. The most demanded destinations are the large metropolises, where density causes creativity to multiply and development to take off. McKinsey (Frem et al., 2018) has studied 13 cities in the world with more that 25% residents born in another country (To mention the largest, Dubai with 83%, Brussels 62%, Toronto 46%. Most cosmopolitan cities are now receiving people from abroad. This movement was not promoted in the past, but now, there is a demand for (talented) foreigners. Vienna should have been included here as well. Our Europe's Eastern gate population has this profile: 50% with a migration background, (they were born abroad or have at least one parent who was), 29 % are non-Austrians and 35% were born abroad. (Vienna, 2019)

And if we look at the net native-born people living abroad, we can check the below Fig. 3.4 from STATISTA. The 2008 economic crisis made a clear impact, but the trend is growing, and that crisis ended by 2012. As we have seen before, many countries are trying to recover all those lost locals. So definitely, people are on the move.

Migrations are no longer driven by unqualified pioneers with nothing to lose, but by well-skilled workers who want to earn what they believe they deserve. People who are very demanding with their salary and evaluate the attractiveness conditions of the possible cities where they plan to develop their lives.

There is a new variable that is conditioning this mobility between cities: the housing price, and the cost of loans that it entails, compared to wages. This means that many professionals are trapped in a city because of the high outstanding debt of their mortgage loan (pre-crisis) against the real value of their home (decreasing) with a stagnant (or non-competitive) salary. In parallel, the most attractive cities raise their housing prices because salaries are higher as they attract the best talents, making them more unattainable. This generates a vicious gentrification cycle

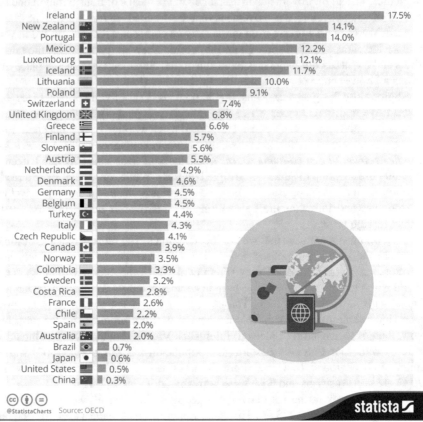

## The Countries With The Most People Living Overseas
Percentage of the native-born population living abroad in 2014

| Country | Percentage |
|---|---|
| Ireland | 17.5% |
| New Zealand | 14.1% |
| Portugal | 14.0% |
| Mexico | 12.2% |
| Luxembourg | 12.1% |
| Iceland | 11.7% |
| Lithuania | 10.0% |
| Poland | 9.1% |
| Switzerland | 7.4% |
| United Kingdom | 6.8% |
| Greece | 6.6% |
| Finland | 5.7% |
| Slovenia | 5.6% |
| Austria | 5.5% |
| Netherlands | 4.9% |
| Denmark | 4.6% |
| Germany | 4.5% |
| Belgium | 4.5% |
| Turkey | 4.4% |
| Italy | 4.3% |
| Czech Republic | 4.1% |
| Canada | 3.9% |
| Norway | 3.5% |
| Colombia | 3.3% |
| Sweden | 3.2% |
| Costa Rica | 2.8% |
| France | 2.6% |
| Chile | 2.2% |
| Spain | 2.0% |
| Australia | 2.0% |
| Brazil | 0.7% |
| Japan | 0.6% |
| United States | 0.5% |
| China | 0.3% |

@StatistaCharts   Source: OECD

statista

**Fig. 3.4** STATISTA Analysis of % people born in a given country but living in another. (McCarthy, 2016)

where two societies and two speeds are created by a Darwinian process. One in unattractive cities, with low wages but still high cost of living and housing.

And another in attractive cities, with high salaries and high living costs, but almost exclusively reserved for talent elites. To simplify very much: the poor are trapped, and talent-elites win it all. This process is described as an economic and social urban *sclerosis* that isolates the most disadvantaged areas, where no one leaves because they are trapped and where no one wants to move to because they are not attractive enough. This process is well analyzed in the U.S. by the International Monetary Forum (Bayoumi & Barkema, 2019), but is happening in comparable ways in other places. If the plus in salary because of living in a large, attractive city doesn't compensate the plus in cost of living, then the model doesn't work, and the potential emigrants have to consider the overall set of conditions, not just work and housing. This is a great opportunity for the mid-sized cities with a moderated cost of living, and which are very well connected to expensive, large metropolises. Again, urban mobility is the most important component and the reason why this is seriously impacting the U.S. and so much of Europe, where distances are shorter and urban mobility is excellent: you can live in an affordable house located 100 km from your job downtown if urban mobility takes you there in reasonable time and cost.

### 3.3.3   SmartCities' Four Evolution Stages

Since its conception in 2010, the term SmartCity has evolved, or better said, it has been *humanized*. Some authors talk about a shift from a SmartCity 1.0 focused on technology to a SmartCity 2.0 focused on citizens. Other experts like Boyd Cohen talk about three generations of SmartCities: 1.0 Technology Leadership; 2.0 Technology-based City Leadership; 3.0 Citizen Leadership. (Cohen, 2015)

Our vision broadens this classification and considers technology (as well as urbanism) as a transversal component, never a destination, but an ever-present mean, and we define four stages.

SmartCities 1.0:

Mr. Cohen explains SmartCities 1.0 as a generation of projects led by large technological multinationals such as IBM and Cisco, with the noble interest of selling their technology and services. In our model, we propose that SmartCities 1.0 use technology to solve cities' main internal problems. With the intensive use of the Internet and the immense computing capabilities available by 2010 in comparison with previous decades, cities understood that computers were no longer just a means of writing letters or collecting taxes. In this generation, technology is used for the city directors' service to solve their fundamental internal problems of management, and financial control. They also begin to consider technology as a possible solver for some physical problems such as traffic management and city elements' geolocation. It is clear that the technological multinationals are here to sell projects, but they also play a fundamental role as catalysts for urban development, providing technology, procedures and methodologies that do not exist within the city's staff. Here is SmartCities' enormous value contribution: before SmartCities 1.0, our cities just used technology for the old concept of *mechanization*, moving administrative procedures from paper to computers.

From the urban point of view, until 2010, urbanism was considered only a bricks & mortar concept, with heavy equipment making hard physical things like buildings, railways, roads, parking, airports, harbors, power plants and energy distribution networks, water reservoirs and pipes). The term *Smart Network City 2010* starts to ring a bell, and technology makes all this world more manageable, able to be planned in advance, and efficient.

SmartCities 2.0:

Mr. Cohen explains SmartCities 2.0 as a generation of City-led, technology-intensive projects. So, the city proposes, and technology delivers. We can observe the increase in SmartCities' solutions industry and an awesome fascination by technology. Other voices talk about the concept of a *Computing City* made up of a *Network City*, that is gathering data from a myriad of sensors combined with a *Software City* that is processing that data in a *Cyborg City* which controls it all. If we add Artificial Intelligence, then we evolve this concept to the *Conscious City* idea, which makes the city work as a self-sufficient, self-conscious living body.

Honestly, I dislike this way of futuristic thinking, which quickly moves from enthusiastically describing the latest technological innovations, to alerting about the potential, scary, sci-fi dystopian worlds. This doesn't help with the ever-complex digital transformation processes, because it is only adding doubts and reducing trust. Technology is always an ally, an enabler for human capabilities' full expression, and it just does what humans program it to do. We must trust technology by default, ensuring it is managed by ethical principles, in skilled hands.

When we talk about SmartCities 2.0, we mainly refer to the new king of the knowledge economy: DATA. Cities are sensorized. Traditional SCADA (Supervisory Control and Data Acquisition) industrial information management is adopted by cities to control the physical environment, creating large data farms, big data.

Available data from IoT (Internet of Things) is massively growing, but it's just a fraction of the human-produced data on social networks. Cities are much better controlled and managed, drastically improving their resilience. Most decisions are based on data, or in other words, all decisions take data into account, because Data is the city's truth, for the good or bad. Knowing the truth makes us/them free to choose what's right. Due to all that data transformed into insight and knowledge, governance accuracy is very much improved. Data comes from different sources: structured (sensors, IoT, existing citizen information, taxes, properties, health records) and unstructured (social networks, posts, tweets, other). To obtain knowledge from all that data, you need analytics tools like Social, Sentiment, Predictive Analytics, BigData or DataLakes. All of them are considered vital tools to manage the city (water, energy, transportation, safety & resiliency, education, health care, tourism, urban planning). Accordingly, cities are developing *smart* plans to build an integrated view of the various city components and create connections between them. This points to the concept of an Urban Operating System, or UrbanOS as an integrated platform to gather all available data and create new solutions and services. This was first proposed by the CityOS model born in Barcelona, but there are many commercial proposals from the main technological providers. This article describes most of them and the potential model's evolution. (Marvin & Luque-Ayala, 2017) Cities are also sharing all public, non-private or PII (Personal Identifiable Information – remember the strict GDPR data protection regulation law) externally, in the concept of OpenData. So, they are collecting data on the city in real time, enriching these and then making them available at the right place and the right time to businesses, governments and citizens (see City Data Exchange (Larsen, 2019) massive OpenData platform from Copenhagen). The aim is to foster the development of new applications and services, improve city management transparency and provide more information to potential investors.

Yet technology is only an enabler, cities are based on people. So. . . where are the citizens? SmartCity 2.0 uses the latest technologies to provide the best services to citizens, but without citizens. We have forgotten about citizens. They are the humans walking the streets there, outside our project's office. Once every four years, we try to connect to them to gain their trust in the form of a vote. This stage is decided and programmed top-down, focusing on the city ecosystem functional procedures rather than citizens real needs, which are treated as passive elements. It is a modern and technological version of XVIII century enlightened despotism, *Everything for the citizen, but without the citizen*. We must change this and place the citizen at the center of all of our actions. If we do not connect to the citizen, we run the risk of simply nullifying them, reducing their city government influence to zero, moving towards the *zero human* paradigm: zero human connection to the real world, as all this can be perfectly managed by IoT; zero human decisions as intelligent assistants will better make them all, flawlessly based on Artificial Intelligence machine-learning algorithms; replacing humans in most tasks, providing maximum comfort and efficiency. There are many dystopian films based on that concept.

The most extreme example of the use of technology to offer better services to citizens could be the Google Sidewalk Quayside Toronto project (Thornhill, 2019). Google promised a completely, built-from-scratch SmartCity from the Internet up. The proposal is based on the idea that real-time data flows can be used to optimize the city's *central nervous system*, making great improvements in transportation, public services, environmental care and land use. This seems very much aligned with the concept of CityOS that we have just seen. But, when citizens have been asked more about the use of their personal data, movements, customs and when they noticed that this real-time monitoring also includes them, protests and strong counter-reactions arose. We encounter, once again, the ethical issue of, personal information vs. protection/knowledge to provide better service or quality of life.

SmartCities 2.0 are therefore implementing the model of *Datapolis*, the city of data, with the plan to evolve into a *Participolis*, where citizens take an active role in city life. (Pisani, 2015)

SmartCities 3.0:

The most advanced SmartCities are in this chapter. Once we have all the data we need, (data is a must-have because without data you don't know your city and you have little to propose to or ask your citizens, basically because, again, you don't know them) we can start engaging, connecting and making the citizens owners and co-creators of their city. It's a big mistake to consider this a non-technological approach. It's not about technology *or* citizens, it's about technology *for* citizens (SmartCity 2.0), and technology *with* citizens (SmartCity 3.0). The plan is to make a Copernican shift and place the citizens at the city center for all activities. We swap from a data-centered city to a citizen-centered city, keeping in mind, we need data (or enough data) first.

We already described the challenge and the main tools we can use to tackle this in Sect. 2.3.2: Connecting/Listening to citizens. City Co-Creation.

There are many alternatives in order to connect/engage with citizens: Apps for smartphones, Citizen Relationship Management tools, Social Listening, Sentiment Analytics, chatbots as *virtual civil servants* you can interact with, eDemocracy tools to provide opinions, feedback or even eVoting in some specific questions. Some cities allow the option of participatory budgets, *ask the Mayor* spheres, or proposals for the cultural agenda and demanded services. Yet, there is a long way to walk till the moment where citizens will feel proud of their city, fully engaged and feeling that *belonging* sentiment. There are some main issues and blockers in making this SmartCity 3.0 paradigm a reality:

- Do we know who our citizens are? We have tons of information on them, (taxes, properties, cars, water-energy consumption, healthcare records, dependencies) but most times all that data is isolated in silos and because of some technical (and sometimes legal) restrictions, we can't integrate it all into a single model, a datalake where we can filter and find the different segments of population with specific conditions that we want to improve. This is the concept of social marketing or citizen segmentation.
- Do we know how to connect to them? If they don't have a virtual identity, a way to uniquely identify each citizen, providing the demanded services with security, authentication, reliability, privacy and obvious compliance with laws becomes a challenge. There are some cities with successful *citizen card* projects. People identify themselves and get a card. That card can be used for multiple city services. This is a physical card, not an electronic way to identify yourself and get access to your city services from your smartphone. Advanced eID Services like those implemented in Estonia and Ireland are needed at the city level.
- Citizens are very reluctant to allow more apps on their smartphones unless they provide advanced services in a way they can trust. Banks are already doing that...just a suggestion.
- Even for basic government services, there is big room for improvement both in the quality of services provided, and the real use of those services. It's not just a question of publishing or making a new service available, you need to make the citizens know it, use it and obtain the expected benefit, otherwise you are wasting your resources. And again, citizens should trust those new services and clearly experience the value, otherwise they simply won't use them. Europe is the most advanced in eGovernment, and even here there are significant differences between countries. If we take this down to the city level, then the gaps are even wider. We can see how the different EU countries are performing in terms of digitalizing the most common services vs the use of those services' penetration in the population. This is improving the 2015 situation (EU DIGIBYTE, 2015), (as explained in Sect. 2.3) where only 27% of public services were mobile-friendly (available on mobile, and using mobile capabilities); only 41% of websites were transparent about the requested process duration, response times, making many citizens to drop before task completion; only 35% were informing

citizens about their chance to participate and provide ideas or feedback about the involved policies; services were not personalized in general, (different people: students, professionals, elders have different needs) not taking into account the available information about the citizen; only 45% forms were pre-filled with citizen data, and finally, only 4% of services were proactively offered and delivered to citizens.

- eVoting? Electronic voting systems are starting to be used in controlled, reduced environments where privacy and voting independence can be guaranteed. If we think of an elderly lady voting on a computer screen, advised (or directed) by her granddaughter, we may have doubts about who is really selecting one option or another. George Washington University is seriously studying the applicability of eVoting to mass elections. Massively criticized, eVoting has failed to improve citizen engagement in politics despite all the investments made to generate public trust in the system. Due to the complexity and questionable election transparency in some cities, and the overwhelming penetration of the Internet and secured smartphones, eVoting is gaining ground and will gradually be adopted everywhere. (Hapsara et al., 2017) Another issue is the nature of the question: to what extent can we ask citizens about advanced urban development topics, for which most of them do not have basic skills, and whose opinion can simply be guided by aesthetic criteria (everyone has the ability to appreciate the beauty and tell whether something looks pretty or ugly), but not considering all the relevant criteria? Sometimes we love the pendulum movement, from not asking anything to asking about even the most minute decisions. Is it an excuse to avoid responsibilities? *You (citizen) chose it, so don't complain now.*

There is a huge set of digital tools to facilitate citizen participation (Creighton, 2017). On the one hand, we can find communication and dialogue tools such as citizen forums, online discussion, chats with the mayor, groups of interest, etc. On the other hand, requests in various formats, reporting tools, direct, grouped, supported by photographs, requests for signatures, volunteer management tools, recruitment for civic social services. There's also participatory financing and crowdfunding, collaboration and crowdsourcing. Massive collaboration tools for popular initiatives. And finally, as we explained, all Opendata tools that share all kinds of city information, both static data, historical data, and real-time info from sensors, always without personally identifying any citizen due to obvious data-protection reasons.

Therefore, we must connect and consult citizens in all that we technically and pragmatically can, with a specific focus on questions of opinion, desire or tendency, questions about familiar topics and where we ensure that there is minimal knowledge and technical criteria required, openly explaining the pros and cons and seeking very high participation, to prevent cyber-ready citizens from having more of a voice than those cyber-*un*ready.

A very well-known project on SmartCities 3.0 is Barcelona's *"Decidim"* or "we decide," an online platform that allows citizens to propose and participate in city decision making. Around 40,000 people use this *civic alternative to Facebook,* which is obviously relevant, although it means only 2.5% of 1,620,000 people, the number of Barcelona's inhabitants in 2018. Anyway, this is a clear way to promote and connect with citizens, but creating other more-viral, cool, must-have tools is still a pending subject. Some initiatives where we ask the citizens for direct participation on specific strategic projects are energy in Vienna, sustainability in Vancouver or the impressive Medellin *sharing* initiatives to help the most vulnerable suburbs with technology innovations. They are leading this SmartCities 3.0 movement.

Apart from technological tools to enable consultations, and citizens' participation in formal decision-making, these new collaborative projects open the scope for more ambitious goals like social inclusion, entrepreneurship-creation and building social capital. Technology remains as a vital component for the SmartCities conversation, but cities that design technology projects around their citizens will be more prepared for the future and more attractive internal and externally.

> *Companies don't disrupt, cities don't disrupt, people disrupt. And as you [the government] think about building and evolving smart cities, you have to have citizens at the center.* (Afshar, 2017)

Although we begin to hear about Citizen-Centric Cities, the reality is that most of the projects and plans are still top-down implementations made for *silent citizens*, who are not asked anything except, rarely, their feedback on the service provided.

Modern SmartCities 3.0 environments confer an active role not only to citizen associations, volunteers and city managers, but also to citizens, in a bottom-up process where they can express their opinions, needs, tastes, preferences and suggestions. Several questions arise when implementing these systems:

- Do the solutions developers take into account the citizens' lifestyle and customs? Are they asked, proposed, do they test solutions before launching?
- Are citizens willing to participate, to get involved, are they ready to help those developers if asked?

We believe that except in a few cities with a strong sense of belonging, citizens are not aware of their responsibility as recipients of services and as collaborators in the city creation. They simply live there and take the opportunity to leave in a hurry as soon as the weekend arrives.

SmartCities 4.0:

Although only a utopia, a happy destination to aim for, we wanted to add this phase, SmartCities 4.0, as the maximum paradigm of collaboration and co-creation. You can start with neighborhoods or small groups, and organize permanent, collective, active-participation projects. It is like a beehive where citizens are almost constantly contributing to the common goal. It is the role of the *smartivist*, defined by the (BeeSmartCity, 2017) association, *"an individual who steps forward to actively support the process of creating a better place on a voluntary basis."* It is an incipient movement, but it is gaining activists as citizens observe that they are heard, and their opinion and contributions really count to improve their city.

Projecting to the future, we could think of a collective consciousness, something like the neural connection of all the tribe members to *mother tree* in *"Avatar"* (Cameron, 2009).

The nearest, real example of this concept would be Bletchley Park, (UK) where a team of people lived as an intelligent community. Led by Alan Turing, all were working focused on collaborating to solve a problem (decoding the Nazi Enigma cypher).

### 3.3.4   SmartCities: The Perfect Solution for Urbanists, Politicians and Technologists

The SmartCities model is the solution to the main motivations of the three main actors: urbanists, technologists and politicians.

- Urbanists faced the model of unlivable megacities, denounced by active leaders such as Jane Jacobs, Rem Koolhaas, Jan Gehl, … and have found in the SmartCities paradigm a way to evolve those megacities from a *generic* City model to a sustainable and livable city; a city for citizens, to enable them to express their creativity and develop their potential.
- Technologists like me are delighted to contribute to the cities development, to inspire our Cities' transformation to cope with XXI century challenges competing in a global context to retain and attract talent to lead the Fourth Industrial Revolution. We want to deliver the enabling technologies to make Cities more sustainable, inclusive, efficient and safer, delivering the most advanced services through a Citizen-Centric model.
- To politicians, who needed new references for human development: there's nothing better than promising livable cities, catalysts of human creativity and competitiveness (economic, artistic, scientific and human rights breakthroughs)

Megacities are mostly described by experts, and experienced by residents as disastrous and inhuman agglomerations when it comes to all progress criteria:

- Disordered or random urban planning that generates a senseless collage of slums, wastelands, racial ghettos in combination with modern districts, financial downtown, green university areas, and, of course, a big airport as an isolated cosmopolitan island…a chaotic complexity.
- Public infrastructure, utilities and services with a chronic inability to respond to a rising demographic rhythm, to the point where they become inaccessible.
- Social segments inequalities that generate violence, riots and crime, social tensions and lack of inclusiveness.
- Abandoned citizens with undesired loneliness in an anonymous crowd of indifferent, numb individuals.
- Natural ecosystem destruction, pollution, inefficient energy generation.

– Wasted time on traffic jams, hectic and stressful lifestyle, work burnout, disease, depression.

It is the *generic* city as described by (Koolhaas, 1997). An empty city, without history; superficial, sedated, as if drugged and numb. A city where the street has died because it is not used and life happens vertically or in a shack, with marked disruption edges (vertical – horizontal), leaving no opportunity for encounter, for creative density. A city that repeats itself in a fractal way, where everything is the same, where everything that is not strictly useful or functional has no place. A formally directed architectural design in the city center, where the wealth is, and a diffuse, wide stain of poor suburbs outside, emphasizing inequality.

To oppose this negative image, the SmartCities model is presented as the solution, the new paradigm, a feasible *utopia*.

The SmartCity is then a convergent ideal that combines the size and density of a modern attractive city, with the manageability, efficiency and livability of its citizens, provided by technology.

## 3.4   How to Develop a Comprehensive and Impactful SmartCity Strategy?

Depending on the different priorities and circumstances, cities define different strategies too. Thus, the strategies of Singapore, (*SmartNation*) or the latest initiatives of Amsterdam or Copenhagen looking for creative alternatives to increase the use of, and make bicycle parking more efficient, are very different.

In any case, a SmartCity plan implies a city huge digital transformation: its citizens, its internal management, its control, and even its organization and its future.

Every digital transformation implies an organizational, change-management process. *"A very big issue in the concept of a Smart City is culture. The technology is easy compared to the necessary culture change. We need to be more agile and have autonomous teams who can get things done."* Mikko Rusama, Chief Digital Officer of Helsinki.

Every change process responds to the famous (Dannemiller & Jacobs, 1992) change formula in order to be successful:

$$\text{Change} = \text{Dissatisfaction} \times \text{Vision} \times \text{First Steps} > \text{Resistance}$$

We would change or update *Vision* by two main areas: Expectations and Leadership, resulting in this modified formula:

$$\text{Change} = \text{Dissatisfaction} \times \text{Expectations} \times \text{Leadership} \times \text{First Steps} > \text{Resistance}$$

Therefore, we have four factors that push change and that are all strictly mandatory. If any factor is limited or scarce, then the final product will also be small and may not be enough to overcome the natural human R resistance to any change or leaving our comfort zone. These four factors are:

D: Dissatisfaction with the current situation. This leads us to first take a picture of our current starting situation, analyzing our assets, our advantages in what we are strong in, and then setting our priorities, with special focus on those areas in which we are not competitive.

E: Improvement expectations. It is clear that technology dazzles us, but here it is about looking at what other cities have already achieved, and designing what technology can do for us. Set achievable expectations in gradual, realistic, approachable steps with our budget and our execution capacity.

L: Leadership. The mayor's role is fundamental. Also, the CTO or SmartCity Strategy Director. They must push without fainting, avoiding the many internal and external obstacles that they will surely face. *"The factor that contributes to smart city success is the willingness of local leadership."* (Collier, 2019)

F: First steps. It is essential to achieve quick wins. They will show all stakeholders the way to walk to an attainable goal, and that these first results are promising. This will achieve additional endorsements and strengthen the strategy execution.

### 3.4.1  Mayor's Leadership. Role of the CTO

A city is not only its mayor, but some mayors' vision and leadership have been instrumental in addressing their city transformation. Some examples such as mayor Azkuna in Bilbao, Mon-soon Park in Seoul, Trias in Barcelona, have led profound transformations in their cities. There is even a (World Mayor, 2019) Prize that recognizes every two years the most transformative mayor, and the one who has contributed the most to all his city's citizens, highlighting the inclusion facet.

It seems clear that a SmartCity requires a Smart Mayor (SmartCityHub, 2019). A mayor who leads, who take risks, who bets and who wins, but also a mayor who listens, who always puts his citizens ahead of any other interest, who is able to travel around the world to promote his city, to make it relevant and attractive.

An excellent mayor who develops an excellent SmartCity should manage the city based on solid and efficient governance. The transparent, effective, reliable and predictable basic government elements are the fundamental pillars of any strategy. On these pillars, you must develop a clear vision of the city, considering and integrating all stakeholders, always with citizens at the center of any initiative. You must have the courage to take risks and experiment, especially within proposals suggested by citizens. Mayor must be open to public-private partnerships (PPP) with technology companies, use all those technologies that demonstrate value and profitability, and lead those that have the greatest impact on the city's main challenges. Mayor must combine technology-based strategies with non-fundamentally technological ones, such as urban planning from a physical point of view, and social services from a human point of view. Finally, Mayor must be very pragmatic, quickly implementing what has been shown to add value and that really works, and immediately stopping what does not, without wasting time or hesitating.

But the mayor cannot devote all necessary time to this plan. Even those very technological mayors can't be leading this transformation. They need a SmartCity plan director. They must be an innovator and a great change manager. We can find them listed as CDO (Chief Digital Officer or Chief Data Officer), CTO (Chief Technology Officer) or Information Officer) or Smart City Manager. It is recommended that they are different from the CIO, because the CIO is very much dedicated to technology as an internal tool that manages the city. Here we talk about going beyond that. A solid IT base is needed in the city, and the infrastructure managed by the CIO will have to be integrated and exploited, but the SmartCity plan implies a city life transformation through the use of technology. Thus, the CDO, CTO or the SmartCity Manager must be a creator, an innovator, planner, strategist, a leader in change management, a city-of-the-future visionary for each case. They need an innovative mayor to bet and provide them with the needed budget, but above all, need trust and leadership. And the other way around: a transforming mayor needs this firm, executive arm so that the impact is real, and together they make the difference.

Any successful SmartCity plan should achieve excellence in four main areas (BeeSmartCity, 2019a):

- Creating a smart city ecosystem
- Planning, Priority Assessment
- Implementing a digital transformation based on those priorities and additional testing tools.
- Delivering measurable, quality-of-life improvements

### 3.4.2   Creating a SmartCity Ecosystem

For the United Cities and Local Governments (UCLG, 2019b) association, the main actors working in a comprehensive SmartCity Plan are: City Council, Universities, Public Services Companies, Technology companies, Other Government and Institutions (like Central Governments) and Entrepreneur companies / individuals.

The city hall, (at the center) public service companies, (especially those providing urban mobility) and other government institutions, especially those above the city metropolitan area, like the region/state or country are fundamental, mainly because of the political support, economic stability and international-context relationship. Universities, research institutes and local companies create the innovation approach by local people, nurturing local talent and fostering the creation of quality employment. Large technological companies are crucial to providing the needed technology and enabling the transformation.

We would add some other main stakeholders: first, the citizens. Citizens as co-creators of a SmartCity, providing inputs, ideas, desires, feedback and using the new projects to obtain the expected outcomes. Other actors to consider are utilities companies (water, energy, waste management and recycling). They are fundamental to achieving the sustainability objectives. Also, very relevant and gaining importance, we can find the construction companies and the urbanism revolution implementers. As we have seen, there is a brick & mortar transformation, and technology has a decisive role in that as well. Additionally, Telcos, with the incoming 5G, play a significant role in the necessary communication infrastructure.

Smart cities are not strictly public sector projects. To reach maximum impact, smart cities must be inclusive by the private sector. The same people are customers for the private sector, and citizens for the public. With the same objective and respecting due transparency and independence, both forces ensure maximum use and impact of projects. At its best moment in projects and initiatives, Barcelona obtained (2014) an additional 1.7€ from external financing (private sector, external institutions like European Union projects) for every 1 € invested by the city.

There is a large SmartCity community of technological solutions and initiative providers (Woods & Lawrence, 2018). We can group them in City Service Providers, Utilities, Telcos, Consultant ICT Services, Mobility Services, and all kind of vertical solutions (Transportation, Buildings, Waste, Streetlighting, Data Analysis, Design/Planning, semiconductors, sensors, energy, water, infrastructure assessment and maintenance, communications infrastructure and Computing&Storage large Datacenter providers). We can understand the variety of proposals from different sectors and areas that contribute to a comprehensive SmartCities plan.

To develop a SmartCity strategy it is not enough to decide on a specific technology or a number of innovative projects in various areas. Many cities make this mistake and end up with a collage of disconnected and isolated systems that add little value. It is necessary to have an integrated urban data platform where all the used technologies are interconnected to simplify the use of all data sources, regardless of the environment from which they come from, and make all components coordinate. From the point of view of actors and entities, this collaboration is also necessary to achieve maximum performance in a system as complex as a city. There are many entities that own relevant information about citizens. Apart from the city hall, other governments, utilities, telcos, health systems, financial and banking systems, and many others have information that can be interesting to better know and understand the citizen and offer a more personalized and advanced service.

From the main technological providers' perspective, the main American digital giants like Microsoft, Google, Amazon, IBM, and Cisco are the most active players. Looking at mid to long-term strategy, GAFAM (Google, Amazon, Facebook, Apple, Microsoft) plus the rising NATU (Netflix, AirBnB, Tesla and Uber) are showing interest. We can't forget their Chinese counterparts (BATX: Baidu, Alibaba, Tencent, Xiaomi) and Huawei all massively investing in Artificial Intelligence and advanced technologies, and clearly wanting to go beyond their Chinese/Asian market, to Europe and Africa. All should be considered as very active players in any broad SmartCity plan. Obviously, top consulting companies are paying attention as well. The main ones in this area are KPMG, EY, PwC, Accenture, Deloitte, CapGemini. A typical plan has a Strategic Consultant as designer, a Technical Office to ensure all data and solutions' integration, and a number of specialized, best-in-class solutions for the different areas, all under the CDO/CTO/SmartCity Manager supervision. An extended plan includes other roles such as marketing, and a Program Manager for other actors' integration, including all city suppliers and providers of physical infrastructure like buildings, roads, streets, bridges, public and private transportation, energy, water and environmental services, and communications (telcos).

Creating the technological ecosystem requires the development of partnerships with high-tech specialized startups, established large companies, universities and research institutes which offer the SmartCity projects' needed skills and knowledge. This plan can also serve to nurture local technology entrepreneurship (BeeSmartCity, 2018a) and university clusters, which will create high-quality employment. A good example of this ecosystem complexity can be found at the (BeeSmartCity, 2019b) Solutions Database, which includes hundreds of services and solutions provided by public and private entities.

So, we clearly have three groups of stakeholders in a comprehensive SmartCity Plan: city leaders and other government authorities, private entities and citizens.

Deloitte (Eggers & Skowron, 2018) proposes some orientation on the main tasks, and guidance for them to cope with the increasing complexity a massive SmartCity plan may entail.

City leaders should prepare a plan with a clear strategy, one which citizens can easily understand. In our opinion, this strategy must be linked to taking advantage of each city's existing assets, and fit its citizens' minds. They should buy in that idea and make it their own. We can use as much technology as we need and be as ambitious as our capacity and budget reach, but we cannot ask citizens to lend their support to something in which they do not believe or with which they do not feel identified. Instead of an all-or-nothing plan as a monolithic project, create a set of smaller projects, but always over a unified integration basis so that everyone takes advantage of the rest and the sum is always bigger than the isolated parts. As we indicated in the change management process, *quick wins* are essential to demonstrate that the chosen path is the right one and gets endorsements. It's fundamental to establish a constant, progressive and convincing communication. This communication means transparency, commitment and leadership, and must be on the political agenda and specially oriented to communicate progress and results.

The private sector, companies, NGOs and nonprofits must seriously consider this revolution in the future of cities within their commercial actions, corporate social responsibility and other activities. The most open and innovative cities are seriously using PPP (Public Private Partnership) agreements. In addition to the noble purpose of selling solutions and services, large companies have the capacity to invest in certain corporate social responsibility programs, where very relevant issues for cities such as sustainability, carbon neutral, equality, ethics in AI, etc. can align with investments in cities. On the other hand, by observing the required ethical and GDPR standards, cities can accept certain concessions from commercial companies in exchange for technological investments. It is about a responsible balance between commercial and public objectives.

Citizens must take on a proactive role in the city, its initiatives and its future strategies as SmartCity co-creators. They must be aware of the change that is taking place, and they must be vocal, asked and be heard. They should use the new technologies with trust, but also with responsibility and with some basic training, to preserve their security and identity/privacy. They must know the central role they are going to take and they must think about what the city does for them, and what they can do for their city, in a non-explicit collaboration agreement. In the development plan, they should be asked for suggestions and ideas, but above all, what's crucial for the plan's success is their participation and use of the new tools that are going to be designed for them.

### 3.4.3 Planning. Priorities' Assessment.

There are several SmartCity planning models. We will describe the most common for new cities, or cities built from scratch as an example and symbol of modernity for their countries. For those that are not new, but are trying to improve existing cities, the model is more complex, slow and restrictive. At the same time, it has the greatest impact on the cities where citizens now live. On the other hand, one of main problems from cities built from scratch is how to fill them with people, avoiding the *Ghost City* fatal destiny. We will also see what main topics to consider when planning a SmartCity, and how to discover what our priorities should be.

The new, innovative and futuristic SmartCities built from scratch respond to a top-down voluntarism model. Fundamentally, country leaders have decided to build these cities for several reasons: to project an external *modern* image, retain talent, develop and export experience in SmartCity technology, develop or improve a depressed area, etc. There are two sub-models according to who is finally investing, whether the state with public money or the private sector. In the totalitarian political regimes, we can find this *Dirigiste* model where a criterion is set and projected down in a pyramidal manner. Its advantage is the innovation-implementation speed, and its disadvantage, the lack of flexibility and reflection of social needs, which in many cases gives rise to a modern *ghost town* which has failed to be attractive even to very country's citizens. There are variants of this model depending on how prescriptive they are. There are many examples in Asia, the Middle East and some in Africa. China is the typical example of large-scale authoritarian voluntarism, with numerous cities developed as well, along with the support of local companies like Alibaba, Baidu and Huawei. The Neom project in Saudi Arabia is also a leader in voluntarism, with an estimated investment of $500 billion in 30 years. The idea is to compete with Dubai, which owns the technological leadership in the Gulf, although it must have its sights set on not repeating the mistakes of failed Masdar (Abu Dhabi). The new project management (by mostly the 2010s' Barcelona former-successful directors) is combining investment directed by the Saudi Kingdom with the investment from technology companies, providing additional flexibility and attractiveness. Morocco is also an example of royal voluntarism with the Tangiers and Zenata projects. Here, apart from projecting the image of a modern country, the intention is to create poles of attraction for the enormous population growth that Africa will experience in the coming years, doubling the urban population until 2030. In this same line, African projects are framed from Diamniadio (Senegal), Yabacon Valley - Lagos (Nigeria), to Benin, e-Madina - Casablanca (Morocco), and Konza (Kenya)- Nairobi's twin.

The intermediate example between a top-down planned city, but which did not start from scratch, is Singapore, with its successful *Smart Nation* model.

The Indian approach is different; although there is a leading country intention to plan 100 new SmartCities, each state has its financial autonomy and has been looking for various private-funding models. An example of the Indian model is Amaravati (new capital of Andhra Pradesh state), designed from scratch in both its location and urban planning.

The second, non-authoritarian voluntarism model is based on private financing. In this case, certain companies want to invest in a new SmartCity as an experiment, laboratory and commercial reference/showcase. It is a fully supported-by-the-authorities commercial strategy, with radical examples of PPP (Public-Private-Partnership). There are many examples of such cities. To highlight the most spectacular, we can look at Songdo in South Korea, with a total investment of about $40 billion from several real estate investment companies. Songdo has everything but inhabitants (Lobo, 2014), becoming the most expensive *ghost town* in the world. The authorities are integrating it into the Seoul metropolitan area with incentives such as a free-economy zone to make it more attractive. Google was investing in its own flagship SmartCity project at Quayside smart district in Toronto (Canada); Panasonic leads the CityNOW project in the Denver (U.S.) area as an extension of its successful project in Fujisawa (near Tokyo in Japan) Yarrabend; a suburb of Melbourne (Australia) is Tesla's testing ground.

For most existing cities that adopt the concept of SmartCity and where the state-directed planning model does not apply, or at least is very restricted because laws and regulations apply or there is opposition and political control, and the voice of citizens individually or organized in associations is heard, we speak of a regulated democratic model. The investments in SmartCities must observe the limitations imposed by democratic audits, transparency and control. Innovation adoption is slower, more gradual and has a much greater weight placed on the social, educational and citizen integration areas. This is the model of modernization that works in the Western world, where in addition, it must take into account the history, old urban centers with obsolete infrastructures, in contrast to a population that especially appreciates their culture and their lifestyle. These audits and investment control are slowing the speed of SmartCity projects' deployment. In Paul McAuliffe's (Dublin's Lord Mayor) words at the Barcelona SmartCityExpo in November 2019, *"Procurement is killing SmartCities,"* explaining how painful it is to run through all the necessary audits, open tenders, investment justifications and transparency checks, stalling the necessary innovation process, creating the paradigm of purchasing innovation that is already obsolete at the moment it can be deployed.

For a good SmartCity strategy planning, it is not enough to have a mayor's leadership and the vision from a CTO. We must have information, be in a good situation, conduct risk analysis, and assess our execution capabilities. We cannot venture to announce such an important plan without having all the information and stakeholders aligned. Nor should we reach paralysis because of analysis. Without hurry, but without pause, we must get going. The rest of the cities in the world compete to attract our talents. Let's look at the main issues to consider.

**Opportunities' and Alternatives' Assessment**
Most of the time, our cities face the *3D blocked state*. They feel disoriented, distrustful, and disconcerted. Disconcerted by the huge amount of available possibilities, solutions and alternatives. The offer is huge, and it is difficult to choose the best for each SmartCity area. Distrustful, because they receive many promises and have seen many deployment failures in cities with a lot of disintegrated, scattered solutions that do not deliver the expected value and generate more maintenance costs than expected. There are large suppliers with strong proposals, but also demanding strong, medium to long-term commitments or *lockdown*. There are small, agile and innovative suppliers, but with little muscle in tackling large projects. It is clear that none can deliver everything by itself. It's also clear that every solution needs to work in-sync on an integrated platform. Disoriented by the large number of inputs they receive and the difficulty of aligning them with the real city priorities, the CTO's vision and the political agenda.

The CTO must combine its vision with the potential solutions' identification and selection. There are multiple sources of ideas and opportunities to explore:

- Citizens, surveys, feedback, crowd proposals, civic technology trials
- From Technology. Companies. Events. Hackathons. Entrepreneurs, innovation labs, university research.
- Regulations to be complied with: GDPR (Data Protection Regulation in EU) and other similar, policies, privacy, security.
- Prize contests. External (like EU Horizon2020) grants for certain SmartCity areas. You can apply, but you must use the funding for what's defined in the call, so better to choose those that fit your strategy, or the other way: adapt your strategy to what the EU Commission is prioritizing.
- Ideas Exchange with other cities. Don't hesitate to look and copy, replicate and mainly, learn from others. But be careful, as everybody shows what shines not what hurts.
- Urgent threats impacting quality of life: human or natural potential disasters. Public health, pandemic, safety, environmental emergencies.
- Disruptive external forces and challenges described in Chap. 2.

**Understanding Who Your Citizens Are. Social Marketing**
You need to provide high-quality services to all your citizens. But not all your citizens are equal or demand the same services. Some cities are just digitizing existing generic services in a one-size-fits-all strategy. While this could be a first step, it neglects the unique needs from your very different citizen segments. On the other extreme, you should be careful to develop very specific, advanced services that only few *hyper-smart* citizens can consume. As an example, watch what the private

sector is offering, especially the most advanced in customer service: retailers and banks. Citizens expect the same, high-quality digital services they enjoy from those private companies. So, you should design advanced services for all, respecting their diversity and differences. If you had to pay special attention to one particular segment, then we would propose two: the elderly and millennials. Elderly people because their special needs and massive future use of digital services, (as explained in Chap. 2) and millennials, because they include a large share of talented citizens you want to retain and attract (Bobman, 2015). But we can find very good news here. You already have massive data on your citizens, so please, use it, and transform it into insights and knowledge. Social Analytics tools can help you in that process. You should be the best in knowing your citizens, and this is a clear advantage. Even more, it's expected that you use that data to identify, and proactively offer the services they need. *Knowing what we know about you, we proactively offer this service because we firmly believe this could logically be your next demanded service.* Imagine you could say that, the same way retail sector leaders do with our data as consumers. Every citizen needs public services according to their current lifestyle. So, if we know you have just had a baby, or want to get married, or have just moved to town, or are looking for a job, or have just reached the age of 18. . .then we can proactively offer you all the services you need because of that particular life fact. Even better, link all those services together, regardless of which entity (local, regional/state, national, international) provides them to you; in other words, put ourselves in citizens' shoes.(Meuris & Noels, 2013) Furthermore, you can seed, nurture, grow and enrich that knowledge (data mining) by using the right tools (apart from Data Analytics) like social networks, civic engagement and all other participation means like surveys, feedback or opinion tools, market research, panels, etc. That way you will use all available data (structured or traditional, and unstructured or from posted info on social tools).

### Dynamic and Agile Smart City Planning
The SmartCity strategic plan must be alive, dynamic and agile. It must be able to establish the fundamental elements in building trust: Discuss how the projects and services that it includes will improve the quality of life, city sustainability and governance; how the city will guarantee the needed resources to carry it out; estimate benefits, costs and risks, and identify contingency measures in case of disruptions or unexpected problems. It must set specific deadlines, but it must be constantly evolving to the citizens' constantly changing needs, and above all, to the emergence of new disruptive technologies, which will have an exponential/viral adoption. It must be a combination of solid strategies with clear paths, but with the ability to self-adapt and manage the ambiguity derived from the speed with which society and technology are changing.

### Innovation Capacity and Skills
Cities need human capital: capacity and culture of innovation, and knowledge to develop the plan. (Greenberg, 2015) They must ensure that they have the necessary innovation capacity, both from a technical point of view (either to implement by themselves or to know how to manage and assess market proposals), as well as from

a political and from an internal-management point of view, to be able to carry out the desired project, overcoming internal and external barriers, always with strict compliance of established regulations. Many projects fail due to the lack of technical skills (many cities are hiring Data Scientists), lack of leadership and political management, or lack of internal agility to make the projects start and develop without stops or blockages (a *champion* is necessary to move through the administration's complicated corridors, and a good communicator that marks the external milestones).

Officials dedicated to this plan must have an innovative culture, exploring alternatives, experimenting, constantly learning and creating new services, with enthusiasm, always from their knowledge of the local culture, needs and possibilities.

**Partnering and Collaborating with Others**
According to the (World Economic Forum, 2017a), cities must maximize collaboration with various entities and co-create public services through:

- Stimulating citizen participation in all areas of the city, both from the citizen as an activist, and from the city, proactively proposing activities and services.
- Partner with universities, research institutes and non-profit organizations, provided they help and collaborate in improving the city, the employability of citizens and innovation.
- Encourage companies and local entrepreneurs to invest in the improvement of urban services. Encourage PPP (Public-Private Partnership) agreements, always with transparency, equality and fair competition principles.
- Share adequate information (OpenData) and other physical assets such as spaces with local companies and entrepreneurs whenever this means attracting investment and talent to the city.
- Actively participating in regional, national and international SmartCity programs. These programs (such as EU Horizon2020) require collaboration between cities from different countries, to ensure that the achieved objectives are replicable across the EU.

Cities can share goods, spaces, buildings, services, data and even residents, all with the purpose of improving the city's quality of life and wealth and under a noble global competition for talent. If citizens are sharing a long list of things and creating multiple new business models because of that sharing, cities should follow the example. There are many ways people share things in the modern, global online *sharing economy*. (World Economic Forum, 2017b) Just to mention some: Urberpool or Blablacar (Mobility), Airbnb (Accomodation/Spaces), Crowdspring (Skills/Talent), CircleUp or Zopa (Financing), CrowdMed (Health), OpenGarden or Gridmates (Utilities), WarpIt or ThredUp (used goods), VizEat or EatWith (Meals), SkillShare or Coursera (Learning)

The SmartCity strategy focuses on the citizen, and it offers a neutral collaborative range where citizens, other governments, industries, investors, entrepreneurs, universities, and NGOs participate.

### 3.4.4  Implementing a Digital Transformation

Minsait/Indra (Gonzalez San Román & Sarmiento, 2019) describes the SmartCity implementation process as a full digital transformation, from long-term vision, short-term impact projects, citizen collaboration, service delivery models, planning to execution involving all stakeholders and finally, sharing the experiences, learning and applying the feedback again to improve the process, so a virtuous, continuous cycle.

A successful innovation project in SmartCity services is basically a process of digital transformation. It is a long, iterative, complex process. Some researchers point to about a 70% failure. (Bendor-Samue, 2018) We find it too pessimistic, although we agree that expectations always exceed the achieved reality. On the other hand, minor or partial objectives are always achieved, and the main idea is: it is a non-optional process; inaction is a guarantee of failure and ruin for the city. BCG states that cities, *"must face digital transformation as a business, review the digital route of public services from start to finish and eliminate all mandatory paper forms, phone calls and non-digital interactions."* (Mourtada et al., 2018) It is about copying the most advanced sectors such as retail, applying social marketing concepts, and taking full advantage of the technological possibilities. All this by translating the concept of customer to the citizen, which means: forget about the ROI and focus on the quality of the service, its real use and associated cost; and obsessively apply respect for the identity, security and privacy of citizens' data.

An innovative project in SmartCities does not imply that it is necessary to take risks, apply a radical renovation or design high-risk services. The reasonable approach is to find proven solutions (Eaves & McGuire, 2018) to try, experiment with models and pilot projects, all with the understanding that our city is unique and so are our needs, although surely applying the best from other cities' implementations will very well match what we want. Run away from *custom* projects. It is a last-century concept, it simply does not scale, it is expensive and has an unattainable maintenance. There are many examples of solution catalogs. To name one, the German organization (BeeSmartCity, 2019b) is the global leader and includes hundreds of them to cover all areas.

(ESI-ThoughtLAB, 2018) describes the SmartCities' investment roadmap as a decisive investment with solid steps, planning citizens' needs, leveraging the best assets we hold: our citizens and city data, working always within the strict compliance and security rules, leveraging and adopting the innovation as soon as it is commercially available, affordable and proven, preparing our infrastructure, (fiber-wiring the city, 5G, etc.), partnering with industry and investing significantly. A SmartCities' process begins with planning, political leadership and coordination of all the actors that will contribute to it. It is necessary to assess existing resources (both human and technical), available budgets and manage expectations. The starting point, the objective or target, the indicators that will validate the progress achieved must be defined. Then you have to look at the market, the previous experience from other cities, the expectations of external grants and begin to test, assess and evaluate alternatives. It's always better to buy existing and proven technologies than to develop ad-hoc solutions. A city is not a software/hardware development laboratory, but it needs software and hardware to achieve its SmartCity goals. The implementation must be constant, agile and adaptive, taking into account the parallel development and evolution of the necessary technologies, incorporating them when possible. It is about taking advantage of everything already done that is commercially available and affordable, without reinventing the wheel or taking on costly developments. We are unique and different, but not so much. . .surely, we'll find elements that give us much more than we need. The process must begin as a pilot, and as soon as its benefits are appreciated, spread throughout the city, and prepare to continue evolving. There is no use in installing 18,000 sensors if half are unusable in a year and there is no continuity, improvement and maintenance plan. (City of Santander noticed and reacted, making the multiple areas providers accountable for them). It is important to pay for what is needed. We need data, not sensors; results, not computers; availability of information, not storage disks; Intelligence, not algorithms. Shift your investments towards pay-as-you-use solutions, in other words, pay for what you use. Here, SaaS, PaaS and Cloud solutions in general demonstrate a tremendous advantage. A typical SmartCity project (in terms of sensors, or IoT devices along with the rest of the city information) starts with the collection of data from the sensors, adding the information we already have from citizens (taxes, properties, utilities, health, identity), and summing up citizens' sentiments reflected in social networks in real time. With this massive amount of information, we feed a complete, predictive, real-time and historical analysis system (Urban Data Platform), determining alerts and behaviors or patterns, providing knowledge about the current state of the city and applying Artificial Intelligence algorithms that generate a city model, which allows us to understand our city, how it behaves now and how it will behave in the future or facing certain unexpected situations (a Digital twin). With this knowledge, directors can make informed decisions and with a solid intelligence base. These decisions should be communicated and shared with the population, to justify investments and improve citizen benefits. It must be proposed, communicate the benefits, seek the collaboration of citizens, making them part of the solution, co-creators of it, not only passive receivers. We must provoke the solutions' propagation virality. Based on the actual use of the proposed solutions and the feedback obtained, model improvements and evolutions are proposed. Public-private collaboration is not only welcome but necessary, as it provides financing for the investment, fitting in with citizens' needs and taking advantage of the natural connection mechanisms established by the companies. We must communicate externally, share with the rest of the world, and learn from the leading cities in each area, all in a fair competition for talent. The international strengthening and recognition of our city will position it as an attractive and innovative place for the rest of the world.

**Citylab Model: Try, Test, Experiment**
In the strategy implementation, a wide range of possible alternatives are available. All SmartCities need to test new solutions, and solution providers need to test their solutions. We can identify three models of *CityLabs*. The most widely available, easy and useful is the *DataCityLab*, where different proposals and solutions are tested with the City Data. Second is reaching further and extending the testing from just data to a real solution (or full strategy plans) implementation in physical, real spaces or neighborhoods: *LivingLab*. The third approach is reaching the extreme, where a new, full city is developed from scratch to serve different purposes, but mainly to validate a strategy *NewCityLab*.

Cities need to test different solutions from the market, run what-if scenarios, test the internal applications' development, and encourage the creation of a local eco-system of start-ups working with universities to start new businesses, create jobs and nurture talent, all developing new SmartCity solutions. They all need real data to test and tune these apps. So, the city is offering a dataset (a snapshot of city data) to test these solutions. The ideal way to make this happen is to use a Cloud environment and protect it with a kind of gatekeeper professional that guarantees the correct use of resources, data, security, privacy and reliability. This is the concept of *DataCityLab*. Linked to it, most cities are exposing aggregated and non-personal-identifiable data to all external stakeholders (OpenData environments).

Many cities have gone beyond that point, not only experimenting with data, but with real city areas, neighborhoods, districts, testing the applicability of the newest technologies, assessing their impact, measuring the benefits before deploying them massively to the whole city. As one can imagine, many technology providers have found this approach very attractive for testing a brilliant solution and obtaining a remarkable reference (the city) as an example or case study to justify the expected benefits to the rest of potential customers. However, at the very beginning, this real *LivingLab* testing started from the academic sector. The growing number of SmartCity LivingLabs is causing turmoil in the urban modernization market. Initially, these test environments were led by laboratories or university and scientific research units that developed technological solutions to test them in real-life situations. Now, more and more, new projects are observed in districts, or small, satellite cities within a large urban area, financed through private initiatives or as public-private partnerships (with the private sector as the main investor).

Those who promote this concept present them as laboratories in real-life conditions; but they are also, above all, showcases, cities similar to the pilot floors produced by real estate developers, models that verify that the strategies and solutions are correct and that seek replicability (to be sold and reproduced). In the years 2000–2010, several innovative cities such as Barcelona came to have more than 100 live projects testing various technologies. The condition was: *test what you want, but leave it installed. If you prove its value, we will evaluate using it for the entire city.*

In the European Union, the European Network of Living Labs (ENoLL, 2019) was created in 2006, with the objective of promoting collaborative developments between cities, research laboratories and co-creating with private companies and citizens. Living Labs tries to serve the citizen, and place him/her at the center of every innovation, and promote the use of all the capacities offered by new technologies to match the specific needs and aspirations from local environments and cultures, leveraging different creativity patterns and potential ones. ENoLL has identified five core components that should be present in any Living Lab: (1) active citizen involvement; (2) clear, real-life setting; (3) multi-actor/stakeholder participation; (4) combined methodologies' approach and (5) co-creation of new city solutions, innovation initiatives. So, ENoLL supports citizen-centric and citizen-driven research, development and innovation.

In the U.S., the concept of a living laboratory was later released by the Massachusetts Institute of Technology (MIT), which opened its first living laboratory in 2010. The objective was to develop new technologies (autonomous vehicles, advanced IoT) in an open, all-welcome, public-private environment, with the city and its inhabitants as end users. Many American university campuses have used the concept of living laboratories to test the practical use of technology solutions, such as *The Big Data Living Lab* at MIT in Boston, Urban Labs in Chicago (social projects like job-seekers and Energy Optimization for low-income households), full university connectivity for students at Nebraska (with kiosks at the smart campus), driverless, cooperative advanced traffic network at University of Wisconsin, or smart metering for anything IoT at the University of Washington in Seattle. International cooperation is also fostered between living labs like *Copenhagen Solutions Lab* (Denmark) and Queensland University of Technology in Brisbane (Australia) in parking space management.

But the best known LivingLab, including the city as a whole, is Singapore, the most advanced smart-solutions *test-bed*. The Asian tiger city-state is the main flagship for this strategy. For business reasons and international awareness, the city is projected as a model of SmartCity, SmartTerritory or SmartCountry, landing over an exceptional, *"highly-connected and wired-up island"*, (Prime Minister Lee Hsieng Loonen in 2014).

Many other cities are developing the concept in association with a private company, as explained before. Another example could be Denver, Colorado, with the *Colorado Open Lab,* focused on IoT, and in association with the specialized company Arrow Electronics.

Now, starting the 2020s we can say that all innovative cities in the world have already started, or are in the process of building a LivingLab matching the local advantages, universities' specialization, companies' investment focus, or political motivations.

For those countries with *Dirigiste* organization, the best, most agile and fastest way to endorse this movement is to create a *NewCity LivingLab*. Examples are Chinese Chengdu Great City satellite district (by 2012, a completely car-free city for the 80.000 inhabitants, now still in development and running the risk of becoming another ghost city); Songdo City (South Korea), a new, made from scratch Seoul satellite-city acclaimed as the *city of the future*; Saudi's huge project, Neom, aiming to create the post-oil economy for the region, attracting the best investors and brains from around the world; nearby, Abu Dhabi's Masdar City, started in 2006, and used as a technology laboratory for sustainable and renewable energies, although not attracting residents as expected. This exercise reaches its culmination in the development of an ideal, theoretically created, designed and implemented city on a 3D model by a laboratory of experts, without any inheritance to keep, without a past, without limitations imposed by history, customs or local culture, like a new colonization on a new planet.

This absolute freedom is a dream for private promoters building a new cyber city, from scratch, both physically and materially as well as culturally and sociologically, to attract relevant, talented, but elitist populations. A theoretical, gentrified city...which normally ends up being a ghost town. They forget that the elites have enough wealth to choose where they want to live and even build their homes with the most advanced technology, while the less rich simply cannot afford to live in such an advanced and expensive new city. In any case, these experiments have stimulated and encouraged the *from scratch* trend: a new concept of urban modernization, developing new urban spaces, even if they are limited spaces, but creating only the physical side, never the human one.

Transforming an old and populated city is much more complicated and expensive, so why not at least to dream of building a new, ex-novo district?

### 3.4.5  Measuring SmartCities Benefits

Before measuring the impact for your project, it's important to define the target: definition and size of who are you targeting, especially considering specific segments of your population, and also external people that you would like to attract. All benefits should respond to clear outcomes, and it's better if they are expressed by figures (improve this topic or indicator from A to B in this period of time, savings, service improvement, extra revenues in some specific area, cost reduction, time savings for citizens, etc.).

Benefits should be calculated as a combination of impact and real usage. It's a waste of resources to improve the quality of a service that nobody or a few people use, and on the other hand, a little and easy improvement used massively brings incredible benefits. In the EU, the European Innovation Partnership on Smart Cities and Communities (EIP-SCC) fosters participating cities to work on collaborative projects to demonstrate how new technology solutions and innovative processes transform current urban environments into smarter and more livable places. (BeeSmartCity, 2018b) categorizes the benefits into six areas (Cost Savings, Environmental Impact, Efficiency Gains, Connectivity, Quality of Life, Economic Prosperity) and we would add a seventh: Recognition/Overall Attractiveness Reference.

As a source for inspiration, this Data-SmartCity Solutions (HarvardKennedy School, 2017) catalog proposes more than 200 solutions available in the U.S., sorted by these expected outcomes: Accountability, Awareness, Civic Engagement, Effectiveness, Efficiency, Social Justice/Equity, Systemic Change and Transparency.

(ESI ThoughtLab, 2019) conducted a 100 world cities' study and the feedback on measurable and significant improvements is notorious: Improvement in citizen satisfaction due to smart mobility is noted by 38% of cities, while 32% associate it to productivity and city service delivery time. The impact on health due to smart environmental and energy initiatives is recognized by 45% of the cities, 44% experience pollution reduction and 43% are controlling energy prices.

**Cost Savings**

In a world with around $4 trillion in public debt, it is comforting to know that instead of increasing taxes, governments have alternatives: a white paper published by ABI Research (Ismail, 2017) pointed out that SmartCity technologies could save over $5 trillion/year by 2022. In 2014, the city of Barcelona published some clear, tangible savings as a result of SmartCity technologies: 75 million euros from IoT smart water, lighting, and more, 36 million due to smartparking fee increases, and creation of 47,000 jobs for the city. (Cisco, 2014)

**Environmental Impact**

Most cities are installing sensors to measure air quality, sound levels, temperature, water levels, traffic. The most advanced cities have a plan to become Carbon Neutral, or to significantly reduce their carbon emissions, as explained in Sect. 2.6. Barcelona has a plan to combat pollution by reducing traffic by 21% and banning cars from 60% of city streets. Antwerp and Malaga have very creative technologies in place to measure air quality by placing sensors on postal service vehicles. New technologies like smart windows on buildings aim to save up to 26% on cooling and 67% on lighting. (Tracy, 2016)

All initiatives on the Circular City explained in Sect. 2.6 are also clearly impacting environmental care.

**Efficiency Gains**

Cities also use technologies, and specifically IoT, to optimize the management of scarce and expensive resources, such as water and energy. The results from the main smart cities in the world are very promising. Some cities have seen approximately 50–60% in energy savings by taking advantage of LED-based smart streetlights, while others have been able to reduce water leaks in the supply network by 20%, saving between 25–80 liters of water per person per day. Optimized traffic flow in some areas is helping citizens save between 15 and 30 minutes a day, reducing traffic congestion by 30%, resulting in a 10–15% reduction in emissions. Up to a 66% reduction in the waste-management operational costs has also been observed due to the optimization frequency of smart garbage collection based on the garbage dumps' capacity and usage sensors. Intel (Juniper Research) estimates that smart city initiatives could save every citizen about 125 hours/year, and from those mostly due to traffic and congestion reductions: up to 60 hours annually. (Nhede, 2018) Carlo Ratti, Director of MIT Senseable Lab, noted, *"cars are idle 95% of time, meaning that every shared car could effectively replace between 10–30 private cars."* (SmartCity International, 2015)

**Connectivity**

As explained in Sect. 2.4, Internet access and good bandwidth is becoming a vital resource for cities' economic growth. But, the European Commission reported in 2017 that an estimated 44% of EU citizens do not have basic digital skills (EU-EPALE, 2019), and 15% do not have access to the Internet. (Carmona, 2019) As people become more aware of the value of technology, they grow in their expectations that the public sector will facilitate a more digital and interactive society that will provide them with better, added-value services. The digital divide acts as a barrier to smart city access for some citizens. Due to the digital divide, citizens without sufficient access to smart devices, broadband networks, wireless connectivity and other technologies (such as the emerging 5G) derive less benefits from the improvements in the quality of life generated by digital solutions. But the digital divide should not be confused with digital inequality. The sociologist Stefano de Marco explains that the digital divide marks the difference between those who have access to the Internet and those who do not, while digital inequality is related to Internet use, and is very much linked to the lack of digital skills. (Carmona, 2019) Digital inequality means that a subset of the online population does not take advantage of electronic services such as shopping, tele-learning, electronic health, telecommuting or Mobility-as-a-Service, e-government, mobile banking, travel planning, etc. Local governments need to develop smart city solutions that continue to narrow the digital divide and the digital equality gap while improving the quality of life. Connectivity between citizens and governments is also more fluid in the SmartCity, where *Fix my City*-like feedback or reporting applications allow citizens to report incidents and problems through their smartphones, and civic forums like *"Better Rekjavik"* or *"DigiTel"* in Tel-Aviv, offer citizens a direct communication line with their authorities, improving relations between citizens and institutions, making better use of available services and initiatives, solidifying the sense of belonging, and improving social cohesion.

**Quality of Life**

The digital divide and differences in quality of life affect the way people interact with the local government. In most situations, citizens with a low quality of life require more local government public services than those who enjoy a high one. (Downey & Jones, 2012) According to the McKinsey Global Institute, digital solutions could improve many indicators of quality of life by up to 30%. (Frem et al., 2018) As an example, the use of predictive analysis applied to real-time crime, finding patterns, modus operandi and conflictive locations, and attempting to anticipate risky situations. Thus, the presence of guards can be reinforced, and avoid these incidents before they occur. The same can be used to predict situations of social divide, vulnerability, energy poverty or gender violence. With the IoT information from all types of systems, small problems can be solved before they could have led to major failures, higher costs and bigger catastrophes.

According to another McKinsey study (Woetzel et al., 2018), cities can achieve quantifiable improvements in the quality of life of citizens through SmartCity initiatives in social services/health, safety, smart mobility, energy, water, air quality, waste management and basic and relationship digital services for citizens. Some figures due to intensive use of SmartTechnologies are: reduced fatalities (from homicide, traffic, and fires) by 8–10%; reduced incidents of assault, robbery, burglary, and auto theft by 30–40%; emergency-response times cut by 20–35%; cut commuting times (SmartMobility by 2025) by 15–20%; potential to reduce DALYs by 8–15% (disability-adjusted life years *DALYs* is the primary metric used by the World Health Organization to calculate the global disease burden, reflecting not only lost years of life due to early death, but also lost productive and healthy years due to disability or incapacity); emissions/pollution can be cut by 10–15% due to applied technology to Smartbuildings, dynamic electricity contracting, and some mobility applications; in water management, leakages can be cut by up to 25%; solid waste per capita can be reduced by 10–20% with solutions such as pay-as-you-throw digital tracking; cities can save 25–80 liters of water per person per day, and reduce unrecycled solid waste by 30–130 kg per person annually; air-quality sensors help identify the sources of contamination to decide impact with further action, (Beijing reduced deadly airborne pollutants by roughly 20% in less than a year by closely tracking traffic and construction), which can reduce negative health effects by 3–15%, depending on current levels.

**Economic Prosperity**
The previously explained concept of CityLab, promoting local startup hubs, such as those in Antwerp (Belgium), Amsterdam, Barcelona, Stavanger (Norway) and many others, contributes to creating qualified jobs and accelerating new businesses around the city. SmartCity technologies serve as the foundation to develop new companies. Those companies can early test their new solutions in the city, as a FabLab, and if successful, they can go to the rest of the world with a first real implementation/reference, and ask for financing not just with an idea, but with a tangible real project.

**Awareness/Overall Attractiveness Reference**
In general, any improvements in Quality of Life because of SmartCity solutions' investment is increasing the City Attractiveness, so talent will better consider that particular city as a target to move to and develop his/her full potential. That way, the benefits from investing in SmartCities are not only for the locals, but for creating recognition of a modern, innovative city, perfect to receive talented citizens from abroad, and to increase prosperity (it's a way to *sell* the city to the world, and become vocal and participative in remarkable international forums and public scenarios). A clear way on how to measure the city's future potential will be to see the level of investment in innovation, and specifically the SmartCity Plan. This will be discussed later.

## 3.5   Humanizing SmartCities

*The intelligence of a city lies in the intelligence of its residents."* J-L Missika, Deputy Mayor of Paris, 2016 (Cathelat, 2019d). *"Cities are not intelligent, citizens are intelligent."* (Morcillo, 2013a)*"We need tools to empower citizens and not simply to administrate cities.* Adam Greenfield-Ideas for Change, 2017 (Morcillo, 2013b).

We have seen how SmartCities use technologies to improve citizens' lives. This should not be interpreted as the complete design of the SmartCity technological scenario. Rather, the SmartCity is above all, how citizens are shaping the city by using technology, from directors to politicians making the best decisions with the acquired information and knowledge, to each citizen with their contribution in the form of data, and the use they make of the services and solutions available to the city. The SmartCity is based on how people are empowered through the use of technology, to contribute to urban change and realize their ambitions. The SmartCity provides the conditions and resources for that change. SmartCity is an agent of change, a living and permanent urban laboratory, an ecosystem of urban innovation that is constantly testing, using and requesting improvements in each and every public service. SmartCity is the city's transformation engine, a generator of solutions for the most important problems and challenges. This is how the city behaves intelligently.

Putting people first and foremost is paramount. Today's challenges require a more holistic approach to problem solving that puts people at the center of innovations, with data and technology around, finally facilitating and improving all the city service areas. *"Cities may be getting smarter, but they haven't noticeably changed from a user perspective. It seems like most of the digital advances in cities have been invisible and focused on city operations, rather than on the parts of the city that people can see, touch, and use. SmartCities are boring. Give us responsive Citie*s." Colin O'Donnell, CIO at Intersection, managing NYC Innovative new Internet-WIFI network, LinkNYC. (O'Donnell, 2017)

### *3.5.1   Creating a City that People Can Co-create, Contribute to and Build Every Day.*

Citizens have a central and crucial role in the city evolution and future. Technology always helps, as an enabler. Citizens should use technology to help cope with the main challenges the world faces today, at the city level. Citizens must take the first personal steps on: decarbonization, circular consumption, city participation and engagement, trusted privacy and Artificial Intelligence use. In this way, citizens must be aware of their personal, daily carbon footprint, in what they use, in the energy they consume and in their mobility means, and they must consider alternatives that produce less emissions from their origin to their final consumption, even if it involves some additional physical, time or economical effort. Things such as circular consumption, reducing the new use of raw materials, especially pollutants such as plastics, awareness of the importance of reusing goods, thinking twice before discarding useful things (without going into problems such as Diogenes syndrome and storing garbage), and encouraging and supporting recycling, a task of intense collaboration between citizens and cities, which will require some additional conscious cooperation. Citizens must have the awareness of the need to contribute to their city, the sense of belonging, of permanent solidarity building, of community. It is not just a matter of paying taxes, but of contributing with opinions, time and above all, with actions to improve your city. The privacy of information is fundamental, and citizens must know how to protect their identity, but they must be generous with their city, providing information that, used collectively and without personally identifying anyone, contributes to a better understanding of the environment, habits and behaviors, and better adapts the services to them, to be more efficient. We must differentiate between allowing access to certain personal information to a private entity that will chase us to sell its products, or something worse; and our city, which will treat that information with care, security and without any motivation for profit, only to improve the service it provides us. Finally, we must rely on technology and its proper use to improve our quality of life. Despite the myths and numerous negative communications about Artificial Intelligence, we must rely on these new solutions and the enormous advantages they will bring us.

We must also work on Design. (Goldsmith, 2019) Cities like L.A. are hiring a Chief Design Officer, trying to make new city urban developments more human and beautiful. So, it's not just about technology, it's about making everything more human, even the new physical locations, and public architecture. Combining both, technology and urbanism, citizens can use some tools to co-create the city. Imagine our citizens using tools as popular as Minecraft to suggest to the city how to design new spaces. Other technologies like augmented reality or even virtual reality like Hololens could help visualize aspects of future spaces and make cities more livable. Mentioned before, Danish urbanist Jan Gehl helped reshape the city of Copenhagen, but also Melbourne and Chicago, by creating urban spaces that fostered social life, cohesion and inclusion, and avoiding many serious mental illnesses due to isolation in big cities.

It seems clear that citizens and their data should be part of how cities design new solutions. Civic participation also allows cities to be more inclusive, as all voices can be heard and taken into account. Therefore, the process of creating a SmartCity must be collaborative (CITIES TODAY, 2019), bi-directional, from city systems to citizens, and from citizens and their devices to the city, in a constant flow of proposals and feedback.

So far, we have seen how the city is proposing new services and solutions to citizens. This is the inside-out way. Analyzing the needs, investing in a solution, proposing that solution for citizens' use.

Yet we have to consider both directions. The *outside-in* is made of innovation landing in the city by other actors, rather than the internal SmartCity team (or city budget). This could be generated by the community or private-sector initiatives.

By studying the EU report (EU Commission D7 Report, 2016a) on analyzing the role of citizens in creating SmartCity Solutions, we can conclude that citizens can provide:

- Information & resources – Citizen feedback is very important in project planning phases, and even more relevant as crowdsourcing information and behavior at the end-user level. In this way, the city can better understand the behavior of its citizens and their reactions to the proposals. This information can be provided proactively and consciously through apps that are popular and known, that provide certain information, (traffic, security, location, payments, etc.) or indirectly through analyzing third-party elements such as social networks or other indicators to determine the so-called *sentiment an*alysis. This interaction also includes awareness, promotion and education, fundamental to the success of any project, which, as we explained, is not only about proposing a new solution, but about being massively used by the population. In this way, citizens are deeply involved, and city moves towards new benefits' achievement and changes in behavior.

- Co-design, co-creation, collaborative research; joint decision-making – These are approaches aimed especially at the design stage. We observe as a trend the direct collaboration in pilots and demos, prior testing on small groups of citizens, as well as the increase in the number of new living labs, where these new services are actually adjusted or fine-tuned. A similar revolution occurs in urban planning and policy generation. Concepts such as participatory planning/budgeting, civic crowd funding, and dynamic master-planning emerge as inconclusive, but unquestionable as support tools. Particularly relevant are applications that permit new ways of democratizing decision-making by collecting data, gathering feedback, and improving solutions' usefulness. Cities are increasingly exhibiting a number of district or neighborhood-level smart spaces such as large-scale demonstrators, living labs or smart streets, which are ideal platforms to explore the needs of citizens as users. In theory, these district-level innovation spaces operate as intermediary platforms among cities, companies, research organizations as well as citizens for joint value co-creation, rapid new services' prototyping or solutions' validation to scale and speed up innovation. Citizens can and should participate in what they can contribute and know: background issues and directions, civic sense or aesthetic elements, where a large majority have an opinion with some foundation. There is an open debate about what methods achieve what results and how representative they are, and from whom are they coming from. Finally, we are seeing new incubation and acceleration techniques, heiresses of successful techniques in the retail sector, such as research laboratories to support the city's service innovation. Joint-decision making is often accompanied by new governance models such as representation of citizens on local city boards, although this is very traditional in many cities through the *district boards* (many local names apply here).

- Cooperative action: social innovation – While this is a new category, it is gaining momentum in specific areas such as social policies, citizen re-skilling, the welfare state and climate change. We can find community-based solutions as a whole, as well as individual contributions to the collective plan. These actions require visionary leadership. Some examples are the community energy co-generation, civic contributions in time and economically, (giving) or Copenhagen citizens' commitment to use public transportation or bicycle in 85% of their commuting to achieve the carbon neutral status target by 2025.

Citizen engagement leads to increased levels of trust on institutions as citizens perceive that their voice is listened to, and their contribution and impact are more direct.

**Ensuring Inclusive Innovation**
In simple terms, inclusive innovation is the means by which technology is used to develop new services for those who have been excluded from the main group of citizens for reasons of wealth, ethnic or linguistic difference, or any kind of disability. New technologies can be included for the base of the social pyramid: mobile phones, mobile services, telecentres, and more accessible services such as sidewalks with wheelchair ramps, audible traffic lights, adapted means of transportation and public facilities, web/mobile applications adapted for people with mobility, visual, auditory or cognitive disabilities, etc. This means the ambition of the future city to be inclusive for all, including the elderly, the marginalized and especially the poor and unemployed, and those who have any degree of disability. Inclusive innovation should focus particularly on the following dimensions:

* Affordable & inclusive social housing
* Social & community innovation. Ensure inclusiveness at the district level, considering all kind of cultural and social diversity.
* Empowering the citizen – marginalized groups often have special needs such as ICT access, interface design simplicity, etc.
* Special solutions for people with any kind of disability

Founded by the UN in 2006, the G3ict or *"Global Initiative for Inclusive Information and Communication Technologies"* merges the United Nations Global Alliance for ICT and Development with the Secretariat for the Convention on the Rights of Persons with Disabilities at UN DESA. (G3ict, 2016) promoted an initiative to secure that SmartCities' development doesn't widen the digital gap for people with disabilities or aging persons with rest of population, just the opposite: try to use the advantages of new technologies to reduce these social differences.

Waag Society (a European consulting firm focused on using technology for social change) provides some guidelines for city officials when designing a Citizen-Centered SmartCity Strategy. (EU Commission D7 Report, 2016b) In summary:

* Your citizens know more about your city than you. Not only do you listen to them, but establish an open dialogue about what could be done, and how.
* Design and development processes must be unified. You have to make rapid prototypes, get continuous citizen feedback, iterate quickly, and be prepared to start over if necessary.

- Combine the fact that the initiatives are civic, with the need to be scalable and sustainable.
- Citizens must have absolute control of their data (comply with GDPR). In order for them to rely on the proposed solutions, they must observe transparency throughout the process of capturing and using the data. Thus, they will rely on the management of the city and provide their data with confidence.

One of most advanced SmartCities in the world, Amsterdam, explains in its SmartCity core values (Amsterdam SmartCity, 2019) the crucial relevance of residents in the city development, directly, or indirectly, through partners or online community of events. They want to stimulate a continuous public dialogue to foster cooperation between public and private organizations in an open and transparent way.

Some well-known examples on strong citizen participation on SmartCity projects could be Medellín (Colombia), Helsinki, Barcelona, Ghent (Belgium) and Tel-Aviv. For LatinAmerica and other areas where available investment is not high, SmartCities' budgets should be very carefully managed, and the projects must be chosen to maximize impact. This requires understanding the citizens first, and then designing the projects. You should understand first who your citizens are, what they do throughout the day, how they are interacting with city services, and then prioritize your proposals accordingly. (Cadena & Ellen, 2018) Citizen-centric is not so different than customer-focused strategies in the private sector, so many marketing techniques can be adapted and used in public service optimization to serve citizens.

Medellín (Colombia) was for many years very famous for being one of the most violent and dangerous cities in the world, due to the Pablo Escobar's cartel. When Federico Gutiérrez (elected in 2016 as the mayor of Medellin) was campaigning, instead of exclusively speaking and explaining his program and trying to convince others, he held constant meetings to listen to citizens and gather their opinions and needs. With this information, he generated a 400-page document that serves as a fundamental government plan, collecting proposals on many topics such as security, urban mobility, environmental problems, and education, employment, and social equality. *"This government plan was built by walking through the streets of Medellín to really listen to each of the inhabitants, and obtain the inputs to elaborate the government plan."* (Cathelat, 2019e) Humberto Iglesias, city pilot, Medellin.

Helsinki is another well-known example where citizens are empowered to participate or *play the game*. Authorities highlight the need to count on good, skilled citizens to ensure the right development.

*"For us, the smart city is also about people. In the past, smart cities were focused on technology, but for us the role of people is key. The inhabitants of the Helsinki region will be active participants. Human well-being is based on the knowledge and skills that competent, open-minded and well-educated inhabitants will require in the future."* Johanna Juselius. Senior Advisor, EU Affairs. Uudenmaan liitto (Helsinki-Uusimaa Regional Council) (Cathelat, 2019f). *"We are working to build a culture of trust. Trust is based on openness, transparency and data exchange and how decisions are made. Fortunately, there is a lot of trust in Finland. People say that data is the new oil, but that is incorrect: trust is the new oil. The data is cheap, but trust is really valuable,"* Mikko Rusama, Chief Digital Officer (CDO)

of the City of Helsinki and Chairman of the Board at the Forum Virium Helsinki. (Cathelat, 2019g)

In Barcelona, Francesca Bria, Barcelona's former CTO and Digital Innovation Officer, claimed an estimated participation of around 40,000 inhabitants, with 70% of proposals being later discussed at city council meetings, turning a *top-down* management into a *bottom-up* built decision flow due to a citizen participation platform.

The Belgian city of Ghent has put people at the very heart of its own definition, *"A smart city reconnects people with their environment and the city to create more efficient relationships. Smart cities need smart citizens to be fully inclusive, innovative and sustainable."* (Pisani, 2015).

The European Union H2020 awarded project *OrganiCity* allowed the cities of Aarhus (Denmark), London (UK), and Santander (Spain) to work together on this concept. OrganiCity tries to define a citizen-centric city-making. They found seven basic principles for citizen engagement:

> *1. Empower Adjacent Communities and Champion Advocates, 2. Design for Trust, Especially Around Change, 3. Facilitate Personal/Community Ownership, 4. Debate and Co-Create Across the Comfort Zones, 5. Use Challenge Areas as Catalysts for Innovation, 6. Respect the Value of Venue: Face to Face, Online, Culture & Collaboration, 7. Provide a Clear Journey and Value Visibility* (Brynskov et al., 2016)

Tel-Aviv is, in our opinion, the model to follow on citizen integration and participation. Known as Israel's *Nonstop City* because of its intense life, and rich variety of opportunities for leisure, entertainment, culture, tourism and dining, the city had the same traditional problems connecting with citizens. Around 2015, the city launched the program "DigiTel" (Tel-Aviv, 2019) to engage with its inhabitants. We like this initiative because it is bi-directional: citizens participating, and the city proposing new ideas and activities in a continuous dynamic. We also love it because it started from citizens' endorsement, from scratch, offering a well-designed, citizen-centered tool and card, and adding more and more as a viral effect till they include most of the 400,000 inhabitants. The city is using its own data, plus the specific citizen preferences. *"We conducted a poll and discovered that citizens really love the city and its dynamic, vibrant, endless day-by-day events. But they weren't so enthusiastic about the government, which they saw bureaucratic and distant. We wanted to change that impression and engage the residents, bring them more value, and create a new kind of city service approach."* Liora Shechter, Chief Information Officer for the city of Tel Aviv-Jaffa. This Digitel Club is open and available for all Tel-Aviv residents aged 13 or older. When registering, citizens provide very relevant information not registered in the *official* city records, like interests, hobbies, and other personal information. So, citizens must trust on the city's correct treatment of this sensitive data. That way, the city can provide a continuous flow of highly personalized services. Those services (sometimes just pieces of information like announcements or invitations to participate in the many city events) are individually personalized, location-based, and sent to smartphones. This is not just for fun, all other *serious services* like tax payments, reporting's, grants, etc. are also available from the application. This way, citizens perceive a living city: nearer, warmer, something like a companion that provides (sometimes surprisingly) all kind of services and opportunities for enjoying a better life. The city government is more transparent and next to citizens, also encouraging proactive citizen participation. With the entire city at the resident's grasp, they appreciate that they can make better choices, observe a more sustainable behavior and become more inclusive. All is there, all city options, all transportation including the Tel Aviv Tel-O-Fun (the bicycle rental system), parking lots information, etc., without the need to use different applications or jump to different providers. Vice-versa, citizens can report whatever needs to be fixed, in a very intuitive and useful way.

In addition to these examples from cities trying to integrate/communicate to citizens, technology also provides new, creative alternatives to mobilize citizens and provoke their participation in city life. These new tools are called *Active Digital Living*, or ADL capabilities. So, apart from the most common tools to communicate with citizens like chats, SMS, etc., we can propose technology-based activities to engage with citizens. ADL could be grouped in Gamification Apps, Wellness habits, Physical exercise, Smart Art (interactive), Learning/Training interactive tools. Cities can take advantage of these tools to become more involved in citizens lives, in the usual and friendly activities. Some examples could be: Gamified Recycling tools; Good-behavior Gamified rewards/city points; Wellness suggestions depending on city parks conditions and weather, a fitness coach chatbot; Virtual-reality tools for biking, for treadmills with city-projected scenarios; Virtual-reality gaming including local traditional sports, local sport teams; use of new technologies like holograms in public spaces to grab people's attention or highlight a place or moment or just for pure artistic intent; Smart art in streets to foster creativity, allowing interactive participation; Drones light shows using LEDs instead of fireworks (polluting less); special streets or monuments Lighting, or just lighting the desert; offer new advanced MOOC (training courses) to improve the population's capacitation/ employability, etc.

### 3.5.2  Possible Cities

Where are our cities going? What is the city model we want to go towards? Does it have something to do with the fictional cities that the movies/narratives pose? Are those cities possible? Our imagination is infinite, but we can link the concept of a possible city to the analysis of possible worlds in literature. When talking about creating a better city, or a new city from scratch, we have to use the concept of a possible world as a reference. A world is any referential entity that our imagination can create and that has related elements. Put another way, a set of semantically referenced elements, with certain established relationships. A possible world includes a series of certain rules, norms, laws, shortcomings or advantages which give it credibility. (Albaladejo, 2018)

What defines a possible city? If we think of our future city model or have the opportunity to design a new city from scratch (either through new investment or territory development or by necessity, as in the case of the city of Kiruna, (Sweden) where the danger of collapse because of the exploitation of the underground iron mine - the second largest in the world - means that they must *move* the city a few kilometers East, (evidently they move nothing except a historical church and the whole city is built again) then we would put a management team composed of an urban planner, a technologist and a humanist, to balance the three fundamental elements of the city's development, as we saw earlier. If from the ontological point of view, a city is a point in space/time where people meet, for there to be a possible city there must be four fundamental components: a place, a moment in time, humans and their relationships. Place and time are defined by the physical dimension of the city and the technological parameters that govern it. Is a city without humans a city? What about the texts about non-human cities? Here we must look at the fourth component: relationships, rational socialization. If that space/time is used to deploy social relationships, then urban magic is created, and we could talk about a non-human-inhabitant city. If there are no rational social relations, then we only talk about animals gathered for certain instinctive purposes, and we end up with the concept of colony, herd, hives or burrows. What would happen to those futuristic cities composed of or dominated by cyborgs? They are not human, but if those machines reach a rational knowledge development through Artificial Intelligence that allows them to establish rational social relationships - scientists are already working on emotions, feelings and self-conscious machines - taking advantage of the physical environment given by a place and time we could think of cities inhabited by machines. As of right now, we are at the concept limit, surely a dystopian limit. They won't be human because they will always be devoid of human dignity, since this is our essential transcendental component, our connection with God, our divine, inherent and inviolable component. If they are simply machines without a social component, then we can't talk about cities, but about warehouses, workshops or hangars. Therefore, the city enables and develops socialization, the encounter, the meeting, the social gathering. If there is a group of humans, but because of the prevailing norms they cannot meet and socialize, then they are not in a city, but in a jail or cages. (Is COVID-19 confinement creating the anti-cities?). Even in the worst concentration camp, humans will always have their dignity, even if that environment is not a city and their capacity for socialization is lacking, severed by repression and violence. There is no sense of collaboration for the development of a better future, there are no social synergies, there is simply basic survival instinct.

A possible city is a possible world where people can live and interact. There may be as many possible cities as places where people have gathered and left their footprints (as constructions, or at least, proof of their experiences). Once we have understood how these possible cities that we want to build and develop can theoretically be, we will know how the real cities we have are, and their different types, to understand our starting point. We can talk about cities of all kinds: large/small, developed/emerging zones, North/South, Western/Eastern culture. We know their parameters: climate, GDP, population, etc., and we could make many classifications.

The most informative classification of the capacity for development, competitiveness and evolution of a city is the one studied by the large construction company, JLL, in its *"Typology of World Cities."* (JLL, 2018)

JLL, from its position as a huge construction and real estate company, finds 10 types of cities in terms of development capacity, mainly urban development, which gives us a good perspective on their strategic position and their development alternatives. It is clear that if a city is attractive to talent, then the first consequence is a valuation of the real estate sector, so we can consider this study a very appropriate and interesting proxy. Note that in this sector, size does matter, as we speak of a combination of physical and economic city footprint, fundamentally.

For Jeremy Kelly, Director in Global Research at JLL, the dynamics, style and amount of real estate required drives the city characteristics, aspirations and priorities, and therefore its ability to grow and attract talent and business. (Kelly, 2018)

**The 10 new city types**
The podium is taken by The Big Seven and the Contenders.

**The Big Seven** are the elite of developed cities and absorb 25% of all globally-invested capital in commercial real estate. They are the by-default option for investors and global corporations. You don't have to think hard to guess which ones: London, New York, Paris, Hong Kong, Tokyo, Singapore and Seoul. They have everything in terms of human capital and real estate.

They are followed by the Contenders, who are experiencing a very important urban development in the last decade, enormous growth in the rental market, growing inhabitant numbers, economic and world leadership that places them in the position of challengers to the elite positions. They include San Francisco, Amsterdam, Toronto, Sydney, Madrid, Los Angeles, Chicago, Washington D.C., Beijing and Shanghai.

From here on, JLL clearly separates two worlds: a Western one, based on economic, scientific and cultural development as an evolution of existing cities, but with strong investment in their future. This investment is fundamentally private and under democratic political standards, with strong citizen participation and ethical evaluation of practices and results; another, fundamentally Eastern, with emerging countries, new Asian cities with rapid developments led by a non-democratic, central government under a planned direction; or emerging countries' mega-cities where the population volume exceeds its economic development.

In the developed, Western democratic countries' side, JLL distinguishes three zones: Innovators, Lifestyle and Influencers. Innovators stand out for their economies of high volume, and great appeal to entrepreneurs and talent. In our opinion, these cities, like Berlin, Tel-Aviv, Dublin, Milan, Seattle, Boston, are solid candidates to jump into the area of Contenders. They lack the population to reach those investment volumes, but they enjoy all the rest of conditions. Lifestyle cities have developed very high-quality-of-life levels and public services for their citizens. They have achieved this with strong investments in technology (they are the best SmartCities), a moderate and orderly population, where inequalities do not impede development. We find here cities like Stockholm, Copenhagen, Helsinki, Oslo, Melbourne, Vancouver, Hamburg. Finally, in this area, JLL talks about Influencers, as cities of great development due to a strategic position for international investments and with cultural and commercial appeal. Here they place Barcelona, Miami, Kyoto, Brussels, Frankfurt. We think that Lifestyle and Influencers are very similar, and we find Barcelona, Vienna and Zurich on the middle border. Perhaps the only difference is from the point of view of international relevance and leadership, which is greater in the Influencers, lesser in the Lifestyle, who devote few resources to this international awareness.

On the other side, we have the emerging world of overcrowded, massively populated cities, or Eastern cities with *Dirigiste* development and planned economies. Megahubs are huge cities in terms of population, where the economy does not have the same level of development. We find Mexico City, Moscow, the Indi Delhi and Mumbai, Sao Paulo, all within the so-called emerging development zone: BRIC. They are the economic centers of their countries, but they fail as investment destinations. The cities in the Enterprisers area have tremendous development and dynamism, although social inequalities sometimes make them messy and chaotic. Among these we find Bangalore, Taipei, and Ho Chi Minh City. By attracting large companies, they hold a very promising future, tending to move to the hybrid area, in between the developing and developed countries. Finally, the Powerhouses are developing rapidly from a state-led economy – fundamentally, we're speaking of Chinese cities - emerging from a low-value economy and innovating to more advanced positions. We have Shenzhen, Chengdu, Chongqing, etc.

Between both worlds, developed and emerging, mainly Western vs Eastern, we find two intermediate exchange areas: The Hybrids area is occupied by medium-sized cities, with a good real estate market transformation, and where transparency in business brings investors' trust. We see here Warsaw, Santiago, Kuala Lumpur, Abu Dhabi, Doha, Dubai.

Finally, on the other end, JLL places the National Growth Engines, as stable, reliable, large, but not very dynamic and innovative cities. They resonate in our head as examples of generic cities (see Koolhaas note on Sect. 1.6). They are Dallas, Atlanta, Houston, Buenos Aires, Osaka, Nagoya. Mega-hubs enter this area as soon as they reach some economic stability.

### 3.5.3  The Beginning of a Social Dystopia?

If the authors of the 50–60s science-fiction literature had been right, today we would travel in flying vehicles or pneumatic trains. We would travel to work in high-speed moving sidewalks and run through the city on horizontal elevators. For short distances, we would use personal jet backpacks or anti-gravity belts. On the contrary, we are at the beginning of the XXI century, and we are still waiting for buses, we are still stuck in traffic jams and trying to cross the street without being hit by a driver who is using their smartphone. Transportation has changed, but not as expected; and many important advances are barely perceived.

Yet, technology's relevance is continuously increasing, taking over more important roles and greater responsibility in our cities' management. Let's think for a moment on the extreme where only technology matters, becoming not a mean or an enabler, but the core component and the exclusive motivation for our SmartCities strategy, with citizens as secondary actors. Some people, like Noël Mamère, Mayor of Bègles, France (Cathelat, 2019h), are already alerting for this risk. When supervision and surveillance is placed over human rights or harmony, then the city moves towards a *Big Brother* concept, when technical progress and advanced technologies take social control. If we turn to this extreme, then we'll see a disruptive modernization model, where:

– It is preferrable to build cities full of sensors and cameras, from scratch, than to modernize an old city, due to the high costs of maintaining history and identity and combining these with the necessary technological progress. This model guides many new, complete, or partially new SmartCities (neighborhoods) and is adopted for its implementation agility and speed. The problem is convincing citizens to move into those new areas. Many times, their high cost leads to gentrification, being only accessible to some elites.
– Instead of allowing citizens and politicians to design and create their city, it is considered more successful to give this responsibility to digital technologists along with highly technical and dehumanized urban planners.
– Instead of respecting and adopting local cultural elements, there is a tendency to adopt a global model derived from technological modernity. Social behavior patterns are marked by an intensive use of technological elements where digital interactions are preferred to social ones. Face-to-face meetings and social festivities are lost, isolation in front of the screen is encouraged, the telematic message is preferred to the phone call, the online purchase to shopping at the neighborhood store (only one physical toy store remains open in Stockholm, all others closed due to online shopping). These global behavior models also reduce costs and speed up the SmartCities implementation.
– Cities' development companies like constructors, couriers, energy, water, and telco companies have to place technology at the frontline of their proposals and products, adding more relevance to IoT, platforms or AI algorithms than any other aspect like aesthetics, human integration, etc. That way, smartbuildings are designed more with technological capabilities in mind, than thinking with a human perspective. Some new technological wonders are horrible and inhuman, where control and monitoring are preferred to ergonomics, and the ability to encourage humans to develop their social facets.

We can talk about CyberCities or Cyborg Cities as a consequence of this Technological Dystopia. Cities run by Cyborgs or intelligent cyber entities.

A Cyborg City would be fully automated and controlled by centralized systems that respond in real time to any circumstance. For efficiency, these automations are left in the hands of systems managed by Artificial Intelligence under certain (or no) expert technologists' supervision (who needs democracy or politicians?). It seems that the increasing complexity of our cities and the need to offer higher and higher quality services made our cities too large and complicated to be managed only by humans. (Kovacic, 2018)

If an elite of engineers plan the future and the machines do everything else, noting that citizens do not disturb or interfere in these plans, and their movements are controlled and monitored to achieve a *perfect*, plain, no-problems city, then democracy makes no sense, individual creativity and freedom cease to exist. We would be in a super-automated *Dirigiste* society (the future China?). At the moment, automations still do few tasks in the city, but as we trust them more, there will come a point where their responsibility and autonomy will be so great that we must ask ourselves what is the limit where we begin to lose control of our development and our destiny, of our creativity and local cultures, and everything begins to be the same, generic, uniform, sad, but efficient and optimal norm. See the last paragraph on Sect. 3.3, about the *Generic Cities* concept by Rem Koolhaas.

Ok, we see this paradigm in the long-term, but we can already perceive some of its aspects today. Some first initiatives of authentic CyborgCities were that the fundamental motivation be technology; said in their words, *A City born and created from and for the Internet,* like the Google Sidewalk Quayside Toronto project, that has been hardly answered by its possible inhabitants, (New World Next Week, 2019) so project is abandoned.

We can also conceive dystopian cities from the urban point of view: megacities. The frequent reality of megacities described earlier in Sect. 3.3 is amplified and generalized by the movies' images and scenarios, television series, novels and comics. Popular culture presents megacities as huge dystopias in a catastrophic and inhuman future world. It is easy to search the list of dystopian films on (Wikipedia, 2019) to find about 200 films where technology, urban planning or a combination of both has reached a dystopian extreme. In these films, this exorbitant, inhuman influence leads to the curtailing of fundamental rights such as freedom of expression, action, identity, culture, etc. Social classes, racism, inequality, are frequent elements, combined with enormous brutality. Super-technological ideal worlds compete with dangerous and violent underworlds. Machines have taken control, have the power, or at least, the fundamental role in society. The human being is displaced to a secondary role, to the point of being just an image in the mind of a body fed to purely serve as an energy-generating stack for ruling machines (Matrix). Humans struggle to survive under technological totalitarianism managed by a dominant entity, like the Plotinus *ONE* in ancient Greece, but as an omnipresent and omnipotent cybernetic superior being. Some examples of these fascinating visions of cities, as shocking as inhuman are: Metropolis, Blade Runner, Welcome to Gattaca, Dark City, Elysium, Total Recall, 1984, Logan's Run, Seven Sisters, Altered Carbon, Ready Player One, Matrix trilogy, Fahrenheit 451, Brave New World, etc.

Figure 3.5 represents a funny meme that describes an extremely inhuman and catastrophic situation. Note the combination of different dystopian films to explain the most disastrous conditions where human values are simply inexistent.

**Fig. 3.5** *Perfect Storm* of
Dystopian films. (Source:
popular meme + author)

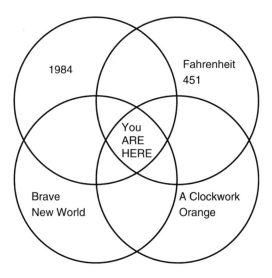

## Zero Human

We could end up in the situation of a *Zero Human* city, where Artificial Intelligence networks, fueled by permanent improvements based on Deep Machine Learning, could completely replace humans in many areas of the city. Without going further than the *"Singularity"* dystopia, where the Artificial Intelligence of a new cyber machine species is superior in all respects to human beings, who are displaced from the status of world owners to become mere slave servers. Of course, human beings show relative incompetence for certain tasks where high precision and reliability are necessary, and where machines already do it better and more unfailingly. If we put a security guard to observe a prohibited or dangerous area for eight uninterrupted working hours, we are sure a human does the job worse, and will end up making more mistakes than if we put in a camera with an intruder-detection AI-based software. If in addition to be more reliable and precise, the solution can work restlessly, 24 hours, without union problems, medical leave and at a very low cost, it seems that the decision is obvious: robots and algorithms can and should replace humans in many tasks. Taken to the extreme, we could think of a complete human replacement, modeling the entire city as a set of objects managed by a common intelligent entity based on Artificial Intelligence. Therefore, a radical digitalization of the city could lead to three clear trends:

– Data has the same (or greater?) value as the reality it represents. The firm belief that the computing platform that manages the city is composed of virtual elements and functions that are as important as the physical elements they handle. That is, the processing of traffic data is as important as the roads and vehicles themselves, the digital electricity smartgrid is as important as the energy production and distribution. We are giving so much importance to virtual management, that it comes to match managed reality. It seems better to have a cyber-controlled system than to have a good physical system; here, we arrive at the paradox of supporting a really poor system, but that is very well-known and managed. Imagine that the water we drink is actually of poor quality, but we can presume that we manage the supply network very well and know exactly how much water we lose in leakages and where the leaks are located.

- Omnicontrol, omni-information. The need to have data about absolutely everything, including humans, through a huge network of sensors, cameras and social network analyzers that allows us to have and cross reference different sources of information for each of the city dimensions (security, air quality, water, energy, waste, infrastructure, vehicles, properties, buildings, etc.) This also includes people, their habits, behaviors, health and vital parameters, all monitored, controlled, watched and measured. At this point, we must ask ourselves where the limit is of what our systems should know to achieve a desired well-being, and balance the impact and ethical cost, privacy, and dignity compared to the economic benefit, health, safety, and well-being...
- Artificial Intelligence is more important than managed hardware. Although it is clear that the really important thing is data over hardware, (sensors, communications' infrastructure, computing, storage) these components cannot be neglected because the data quality, the security and privacy and the availability and resilience of the whole strongly depend on them. There is no point in having powerful Artificial Intelligence if the data it uses is biased by poor communications' infrastructure or poor information acquisition. There is Artificial Intelligence that tries to solve this problem, but never to the point of fixing it entirely. That is, one thing is to correct occasional, spurious errors, and another thing is to correct all the data because all (or a large part) are basically false. Therefore, although the software, the algorithm, the Artificial Intelligence always seem more attractive, we cannot neglect the physical infrastructure that supports the system and the humans who install, manage and maintain it with their hands.

Although we may not realize it, we are using and relying on Artificial Intelligence (AI) every day, every time we use Internet search engines, personal computing tools, any identification system, dictation, etc. We can say that Artificial Intelligence is already omnipresent in our lives. (Gartner, 2019) estimates that virtually all large companies will massively trust their main systems on AI in three years, although only a third are currently doing so. The study also suggests that all companies want to start using AI now, although they face challenges related to strategy and execution. Despite this enormous potential, AI is probably one of the most unknown technologies, mainly because it works discreetly, hidden from users' eyes, in the backoffice, and is not something that can be touched. Many times you do not recognize that it is there; you just understand that its effects are natural, or a consequence of others' actions, or just the result of good programming, because essentially, AI tries to simulate human reactions and behaviors. This makes us scared. In the same study, 79% of the participants indicated fear of the unknown as the main challenge in the adoption of AI.

It is clear that it scares us, and it is clear, as we saw in Sect. 2.5 when describing the "Moral Machine" MIT experiment, that the AI adoption implies moral consequences, since we are leaving fundamentally human issues in AI's hands. The AI will do exactly what it has been programmed or prepared for, but in these matters, it will act according to the programmer's moral code. As we saw in that experiment, the problem is that there is not a single, global morality or a single moral code on the planet, but one for each civilization, so that the decision-making that we leave to AI will be marked by the morality or the civilization which directs it (or coded it) in every moment.

The consequences of AI misuse could be disastrous (Dent, 2019), and there is no legislation in place yet. Programmers include ethical decisions into their developments without any rigor or control, simply using their common sense and scale of values, which will be different according to their culture or civilization. Moreover, these decisions and the data used to train the systems are considered trade secrets and are not published. In companies' commercial competition to offer the best performance at the lowest price, are ethical considerations included? What human sciences' skills do programmers hold or what ethical control/audits do these developments pass? Can we lose control and come to situations like those described in the dystopian films of Fig. 3.6?

AI tries to replicate human behavior in two fundamental areas: sensorial perception and rational knowledge. In sensorial perception, during the years 2016–2019, we can affirm that modern AI systems have reached and exceeded parity with human capacity; that is, they are comparable or better to their human equivalents in vision (object recognition), speaking (recognition of spoken language and speech synthesis), reading and its syntactic and semantic understanding, and simultaneous translation in multiple languages. Precision in object handling (touch), shapes recognition, odors and gases (electronic nose) and flavors have already surpassed those of humans for a longer time.

The next issue is rational knowledge. In this area we talk about four phases or seven types of stages in the Artificial intelligence evolution (Joshi, 2019). We start with Reactive AI, in which the system reacts to stimuli or simple information entries by applying established rules (i.e., we program the chess rules, and the system can play chess looking for the best movement in each case by developing a huge amount of steps forward and determining possible combinations from the current position). The next step is called Limited Memory AI (similar to the previous one, but with a certain amount of memory, as a source of experience or a knowledge base for the known actions' consequences).

If this knowledge base is constantly fed in each iteration and new situation, then the system learns (machine learning). So far, we have covered the current systems, also called ANI (Artificial Narrow Intelligence), in which the system strictly and exclusively does what the programmer has previously established. The next phase is the Mindful, Emotional AI, in which the systems have feelings and emotions (it is clear that their original definition on what's an emotion or a feeling is done by humans, but once in operation, their decisions and behavior will depend in some way on their mood. The obvious evolution is the Self-Aware, self-conscious AI, where AI becomes aware of its own existence, identity, which opens a nice discussion about. . .rights? Obligations? These more advanced forms are called AGI, (Artificial

Blade Runner 2049:
No hope in this dystopia

**Fig. 3.6** Dystopian Cities in the movies. (Source NETEXPLO/UNESCO (Cathelat, 2019e))

General Intelligence) and we find the machines with these learning functions, perceptions, knowledge and behavior are completely indistinguishable (Turing test[1]) from humans'. Finally, the constant evolution and improvement will lead to ASI (Artificial SuperIntelligence), where all functions will be superior to human ones.

**Conscious City**

This AI evolutionary and capacity improvement line brings us to the concept of *Conscious City*: a city as a self-aware, technological entity, not far from the paradigm presented in *"Singularity,"* (Kouba, 2017) where the city behaves as an autonomous entity which self develops its capacity without any human intervention, excluding humans at all decision levels, as they are considered hazardous for the planet and themselves. Without reaching that dystopia, Sensitive (better to say *Senseable* (MIT, 2020)) Cities or cities that automatically orientate its actions towards objectives such as welfare, environmental sustainability or citizen health or safety, are already in the mind of AI developers. Thus, through the capacity to feel, and a certain form of self-awareness, the systems are oriented towards achieving those objectives, marked and supervised by human management. There is a research path around the idea of *persuasive cities*, through the application of psychosocial theories integrated in new urban designs. The intention is to integrate cognitive neuroscience elements into the city's daily operations, so that Conscious Cities better adapt themselves to offer the best citizen well-being and happiness, while achieving excellent sustainability.

A conscious city could use real-time data, historical planning and citizens known behavioral patterns to dynamically react and adapt itself to exceptional situations, (resilience) or to just evolve according to an established plan, by changing the urban landscape. (Palti & Bar, 2015)

Imagine a large lighting plate on a city ring road depicting that in last hour, cars average speed has been 9 mph and motorbikes 12 mph. The city tries to persuade citizens to think twice next time they plan to use the car during rush hour to approach the city center. Other alternatives like moto, bike or public transportation seem faster. As explained before, with an average car speed of 6 mph in Dublin's downtown, it might be worth a commuting-pattern reconsideration. . .

Created in 2014, the concept establishes that, through AI, the city manages not only the data coming from sensors (IoT world) that mark the city's physical parameters, but also citizens' available information, their interactions on social networks, etc.

---

[1]The Turing's test sets a challenge where a human can't differentiate whether he is talking to a computer or another human (by electronic chat). Although Google claimed for a basic pass with a 2018 test with a 13year-old human and his system, other researchers like: KAPOR, M & KURZWEIL, R. *"By 2029 no computer – or 'machine intelligence' – will have passed the Turing Test", The Arena for Accountable Predictions: A Long Bet,* betted a wager of $20,000 about computers passing a full Turing test not before 2029.

Furthermore, (and here is where innovation shows up), the city knows about the citizens' psychological state, both individually, and collectively, to determine their needs, satisfactions or frustrations, moods, and responds by adapting the city and its resources: information, benefits, services, etc. The use of this new type of information, (psychological) even if it is intended for good purposes, raises serious ethical questions about respect for citizens' psychological privacy, as it leaves room for its possible misuse like mass mental control (populism taken to the extreme?, Big Brother, etc.).

### 3.5.4 The Future is a Mixed Model for SmartCities

The most common criticisms of current SmartCities strategies point at the fact that implementations and designs are too *top-down* from city managers to citizens; that the evaluation of success is too purely economic or financial; there's too much technology narcissism; data is elevated to a gold-like status; psycho-sociological impacts are unattended; we create a dehumanized vision, too virtual and proof-of-concept driven, (PoCs are excessively frequent) and not citizen-centric.

The model should evolve to strategies more focused on:

- Human: Citizen-centric with welfare and quality of life as the major goal.
- Sense of community (ideally a beehive) with all citizens cooperating around a collective task or project, with a strong sense of unity, belonging and identity. Multiplicity as the new city social paradigm, where the total sum of ideas, opinions, and preferences set the city's evolution.
- Self-everything: sufficient in water, energy, matter, people-talent, funding, resiliency...
- Zero-everything: car fatalities (zero vision), pollution, carbon, violence, unrecycled waste, unmanaged water, non-renewable energies, crime, inequality, poverty.
- Sustainability: social, economic, and eventually environmentally: Carbon negative, Circular.
- City as a social enabler: relationships facilitator, inclusive, social diversity, livable, leisure-fostering and shared activities.
- Citizens as co-creators: permanent engagement, proud to contribute. City as an expression of collective experience. SmartArt as a combination of technology and creativity.
- Megalopolis broken: walking-distance suburbs/districts, making them next-to one another, spaces for humans, soft heights gradient, boulevards as an urbanism principle, walkable city, bike-friendly.
- Smart-DataSphere: AI-driven Digital Twin models monitoring the physical city (from sensor to IoT to Edge to Cloud Analytics to AI), simulating potential improvement alternatives, but always understanding living humans. A respectful

**Fig. 3.7** SmartCities
Concentric Vision. (Source:
Author)

and ethical technological city, conscious and persuasive city by tracking citizens' psychologies.

- Agile, Dynamic and Versatile: Always creating projects, experimenting, listening to citizens, applying feedback, adapting to new circumstances and needs, developing new solutions and starting over again and again. Creativity always as the leading motion.

*Create opportunities, solve problems, innovate. All three are inseparable. Jane Jacobs* (Lawrence, 1989)

- Open, Respectful, Ethical, based on a strong identity and values.

From the technology point of view, experts think about a future where we balance a cybernetic, centralized governance, where the city resiliently manages all the environment, and responds with self-adaptation to human needs, (managed by some technocratic experts, so who needs politicians?) with a distributed, human-collaborative intelligence, where citizens are permanently connected (through a digital symbiosis) to the city, contributing and co-creating.

Our short-term vision (Fig. 3.7) is made up of three concentric and permanently interrelated areas: Citizens, Spaces, Data, or a combination of Humanism, Urbanism, and Technology.

While the citizen must be at the center of all activities and initiatives, everything happens in a place or space, and technology is always present to help achieve the welfare objectives or act as an enabler for other areas' actions. Placing the citizen at the center implies permanently keeping in mind the city's cultural values and the larger civilization's ethical principles, with full respect for human dignity. But a city is *a place where people meet*, we said, so to talk about a city, we must include the spatial dimension, because everything happens in spaces: open spaces, or thinking

**Fig. 3.8** Example of wrong design for humans. (Author)

about the whole planet (environmental sustainability, as we have one single planet, sharing the same atmosphere, etc.); or closed spaces like buildings, homes, transportation vehicles. In the urban area, spaces must be designed by technology, but being put to citizens' service as the main, core objective. Look at Fig. 3.8: citizens are telling us with their behavior what's the right design. I still remember my childhood and the endless amount of time I spent on the streets, playing with my schoolmates. Numbers suggest that 75% of children played on the streets in 1975, and less than 15% do so today. We need to reconquer streets for humans, because currently, cars are ruling them. Only benefits flow from that: physical activity, sense of community, social activities, business growth,...

Everything is producing data, continuously; data that can be monitored by technology to increase city welfare, controlling the physical city and understanding citizens' needs, converting all that massive, raw data into insights, to make well-informed and right decisions, and to fully engage with citizens in the future city construction.

So, a SmartCity's design should continuously flow through these three concentric concepts, in-out and out-in, but always considering the citizen, the user of any city service, the Lord to serve, in a space that must be carefully adapted and leveraged, always with the most advanced technology, and taking advantage of the incredible innovations and new possibilities they bring.

### 3.5.5   SmartCity Ethics principles

As technology accelerates innovation, it becomes more and more inevitable, omnipresent and indispensable. So, the adoption of technology is a matter of time and investment capacity, as Bill Gates once said, *"It's neither easy, nor cheap nor optional."* Then, the question is to define the ethical limits and choices for that technology's operation.

The increasing role of technology in SmartCity strategies is raising criticism from different angles:

- Concerns about technology's impact: usefulness of Big Data and Opendata, credibility of algorithms and their applicability to everything, an innovation speed that makes humans lose control. Innovations' improvements and citizens' real use of them.
- Concerns about technology's displacing socio-cultural assets. Interest in culture is declining; for reading, for arts, as everything can be found immediately on the Internet. Cities are losing soul, humanity, charm, becoming generic, grey, unhuman, huge amounts of concrete.
- Concerns about technology's accelerating the economy's globalization, paying no attention to micro-economy, inhabitants' real concerns.
- Concerns about technology gaining power to the detriment of elected officials and politicians. Algorithms make less mistakes, better manage the city, so politicians are less relevant. This leaves no room for creative governments, as every initiative should be the informed consequence of analyzed data.

With technology in all city aspects, we should balance the Non-human City's (*Robot City*) automatic operations, where technology could work in an automatic way, and the *Human Collaborative City*, where digital citizens use technology to contribute and influence the city's evolution, as co-creators of the city's future. Both worlds could coexist depending on the city's complexity, always seeking the best future quality of life. Some areas must be automatic or semi-automatic as technology can manage it much better than humans, while others will use technology as an enabler, a companion, a facilitator for pure human decision making. This will turn the SmartCity strategy/plan as a core component of any electoral campaign, an attractive promise in gaining voters and winning elections.

The main ethical discussion about AI applied to cities is the use of citizens' data. Citizens' identity, personal circumstances, preferences, sexual options, race, gender, mobile phone number or other identification systems like an ID-card, Social Security Number or driver's license, face recognition, fingerprint, iris scan, properties, wealth level, and healthcare conditions, DNA, define a person, but all these data are PII (Personal Identifiable Information) and must be protected. EU GDPR and many others are strictly forbidding the use of this kind of data without explicit owner consent, and fines for lack of compliance are huge.

Non-PII, or collective information, patterns, and aggregated information is very valuable for making the right decisions and offering the best city services. However, this kind of information is based on different sources of PII. . .To what extent should citizens be forced by some Internet solution providers to give access to PII information, in exchange for some popular services, sources of information, or useful tools? In other words, do they have alternatives or options, or must they accept or assume that they will be considered a-social, weird citizens?

We must balance the real need to make all citizens traceable, for good (need to know my citizens in order to deliver better service), while avoiding the evil (espionage, Grand-Father repression, intrusive marketing). So, we need to operate in a triangle that is always looking for: (a) Full respect for privacy, (b) Understanding citizens' behavior, (c) Fostering economic and human growth by collecting all needed data, and properly managing it in an anonymous, aggregated, secured, and trusted way. All SmartCity strategies must combine these statements, and working with the three main actors: (a) Citizens, always under pressure, need basic training to protect their virtual identity from Internet sharks, while allowing city officials to properly use it, (b) City Managers, defining the data management rules, compliant with regulations, and obsessive about data misuse and potential leakages, (c) Data Providers, from those managing sensors and cameras, to those processing software and data, who must be very respectful with the data they manage, or otherwise prepare to receive fines and critics (remember the recent Facebook and Google scandals). The problem arises when some of those companies' business is precisely based on making money by means of the data they grab and process, so they are permanently gambling with soft regulations in some data acquisition methodologies vs strict rules like EU GDPR.

The data use discussion moves around concepts like OpenData (freely-published, anonymous data to foster economic growth based on a better city knowledge), City Data Control (IoT Data to manage physical parameters), Civic Data (data on citizens' behaviors, mostly coming from social networks analysis), Data Privacy (related to all PII information and trading, companies, safety secrets or Intellectual Property), Data Business (all related to economic and business trends, but mainly fed by personal investments, transactions, and wealth status), Data Concession (patterns and methodologies to get citizen consent to allow some private data), Data Safety (Cryptography, Blockchain, other technologies). All these concepts move between the constant fight between good and evil. Other dimensions like time, (old or fresh data), truth (true or false), accuracy (biased or exact data, error margins), ownership (who controls or owns it) are forgotten or not taken into consideration, and then, all analytics and conclusions based on that data could be false, manipulated, inaccurate, inexact, and lead to wrong decisions.

So, legislation about data acquisition, use and management needs massive improvement, and lawmakers are not skilled enough to create it while technology is continuously accelerating in terms of performance and possibilities. Countries make laws, not cities, but cities are responsible for citizens' data, and they are reacting. Amsterdam, Barcelona and New York City formed the *Cities Coalition for Digital Rights* (CITIES FOR DIGITAL RIGHTS, 2019) in November of 2018 with UN-Habitat support. Many other cities, (aiming to soon reach 100), the UCLG, (World Organization of United Cities and Local Governments) and EuroCities

Associations have joined as well. Participating cities agree on signing a five key-principles declaration on Digital Rights:

- *"Universal and equal access to the internet and digital literacy.*
- *Privacy, data protection, and security.*
- *Transparency, accountability, and non-discrimination of data, content, and algorithms.*
- *Participatory democracy, diversity, and inclusion.*
- *Open and ethical digital service standards."*

This initiative demonstrates cities' concern for the lack of legislation that is seriously compromising ethical values (especially Western ones) when applying certain digital technologies. Universal, inclusive access to these technologies is defended as humanity's progress, but it is undeniable that such use must offer due protections. Any activity or action's ethical problem (as we saw in the MIT Moral Machine problem) is the fact that there are different ethic AI standards according to the different civilizations that dwell on our planet, although many considerations might emanate from the Universal Declaration of Human Rights, signed by all nations. As an example, Western Civilization is based on three fundamental pillars: Reason (with Athens as a reference), Rights/Law (Rome) and the Christian religion (Jerusalem); but there are other civilizations and other lighthouse cities.

This lack of legislation also presents a challenge for technology providers, who must determine the limits to impose on their developers and balance the business opportunity with the underlying ethical impact. Some companies like Microsoft have publicly stated that they will never put business before ethics. But the fierce competition from companies based in countries with a lax ethical code in this regard makes companies have to consider what is ethical and what is not, and assess whether they invest in certain technologies, or just lose those business opportunities. As an example, facial recognition systems are on hold and under question by many Western companies, while some Chinese ones are accelerating and leading that market. The leading technology companies' relevance is increasing as they become ethical judges, due to the international organizations' lack of consensus or even basic guidance. Users (cities) will decide with their investments whether they will reward these ethical considerations or punish them (by investing in their competitors). As an example, let us include here the *"Microsoft AI Ethical principles"*: (Microsoft, 2018)

- *"Fairness. AI systems should treat all people fairly.*
- *Inclusiveness. AI systems should empower everyone and engage people.*
- *Reliability & Safety. AI systems should perform reliably and safely.*
- *Transparency. AI systems should be understandable.*
- *Privacy & Security. AI systems should be secure and respect privacy.*
- *Accountability. AI systems should have algorithmic accountability."*

We would like to highlight the deep reflection on human dignity, equality and social inclusion that these series of principles raise. The main AI problem must be taken into account: the data licit origin and accuracy, avoiding bias. Biases are practically inevitable and may compromise the usefulness of the entire AI application. Another main topic to think about is transparency in developments: should software companies report on the algorithms they are working on, how they work (to verify their information ethical management) and their purposes or the purposes for which they are being created? Should there be an UN-dependent body that knows about these latest innovations? Or, on the contrary, should legislation be established that defines what constitutes abusive AI use? Should they be considered crimes against humanity and judged by The Hague Human Rights Court? Cities are, again, leading by example, and we can study the first initiative from Helsinki and Amsterdam to create an *AI Algorithms Register* (Wray, 2020) to provide the needed knowledge and transparency over the AI tools used by the city, making them *trustful and human-centered.*

### 3.5.6 Cities' Ethics under Lopez-Quintas' Reality & Conduct Levels Analysis

Universal history is citizens' history. The city gathers everything that refers to mankind, and none of its competencies are alien to it. (Chueca Goitia, 1968) The city is multiple, diverse, constantly changing, it is the place where humans develop and exercise their social facets. They do it fundamentally through encounter. The encounter gives human meaning to the city, turns humans into persons, so they collaborate, and develop their creativity. The philosopher Alfonso (López Quintás, 2009) develops his theory about human levels of reality and behavior on this fundamental question: the encounter. Since the encounter, men enrich their lives through ecstasy, as a creative expression, and from the growth of knowledge (growth mindset). Below encounter, we can find the vertigo spiral that begins with objectification and individualism, leading to violence, anguish, despair, and death.

Encountering (as in social) is far more than just formal meeting. By means of the encounter, people grow, both personally and collectively.

In the (EU Urban Charter, 2020) Manifesto, cities are considered the ideal place for meeting, for gathering, the best place where social life fully deploys, and without which, as Thomas Hobbes once said, *"life is nasty, poor, solitary, brutish and short."* (Hobbes, 1651)

*There is nothing more attractive in cities than other people.* (Gehl, 2010)

In López Quintás' theory, we can find positive and negative levels of reality and behavior. Positive levels express human development, from people as things (level 1), to encounter and socialization (level 2), to the maximum expression of human values (level 3) reaching the transcendent (level 4). This positive progression is called ecstasy by the author. Guided by the expression of human values of dignity, and cultivated by knowledge, it arises, developing all human potential. It is a positive spiral. In the other way, we find a negative spiral, a vicious circle that leads to anguish, despair and the worst-known human expressions. This path is described by the author as vertigo, giving the sense of falling, self-destruction. We start from insensitive selfishness (level -1) to possession, domination, including violence and phycological and physical abuse (level -2). The next phase (level -3) reaches death and war, the denial of life. The author comes to describe (level -4) as outrage towards the dead's memory, the supreme expression of human evil.

We must not confuse ecstasy/vertigo with good/evil, vice/virtue. Ecstasy is supported/fed by creativity (López Quintás, 1992a) and knowledge (López Quintás, 1992b); vertigo is an expression of moral evil (López Quintás, 1992c) in all its degrees. Ecstasy's attributes are: Humility, Love, Stability, Realism, Creativity, Respect, Responsibility, Perseverance, Leisure, Relationship, Trust.

Vertigo's attributes are marked by: Arrogance, Egomania, Hedonism, Instability, Arbitrariness, Pragmatism, Reductionism, Indolence, Sadomasochism, Greed. (López Quintás, 1992d) In cities, as places where many humans live, we can find all these levels of reality and behavior. We can match different city areas, places, buildings to those levels, depending on their function and the human values expressed there. (Casado, 2019) But, like humans, cities as a whole can also develop levels of reality more pronounced than others, and could be clearly identified with levels of reality and behavior (city ethics). We will apply these levels to cities to find role models for inspiration in their development and strategy, and to know what we should *not* look for, or the abyss in which some cities sink.

**Level 1**  describes a physical reality. It's the world of things. People here simply live as individuals, doing basic functions like working, moving, resting.

Values: Efficiency, savings, time-speed. The human being is reified. Vice as a lifestyle such as gambling, or prostitution is also included in this category. People are just elements to be used. If there is dominion or repression, then we would fall into level -1.

Cities in Level 1: This is the level of Koolhaas' Generic Cities. Inhuman, functional, concrete cities. No human touch, no history, no traditions, no flavors, no spaces for connection, meeting. Just things managed by IoT, all under control. Efficiency for citizens, but without the citizens. Those large cities are numb, petrified, cement monsters. Those mid-sized are typically suburbs. It's very unlikely to find a small city in this stage, as small size fosters citizens' cooperation and sharing. These cities are not fostering social behavior. It exists, true, citizens are finally humans, but there is no affect or human relationships in these city models. In these cities' definition, love doesn't exist, (Gräf, 2015) like in the most famous dystopian novels: *Brave New World* by Aldous Huxley and *1984* by George Orwell. It's a city of Data, not of Humans. The IoT Kingdom with Data as the city center, The Generic, cold City.

City Examples: It's hard to assign cities to this level, as all of them include some human aspect, although most times it is hidden behind all the cement walls. It brings to mind long walks over long, grey cement streets in Atlanta or Los Angeles. Could we interpret (L.A. beautification, 2019) (initiative, as a reaction to this Generic City image?

We had a similar experience in Helsinki, but that because of cold climate: functional, ugly, soviet-like urbanism. Also, in some Swedish mid-sized cities neighbors don't know or talk (Gee, 2013) to each other, and this reality combined with the cold weather makes streets appear empty like ghost cities. Another vision comes from the very famous *sin Cities* like Las Vegas (U.S.) or Macau (China) which promote the worst human vices like gambling, sex, possession, prostitution, etc. Humans are only customers, with the aim to make them spend the largest amount of money: the false idol.

Historical City: Looking back to history to find models in this stage when technology was not present, we could point to Tomas More's Utopia (More, 1516), an ideal, dehumanized, perfectly organized city. That way, we can't point to technology as the only precursor for this model; the Spartan inhuman city model was invented a long time ago. There, citizens were just doing and complying with basic functions and activities like working, resting, moving, fighting (defending the city), trading. To match *sin cities*, the obvious historical reference are the biblical cities of Sodom and Gomorrah.

**Level 2** City as a person, real and with a certain conduct/behavior. This is the main model: a city where citizens can develop their creativity and express the human social dimension. Here, the main socializing driver is encounter, not mere meeting, but more like an engagement, a joint desire to collaborate and do things together.

Values: Basic values lean on respect, generosity, regard, esteem, friendship, love.

Cities in Level 2: The City fosters these behaviors with the right spaces for leisure, for meeting, trading, agoras to talk and discuss, theatres to dream together, to express creativity, open spaces in which to play, enjoy and kindly compete, all over a base of freedom. A city model where citizens are treated with equity, respecting rights and dignity. These cities create the sense of belonging, and citizens feel proud of living there.

We can see in Fig. 3.9 an example of these spaces that promote social integration and share knowledge. Traditionally, these spaces have mainly been religiously-driven meeting spaces like churches, abbeys, monasteries or civil squares, markets, and occasionally theatres, stadiums, then universities, schools, bars, boulevards. Now we are finding open, smart spaces in urban parks, recreational areas, natural parks, smartworking spaces where nomads and start-ups shine, and virtual social spaces. By the 80's, many experts pointed to technology adoption as a dangerous, a-social isolation driver, leading to scattered cities with almost no human face-to-face connection. Reality has proven this idea wrong, with social technologies connecting people from distant places, but eventually they meet and greet, and these technologies never replace social life with nearby people (family, coworkers, neighbors, etc.).

Historical City: Many cities like NYC, Paris, London, San Francisco, have promoted social human expression, mainly as a consequence of intense attraction because of the three Industrial Revolutions that happened there.

**Level 3** The next step forward means reaching the ideal of Beauty, Truth, Justice, Good-Goodness. Citizens reach full personal development. It is the apex of human creativity, in freedom, and always over the basis of respect for human dignity.

**Fig. 3.9** Cities are meeting spaces. Photo by Kampus Production from Pexels

<u>Cities in Level 3</u>: The city flourishes in the sciences and arts, with maximum expression of human creativity. The city offers the optimal conditions for human qualities' boosting, and we can say that its inhabitants are very happy.

<u>Historical City</u>: Although several cities have hosted very notable groups of artists and scientists who have contributed to mankind's progress (to mention a few: Paris, London, Madrid, NYC, Los Angeles-Hollywood, Boston, Geneva, Stockholm), these have shone in one or several disciplines, partially. Only two cities have been able to, in a single historical moment, gather all the best experts and geniuses of that time, in all disciplines, and get them to live and work together: Aristotle's Athens (around 350 BC) and Wittgenstein's Vienna (around 1900). Already explained in Sect. 2.1, these two cities at that exact time could be considered the richest expression of human creativity. We also find at this level the concept of community, collective effort, unity around a common goal. We would be at the stage of SmartCities 4.0, already explained, of collective consciousness. Several cities lived this communion forcibly due to the circumstances (fighting for freedom or achieving an extraordinary goal). We could mention cities besieged in various wars, or Sausalito, (CA) with men and women tireless building destroyer ships in WWII, Bletchley Park (UK) (decoding the Nazi Enigma cypher), Dubrovnik's (Croatia) reconstruction, Cape Canaveral (FL), Houston in the space race, MIT headquarters (MA), CERN (Switzerland) and many other cities where citizens have lived in community. The Copenhagen Carbon-Neutral status objective including citizens (the entire city) implies that everyone must use their bicycle / public transportation

for at least 85% of their commuting, demonstrating how a collective effort towards a common goal achieves extraordinary human development.

**Level 4** Above level 3, only the concept of transcendence can be described. The human being connects with the divine from its deepest essence, from its dignity.

Values: Unity, transcendence

Cities in Level 4: Many cultures such as the Islamic, Jewish, Buddhist ones, consider the city a sacred place. For centuries, the development of human activity has been centered around the city temple, and human knowledge has been generated and transmitted in monasteries, the precursors to current universities. Some cities inspire mysticism, inviting us to elevate our thinking and abstract ourselves above our crazy life and the speed with which we do things, without reflecting, often without a clear sense and without contributing anything to our personal development.

Historical Cities: Several cities at different times seem clear expressions of this level: Rome, Toledo (Spain), Jerusalem, Mecca. The clinking of the candles at the temples, together with the dim light creates the atmosphere that brings on memories and personal reflection. The sound of Tibetan bells and prayer wheels in Buddhist cities, the song of the muezzin in the Islamic ones, the incense in the Shinto Japanese shrines and at Santiago de Compostela's (Spain) cathedral, welcoming pilgrims to create a mystical halo, a relaxing and sublime atmosphere in which to achieve complete meditation. One hundred and seventy cities around the world can be found named as *Holy Cities*. It seems clear that this concept of a transcendent city makes no sense without observing man's religious dimension, something very important for some and less for others. In any case, this classification as a sacred city means a reference, a historical branding, a powerful city attraction for some. If a city attracts pilgrims, it holds the opportunity to make itself known from a different dimension than just the purely touristic or business one.

**Level 0** Not in the López Quintás' theory; we would like to add this level as a tipping point.

From an individual point of view, level 0 marks the border between falling into the spiral of depression, anguish, despair, which can end in suicide, or initiating a vital ascent towards socialization, friendship, love and human values. This level 0 is brutally illustrated in Pink Floyd's *The Wall* (Gilmour & Waters, 1979) That wall is precisely that threshold: level 0.

This artwork is a double *Waters'* autobiographical album and is the best-selling double album in music history. It describes the life of a rock star named Pink. Since his childhood, Pink has been building a defensive *wall* against a hostile outside environment that constantly mistreats him. His various fears and traumas constitute the bricks with which he is forging it: the death of his father in World War II, sacrificed in a key battle in Italy, the dominant maternal overprotection, childhood without a father, the British post-war oppressive education system, a government that treats its citizens as chess pieces, his tyrannical and superficial ego as a famous artist, his sentimental failure with his unfaithful wife, the drug world that surrounds the stage, his asthma...

Yet this wall, instead of protecting and isolating from what oppresses him, leads him to a spiral of self-destruction that comes to question and attempt suicide. A friend's help and self-reflection lead him back, to explore if there is something/ someone beyond that wall and finally, to tear it down to find a new life. Pink builds his wall exactly between Vertigo and Ecstasy and chooses the descending path of anguish and despair to fall into the ditch of dehumanization. He is the antihero. The suicide attempt with drugs marks the bottom of this abyss of self-destructive loneliness and isolation, the point of embracing madness. But here Pink is subjected to a trial of self-analysis and reflection. This judgment condemns him to tear down the *wall* and explore the outside world: to *flow* again, like a *fluid* in allegory to *Floyd*, and rediscover the new reality as a liberation, a catharsis, a reinvention, a rebirth, the discovery of Ecstasy. (PINK FLOYD, 2018)

It is a masterpiece developed from a situation of anguish, constantly going up and down the vertigo slide towards destructive loneliness. The wall separates and isolates from reality, and prevents glimpsing the possibility of ecstasy, of a positive construction of a happy life. It is a tremendous social denunciation of the post-war situation and the conditions in which those generations lived. The creative tone is surrounding level 0, between -1 and 1. It's about people's objectification by an accepted order, seen as necessary to trace and rebuild a society destroyed by war. At that zero-point, Pink builds his wall based on traumas and fears, as a barrier to the outside. There are a few references to a level 2 with the relationship of love/hate with his mother and the love for his wife, although she is unfaithful. There are very few at a level 3, although the denunciation of the unjust and the oppressive aims at the ideal of justice and truth. In the video, there is a stroke of the transcendent, when it seems that Pink falls into the acceptance of suffering looking like a bereaved Christ. Finally, self-reflection and external help make their judgment known, and the wall falls, beginning to show that there is another world, a world that starts in ecstasy and leads to happiness. It's too bad the work ends when Pink begins to look at it with enthusiasm, because we are left without knowing it. The work is wonderful from a musical point of view, but it immerses us in a permanent situation of denunciation and anguish, of pain. Just when we see the light, the wall falls, and it all ends, and we are left with only expectations, but at least, with the satisfaction that the wall has finally fallen.

This allegory has been adopted as a symbol by numerous social demands, such as apartheid, the reaction to the Argentine dictatorship and the fall of the Berlin's wall, the city's liberation and unification. It was not thought in that line, but the Pink Floyd's concert in Berlin in 1990 was really epic, celebrating the anniversary of its demolition.

From the city perspective, level 0 makes the difference between respecting the law, verifying minimum standards of democracy and ethics in the city, in contrast to places where living poses a risk to people's life and basic elements such as democracy, freedoms and ethical values are seriously threatened or subjected to dictatorial power.

In The Economist's Liveability Index, (The Economist, 2019) we can find that cities scoring under 50 have severe limitations on normal human development. Those under 80 have aspects of normal living impacted, and the consultant suggests to companies that want to hire employees there to compensate them with an allowance. This Liveability Index score of 80 would correspond to level 0 of this reality/behavior scale.

**Level -1** In the opposite direction, the negative, that of vertigo, we begin with level -1 as people showing a selfish behavior, exercising others' explicit domain through threats and repression. Another expression of this level could be good people that have fallen into vice, which can only lead to bad consequences for their lives and relatives.

Anti-values: There is no freedom, there are no voluntary activities, everything has a directed purpose. There is no personal time or spaces, there is no place for leisure or creativity, everything has a pre-defined purpose. The selfishness and irresponsible consumption from some means poverty and despair for many others, in situations close to slavery.

Cities in level -1: Cities at level -1 are cities with a poor or non-existent democracy, no/few freedoms, where human rights are very limited. *Dirigiste* cities, where the omnipresent authoritarian regime decides absolutely everything, what can be done, said, learned, listened to, etc. They are Asian cities with communist regimes, and other cities in places where a military or royal dictatorship prevails. In these cities, individual privacy is not a right, and video surveillance reaches its maximum expression by observing and evaluating citizens' behavior, as a Big Brother. Some Chinese cities are examples of this. We can also apply this level to cities with a very unbalanced society, with high levels of poverty, underworlds or slums, such as Cape Town and many Latin American cities like Rio de Janeiro's favelas or Africa's Accra's beachfront slum, Kibera in Nairobi, India's Delhi, Karachi or Gecekondu in Istanbul. In these suburbs, the law of the best-armed prevails and life has little value.

Historical Cities: Most cities went through this phase totally or partially, especially during the Middle Ages. The periodic famines that hit Europe brought their inhabitants to these situations. As we enter the Modern Age, improvements in health, and industrial development have resulted in very significant advances in social welfare. We can observe how many cities went from a -1 to +1 status, with some reaching +2. As an artistic reference, we can think of Victor Hugo's *Les Miserables* (Hugo, 1862) to illustrate this level.

**Level -2** Linked to the previous level of anti-values, we have level -2, where violence, abuse and extortion are common, and fear of others is a daily reality.

Anti-Values: Contempt for life, physical and psychological violence, fear, frustration. Injustice, insecurity, racial, social and gender segregation. Fear drowns creativity and any other human form of socialization; surviving is the only thing that matters.

Cities in Level -2: An example would be Ciudad Juarez (Mexico) at the time of the Juarez drugs cartel, where just surviving was a constant challenge. We could indicate Caracas (Venezuela) as the city with the highest number of homicides or 120 deaths per 100,000 in 2015. (Insight Crime, 2016)

Historic Cities: The history of the city is associated with the sad story of murders and violent acts that happened in it. It's easy to find the most famous murders in history to find the moment that these cities lived, and the panic its citizens felt.

**Level -3** It is an evolution of the previous level, where death and murder are usual.

Anti-values: Evil, injustice, violence, murder. Destruction, war.

Cities at level -3: Continuous and long-term war location. Damascus (Syria) here.

Historic Cities: We live in peaceful times. Although the XX century saw World War II with 66 million dead and the horror of the Holocaust, the worst massacres in the history of mankind happened before the XX century. These episodes of extreme cruelty happened especially in Asia, where the Mongol conquests of the XIII century, or the civil war of the Tang Dynasty killed 35 million people in eight years in the VIII century. Genghis Khan in his conquest of China in the XVII century killed 25 million people. The two Opium Wars in the XIX century ended with 60 million dead. Perhaps the example of a city with maximum horrors could be Nanjing, (the capital of China then) when in 1937 the Japanese army killed 300,000 in two weeks, with a barbarism and cruelty never seen in the mankind history. Basically, they wanted to annihilate the base of the Chinese civilization. It was done viciously, in front of horrified international observers. (Chang, 1997)

**Level -4** Finally, this level puts us in cities at war, where destruction is the objective, death is the path for victory at all costs. The greatest degree of vileness is reached, destroying the defeated memory, as the Taliban did with ancient monuments.

Anti-values: Destroying even the enemy's memory to attempt to kill others' dignity.

Cities at this level -4: Palmira (Syria) was destroyed and wrecked by the Taliban; even historical places were devastated, in an attempt to erase the memory. The Taliban also destroyed the Buddhas of Bāmiyān, two monumental statues of Buddha carved on the sides of a cliff in the Bāmiyān Valley in Afghanistan. Eight world heritage cities have been destroyed by ISIS in the XX century. (UNHCR/ACNUR, 2017)

Historical Cities: There have been many cities completely destroyed to erase the culture that flourished there, and from which, we only have few ruins, or even worse, the original location is still a mystery. To highlight one of the most famous, we will talk about Troy, in ancient Greece. In the Iliad, Achilles killed the Trojan prince Hector, tied his corpse to his carriage, and dragged him wildly on the ground in view of all, to leave him without burial and to be devoured by vermin, as a method of post-mortem humiliation. Priam, king of Troy and Hector's father, offered numerous goods and begged Achilles to return his son's body to bury him. Achilles, moved by the pain of the king, his courage and his dignity, returned the body of Hector amidst a long cry, for there were so many terrible tragedies war had brought to Greeks and Trojans. (Homer Iliad)

Artistic expressions generally impact the viewer by playing with situations or actions that go through these different levels of reality, causing a strong impression and, therefore, a better message fixation. Thus, a novel includes passion, love, violence, domination or even murder, and rises to supreme values such as Beauty or Truth. That oscillation across the levels of reality and behavior makes a sublime and human artwork. These contrasts can be seen in all kinds of art. Let's look at an example in a song dedicated to the city. There are many songs dedicated to cities, because cities inspire us and contain most of the levels explained above. In the song *Neon Heart* (Gurruchaga et al., 1995) by the Mondragón Orchestra, we can see those levels, those contrasts, that love/hate relationship that we often feel for our city.

*"The city where I live has grown with its back to the ground*
*The city where I live is the map of loneliness.*
*The one who arrives receives a candy with the poison of anxiety.*
*The city where I live is my prison and my freedom.*
*The city where I live is an ogre with gold teeth.*
*A fancy lover that I always wanted to seduce.*
*The city brings together God and the devil, the official and the transvestite.*
*The city where I live is a boy cleaning a rifle.*
*Heart, heart, heart, cement heart // Heart, heart, heart, concrete heart*
*Heart, heart, heart, pollution heart // Heart, heart, heart, neon heart*
*The city where I live is a seven-headed monster.*
*It's a wounded bird wrapped in cellophane paper.*
*A huge barrel of beer that will suddenly burst.*
*The city where I live is the temple of good and evil.*
*Barcelona, Moscow, Casablanca, Brussels, Madrid, Rome, Tokyo, Los Angeles,*
*    Naples, London, Berlin, New York, Stockholm, Donosti (San Sebastián), Mexico,*
*    Rio, Tangier, Paris, New Delhi, Caracas, Cairo, Warsaw, Madrid"*

These contrasts can be observed in all cities. To highlight a city where they are spectacular, I recall a tourist excursion in NYC called *Contrasts in Manhattan*. It consisted of an explanation of the wealthiness, lifestyle, and customs of lower Manhattan with China Town, Little Italy, the financial district, the very expensive mid-Manhattan, Central Park, the impressive MOMA, the Dakota Hotel where John Lennon was assassinated, arriving in Upper Manhattan with the Bronx, Harlem, graffiti, the burned buildings, the gospel, then into multicultural Queens. . .it was an incredible experience of aesthetic and cultural contrasts.

This aesthetic richness that the city brings reached incredible notoriety and expression in the work of Chesterton (Beaumont & Ingleby, 2013), with London at the center, establishing a continuous dialogue between his characters and the City, imaging the modern metropolis.

### 3.5.7  City Psychology

With the new technologies and advanced information collection systems, we could try to understand citizens' reaction to the environment, to urban space, the climate, the culture, and to the interesting, exciting, dramatic and stressful events that happen every day in the city. We could interpret your mood on social networks, or even measure your vital signs reacting to those situations with smartwatches.

Australian researchers Chris Murray and Charles Landry (Murray & Landry, 2019a) have been working to find the connections between the city, and the minds of the humans that inhabit it. Following the natural and human tendency to personify all things, these researchers wonder about a city's personality and have even developed a test to evaluate it. (Murray & Landry, 2019b) It seems clear to us that cities are more outgoing, introverted, more open and friendly with the visitor or expat, more direct or more complicated to understand, more aggressive or more inclusive, more detailed with the rules, or laxer. Yet the most important thing: how to use neuroscience tools to understand how citizens' way of being is conditioned by city conditions and activities, and vice versa, how citizens, especially new, incoming ones, are transforming the city. As we said before, we can explain that the city acts as the sum of the collective attitudes, experiences and lifestyles of its inhabitants, and those are influenced by the environment and the urban layout, also by the city directors (mainly the mayor's leadership) decisions. It's clear that we are in front of a dynamic ecosystem. Charles Landry has been especially prolific on this subject, publishing 13 books about it. (Landry, 2017)

### References

Afshar, V. (2017). *Salesforce chief digital Evangelist at smart cities connect conference*, AUSTIN, Texas, US.

Albaladejo, T. (2018). *Teoría Literaria de los mundos posibles.* Conference 25 May 2018, Universidad Francisco Vitoria, https://www.youtube.com/watch?v=d_eLlOs76w86'ss. Accessed 11 Nov 2019.

Albino, V., et al. (2015). Smart cities: Definitions, dimensions, performance, and initiatives. *Journal of Urban Technology, 22,* (1) Routledge. Taylor&Francis Group, pp. 4–8 doi:https://doi.org/10.1080/10630732.2014.942092

Allas, T., et al. (2019). *Confronting overconfidence in talent strategy, management, and development.* McKinsey https://www.mckinsey.com/featured-insights/talent-management. Accessed 2 Aug 2019.

Alphonse, L. (2018). New York City CTO Miguel Gamino Aims to 'Make Sure Technology Is Working for People' *USNEWS* https://www.usnews.com/news/best-states/articles/2018-03-16/new-york-city-cto-miguel-gamino-aims-to-make-sure-technology-is-working-for-people. Accessed 23 Aug 2019.

Amsterdam SmartCity. (2019). https://amsterdamsmartcity.com/network/amsterdam-smart-city. Accessed Oct 2019.

Aravena, A. (2016). *Blogspot.* https://comover-arq.blogspot.com/2016/01/alejandro-aravena-o-pritzker-de-2016.html. Accessed 10 July 2019.

ArchitectMagazine. (2019). Quinta Monroy Housing. Iquique (Chile) https://www. architectmagazine.com/project-gallery/quinta-monroy-housing_o Accessed 16 July 2019

Author. (2019). *Attractive smartCities: Contest for talent*. TED Talk. https://www.ted.com/talks/ jose_antonio_ondiviela_attractive_smartcities_contest_for_talent (SPANISH) or https://www. youtube.com/watch?v=DAABkQRIcM8 (ENGLISH) Accessed 6 Dec 2019.

Bayoumi, T., & Barkema, J. (2019). *Stranded! How rising inequality suppressed US migration and hurt those left behind*. IMF WORKING PAPERS. https://www.imf.org/en/Publications/WP/ Issues/2019/06/03/Stranded-How-Rising-Inequality-Suppressed-US-Migration-and-Hurt-Those-Left-Behind-46824. Accessed 22 Aug 2019.

Beatty, S., & Mitchell, A. (2017). *Benchmarking city services* (p. 7). KPMG International. https:// assets.kpmg/content/dam/kpmg/xx/pdf/2017/10/benchmarking-city-services.pdf. Accessed 28 Aug 2019

Beaumont, M., & Ingleby, M. (2013). *G.K. Chesterton, London and Modernity*. Bloomsbury Academic.

BeeSmartCity. (2017). *Redefining the SmartCity: A new definition*. https://hub.beesmart.city/ strategy/en/towards-a-new-smart-city-definition. Accessed 24 Aug 2018.

BeeSmartCity. (2018a). *Building and planning the citizen-centric SmartCity-part1*. https://hub. beesmart.city/strategy/building-planning-citizen-centric-smart-city-part-1. Accessed 10 Aug 2019.

BeeSmartCity. (2018b). *The 6 key benefits of transforming a municipality into a Smart City*. https:// hub.beesmart.city/strategy/en/6-key-benefits-of-becoming-a-smart-city. Accessed 10 Oct 2019.

BeeSmartCity. (2019a). *Smart cities and the promise of innovative public services*. https://hub. beesmart.city/strategy/en/smart-government/smart-cities-and-the-promise-of-innovative-pub lic-services. Accessed 3 July 2019.

BeeSmartCity. (2019b). https://www.beesmart.city/. Accessed 20 July 2019.

Bendor-Samue, P. (2018). *Where most companies go wrong in digital transformation*. FORBES. https://www.forbes.com/sites/peterbendorsamuel/2018/07/18/where-most-companies-go-wrong-in-digital-transformation/#7bf1817d6884. Accessed 12 Sept 2019

Berger, S. (2018). *These towns will help pay off your student loan debt if you move there*. CNBC Make it. https://www.cnbc.com/2018/01/03/us-towns-that-offer-financial-incentives-to-live-there.html. Accessed 28 Aug 2019

Bloomberg. (2019). *Trump's next trade war target: Chinese students at Elite schools*. https://www. bloomberg.com/news/articles/2019-06-03/trump-s-next-trade-war-target-chinese-students-at-elite-schools. Accessed 28 Aug 2019.

Bobman, M. C. (2015). *Effects of smart city infrastructure on Millennials*. Arizona State University Digital Repository. https://repository.asu.edu/items/28740. Accessed 21 Aug 2018

Brynskov, M., et al. (2016). Co-creating smart cities of the future. We are all OrganiCitizens Interim Engagement Strategy. H2020 No. 645198. *FutureCities Catapult*, http://organicity.eu/wp-content/uploads/2017/05/D1.2_We-are-all-OrganiCitizens_Interim-Engagement-Strategy.pdf. Accessed 12 Oct 2018.

BSI. (2019). Making Cities smarter. Guide for city leaders: Summary of PD8100. p.2 *BSI group for UK Department for Business, Innovation & Skills. London*. https://www.bsigroup.com/ LocalFiles/en-GB/smart-cities/resources/BSI-Making-cities-smarter-Guide-for-city-leaders-UK-EN.pdf. Accessed 11 Jan 2019.

Business Facilities. (2019). https://businessfacilities.com/state-by-state-incentives-guide/. Accessed 22 Aug 2019.

Cadena, A., & Ellen, P. (2018). *Putting citizens first: How Latin American cities can be smart*. McKinsey&Company, https://www.mckinsey.com/industries/capital-projects-and-infrastruc ture/our-insights/putting-citizens-first-how-latin-american-cities-can-be-smart. Accessed 13 Jan 2019.

Cameron, J. (2009). AVATAR

Carmona, M. J. (2019). What will it take to close the digital divide? *EQUALTIMES* https://www. equaltimes.org/what-will-it-take-to-close-the#.Xg9TjnOSkvj. Accessed 24 Nov 2019.

Casado, M. (2019). *Cf. Trabajo Fin Máster de Humanidades*. UFV.
Cathelat, B. (2019a). *Smartcities shaping the society of 2030*. UNESCO/NETEXPLO p. 106 Paris: UNESCO and NETEXPLO
Cathelat, B. (2019b). *Smartcities shaping the society of 2030*. UNESCO/NETEXPLO p. 99 Paris: UNESCO and NETEXPLO
Cathelat, B. (2019c). *Smartcities shaping the society of 2030*. UNESCO/NETEXPLO p. 103 Paris: UNESCO and NETEXPLO
Cathelat, B. (2019d). *Smartcities shaping the society of 2030*. UNESCO/NETEXPLO p. 208 Paris: UNESCO and NETEXPLO
Cathelat, B. (2019e). *Smartcities shaping the society of 2030*. UNESCO/NETEXPLO p. 154 Paris: UNESCO and NETEXPLO
Cathelat, B. (2019f). *Smartcities shaping the society of 2030*. UNESCO/NETEXPLO p. 208 Paris: UNESCO and NETEXPLO
Cathelat, B. (2019g). *Smartcities shaping the society of 2030*. UNESCO/NETEXPLO p. 292 Paris: UNESCO and NETEXPLO
Cathelat, B. (2019h). *Smartcities shaping the society of 2030*. UNESCO/NETEXPLO p. 142 Paris: UNESCO and NETEXPLO
Cathelat, B. (2019i). *Smartcities shaping the society of 2030*. UNESCO/NETEXPLO p. 38 Paris: UNESCO and NETEXPLO. ISBN 978-92-3-100317-2 IGO (CC-BY-SA 3.0 IGO)
Chang, I. (1997). *The rape of Nanking* (pp. 90–100). Basic Books.
Chueca Goitia, F. (1968). *Breve Historia del Urbanismo* (p. 8). Alianza Editorial.
Cisco. (2014). *The impact of internet of everything on Barcelona* https://www.cisco.com/assets/global/ES/tomorrow-starts-here/Barcelona_Jurisdiction_Profile_final.pdf and http://www.youtube.com/watch?v=p34YUzCyz0A. Accessed 2 Jan 2019.
Cities for Digital Rights. (2019). https://citiesfordigitalrights.org/. Accessed 20 Dec 2019.
Cities Today. (2019). *Creating better lives in our cities of the future requires collaboration*. https://cities-today.com/industry/creating-better-lives-in-our-cities-of-the-future-requires-collaboration/. Accessed 10 Aug 2019.
Cohen, B. (2015). *The 3 Generations of Smart Cities*. FASTCOMPANY. https://www.fastcompany.com/3047795/the-3-generations-of-smart-cities. Accessed 15 May 2018.
Cohen, B. (2019). *SmartCities Wheel*. https://www.smart-circle.org/smartcity/blog/boyd-cohen-the-smart-city-wheel/. Accessed 28 Aug 2019.
Collier, C. (2019). *The one factor that determines if your city will be a smart city*. *SmartCitiesConnect*. http://smartcitiesconnect.org/the-one-factor-that-determines-if-your-city-will-be-a-smart-city/. Accessed 7 Aug 2019.
Contreras, M. (2017). Holanda instala semáforos en el suelo para despistados con móvil. *Clipset*. https://clipset.com/semaforo-en-el-suelo-paises-bajos/. Accessed 24 Aug 2018.
Creighton, J. L. (2017). *La participación ciudadana en la era digital*, CIVICITI (pp. 44–45). OpenSeneca
Dannemiller, K. D., & Jacobs, R. W. (1992). Changing the way organizations change: A revolution of common sense. *The Journal of Applied Behavioral Science, 28*, 480–498.
Dent, K. (2019). *The risks of amoral AI*. TechCrunch. https://techcrunch.com/2019/08/25/the-risks-of-amoral-a-i/. Accessed 22 Oct 2019.
Downey, E., & Jones, M. (2012). *Public Service, Governance and Web 2.0 Technologies: Future Trends in Social Media* (p. 102). IGI Global.
Eaves, D., & McGuire, B. (2018). The fast-follower strategy for technology in government. *GOVERNING*. http://www.governing.com/blogs/bfc/col-fast-follower-strategy-technology-government.html. Accessed 10 Sep 2019.
Eggers, W. D., & Skowron, J. (2018). *Forces of change: Smart cities*. Deloitte Insights. https://www2.deloitte.com/insights/us/en/focus/smart-city/overview.html. Accessed 16 July 2019.
Elliot, D. (2019). *Portugal wants its emigrants back – So it's paying them to return*. World Economic Forum. https://www.weforum.org/agenda/2019/08/portugal-emigration-incentives-population/. Accessed 4 Aug 2019.

ENOLL. (2019). *European Network of Living Labs.* https://enoll.org/. Accessed 2 Jan 2019.

ESI-ThoughtLAB. (2018). *Smarter Cities 2025 building a sustainable business and financing plan* (p. 8), also https://econsultsolutions.com/wp-content/uploads/2018/11/ESI-ThoughtLab_Cit ies_2025_Whitepaper_FINAL.pdf. Accessed 13 Sep 2019.

ESI-ThoughtLAB. (2019). *Building a Hyperconnected City. Improved public safety, health, business productivity, and economic growth are just some of the benefits.* https://econsultsolutions. com/esi-thoughtlab-study-reveals-measurable-roi-on-smart-city-investments/. Accessed 1 Nov 2019.

EU – EPALE. (2019). *Electronic Platform for Adult Learning in Europe.* https://ec.europa.eu/ epale/en/content/nearly-half-europeans-dont-have-basic-digital-skills. Accessed 7 Aug 2019.

EU Commission. D7 Report. (2016a). *Analyzing the potential for wide scale roll out of integrated Smart Cities and Communities solutions.* https://ec.europa.eu/energy/sites/ener/files/documents/ d2_final_report_v3.0_no_annex_iv.pdf. Accessed 8 Aug 2019.

EU Commission. D7 Report. (2016b). *Analyzing the potential for wide scale roll out of integrated Smart Cities and Communities solutions.* https://ec.europa.eu/energy/sites/ener/files/documents/ d2_final_report_v3.0_no_annex_iv.pdf. Accessed 8 Aug 2019. p.24

EU DIGIBYTE. (2015). *EU eGovernment Report 2015 shows that online public services in Europe are smart but could be smarter.* https://ec.europa.eu/digital-single-market/en/news/eu-egovernment-report-2015-shows-online-public-services-europe-are-smart-could-be-smarter. Accessed 30 Aug 2018.

EU Horizon2020. (2018). https://ec.europa.eu/programmes/horizon2020/en. Accessed 6 Aug 2018.

EU Urban Charter. (2020). *Manifesto for new urbanity.* p. 44. https://rm.coe.int/urban-charter-ii-manifesto-for-a-new-urbanity-publication-a5-58-pages-/168095e1d5. Accessed 12 Jan 2020.

Eurocities Association. (2018). http://www.eurocities.eu/. Accessed 6 Aug 2018.

European Union. (2019). *Digital Single Market. Policy. Smart Cities.* https://ec.europa.eu/digital-single-market/en/smart-cities. Accessed 24 July 2019.

Forum Virum. (2019). *Helsinki's citylab.* https://forumvirium.fi/en/. Accessed 3 Aug 2019.

Frem, J., et al. (2018). *Thriving amid turbulence: Imagining the cities of the future,* McKinsey & Company, https://www.mckinsey.com/industries/public-sector/our-insights/thriving-amid-tur bulence-imagining-the-cities-of-the-future. Accessed 3 Aug 2019.

Future City Catapult. (2018). Smart City Demonstrators. Hyperconnected. https://cp.catapult.org. uk/wp-content/uploads/2021/01/SMART-CITY-DEMONSTRATORS-A-global-review-of-challenges-and-lessons-learned.pdf. Accessed 11 Dec 2019

G3ict. (2016). *Newly launched accessible Smart Cities initiative to promote Access for persons with disabilities and aging communities.* https://g3ict.org/news-releases/newly-launched-accessible-smart-cities-initiative-to-promote-access-for-persons-with-disabilities-and-aging-communities. Accessed 19 Mar 2019.

Gartner. (2019). Gartner Survey Shows 37 Percent of Organizations Have Implemented AI in Some Form. *Gartner Press Release.* Also https://www.gartner.com/en/newsroom/press-releases/ 2019-01-21-gartner-survey-shows-37-percent-of-organizations-have. Accessed 10 Oct 2019.

Gee, O. (2013). Swedish people just don't understand small talk. *The Local.* https://www.thelocal. se/20130702/48816. Accessed 3 Dec 2019.

Gehl, J. (2010). *Cities for People* (p. 68). Island Press.

Gil-García, J. R., et al. (2015). *What makes a city smart? Identifying core components and proposing an integrative and comprehensive conceptualization Information* (Information Polity, vol 20, no 1) (p. 64). IOS Press.

Gilmour, D., & Waters, R. (1979). *The Wall.* Pink Floyd.

Goldsmith, S. (2019). *Designing the Human-Centered City,* DATA-SMART CITY SOLUTIONS, HarvardKennedy School, ASH Center for Democratic Governance and Innovation https:// datasmart.ash.harvard.edu/news/article/designing-human-centered-city. Accessed 7 Mar 2019.

Gonzalez San Román, M. A., & Sarmiento, D. (2019). The Digital City at the Service of the 21st Century Citizen. p. 61. *Minsait/Indra* https://www.minsait.com/en/news/insights/digital-city-service-21st-century-citizen. Accessed 12 Jan 2020.

Government of India. (2019). *SmartCities Mission*. https://www.india.gov.in/spotlight/smart-cities-mission-step-towards-smart-india. Accessed 22 Aug 2019.

Gräf, L. (2015). *Love and Sexuality in Dystopian Fiction. An Analysis of 'Brave New World' and 'Nineteen Eighty-Four'*. GRIN, https://www.grin.com/document/319788. Accessed 23 Oct 2019.

Greenberg, S. (2015). *Using innovation and technology to improve city services*. University of Texas at Austin, US, IBM Center for The Business of Government. pp. 30–36. Also as http://www.businessofgovernment.org/sites/default/files/Using%20Innovation%20and%20Technology%20to%20Improve%20City%20Services.pdf. Accessed 10 Oct 2019.

Gurruchaga, J., et al. (1995). *Ellos las prefieren gordas*. ORQUESTA MONDRAGON.

Hapsara, M., et al. (2017). *E-voting in developing Countries current landscape and Future Research Agenda*. University of New South Wales, Canberra, Australia. https://www.researchgate.net/publication/312923714_E-voting_in_Developing_Countries. Accessed 23 July 2019.

HarvardKennedy School. (2017). *Data-Smart city Solutions*. ASH CENTER. https://datasmart.ash.harvard.edu/civic-analytics-network/solutions-search. Accessed 5 Nov 2019.

Helsinki. (2019a). From Agenda to Action The Implementation of the UN Sustainable Development Goals in Helsinki 2019. p. 2 *City of Helsinki* https://www.hel.fi/static/helsinki/julkaisut/SDG-VLR-Helsinki-2019-en.pdf. Accessed 20 Aug 2019.

Helsinki. (2019b). *City of Helsinki*. https://www.hel.fi/helsinki/en/administration/strategy/strategy. Accessed 30 Aug 2019.

Hobbes, T. (1651). *Leviathan*, Part I: Of Man, Chapters 10–16. Andrew Crooke

Homer, *Iliad*, II, 24, written: 750 BC, first published 1844

Hugo, V. (1862). *Les Miserables*, Paris

IBM 100. (2018). *Icons of Progress*. https://www.ibm.com/ibm/history/ibm100/us/en/icons/smarterplanet/. Accessed 5 Aug 2018.

InsightCrime. (2016). *Caracas World's Most Violent City: Report*. Insight Crime. https://www.insightcrime.org/news/brief/caracas-most-violent-city-in-the-world-2015-report/. Accessed 28 Nov 2019.

Ismail, N. (2017). *Smart cities could lead to cost savings of $5 trillion – Report suggest*. INFORMATION AGE, https://www.information-age.com/smart-cities-lead-cost-savings-5-trillion-123469863/. Accessed 2 Oct 2019.

JLL. (2018). *Cities research*. https://www.us.jll.com/en/research/cities-research. Accessed 1 Aug 2019.

Joshi, N. (2019). *7 types of artificial intelligence*, FORBES, https://www.forbes.com/sites/cognitiveworld/2019/06/19/7-types-of-artificial-intelligence/. Accessed 23 Nov 2019.

Keeton, R. (2019). When Smart Cities are Stupid. International New Town Institute. http://www.newtowninstitute.org/spip.php?article1078. Accessed 24 Feb 2019.

Kelly, J. (2018). JLL rethinks global city competitiveness for the futur. *Cities Today*. https://citiestoday.com/industry/jll-rethinks-global-city-competitiveness-future/. Accessed 16 July 2019.

Koolhaas, R. (1997). *Acerca de la ciudad*, GG, Barcelona, 2014 from "*The Generic City*", núm. 791, pp. 8–12. Domus

Kouba, R. (2017). *Singularity*

Kovacic, M. (2018). Robot Cities: Three Urban Prototypes for Future Living. *SingularityHub*. https://singularityhub.com/2018/04/13/robot-cities-three-urban-prototypes-for-future-living/. Accessed 21 Jan 2019.

L.A. Community Beautification. (2019). Los Angeles Office of community beautification http://laocb.org/. Accessed 11 Nov 2019.

Landry, C. (2017). *Psychology & the City: The hidden dimension. Comedia* Perth – Australia: Comedia Publications Limited and his blog: https://charleslandry.com/blog/psychology-the-city-the-hidden-dimension/. Accessed 3 Nov 2019.

Larsen, P. B. (2019). *Open Data Exchange*. Copenhagen. Hitachi. http://live.industrienshus.dk/files/12915716/5b960afa2b3062d.pdf. Accessed 7 June 2019.

Lawrence, F. (1989). *Ethics in Making a Living*. The Jane Jacobs Conference Edited. Boston College, p. 135. Scholars Press.

Lobo, R. (2014). Could Songdo be the world's smartest city? *World Finance*. https://www.worldfinance.com/inward-investment/could-songdo-be-the-worlds-smartest-city. Accessed 4 June 2019.

López Quintás, A. (2009). *Descubrir la grandeza de la vida* (pp. 93–123). Desclée de Brouwer.

López Quintás, A. (1992a). *Vértigo y éxtasis. Bases para una vida creativa* (p. 77). Asociación para el Progreso de las Ciencias Humanas.

López Quintás, A. (1992b). *Vértigo y éxtasis. Bases para una vida creativa* (p. 338). Asociación para el Progreso de las Ciencias Humanas.

López Quintás, A. (1992c). *Vértigo y éxtasis. Bases para una vida creativa* (p. 43). Asociación para el Progreso de las Ciencias Humanas.

López Quintás, A. (1992d). *Vértigo y éxtasis. Bases para una vida creativa* (pp. 327–331). Asociación para el Progreso de las Ciencias Humanas.

Major Cities of Europe. (2018). *Association*. https://www.majorcities.eu/. Accessed 6 Aug 2018.

Marvin, S., & Luque-Ayala, A. (2017). Urban Operating Systems: Diagramming the City. *IJURR (International Journal of Urban and Regional Research)*. https://onlinelibrary.wiley.com/doi/full/10.1111/1468-2427.12479. Accessed 17 July 2019.

McCarthy, N. (2016). *The countries with the most people living overseas*. STATISTA https://www.statista.com/chart/4237/the-countries-with-the-most-people-living-overseas/. Accessed 31 Aug 2019.

Mendoza, A., & Dessibourg-Freer, N. (2019). *Talent makes the city*. THE HILL. https://thehill.com/opinion/finance/448371-talent-makes-the-city. Accessed 7 Aug 2019.

Meuris, F., & Noels, B. (2013). *Customer Insight Profiling and Service Design Guide*. SmartCities (EU. The Interreg IVB North Sea Region) (p. 17). Edinburgh Napier University.

Microsoft. (2018). Microsoft: Our Approach to AI https://www.microsoft.com/en-us/AI/our-approach-to-ai. Accessed 12 Dec 2019. Also at: *The Future Computed. Artificial Intelligence and its role in Society*. pp. 57–73. Microsoft

MIT. (2020). *Senseable City Lab*. http://senseable.mit.edu/. Accessed 17 Oct 2020.

Morcillo, F. (2013a). Sostenibilidad urbana, ciudad y ciudadanos inteligentes. UNESCO Extremadura, slide25 http://unescoextremadura.com/unesco/upload/ent10/1/9%20Francisco%20Jose%20Morcillo.pdf. Accessed 12 Sept 2019.

Morcillo, F. (2013b). Sostenibilidad urbana, ciudad y ciudadanos inteligentes. UNESCO Extremadura, slide21 http://unescoextremadura.com/unesco/upload/ent10/1/9%20Francisco%20Jose%20Morcillo.pdf. Accessed 12 Sept 2019.

More, T. (1516). *Utopia*, London.

Mourtada, R., et al. (2018). *How to Supercharge Your National Digital Transformation*. Boston Consulting Group. https://www.bcg.com/publications/2018/how-supercharge-your-national-digital-transformation.aspx?linkId=55243049&redir=true. Accessed 21 Sept 2019.

Murray, C., & Landry, C. (2019a). *Psychology of the city*. https://charleslandry.com/themes/psychology-the-city/. Accessed 5 Nov 2019.

Murray, C., & Landry, C. (2019b). *Urban Psyche assessment and city personality test*. https://www.urbanpsyche.org/. Accessed 12 Dec 2019.

Neirotti, P., et al. (2014). *Current trends in Smart City initiatives: Some stylized facts*. CITIES (Vol. 38, p. 25). ELSEVIER. https://doi.org/10.1016/j.cities.2013.12.010

NewWorld Next Week. (2019). Toronto Resists Google SmartCity Dystopia. *Youtube*. https://www.youtube.com/watch?v=L0fLEiEzlY8. Accessed 11 Sept 2019.

Nhede, N. (2018). *Smart cities technologies to save citizens 125 hours*. Smart Energy International. https://www.smart-energy.com/industry-sectors/iot/smart-cities-intel-juniper/. Accessed 1 Feb 2019.

O'Donnell, C. (2017). *Smart cities are boring. Give us responsive cities*. TECHCRUNCH, https://techcrunch.com/2017/10/14/smart-cities-are-boring-give-us-responsive-cities/. Accessed 12 Oct 2018.

Palti, I., & Bar, M. (2015). A manifesto for conscious cities: should streets be sensitive to our mental needs? *The Guardian* https://www.theguardian.com/cities/2015/aug/28/manifesto-conscious-cities-streets-sensitive-mental-needs. Accessed 12 Nov 2019.

Pink Floyd. (2018). Cf. *Pink Floyd. The wall. A complete analysis.* http://www.thewallanalysis.com/. Accessed 22 Dec 2018.

Pisani, F. (2015). *A journey between SmartCities: From Datapolis to Participolis* p. 163 Paris: UNESCO / Netexplo. https://unesdoc.unesco.org/ark:/48223/pf0000234422. Accessed 20 June 2019.

Ratti, C. (2019). *Carlo Ratti's website.* https://carloratti.com/. Accessed 12 Aug 2019.

Rosenbaum, D. (2018). *All hail the AI overlord: Smart cities and the AI Internet of Things.* ARSTECHNICA. https://arstechnica.com/information-technology/2018/12/unite-day3-1/. Accessed 20 Jan 2019.

Rubel, H. (2014). *Smart cities – How to master the world's biggest growth challenge.* Boston Consulting Group. Slide 14.

SmartCities Council. (2018). https://smartcitiescouncil.com/. Accessed 18 Oct 2018.

SmartCity Expo. (2018). http://www.smartcityexpo.com/en/home. Accessed 7 Aug 2018.

SmartCity Hub. (2019). *Smart city? Smart mayor!* Smart City Hub. http://smartcityhub.com/governance-economy/smart-city-smart-mayor/. Accessed 10 Aug 2019.

SmartCity International. (2015). *SmartCircle.* https://www.smart-energy.com/industry-sectors/iot/smart-cities-intel-juniper/. Accessed 23 Feb 2019.

Snyder, S. (2019). *Talent, not technology, is the key to success in a digital future.* World Economic Forum https://www.weforum.org/agenda/2019/01/talent-not-technology-is-the-key-to-success-in-a-digital-future/. Accessed 21 Aug 2019.

Techtarget. (2019). *IoT World SmartCities Components.* IoT Agenda.. https://internetofthingsagenda.techtarget.com/definition/smart-city. Accessed 22 Aug 2019.

Tel-Aviv. (2019). Website. https://www.tel-aviv.gov.il/en/Live/ResidentsCard/Pages/default.aspx. Accessed 6 Aug 2019.

The Economist. (2019). *The Global Liveability Index,* p. 5. Also at https://www.eiu.com/n/the-global-liveability-index-2019/. Accessed 5 Jan 2020.

Thornhill, J. (2019). Smart cities still need a human touch. p. 1. *Financial Times.* https://www.ft.com/content/67c52480-b51f-11e9-8cb2-799a3a8cf37b. Accessed 21 Aug 2019.

Tracy, P. (2016). Smart building technology helps reduce energy costs. *CRWirelessNews,* https://www.rcrwireless.com/20160725/business/energy-costs-smart-building-tag31-tag99. Accessed 23 Aug 2019.

UCLG. (2017). *SmartCities Study 2017.* p. 13 Bilbao: UCLG Committee Digital and Knowledge-Based Cities

UCLG. (2019a). *United Cities and Local Governments.* https://www.uclg.org/en. Accessed 20 July 2019.

UCLG. (2019b). *Factors that define a SmartCity.* http://www.uclg-digitalcities.org/en/factors-that-define-a-smart-city/. Accessed 16 July 2019.

UNHCR/ACNUR. (2017). 8 Patrimonios de la Humanidad destruidos en el siglo XXI. https://eacnur.org/es/actualidad/noticias/eventos/8-patrimonios-de-la-humanidad-destruidos-en-el-siglo-xxi. Accessed 14 May 2019.

Vienna. (2019). *Vienna facts.* https://www.wien.gv.at/english/social/integration/facts-figures/population-migration.html. Accessed 20 Aug 2019.

Walker, B. (2018). Big mayors talk big plans at Smart Cities New York 2018. *HERE360.* https://360.here.com/big-mayors-talk-big-plans-at-smart-cities-new-york-2018. Accessed 4 May 2019.

Welch, D., & Dadaglio, F. (2015). ISO Smart Cities Key Performance Indicators and Monitoring Mechanism ISO, *ITU Forum on Smart Sustainable Cities,* 2015, p.17 Abu Dhabi. https://www.itu.int/en/ITU-D/Regional-Presence/ArabStates/Documents/events/2015/SSC/S6-MrDWelsh_MrFDadaglio.pdf. Accessed 12 Mar 2019.

White, M. (2017). 5 U.S. Cities That Will Actually Pay You to Move There. *Moving.com* https://www.moving.com/tips/5-us-cities-that-will-actually-pay-you-to-move-there/. Accessed 2 Aug 2018.

Wikipedia. (2019). *List of dystopian films.* https://en.wikipedia.org/wiki/List_of_dystopian_films. Accessed 3 Oct 2019.

Woetzel, J., et al. (2018). *Smart cities: Digital solutions for a more livable future.* McKinsey & Company. https://www.mckinsey.com/industries/capital-projects-and-infrastructure/our-insights/smart-cities-digital-solutions-for-a-more-livable-future. Accessed 4 Jan 2019.

Woods, E., & Lawrence, M. (2018). *Smart City Platforms* (p. 14). Navigant Research.

World Economic Forum. (2017a). *Collaboration in Cities: From Sharing to 'Sharing Economy'* p. 12. Also http://www3.weforum.org/docs/White_Paper_Collaboration_in_Cities_report_2017.pdf. Accessed 12 Oct 2019.

World Economic Forum. (2017b). *Collaboration in Cities: From Sharing to 'Sharing Economy'* p. 11. Also http://www3.weforum.org/docs/White_Paper_Collaboration_in_Cities_report_2017.pdf. Accessed 12 Oct 2019.

World Mayor. (2019). *Honouring Outstanding mayors since, 2004.* http://worldmayor.com/. Accessed 12 Aug 2019.

Wray, S. (2020). Helsinki and Amsterdam launch AI registers to detail city systems. *CitiesToday.* https://cities-today.com/helsinki-launches-ai-register-to-detail-city-systems/. Accessed 13 Oct 2020.

# Chapter 4
# Main Cities Objective: Becoming the Most Attractive City for Talented Citizens and Investors

## 4.1 Concept of City Attractiveness

We explored in (Sect. 2.2) how the consecutive Industrial Revolutions have meant a competition for talent. Talent is attracted to a new, disruptive technology that flourishes in a city or area. If this city is open enough to admit and collect the talent that wants to go there, we arrive at the magic formula of the 3 T's: Technology + Talent + Tolerance (first described by Pf. Florida) (Florida, 2007), as a recipe that has made the most successful cities prosper. We also analyzed that Artificial Intelligence needs three fundamental components: Data (a huge amount, and rapid availability), Cloud Computing (a massive capacity for processing and data analysis), and? Talent, yes, talent again, to develop algorithms that achieve spectacular results (Sect. 2.2). It is clear, then, that talent is the key component of the city's development.

Let's create the conditions for this talent to stay or go to a particular city. What's making a city attractive, or not, for those talented citizens and investors?

Let's start by understanding what attractiveness means. According to (Cambridge Dictionary, 2019), the word attractiveness has two meanings:

- *the quality of being very pleasing in appearance or sound*
- *the quality of causing interest or making people want to do something*

We want to focus this study around the second meaning; that is, attractiveness is not just a matter of beauty. In our approach, attractiveness means attraction more than something nice or beautiful. It is the attraction that makes a talented person consider a city as a possible destination to develop their life, their potential. It is a decision among many alternatives, like a marriage, like a life option.

We could consider the word attractant, which has the meaning of tempting, inviting, attracting like a magnet, but this word is very unusual, and *attraction* is preferable because of a beauty, personal taste, emotional component involved.

Retain vs attract. The cities and in particular, mayors, must balance the daily effort in offering the best services in an orderly, safe and sustainable city to retain the talent that lives there by investing in the concept of an attractive city to attract possible talents. That is, provide good governance for local's vs *selling* the city advantages to attract outsiders. In this process, they must combine providing a good service with having enough appeal for the millions of millennials who are out there evaluating and considering the city of their dreams. As in many companies, it makes the mistake of giving better conditions to attract new customers than to retain good existing ones. This issue is irritating and should be treated with great care so that local taxpayers do not think that their taxes are being spent on superfluous ornaments to woo outsiders. On the other hand, having good internal governance does not guarantee being attractive. Good governance is a basic condition, but just one more among the many that we are going to study.

The most successful cities will be those that retain and attract the best talent, by creating an attractive city for humans with the physical and economic conditions that stimulate the growth of companies, entrepreneurs, universities and investors.

When talking about Cities of Future, The European Urban Charter (The Council of Europe) states that:

> An ideal city is one which succeeds in reconciling the various sectors and activities that take place (traffic, living working and leisure requirements); which safeguards civic rights; which ensures the best possible living conditions; which reflects and is responsive to the lifestyles and attitudes of its inhabitants; where full account is taken of all those who use it, who work or trade there, who visit it, who seek entertainment, culture, information, knowledge, who study there (Council of Europe, 2008).

Then, when we think about how to create an attractive city, we should consider that we are serving citizens (humans first and foremost), developing advanced public services and enhancing economic factors.

The consulting company Mercer, very famous for its *Quality of Living Cities ranking* (Mercer, 2019a) analysis, highlights attractiveness as the pre-condition for economic success, attracting investors, and becoming more competitive in the globalization era (Mercer, 2019b).

Unfortunately, academic literature does not provide a solid, detailed description of a city attractiveness concept, nor has it ever been addressed in its complexity (Sinkene & Kromalcas, 2010). The European Commission describes attractive city elements such as excellent economic development, mobility, accessibility, sustainability and an inspiring and pleasant natural, cultural and touristic environment. Urbanist Irma Neminei also addresses the issue as a combination of city benefits: economy, housing, supplies, transport and traffic and a pleasant environment, together with a *secret* ingredient that she calls *something special*. The UK government focuses this definition of an attractive city into quality of life: environmental quality and public spaces, and adds human elements such as habitability, vitality, livability and city image.

These approaches suggest that what makes a city attractive is not just the portfolio of services it offers to citizens. There is something else, there is an aesthetic component, a human perception, a personification of the city into something that attracts us.

VALUER.ai, (Valuer, 2019) an important Danish start-up incubator that has also developed an AI tool to find market opportunities and connect with corporations, has conducted a study to determine the 50 most attractive cities to start a new business. Using the experience of its associated companies' extensive network in more than 25 countries, they determined that the elements that make an attractive city for entrepreneurs are, apart from the obvious ones such as regulations, access to capital, market, infrastructure, some more related to the existing human capital such as talent, culture, communication skills or global mindset.

It is clear that it is not just about attracting investors or new companies, but attracting humans. We have already seen the problem of building new, gentrified cities that nobody wants to live in. Cities must also be attractive from an aesthetic and human point of view. The School of Life addresses this issue and defines six principles that a city must meet to be attractive from those angles. It seems that the art of building beautiful cities has been lost, although few dares to say that modern architecture is fundamentally horrible. This is true, simply if we understand the association that exists between an appealing city and its age. It is difficult to find new cities with charm, that are cozy and pleasant, and this is due to modern architecture, which has built generic cities, without identity, without soul, that are homogeneous, functional, fractal, and which lead to deep boredom (Koolhaas, 2014). Mostly urbanistic suggestions, the School of Life shows a nice video-tutorial on these six principles to create beautiful cities (The School of Life, 2019):

- Neither too chaotic nor too orderly. Both extremes are horrible, one because of the disparity of heights and styles, without harmony, without beauty. Another because it seems a fractal succession of the same pattern, as directed by a communist regime. It is about finding harmony from the diverse, the vividness, the color, but within an order, as a whole, as a musical symphony. The ancients constantly used the aurum ratio as the basic element of beauty, because it offers a display of dimensions that please us, that seem harmonious to us. This relationship is found from the Parthenon to the credit cards that we carry in our pockets. It consists of a rectangle where the short side compares to the long as the long side compares to the sum of the long plus the short. Its resolution is 1: $\left(1 + \sqrt{5}\right)/2$ or 1: 1,618.
- Find visible life. See that the city is alive, vibrant, with people doing things in the streets, with places to socialize, to meet, with public activities, with urban furniture that citizens can use and enjoy, with smart spaces.
- Compact a city with a correct combination of distances that allow human communication and integration. Neither claustrophobic, nor with enormous insurmountable walking distances. And all this with artistic elements that recreate the look and inspire creativity. Compact also refers to high density, a positive component as described in Sect. 2.1.
- Combine orientation and mystery. A city that is neither a labyrinth, closed or impossible to understand, nor flat, basic, or boring. With a certain mystery, with a story to tell associated with each corner, to the collective experiences of those who previously lived there.

- Scale. Joseph Campbell said that, *"to understand the true beliefs of a society, you just have to look at what the tallest buildings are dedicated to"* (Cambell, 1988).
- If we look back some centuries, the answer is clear: the cathedral or mosque's minaret or similar main tower as an inspiring element of that society, marked by religion and dedication to God (each one with its own name). If we look now, we find that the most important buildings are dedicated to financial, oil, pharmaceutical or sports companies. Our fundamental aspiration is money, wealth, notoriety. Our city managers have entrusted their development to private investment, and wealth owners have built these huge buildings. The city management has been reduced to transparent and efficient governance. Has the city aspiration and identity passed into private hands? No public money to build what should be the symbol of the city? We see examples such as Bilbao (Spain), which have taken the right direction when betting on a public urban transformation that marks the new city image (see Guggenheim Museum), but we also see other cities whose identity is a downtown conglomeration of commercial brands. Citizens remain indolent, mute and numb, afraid to get out of their intellectual confusion about what is beautiful or not, and raise their hands proclaiming that all those buildings are simply ugly!
- Make it local. It is important to lead the world and observe best practices, but you have to adopt them and make them your own without losing the city personality and identity. The same with innovation and technology: use it to the fullest for the benefit of citizens, but adapt it to respect for local customs and to strengthen local identity.

Coming back to the competition for talent, we can see that cities (and mainly their universities) are the center for skills' generation, human capital, creativity and innovation. These creative-class citizens characterized by their enthusiasm to search for something new, have historically been gathered in cities. Those cities have set the pace of economic growth. Cities bring together activities, businesses and investments that create wealth and, therefore, are and will be the main driving force behind the future economy. This makes cities the new centers of power and hubs of global influence, way beyond their countries. They compete to develop an attractive image to attract creative classes which are not too tied to their birth places, to nomadic elites, and obviously, the new digital nomads. Cities are creativity workshops, driving forces for sustainable economic development. The peripheral rural areas are integrated into the metropolis because of increasing public transportation efficiency. The furthest ones will disappear, losing talent little by little, without access to good Internet bandwidth due to the telcos' lack of economic interest in those areas, and without the necessary human density to generate wealth and attractiveness (create another metropolis). Only those with a special natural attraction can survive.

Cities already rule the world. It is no longer countries that compete, but cities (Bodur Okyay, 2018). Each city must create a competitive advantage to differentiate itself from the rest. Agile, creative and competitive cities that can diversify their resources and offer cultural, social and economic opportunities to their citizens will succeed. Cities that are better equipped to produce innovative, inclusive and ethical solutions to face the increasing challenges will better cope with them and emerge as leaders. Cities will compete and collaborate globally as interdependent entities, compete for talent, collaborate for the planet and other UN SDGs.

Cities are embarked on a hidden (not public) war/competition to attract the most talented citizens/investors (Kneeshaw, 2017). Cities which fail will become bedrooms for the elderly, homes of people with dependent ties due to different reasons, (personal, family, unpaid mortgage,...), and eventually disappear.

People move. New generations (mainly Millennials) are world citizens. Mobility is very affordable. The world is getting smaller. People movements/flows are faster than ever before. War/famines/conflicts are no longer the main reason why people move, but rather the desire to live in the best possible place, in the most appealing city to deploy your full potential, a city where you will be happy, safe, healthy and with an excellent personal realization.

For some cities, and due to the high cost of mortgages, it happens that the poor cannot move because they have to pay for their home, and if they leave or do not pay, they will lose their home and what they have already paid. They are *stuck* because of their loan. Thus, being able to emigrate is considered a privilege only available to independents, without family dependents and without loans to pay. This IMF (Bayoumi & Barkema, 2019) study highlights these areas where people are tied to a place because of housing. If we look at the destination cities, then we see the same problem: the price of housing is proportional to city attractiveness, so that the best destinations also have the highest prices. We reach the situation where the premium we make from a good employment in a star city does not compensate for the extra housing cost. Only the highly qualified can withstand this situation with a very high salary. In addition, this situation has a positive feedback: high salaries, higher living standards, higher housing prices. On the contrary, those who have not been able to move, see how their properties are worth less, even passing the limit where they are worth less than the mortgage's outstanding capital. This is producing a social fracture in areas like Silicon Valley or Seattle in the U.S. An authentic urban sclerosis, where emigrants are highly skilled young people from the upper & middle classes, seeking high salaries in line with their qualification.

The best possible City is idealized/imagined:

Theoretically: By Mayors, Citizens, mainly by immigrants.
Practically: By Urban Planners/Designers, and Technology Implementers.

If this process is like a wooing between the city and the talented person, then global easy mobility is making possible some previously impossible marriages.

See in Fig. 4.1 the dynamic map of Migrations (Metrocosm, 2016). In figure, we can observe the planet's main migratory flows. In blue, countries with positive balance and in red, those with negative balance, or losing net population. The large red circle in the middle shows the strong migration that happened in Syria due to the war.

If this study could eliminate migratory movements due to precarious situations such as poverty, famine or fear of war/violence, and we took only the voluntary movements of citizens in search of the best city to realize their potential, this research

**Fig. 4.1** Global immigration paths and volumes. Metrocosm

would not make sense. Simply by observing the cities with the greatest positive balance we would have the most attractive ones based on an aggregation of citizens' decisions. We could, for example, conclude that Australia is a highly attractive place, since it has a positive balance even with the U.S. We assume the fact that, as rational humans, these decisions are the result of the benefits moving could offer, and how attractive that city is for living. As such an analysis does not exist, because it would mean asking all migrants (about 244 million in 2015, with an increase of 41% since 2000) (UN SDG, 2019) about their reasons for emigrating and accounting only for those who have done so voluntarily, without being forced by circumstances, just putting their talent as a value for the target city to open its doors, then let's analyze what makes an attractive city. Thus, we can help many citizens to make an informed decision with a series of evaluative criteria, and on the other hand, help many cities to prepare, to be more attractive in this global competition for talent.

A few decades ago, the companies' location or job availability was the most important factor, and many people made their choice of a city subject to this fundamental issue. Today, it is not like that. Companies decide new offices looking at where talent is, not the other way around. We have recently seen Amazon deciding where to base its second HQ. This was a race to get the maximum public grants and offerings to choose the location. Many U.S. cities and states offered exorbitant aid, low taxes, and almost insulting conditions for companies that are already based there and don't enjoy those benefits. All with the aspiration of attracting the giant, to settle in talent and generate wealth in the city. Finally, the company decided to move to a place with guaranteed talent provision (The Guardian, 2018). Well, two locations to be more accurate: Arlington (Virginia) and Long Island City in Queens, New York City.

Imagine the extreme situation of a super-attractive company placed in a desert... people (especially new millennials) won't even consider it. Access to good employment is an important component, especially for young people, but it is not the only one, nor is it the determinant in most cases. It is, therefore, an important effort for cities to become attractive to citizens, especially for the talented, for the creative class, which will generate wealth in the Fourth Industrial Revolution.

Global competition is here to stay: hidden, fierce but bloodless, leading to even larger urban areas vs non-so-attractive cities' extreme decline or depopulation.

This issue is becoming dramatic for cities or metropolises that see how they are losing talent after having invested a lot of time and resources in nurturing it. It's about *hunting* talent and retaining it in the city to generate wealth, contribute to improve the city performance, then attract more talent, in a virtuous cycle. The opposite is to lose: lose talent, wealth, investment and therefore the ability to be attractive, which leads to greater loss of talent, in a vicious circle. In origin, talent is distributed homogeneously across the planet by birth or DNA, so that the areas with a greater population, or rather, with a larger birth rate, have greater talent in origin. This talent in origin can be missed if there are no conditions that develop it, with education from, for example, universities. The education system converts that raw talent into operational, useful, updated and desired talent. Here comes the fundamental question: at that point where talent is formed and ready, is when people look at the world and the cities that shine in it, and decide where they can reach the maximum. This is where the issue of City Attractiveness is mainly evaluated and where cities bid for those talents, like in an art auction: paying (Harrison & Raice, 2018) money, grants for paying back student loans, home purchase helps, and other aids, only for those with great potential.

In that way, Cities are becoming large HHRR departments, trying to nurture the local talent retention while attracting the foreign.

Cities must also compete locally with the private sector to hire talent (Andrews, 2020). They try to compensate for their disadvantage in lower wages with the plus of working for the common good and for improving the city. In any case, cities need very good professionals to address the challenges we have previously detailed. Specifically, they need data analysts and scientists, urban planners and humanists (psychologists, neuroscience experts) and specialists in social networks and community management. Otherwise, they will simply be unable to cope with these challenges, no matter how much technology they use, because they will not understand their own data or their own citizens.

Let's look at some examples of this *talent hunting*. We like the following examples, where countries and mainly cities are openly offering advantages to those talented citizens seriously considering moving there:

- The UK has offered *Exceptional Talent* (Gov.UK, 2019) visas aimed at attracting workers from the tech sector and providing additional opportunities to apply for UK settlement after three years of citizenship probe (work or study). This has changed with Brexit, but the new plan keeps trying to directly attract talent.

- China (Barry & Kolata, 2020) launched a high, economic value plan to attract American scientists. Now it is accused of taking advantage of this to get intellectual property.

Many cities and American states have launched ambitious plans to *hunt* talents as soon as they leave the *talent factory – University*, especially those who leave the Boston area, offering financial aid to pay for student loans, housing aids, moving costs, etc., only with the commitment to settle down in the area. Other examples: Indianapolis (Indianapolis, 2015), Wisconsin (Wisconsin Economic Development Corporation, 2020), Virginia (Virginia Tobacco Region Revitalization Commission, 2020), Michigan (Michigan Workforce Development Agency , 2020), Hamilton Cincinnati (James, 2018) or Queensland (Australia) (Advance Queensland, 2020).

More discreetly, other places do not offer such direct advantages, but they invest in generating the conditions for the expatriate who arrives there to be welcomed with open arms. If you decide on Sweden, the cities there will help you with all the information you need. When we see a website in 33 languages, we would think of a tourist motivation. Not at all; the motivation is to explain to the foreign talent the advantages that they are going to get: access to housing, employment (and Swedish classes, of course) that you will enjoy if you choose Sweden as a destination to establish yourself. Swedish cities are ready for immigrants in 33 languages! (Swedish Migration Agency, 2020).

When we create an attractive city, it is attractive to all kinds of people. So, the question is how to filter only those who are talented? They need new workers to pay for welfare society with their taxes, but talented ones. This question is obviously, classist. Yes, but you cannot deny the right of a city to choose or try to find the best future citizens. Nobody wants beggars, homeless people, or people who are not going to contribute taxes, and especially with wealth generation, with creativity, with talent. They prefer and fight for talent. It is not a matter of sex, race, religion, etc. It is simply talent, the ability to have basic languages, skills and creativity to generate value. As we said before, the repetitive, mechanical, routine work is left for the robotization that the Fourth Industrial Revolution brings us. Filtering creative vs non-creative classes is not an easy task. We are all creative in one way or another, a lot or a little, what is not creative for many is their job! So, we should better make creative jobs, but the problem will come when it is not growing as fast as job destruction due to robotization. It is clear that work must also evolve towards being more creative, with more human environments, where social relations, empathy, the ability to innovate, creativity are more important and where routine, and the sequence of rules are less important.

Cities (or countries, as we still have borders) can set a test or exam and admit with a visa only those that are talented enough. This is socially inadmissible, classist and discriminatory, although each country is sovereign in deciding who gives a residence permit to and who does not, and can set the criteria they want. We are starting to see movements in this regard: The United Kingdom is implementing a points/scorecard system for immigrant workers' admission, starting from January 1, 2021 (Gov.UK, 2020). It seems a plan inspired by a social Darwinism and is being pushed back by important economic and social-services sectors. It is about only incorporating workers with high professional preparation and good English skills. Employment has increased a lot, but without raising productivity. There are many entrepreneurs who need labor and are not willing to pay a bonus because the immigrants must be more qualified. The most relaxed EU position frontally clashes with this plan.

Others are more discreet and moderate, and simply demand knowledge of the local language. This seems less classist and more reasonable, although if we consider how difficult it must be to learn languages like Finnish/Suomi for a non-native, it is also a filter for people with high intellectual capacity and that are obviously talented (Infofinland.Fi, 2019).

In Australia, they are more direct and pragmatic. There, within the new Global Talent Independent program (GTI) (Government Australia, 2019), if you expect that you will get a high salary, (the level is set at AUD 148,700 or 87,800 €/year) either with a job offer or with a high academic qualification, getting a visa and subsequently a permanent residence has many facilities and is quite simple. What's more, Australian talent recruitment offices have been opened in Berlin, Dubai, New Delhi, Santiago, Shanghai, Singapore, and Washington DC. It is about letting the companies' HHRR departments act as a filter. It is assumed that if they offer a high salary to a foreigner, it is because they have the talent they are looking for, so, open the doors to those.

## 4.2   Problem: How to Measure/Track City Attractiveness

Worldwide competition for talent is clear. Therefore, we must improve and adapt our cities to be attractive, in the ways explained before. Let's try to find what makes a city an attractive one. The attractiveness components will be those that we must improve or maximize to increase our success at attracting talent.

### 4.2.1   A Dozen Reasons for Denver

Last 20 March 2019, I received this (Fig. 4.2) email in our inbox.

The U.S. organization Smart Cities Connect was announcing its next big event in Denver (CO) (Smartcities Connect, 2019). In the decision justification for Denver as host city for this innovative event, they made a summary assessment on why Denver is a very attractive SmartCity. Are those 12 reasons clear indicators of what's making a city attractive? Maybe they are not the only ones, but they are definitely contributing to making Denver as one of most attractive cities in the U.S.

Let's analyze them:

There are reasons or facts defining Denver and describing the city's main characteristics: mile high, sunshine hours, parks. We would add other attractions such as

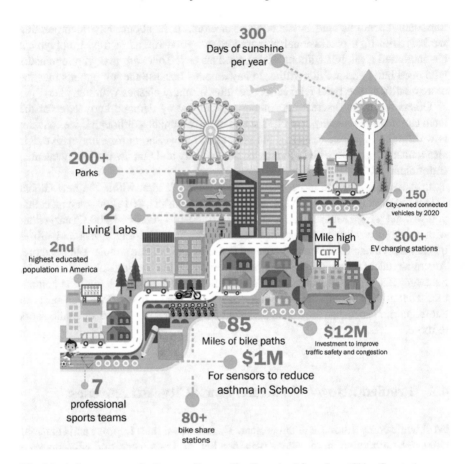

**Fig. 4.2** A dozen reasons for Denver. (Source: Email received from SmartCities Connect)

the mountains, the amazing natural *Red Rocks Park and Amphitheatre*, or for being founded as a gold mining town, always a meeting place for miners, workers, and travelers, mainly pioneers who went to explore the American West. It is interesting to see the mention of sports teams, as a projected city image and as a leisure attraction. These elements mainly make up Denver's identity, and it can't be changed overnight, and they are not related to city services, or SmartCity plans.

This is an American event, so the choice of which American city is going to host it does not take into account the living conditions in that city compared to the entire world. If we talk about Denver in a global context, we should consider the political system, conditions of equality, opportunity, social services, respect for diversity, etc.

These living conditions are quite similar for many U.S. cities, and therefore are not considered in this internal election, but they are very important in a global context.

Most of the reasons are focused on the quality of public services such as transportation, education, traffic, safety, health, and these are very differentiating elements where the results of a good investment in your SmartCity plan are paying off. The mentions of sustainability, decarbonization/electrification make a clean and sustainable city stand out.

The orientation to the UN SDGs is clearly appreciated. These topics are obvious Denver attractions if compared to other American cities. If we thought about Denver from a global context, we should also consider economic issues such as average salary, taxes, cost of living, etc. Again, these components are similar for many American cities, so they are not too important from an internal decision perspective, and therefore we do not find reasons of this kind: low taxes, high salaries, high net-purchasing power, low cost of living, etc.

Anyway, these twelve reasons mean a good scorecard for how attractive Denver is presented to us (within an American context) and gives us many clues about the indicators to be considered in a global study.

If we think about a city that tries to be attractive in an international context, and from a highly competitive area like Asia, then Singapore could be a great reference. Let's see how they are *selling their city/state*, how they use their branding to attract the 1.7 billion millennials that are looking around the world for the best city to develop their full potential. We see that the authorities are marketing Singapore mainly to companies: ease of doing business, taxes, protection of intellectual property, access to financing and some attractions that indirectly stand out for citizens, such as low taxes and excellent security. In the images used by Singapore Economic Development Board (EDB) we can find the 5G logo placed over the bay as an added sticker, indicating the city leadership's adoption of this connectivity revolution. (Singapore Government, 2019)

We are missing important attractions such as the avant-garde image in architecture, sports events, excellent urban mobility: wonderful public transportation combined with the pressure to eliminate private traffic.

In my trips, I have found cities that did not dedicate efforts (not even a good website) to present their city and its attractions to potential talented foreigners. They are cities that either do not compete in this race because they have many other basic problems to fix, or

because they think they do not need it: they are attractive enough without having to promote the city or invest in an advanced SmartCity plan. No longer. These arrogant or narcissistic cities are realizing that they need to attract talent. Their high living standards and low birth rates indicate that they must welcome emigrants to sustain their societal model. Thus, we can say that there are only two groups: the cities that struggle to achieve minimum quality of life standards, and all others, which are embarked on the global competition for talent. If a city does not identify itself in any of these two groups, it should be concerned about the quality of its managers/politicians, isolated from the world or carefree, asleep in ephemeral laurels. Time to wake up and react!

## 4.3 City Attractiveness = City Magnetism × City Profitability (Yield)

By how cities are prepared and presented to talented citizens and investors, and on the other side, how citizens decide whether or not to move to another city to improve their quality of life and opportunities, we can conclude that we are ahead of a similar decision process to a marriage or to a purchase. It looks like a marriage because there is a certain compromise between the parties, some love is necessary, or at least attraction, and it is not a decision that lasts a short time. It is not exactly a marriage because one part, the city, simply sets minimum conditions: talent, and perhaps, language skills or a certain period of cadence time until the expected visas are granted, and these conditions are for anyone who wants and can take advantage of them. It is more like a purchase. The talented citizen *buys in* to live in a city and contribute to its economic and human development, and the city *sells* its attractions, advantages, and even offers special advantages, as we have previously seen. There is no economic transaction, although it is clear that a price is paid due to differences in purchasing capacity (net-purchasing power) for the same citizen with the same kind of job, but done in different cities. We have, therefore, that it is a human decision process among many alternatives, where mercantilist/trading benefits are involved, but also aesthetic and ethical questions about the possible destination cities. Do I like that city? And what about that city's lifestyle? These seem to be previous questions to those related to conditions (wage, safety, taxes, environmental care, services.)

If we analyze the components of every human decision, we can observe two main components: the emotional and the rational (Tybout & Calder, 2010). In the rational arena, there are no emotions, but pure functional and economic arguments/facts. But humans are emotional beings, so the emotional component is very relevant, very frequently the most. For Kellogg's marketers, it is very hard to assess before they prepare a campaign or a new product launch, because emotional goals very often come from the subconscious. If we distinguish the rational part by observing the benefits or functions' component, and the economic component or price, and maintain the emotional component, we conclude that the combination of those three areas (Performance, Economy, Emotional) are leading the final decision making.

Then, if we talk about what makes a city attractive, we must think about an emotional component and a rational double-component (Services and Benefits of the city, and the *price* or cost of living or opportunity cost due to living in that city). Let's go deeper into these concepts:

**Emotional Arena**

We can say that this is the decision-making part based on emotions. It is a first step or pre-condition: from all the cities that I have some good feeling with, I will choose the best in terms of performance and my self-convenience. Let's call it City Magnetism, because it works as a magnet, attracting or repelling me.

CITY MAGNETISM = *I like it*. This is the Emotional part of the assessment.

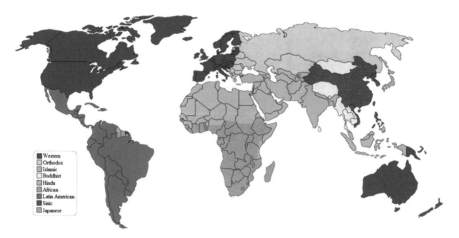

**Fig. 4.3** Map of Major Civilizations according to Huntington's Clash of Civilizations Theory. (Source: Wikipedia. By Kyle Cronan and User:Olahus – imported from enwiki, GFDL, https:// commons.wikimedia.org/w/index.php?curid=18187203)

A human will not even consider living in a city that they do like at all unless they are forced by circumstances. Each person has an idealized image of a city. It is an image formed by what you know about that city, its projected image, what you have been told about that city, what you can deduct from outside about its living style, basic questions about the economic and political stability; above all, what you know from citizens who live there and know that city very well and act as ambassadors for you. This generates a positive or negative emotion about an unknown city. Sometimes it is a broad filter and we can simply eliminate the cities in which we would never live because their living conditions do not meet my minimum standards, or are simply lower than those I already enjoy where I currently live. There are also previous or boundary conditions / determining factors. Basically, we can identify three mains:

- Language: Language is an advantage or a barrier. If a city is a meeting place and I cannot communicate with my fellow citizens, then I will not be able to properly develop my life there. There are three languages that can be heard anywhere in the world: English, Spanish and Chinese. These three top the list of native speakers and total number of speakers (James, 2019). If I can speak any, or some of them then I will have a great ease of communication wherever I go. Or simply, I must demand that my possible destination city has a good percentage (>50%) of people who can speak English as a universal language. Thus, I will be able to consider that city because I will have the opportunity to develop my human social aspect: communication.
- Civilization/Religion/Ethics: The city ethics or scale of values intrinsically depends on the civilization in which it is framed. Each civilization has a different ethic, justice, equality concept and idea of human rights. (Huntington, 1996) describes nine great civilizations in his book on "*Clash of Civilizations*," (see Fig. 4.3) where he argues that the great post-Cold War conflicts will happen

**Fig. 4.4** World of Cities. Vienna's Airport. Dec2017. (Source: Author)

between civilizations and not between countries. Analyzing these nine civilizations, which we could reduce even further, down to seven, assuming Orthodox and Latin American are classified as Western, we see their close correspondence with the major religions. In that way, the consideration of the city's majority religion will identify with a civilization, and therefore a scale of values. For many people, when choosing a city, analyzing the preferred ethics will be determinant in a negative way, choosing which civilization's ethics are unacceptable for your basic principles.

- Landscape (aesthetic question about the environment): Sea/Coast, Mountains or both? I like the sea (Barcelona, Sydney), or the Mountains (Denver, Zurich) or I want to get both nearby (Seattle, Santiago). . . Or on the contrary, if I need to do scuba-diving every day, then I can't live in Madrid, or if I have rheumatic problems and I must flee from wet places, I cannot live by the coast. After that, there is a landscape aesthetic component.

These pre-conditions are filters when choosing the most attractive city amongst all possible ones.

We see how this emotional component has a lot to do with our tastes, preferences and emotions, and fits perfectly into the city aesthetic and ethical facets.

If we humanize the concept of the city -obvious, as it is a living ecosystem-clearly this component would be the city soul, while the rational part would be the physical part, the body. Cities are not just places and spaces in which you can live, they are living entities with emotional components, they have *souls* (Alcalde, 2017). This concept of soul can be perceived, breathed and appreciated in most cities. It is what makes a city *special* (look back at *secret component* in City Attractiveness definitions). It is part of its essence, the series of emotional, intangible, qualitative elements that make a difference and distinguish them. It has to do with the environment, and above all, with the people who live there and their lifestyle. This personification of the city is clear in very famous works of literature; cities like Paris, as one main character of Victor Hugo's *Notre Dame de Paris* (1831), Dublin at James Joyce's *Dubliners* (1914) and *Ulysses* (1922), New York in Jacques Tardi's and Benjamin Legrand's novel *Roach Killer* (1984), London in Peter Ackroyd's book *London-The Biography* (2000) (Vanderbeke, 2007).

**Rational Arena**
This is related to the world as a Cities' marketplace where citizens, depending on their preferences at that moment decide to *buy* a city and dedicate their lives to that city since then. We want to point out the concept of time. Citizen preferences may change over time. Depending on the time when you plan to change cities, you may have some preferences or others. Thus, you can give more value to employability when leaving university, or to social services when you reach your retirement age. Depending on your family dependencies (children or seniors), your priorities may vary as well.

We studied that the rational arena consists of: city benefits or city performance, (functions, services, variable elements that the city provides to the citizen and that are tangible and valuable) and an economic component (the ability to acquire things or the net-purchasing power that the citizen will achieve in that city, compared to others). It is, in short, a deal. We will name that deal City Profitability, in the sense of yield.

CITY PROFITABILITY = *I want to Live/Work here*. This is the non-emotional part, more related to city merits (Economic and Performance indicators).

Based on that, the decision about our preferred City for living/working (temporarily or long-term) follows these steps:
First: Select cities with an acceptable City Magnetism (I could live here). No initial blockers. (Cities scoring over 50 in The Economist's Liveability Index (The Economist, 2019), which means no severe limitations on normal human development there). Then select those with which I have some good feeling with, attraction, some magnetism.

Then, assess City Profitability = Services I get from City/Cost associated to living in that city.

Services: The services received can be weighted as well per my perceived scale of values and specific time circumstances, as explained. We can group them into 10 main AREAS (as per studied SmartCity main components): GOVERNMENT

ADMINISTRATION (Governance) – EDUCATION – EMPLOYABILITY – HEALTH/SOCIAL SERVICES – SAFETY – ENVIRONMENTAL SUSTAINAB ILITY /UTILITIES – CONNECTIVITY – URBAN MOBILITY/TRANSPORTA TION – TOURISM/CULTURE

So, we have a clear definition of city Services and we can assess them, then weigh each one depending on its relevance to us according to our scale of values.

Cost associated to living in that city: On the other hand, we must measure the associated cost to our personal economies from living in that city. Imagine we have the same kind of job and living standards in two different cities. At the end of the month, we'll make different net money to buy what we want. That's the price we pay because of living in that city in comparison with other. We can consider the opportunity cost as well, or how much we are losing today because of not moving immediately to a better place with better opportunities and possibilities to develop our full potential. A good approach will be based on AVERAGE WAGE – (DIRECT TAXES + INDIRECT TAXES + SOCIAL CONTRIBUTIONS ) – COST OF LIVING (Net Purchase Power) = NET INCOME.

In other words, working the same kind of job, and after purchasing my needed things according to my lifestyle status like food, housing, education, healthcare, mobility, utilities, how much money will remain in my pocket at month's end? It's important to note that some cities offer high salaries, but also high taxes or high cost of life. Some others may pay you fewer wages, but if taxes and cost of life are more affordable, then your numbers will be better.

So, our intention is to create a City Attractiveness Annual report, as a WW Observatory. But the objective is not to create another ranking. Every citizen will provide their preferences for Magnetism's main Areas and their sorted priorities on the 10 main Profitability City services. Then, the tool will provide a list of top cities matching those criteria, as the best references to explore. This will be available by a smartphone app.

## 4.4   City Attractiveness & City Metaphysics

We said that to the city, *"there is nothing human which is alien to it"* (Terence 163). We could also say that to the city, nothing beautiful is alien to it, and nothing true is alien to it, or nothing good is alien to it. As a city is essentially human, all human being essential transcendentals are also city components. So, we study the city personified by a physical, urban body and the soul of its dwellers.

If we think about the transcendentals of being a *City*, then we would start with Beauty. The Beauty of the city is associated with its shape as a result of its constant transformation through the passage of time (history), with the addition of collective experiences from its inhabitants, and also the constant destruction or erosion from most city components. Beauty is also associated with its climate, its landscape, its smell, colors, slopes and hills, rivers, its gastronomy, customs and events; in short, its Identity.

The Truth of the city is expressed in its present, in its social and economic sustainability, its creativity and competitiveness, its citizens' human quality, its equity and equality. We could very well associate the Truth of the city with its Dynamism. And what about the City Strategy (Future)? It is about the potential, the hope of reaching new goals, it is a projection of the expected truth; the City Strategy could also be associated with the Truth. All religions turn to the Truth as a guide to facing the future (Psalm. The Bible 43:3–5). Then the Truth of the city guides its development, its strategy and its future.

The Good, the goal of goodness, of justice, is reflected in our citizen contract with the city, because the city does good with the services and benefits it offers us, because it protects, encourages, stimulates, connects, heals, educates us, and it allows us to move and develop. Let's remember again the essential City principle: it makes it possible us to meet and encounter each other. And in fair consideration we pay our price for it, for living in that particular city and not in any other. We could therefore associate the Good of the city with city Profitability. We might think now, ok, but social equity and equality are part of this Dynamism model, and they are also basic components of the social good concept. True, but without economic sustainability there is no social justice, so what is Good is well mirrored by City Profitability.

Unity. Although we know that the city expands as urban mobility becomes more efficient, and we see that the city blurs with its region becoming a metropolitan area, it is clear that from a human point of view, the city is a unit of coexistence and social development. After the family, as a basic social element, the city is the unit of synergy and social expression par excellence, and even more in a global context with economic stability and peace, where countries cease to make much sense. The city dwellers share their destiny, they travel to the future in the same ship, with its advantages and possibilities and also with its uncertainties and problems. In our model, unity is associated with the overall concept of City Attractiveness. Talent takes or leaves the option to go live in a city. As we said, it is like a marriage's commitment. We commit to the city in the same way that we marry our partner, with everything that person is, means and has (not partially, but altogether). As it is said in weddings, for better and for worse...

The sense of unity is found in the city as a whole world. As we discussed earlier, as a possible world of people and things interconnected by relationships. We speak of a city as one whole world concentrated in one place. It's a world within the world, like a world-in-world. The city is the place where the world takes place (Marín, 2019a). It is the place where things happen. The city unifies the world's people and things since the moment it integrates, connects and relates them, making them unite, adding to and multiply their creativity and development.

Uniqueness. Each city is different. It includes, cultivates and develops its hallmarks, its branding, its offers and its proposals for internal and external talent. No two cities are the same because of their history, and their inhabitants are always different. The concept of uniqueness would be closely associated with Identity, although all of City Magnetism describes a specific city. However, there are many similar services and benefits between cities, and many share a similar model of wages and taxes (by country or economic block). Therefore, the uniqueness of being a certain *city* would be associated with all of City Magnetism.

Each city is different; but for a city to be such, to be complete, it must have a universal meaning. The city must have a vision of the world, its vision, its reality, its way of developing human potential. For this world view, the city must have developed a series of attributes. It must have a great capacity for connection with the rest of the world, such as the neural projection of its brain. *All roads lead to Rome*, it was said at the time of imperial Rome; and it was said because Rome was in fact, the center of the world. It must have a market, a place where economic relations develop. The city is a market (Marín, 2019b). This concept of a market-city was already present in imperial London, and Seville as a Spanish-American market; Babylon, or the Xanadu that Marco Polo visited in China. It is the concept of a world trade center that we have today in many modern cities. It is the city's wealth and economic-power, dynamic heart. To attack the heart of the U.S., the NYC World Trade Center was sadly selected. It must have a stadium, a podium on which to place the champions, the best, those who lead the city by example, its favorite children. Let's remember the song about NYC that placed it on top of the world, as a lighthouse for the rest. The city must have a place for victory, for glory (Marín, 2019c). The Greek goddess Niké had it on top of the Acropolis. And our flags have it, with their meaning of pride, patriotism, and glory. That is the reason why all main great cities have their 'arches of triumph', to give glory to their best sons. All modern cities are paying special attention to their main stadium, as a place where the city's achievements are celebrated, as they were at the Colosseum in Rome. The city must have places to be visible, to project art, culture, to improve and educate its children as a mother does. It must have theaters, opera houses, museums. If the city is a world unto itself, it needs a place where it represents itself, it needs a theater. The city is a theater of the world (Marín, 2019d) because everything that happens, anything human, all that is represented, is done there. The city also needs an agora, a public place where everyone speaks, anything is discussed, is fought with words. Nowadays, and with new technologies, the agora is in the media, and especially on social networks, which allow for any citizen expression. The city must also have its temple, its place of expression of the transcendent, of the connection between the world and the cosmos, the projection towards the divine, as we already explained in cities that enjoy high levels of human values. We said that a city is a point in space/time where humans meet/encounter each other. That point is a cross (Marín, 2019e). It has a horizontal mundane dimension, with its market, its stadium, its agora, its mini worlds, all embedded in the city. It also has a vertical, universal dimension, connecting to the cosmos from the temple, radiating energy, attracting the world's attention.

Other transcendental beings like Entity, Reality, and Aliquant (it is something, it is not nothing) are obvious for a City and cover all the many studied dimensions.

Finally, the idea of a universal city (Marín, 2019f), an open city, a city that seeks the best people in the world, regardless of their origin. Are we talking about talent? Tolerance? Of course, please remember the chapters dedicated to the 3 T's (Technology, Talent, Tolerance). Without that *universal place* character, a world city where the best happens, where the champions go, where talent is fascinated and empowered, where you can elevate from the world to the universe, it would not be a city written in capital letters, but just a project. If it had not been for that character of universality, the philosophers would not have gone to Athens, nor the best and brightest scientists and artists to Vienna in 1900, nor Picasso and many other artists to Paris, nor Nicola Tesla (a Croatian immigrant, and my favorite inventor) to NYC to create amazing energy machines, nor the best talents of interpretation to Hollywood. Half of Fortune100 companies were founded by immigrants (Shoot, 2019). This is the meaning of this analysis: to find out how to make Attractive cities shine in their fullest expression. Universal and transcendent cities, where human talent becomes sublime, and where all humans can reach their highest levels of development, well-being, equity and equality.

## 4.5  Cities Selection. Criteria

We already have the master areas to research on what makes an attractive city. Now we have to select a list of cities and study their attractiveness.

There are many city rankings, according to different indicators. Professor Ayyoob Sharifi, from Hiroshima University has studied most rankings, finding as many as 34 (Ayyoob, 2018), grouping all available information into seven main themes, and 44 sub-themes. Most are partial in subject or geography, many only provide the top 10 list, which is not long enough for our research. Some others are based on surveys, not facts. The seven most important city indexes are (according to IESE Cities in Motion) (Berrone & Ricart, 2018): Cities in Motion (IESE), Global Cities Index (AT Kearny), Global Financial Centers (Z/Yen), Global Power City (MMF), Quality of Living City (Mercer), Global Liveability (The Economist) and Sustainable Cities (Arcadis) (some of which were not included in Prof. Ayyoob extended list!) Of those seven main rankings, we chose two that cover most of the areas to study, and with which we can get access to a long list of cities and detailed information.

These two indexes are the Mercer Quality of Living 2018 and the IESE Cities in Motion 2018. Then, we can approach the world's most Attractive cities based on:

- Selection Criteria: Top cities in Quality of Living (Mercer, 2018) AND Cities in Motion (IESE) AND scoring over 50 (no personal risk or severe living restrictions) in the Global Liveability Index (The Economist, 2018). The first two are reports of superior quality in detail and richness of components (indicators), coming from very well-known, highly reputable sources. The addition of the Liveability Index minimal threshold responds to a basic fact: nobody wants to live in a city where his/her life will be threatened, or basic living conditions are severely restricted. Those cities are not attractive at all!
- Quality of Living (Mercer) index included 180 cities, and Cities in Motion (IESE) analyzed 200. We took the top 140 cities, overlapping both main sources, to include as many countries as possible including all continents, while not

increasing the complexity too much. We did that for analysis diversity and globalness. It would have been easier to take only the top 50 (or fewer) modern world cities, but let's include the emerging ones as well to show them the path to becoming attractive, fix the basics and then compete globally. All indicators used must be available for all, or most, so if we add more cities, then the study could be biased because of a lack of data on them. So, these 140 are very representative, and quality data is available for them from most sources. Ok, let's get to studying the 140 Main Most Attractive World Cities! (See at APPENDIX II for the full list)

- Like any good/useful set of indicators, all information included from external studies/rankings must comply with some basic principles: It must be benchmark-able, replicable, with data acquisition costs near zero, facts/data-based (no surveys, rumors, opinions, subjective topics), relevant to the analyzed topic, fair, manageable, so we can compare apples to apples (based on cities in same situation), and dynamic/evolving (planning to update it yearly), as cities change, and a new indicator could show up and better describe one particular topic. As new services and tools also become available, for example, 5G, we should incorporate them as they become deployed.

The selection of indicators to use follows the Metanalysis methodology: researching all available documents and indexes, then choosing those matching previous criteria, and avoiding biases. The main source of bias is the lack of information for all the 140 researched cities. All used indicators must be available for at least 75% of them. When not, the remaining 25% must be easily extrapolated from other cities from same country, or from general country or region information. Some very important indicators are only available for countries. The information by city does not add significant detail or differences, for example, the government model or level of democracy.

# References

Advance Queensland. (2020). *Recruitment/talent attraction.* https://advance.qld.gov.au/can-we-help/recruitment-talent-attraction. Accessed 22 Jan 2020.

Alcalde, I. (2017). Ciudades con Alma en la Era Digital. *Citizen.* http://thecitizen.es/cultura/ciudades-con-alma-en-la-era-digital. Accessed 20 June 2019

Andrews, J. (2020). How cities are attracting tech talent. *CitiesToday.* https://cities-today.com/graduating-to-a-city-job/. Accessed 2 Feb 2020.

Ayyoob, S. (2018). *A critical review of selected smart city assessment tools and indicator sets.* Hiroshima University. pp. 6–8. Elsevier Editorial System(tm) for Journal of Cleaner Production.

Barry, E., & Kolata, G. (2020). China's lavish funds lured U.S. scientists. What did it get in return? *The New York Times.* https://www.nytimes.com/2020/02/06/us/chinas-lavish-funds-lured-us-scientists-what-did-it-get-in-return.html. Accessed 12 Feb 2020.

Bayoumi, T., & Barkema, J. (2019). *Stranded! How rising inequality suppressed US migration and hurt those left behind.* IMF Working Papers. https://www.imf.org/en/Publications/WP/Issues/2019/06/03/Stranded-How-Rising-Inequality-Suppressed-US-Migration-and-Hurt-Those-Left-Behind-46824. Accessed 31 Aug 2019.

Berrone, P. & Ricart, J. E. (2018). *2018 Cities in motion index*. IESE. https://media.iese.edu/research/pdfs/ST-0471-E.pdf. Accessed 15 Mar 2018.

Bodur Okyay, Z. (2018) This is what a Smart City should do for its people. *NEWCITIES, 2018.* https://newcities.org/the-big-picture-this-is-what-a-smart-city-should-do-for-its-people/. Accessed 4 Jan 2020.

Cambell, J. (1988). *The power of myth, episode 3*. PBS Documentary.

Cambridge Dictionary. (2019). *Attractiveness*. https://dictionary.cambridge.org/es/diccionario/ingles/attractiveness. Accessed 12 Oct 2019.

Council of Europe. (2008). Manifesto for a new urbanity. European Urban Charter II. Council of Europe Publishing. p. 49. Also at: https://rm.coe.int/urban-charter-ii-manifesto-for-a-new-urbanity-publication-a5-58-pages-/168095e1d5. Accessed 13 Nov 2019.

Florida, R. (2007). *The flight of the creative class* (p. 37). Collings.

GOV.UK. (2019). *Exceptional talent visa*. https://www.gov.uk/tier-1-exceptional-talent. Accessed 24 Aug 2019.

GOV.UK. (2020). *The UK's points-based immigration system: Policy statement*. https://www.gov.uk/government/publications/the-uks-points-based-immigration-system-policy-statement/the-uks-points-based-immigration-system-policy-statement. Accessed 4 Feb 2020.

Government Australia. (2019) *Global Talent Independent program (GTI)*. https://immi.homeaffairs.gov.au/visas/working-in-australia/visas-for-innovation/global-talent-independent-program. Accessed 22 Dec 2019.

Harrison, D., & Raice, S. (2018). *How bad is the labor shortage? Cities will pay you to move there, WSJ*. https://www.wsj.com/articles/how-bad-is-the-labor-shortage-cities-will-pay-you-to-move-there-1525102030. Accessed 2 Nov 2019.

Huntington, S. (1996). *The clash of civilizations?: The Debate*. p. 26. Foreign Affairs. Simon & Schuster.

Indianapolis. (2015). *$1.4 million Lilly endowment grant to support TechPoint talent attraction and development initiatives*. Central Indiana Corporate Partnership. https://www.cicpindiana.com/1-4-million-lilly-endowment-grant-support-techpoint-talent-attraction-development-initiatives/. Accessed 3 Jan 2020.

infoFinland.fi. (2019). *How to apply for Finnish citizenship?* https://www.infofinland.fi/en/living-in-finland/settling-in-finland/finnish-citizenship/how-to-apply-for-finnish-citizenship. Accessed 22 Nov 2019.

James, A. (2018). Hamilton gets back to business with innovative talent attraction efforts. *Hamilton Cincinnati*. https://redicincinnati.com/blog/articles/hamilton-gets-back-to-business-with-innovative-talent-attraction-efforts. Accessed 11 Jan 2020.

James, L. (2019). The 10 most spoken languages in the world. *Babbel Magazine*. https://www.babbel.com/en/magazine/the-10-most-spoken-languages-in-the-world. Accessed 17 Jan 2020.

Kneeshaw, S. (2017). *The war for talent in cities*. EU URBACT. https://newcities.org/the-big-picture-this-is-what-a-smart-city-should-do-for-its-people/. Accessed 22 Nov 2019.

Koolhaas, R. (1997). *Acerca de la ciudad*, GG, Barcelona, 2014 from "The Generic City" Domus, núm. 791, pp. 35, 44, 63. Domus.

Marín, H. (2019a). *Mundus. Una arqueología filosófica de la existencia* (p. 145). Nuevoinicio.

Marín, H. (2019b). *Mundus. Una arqueología filosófica de la existencia* (p. 146). Nuevoinicio.

Marín, H. (2019c). *Mundus. Una arqueología filosófica de la existencia* (p. 152). Nuevoinicio.

Marín, H. (2019d). *Mundus. Una arqueología filosófica de la existencia* (p. 158). Nuevoinicio.

Marín, H. (2019e). *Mundus. Una arqueología filosófica de la existencia* (p. 189). Nuevoinicio.

Marín, H. (2019f). *Mundus. Una arqueología filosófica de la existencia* (p. 169). Nuevoinicio.

Mercer. (2018). 2018 Quality of living mercer index. https://mobilityexchange.mercer.com/Insights/quality-of-living-rankings. Accessed 16 Mar 2018.

Mercer. (2019a). *Quality of living cities ranking*. https://mobilityexchange.mercer.com/Insights/quality-of-living-rankings. Accessed 20 Nov2019.

Mercer. (2019b). Mercer city attractiveness. *How competitive is your city?* https://www.mercer.com/what-we-do/workforce-and-careers/city-attractiveness-index.html. Accessed 30 Aug 2020.

Metrocosm. (2016). *All the world's immigration visualized in 1 map.* http://metrocosm.com/global-immigration-map/. Accessed 20 Sept 2019.

Psalm. The Bible. 43:3–5

Regional Workforce Development Agency. (2020). *Michigan works!* (p. 2). http://www.discovernortheastmichigan.org/downloads/final_report_for_workforce_talent_development_and_retention_112014.pdf. Accessed 24 Jan 2020.

Shoot, B. (2019). Immigrants founded nearly half of 2018's fortune 100 companies, new data analysis shows. *Fortune.* https://fortune.com/2019/01/15/immigrants-founded-half-fortune-500-companies/. Accessed 12 Jan 2020.

Singapore government. (2019). *EBD Singapore.* https://www.edb.gov.sg/en/why-singapore/discover-the-singapore-difference.html. Accessed 9 Aug 2019.

Sinkene, J., & Kromalcas, S. (2010). *Concept, Direction and practice of city attractiveness improvement* (pp. 148–150). University of Technology. *Kaunas.*

SmartCities Connect. (2019). *Spring conference & expo.* https://spring.smartcitiesconnect.org/. Accessed 14 Apr 2019.

Swedish Migration Agency. (2020). https://www.migrationsverket.se/Other-languages.html. Accessed 21 Jan 2020.

Terence. (163) (Latin: Publius Terentius Afer) *Heauton Timorumenos* (The Self-Tormentor), Act I, scene 1, line 25 (77). "Homo sum: humani nihil a me alienum puto."

The Economist. (2018) *2018 global liveability report.* https://store.eiu.com/article.aspx?productid=455217630 and https://www.eiu.com/public/topical_report.aspx?campaignid=liveability2018. Accessed 22 Mar 2018.

The Economist. (2019). *The global liveability index 2019* (p. 5). Also at https://www.eiu.com/n/the-global-liveability-index-2019/. Accessed 23 Jan 2020.

The Guardian. (2018). *Amazon to split second headquarters into two locations – report.* https://www.theguardian.com/technology/2018/nov/05/amazon-second-hq-two-locations-cities. Accessed 21 Oct 2019.

The School of Life. (2019). The book of life. On how to make an attractive city. https://www.theschooloflife.com/thebookoflife/how-to-make-an-attractive-city/. Accessed 12 Dec 2019.

Tybout, A., & Calder, B. (2010). *Kellogg on marketing* (p. 8). Wiley.

UN SDG. (2019). 17 goals to transform our world. https://www.un.org/en/development/desa/population/migration/publications/migrationreport/docs/Migration_increase_digitalcard.png. Accessed 22 Nov 2019.

Valuer. (2019). 50 Best startup Cities in 2019. https://valuer.ai/blog/top-50-best-startup-cities/. Accessed 22 Nov 2019.

Vanderbeke, D. (2007). *The city as a superorganism. The mighty heart or the desert in disguise? The metropolis between realism and the fantastic* (pp. 162–165). Tübingen Stauffenberg Verlag.

Virginia Tobacco region Revitalization Commission. (2020). *Student loan repayment talent attraction program.* https://www.revitalizeva.org/grant-loan-program/student-loan-repayment/. Accessed 3 Jan 2020.

Wisconsin Economic Development Corporation. (2020). *Talent development, retention and attraction.* https://wedc.org/business-development/talent-attraction-and-retention/. Accessed 11 Jan 2020.

# Chapter 5
# City Magnetism

## 5.1  Introduction. Defining and Unearthing a City's Magnetism

*I hope I go to Heaven, and when I do, I'm going to do what every San Franciscan does when he gets there. He looks around and says, 'It ain't bad, but it ain't San Francisco'* (Caen, 1957). Herb Caen, American newspaper columnist for the "San Francisco Chronicle."

We talk about the emotional component. That magnetic part that attracts us to the city. It is difficult to explain if you have not lived there, so the exercise is extremely difficult, because it is about emotions, a kind of love-relationship with our city that is associated with the elements that define that city, its essence.

Cities know this, and try to cultivate that relationship of belonging, even with direct symbols or messages, like the ones we can see in the composition in Fig. 5.1. Ok, but what makes up this city essence that attracts us like a magnet? If we have on the one hand that the essence of things is fundamentally the invariable and permanent nature that constitutes them, and the city is in essence, a point in space/time where humans meet/encounter, then the city essence is determined by the humans who have previously lived, and currently live there. Every minute we live in the city we can observe it, we can understand that there are things behind everything we see, more lost sounds behind what we hear, there is a point of view waiting to be explored. We perceived the extreme of this situation in Rome, where each corner has a rich history behind it, and suggests to you to try to discover it, challenging. Nothing is isolated, or constitutes a comprehensive experience by itself, but always in relation to what surrounds it, to the sequence of events that happened there, the memory of past experiences (Lynch, 1960a). The city is like that: it has been designed, built, destroyed, modified and changed by the humans who have lived there and continue transforming it every day. There is, therefore, a direct relationship between the elements that make a city magnetic, and its evolution over time, from its foundation till today. It extended even beyond, projected into the future, because its

© The Author(s), under exclusive license to Springer Nature Switzerland AG 2021
J. A. Ondiviela, *Beyond Smart Cities*, https://doi.org/10.1007/978-3-030-83371-8_5

**Fig. 5.1** Love Cities Collage. (Source: Author)

future as a city depends on its ability to retain and attract talent, to the point of compromising its development, prosperity or decline and disappearance.

Also, we can observe the evolution of a city according to the notion of time that its inhabitants hold. There is a very Western conception that reaches its maximum expression in the U.S. in terms of time as a push forward, towards the future, never looking back. It is easy to understand why this happens when your history is very limited and not rich in relevant cultural contributions. In general, in the Western civilization, we look to forward as the future and backward as the past, as we see a river going in one direction and passing in front of us.

However, the Jewish tradition thinks just the other way around: the past is in front of us, we face it, in Hebrew: '*lefanim*' (literally: in our face), while the future is placed behind us, in Hebrew: '*leajor*' (literally: what is behind). This has a certain logic, because you know and see and you can study the past, while nothing, or very little is known about the future, like what you have behind, is unknown, because you do not see it. The future comes from behind, it shows up to us in the present, and we see it moving away to the past.

We also see time as a cyclical element in the Jewish tradition, where great stages and movements are repeated. Many times, we have thought about this concept when talking about climatology, migratory movements, stock market developments, history, everything we repeat at the same date every year, every month, week, or even every day, and especially when talking about human behavior, good and evil, human progress and corruption. An ancient description of this conception is found in the Bible, "*what it was is what it will be, and what was done is what will be done, and there is nothing new under the sun*" (Ecclesiastes).

Therefore, the concept of time (Shteinsaltz, 2019) in Judaism combines the idea of periodicity, of the cycle, and the conception that the world is moving towards a certain goal. We can say that the timeline describes a helix, such as a hair ringlet, the vines' tendrils or a DNA chain.

The historical methodology will be able to offer us an accurate analysis of any hypothesis about the city, because in itself, it is the repository of history (Rossi, 1978). This will help us understand its foundations as a physical structure and as a synthesis of values, and as a collective imagination, as if we could see past, present and future intertwined in the city. Therefore, cities are living history. They are a constant historical evolution, a reflection of the passage of time. The city must respect and balance modern development with the preservation and retention of its historical heritage (Pinto, 2009). It is a sustainable development, where new things are added and integrated without destroying or ruining the old, but constantly learning from them. A city without history is like a man without memory. Humans leave traces of their lives, their experiences and their effort and work, their history in the city. They do it in the form of monuments, neighborhoods, trees, constructions, spaces, parks, churches, libraries, institutions, universities...all this constitutes the city's collective legacy and allows a sense of continuity to be established for its inhabitants, understanding where they come from and getting them prepared for the future. Therefore, the City Magnetism is the result of human action, and will cover three moments: past, present and future, both progress and prosperity in ascending line, or destruction and decline in a descending one, as we studied in López Quintás' theory: ecstasy vs vertigo. This evolution will follow the human cycles: life and its behaviors, in a perfect and infinite helix. We therefore see the city in its evolution from an entirely human perspective. We could say that to the city, "*nothing human is alien to it*" (Terence). This absolutely humanistic conception has been adopted by the Autonomous University of Mexico City as its main motto.

For KPMG (Haynes, 2014a), *Magnet Cities* have strong leaders, great ability to raise funds (fundraisers), attract young wealth creators (talent), experience a constant physical renewal, and have thus generated a new, definable city identity.

Let us study these three groups of magnetic components.

## 5.1.1   Cities' Past

The Past marks, defines and writes the city identity in stone. It is like its DNA, the addition of collective contributions from its former inhabitants, all adding parts of that DNA: evolving, constantly recombining itself. It can evolve, but slowly. It can be transformed by a long, complex process. It will take, with a well-defined, well-funded and widely-agreed plan, at least 15 years to start watching new identity traits, which will not be consolidated until they are adopted by the citizens as their own, as part of themselves. Bilbao's (Spain) famous full reinvention took 20 years. See Fig. 5.2.

From a full industry collapse (1970) and a devastating flood (1983), city revamped, regenerating the riverfront (1991), building the Guggenheim Museum

**Fig. 5.2**  Bilbao's new identity symbol: Guggenheim Museum. Source: Wikipedia

as City symbol (1997), Euskalduna Music and Conference hall (1999), new airport (2000), tramline (2002) and many more since then. (Haynes, 2014b).

The City identity is thus defined by those elements that make up its essence, and that have been defined throughout history, such as its culture, customs, gastronomy, type of society/government. In addition, we can include fixed determinants such as geographic location, climate and environment, green spaces, or the risk of natural disasters. Finally, the city has been nurturing its reputation, its external or projected image, its branding, through the impacts it has brought in the media, in history, and continues to provide in the present, such as through cultural or sporting events.

Here, we are talking about Culture as identity (past) expressed in the city (monuments, museums, events, etc.), but not as a service or benefit.

## 5.1.2  Cities' Present

The city's present moment is defined by citizens' daily activity. This is ever-changing, and different activity every day is also a magnetic element. We talk about the cities' psychology, about their ethics, about how people live in them, how they make a living. The present is the City Dynamism, how are the relations like between its inhabitants. If Identity laid the foundations for Magnetism, Dynamism establishes the actions. The city attracts me by its Identity, when I arrive it delights me, welcomes me, motivates me, encourages me, moves me, helps me (or not), with its Dynamism, or its lack thereof. The Identity would act like the brochure of a holiday vacations' agency, the Dynamism is the excursions that I can do at the destination.

City Dynamism will be marked by its activity, creativity, competitiveness in business and in human activities, attracting investors, promoting entrepreneurship and generating employment. Also, in the way of human relationships, participation, accessibility of all, inclusion and integration. It will be noticed in the citizens' happiness, all in a city with ethical values, marked by parameters of equality and tolerance. It is about how vibrant the city is. In the era of the acceleration of new technologies' adoption, speed is attractive, immobilism is boring. The main difference between our society's model and the previous ones is the speed of change.

### 5.1.3 Cities' Future

And the next obvious question is about Future. How can the future become an attraction driver for the city? When we fall in love with someone, we cannot predict how that person will evolve in the future, but we are attracted by their potential, or at least preparation/skills, strength, motivations…various indicators on how that person will face the future and seize opportunities. This is unpredictable, of course, and has a large degree of pure risk. We all know people who have surprised everybody by their achieved level of development from a modest position, and others who have just wasted their potential.

Therefore, the city's planned future is also a strong component of Magnetism. It is always more beneficial to get on a wave of progress and innovation when it starts to lift off than when it is already consolidated. Yet, it also implies betting, and involves the risk of being wrong.

So, what do we expect from a city with a bright Future? We expect it to have a solid plan (a SmartCity Plan), which includes the components we have already studied (leadership, projects, ambition, financing, strategy, and above all, enthusiasm and hope, desire to progress). What makes that plan work? Remember the rule of City prosperity, (Chap. 2), the 3 T's (Technology, Talent, Tolerance). We need investment in Innovation as a fundamental and permanent driver and, of course, talent, human capital.

Then, we can conclude that the City Magnetism model can be approached by three groups of indicators:

- Identity (Past)
- Dynamism (Present)
- Strategy (Future)

We are going to study them by using the best available and accurate proxies matching the criteria selection definition.

## 5.2   City Identity (Past)

The City Identity is a sum of all contributions derived from its place and physical conditions, its history, its past inhabitants and all the imprint they left in the city which created and built, for good or bad, its current shape. Most times, the environment strongly marks this identity.

*I was born in Cartagena, a city on the shores of the Mediterranean with more than three thousand years of history. I was born in a library, in my grandfather's, where are the stories of that sea; the stories of the Crusades and the Greeks and the Peloponnese and the battle of Salamis. Of the corsairs, of the Berbers...for me, the sea is school, it is memory, it is history. And it is my city* (Pérez-Reverte, 2019).

We studied in the reflection from Rem Koolhaas (Koolhaas, 1997) how the lack of identity leads to generic, soulless, inhuman cities, as a repetitive, fractal collection of the same gray, horrible constructions, where humans voluntarily live in little apartments, caged like rabbits. The generic city eliminates human creativity, cancels it out, and humans become productive robots wandering in a sea of cement.

Each city must work with its unique geographical location, political, demographic, economic, fiscal and historical/cultural characteristics.

Identity crisis. The City Identity must be preserved. Otherwise, it can be deteriorated, damaged or even lost, except for in archaeologists' memory. Cultural singularity is lost as the lack of inclusion grows, because the traditional inhabitants are displaced from the center to the periphery, which is empty of people, but full of expensive offices, some gentrified luxury neighborhoods, or sub-housing areas that emigrants occupy offering basic services or Historic places preserved only for tourists, because local young citizens don't even know them. The sense of community that fed the city's identity for decades or centuries is disappearing. Creative density is lost, citizens no longer meet, the city ceases to make sense, making it lose its essence. People's housing looks more like a set of closed boxes, linearly arranged in a warehouse called *urban area*, with space to access each independently. The city is less and less inclusive, pushing low-income citizens to the outskirts, near the industrial estates.

Identity takes many years to develop and be perceived. This happens for planned cities, built from scratch. Some cities planned in the 60's and 70's such as Chandigarh (India, 1966), Bhubaneswar (India, municipality since 1979, although it is the city of temples, some as old as the I century), Almere (Netherlands, 1975, gaining land from water) or Milton Keynes (UK, created in 1974, independent since 1997), are now beginning to project something similar to a specific urban character (Keeton, 2020). We could conclude that a new city takes a minimum of 50 years to develop a perceptible identity. Or the other way around, Identity can't be changed overnight, it takes a long time, and invested resources.

To better illustrate the City Identity concept, let's take a look at Fig. 5.3. Which city is behind those symbols, photos? We are going to make a small quiz. Looking from top to bottom, we find:

**Fig. 5.3**  City Identity Quiz. (Source: Author)

An artifact with balls that looks like a molecule of united atoms. A large door as a monument. A statue of a boy peeing. And a comic character face. Have you already guessed? No?

Let's look at the gastronomy: chocolate with a flag, cabbage, waffles, beer, and a pot of mussels. At least you will be clear about the country, right? Not yet?

If you still have doubts, look below, and find a very large building full of European Union flags, and a football team flag called Anderlecht.

Yes now? Ok, it is clearly Brussels, the capital of Belgium and the European Union.

The artifact with balls is a unique building: the Atomium, symbol of Brussels since the World Exhibition of 1958. The door is the triumphal arch at the Cinquantenaire Park, built for another world exhibition in 1880 commemorating 50 years of Belgian independence. The peeing boy is the famous Manneken pis, a symbol of the city, together with the Atomium and the Grand Place. The comic is... Tintin, the very well-known character of the amazing Belgian artist Hergé, which was published from 1930 to 1976, becoming one of most influential European series.

Then, Belgian chocolate, Brussels sprouts, waffles, beer from one of about 180 Belgian breweries (many of them former abbeys with more than 1150 different beers), mussels: the famous and traditional *moules-frites*. The European Commission headquarters in Schuman Square, and the most important local football team,

Anderlecht. Anderlecht is one of the 19 small towns that make up the Brussels region, or rather, the Brussels metropolis.

It seems clear that the identity of a city is composed of unique symbols, places or special people that are strongly associated with that city, entrenched customs, gastronomy and events or elements that frequently project its image to the rest of the world. The City Identity model includes all relevant known components which provide information and help describe that identity. A model is always a simplification of a complex reality. The list of components that can be used as a proxy to uniquely identify a city is not exhaustive, it's the best approach using the available sources of information and respecting the criteria selection rules described before.

The best-known City Identity proxies:

## 5.2.1   Identity: History/Culture as Identity

### Why Is This Proxy Relevant?

As we explained earlier, a city needs at least 50 years to start creating certain identity marks in the minds of its citizens. The city's permanent construction or destruction by its citizens in a historical process means that the city is like a history archive (Chueca Goitia, 1968a), like a book that has been written day by day since its foundation, with happy and sad episodes, glorious and painful ones, of brilliant splendor and decay. The cities, more-than-linked to history or to the events that have been happening, are history in themselves, it's part of its essence. The city is a changing, physical structure and it has a spirit (soul), so it is a historical being (Chueca Goitia, 1968b). By establishing itself as a historical being, a two-way relationship is developed with History: History is made in the city, and this forces the city to become History. Universal history is urban history (Sprengler, 2013). Therefore, the city's history will give us a lot of information about its identity, so much so that we can establish a direct relationship between both concepts.

Intimately linked with history, we have cultural development, as a human expression during all that past time. We are going to try to approach this concept as an identity generator, *not* as a public (cultural) service (it will be studied as such in Chap. 6). It is very difficult to measure the cultural impact on the city Identity, although its enormous relevance and permanent footprint are relevant. Should we count the monuments, the pieces of artwork that were made there, or using the city's inspiration? Let's not lose focus: it is about valuing what a talented person can appreciate, and what can be compared with other cities. There are two elements that give us a good proxy of this cultural impact: the UNESCO-World Heritage consideration, and the presence of important museums. There are many other elements that we could consider as historical contributions to the city identity, such as important events, battles, treaties, agreements, mentions in history books, but a model must be simple, and with great descriptive power. Trying to add many more elements would make it complicated and provide very little added value.

To be included in the UNESCO World Heritage List (UNESCO, 2019a), cities must meet at least one of the 10 selection criteria. These criteria specify that the city must be/contribute a unique universal value, exceptional in terms of history and culture. The list includes 1121 places/cities (869 cultural, 213 natural and 39 mixed). To summarize them, the candidate cities must be an outstanding example in one of these areas, always related to the culture-history binomial (the first six are human creations, while the additional four are natural spaces):

1. Masterpiece of human creativity.
2. Exchange of human values in an era/time.
3. Testimony of a cultural tradition or a civilization.
4. Architectural or landscape environment.
5. Human settlement in relation to the environment.
6. Associated with events, traditions or artistic works of universal importance.
7. Nature-Aesthetics.
8. Nature-Earth History. As Registry.
9. Nature-Evolutionary Earth history. Ecology and Biology.
10. Nature-Conservation-Preservation biological diversity.

Museums have traditionally been dedicated to the protection, preservation, collection and exhibition of objects with high cultural and historical value (Werner, 2019). They are, therefore, history storehouses. In the last decades, the sense of research has been greatly developed, from disclosure/cultural dissemination, with continuous activities such as thematic exhibitions, to interpretation sessions, conferences, auditions with experts, etc. A clear expression of the relevance of museums is their growing number, which means that cities are investing in these spaces to improve their attractiveness (some have based their transformation around a museum, such as Bilbao (Spain) with its new Guggenheim Museum). On the other hand, the importance that is being given to old museums that were falling into oblivion due to Western society's cultural decline is noticeable. These museums are being recovered, revitalized and promoted, to reinforce their role as cultural icons and hallmarks. This accelerated growth in the number of museums that have opened its conception to an incredible variety of subjects, some with relatively little cultural value, offering just information on a curious topic or becoming an evolution of collecting. Therefore, we are going to select the most important ones. As it is complex to determine what is important or not in a cultural environment, we will select the most visited. Although these lists are summarized on Wikipedia, they come from reliable sources such as the annual Art Newspaper exhibition, and the TEA/AECOM Museum Index, a Fortune 500 consulting company. The list includes museums related to art, history and science, but does not include archaeological sites or historical monuments such as palaces, unless those palaces include important museums.

**How to Measure It?**

We have to rank from one to 10 the 140 cities considered according to their history/ cultural history.

Age. The age of a city is a key indicator in its history. The older the better, the longest history, obviously. We will take, then, the year of its foundation as a starting date. As there is a wide variety and dispersion, from relatively new cities to multi-millennial cities, and there were dark times in history such as the low Middle Ages with little cultural contribution, instead of taking that data as an absolute value, we will make a ranking. This ranking is grouped into eight groups, with group one being very old cities, and group eight very modern ones. We assign one point to each group number, so we give zero to seven points.

UNESCO. We will add two points to those on the (UNESCO, 2019a) list.

Museums. We will add an extra point to those that appear on the list of cities with top-visited museums (62 museums with more than 2 million visitors/year (2018)) or top art museums (77 museums with more than 1 million visitors/year (2018)).

Weights. The most important indicator is history. UNESCO's consideration is very important and has an enormous correlation with historical human activity, although it is also given to unique natural spaces. These spaces also make the city unique, singular and attractive. We consider this indicator an enhancer of the history indicator, as it is a recognition. Museums' quality is also strongly correlated to history, although some respond to a modern effort by some cities to improve their attractiveness. We then assign 70% of weight to Age, 20% to the UNESCO indicator and 10% to Museums.

(See History data Ranking at APPENDIX III)

## 5.2.2   Identity: Climate

**Why Is This Proxy Relevant?**

The climate of a city is a fundamental component of its identity and its attractiveness. Although the human being is the only animal adapted to any climatic situation, the human development living conditions are highly conditioned by climate. Within the climate, we can evaluate the temperature (too-hot and too-cold places prevent outdoor social life development, the city's essence). Also, precipitation (here we also see the extremes that make cities too dry or too rainy/humid) also inhibits social development and economic growth). Additionally, a social life determining component is the number of sunshine hours. Luminosity (real sun hours, not those related to latitude, but those with clear skies) invites you to enjoy the city, social relationships, outdoor activities, go out for leisure activities, socialize, shop, etc. It is even a psychological component that provides emotional stability and happiness. This is very well studied in Psychiatry. Decreased sun hours or exposure has been linked to a drop in serotonin levels, leading to a higher depression with a seasonal pattern incidence. The serotonin production is induced by light entering the eyes. This light impacts certain areas of the retina which cue the release of serotonin. Thus, this type of depression is associated with winters and areas with low levels of sun exposure (Nall, 2018). Seasonal affective disorder (SAD) is a major disorder, a subset of mood disorder in which patients exhibit depressive symptoms at the same time every year, usually in winter. Common symptoms include low energy, reluctance, overeating, and sleeping too much. The term was coined by Dr. Normal Rosenthal at George-town University to describe the so-called winter sadness/gloom/blue: feelings of sadness, hopelessness, and listlessness, the lethargy that occurs when the external weather forces people to spend more time indoors and there are few opportunities for natural light exposure. Rosenthal wondered why he slowed down during the winter after moving from sunny South Africa to New York. When he experienced increased exposure to natural, non-artificial light again, he observed a clear improvement in health. Some people have speculated that our modern lifestyle, which keeps people under artificial light for so many hours, may be encouraging a form of permanent SAD throughout the year. The main therapy is simply light; bright-light therapy as a common treatment for seasonal affective disorder and circadian rhythm sleep disor-ders (Wu, 2017). Winter depression is a common depression in most Nordic countries. In Alaska, it has reached a rate of 25%, falling to an approximate estimated 10% in the Netherlands, and reaching only 1.4% in Florida. In Spain, there are hospitals and tourist resorts specialized in receiving Norwegians for 2 weeks as a cure for their depression. The Norwegian government pays for these health vacations as they are more effective and cheaper than the use of drugs and expensive hospital rooms. Aside from better mental health and sleep quality, sun-light has other very beneficial health effects like Vitamin D production, which improves bone strength by fixing calcium and improving blood pressure (Tri-City Medical Center, 2018).

Hurricane risk, or other unique meteorological elements will be included in the risks section – GeoRisks.

## How to Measure It?

As we have seen that in climate, extremes are bad, therefore we will use the difference between each city's data vs the world average in temperature (about 15 °C) and in rainfall (884 mm or liters/m$^2$) as the main indicator. On top of this, we will add a corrective factor relative to the gradient of that indicator, since it is not the same to have an average temperature without great variation, than strong heat/cold waves/spells, or in a matter of rain, having frequent soft rains or periods of high drought combined with downpours.

This data about city average temperature, rain precipitation and daily sun hours is available from Climatemps (Climatemps, 2018).

The world's average temperature is 15 °C. It's the same result we got as the average from our 140 cities, so that means we have a good balanced sample. We will always take average temperatures. So, we will take the city's annual average temperature difference at 15 °C. This number will be amplified with the gradient, which is the difference between the average temperature in the hottest month vs the coldest. This difference is ranked for all 140 cities to get a % (from 0 to 1). This percentage will be added to the previous indicator as deviation. So, the best cities will be those with average temperatures nearest to 15 °C, and with the smallest range of temperatures between hottest and coldest months. In other words, mild weather, wonderful to stimulate human activity. On the other extreme, a city that is very hot or very cold with extreme differences between months' averages will have a very bad indicator and be amplified by close to 100%, or multiplied by 2.

The world's average rain precipitation is 990 mm. Our 140 cities' average is 884 mm, meaning that we have less cities from humid, tropical areas than cities from drier areas. Here, we'll follow the same method: the difference in precipitation vs the average will be weighted by the % of gradient obtained by the difference between the month with the highest precipitation and the month with the lowest.

The sunlight hours/day can be directly obtained from Climatemps, then normalized. Note that this indicator refers not only to the presence of sun due to Earth's rotation and latitude, but to the availability of direct (cloudless) sunlight.

Weights. Daily sunshine is more impactful on citizens' mood, but temperature and rain precipitation are more important to city activities and rhythm, so we will treat all three as equally weighted.

(See Climate data Ranking at APPENDIX III)

## 5.2.3   Identity: Space. Green Areas. Density

### Why Is This Proxy Relevant?

The extension and space available are other basic hallmarks. Here we find a contradiction: we want ample spaces to develop our lives, but, as we said previously in Chap. 2, maximum human density is necessary to strengthen economic and social development. How do we solve this dichotomy? Easy; we need large, green spaces for leisure, like a forest city *lung*, cleaning the air and contributing to the carbon neutral objective. These are spaces associated with the city, but without/or with little urban population. The population must be concentrated in high densities (but without abusing from verticality). That is, located at short distances, or rather short periods of time with an efficient public transport system. (15-minute City).

The environmental policy dimension of green cities addresses the problems of sustainable urban development through pollution control, the reduction of carbon dioxide emissions, and the limited consumption of resources, highlighting the important role of urban vegetation, and ensuring a high quality of life. The development of a green identity aims to achieve a better position in the general context of cities, as an advertising slogan for potential external citizens that we want to attract, and as an indicator of a greater environmental policy for existing citizens (Gulsrud, 2015).

The urban form and spatial pattern of land and space use determines how cities use and generate matter, resources, and dispose of waste. This also conditions and impacts the quality of life of its inhabitants (Dempsey & Jenks, 1978). The World Bank indicates that the most compact and contiguous cities enjoy efficiencies and advantages in transportation and infrastructure. Likewise, density, agglomeration and proximity are fundamental for human progress, economic development and social equity (Swilling et al., 2018).

Therefore, we must measure the percentage of green space and its density.

**How to Measure It?**

The data referring to the percentage of space dedicated to green areas is sometimes found directly in the information related to the city, while other times it must be calculated directly as green spaces out of the total city space. With the new concept of city dimensions that brings us increased efficiency in urban mobility, (see Chap. 2, Fig. 2.5, where we associated to a single metropolis everything reachable in less than 90 minutes commuting time) we must be very careful and consider as urban green spaces only those enabled for its use as such; that is, parks and gardens. We can't fall into the mistake of adding the natural spaces and countryside that surround the city. The main source of information will be from the World Cities Culture Forum (World Cities Culture Forum, 2018). To add needed data for additional cities, we'll take it directly from Skyscrapercity, World Cities Culture Forum and others (Skyscrapercity, 2018), and do calculations.

The main source for Density will be (Demographia, 2019). Demographia includes metropolitan areas in an exhaustive analysis. Data is taken in terms of inhabitants/km$^2$, then normalized.

As both indicators are complementary, we consider both as equally relevant, then we assign a 50–50 weight. Then, a perfect city should have both in high levels, or a balanced use of space for green areas and its associated objectives, and a high density for human development.

(See class Space, Density data ranking at APPENDIX III)

## 5.2.4  Identity: GeoRisks

**Why Is This Proxy Relevant?**

Each city, due to its geographical position, its type of construction and preparation for possible natural disasters, will experience a more or less significant risk. This risk is measured as: their exposure to these natural phenomena weighted by their vulnerability or potential damage, and resilience to minimize their impacts. This natural risk and its possible impact mark the lives of the citizens of that city. The citizens of Seattle know what an earthquake is, the Japanese are very used to and prepared for them. In Santiago, (Chile) they know that every few years they will suffer an important one. Other natural disasters such as droughts, floods, hurricanes, are increasingly frequent due to the impact of climate change. The Dutch know that they live below sea level, and many coastal cities in the world fear that sea levels could rise, just as many cities near a volcano do not stop thinking about its danger. These events are part of the city life; they have historically marked it, and will continue to impact it. They are part of its identity, unfortunately not as an attractive topic, but as an obstacle. On the other hand, citizens who are considering that city should know the associated risks.

We are not considering here the economic, geopolitical, societal or technological risks, as those will be evaluated in the City performance in Chap. 6. We only consider here the environmental/natural risks. To see a full report on Global Risks, we recommend the one from the World Economic Forum, 2020 (World Economic Forum, 2020).

**How to Measure It?**

The WorldRiskIndex (Institute for International Law of Peace and Armed Conflict, 2020) was developed by the Institute for Environment and Human Security at the United Nations University (UNU-EHS). It has been published annually since 2011 by Bündnis Entwicklung Hilft. Since 2017, the Institute of Peace, Law and Armed Conflict (IFHV) of Ruhr University Bochum has been the responsible entity for its scientific research, management and calculation. The WorldRiskIndex is calculated using 27 indicators, and it rates natural disaster risk for 180 countries due to five main, natural hazards: cyclones, floods, droughts, earthquakes and rising sea levels. The WorldRiskIndex does not predict when and with what probability the next natural disaster will occur, nor its magnitude, but it does tries to assess the potential risk in terms of material damage and victims, depending on its nature and the exposed territory preparation. It is calculated country by country by multiplying Exposure by Vulnerability. The Exposure covers threats to the population, and material damage due to those natural disasters. Vulnerability encompasses the impacted social and structural sphere, and is made up of three components, which are equally weighted in the calculation:

- Susceptibility describes the structural characteristics and framework conditions of a country in relation to possible damage. It is the likelihood of harm.
- Resilience, or coping, includes the skills, experience and reaction conditions to minimize negative impacts and damages. Capacities to reduce consequences.
- Preparation and adaptation include measures and strategies in anticipation of this risk and it is understood as a long-term process that includes structural changes.

The maximum value deviates a lot: Manila is at 20.69, and using it would mean a large data concentration and loss of relevance for all others, being the second largest Montevideo with 12.52. To avoid this loss of meaning by data dispersion, Manila is not used and set to zero.

(See GeoRisk data ranking at APPENDIX III)

## 5.2.5 Identity: Government Type (Basics)

### Why Is This Proxy Relevant?

Governance is a kind of city performance and will be covered later, but Government Basics and Safety are strongly marking the type of City Identity. In a city without democracy, or with basic security problems, with restrictions on freedom of expression and assembly, the city is restricted in its capacities for economic and social development, and cannot express itself in its essence, in its abilities as a place of encounter. The city identity is also marked by these living conditions. You can still see the difference in the buildings on both sides of the former Berlin wall. The identity of cities under harsh communist or dictatorial regimes is highly influenced by the political and security situation in which they find themselves. As we said in the selection criteria, we do not contemplate studying cities that do not meet a minimum score in livability: they are simply cities where nobody would want to go, and their innate talent will very likely want to leave as soon as possible. But the level of democracy and basic safety are issues to value as a city's perceived identity. In next chapter, we will study the services the city offers as performance, and we will return to studying citizen security services. Here, we include the basics, customs in terms of safety, not as services, but as characteristics of the city, as components of its identity. It's mainly about the perceived sense or image of safety associated with a city, not the real security/safety processes or efficiency of services in place. We want to assess cities as safe places to move and live, Safety services' performance will be evaluated in Chap. 6.

### How to Measure It?

Ranging from top full and best democracy in Norway, to the worst conditions in North Korea, The Economist's Democracy Index 2019 (The Economist, 2020a) provides a snapshot of democracy development status for 167 independent countries/territories. From full democracy to authoritarian regime, all countries are assessed on government style. The Democracy Index is based on the assessment of five categories: electoral process and pluralism; government functioning; political participation; political culture; and civil rights/liberties. Using this range of indicators, each country is classified into one of four regime types: *full democracy, flawed democracy*, and *hybrid regime*, or *authoritarian regime*. Only 45.5% of all studied countries can be considered democracies.

The Economist's Safe Cities Index (The Economist, 2020b) summarizes the multi-dimensional components of urban safety, approaching the concept using 57 indicators and four different areas: digital, infrastructure, health and personal security.

It should be noted that the concept of safe city as a key component of its identity does not lean on solely on the traditional personal security provided by the armed forces and the police. The idea is much broader, encompassing the security of the whole city's infrastructures and their resilience, safety and guarantees in the health service, and, in an increasingly relevant sense, in the digital environment, protecting identity, privacy and communications with citizens. This expanded and comprehensive concept of safe city will attract or inhibit talent preferences for it.

Both are basic principles of an attractive City Identity, so we are equally weighing them. (See Government Basics data ranking at APPENDIX III).

## 5.2.6   Identity: GeoEconomics (Due to Location)

### Why Is This Proxy Relevant?

The term geo-economics was first used by the American economist Edward Luttwak. It tries to connect economies and resources with a place in geography, time and specific politics. Luttwak postulates that there is a change in global power from politics (military strength, diplomacy or propaganda) to geo-economics, where governments are using economic power to invest in research, market control, production intervention and other to gain significant advantage against other competitors' areas. Winners take massive profits, losers will take, if the local market is large enough, only some assembly lines to create jobs, but nothing creative or business with added value. He names this politics style the *turbo-capitalism* (Luttwak, 1999). This association of economic power capacity with a geographical area makes the city more or less attractive, in terms of economic development capacity, or in terms of the achievable/accessible market at a close/cheap range. This is part of the city Identity because it is inherent to its geographical location, the economic bloc to which it belongs. From the talent-attraction point of view, it is a matter of evaluating the development capacity of your job/activity in relation to the economy of the surrounding area where you would live. In other words, if I live in a place where there is great wealth around me, the impact of my work will be greater than if I live in a more isolated area, away from main economic power circuits. We must therefore evaluate the influence or the weight of our city in the world economy. It is clear that if we can influence a greater economic area with our talent, we will obtain an important number of advantages and we will be able to better develop our potential.

**How to Measure It?**

It is not easy to find an indicator of the area of economic influence centered on a specific city. If we think about how many customers I can connect with or visit in the same day, then we should think about flying and returning home in the same day. That puts us on less than 2.5-hour flights. Well, how much world GDP percentage is located at less than a 2.5-hour flight from my city? That is the area of direct economic influence. It's true that we have the Internet, and that flights are becoming faster and cheaper, but it is clear that distance is still an important handicap in foreign trade, and the world continues to be governed by large blocs or areas of influence. There are areas that accelerate their development due to proximity to other more powerful ones, such as Mexico; and there are others that, although very attractive due to their excellent conditions, are far from major economies and clients, such as Australia.

We will measure the sum of GDP of all achievable regions/countries within less than 2.5 h flight from our city as percentage of the world total. In the case of large countries like the U.S., we will use the GDP of each reachable state. It is like measuring the area of economic influence with a compass centered on the city and a radius of a 2.5-hour commercial flight. The way to do it will be with our own research work with flight data and GDPs.

For world total 2017 GDP in millions ($), we take Worldometers data (Worldometers, 2019).

(See GeoEconomics data ranking at APPENDIX III)

## 5.2.7   Identity: Gastronomy (Food)

**Why Is This Proxy Relevant?**

Gastronomy is one of the most important city hallmarks. When we plan a trip to discover a city, we previously study what to see, but also what to eat and drink. We must eat to live, but the act of eating becomes in many cultures a fundamental social experience. It is about meeting others, sharing experiences, enjoying life, it's a social ritual (Kowalczyk & Derek, 2020). It is the first cultural component exported to other places, and for this reason, cities with a rich cultural diversity are full of restaurants with diverse cuisines. Many dishes and types of food and drinks are intrinsically associated with a city. Spaghetti Bolognese, Calamari a la Romana, Brussels Sprouts, Hamburgers, Port Wine, or Sherry wine, or some brands of beer specifically associated with Dublin, or Amsterdam, or Scotch whiskeys, Kentucky Bourbon have a distinct denomination associated with specific cities or metropolises. The *designation of origin* is considered a synonym of quality and originality: thus Identity. On the contrary, international fast food represents a loss of identity for the city. From the point of view of a foreigner who considers moving to a city, the gastronomic offering will have an important weight depending on his standards and tastes. Cities with awful, or expensive, or very artificial/unnatural food will have a drawback in attractiveness. The city's usual food is also an indicator of health, since it affects very important diseases like obesity, diabetes, hypertension or other cardio-vascular ones. This association is very well studied in areas with a high incidence of these diseases.

**How to Measure It?**

We will first study the overall quality of nutrition in a city. We will use the Oxfam indicator, The Food Index (Oxfam, 2018). The global philanthropic organization Oxfam, dedicated to eradicating poverty and famine, publishes this index studying 125 countries. For each country, it analyzes the quantity of food, its affordability, its quality and healthy eating habits (to be precise, it studies them from their negative impacts; that is, it studies the impact of diseases most commonly associated with disorders derived from poor food quality, like diabetes and obesity). The ranking is obtained by combining these four elements. It indicates the best and worst places in the world in which to eat, and the challenges of living there in terms of access to quality and quantity of good food.

Ok, if we have food in sufficient quantity and quality, now let's try to turn it into dishes with excellent flavor, dishes and cuisines that mark the city Identity, as a cultural element and as a city attraction. To measure this ability to covert food's raw materials into delicious dishes, some authentic artworks, we refer to the Michelin Guide. We will take how many restaurants are outlined in that guide (which means the restaurant has one or more Michelin Stars, or The Plate Michelin, or Bib Gourmand categories, and therefore deserves its consideration) (Michelin Guide, 2018) per million inhabitants in that metropolitan area. This will give us a good approximation of the city's culinary level. If there are many restaurants of this type, we will understand that gastronomy is very important there, and this is because it is, in fact, a strong city hallmark. The indicator works, as famous gastronomic areas like the Spanish Basque Country (Bilbao) or French traditional areas like Lyon or Nice are very well scored.

We should balance quality of raw food with prepared food, so we conclude on equally weighing both indicators.

(See Gastronomy data ranking at APPENDIX III)

## 5.2.8   Identity: Reputation

**Why Is This Proxy Relevant?**

Reputation is an emotional perception and assessment of a specific thing. It is based on admiration, esteem and respect. It also inspires confidence, and it is a fundamental driver when making a decision about an issue with many alternatives. Applied to a city, it has a strong relationship with the evaluation of success and prosperity, and also about the applied ethics in that city. People's behavior and their preferences about which city may be best for them has a strong emotional component based on that city's reputation. A city's reputation is built on a long-built perception, and like personal reputation, it can easily be ruined in short time. As an example, the Institute that studies the reputation of cities and countries has highlighted the decline in the reputation of Barcelona after the recent independence revolts. It is not easy to measure, as it is not measurable in specific parameters or data. The studies described are based on surveys, on evaluating that personal perception from a large group of people (Reputation Institute, 2018a).

**How to Measure It?**

City RepTrak (Reputation Institute, 2018b) is a survey based on more than 22,000 people in the G8. Thirteen attributes grouped into three dimensions are evaluated: *Effective administration, Advanced economy* and *Attractive environment.*

What drives city reputation? Cities' reputation is evaluated based on these three dimensions:

- Governance: how effective is city organization? What's city reputation regarding safety, leaders, transportation and infrastructure, social and economic policies, and overall political and legal institutions.
- Environment: is it an aesthetically attractive/beautiful city? Can you find there exciting experiences and well-known attractive personalities?
- Economy: Does the city have a robust economy with a promising future? Stable, well-respected financial institutions. Base for technology companies.

For a city to achieve a higher score, it must attain a balanced profile among those three, but from the effective-government perspective, since recent years' surveys, the Governance aspect has dominated the other two in determining a city's reputation.

When we study Governance, we analyze: how developed are the legal institutions, the adequacy of the infrastructure, the social policies' progressivity, how respected are the leaders and what is the level of city safety. When we delve into the attributes that make up these three dimensions, the three most important in building a city's reputation are: being a beautiful, safe place, and offering a wide range of engaging/attractive experiences. While safety and beauty have always been key attributes in determining a city's reputation score, it is interesting to see that beauty has recently declined in importance, surpassed by safety as the primary reputation attribute. Leadership is also a primary driver after these three.

We take the city index when available. When not, we take the country index associated with that city, so we get credible information for all.

(See Reputation data ranking at APPENDIX III)

## 5.2.9   Identity: Branding (Projected Image)

### Why Is This Proxy Relevant?

We have seen how cities are engaged in a global competition to retain and attract talent. In this competition, we have seen how cities prepare themselves to become more attractive from many points of view; in short, cities are offered in the global market as a product. Like any product, it needs a powerful branding, based on a strong, consolidated and attractive projected exterior image.

The City branding is based on three fundamental pillars, which are uniqueness, authenticity and image (Riza et al., 2012). The uniqueness of a city is determined by its culture, its geographical position and its history, that which makes it special, unique, different, what makes its hallmarks and what doesn't exist in any other city.

Authenticity speaks to us about truth, a city we can trust, with clear civic and ethical standards. An open and inclusive city, respectful, but without relativisms that blur its Identity, which welcomes the outsider and integrates them, without modifying its authentic being, its character.

Finally, the image, the image projected outwards, its advertising claim in the minds of those who do not live there. Highly imageable (apparent, readable, visible). A city with a high chance of evoking a strong image in the mind of an external observer (Lynch, 1960b). We saw in the exercise on Brussels' identity those unique symbols associated with the city, combined with elements made by images, with a clear appearance, legible, visible elements that clearly identify the city to the rest of the world. We are going to understand the city image not as a physical, visual element, but as a mental process that analyzes and incorporates city components and their use by its inhabitants. It is a projection of the city's physical and social urban environment, seen from the people who daily produce and live those images and experiences (Ierek, 2018).

The elements of singularity and uniqueness are impossible to quantify and were collected in the reputation (its aesthetic part), its history, museums, climate and other elements that we have previously discussed. We need to try to measure the impact on an external image, as a fundamental component of your city's marketing, of your city's branding. We must measure how many times the city is in the global press every week, due to events or activities that contribute and improve its branding, its attractive perception.

The main objective in the creation and development of branding for the city is the presentation and articulation of the city in a globalized world. To be successful in this global competition, the city needs a good economy, wealth and an attractive image. Therefore, *"the city's branding will have to be seen as a set of elements, (culture and history, infrastructure and architecture, economic growth and social development, landscape and environment, among other things) combined in a saleable identity, acceptable and attractive to all people"* (Zhang & Zhao, 2009).

Quality of life also influences the city's promotion, its ability to attract capital and talent. The quality of life tries to create a distinct image and atmosphere, an environment, a distinction and recognition that acts as a magnet for both (capital and talent).

## How to Measure It?

To try to approximate a model of measurable variables that inform on a city's projected image, about main city's creations abroad, we will look at the different specialization areas that UNESCO attributes to a possible creative city, "*Crafts & Folk Art, Design, Film, Gastronomy, Literature, Music and Media Arts*" (UNESCO, 2019b). Measuring art that emanates from a city is very complex. We have seen some indexes that value the number of art galleries, but they do not seem adequate due to their mercantile nature. We have already measured the ability of becoming a UNESCO World Heritage city and hosting important museums. We also measured gastronomy. We have tried to find how many songs, or pieces of music with a particular city as part of the song title or as an inspiration exist, but there is no such information available. Yet, we will understand a city's projected image from various approaches. On the one hand, the number of films set in the city (it is obvious that these films sell the city and place it in the minds of all spectators). This is why Barcelona commissioned Woody Allen to make a film with Barcelona in its title. The famous director decided to mainly film it in Oviedo (Spain), because of his love for that city that rewarded him the Prince of Asturias Award, and at the end of filming, someone had to remind him of his commitment to branding, which is why he called the film "*Vicky, Cristina, Barcelona*" (Allen, 2008). Let's think about the enormous importance of the movie "*Casablanca*" (Curtiz, 1943) for city of Casablanca, (Morocco) which was entirely filmed in the U.S. On the other hand, we are going to measure the appearance of the city in the world press in a positive sense, not due to accidents or crime reports. This is the consequence of the organization of main cultural or sporting events. To have a top-level sports event, you must have top-line sports teams/brands in some sport with a massive audience. Thus, we will analyze the number of cities with local teams in international competitions for soccer, basketball, and other main sports, including large marathons. The analysis will also include those which have previously organized unique, worldwide events that have projected a permanent city image such as the Olympics, Universal Exhibitions and other globally relevant periodic cultural events.

Movies: There is a lot of information about films and where they were set. A film based in a city is telling about many things, and at least is projecting the city's identity to all who watch it. A movie is like a large, live city ad. We found information about most of the analyzed cities in a wonderful list from Wikipedia (Wikipedia, 2018a). For those not on that list, we searched the web using the key words *films set in City X*. We always tried to find internationally available films, or films that are city ambassadors over local, limited-scope films.

Main Sports: Soccer: We add a point per team which played in international leagues like the European Cup by 2018. There are cities like London which score three extras because of Chelsea, Tottenham Hotspur and Arsenal. We compare this with the list of the world's top 50 football teams (Soccer Clubs Ranking, 2018). As an idea of the importance of this indicator, let's think about the image of Madrid (Spain) projected by the soccer teams Real Madrid and Atlético de Madrid with their almost constant, worldwide presence. Real Madrid has more than 700 million online followers, worldwide. Its stars are more popular on social networks than the most important players in the NBA or the best tennis players.

Basketball: Same, international leagues + all NBA brandings (NBA Teams, 2018).

Other Sports: Main Athletics, Formula I, Tennis, Cycling, Golf, Horse races...there are many. To not exclude the main ones, we take the top 100 *must-see* Sporting Events (Topendsports, 2018). Hosting main marathons also adds a point. Marathons are events of a very rich sporting and cultural interest, and are an excellent international city showcase.

We eventually obtain a list of cities and scores ranging from zero to seven (again, London topping it). We are capturing those cities with a strong international presence in the press/media because of these large sports events' organization.

There are other series of events which have marked the Identity of the city, and that have projected a very persistent image at the international level. We are talking about the organization of the Olympic Games and Universal Exhibitions. These massive events involve preparation, urban planning and new developments, and permanent presence in the eyes of the whole world during its celebration. Therefore, they are coveted by many cities, since they find in their organization not a business but an incalculable investment in branding and city reshaping, with new buildings and constructions. As an example, let us remember the impact of the 1992 Olympic Games organization on Barcelona, or the Universal Exhibition on Paris in 1889, which marked the city forever with the Eiffel Tower. The official list of Olympic Games (Official List of Olympic Games, 2018) and World Expositions (Wikipedia, 2018b) are used.

We should add cultural events with important international projection. There are many, and it is difficult to select, but we will look only for those with significant relevance in the world press, and which really mean a clear city promotion and identification, a city branding main component, such as the Rio's Carnival or the New Orleans' Mardi Gras. DayZero (Dayzero, 2018) offers us the complete list of the Top50 Festivals & Cultural Events.

How should we assign weights in this score to these different components?

The most appropriate way is an allocation proportional to its impact, or to the time consumed on international television during the year. We group this information in movie setting/reference in the city; international, city-based sports teams; and the rest of past international events (if they were so important and left a permanent mark such as an Olympics or a Universal Exhibition, or those traditional annual events such as cultural festivals). Of these three groups, Sports teams is the main one, the one which provides the greatest presence and impact, so we give it 50% of weight, distributing the other 50% between movies (25%) and important historical or cultural events (25%).

(See Branding data ranking at APPENDIX III)


## 5.2.10   Identity: Integration of All Data Sources

To create a consolidated Magnetism Identity indicator, we need to combine these nine explained Indicators/groups.

Although it is not the intention to develop another fixed City index, but rather, that each citizen evaluates the cities and their attractiveness according to their scale of values and preferences, we cannot leave the model as open as possible, asking to enter a personal value to the more than 100 indicators used. We will allow the choice of these preferences from a high level; that is, City Identity, City Dynamism and City Strategy. In our City Identity case, we must build a fixed model based on combining the studied indicators.

When we look at these nine groups, we can find that their influence is always very remarkable, but we can group them into five areas, each with a similar contribution to the concept of City Identity. Each area will take 1/fifth of total or 20% weight.

Area 1: Identity: History/Culture as Identity. Receives 20% weight.

Area 2: Here we are grouping: Government Type (Basics) and Reputation. We have seen that perceived government efficiency is the main driver for Reputation, so we take this as Extended Reputation Group. We assign its 20% equally split among Government Basics/Security Basics and Reputation Index, 10% each.

Area 3: Geo Natural Conditions, and we split its 20% among 15% Climate and 5% GeoRisks. Climate is more determinant than GeoRisk, more avoidable, and less permanently impacting (most of the time).

Area 4: Geo Human Conditions, and we split its 20% among Green Spaces/Density and GeoEconomics, 10% each.

Area 5: Branding, assigning 5% to Gastronomy and 15% to Branding/External Image, because of the huge relevance of this projected external image/international events and massive audiences sports.

So, this is the schema (Table 5.1) for City Identity model: (W means weight). (See Integrated City Identity Data ranking Summary at APPENDIX III)


## 5.3   City Dynamism (Present) People

*To make the portrait of a city is a life's work, and no one portrait suffices because the city is always changing. Everything in the city is properly part of its story-its physical body of brick, stone, steel, glass, wood, its lifeblood of living, breathing men and women. Streets, vistas, panoramas, bird's-eye views and women's-eye views, the noble and the shameful, high life and low life, tragedy, comedy, squalor, wealth, the mighty towers of skyscrapers, the ignoble facades of slums, people at work, people at home, people at play- these are but a*

**Table 5.1** City Identity model

| W | Class | W | Indicator | Subindicator | Entity |
|---|---|---|---|---|---|
| 20 | History. Culture | 70 | Age | | Own work |
| | | 20 | UNESCO | | UNESCO |
| | | 10 | Top museums | | Own work |
| 10 | Government basics | 50 | Democracy index | | The economist |
| | | 50 | Safe City index | | The economist |
| 10 | Reputation | 100 | Reputation | | Reputation institute |
| 10 | Space. Density | 50 | % natural space | | Own work |
| | | 50 | Density (inh/km2) | | Demographia |
| 15 | Climate | 33,3 | Avge. Temperature Desviation | Gradient | Climatemps |
| | | 33,3 | Avge. Precipitation Desviation | Gradient | Climatemps |
| | | 33,3 | Avge. Daily sunshine | | Climatemps |
| 5 | Geo risk | 100 | Natural disaster risk | | WorldRiskReport |
| 10 | GeoEconomics | 100 | GDP proximity | %WW | Own work |
| 5 | Gastronomy | 50 | RK food index | | OXFAM |
| | | 50 | Michelin guide | #rest/mInh | Via Michelin |
| 15 | Branding. External image | 25 | Movies | | Wikipedia |
| | | 50 | Sports | Soccer, basketbal, lother sports events, marathons | Football databaseNBATopendsports |
| | | 25 | Main events | Olympics | Olympics org |
| | | | | Universal expo | Own work |
| | | | | Cultural events | Day zero project |

*small part of the city. Nothing is too humble for the camera portraitist.* — Berenice Abbott (American Photographer) (Abbott, 1942).

The city lives, constantly changes: it is a dynamic ecosystem. There is a constant feedback between past and present, between the identity that marks its behavior and the present, which creates history and then, builds identity. This dynamism, or its lack thereof, marks the rhythm and lifestyle of the city. We can choose vibrant cities, cities that do not stop, *that never sleep*, as Sinatra sang, that make us wake up every morning with the expectation that today, the city is going to suggest to us activities that we had not planned, that will allow us to boost our social facet, perhaps too frantic for many, but purely human for others. Or just the opposite, it will be a boring place for many, or a place of rest, reflection and meditation for others. In the Internet age, the city tries, and sometimes fails, to keep up with the acceleration at which technology advances. As we saw before, this is not good; the city must use technology for its development, we cannot put technology to lead, but people, using technology as a means, never as an end.

> *The city is not about houses, porticos, or public squares: it is men who form it.-* Eugenio Espejo (Ecuadorian doctor and writer) (Astuto 1747–1795).

> *What is the City but the people?* William Shakespeare (Shakespeare, 1609).

Therefore, when we explore the present of the city, its dynamism, we must speak of its people, of their competitiveness, of their behavior, of their ethics, of how they welcome the expatriate who has just arrived to stay, how warm and welcoming they are, and of the social equity conditions the city holds.

> *He who is unable to live in society, or who has no need because he is sufficient for himself, must be either a beast or god,* (Aristotle).

It is, therefore, in the city, where man becomes social. The city creates the conditions for men to collaborate, build, create and advance in human and scientific disciplines. Isolation dehumanizes, pushes us toward the beast within us, mentally impoverishes us and limits us in all our performance and works. Living together, in society, brings the advantages, synergies that made the city possible from its origins. Life in society is a catalyst for human development, but living together implies observing standards of coexistence, respect, equality, an ethical platform that sets the way of living in that city. This lifestyle is a magnet or a repellent, because it will attract talent that feels comfortable, free, stimulated in their creativity by that type of society; or it will be a blocker to talent that is not comfortable in that lifestyle, making the other evaluated considerations provide an important addition, to even consider these alternative cities as a possible destination.

These conditions and lifestyle can't be changed in a short period of time, or by investing in a short-term plan: they are inherent and make up a city's distinctive element. We have cities from various civilizations, marked in their ethics by their religious values. We have cities with a strong ethical code, and very consolidated human values, and others with greater relativism and relaxation in ethical questions; demanding and strict cities adhering to certain social behaviors due to a strong religious presence, and other non-denominational ones, that do not attach any importance to man's religious dimension.

We are observing a growing social deficit in the cities (Montgomery 2013a). People who live more isolated from others, from their neighbors, from their family, even in massive cities. This makes them more distrustful of others and of institutions, they become *lone wolves*, which exacerbates their selfishness and lack of solidarity. This isolation is accompanied by the rise of mental illness and sleep problems. There is also a correlation between the shape and size of cities and this social deficit. People with long commuting times are also more prone to anger, divorce, and gender violence. On the other hand, we have studied that there are very serious problems that require a collective social effort, such as security, climate change, pollution.

It is also necessary to consider, as a city magnetic component, the set of values and action guidelines that people adopt there and that they assume as their own, not as a result of a *origin appeal*, but as an awareness of belonging to that community. This sense of belonging is a great energizer for different forces in an open system which determine the city's collective personality. The city is constantly moving (Chueca Goitia, 1968c). It is a piece of artwork in permanent production, in constant growth and destruction. A balance between construction and destruction must be maintained, respecting history and traditions, identity, but adding dynamism, constantly growing at a rate that consolidates identity without wrecking it.

The American urban planner Jane Jacobs always proposed the city as a dense mesh of intertwined social relations, where the diversity of forms and people mix in community. As early as the 1990s, she criticized that cities were divided into a wealthy business centers and endless, inhuman, remote suburbs, like ghost towns during the day. Cities cannot include these artificial boundaries. Cities are pure life in its most intense and complex form, its maximum social development. They cannot be a static artwork (Jacobs, 1961); they are constantly changing.

The city evolves, becomes the sum of intelligences, a consolidated summary of the collective experiences of its past and present dwellers, with a constant, dynamic flow of people. It is a platform for mixing and developing new cultures, for change. Many cities have, as a key element of their development, the agility to open up to talent (tolerance), and to quickly adapt to a new wave of global change, to a new social or industrial revolution.

As we saw in Chap. 3, to understand the city's behavior and dynamism, we must understand its shape and its psychology (Murray & Landry, 2019). This will try to anticipate how the city will receive us, how it treats the expatriate, and how we must adapt to the city's particular idiosyncrasies if we decide to live there.

Jan Gehl noted pointedly, *"It is ironic that we know more about the habitat of mountain gorillas than we do about the habitat of people"* (Gehl, 2019). True. We have studies, academic research and programs for SmartCities: sustainable, safer, green, healthy, resilient cities, but citizens are very rarely at the center of them. Too often, cities are seen as an artificial Meccano, with inanimate sets of buildings and technology, like elements of a construction game. This forgets its essentially human nature. We should not ignore that although infrastructure, architecture and technology are of fundamental importance, cities are substantially a lived emotional experience (Murray & Landry, 2017).

Cities are the citizens' closest administrative link. The expected quantity and quality of municipal services is increasing, and on the contrary, the funds provided by the central government are more insufficient. Central governments are huge deficit monsters, incapable of giving cities the budgets they need. Thus, cities must find creative ways to deliver more with less. To make this happen, they must rely more on private initiatives and give more power to residents. This requires greater trust on citizens and the ability to innovate, contribute and co-create. However, cities have lost contact with their citizens. They must recover it by creating strong social dynamisms and community awareness (Beachler, 2019).

We are going to try to model the city dynamism as a magnetic force, based on its daily effect, on people's relationships. We will group into four the various indicators of this area. On the one hand, Competitiveness: those elements that measure the action, relationships, city creativity and motion, those which turn it into a social and economic hotbed, into a complex interrelations' machine, of human development. On the other hand, we must measure how the city treats those who come from outside, like expatriates, how easy or difficult city social integration is. We will also measure the city's ethical values and finally, its social equality. The city may be perfect from the point of view of development, and offer an exquisite treatment to the newcomer, but additionally we must consider its value scale, its ethical principles and social equity, inclusiveness and justice.

## 5.3.1   Dynamism: Competitiveness

### Why Is This Proxy Relevant?

What makes a city attractive from the perspective of dynamism, competitiveness? We must talk about creativity and competitiveness. Creativity as a generator of wealth, prosperity and as a talent attracter. It's about combining creative talent, what Prof. Florida called a *creative class*, with the right conditions and technologies. We return to the city prosperity recipe: to the 3 T's that we explained in Chap. 2, to Technology as a catalyst, as a disruptive trigger of new opportunities and innovation, to Tolerance, towards the foreigners that will approach the city attracted by that technology, and to the existing or attracted Talent. With these three T's, Prof. Florida measures creativity applied to the prosperity generation, to the City's current magnetism status, to its dynamics. Prof. Florida's Creative Class definition includes the *"jobs spanning the fields of science, technology, and engineering; business, management and finance; design and architecture; arts, culture, entertainment, and media; law, healthcare, and education"* (Florida, 2011). We would say that it includes all jobs not replaceable (or not easily replaceable) by robotics or the Fourth Industrial Revolution technologies.

**Fig. 5.4** Six main pillars for SmartCity and three C's of a Creative City. (Source: Maurizio Carta. Creative Commons Attribution 3.0 Unported license. Wikipedia)

Creative and cultural professionals change and transform the city. We live in a demanding time for new projects, and they must demonstrate more than ever a clear concern to respond to that call for change. As Andy Warhol (Warhol, 1975) once said, *"They always say time changes things, but you actually have to change them yourself."* The creative business activity leans on those entrepreneurs who have a project in the field of arts or technological innovation.

On and around this basis of City prosperity provided by the 3 T's (Technology, Talent, Tolerance), Prof. (Carta, 2011) develops the concept of Creative City (see Fig. 5.4) by adding 3 C's (Culture, Cooperation, Communication) as an evolution of those basic 3 T's. Culture as development and consolidation of creative talent. Cooperation as an expression of tolerance, cooperation between people in the city, advancing in the creation of a sense of community, between companies, and even between cities. Communication implies the use of technology to reach all citizens with advances and new city services, as an expression of creativity.

The Cities' competitiveness performs as a key informative element about their livability, their citizens' happiness, or their ability to become a phenomenal place to do business (European Commission, 2016). Another indicator to compare will be the progress capacity, movement and dynamism, for human growth, and how the city is associated with these characteristics.

Considered as a worldwide symbol of success, New York City is the paramount of Competitiveness/Motion/Progress. Let's read one of the city's many icons, its main song, very famous because of Sinatra's amazing performances.

*Start spreadin' the news, I'm leavin' today // I want to be a part of it // New York, New York.*
*These vagabond shoes are longing to stray // Right through the very heart of it //*
*New York, New York.*
*I wanna to wake up, in a city that doesn't sleep. // And find I'm king of the hill // Top of*
*the heap.*
*These little town blues // Are melting away // I'll make a brand-new start of it // In old*
*New York.*
*If I can make it there, I'll make it anywhere // It's up to you, New York, New York //*
*I want to wake up in a city that never sleeps // And find I'm a number one, top of the list //*
*King of the hill, a number one.*
*These little town blues, are melting away // I'm gonna make a brand-new start of it*
*In old New York // And // If I can make it there.*
*I'm gonna make it anywhere // It's up to you, New York.*
*(alternative end):*
*If I can make it there, I'll make it anywhere, // Come on come through, New York,*
*New York. // New York // New York* (Ebb & Kander, 1977).

This song is associated with the image of New York City. It is a song that expresses enthusiasm, leadership, success, superiority, initiative, entrepreneurship. Also, joy, fun, compensation after having done a good job. A great symbol that describes very well the concept of competitiveness, creativity, incessant movement, growth, progress, and prosperity often associated with New York City. Let's remember how NYC has been a benchmark in talent attraction, innovation and multicultural tolerance. (Clear demonstration of 3 T's in execution).

We must also analyze the cities' Economic Competitiveness link to productivity. Finding a balance between technology adoption and human capital investments will be critical to improving productivity.

Finally, the competitiveness associated not only with economic growth, but with the competition for Talent attraction, its development, and retention.

**How to Measure It?**

Creativity. To measure City Creativity, we will use the Martin Prosperity's Global Creativity Index (Florida et al., 2015). This indicator makes an assessment of 139 countries around City Creativity, approached from the 3 T's. Technological adoption is evaluated by R&D Investment, Number of researchers and patents per Capita. It is important to notice that it doesn't include technological creation, because that technology could have been created in another city/country. It tries to understand the city/country capacity for creating new technologies that will attract talent. Talent's presence in the city is approached by Educational Attainment (internal talent generation) and the net Creative Class present at the city. Finally, Tolerance is measured by Gallup surveys (Gallup Advanced Analytics, 2019) studying immigrants, diversity, (racial, ethnic, or other minorities' presence) rights and given treatment. Each country is ranked for Technology, Talent and Tolerance, then aggregated in the Global Creativity Index.

Economic Competitiveness.

The World Economic Forum's Global Competitiveness Index GCI 4.0 (World Economic Forum, 2019) provides a detailed map of the factors and characteristics that promote growth, productivity, and human development. The 2019 edition studies 141 countries, which accounts for 99% of global GDP. The index is mainly focused on measuring long-term growth expectations, over immediate production factors' growth. GCI 4.0 aggregates data from 103 indicators developed by international forums and organizations. They are organized into 12 thematic pillars: "*Institutions; Infrastructure; ICT Adoption; Macroeconomic stability; Health; Skills; Product market; Labor market; Financial system; Market size; Business dynamism; and Capacity for innovation.*" Measuring this economic competitiveness is extremely relevant because an improvement in city attractiveness will balance technological integration and human capital nurturing. As a conclusion, the analysis points to Competitiveness, Sustainability and Equality as the way forward for a brilliant attractive city facing the Fourth Industrial Revolution challenges.

To help achieve the objective of creating a global Attractive city ranking, IESE proposes the Cities in Motion Index (Berrone & Ricart, 2019). The Cities in Motion (CIMI) model is based on four main factors: "*sustainable ecosystem, creative activities, equality among citizens, and connected territory.*" CIMI studies the performance of ten fundamental dimensions of a city, "*human capital, social cohesion, the economy, public management, governance, the environment, mobility and transportation, urban planning, international outreach, and technology.*" In the 2019 edition, the study covered 174 cities and 96 sub-indicators. The plan is to analyze these 10 main drivers for city prosperity and compare them with others, so a prioritization plan can be defined. The leading CIMI cities will show a vibrant economy combined with the human potential and respect for the environment that will project the city towards the highest achievements and obviously, turn the city into a lighthouse for talent.

Yet, if we want to measure how competitive a city is in attracting talent, we must include in our research the INSEAD Global Talent Competitiveness Index (Lanvin & Monteiro, 2020a). This index measures the capacity of a city to produce, grow, retain and attract talent. Based on 70 indicators, the GTCI studies 132 countries and 155 cities with the aim of helping cities create a talent development strategy to become more competitive in the global context. These 70 indicators are grouped into six pillars or areas of study: Four analyze the flow and generation of talent (Enable, Attract, Grow and Retain) and two additional ones observe the external output: the city global position in technical/vocational skills, and the capacity to generate knowledge and global innovation.

So, we have finally four indexes, two country-based, two cities-based, to help us understand the city as a global lighthouse for talent, rampant creativity, paramount to thriving and activity. It is the magnetism of prosperity.

We should balance these four areas measuring human activity, development and prosperity, so we conclude on equally weighting them.

(See Competitiveness data ranking at APPENDIX IV)

## 5.3.2 Dynamism: Expat Social Experience

**Why Is This Proxy Relevant?**

We have studied what the city is like in its dynamism and activity, especially economically, as an attractive magnet for talent. We will now see the expatriate experience from the social point of view when they arrive in the city. We want to understand the city psychology applied to the stranger. Is there an attractive lifestyle, the ability to establish social relationships and friendships, and if those relationships are trustworthy, inclusive and respectful of foreigners? In short, we are going to see how welcoming a city is, how open and inclusive it is. This is the main characteristic that the city of Madrid wanted to highlight with its "Madrid hugs you" (Madrid, 2019) campaign. When we arrive in an unknown city to settle ourselves, we can say that it is a friendly city, or a closed, complicated, hard city, where there are few, unreliable relations, and where it is really difficult to get ahead and simply know where the basic necessary things to live are.

**How to Measure It?**

To analyze the social experience that the city offers expatriates, we will use the HSBC Expat Explorer study. It is a global study, which has been going on for more than 10 years and with some 100,000 participants, all of them expats who explain their experience. The study that we will use is the 2017 version because it contains a series of highly interesting indicators that are not reflected in the 2019 version. Expat Explorer (HSBC, 2017) studies the inanceial and social aspects of integrating an outsider into a city. This latest report includes information obtained from about 28,000 expatriates in 159 countries. Expat Explorer's final score is made up of three fundamental areas: the economy, the social experience and the family experience, and is obtained from combining 27 subtopics.

The economic area is covered with the impact on personal finances, the local economy's style and the expat's working life. We will not use these indicators because the economic component has been collected extensively in the Competitiveness aspect that we studied in the previous indicator.

The social experience area covers lifestyle (quality of life in general); social integration with people around you; and the ease of settling down (finding accommodation, housing, papers, permits, etc.). We will use lifestyle and social integration with people because they explain very well what we are looking for.

The Family area covers the expatriate's social relations (it measures if their social life is more active); the education and care of children; and the capacities to raise them. From these three, we will only use the first, since it measures social relations. Education will be studied as a city service in the next chapter. Therefore, we will use these three indicators to measure the city sociability, or how open, friendly, welcoming and inclusive the city is with newcomers who are trying to settle in. Thus, we will use:

- Lifestyle: local culture, healthy customs, perceived quality of life.
- People around: ease of making friends, integrating into the local environment, trust in relationships.
- Social relations: how welcoming is the place, inclusive, and diversity respectful.

We should balance these three areas measuring a City's Expat social experience, so we conclude on equally weighing them all.

(See Expat Experience data ranking at APPENDIX IV)

### 5.3.3  Dynamism: Ethics. Well-Being

**Why Is This Proxy Relevant?**

The city is in itself a project of and for happiness. We studied that its essence is to serve as a place and time for humans to encounter each other, but the meaning, the *for what* these citizens meet is to develop their social sense, their freedom, to collaborate and progress; in short, to be happy. Therefore, the objective of the city is to make us happy. Thus, if we can measure how happy the city's inhabitants are and how well they live, we can also quantify its magnetism, its attractiveness. As much as we have a good job and economic conditions, nobody will want to go live in a city where they are not happy or have a questionable well-being. It is not a question of money (Montgomery, 2013b). Mayor Peñalosa greatly improved the happiness of his city, Bogotá, by basing his leadership on listening to citizens and responding to what they needed to be happy, without large financial investments. It is not about having more than one bathroom per person or more than one car; one in every 10 U. S. citizens suffers from depression.

Thus, the ethics of the city are very clear to us: doing what leads us to be happy and avoiding what does not, understanding happiness as a city-collective objective, not an individual or selfish one.

> *Whatever creates or increases happiness or some part of happiness, we ought to do; whatever destroys or hampers happiness, or gives rise to its opposite, we ought not to do.* (Aristotle, Rhetoric).

What makes a happy city? Division of labor created efficient specialization and brought to cities the advantages of density/agglomeration and increased productivity, fostering innovation, and achieving tremendous improvements in living standards. In our current city, for many, the concept of a happy city would be associated with the proximity of necessary resources, with human and material density, that is, reaching in less than 15-minutes walking or by microEV vehicle, 95% of everything necessary, including work location. In this approach, the distance and the time that we lose in commuting, the urban mobility efficiency, prevails, although we must try to define what we consider as *necessary*.

For many others, happiness is correlated with being healthy, connected with friends and family, and being in good financial situation. Furthermore, happiness also depends on daily variables that are intrinsically dependent on our SmartCity plan, (Citiestoday, 2018) such as stress-free, efficient mobility, security, sustainability, reliable and transparent governance, or basic things like a clean city, access to natural environments and a comfortable and easy life. At the same time, however, cities generate negative issues in their development and operation such as disorderly urban sprawl, insecurity and crime, pollution, noise, stress, social isolation, etc.

The Happy City model by Boyd Cohen and Rob Adams: *"HAPPY CITIES HEXAGON"* (Boyd & Adams, 2020) frames in six areas the elements that contribute to happiness from the point of view of the city-offered services and activities. It is a humanistic and urbanistic approach, where technology is intrinsically enabling each of these areas. As we will see when studying the set of services that the city offers in the next chapter, all of them are considered positive or even essential because they precisely contribute to that state of citizens' happiness. There are elements derived from the city urban planning and from city psychology or the way citizens think, act and overall, relate to others, which are also fundamental components of this *Happy City*. These elements are the ones that most influence its magnetism, since they have a strong persistence over time, shape the city lifestyle and differentiate it. That way, the hexagon perfectly balances the basics (Safe and Healthy) with Economics (Shared prosperity, which includes Education, Housing and respect for Diversity). Urbanism and Inclusiveness are including at (Clean and Green) and (Walkable and Accesible, which includes the Urban Mobility Services). Model adds two main Humanistic areas like (Socially Connected) and (Culture & Civic Pride, which includes Democracy and citizen co-creation). So, two pure humanistic areas, two covering the basics and two related to the environment and mobility, pointing to a very human concept of happiness, associated to well-being and personal development.

From a technological point of view, a smart city aims to improve citizens' well-being by making each dimension of their lives work in a more efficient, sustainable, safe, healthy and transparent way: governance, health, environmental sustainability, urban mobility, connectivity, planning/infrastructure, education, employability, security and culture. In each city, the Chief Technology Officer/SmartCity Manager will develop a comprehensive plan, using all available data and technologies to maximize citizens' happiness and well-being.

What is the recipe for happiness? What does a city have to achieve to become a happy city? Apart from the basic elements such as food, shelter and security, a city must develop the policies, activities, and investments that promote that state of happiness. Cities must foster joy and minimize problems and difficulties. Promote health and help prevent diseases. Create the environment and conditions so that citizens enjoy real freedom to live, move, relate and develop their lives as they wish. It should build resilience against the threats of economic crisis, or human or environmental disasters. It must be fair in the distribution of space, aid/grants, services, mobility, and its associated costs (taxes) depending on the possibilities and conditions of accessibility and inclusiveness. It must establish the conditions that allow citizens to build and strengthen the bonds between family, friends and strangers, those that give meaning to the city in its role as a platform for social relations (Montgomery, 2013c). In the same way we have medical practice Ethics, we could talk about City Ethical principles as:

Three basic ones: Do good (Citizen benefits, efficiency, quality of services, quality of life improvement), Avoid hardship/Do not harm (safety, privacy), Equity (equality, fairness, justice, social cohesion, solidarity);

Six about how city work/deliver services: Respect (diversity, accessibility, inclusiveness), Empowerment (community development, cocreation, cooperation), Social responsibility (solidarity, sense of belonging, citizenship), Sustainability (carbon neutral, clean energy, circular city), Participation (listening, democratic, citizen engagement) and Openness (transparency, trustable).

And as mandatory for any public sector organization, the expected Accountability (resources, costs, investments on time, amount, efficiency, avoid corruption) in the used resources and achieved targets (Tannahill, 2008).

A happy city is also one where citizens are generous and altruistic, with high level of giving. Citizens do not contribute only with their taxes, but with their time, donations, ideas, proposals. A city where the foreigner is helped and those who need it for humanitarian reasons; a caring city, as we said before, a welcoming, a close and friendly city. A city where citizens help maintain it, repair (Montgomery, 2013d) what they can, and make it more beautiful, as we saw in the example of Los Angeles and the beautification movement (see Chap. 3), a city where citizens treat the outdoors, the street, with same care they treat their house, because they consider it as their own, as part of their life.

An attractive city must be fundamentally democratic. The city has the responsibility to promote and generate a democratic organizational culture. Only within a democratic society, people learn the civic and ethical values of a democracy, such as participation in conditions of equity; open dialogue without censorship, coercion or retaliation; tolerance with all diversity, attitudes and all different conceptions of good (Solarte Rodriguez, 2003). Trust in government is fundamental for well-being and social cohesion. Excellence in transparency is not only key to maintaining integrity in the public sector, but it also consolidates a better government, avoiding corruption, fraud, and public funds' mismanagement.

Finally, there is a strong association between well-being, satisfaction and quality of life that is indicated by work-life balance. The balance between professional life in a fairly paid job, and social, personal, family life, the amount of hours dedicated to leisure and personal care, to loved ones, and those activities that fill us with satisfaction and realization (Montgomery, 2013e). Governments can help tackle the problem by promoting time-flexible and family-caring work practices.

**How to Measure It?**

It is not easy to measure or evaluate the City ethics and well-being by objective indicators that meet the established criteria. We are going to model the concept with an evaluation of city happiness, the level of giving, civic engagement and work-life balance.

Happiness:

The World Happiness Report (University of British Columbia, 2020) offers a ranking of city happiness based on both objective indicators and subjective well-being perception surveys, provided by the global Gallup survey. At the same time, the current life situation and the expected future are observed. They are also weighted with experience-based elements, according to how positively or negatively citizens evaluate their lives in the city. The best-ranked countries and cities obtain high values in indicators as fundamental to a happy city as income, clean environment, mobility, life expectancy, infrastructure, and transparency and efficiency in governance.

This way, the World Happiness Report uses objective indicators such as GDP per capita, life expectancy at birth. It adds subjective elements such as social support, or help you can count on from friends or family, freedom of choice in your life, generosity (charity), perception of corruption, and elements of positive affect such as laughter or joy that you remember from yesterday; and on the contrary, negative elements such as fear, sadness or anger also from the previous day (WHR, 2020).

Giving: CAF has been producing its World Giving Index (CAF, 2019) for the past 10 years. It is the result of the largest Giving survey ever produced, with around 1.3 million people interviewed from 128 countries. The report's fundamental questions focus on evaluating citizens' altruistic and charitable behavior based on three possible actions taken in the last month: Have you helped a stranger or unknown who needed help?, Have you made donations to any charitable organization?, Have you dedicated time to any non-for profit organization?, all again made by Gallup World Poll.

Civic Engagement:

We will use the OECD Better Life Index (OECD, 2020a) to measure citizen participation and involvement in public life. Within this comprehensive study, we take the Civic Engagement indicator. It is made up of two fundamental areas: Electoral participation, and Participation in the development of norms and laws.

Electoral participation. Voter turnout is measured as the percentage of the population (census) that voted during the last elections. High participation indicates trust, involvement in public action, and commitment to city progress. It also indicates the sense of belonging, cooperation and contribution to the common good.

Participation in the development of norms and laws. Measures the extent to which a country's executive power involves citizens in the development of laws and regulations. Listening to public petitions and proposals, and turning them into laws is another way of participating in public life and co-creating the government.

Work life balance:

We will again use the OECD Better Life Index (OECD, 2020b), but now we examine Work-Life Balance. Two parallel concepts that contribute to improving this balance are evaluated. On one hand, the percentage of employees who work a large number of hours; that is, time citizens spend at work. An excess of worked hours negatively impacts physical and mental health, mood and happiness, increases stress and can even jeopardize safety while using machinery or vehicles. On the other hand, personal quality time is measured; that is, time dedicated to leisure and personal care. Contrary to the other, this measure is positive since free time quantity and quality contribute to citizens' general well-being, their happiness, joy and hope, and provides additional benefits for mental and physical health.

The happiness indicator is more comprehensive and relevant, and it's based on a combination of facts and citizens' direct perceptions, so we assign it a 40% weight, completing the model with the other three being equally weighted as there is not clear evidence which could lead us to assign a larger weight to any.

(See Ethics. Well-Being data ranking at APPENDIX IV)

### 5.3.4   Dynamism: Equality

**Why Is This Proxy Relevant?**

*We get used to getting up every day as if it couldn't be any other way, we get used to violence as something inevitable in the news, we get used to the usual landscape of poverty and misery walking through the streets of our city.* Pope Francis (Bergoglio, 2013).

Equality is a fundamental indicator about city social life. It marks the moral standing of its inhabitants and determines the way in which the city will develop, with respect and collaboration, or with inequality and inequity, unbalanced and disordered. The European Union, in its Manifesto for a new urbanity, stresses that equality is essential for local authorities to ensure the rights of citizens, regardless of their characteristics and diversity (sex, age, belief, origin, economic, political or social position, or physical or mental disabilities). It also sets out some basic principles that cities must ensure for people with any type of disability, such as access to any place, integration and adaptation of homes, work places and means of transportation to their possibilities (EU Urban Chapter, 2020).

The city life dynamism, its ability to progress and attract talent is also marked by the equality with which social life develops there. Local talent needs development opportunities regardless of its diversity. As we said in the 3 T's recipe, external talent needs tolerance conditions that allow it to settle and generate wealth in the city. If the city is not egalitarian, inclusive, its own talent will migrate as soon as it can, and the outsider will not even consider that city as a possibility. Talent does not know about race or social conditions; it just needs the right environment in which to be nurtured. Equality in wealth distribution and opportunities, especially in terms of gender equality, are fundamental elements for building, with diversity, a vibrant, attractive city or, on the contrary, an intolerant, aggressive and hard city.

However, despite the recent years' economic development and the notable reduction of poverty worldwide, our cities are not improving in equality. Just the opposite: the gap between rich and poor has widened from 1990 until today. If we compare these differences, we see that the richest 10% own 50% of the wealth, while the poorest 50% only own 5% (Cathelat, 2019a).

Economic inequality has increased in almost every city in the world in the last 30 years, but at different speeds. We can see in the Fig. 5.5 how in the U.S., the top 1% of the richest had 11% of wealth by 1980, reaching 20% by 2015, while in Western Europe, this segment barely rose from 10 to 12% in the same period. This suggests the very important role that national and local governments and policies play in inequality's consolidation or acceleration.

Within the most innovative cities, a growing division is taking place between the center and the periphery/suburbs. If exquisite care is not taken when developing the city, paying attention to all areas, we find that when most advanced creative class grows and lands, it takes over the center and the most modern neighborhoods. Due to its greater purchasing power, it causes property prices to rise in that area and displaces lower-income creative layers and service-sector workers to peripheral areas and suburbs, fostering social division (Barnés, 2017).

Prof. Florida's creative class model we studied before, in his own words, becomes a 'time bomb' if the city's investment in modernization benefits and SmartCity projects only reach an elite who live downtown. If that happens, that elite enjoys even greater benefits and a better quality of life, while the others have it worse. Toronto underwent this innovation process with that consideration, but this has not happened in many other cities. At the national level, some see this separation as the origin of populism, where a broad social base that cannot access those innovation social benefits revolts, and votes for change, even if it leads to the consequences that we have observed in the UK, U.S. and other countries. It is important to consider that this social division begins in the city, with the neighborhoods' separation, so inequality has its origin in the city, and hosts there its maximum expression.

We already studied in Chap. 2 the importance of counting on a city's balanced class stratum. We mentioned Plato, who stressed that the best model for a city is one with the largest middle class. The middle class does not fight for power or survival, but is the real, great city builder, with creativity and through social relationships. Other authors such as Kant, position the middle class as the guarantee of peace, against the aristocracy. In *Perpetual Peace*, Kant explains how a strong middle class facilitates the ending of wars and the establishment of constitutional republics (Kant, 1795).

Globally, inequality is declining, as developing countries like China and India and middle countries like Indonesia and Mexico have declining inequality rates and are growing faster than wealthy countries, taking a larger share of the global economy. However, inequality in rich countries continues to grow, as we have already seen.

**Top 1% vs. Bottom 50% national income shares in the US and Western Europe, 1980–2016**

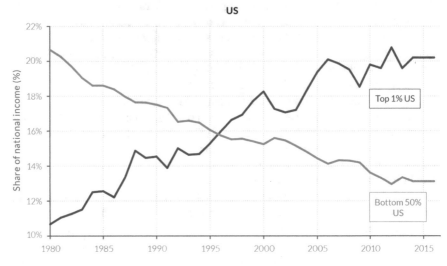

Source: WID.world (2017). See wir2018.wid.world for data series and notes.

In 2016, 12% of national income was received by the top 1% in Western Europe, compared to 20% in the United States. In 1980, 10% of national income was received by the top 1% in Western Europe, compared to 11% in the United States.

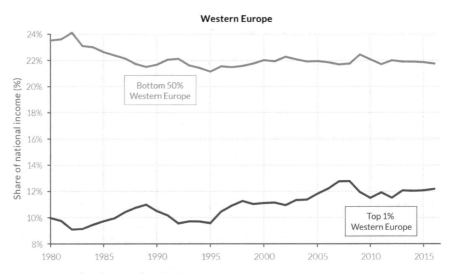

Source: WID.world (2017). See wir2018.wid.world for data series and notes.

In 2016, 22% of national income was received by the Bottom 50% in Western Europe.

**Fig. 5.5**  Income inequality evolution. US vs Western Europe (Alvaredo et al., 2018)

Some experts explain that economic inequalities seriously harm economic growth in the medium and long term by blocking skills improvements and talent development, inter-generational mobility and generation of human capital. Furthermore, when incomes go primarily to the wealthiest, some suggest that little is left to motivate those with lower incomes. If we add the pressure that robotics and the Fourth Industrial Revolution bring, the lower-income classes see their development as almost impossible, then radicalize their political options (populism). We can improve outcomes by continuous skill improvement, harnessing social creativity, adopting a culture of inclusiveness, and facilitating greater prosperity for younger generations (Fina et al., 2019).

The current district model is outdated. Based on citizens' zip codes, we can group them by income, and we can even know the predominant race, age, religion and class in each district. According to Hannah Beacher, designer at Black Panther (Beachler, 2019), this also means that each district receives different services in quantity and quality (health care, type of education, public transport, access to employment and opportunities for entrepreneurship, etc.). Residents have little chance to be heard. The city should restructure and reinvent current urban spaces and offer services in a more equitable way. It is not a matter of building futuristic buildings or flying cars, but rather reorganizing the city and the distribution of services. It is also very well known that inequality inside cities leads to higher crime rates and violence (Montgomery, 2013f).

The SmartCity model that started in 2010 as a cutting-edge social development led to gentrified cities that were only accessible to an elite of high-income people. The evolution through 2020 leads us to more of the same in private cities or districts built from scratch. We have seen cities with smart zones in exclusive districts creating more inequality, designed to attract large, high-income multinationals rather than use those resources to serve permanent residents. Only in traditionally innovative cities such as Barcelona, Copenhagen or Helsinki, have we seen a positive impact as a result of SmartCities' investments for the entire city. While the *Dirigiste* models and those where a large company chooses a city as a technology lighthouse continue to promote neighborhoods' inequality, we see that the slower but more inclusive model applied in traditional cities is spreading to many others in Europe, America and Asia, making SmartCity-plan technology and innovation really have a positive impact on generating attractiveness and wealth, but in a balanced way. It is for the whole city, with special attention to those less-integrated neighborhoods, not only to the downtown or to the wealthy elite neighborhoods. Only developments based on an equitable distribution of services and innovations lead to a smart modernization accessible to all districts, without creating divisions. Although it seems like a utopia, there is a growing awareness of the Inclusive City concept, where investment is being made in progress and modernization, but offering new services and facilities to all and at affordable costs for all (Cathelat, 2019b). These new models apply creativity and imagination to create a friendly city for everyone, especially for women. However, these objectives are not always the priorities for private investment.

We must therefore think of a SmartCity to attract strangers or residents? For men or for women? A SmartCity that also cares for the vulnerable and the disabled.

The super-advanced, hyper-connected city, run by and for technology and with huge sums of private capital invested, seeks to achieve a prestige that appeals to business elites. It is about creating a kind of Eden for an elite of globalized nomads, but it falls into an exclusive model, in gentrification, in inequality.

According to Seoul mayor Park Won-Soon, the SmartCity should be citizen-centered, with the overall goal of improving the quality of life and helping the most deprived, an exclusive but equitable city. Mayor Won-Soon talks about *a people and welfare-oriented* city, with special peculiarities such as *"Seoul-style social security program, worry-free hospital beds, and free school lunches"* (Cathelat 2019c).

We have already discussed the example of social transformation in Medellín. The city received the *"Lee Kuan Yew"* award at the World Cities Summit in 2016 for its *"Citizen Community Inclusive City,"* a program that helped the city, which was considered one of the most dangerous on the planet and dominated by drug cartels, reduce the crime by 90%, and extreme poverty from 8% to 3%. Therefore, a good SmartCity plan is not a question of constructing many modern and futuristic buildings, but an improved quality of life in a safer and more inclusive city.

Regarding gender inequality, many sociologists explain that our cities are places designed by and for men, as even recreational places have 75% of the budget oriented to men's activities. In addition, there are certain places notorious for being dangerous for women, especially at times when there are few people around. Should we think about the concept of a women-friendly city? Corrective measures rather than innovative solutions have begun to be taken in some cities in the U.S. Once again, cities with greater gender equality like Stockholm have taken the initiative by identifying places where women do not feel safe and adapting or replacing them in what has been called a feminist urban planning. Also in Sweden, in the city of Umeå, one can enjoy the *Gendered Landscape Tour* where the city is shown, especially the progress made in gender equality urban planning, with important achievements like a park especially designed by and for women, priority in the use of the football stadium, priority given to cultural events with parity of actors on stage, etc. (Cathelat, 2019d). In many places there is a public transportation, mainly taxis especially prepared for women, where they can feel safer. It is the idea of the *pink taxi* or *taxi rosa* in Milano, where apart from additional security guarantees, unaccompanied women enjoy discounts; or in Rome, where they are painted pink and are driven by women.

We must advance to a city with equity, with a fair and equal distribution of opportunities, public services, and even spaces split between humans and vehicles. The opposite is segregation, a divided city not attractive to anyone, neither the inhabitants themselves nor the visitors or foreigners (Montgomery, 2013g).

It is relatively easy to look at our cities and find racial, ethnic, and economic class segregation. We can clearly distinguish the neighborhoods occupied by each of those segments. On the contrary, it will be difficult for us to find spaces where we cannot differentiate this segregation, or places that contribute to the cohabitation of a wide range of social groups, places that allow and foster integration. This physical segregation also happens on another plane, with social isolation of some, and the triumph and social notoriety of others, all within the same city (Yang & Ratti, 2018).

If we add the equity component to our SmartCity definition, then we can start talking about a "SENSEable" city, a SmartCity which encourages an open dialogue between all city actors and players to make better-informed decisions and achieve an equitable use of available resources. So, equity completes the SmartCity concept by creating a SENSEable city, a smart and fair city (Greco & Benardino, 2014).

Cities are the center of the new digital economy brought by the Fourth Industrial Revolution, attracting the best talent by means of a high level of wages and excellent lifestyles with greater spending capacity or purchasing power. A greater desire to live in certain areas arises, which leads to an increase in rental prices, and a greater number of homeless people, which increases the gap with the most vulnerable citizens. In King County, (Seattle area, U.S.) a correlation has been clearly established between increased income and homelessness (Stringfellow & Wagle, 2018).

City equity should aim to ensure an equitable distribution of the benefits that prosperity brings. These benefits should provide high standards of living for some, but also reduce poverty and the amount of slums, protect the rights of vulnerable groups and minorities, improve gender equality and guarantee the equitable participation of all in social, political, economic, and cultural areas (Unhabitat, 2019).

**How to Measure It?**

We will model the City Equality with four main sets of indicators:

Economic classes and equality in the wealth distribution: GINI Index; Genre Equality through different components, Tolerance with minorities and immigrants and Poverty. We would have liked to include some indicators to measure city accessibility (for elderly or people with disabilities), but although there are some associations and groups of interest on that topic, there hasn't been any formal, wide study and analysis.

GINI Index. The GINI Index owes its name to the Italian statistician and sociologist Corrado Gini who first proposed it in 1912. This index measures the wealth distribution in a country. If that distribution were perfect, a percentage of the population, X%, would also have wealth of X%. As we have seen previously, our modern countries have a very uneven distribution, which will lead to lower GINI index scores. To measure this, when comparing wealth, we talk about all the annual disposable income that a family gets, including all its members, after deducting direct taxes and social contributions. When comparing the percentage of the population with the percentage of accumulative income, we obtain a curve, called Lorenz' curve. If this curve were linear, meaning a certain percentage of the population had that same percentage of income, we would have an index of 1, or perfect. The greater the inequality, the closer to zero. Mathematically, the Gini index is calculated as the area A, (in Fig. 5.6) between a perfect line, and the real distribution divided by the whole area under the perfect line or A + B, i.e. $G = A/(A + B)$. As A + B = ½, then $G = 2A$.

For our purposes, we take the official data by WorldBank for 264 countries and dated 2019 or before (World Bank, 2020).

**Fig. 5.6** Lorenz Curve and
GINI Index Calculation.
(Source: Wikipedia, 2020)

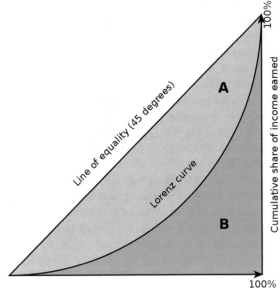

100%
Cumulative share of people from lowest to highest incomes

Gender Equality. To measure this, we go to INSEAD Global Talent Competitiveness Index. This index tries to evaluate talent nurturing in a country or city. In this way, the same as any corporation with a complete HHRR management program, the intention is to see how cities manage talent as large HHRR departments. The purpose is to assess how they implement policies and generate the conditions for Enabling, (legal and labor conditions) Attracting, (openness to immigrants and internal inclusion) Growing (education and training) and Retaining (sustainability of work and lifestyle) talent. The study has 6 years of experience and knowledge and includes 132 countries and 155 cities. For our analysis of equality in the Gender and Tolerance part, we will use the analytics available in the Attract area (internal inclusion) (Lanvin & Monteiro, 2020b). Gender equality will be measured by three main indicators:

- Graduated women (updated data for 2018): refers to the percentage of women who reached tertiary education level (level 5–8 according to the International Standard Classification of Education (ISCED)). Source: UNESCO Institute for Statistics (UIS.Stat, 2020).
- Gender development gap (updated data for 2017). Based on the Gender Development Index (GDI), it measures the differences and disparities between the level of human development achieved by men and women in three basic dimensions: knowledge, health and living standards. It is based on the Human Development Index (HDI) and is expressed as the female HDI as a percentage of the male one. Source: United Nations Development Program (UNDP, 2020), Gender Development Index.

- Leadership opportunities for women. (data from 2018). It is based on The Executive Opinion Survey (EOS) from the World Economic Forum survey on the question: *"In your country, to what extent do companies offer women the same opportunities as men to achieve management/leadership positions?"* Source: World Economic Forum, Executive Opinion Survey (Economic Forum 2020).
- (See class Gender Equality data ranking at APPENDIX IV)

To address tolerance, we have added two reports: one on Tolerance for minorities and one on Tolerance for immigrants.

- Minority tolerance. (data updated for 2019). The analysis on the discrimination and violence against minorities is based on the indicator of group complaints within the Fragile States Index published by The Fund for Peace. The group complaint focuses on pressures based on social or political characteristics, and the subsequent response to conflict, divisions, inequality and community violence. Source: The Fund for Peace, Fragile States Index 2019 (The Fund for Peace 2020) C3: Group Grievance.
- Immigrant tolerance. (updated data in 2018) It is based on the famous Gallup survey, and specifically on a question related to the indicator associated to tolerance with immigrants: *"Is the city or area where you live a good place to live for immigrants from other countries?"* Source: The Gallup World Poll (Gallup World Poll, 2018).
- (See Tolerance Equality data ranking at APPENDIX IV)

Finally, we are analyzing Poverty. Poverty studies show the percentage of the population living under the poverty line for any given country. We are taking this data from IndexMundi (Indexmundi, 2020), which is also taking it from different sources, mainly from CIA World Factbook (World Factbook 2019 and before). This is probably one of the data sources that we consider most relevant, but honestly, with poor data quality. Definitions of poverty lines vary very widely from different groups of countries. All want to show good numbers, so rich countries use ample standards and poor ones use narrower definitions, so we have found surprisingly large numbers for some modern countries and some unbelievably small numbers for some under-developed ones. Anyway, if clusters of similar countries are hopefully using same criteria, then the study is not so biased, and the information makes sense.

Finally, we want to indicate that we would have liked to add a city or country indicator that measures how much the city is more inclusive towards people with disabilities/elderly people through the use of technologies. It is obvious that Information Technologies are playing a fundamental role in removing barriers of social isolation, communication, integration, eliminating distances and physical barriers, by allowing the same tasks to be done online or teleworking. Each city has a greater or lesser degree of investment in new technologies to improve the quality of life of its citizens with disabilities/elderly people. But there is no such information. The G3ICT (G3ICT, 2013) entity works in this regard and publishes aggregated information on this adoption of new technologies. Also, a SmartCities4All Playbook (G3ICT, 2019) shows guidelines and good practices in this regard.

We should balance these four areas (GINI Index, Gender, Tolerance, Poverty) measuring Cities' Equality, so we conclude on equally weighing them all, as all are very relevant, and no evidence points us to give extra weight to any of them.

(See Equality data ranking at APPENDIX IV)

### 5.3.5  Dynamism: All Data Sources Integration

To create a consolidated Dynamism indicator for Magnetism, we need to combine these explained four Indicators/groups. When we look at these four groups, we can find that their influence is always very remarkable, and again, there is no evidence to lead us to especially differentiate any of them from the City Attractiveness point of view, so we equally weigh them all. So, this is the schema (Table 5.2) for the City Dynamism model: (W = Weight).

## 5.4  City Strategy (Future)

*A city is not gauged by its length and width, but by the broadness of its vision and the height of its dreams* (Caen, 1967).

Herb Caen was a famous journalist and reporter. He loved San Francisco, and it was one of his works' core topics. City, dream, vision. . .let's combine these three words, let's think about what's making a city attractive for its future, potential, readiness, planning, promising development points of view.

Many cities take advantage of their future plans' announcement to promote themselves. Fair. They are selling a future, hope in a better city and society. They are selling their project, what they want and aspire to be for years to come. A city, like any dynamic human ecosystem, must have a sense, a direction to move to, a strategy. If it does not, then it is very difficult to evolve in a correct direction, simply by chance; serendipity is not acceptable. Cities developed without a plan are complete chaos, just as cities that are *only* a plan are absolutely inhumane. A compromise is therefore necessary between what I want to do, and how I am going to make it happen, as we saw in the conception and development of the SmartCity plan.

Cities must be bold and take risks, always using what they know about their citizens, taking advantage of technology and urban planning, always putting the citizen in the spotlight, at the very center, as a participant and as a recipient of city services. When we search for a city's SmartCity plan and can't find it, or simply see a lot of headlines on a website without significant actions, we think that city is at risk; what's more, we think it's wasting precious time, missing the train of innovation, and that will pay for it in loss of attractiveness and talent. It's a city without a dream or a vision. . . is it still alive? Or it is its managers who are dead or dormant.

**Table 5.2** City Dynamism model

| W | Class | W | Indicator | Subindicator | Entity |
|---|-------|---|-----------|--------------|--------|
| 25 | Competitiveness | 25 | Creativity index | | Martin prosperity |
| | | 25 | Global Competitivenes | Economic | World economic forum |
| | | 25 | Cities in motion | | IESE |
| | | 25 | Global talent competitiveness | Talent | INSEAD-GTCI |
| 25 | Expat social experience | 33,3 | Life style - quality | | HSBC expat explorer |
| | | 33,3 | People around | | HSBC expat explorer |
| | | 33,3 | Relationship - social life | | HSBC expat explorer |
| 25 | Ethics. Well-being | 40 | Happiness | | Happiness report |
| | | 20 | World giving score | | Charities aid foundation |
| | | 20 | Civic engagement | | OECD-better life index |
| | | 20 | Work-life balance | | OECD-better life index |
| 25 | Equality | 25 | GINI index | | WorldBank |
| | | 25 | Gender | Female graduates | INSEAD-GTCI |
| | | | | Gender development gap | INSEAD-GTCI |
| | | | | Leadership opportunities for women | INSEAD-GTCI |
| | | 25 | Tolerance | Tolerance minorities | INSEAD-GTCI |
| | | | | Tolerance immigrants | INSEAD-GTCI |
| | | 25 | Poverty | | IndexMundi |

(See Integrated City Dynamism Data ranking at APPENDIX IV)

As the thinker born in my homeland, Baltasar Gracián (Gracian 1647), once said: *"Courage or wisdom are not enough, we must combine both"*. You have to know your city and the citizens' past and present, to fully understand it, analyze its parameters, indicators and customs. You have to take its pulse and decide the direction in which to work, run fast, rethink, restart, but never stop; your citizens want to see action, modernity, they want to feel proud of their city and that will retain them there and make them co-creators of the new city. It is a collective effort, where everyone must have an awareness of the future, where everyone has the ability to contribute or invent something, and that sum of intelligences will allow us to build the city of tomorrow, from the foundations of the past and the actions of the present.

It is a permanent dynamic of innovation, construction combined with some destruction/correction of errors, but with an excellent net positive progress. The opposite is to languish; it is a static, generic city, dead in life, inert, numb...better to close it and found another one, for the good and happiness of its inhabitants.

McKinsey (Frem et al., 2018) recommends that city governments consider several key issues as they look to the future (Talent competition, Connected world and globalization, Sustainability and Technology permanent role, all serving the citizens). Let's discuss them.

Cities play in the global competition for talent. The talent net balance is the measure for a city's success or failure.

Technology has, in our opinion, two speeds: one of permanent innovation that cities must incorporate into their SmartCity plan; and another made of disruptive advances that are accelerating in various areas. A perfect plan means permanently incorporating current and proven technology while looking at the following possible disruptions that we are about to trigger and will change everything. For example, you have to invest in IoT, knowing that 5G will be a disruptor in the capabilities and possibilities that it will bring us.

We must give important attention to sustainability and the environment. The city plays a fundamental role in the global task of coping with climate change. It is a possible component of future stress for the city (the main potential stresses are: resources, climate, social) (most forgot the possible pandemic due to a virus...). On the subject of sustainability and the future, let us remember that the very famous Greta Thunberg's activity is named *"Friday for future"* (Fridays for Future 2020).

We live in an increasingly globalized and open world, a super-connected world of cities. The city must be prepared and understand that there is a constant flow of people, who are simple tourists, who are exploring to stay, or who are leaving to other places looking for new opportunities.

Citizen well-being will be the key for cities' success. It is linked to talent attractiveness, and as a precondition, our citizens' well-being and happiness should be our goal, with the net talent lost/won as our metric.

Finally, all this must be done by placing the citizen at the center, collaborating on the initiatives and co-creating the future of the city.

Every city has a future, so how can we imagine a city without one? Without considering cities with serious economic or social development problems, at war or with recent natural catastrophes, what would a modern city with no future be like? When we think about this, the Spanish city of Talavera de la Reina (Toledo) always comes to mind. Located just 115 km from Madrid, and with some 90,000 inhabitants, this city has observed a permanent economic and social decline in the last 30 years, to become a distant Madrid's town. Talavera de la Reina is too close to Madrid to stop its talent from migrating, and too far/poorly connected to become a Madrid smart suburb. Talavera was losing its thriving service economy, commerce, in a large region. Within it included a national cattle market, and strong industries in artistic tiles and textiles, because the administrative center of its region was established in another city: Toledo; nearby regions such as Extremadura and Madrid were competing hard in the trade area with the best markets and outlets. The dream

**Fig. 5.7**  City of Talavera de la Reina (Spain) fighting for its future. (Photo: Author)

of a high-speed train to *bring* the city closer to Madrid was cut short by the economic crisis and because the final destination of such a journey, Lisbon, could not commit the funds to build the Portuguese part. Without good connection, without industry, Talavera was languishing to what it is today: a dormant city for workers who must travel 90 minutes to reach work in Madrid and therefore, leaving a good share of their salary in transportation. Another indicator is that it is the city with the cheapest real estate cost in Spain, which shows the city degradation and the loss of talent. Add to this a lack of history and important touristic attractions, the arrival of a large department store killing the local, small supermarkets and stores, wrong policies like not taking advantage of its huge riverbank as a natural attraction, inadequate investments like building one of the highest bridges in Europe to cross the river but with nowhere to go to the other side, letting the ceramic art industry die; this all completed the disaster, and marked the trend of unstoppable decline. On the social level, there is higher inequality and security problems, making the city even less attractive to locals due to terrible, high unemployment and a large percentage of unskilled labor. On March 11, 2017 (Europa-Press 2017), a demonstration of more than 30,000 people simply asked for a FUTURE, a future for their city, for their children, including connectivity (a high-speed train), to develop the few assets they still had left. We did not understand that demonstration as a particular political demand: they just asked for an opportunity. When more than 1/3rd of a city spontaneously asks for help, asks to have a place, a space in the future, it is because clearly the city is about to die, about to stop having a meaning, a differentiation; it's on its way to becoming an elderly person area whose children (all of them living in Madrid) are going to visit then every weekend.

We loved how they used the Delacroix's painting *"Liberty leading people"* (Delacroix, 1830), who championed the French Revolution. (Fig. 5.7) They dressed her in Talavera's traditional costume with the local flag, and used her as a symbol of that fight, not for freedom, but for a future.

To measure how attractive a city is in its Future, its potential or strategy, we'll measure the Human Capital as potential to activate, the Strategy shown in a powerful SmartCity Plan, and the investment in innovation required to activate that human capital and implement that SmartCity Plan.

### 5.4.1   Strategy: Human Capital

**Why Is This Proxy Relevant?**

The prosperity of the most competitive cities in the world, such as New York, Singapore, Amsterdam or San Francisco, are not so by chance, but by constant investment and policies that have long focused on human capital. This, together with attracting investments from large corporations and developing a future based on technology, have turned these cities into *global* cities with enormous attractiveness for individuals and companies.

The ATKearny Global Cities Report (ATKearny, 2019) measures human capital as a combination of factors related to the kind of population: people who have been born abroad, number of international students; and the city's ability to build talent in the educational system: first-rate universities, population with a tertiary degree, and number of international business schools.

Therefore, human capital is the base on which to build the future of our city, it is the engine that will move our city along the complex paths that destiny and the future will bring us, and that will successfully or unsuccessfully manage the city prosperity from its social, economic and environmental facets.

**How to Measure It?**

We are going to analyze human capital from its creation to its maximum splendor. Raw human capital is born and is distributed homogeneously throughout the world, by DNA; we could say that it is a divine gift. To measure how much raw human capital we have in a city, we must consider the average age of its citizens. Obviously, a city with a young population has more opportunities to generate its own talent than an aging city, which must strive to import it from outside. To measure this, we will simply use the population's average age.

This raw human capital must be cultivated through education from its earliest stages through university, fostering international experience and exchange to generate the greatest human capital capacity, ready to develop the city in the near future. To measure this finished human capital, ready to contribute, we turn to a consolidated index. As we have no Human Capital information from the last index we have just mentioned, Global Cities, we use another well-known and highly prestigious one: IESE Cities in Motion 2019 (Berrone & Ricart, 2019).

IESE Cities in Motion studies human capital from a great wealth of angles, including: Education: Higher education %; Business schools; Student international movements; Top 500 Universities; Schools; Expenditure on education; and Culture: Museums and art galleries; Theaters, Spending on leisure and recreation.

Given the richness of IESE Cities in Motion Capital and the fact that Population Age is only referring to raw human capital, then we assign a higher weight (80%) to IESE Indicator, and 20% to citizens' average age in a given city.

(See Human Capital data ranking at APPENDIX V)

## 5.4.2   Strategy: SmartCity Plan

### Why Is This Proxy Relevant?

A City's strategy and future plan are described in its SmartCity plan. This is so because nobody conceives a strategy where technology is not present as the enabler, as the essential means for all plan components to be put into operation, taking advantage of, and maximizing the assets of the city, and developing and remediating those areas where the city needs improvement. New problems, complex and unknown to those responsible for the city today, constantly arise and need to be addressed with a short-term plan. In parallel, it is time to design a long-term plan, an ambitious plan to transform the city. Cities are going to be the most important locations of economic transformation known to date. When we ask ourselves about the future of a city, we look at its potential and its capabilities, but that is not enough; we must put it into action, we must have a strategy and plan for urban transformation in the medium/long term. This change process was detailed in Chap. 3.

On the contrary, we have very serious doubts about the city's success capacity without a short-term plan as a SmartCity, or without a strategy for five and 10 years. We have seen 30-year plans in the most advanced and innovative cities. We have already seen that these plans are there to be changed, modified and adapted as new disruptive technologies appear. We know it's a trial-and-error, often a restarting process, but without a plan, the only thing that is guaranteed is the loss of opportunities and the failure of the city to attract/retain talent.

### How to Measure It?

Current city challenges were described in Chap. 2, the SmartCity plan areas were detailed in Chap. 3, the city performance indicators will be described in Chap. 6. In this section, we are evaluating the city's future by means of its SmartCity plan. The first approach to that model is to verify that such a plan exists. If it is not published, and therefore the citizens do not know it, we will assume that it does not formally exist. Sometimes, there are cities that do not have a plan as an integrated document, but rather have different smart actions within the services it offers to citizens. It is a bad indicator not to have a complete comprehensive plan because it shows a lack of strategy, investment, and agreement by all parties/stakeholders, with a lack of coordination and lack of leadership. However, we search the main city's website to try to find these smart actions.

We are going to study the city's SmartCity plan or actions looking at two places: On the one hand, the website and its services' offering, and on the other hand, the specific SmartCity plan or closest thing to it.

On the analysis from those websites/documents, we try to find evidence about the plan/real implementation of these 15 different SmartCity Concepts:

- Traffic. Traffic management, Analytics, Urban Mobility. Mobility-as-a-Service.
- Energy Efficiency. Savings. Fossil energies reduction. Renewables.
- Water. Avoid leakages. Water Quality. Air Quality control applied technology.
- Tourism. Destiny. Info for tourists while at destiny. Post-Social sharing.
- SmartBuildings. Efficiency. Energy, Water, Safety, Spaces, Productivity.
- $CO_2$ Emissions Reduction-Carbon Neutral. Carbon Neutral target, Plan.
- Safety-Resilience. First Responders. Emergency Plan.
- Social Services. Remote/Home Care. Vulnerable population.
- Transparency. Governance. Quality of eGovernment Services.
- Citizen Engagement. Participation. Cocreation.
- Civil Servants tools. Modern Workplace. Teleworking. Hybrid way of work.
- Cloud enablement. Technology adoption. Transformational Capacities.
- Mobile enablement. Mobile ready. Citizen Communication tools. 5G Deployment.
- City Data Management. Urban Data Platform. Datalakes. OpenData. Digital Twin models.
- Social Analytics. AI for City modelling, Citizen Sentiment Analytics.

It's a very wide and diverse number of topics to analyze, and every city is prioritizing some areas or others, dedicating different budgets. To enable comparisons and have an overall view, we are assigning for each concept:

0: If no mentions, nothing found.
1: If mentions, scattered actions, light investment/dedication.
2: If clear evidence for investment, solid actions are found.

Then we are adding the 15 scores, so we are measuring the depth and real implementation SmartCity actions from 0 to 30. Finally, we are normalizing all cities scores from 0 to 10, as usual.

(See Appendix V for SmartCity Plan ranking)

### 5.4.3   Strategy: Innovation

**Why Is This Proxy Relevant?**

Investment in innovation makes talent flourish and develop its creativity to generate wealth and property for the city. It is the gasoline that makes the engine of human capital work. SmartCity's strategy is the road, the direction and the priority we want to set in our city's development.

As Jaime Lerner, Mayor of Curitiba, Brazil, once said, *"cities are not the problem, they are the solution"* (Sim 2019). They are the solution for global warming, for aging populations, for all the challenges we studied in Chap. 2. Cities are the solution because they exchange knowledge, intelligence, creativity and innovative ideas; they set the place, the time and the conditions where innovation can easily thrive.

Cities are the demonstration of how human societies are articulated within the continuous process of searching for new opportunities. For this, humans meet in the city, to seek and develop progress and wealth. It is the essence of the city, as we saw. As cities are the largest production centers, they are also the places where new opportunities are searched and found, and greater wealth is generated (Yang and Ratti 2018). The main engine for long-term economic growth is innovation. Cities facilitate the interaction between humans and the exchange of ideas that trigger the generation of social, economic and technological advances and new opportunities.

We think we are at the beginning of the greatest acceleration in city innovation ever. This is justified, according to Prof. Florida (Florida, 2019), by central governments' ineffectiveness, partisanship, populism and immobility, incapable of articulating changes in society, in contrast with closer, pragmatic, effective and much more depoliticized local governments. On the other hand, even the largest cities are still creative and alive, with enormous dynamism and innovation. In parallel, there is a global decentralization process that encourages innovation at the local level to solve the problems and challenges that arise, most just transferred or delegated by central governments. Finally, we see the emergence of a new city-specific technology sector, (Prof. Florida calls it *"urban tech"*) with a huge investment in technological development, capital contribution, social and institutional funds, and the creation of urban innovation platforms combining local agents, local technology companies, universities and multinationals. The great innovations that we are envisioning, are focused and will be developed in and for cities (autonomous cars, 5G, electric vehicles, IoT, Artificial Intelligence, etc.)

**How to Measure It?**

The first step will be to measure the country R&D investment as a percentage of Gross Expenditure. This data is available by country, is generic, but gives us a first approach on how relevant innovation is for a country. We'll take this data from the very well-known INSEAD Global Talent Competitiveness Index (GTCI) (Lanvin & Monteiro, 2020c).

Then, we'll go deeper into innovation radiography by country. The Global Innovation Index (Dutta et al. 2019) study provides an in-depth analysis of the capacity and investment in innovation in 129 countries, which accounts for 92% of the world population and 97% of world GDP. It uses a total of 80 indicators and groups the innovation inputs into five fundamental pillars: institutions, infrastructure, human capital and sophistication in the local market and companies/businesses.

Yet, if we are looking for specific information in each city about innovation, we should look at the Innovative Cities Program (2thinknow, 2019), from the consultant 2ThinkNow.

The Innovation Cities Framework studies more than 1500 cities grouped into 31 market segments. It uses a set of 162 city indicators. This framework provides a comprehensive and structured way of measuring and comparing the innovation status of cities, and provides suggestions and guidance on how to prepare a city for innovation attraction and development. The report evaluates the performance of cities in three major areas that foster innovation: Cultural assets, human infrastructure and network markets. Cities are grouped into 31 segments for better comparison.

We are assigning a larger weight (50%) to Innovation Cities Program as it is much more city specific and rich in details. R&D Investment and Country Innovation are very relevant but less informative for this indicator, so they share the other 50%.

(See Appendix V for Strategy. Innovation data ranking)

### 5.4.4   Strategy: Integration of All Data Sources

Finally, we consolidate in City Strategy (Future) these three areas that constitute the future of the city and its attractiveness as potential. Human Capital, SmartCity Plan and Innovation intertwined complement, reinforce and develop one another, as all need each other for their implementation, activation and creation of wealth and city prosperity.

So, this is the schema (Table 5.3) for the City Strategy model: (W=Weight).

When evaluating these three areas, we must bear in mind that the most important is the SmartCity Plan, since without a solid plan or an structured, integrated or well-planned way of guiding innovation, we will not achieve the achievements that the city, and most importantly, its citizens, aspire for. For this reason, we give the Plan a greater weight (50%). Innovation is essential, but it is more generic than the city plan and fits more in the capacities than in practice, that's why we give it a lower weight (30%). Finally, we assign the lowest weight (20%) to Human Capital, as it is the raw material we need and although very important, is less indicative of the city's strategy and its ability to achieve excellent goals in the future.

(See Appendix V for Strategy rankings. Summary)

**Table 5.3**  City Strategy model

| W | Class | W | Indicator | Subindicator | Entity |
|---|---|---|---|---|---|
| 20 | Human capital | 20 | Population age average per country | | Own work |
| | | 80 | Ranking human capital | | IESE cities motion |
| 50 | Smart cities plan | 100 | Plan smart cities | 15 areas | Own work |
| 30 | Innovation | 25 | R&D (% GDP) | | INSEAD - GTCI |
| | | 25 | Global innovation index | | Cornell INSEAD WIPO |
| | | 50 | Innovation cities | | 2ThinkNow |

# 5.5  City Magnetism Indicators Summary

It's very important to notice that we are not assigning any weight to these three main areas. Users of the app will do. They will provide their inputs. In other words, we are giving the users (citizens, cities) the freedom to tune the tool to match their preferences.

Thus, we will ask the user to assign some weights (which will be normalized to total 100) for each of those three areas. The questions to ask would be:

Evaluate and assign your preferences on which characteristic of the city attracts you the most (without evaluating city services or cost of living).

- If you value the most a city with a Past, with a strong Identity (history, culture, invariable elements derived from its geographical position such as climate, its gastronomy, its image or branding or its international projection) then you should especially value the City Identity indicator.
- If what you value most is the Present, the dynamism of the city reflected in its creativity, competitiveness and the way it treats expatriates, its lifestyle and its ethical values, equity and equality, then assign greater value to the City Dynamism indicator.
- And finally, if what you value most is the Future, a city with a strategy and a promising future based on rich human capital, strong investment in innovation and a solid and comprehensive SmartCity Plan, then assign bigger value to the City Strategy indicator.

Then, we can draw the complete City Magnetism Area with these indicators / descriptors:

W=Weight (see Table 5.4).

(See Appendix VI for Magnetism. Summary. Ranking). Note that the weights used for the three main areas come from a large survey. To be explained in Chap. 7.

So far, the model includes 27 indicators for Identity, 18 for Dynamism and 22 for Strategy, for a total of 67 for Magnetism. The number of sub-indicators inside them is very large, as some include more than 100 subcomponents.

**Table 5.4** City Magnetism model

| W | Subarea | W | Class | W | Indicator | Sub indicator | Entity |
|---|---|---|---|---|---|---|---|
| User input | Identity | 20 | History. Culture | 70 | Age | | Own work |
| | | | | 20 | UNESCO | | UNESCO |
| | | | | 10 | Top museums | | Own work |
| | | 10 | Government basics | 50 | Democracy index | | The economist |
| | | | | 50 | Safe City index | | The economist |
| | | 10 | Reputation | 100 | Reputation | | Reputation institute |
| | | 10 | Space. Density | 50 | % natural space | | Own work |
| | | | | 50 | Density (inh/km2) | | Demographia |
| | | 15 | Climate | 33,3 | Avge. Temperature Desviation | Gradient | Climatemps |
| | | | | 33,3 | Avge. Precipitation Desviation | Gradient | Climatemps |
| | | | | 33,3 | Avge. Daily sunshine | | Climatemps |
| | | 5 | Geo risk | 100 | Natural disaster risk | | WorldRiskReport |
| | | 10 | Geo economics | 100 | GDP proximity | %WW | Own work |
| | | 5 | Gastronomy | 50 | RK food index | | OXFAM |
| | | | | 50 | Michelin guide | #rest/minh | Vía Michelin |
| | | 15 | Branding. External image | 25 | Movies | | Wikipedia |
| | | | | 50 | Sports | Soccerbasketballother sports events, marathons | Football databaseNBATopendsports |
| | | | | 25 | Main events | Olympics | Olympics org |
| | | | | | | Universal expo | Own work |
| | | | | | | Cultural events | Day zero project |
| User input | Dynamism | 25 | Compe titiveness | 25 | Creativity index | | Martin prosperity |
| | | | | 25 | Global Competi tiveness | Economic | World economic forum |
| | | | | 25 | Cities in motion | | IESE-CiMI |

| | | | | | Talent | |
|---|---|---|---|---|---|---|
| User input | 25 | | 25 | Global talent Competitiveness | | INSEAD-GTCI |
| | 25 | Expat social experience | 33,3 | Life style - quality | | HSBC expat explorer |
| | | | 33,3 | People around | | HSBC expat explorer |
| | | | 33,3 | Relationship - social life | | HSBC expat explorer |
| | 25 | Ethics. Well-being | 40 | Happiness | | Happiness report |
| | | | 20 | World giving score | | Charities aid foundation |
| | | | 20 | Civic engagement | | OECD-better life index |
| | | | 20 | Work-life balance | | OECD-better life index |
| | 25 | Equality | 25 | GINI index | | WorldBank |
| | | | 25 | Gender | Female graduates | INSEAD-GTCI |
| | | | | | Gender Develo pment gap | INSEAD-GTCI |
| | | | | | Leadership oppor tunities for women | INSEAD-GTCI |
| | | | 25 | Tolerance | Tolerance minorities | INSEAD-GTCI |
| | | | | | Tolerance immigrants | INSEAD-GTCI |
| | | | 25 | Poverty | | IndexMundi |
| | 20 | Human capital | 20 | Population age average per country | | Own work |
| | | | 80 | Ranking human capital | | IESE cities in motion |
| Strategy | 50 | Smart cities plan | 100 | Plan smart cities | | Own work |
| | 30 | Innovation | 25 | R&D (% GEx) | 15 areas | INSEAD - GTCI |
| | | | 25 | Global innovation index | | Cornell INSEAD WIPO |
| | | | 50 | Innovation cities | | 2ThinkNow |

# References

2ThinkNow (2019) *Innovation cities program.* https://www.innovation-cities.com/index-2019-global-city-rankings/18842/ and also at https://report.innovation-cities.com/about-the-innovation-cities-framework/758 Accessed 22 Jan 2020.

Abbott B. (1942) *Documenting the City* (pp. 25–26). New York Public Library.

Allen, W. (2008) *Vicky, Cristina, Barcelona.*

Alvaredo, F. et al. (2018) World Inequality Report, *World Inequality Lab, Paris School of Economics* (p. 70). https://wir2018.wid.world/files/download/wir2018-full-report-english.pdf Accessed by 4 April 2020.

Aristotle, Rhetoric, 350 BC, Book1, Part 5.

Aritotle. Politics Book 1 Section 1253ᵃ. 350 BC.

Astuto, P. (2003) *Eugenio Espejo 1747–1795 : reformador ecuatoriano de la ilustración.* p.102 Quito:Campaña Nacional Eugenio Espejo por el Libro y la Lectura.

ATKearny (2019) *A question of talent: how human capital will determine the next global leaders.* 2019 Global Cities Report https://www.atkearney.com/global-cities/2019 Accessed 22 Jan 2020.

Barnés, H. (2017) Así serán nuestras ciudades: 'Una bomba de relojería'. Alma, Corazón y Vida. El Confidencial. https://www.elconfidencial.com/alma-corazon-vida/2017-04-15/clases-ciudades-richard-florida_1365496/ Accessed 22 Oct 2019.

Beachler, H. (2019) *A whole city is a more equitable city.* The future of city innovation. Bloomberg Cities. MEDIUM Future. https://medium.com/@BloombergCities/the-future-of-city-innovation-99a0950a76c3 Accessed 22 Jan 2020.

Bergoglio, C. J. M. (2013). *Pilares de un pontificado, Mensaje Cuaresma 2012* (p. 39). Ed.San Pablo.

Berrone, P., & Ricart, J.E. (2019) *Cities in Motion 2019.* IESE. https://media.iese.edu/research/pdfs/ST-0509-E.pdf Accessed 25 Jan 2020.

Boyd C., & Adams, R. (2020) *Happy cities hexagon.* HAPPY CITIZENS, http://www.happycitizendesign.com/ Accessed 21 Jan 2020.

Caen, H. (1957). *Herb Caen's Guide to San Francisco.* Garden City, New York: Doubleday & Company.

Caen, H. (1967). *San Francisco, City on Golden Hills* (p. 5). Garden City, NY: Doubleday.

CAF (2019) *World giving index.* CAF (Charities Aid Foundation). London https://www.cafonline.org/docs/default-source/about-us-publications/caf_wgi_10th_edition_report_2712a_web_101019.pdf Accessed 4 Feb 2020.

Carta, M. (2011) *Città Creativa 3.0. Rigenerazione urbana e politiche di valorizzazione delle armature culturali. Citymorphosis. Politiche culturali per città che cambiano* (pp. 213–221) Giunti.

Cathelat, B. (2019a) *SMARTCITIES SHAPING THE SOCIETY OF 2030* (p. 35). UNESCO and NETEXPLO.

Cathelat, B. (2019b) *SMARTCITIES SHAPING THE SOCIETY OF 2030* (p. 174). UNESCO and NETEXPLO.

Cathelat, B. (2019c) *SMARTCITIES SHAPING THE SOCIETY OF 2030* (p. 177). UNESCO and NETEXPLO.

Cathelat, B. (2019d) *SMARTCITIES SHAPING THE SOCIETY OF 2030* (p. 188). UNESCO and NETEXPLO.

Chueca Goitia, F. (1968a) *Breve Historia del Urbanismo* (p. 9) Alianza Editorial.

Chueca Goitia, F. (1968b), *Breve Historia del Urbanismo* (p. 43) Alianza Editorial.

Chueca Goitia, F. (1968c) *Breve Historia del Urbanismo* (p. 250). Alianza Editorial.

CIA World Factbook (2019) *Population under poverty line.* https://www.cia.gov/library/publications/resources/the-world-factbook/fields/221.html Accessed 28 Jan 2020.

CitiesToday (2018) *How SmartCities can make you happier.* CitiesToday. https://cities-today.com/industry/how-smart-cities-can-make-you-happier/ Accessed 22 Aug 2019.

CLIMATEMPS (2018). http://www.madrid.climatemps.com/index.php Accessed 22 June 2018.

Curtiz, M. (1943) *Casablanca*.

DayZero (2018) Top50 Festivals and Cultural Events. https://dayzeroproject.com/festivals/ Accessed 27 Oct 2018.

Delacroix, E. (1830) *Liberty leading the people*. Oil on canvas. Romantic. Louvre-Paris.

Demographia (2019) Demographia World. *Urban Areas. 15th Annual Edition: 201904* (pp. 81–123). Also at http://www.demographia.com/db-worldua.pdf Accessed 19 Oct 2019.

Dempsey, N., & Jenks M. (1978) The Future of the Compact City. *Built Environment* (Vol. 36. No. 1 pp. 116–121). Alexandrine Press.

Dutta, S. (2019) The Global Innovation Index 2019 (p. 35) *Cornell University, INSEAD, and WIPO* https://www.globalinnovationindex.org/ Accessed 24 Jan 2020.

Ebb, F. and Kander, J. (1977) Theme From *New York, New York* Martin Scorsese film. Sony/ATV Music Publishing. First Singer: Liza Minnelli. Most famous: Frank Sinatra.

Ecclesiastes, 1,9.

EU Urban Chapter (2020) *Manifesto for new urbanity*. pp.39–53. https://rm.coe.int/urban-charter-ii-manifesto-for-a-new-urbanity-publication-a5-58-pages-/168095e1d5 Accessed 5 Jan 2020.

EuropaPress (2017) Más de 30.000 personas en la 'histórica' manifestación del 11-N 'Talavera por su futuro'. https://www.europapress.es/castilla-lamancha/noticia-mas-30000-personas-participan-historica-manifestacion-11-lema-talavera-futuro-20171111150531.html Accessed 18 Nov 2018.

European Commission (2016). *Analyzing the potential for wide scale roll out of integrated Smart Cities and Communities solutions. Report D7*. p.5 Directorate-General for Energy.

Fina, D. et al. (2019) *Inequality: A persisting challenge and its implications*. McKinsey, https://www.mckinsey.com/industries/public-sector/our-insights/inequality-a-persisting-challenge-and-its-implications Accessed 22 Jan 2020.

Florida, R. (2011) *The World's Leading Creative Class Countries*. CityLab. https://www.citylab.com/life/2011/10/worlds-leading-creative-class-countries/228/ Accessed 9 Oct 2019.

Florida, R. (2019) *Cities will become platforms for innovation and creative destruction*. The future of city innovation. Bloomberg Cities. MEDIUM Future. https://medium.com/@BloombergCities/the-future-of-city-innovation-99a0950a76c3 Accessed 22 Jan 2020.

Florida, R. et al. (2015) *Global creativity index*. Martin Prosperity. http://www.martinprosperity.org/media/Global-Creativity-Index-2015.pdf Accessed 11 Oct 2018.

Frem J. et al. (2018) *Thriving amid turbulence: Imagining the cities of the future*. McKinsey. https://www.mckinsey.com/industries/public-sector/our-insights/thriving-amid-turbulence-imagining-the-cities-of-the-future Accessed 12 Oct 2019.

Fridays for Future (2020). https://www.fridaysforfuture.org/ Accessed 12 Jan 2020.

G3ICT (2013) *Global Initiative for Inclusive ICTs*. https://g3ict.org/publication/convention-on-the-rights-of-persons-with-disabilities-g3icts-2013-ict-accessibility-progress-report-survey-conducted-in-cooperation-with-dpi Accessed 22 Oct 2019.

G3ICT (2019) SmartCities4All https://smartcities4all.org/wp-content/uploads/2019/05/I2-Playbook-XT.pdf Accessed 21 Oct 2019.

Gallup Advanced Analytics (2019). https://www.gallup.com/analytics/213617/gallup-analytics.aspx Accessed 3 Oct 2019.

Gallup World Poll (2018). https://www.gallup.com/analytics/232838/world-poll.aspx Accessed 24 Jan 2020.

Gehl, J. (2019) *Year or Monkey*. GehlPeople https://gehlpeople.com/announcement/year-of-the-monkey/ Accessed 30 Oct 2019.

Gracian, B. (1647) *El Arte de la Prudencia*, Aforismo 4, p.8. Menorca:textos.info. also at https://www.textos.info/baltasar-gracian/el-arte-de-la-prudencia/descargar-pdf Accessed 3 Oct 2019.

Greco I., & Bencardino M. (2014) *The Paradigm of the Modern City: SMART and SENSEable Cities for Smart, Inclusive and Sustainable Growth*. In: Murgante B. et al. (eds) Computational Science and Its Applications – ICCSA 2014. ICCSA 2014. Lecture Notes in Computer Science, vol 8580. p. 587. Springer. https://doi.org/10.1007/978-3-319-09129-7_42.

Gulsrud, N. (2015) *The Role of Green Space in City Branding: An Urban Governance Perspective* (pp. 26–27) Thesis. University of Copenhagen.

Haynes, C. (2014a) Magnet cities. Decline | Fightback | Victory, (pp. 4–32) *KPMG.UK* https://assets.kpmg/content/dam/kpmg/pdf/2015/03/magnet-cities.pdf Accessed 3 Nov 2019.

Haynes, C. (2014b) *Magnet cities*. Decline | Fightback | Victory, (pp. 56–57) *KPMG.UK* https://assets.kpmg/content/dam/kpmg/pdf/2015/03/magnet-cities.pdf Accessed 3 Nov 2019.

HSBC (2017) *Expat Explorer*. HSBC Holdings plc. London https://expatexplorer.hsbc.com/global-report/ Accessed 22 Oct 2018.

IEREK (2018) *The Identity of the City* https://www.ierek.com/news/index.php/2018/10/29/the-identity-of-the-city/ Accessed 13 Dec 2019.

IndexMundi (2020) *Population below poverty line.* https://www.indexmundi.com/g/r.aspx?v=69 Accessed 25 Jan 2020.

Institute for International Law of Peace and Armed Conflict (2020) The WorldRiskReport. Bündnis Entwicklung Hilft and Ruhr University Bochum – *Institute for International Law of Peace and Armed Conflict (IFHV)*, pp.56–61 Berlin. https://weltrisikobericht.de/english-2/ Accessed 3 Jan 2020.

Jacobs, J. (1961) *The death and life of great American Cities*, New York:Random House, 2002 (first published 1961) p. 372, republished Entrelíneas, 2013.

Kant, I. (1795) *Perpetual peace. A Philosophical Essay.* Zum ewigen Frieden. Ein philosophischer Entwur. Germany:F.Nicolovius. Translated by Smith, Mary C. Project Gutenberg. 2016. pp. 120–137.

Keeton, R. (2020) *When Smart Cities are Stupid.* International New Town Institute. Rotterdam http://www.newtowninstitute.org/spip.php?article1078 Accessed Feb 2020.

Koolhaas, R. (1997) *Acerca de la ciudad* GG, Barcelona, 2014 from "The Generic City", núm. 791, p.35 Milano:Domu.

Kowalczyk, A., & Derek, M. (2020) *Gastronomy and Urban Space. Changes and challenges in geographical perspective* (p. 108). Springer.

Lanvin, B., & Monteiro, F. (2020a) *Global City Talent Competitiveness Index 2020.* INSEAD. https://gtcistudy.com/ and https://gtcistudy.com/special-section-gctci/ Accessed 4 Jan 2020.

Lanvin, B., & Monteiro, F. (2020b) *INSEAD Global Talent Competitiveness index (GTCI), Global Talent in the Age of Artificial Intelligence* (p. 354). Fontainebleau, France:INSEAD https://www.insead.edu/sites/default/files/assets/dept/globalindices/docs/GTCI-2020-report.pdf Accessed 11 Feb 2020.

Lanvin, B., & Monteiro, F. (2020c) *INSEAD Global Talent Competitiveness index (GTCI), Global Talent in the Age of Artificial Intelligence* (p. 274). Fontainebleau, France:INSEAD https://www.insead.edu/sites/default/files/assets/dept/globalindices/docs/GTCI-2020-report.pdf Accessed 11 Feb 2020.

Luttwak, E. (1999). *Theory and practice of geo-economics from turbo-capitalism: Winners and losers in the global economy* (p. 134). New York: HarperCollins Publishers.

Lynch, K. (1960a) *The Image of the City* (p. 1) The MIT Press.

Lynch, K. (1960b). *The Image of the City* (pp. 9–10). The MIT Press.

Madrid (2019) Madrid te abraza. Madrid https://www.esmadrid.com/madrid-te-abraza Accessed 20 Aug 2019.

Michelin Guide (2018). https://guide.michelin.com/en/restaurants Accessed 10 Oct 2018.

Montgomery, C. (2013a) *Happy City* (p. 53). Penguin Books.

Montgomery, C. (2013b) *Happy City* (pp. 7–9). Penguin Books.

Montgomery, C. (2013c) *Happy City* (pp. 42). Penguin Books.

Montgomery, C. (2013d) *Happy City*. p. 317 London, UK: Penguin Books.

Montgomery, C. (2013e) *Happy City* (p. 33). Penguin Books.

Montgomery, C. (2013f) *Happy City* (p. 244). Penguin Books.

Montgomery, C. (2013g) *Happy City* (p. 237). Penguin Books.

Murray, C. and Landry, C. (2017) *How urban psychology could radically transform city living.* CitiesToday https://cities-today.com/the-city-in-mind-how-urban-psychology-could-radically-transform-city-living/ Accessed 21 Jan 2020.

Murray, C. and Landry. C (2019) *Urban psyche assessment and city personality test.* https://www.urbanpsyche.org/ Accessed 20 Dec 2019.

Nall, R. (2018) *What are the benefits of sunlight?* Healthline https://www.healthline.com/health/depression/benefits-sunlight#mental-health Accessed 10 Aug 2019.

NBA Teams (2018). https://www.nba.com/teams Accessed 16 Oct 2018.

OECD (2020a) *Better Life Index.* Civic Engagement. http://www.oecdbetterlifeindex.org/topics/civic-engagement/ , also https://stats.oecd.org/Index.aspx?DataSetCode=BLI Accessed 22 Jan 2020.

OECD (2020b) *Better Life Index.* Work-Life Balance. http://www.oecdbetterlifeindex.org/topics/work-life-balance/ Accessed 22 Jan 2020.

Official List of Olympic Games (2018). https://www.olympic.org/sports Also here: https://en.wikipedia.org/wiki/List_of_Olympic_Games_host_cities Accessed Oct 2018.

OXFAM (2018) The Food Index. https://www.oxfam.org.uk/what-we-do/good-enough-to-eat Accessed 20 Oct 2018.

Pérez-Reverte, A. (2019). https://akifrases.com/frase/125400 Accessed 17 Aug 2019.

Pinto, C.A. (2009) Manifesto for a new urbanity. European Urban Charter II. p.49 *Council of Europe. Strasbourg.* https://rm.coe.int/urban-charter-ii-manifesto-for-a-new-urbanity-publication-a5-58-pages-/168095e1d5 Accessed 11 Aug 2019.

Reputation Institute (2018a) World's most reputable cities. https://insights.reputationinstitute.com/blog-ri/the-world-s-most-reputable-cities-explained Accessed 13 Oct 2018.

Reputation Institute (2018b) Cities 2018 https://insights.reputationinstitute.com/north-america/city-reptrak-2018 Accessed 22 Oct 2019.

Riza, M.et al. (2012) *City Branding and Identity. Procedia - Social and Behavioral Sciences* vol 35, p. 294 Malaysia:Elsevier B.V. Universiti Teknologi MARA. doi:https://doi.org/10.1016/j.sbspro.2012.02.091.

Rossi, A. (1978) *La arquitectura de la ciudad.* pp. 148–149 Barcelona:Ed. Gustavo Gili.

Shakespeare, W. (1609) *The tragedy of Coriolanus* Act3 Scene1. England http://www.literaturepage.com/read/shakespeare-coriolanus.html Accessed 20 Jun 2019.

Shteinsaltz, Rab. Adin. (2019) El concepto del tiempo en el pensamiento judío. pp. 2–4 *Bama* http://www.bama.org.ar/sitio2014/sites/default/files/_archivos/merkaz/Jomer_on_line/ST_conceptoTiempo.pdf Accessed 10 Oct 2019.

Sim, D. (2019) *Soft City: Building Density for Everyday Life,* p.6 Washington DC:Island Press.

SKYSCRAPERCITY (2018) Cities with the most % of public green space (parks and gardens). http://www.skyscrapercity.com/showthread.php?t=1660203 Accessed 9 Oct 2018.

Soccer Clubs Ranking (2018) World Football / Soccer Clubs Ranking http://footballdatabase.com/ranking/world/1 Accessed 16 Oct 2018.

Solarte Rodriguez, M.R. (2003) *Moral y ética de lo público.* p.29 Bogotá:Facultad de Teología. Pontificia Universidad Javeriana.

Sprengler, O. (2013) *La decadencia de Occidente,* vol II, p131 Barcelona:Editorial Austral.

Stringfellow, M. and Wagle D. (2018) *Booming cities, unintended consequences.* McKinsey, https://www.mckinsey.com/featured-insights/future-of-cities/booming-cities-unintended-consequences Accessed 22 Nov 2019

Swilling M. et al. (2018) *The weight of cities.* Resource requirements of future urbanization. p.53 *United Nations Environment Programme* also at UN-20180906-peso-ciudades-informe-weight-of-cities.pdf Accessed 12 Oct 2019.

Tannahill, A. (2008) Beyond evidence—to ethics: a decision-making framework for health promotion, public health and health improvement. *Health Promotion International* 23(4): 380–390, also at https://doi.org/10.1093/heapro/dan032 Accessed 20 Dec 2019.

Terence (163) (Latin: Publius Terentius Afer) Heauton Timorumenos (The Self-Tormentor) written 163 BC, Act I, scene 1, line 25 (77). "Homo sum: humani nihil a me alienum puto."

The Economist (2020a) *Democracy Index 2019*. A year of democratic setbacks and popular protest. pp.10–14. London. Also from https://infographics.economist.com/2019/DemocracyIndex/ Accessed 11 Feb 2020.

The Economist (2020b) *Safe Cities Index 2019*. Urban security and resilience in an interconnected world. p.15 London. Also from https://safecities.economist.com/safe-cities-index-2019/ Accessed 12 Feb 2020.

The Fund for Peace (2019) Fragile States Index 2019. https://fragilestatesindex.org/indicators/c3/ Accessed 23 Jan 2020.

TOPENDSPORTS (2018) *The 100 Sporting Events you must see live*. https://www.topendsports. com/world/lists/must-see-events/top100.htm Accessed 11 Oct 2018.

Tri-City Medical Center (2018) *5 Ways the Sun Impacts Your Mental and Physical Health*, Oceanside, CA https://www.tricitymed.org/2018/08/5-ways-the-sun-impacts-your-mental-and-physical-health/ Accessed 21 Aug 2018.

UIS.Stat (2020) UNESCO Institute for Statistics http://data.uis.unesco.org/ Accessed 28 Jan 2020.

UNDP (2020) *Human Development Index*. Gender development index. United Nations Development Program (UNDP) http://hdr.undp.org/en/content/table-4-gender-development-index Accessed 20 Jan 2020.

UNESCO (2019a) *World Heritage Centre (2019) World Heritage List* - https://whc.unesco.org/en/list/ Accessed 22 Aug 2019.

UNESCO (2019b) *Creative Cities* p.1. http://www.unesco.org/culture/culture-sector-knowledge-management-tools/09_Info%20Sheet_Creative%20Cities%20Network.pdf Accessed 28 Oct 2019.

UNHabitat (2019) *The Six Dimensions of Urban Prosperity*. UNHabitat. http://urbandata.unhabitat. org/six-dimensions-urban-prosperity Accessed 3 Nov 2019.

University of British Columbia (2020) World Happiness Report 2020. University of British Columbia. Vancouver. The World Happiness Report is a publication of the Sustainable Development Solutions Network, powered by data from the Gallup World Poll, and supported by the Ernesto Illy Foundation, illycaffè, Davines Group, Blue Chip Foundation, the William, Jeff, and Jennifer Gross Family Foundation, and Unilever's largest ice cream brand Wall's. https://worldhappiness.report/ed/2020/ Accessed 5 Feb 2020.

Warhol, A. (1975) *The Philosophy of Andy* Warhol (From A to B & Back Again). Chapter 7. Harcourt Brace Jovanovich.

Werner, A. (2019) *Making history*. Museums and history. Archives UK https://archives.history.ac. uk/makinghistory/resources/articles/museums_and_history.html Accessed 3 Oct 2019.

WHR (2020) *World happiness report 2020*. p. 22. https://happiness-report.s3.amazonaws.com/2020/WHR20.pdf or https://worldhappiness.report/ed/2020/cities-and-happiness-a-global-ranking-and-analysis/ Accessed 20 Feb 2020.

Wikipedia (2018a) *List of films based on location*. https://en.wikipedia.org/wiki/Lists_of_films_based_on_location Accessed 20 Oct 2018.

Wikipedia (2018b) *List of World Exhibitions*. https://en.wikipedia.org/wiki/List_of_world_expositions also here: https://en.wikipedia.org/wiki/World%27s_fair Accessed 20 Oct 2018.

Wikipedia (2020) *Lorenz Curve*. https://en.wikipedia.org/wiki/Lorenz_curve Accessed 10 Jan 2020.

World Bank (2020) *GINI Index*. https://data.worldbank.org/indicator/si.pov.gini Accessed 9 Jan 2020.

World Cities Culture Forum (2018) *Global Leadership on culture in cities*. Bop Consulting. http://www.worldcitiescultureforum.com/data/of-public-green-space-parks-and-gardens     Accessed 11 Oct 2018.

World Economic Forum (2018) *Executive opinion survey*. World Economic Forum, https://reports. weforum.org/global-competitiveness-report-2018/appendix-b-the-executive-opinion-survey-the-voice-of-the-business-community. Accessed 14 Jan 2020.

World Economic Forum (2019) *Global Competitive Index*. http://reports.weforum.org/global-competitiveness-report-2019/ Accessed 2 Jan 2020.

World Economic Forum (2020) *The global risks report 2020.* 15th Edition. Geneva. Also at http://www3.weforum.org/docs/WEF_Global_Risk_Report_2020.pdf Accessed 7 Feb 2020.

Worldometers (2019) *GDP.* https://www.worldometers.info/gdp/ Accessed Aug 2019.

Wu, D. (2017) *Let the sun shine: Mind your mental health this winter.* Harvard Health Publishing https://www.health.harvard.edu/blog/let-the-sun-shine-mind-your-mental-health-this-winter-2017012311058 Accessed 28 Aug 2019.

Yang, X. and Ratti, C. (2018) *A la conquista de las ciudades divididas. Hacia una nueva ilustración. Una década trascendente* (pp. 375–379) Madrid:BBVA-Openmind. also at https://www.bbvaopenmind.com/wp-content/uploads/2019/02/BBVA-OpenMind-libro-2019-Hacia-una-nueva-Ilustracion-una-decada-trascendente.pdf Accessed 3 Jan 2020.

Zhang, L., & Zhao, S. X. (2009). City branding and the Olympic effect: A case study of Beijing. *Cities, 25,* 245–254.

# Chapter 6
# City Profitability (Yield)

## 6.1  Introduction. The Citizenship Contract

Cities were born as meeting places where living together provided people with an indisputable series of advantages and synergies. As soon as we live together, we develop a society. In every society, each member contributes and obtains in return a benefit from the whole. This basically works by the principle of union; the union of individuals is stronger and achieves many more goals in every subject than the sum of individualities. From the beginning of cities, a series of norms of coexistence was established, an ethical code.

It is the so-called *social contract*, where individuals give up part of their individual freedom to the state, in exchange for protection, generation of opportunities and well-being. This concept began in ancient Greece. The social contract is not a static concept, like the stone tablets of the law, but has evolved. There was talk of a kind of legal system between the individual and the state from the first Greek city-states. Plato mentions this kind of contract in *"Crito"* (Plato Crito) and *"The Republic"* (Plato Republic) around 375 BC.

Since then, cities have ceased to be states; they've evolved as places for life and commerce, and the social contract has evolved in parallel to become an agreement between the state and individuals. The evolution of the state as Absolute Monarchies reinforced that sense of vassalage in which citizens basically contributed taxes in exchange for protection. The entire dark Middle Ages ran through this forced relationship. As a remnant of light over a relationship of coercion and violence between state and citizen, voices appeared demanding a relationship more focused on human values. Saint Augustine (Augustine, 1958) and Saint Thomas Aquinas (Mirete, 1998) studied from Christian ethics what it meant be a good citizen and explored individual autonomy as an exercise of human dignity, which emanates from and reflects the divine dimension of our existence. This was the only question, the sphere of the divine, which could not be under the monarch's absolute control, and the only loophole through which to argue and defend certain inalienable human

J. A. Ondiviela, *Beyond Smart Cities*, https://doi.org/10.1007/978-3-030-83371-8_6

rights. With the decline of monarchic power, the relationship between individuals and the state resumed by the XVII century. A more powerful civil society based on the emerging mercantile economy and the Christian Church's humanistic support opened the debate on the terms of this relationship. Thomas Hobbes and John Locke studied and debated it notably in England by the mid XVII century and later, Jean-Jacques Rousseau in France in his 1762 book *"On the social contract,"* (Rousseau, 1762) a whole rethinking of the individual-state relationship when the French Revolution was brewing. Thomas Hobbes, wondered how a serious, predictable, reliable and stable social order could emerge from the contributions of an enormous number of isolated individuals, who do not even know each other and among whom only some skilled elites are able to agree and coordinate through tacit or explicit agreements. Hobbes's proposal, known as the social contract and, *"a mutual transferring of right"* (Hobbes, 1651), says that order is produced by the laws and authority of an almighty ruler, whose power lies in the use of coercion and the force with which he punishes lawbreakers, or to those who oppose its infallible judgment (Solarte, 2006). This force is nothing more than the capacity to exercise violence, expressed in the reduction of freedom, that each individual has ceded to the ruler (Habermas, 2006).

The fundamental problem, in our opinion, of this social contract was to consider other human beings as enemies, as competitors for survival or wealth, and to consider that the only remedy to impose a social order was a strong state that allows us to regulate life in common thanks to the fact that it has all the power to exercise against us the violence that we as individuals renounce. It is a repressive but desired state to establish and guarantee compliance with our society's norms.

From there, the concept of social contract has been associated with workers' demands, to determine the terms of the labor relations between citizen and company and the rights of workers, all of them highly influenced by the XIX century social revolutions. The end of empires at the end of the WWI by 1919, the definition of our world as made of countries after the WWII, associated with the United Nations, opens the discussion on workers' civil rights to the broad concept of human rights, and the social contract incorporates not only the rights of workers, but also their civil rights, all of this under a constant struggle for equity and demands for equality. The debate continues today, as there are still inequalities to tackle such as gender equality, poverty, ethnicity, sexuality, emigrants' rights, etc. In *"A Theory of Justice,"* John Rawls (Rawls, 1971) studies the principle of social justice as equity, as cooperation between citizens, whatever their characteristics of wealth, ethnicity, religion, etc. are, to achieve the common good of development, peace and welfare (Manyika, 2020).

As states become decentralized and cities take over the power in terms of economic and social development, we return to the starting point: the old city-state model. In a context of world peace and economic stability, it is the cities that direct the fate of humanity, and specifically the destiny, opportunities and aspirations of its citizens. The social contract with the state is marked by human rights and the Sustainable Development Goals developed by the United Nations (UN SDG).

It is time to redefine our relationship with the city. Modern cities increasingly resemble Greek city-states, overcoming the distances that social achievements have brought to our society during these 25 centuries; cities want and must redefine the terms of the contract with their citizens: *the citizenship contract.*

The citizenship contract is a virtual contract that we all implicitly hold with our city. It is the value proposition that the city makes to us and to the possible talent that wants to establish in a city. It is the list of *gives and gets* that the city offers, like a billboard of city's menu. It is a contract because the city offers us a series of services, benefits, and development opportunities, in competition and in differentiation with other cities in the world. For our part, we make our contribution to the common project of that city. This contribution has many facets, not only our taxes, but our contribution to the generation of wealth, creativity, competitiveness, values, experience, co-creation, development of a new city and impulse to achieve the goals set for the future.

It is this citizenship contract that millions of millennials are evaluating now, and what local, talented citizens weigh before deciding to emigrate looking for better opportunities.

In summary, the Citizenship contract sets the *gets*: the long list of services the city offers to you, all with different performance and possibilities to improve your life, realization and wellbeing. But also there are *gives*: when you decide to live in that city, you will get a wage for your job according to that city's salary standards (different from same job wage in other cities), and you will have to pay direct taxes and social contributions. With the final salary in your pocket, you use it to buy your preferred things, some basic, some very personal. At that purchase's moment, you pay indirect taxes, and depending on which city you live in, you have different net purchase power, i.e.: you can buy different things because of different prices. Net, depending on your city choice, at month's end, you can obtain different things in quality and quantity: that's the price you pay for living in that city. You pay also the opportunity cost because of the different cities' potential, but that's part of city services.

This is the question all those talented millennials, and not just millennials, are asking themselves today: Would it be a *good deal* for me to move to that city? That's the short evaluation of the proposed citizenship contract. For locals, it's the same evaluation but better informed, comparing that list of *gives and gets* with the known propositions from other cities. A good deal matters, but as we explained in the previous chapter, this decision is also emotional, and Magnetism components matter too.

### 6.1.1 City Profitability Definition

As we already explained in Sect. 1.1, my friend Pablo decided to emigrate for two to three years to Singapore from Madrid. In that decision, Pablo evaluated his citizenship contract with Madrid on the one hand and Singapore's proposal on the other. At that moment in his life and with his personal and family circumstances, he decided that the best deal for his professional career was to emigrate. He explained to me in detail the conditions and lifestyle expected from Singapore. *It rains a lot, but it is a very safe city, with excellent public transport, open to Westerners. I'll be able to learn how the Asian market works and add to my CV some very valuable and differentiating characteristics. The work is very good, for a very prestigious American multinational company, high salary, and low taxes. Apart from developing my employability, I am going to make a lot of money to buy a house when I return. I do not like the political local regime or how they treat those who make mistakes, but I do not plan to commit any, so I'm not worried about that. There are no problems with language, I can use my English and be understood. The food is different, but I'll get used to it. And the Real Madrid games can also be watched there.* Pablo was unknowingly explaining to me the details of the citizenship contract.

Therefore, to define the citizenship contract, we must detail the series of benefits and services the city offers us, which must be evaluable, measurable, comparable, benchmarkable and that allows consideration of city merits. We are not talking about aesthetic topics, customs or emotional components, (we have already addressed them by means of City Magnetism) we are talking about quantifiable, rational benefits. We are not talking about emotions, but about a contract. This will be the list of performance indicators to evaluate and where we group into 10 areas all the quantifiable services that the city delivers us. We are measuring the areas of a complete SmartCity Plan as we saw in its different definitions/proposed areas in Sect. 3.2. These 10 areas will be:

- DIGITAL GOVERNMENT: Democratic, efficient, transparent, participatory, digitalized city Government. Digital government-as-a-Service.
- EDUCATION . Lifelong Training: Quality Business Schools, Training and Development on the job.
- EMPLOYABILITY: Talent Demand
- CONNECTIVITY: Internet infrastructure. 4G/5G Deployment
- HEALTHCARE/SOCIAL SERVICES
- ENVIRONMENTAL SUSTAINABILITY: Water, Energy efficiency. Air quality. Carbon emissions reduction, Carbon Neutral Plans. Circular City.
- CULTURE-TOURISM: Culture as a City Service, not as customs/traditions, again, not emotions, but valuable services.
- URBAN MOBILITY: Traffic. Public Transportation. Mobility as a Service.
- URBAN PLANNING: Urbanism as a City Service. Design and functionality.
- SAFETY: Physical and Virtual Safety.

These are the services that I obtain from the City. Then, I have to balance or weigh them with the cost of living in that city, or in other words, the final net purchasing power (the amount of things that I could buy with my final salary after taxes) that I will get because of doing my job/work or professional activity, after deducting the local taxes and paying the cost of life. Then City Profitability (Yield) will take both concepts: city services compared to cost of living, in other words:

SERVICES to obtain from City / COST OF LIVING in that City.

It is not a simple division, it is not exactly the amount or quality of services I receive divided by the price I pay for them, as if it were a transaction. As we have seen, the *price* that I pay is what I could buy at the end of the month due to my salary, after taxes and according to the cost of living in that city. Therefore, it is about comparing what I get from the city with what I get for my professional activity because I develop it in *that* city. It is, accordingly, more a multiplication of two positive quantities. The higher the result, the more appealing the option is of living in that city. We speak of an objective assessment, the same one that so many talented citizens are considering nowadays when deciding to move or stay. In fact, one of this research objectives is to help them make that decision better-informed, and with the appropriate data.

Nordic countries are traditionally offering the highest quality of city services. True, but also the cost of living there is among the highest. It is easy to drink a very good wine if we pay a lot of money for it. The difficult thing is to drink an excellent wine for an affordable price. You have to know a little about the world of wine, the producers, the market and access authentic unknown jewels, which have not yet been exaggeratedly valued by experts and which keep a low price.

Translated to the cities, it is about offering the best possible set of services at the smallest citizen expense. All Cities want to offer the best set of Services, of course, BUT at what cost for citizens? The best services most times mean the biggest contributions from citizens, so the City Director should try to wisely invest the resources to maximize this efficiency. All cities are different, and start from different baselines; prioritization, comparison with others is necessary, deciding where, from the wide list of potential areas, the next invested dollar will make the biggest impact.

Therefore, creating the most effective plan, with the lowest cost, prioritizing the preferences of citizens and always putting them at the center is a true work/art of financial and social engineering. All this with a future plan, with a strategy, fulfilling the promises and explaining the investments and objectives achieved with transparency.

For this reason, this study also aims to help our mayors and city directors to assess where they are in the global competition with their city, where the cities in their same cluster are, which areas they are in an advanced position to take advantage of, and in which they are lagging behind and urgently need investment.

We are not talking about basic infrastructure services or basic problems to access utilities such as water or energy, or cities with serious security problems. As we defined in Chap. 4, we have ruled out cities where living poses a risk to our health and physical integrity. Those cities must first fix the basics, in order to compete in the global landscape of attractive cities. We are talking about advanced, modern services always backed by a strong technological component.

The city must also balance investments towards its citizens with investments to create an attractive city for potential new outsiders, just as a company must balance its marketing investments between maintaining and retaining its current customers, (loyalty programs) while attracting new ones.

It is also very important to balance the services offered by the city with the tax burden. In some cities we are reaching a point of *capitalist-communism*, where the sum of total taxes is close to 100%. It is okay to give the citizen all the services that we can, but it comes to a point where the citizen asks to pay less, to have more money in their pocket and to allow to decide themselves, not always the city/country, in which services they will use the resources. We already studied it in Chap. 2, but we'll simply add here that when direct taxes are greater than 50%, then citizens begin to think about their excessive contribution and their lack of freedom when deciding what they use their salary for. It's about valuing *my* things, the things I can buy with what I have left after paying all my taxes: my car, my house, my leisure, my hobbies, my cultural services, etc.

We are not talking, therefore, about forced migrations due to human calamities, wars or natural disasters, but of voluntary movements with the noble purpose of simply seeking the best place for personal and professional development.

As an example of these talent migrations, let's look at Fig. 6.1, which shows the internal migrations within the European Union from the last economic crisis in 2012 to 2017. Thousands of citizens, especially qualified young people, took advantage of the single unified labor market to assess and decide their vital destiny within Europe. The ease of getting around, cheap mobility, to *go back home for Christmas*, but also to be able to develop their profession, their talent and access a decent, well-paid job and a new life in a new city made this decision easier.

It is important to note the strong impact in many small and medium-sized, non-capital cities, which have been losing population in recent decades in what is called urban contraction. This is also a consequence of global competition for being attractive to talent. These cities, if they are not located close to other large ones, have great disadvantages in the quality and quantity of services they can offer, simply because of their size, so they compete poorly. As examples, to have a well-connected airport you must hold several million people in the metropolitan area, same as supporting an Opera house. This phenomenon generally impacts the entire European Union and, in particular, eastern and southern European countries.

The Eastern countries turned towards their natural entry door in the heart of Europe, Vienna, from the South. From the North, the Nordic countries received a strong arrival of talent, especially from the Baltic countries. Spain and Portugal observed heavy talent losses to the Center/North Europe. France and Italy experienced a concentration from small cities into few large cities, with enormous attractiveness and rich metropolitan areas.

## 6.2   City Services Performance

We are going to describe our 140 cities according to their performance in this group of 10 city service areas. It is very important to highlight that we will leave the weight assigned to each group to the info/tool user, so we are not creating another absolute ranking. Why? Because each citizen, depending on their personal situation, age,

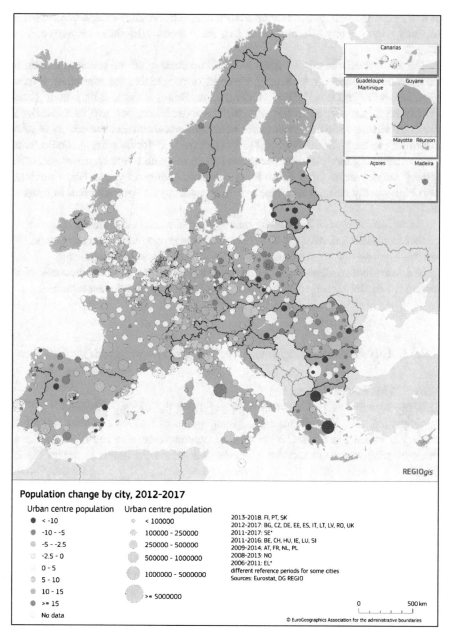

**Fig. 6.1** Impact of recent 2012 economic crisis in EU migrations. (Eurostat, 2018)

dependencies of children or the elderly, will assign greater or lesser importance to each of them. For example, the same single person preparing to explore the world will give much importance to Employability and Education, while that same person at retirement age will give more importance to Health/Social Services. We are going to study what the city offers us in each of these areas. Why these 10 areas and no others?

For any citizen, the city attractiveness will be made of all the elements that bring them well-being and all the family members or people that are important to them (Sinkene & Kromalcas, 2010). According to Braun (Braun, 2008), it is about evaluating things related to the city, such as its services, but also its educational facilities, leisure or other services such as cultural ones, and also the quality of jobs. According to Berg (Berg et al., 1999), an attractive city for its citizens should focus on providing a good, pleasant, accessible, clean and safe living environment; offer quality employment; good educational services; high-quality healthcare services; also high-quality cultural services; excellent security; and pay attention to religion and arts.

As we saw in Sect. 3.2, there are many different models, definitions and components of a perfect SmartCity. We can say that there is one model for each author, but we can also say that most of them share 80–90% of the same components.

We have chosen these 10 because they integrate all of them, and because when testing the model with many cities, it appears to include all relevant aspects.

## 6.2.1   City Services Performance: Digital Government

### Why Is This Proxy Relevant?

One of the services that we must demand from the city government is citizen participation; that is, collaborating, giving opinions and co-deciding the city's destiny between elections. To do this, to communicate and learn what citizens think or wish, we must use the language and the media they use today: digital media. We should talk to digital citizens and even more, if we are thinking about attracting talent, which will surely use these communication technologies by default. We are considering a Digital government-as-a-Service, that is, how effective is this participation mechanism.

Digital participation can achieve all kinds of interaction, often in the form of ideas, opinions, points of view, proposals or simply votes, which allow citizens to influence the city's decisions. That is why the success of digital participation requires a wide, permanent, open and well-oriented approach to what can be done in the city, taking into account the citizens knowledge and skills (we cannot consult technical questions, as only a minority would be qualified enough to answer, or naive basic issues, as we cannot treat citizens as idiots). If we ask too much, they can think we don't know how to make decisions; if we ask too few, then we are not counting on them. Again, a balance is advisable.

The great contribution and the base for digital democracy in a city through a participation platform is based on the principle of collective intelligence (Citizenlab, 2019). That is, it is assumed that the sum of ideas and arguments from all (or from a strong participation) citizens will always be more important and appropriate to the city's destiny than the ideas from a very limited number of directors or decision makers, always, we repeat, that we ensure a series of guarantees, good mechanisms and a very wide participation, avoiding the concept of the *same 10 activists shouting all day on the social networks*. It is a permanent democracy, not a single connection every four years. It can be adapted to a general city theme, or to a particular neighborhood or to a specific moment, or just to value an interesting idea.

Benefits:

- We can listen to a wider and more diverse audience, at a much lower cost than other methods, and in a short period of time. Some forms of participation can be recurring and permanent.
- Using participation will give more public support for our decisions. Building consensus will justify complicated decisions and citizens will accept these difficult issues as their own.
- Greater efficiency and responsiveness. We can pulse the citizenship feeling in a very short time, obtaining very valuable information, and reducing the error risk or receiving a strong pushback.
- Obviously, we improve the quality of decision-making and administrative services in general. It is a boost for administrative innovation.
- Avoid the worst-case scenario of confrontation (Creighton, 2017). We can anticipate and avoid it, saving us many annoyances, citizens' disconnection and loss of prestige. Thus, we will make controversial decisions measuring risk and impact beforehand.
- Maintain credibility and legitimacy. Promote the feeling of closeness, of empathy.
   Development of civil society by empowering citizens. Promote a sense of belonging and co-creation.
- Anticipation of citizens' concerns. If we analyze what they tell us and the data we already have, then we can predict reactions and future demands for services, offering a proactive administration.

Apart from citizens' digital participation, the city government itself must be digital and offer its services online to citizens. It is the other way, from the administration to the citizen, offering the services in an easy, intuitive, personalized digital format, using the same communication mechanisms that citizens use daily (social networks, instant messaging, chats, etc.). We must therefore measure to what extent city management uses technology internally, and how accessible the services offered are online.

**How to Measure It?**

To measure online administration services, we will take the Online Service Index (OSI) developed by UNITED NATIONS E-GOVERNMENT SURVEY 2018 (United Nations, 2018a).

The study was carried out in 193 UN member states and evaluates a series of benefits offered as online services, including multi-channel services, mobile services, and opendata. Electronic participation, online applications use, the digital divide, and others related to the use of ICTs in public services are also measured. The Online Service Index is a component for the very well-known E-Government Development Index (EGDI).

Even more important than offering public services online is to get citizens use them. To measure the actual and effective use that citizens make of these services, we will use the Electronic Participation Index. The Electronic Participation Index (EPI) is an addendum to the United Nations Electronic eGovernment Survey. Citizen participation is the key for a socially inclusive government because it allows all citizens to be co-participants in management, without differences and without barriers. Participation improves social and individual well-being by fostering team building, collaboration and community awareness. To help in this participation, the online service feature makes these electronic services especially suitable, because of their ease of use and their all-included reach.

This index evaluates all the ways of electronic interaction: on the one hand, communication from the government to citizens in electronic format, (*electronic information exchange*) proactively providing public information without prior request; on the other hand, interaction with citizens, (*electronic consultation*) involving citizens in deliberations or matters of their concern; and finally the direct participation of citizens in decision-making processes (*electronic decision-making*) with the appropriate tools (United Nations, 2018b).

We have already studied the provisioning of online services and the use that citizens make of them, but do we really enjoy an electronic administration? We must study the use of digital technologies within the city administration. To face this, we will use the indicator *Digitalization of Government*, within the "EasyParkGroup SmartCity Index 2019" (Easy Park Group, 2019). This index is one of the most comprehensive at the time of studying benefits of SmartCities, and gives us information about cities, not only at country level like the previous ones. This index is based on the "Digital City Rank" (Bloom Consulting, 2017) and on measuring the use and traffic generated by the cities' websites as a percentage of their total population.

When evaluating these three areas, we consider that e-Participation is the most relevant as a Service to attract & retain talent because it measures the level of civil engagement and government co-participation in that city. It is a bottom-up metric and observes citizen involvement in the city management. Because of that, we assign it half relevance, or a 50% weight. How digital the city government is and the availability of online services are also very important but measured the other way (top-down); so, we split the other half or 50% weight among them (25% each, Online Service Index and Digitalization of Government).

(See Appendix VII for City Profitability. Services. Digital Government Ranking)

## 6.2.2   City Services Performance: Education. Lifelong Training

### Why Is This Proxy Relevant?

With this indicator we cover the area of Education services. It is not about evaluating the basic education services available in the city or the status of the educational system. We talk about the attractiveness for talent, and therefore, we assume that talented citizens do not need basic educational services, but rather advanced, complementary, postgraduate services and opportunities for development and continuous training on the job, offered and facilitated by the company itself. This will be an important attraction for talent, keep updating and training in new disciplines and technologies as they become available.

### How to Measure It?

To measure these items, we go back to INSEAD Global Talent Competitiveness Index (GTCI) (2017) (Lanvin & Monteiro, 2020a) where we can find the appropriate information called Lifelong Learning. This concept measures the postgraduate, on-the-job training available for talented citizens in the form of attending additional training from business or management schools, or on-the-job training facilitated by the company, helping the employee development.

We will use three available indicators for Lifelong Learning:

Quality of management/Business schools.

This indicator is based on the "World Economic Forum Executive Opinion Survey" (World Economic Forum, 2018) (EOS) as a complementary work to reinforce The Global Competitiveness Report.

It measures the quantity and perceived quality of the available business and management schools. It is an important fact to attract talent, especially those looking for a first job and wanting to improve their skills with an additional master's degree or other postgraduate training.

Prevalence of training in companies.

The proportion of companies that offer formal training to their employees, either directly, co-financed or at least, facilitated. We measured the percentage of total companies by 2019. It is based on the Enterprise Survey that is carried out at the company level by the World Bank Business Analysis Unit (World Bank, 2020a). Over 135,000 interviews in 139 countries are analyzed.

Employee development.

Once again, in the "World Economic Forum's Executive Opinion Survey" (World Economic Forum, 2018) (EOS), it asks about how much and how companies invest in employee training and development. Although it is something that every HR department should do, there are different degrees and levels of investment. For young talent, this is an important indicator when developing a promising career.

Just as INSEAD Global Talent Competitiveness Index does for calculating the Lifelong Training indicators, we assign the same weight to all three reports.

(See Appendix VII for City Profitability. Services. Education. Lifelong Training)

### 6.2.3  City Services Performance: Employability

**Why Is This Proxy Relevant?**
Employability is one of the fundamental elements in making a city attractive for talent. Many times, we think that it is the only one, and that people move mainly due to labor issues. This main motivator decreases as the new generations consider work as an important, but not definitive driver, and the other components gain weight. On the other hand, companies no longer decide where to set up or open new offices without considering the availability of abundant local talent as a critical decision-making criterion. That is, companies are looking for talent, while a few years ago it was the other way around.

In any case, the question of employability remains a fundamental attractive component for any city. Citizens will stay or think twice about emigrating if employment is good and abundant, and the potential new citizens need their target cities to have good employability to develop their potential, their professional career and maximize their possibilities.

**How to Measure It?**
With hundreds of millions of CVs and companies' jobs offering, LinkedIn platform is the largest employability tool in the world.

Within this platform, we use the LinkedIn Talent insights application, Talent Pool Report (Linkedin, 2020) to analyze the employability of each of our studied 140 cities (metropolitan areas). In this way, we will investigate if they had a low, medium, high or very-high hiring demand during the last year. This data comes from each area's actual count of published job offers compared to its population. We will add as an additional reference whether the number of qualified professionals has grown during this past year. This data indicates the gain or loss in talent that this metropolitan area is experiencing.

With these two parameters, we will assign a score according to the Table 6.1.

We see how the base parameter is the Hiring Demand and the Growth in Talent has been added as an additional +1, with which we obtain a range from 0 to 7 for our cities.

We are going to make two queries varying the job function/matching professionals:

Query 1: We use all types of functions for any professionals. We are analyzing 122,310,193 professionals in our 140 metropolitan areas.

**Table 6.1**  Talent flow scoring as per LinkedIn Talent Pool Report data

| Hiring demand | Growth in talent-professionals / y | Score |
|---|---|---|
| Low | Negative | 0 |
| Low | Positive | 1 |
| Moderate | Negative | 2 |
| Moderate | Positive | 3 |
| High | Negative | 4 |
| High | Positive | 5 |
| Very High | Negative | 6 |
| Very High | Positive | 7 |

All available Functions:

Operations, Business Development, Sales, Education, Engineering, Information Technology, Administrative, Healthcare Services, Arts and Design, Finance, Support, Media and Communication, Accounting, Marketing, Community and Social Services, and Human Resources.

Query 2: We restrict the type of jobs/matching professionals, and eliminate those functions that the approaching robotization could impact/eliminate (Fourth Industrial Revolution). We take only the eight types more associated to creativity or creative jobs as defined by Prof. Florida. (see previous multiple references).

Only the top eight very creative functions: Business Development, Sales, Engineering, Information Technology, Healthcare Services, Arts and Design, Media and Communication, and Marketing.

We have eliminated almost half of the professionals and now we have 68,412,947 analyzed professionals.

We do not want to take only Query 2 as it is clear that the effects of robotization won't be as dramatic as some predict. Our perspective is that all humans are creative by DNA, what are not creative are many of our jobs; therefore, it is expected that many jobs will be replaced by others with a higher creativity component and that cannot be easily done by robots, and job losses won't be so high, if any. Therefore, we add (we value both queries at 50%) and we will have a ranking of cities scoring from 0 to 14.

If we look at the available studies on employability, then we find that the most complete one is the INSEAD Global Talent Competitiveness Index (GTCI) (2017) (Lanvin & Monteiro, 2020b). After analyzing the job offer in cities, we will study the employability of citizens as a result of living in that city. The GTCI, within its Output section, Vocational & Technical Skills, studies the employability of the city from the perspective of its citizens. It studies how the city has developed talent and how that talent is associated with the job opportunity.

To address this topic, the GTCI uses four concepts:

All four are based on data obtained from the Executive Opinion Survey (EOS) of the World Economic Forum conducted as a supplement to The Global Competitiveness Report (World Economic Forum, 2018).

- Ease of finding qualified employees. To what extent do companies easily find people with the skills they need?
- Adequacy of the educational system for the economy. Is the education system adequate for the needs of a competitive economy?
- Compatibility of skills and abilities developed with secondary education. Are graduate students at this level prepared to respond to the needs that companies require?
- Compatibility of skills and abilities developed with tertiary education. Are graduate students at this level prepared to respond to the needs that companies require?

With these four indicators, GTCI calculates the average and reports it as Employability. So, Employability shows as balance between Hiring Demand and Citizen qualification to match that demand.

For that reason, we equally weigh both sources of information, LinkedIn Talent Hiring Demand and Employability.

(See Appendix VI for City Profitability. Services. Employability Ranking)

## 6.2.4  City Services Performance: Connected City

### Why Is This Proxy Relevant?

The connectivity possibilities from communication networks are an essential technological component in the city's development. In the same way that the construction of streets and highways facilitated the development of transport and commerce, as well as the mobility of people and then, their ideas, creations and inventions, turning urban mobility into the bloodstream's city, now, in the digital age, those digital highways are our digital communication networks. We could compare those network of cables, fiber optics and wireless connections as the city's nervous system, through which signals are sent: the city's data, what the city feels, thinks, what happens. The citizens are also digital and are permanently connected to that network with multiple devices, especially with their smartphones, as the fundamental doors/switches that turn the digital world into analog realities; bits into sounds, images, ideas, emotions, feelings and vice versa.

This network quality conditions the city's development, creativity and competitiveness, attractiveness for people and for companies. Without a good connection, there are no possibilities to communicate with the world, to compete, to make yourself known.

Speaking with political leaders in rural areas, we came to the conclusion that without good Internet bandwidth there is no future for these areas. This is a radical concern. Without good bandwidth they have no chance of development, so this question is posed as a sine qua non.

It is clear that a talented citizen will evaluate the communication and connectivity possibilities of a city before deciding on it. We are going to model them.

**How to Measure It?**

First, let's evaluate Connectivity Services from a user point of view, from the individual received performance.

So, first, let's evaluate the mobile connection performance. We are assessing 4G LTE knowing that 5G is here and we'll soon replace this term when 5G deployments can be quantified. We'll use the "EasyParkGroup SmartCity Index 2019" (Easy Park Group, 2019) taking the 4G LTE Indicator. It measures the *average 4G download speed (in Mbps)*, adjusted to each city's internet speed. Data obtained from speed test.

Next relevant data will be the average City Internet speed (wired). To obtain them, we'll use the INSEAD Global Talent Competitiveness Index (GTCI) (2017) (Lanvin & Monteiro, 2020c) applied to cities, or the Global Cities Talent Competitiveness Index (GCTCI), taking the Internet Speed indicator, which measures it in Mbps, using data from Nomad List.

One of most appreciated city services by citizens and visitors is the availability and connectivity from city Wi-Fi Hotspots. These connectivity points foster communication, business, trading and continuous Internet access at better speeds than the 4G network. In the near future, 5G deployment will make them irrelevant because of its speed, or maybe not, if they provide improved bandwidth for free. Today, a city with a large network of high quality Wi-Fi hotspots is a good indicator of a modern, advanced city taking care of its citizens and visitors and providing good connectivity to help them be successful in their lives wherever they are. To measure this, we'll use again "EasyParkGroup SmartCity Index 2019" taking the Wi-Fi Hotspots indicator (it measures free Wi-Fi hotspots using data from Online Wi-Fi databases and adjusting in every case to the city area.

So far, we have measured the user experience, using their smartphone, computer-connected wireless or directly wired, a home or office or at public space.

To evaluate the overall city Connectivity infrastructure, we reinforce this analysis with the whole city ICT (Internet/Information Communication Technologies) infrastructure info. We come back to the INSEAD Global Talent Competitiveness Index (GTCI) (2017) (Lanvin & Monteiro, 2020d) to take this ICT Infrastructure indicator. The ICT access Index (2017) measures the actual use and penetration of new communication technologies in a city. It is a composite indicator that adds five equally weighted ICT components: 1 Fixed telephone lines/100 inhabitants, 2. Mobile phone lines/100 inhabitants, 3. International Internet bandwidth (bit/s) per user, 4. Percentage of households with an available personal computer, 5. Percentage of households with cable internet access. The information comes from the ITU ICT Development Index (IDI) report (International Telecommunication Union, 2017).

In then model, the first three (4G LTE, Internet Speed, WIFI Hotspots) measure the individual user experience and will take 20% weight each, and the last one (ICT

Infrastructure) evaluates the collective use of these resources, so we give it double weight, or 40%.

(See Appendix VII for City Profitability. Services. Connectivity Ranking)

## 6.2.5   City Services' Performance: Health/Social Services

### Why Is This Proxy Relevant?

It is an obvious question for anyone to think about the healthcare/social services that are available in a city before considering it as a permanent destination. Health and associated services are obviously a fundamental question to decide even on few days' tourist trips. Depending on our family situation, and dependence on children and/or elder adults, this issue becomes more or less fundamental.

But the concept of Healthy city is wider, not just limited to healthcare services available, but the creation of city conditions that allow healthier human conditions. This may include building a park for citizens to do some exercise or connecting existing parks in a longer circuit (we saw that in Barcelona's future planning). These initiatives should foster healthier habits and help others (the city is social by essence) to stay or improve healthy conditions.

In words from UN World Health Organization, (WHO):

*A healthy city is one that is continually creating and improving those physical and social environments and expanding those community resources which enable people to mutually support each other in performing all the functions of life and developing to their maximum potential* (World Health Organization, 1998).

So, we should think about that physical, social and phycological conditions that allow humans to improve their health.

To go deeper, the WHO also suggests a checklist for City managers to analyze their City plans in order to improve City healthiness (World Health Organization, 2020). Thus, a healthy city must provide:

Environment and ecosystem issues:

- a safe and clean (and healthy?) physical environment, with high quality infrastructure (including housing), within a sustainable ecosystem.

Socioeconomic issues:

- a strong, inclusive and supportive community. Intense social contact, interaction and communication.
- a high degree of participation and control of public decisions, and especially those that impact their health and well-being.
- have basic needs (such as food, water, energy, housing, security and work) satisfied for all citizens.
- a powerful, balanced and innovative economy.

- respect for cultural heritage, and for the city's inhabitants' culture and other groups.

Health issues per se:

- an excellent level of health services accessible and affordable to all.
- a high status of health in general, with low levels of disease.

The "EU Urban Manifesto for New Urbanity" (EU Urban Charter II, 2008a) also explains the principles for Health in towns, highlighting the fact that the city must ensure good health for all citizens, as well as a reliable supply of goods that ensure basic needs, encourage healthy community initiatives and participation, and collaborate internationally in programs dedicated to it.

We have already studied and covered in the City Magnetism discussion (Chap. 5), all the social, economic and psychological conditions that the city offers, including the multiple factors that impact physical and mental health. We are going to concentrate in this city services' section on those that are properly Healthcare/Social Services.

Social services and grants are very popular and broad concepts. They are provided by all governments (central, regional and local), even sometimes with overlaps and duplications between them. We can say that a social service is any monetary or assistance aid that a citizen receives due to an existing particular condition of need, vulnerability, inequity or inequality, and that is not provided within a healthcare building or institution (pharmacy, clinic, hospital, ambulatory, etc.). When you receive this assistance in one of these buildings, then you are a healthcare system patient, while if you receive any help at home then it is a social service. There are many, from unemployment and social security benefits, (which are usually provided by the state) to any kind of help for dependency situations, which may be given by the regional or other government, to receiving a caregiver at home to monitor situations of mild dementia or simply unwanted loneliness, usually provided by the city.

In this study, for simplicity, and honestly, in the absence of better detailed data, we will study the whole set of social benefits.

**How to Measure It?**

We are measuring social spending as a total expenditure of Social Services as a percentage of GDP/capita. This OECD indicator (OECD, 2020a) includes all benefits including cash, direct provision in kind of goods and services, and tax exemptions for social purposes. Benefits may be directed at the unemployed, low-income households, the sick, the elderly, the disabled, or youth and must meet certain conditions and circumstances. To be considered social, programs must include the redistribution of resources and the search for social equity. Total net social spending includes both public and private spending.

As an indicator in between Social Services and Healthcare, Life Expectancy offers us a good approach about city quality of life, and also shows the aging population problem described in Chap. 2.

We will use UN Data measuring Life Expectancy at age 60, (years) for both sexes, from 2012 (UN DATA, 2012).

To measure pure Healthcare services, we'll use two indicators:

First, we take the INSEAD Global Talent Competitiveness Index, (GTCI) (2017) (Lanvin & Monteiro, 2020e) measuring the number of doctors per 1000 inhabitants or *Physician Density*. Thus, this 2016 updated indicator reports the number of doctors, including generalists and specialists. Data comes from these different sources: The World Bank, World Development Indicators (World Bank, 2020b) based on World Health Organization, OECD, Global Atlas of the Health Workforce and country data.

Second, we will measure the total public health expenditure to understand the quality of services provided as a percentage of GDP. The best source for this will be the World Health Organization – Global Health Expenditure Database (World Health Organization, 2017), providing 2017 information for 190 countries. We take (GGHED or Domestic Public Health Expenditure as a percentage of GDP) 2017.

To assign weights, we consider two main areas: Social Services and Healthcare, with a bridge topic in between: Life Expectancy.

So, we assign 40% to Social Expenditure, 40% to Healthcare (split in 20% for each topic: Number of Physicians and Public Health Expenditure) and another 20% to Life Expectancy as a generic, all-connected indicator.

(See Appendix VII for City Profitability. Services. Health/Social Services ranking)

## 6.2.6   City Services' Performance: Environmental Sustainability

### Why Is This Proxy Relevant?
The concept of sustainable city includes three facets: Social, economic and environmental sustainability (Akande et al., 2019).

The United Nations defines an intelligent and sustainable city as one that uses new technologies and other means to achieve the highest levels of well-being, quality of life, efficiency in city operations and economic competitiveness, thinking about the present but especially about the future, in the sense of guaranteeing these optimal conditions from the economy, social development and the environment (CEPE, 2015).

The city's social and economic sustainability was studied in the previous chapter within the concept of City Magnetism as part of the City Dynamism, its competitiveness, and its equity and equality. They are city components that result from a long process of investment and proper development, and mark the city from the point of view of its attractiveness. In this chapter we talk about city performance, and we

**Fig. 6.2** UN Sustainable
Development Goals. Goal
11. (United Nations
Development Programme,
2020)

will focus on the services it offers from the point of view of environmental sustainability.

The concept of environmental sustainability was first introduced into urban development and planning in the early 1990s. It emerged from an understanding of the risks that uncontrolled urban development poses to the environment and that can lead to a future full of dangers and threats (Bibri & Krogstie, 2017).

We can also find this concept from the first UN definition (UN, 1987) about the sustainable city development as one that meets the needs of the present without compromising the future of later generations when they must face the same challenges. Regarding this development, and specifically in environmental sustainability, factors such as anti-pollution policies, support for the green buildings construction and adaptation, alternatives for the use of renewable energy, efficient management of water and energy consumption, the adequate treatment of waste and actions that generally combat climate change's worsening and potential impacts are essential to this long-term objective of sustainability for cities.

The United Nations, within its famous 17 Sustainable Development Goals, dedicates a special one to cities and communities (see Fig. 6.2). It is about cities fulfilling their mission as human spaces that facilitate prosperity by creating professional and economic opportunities, in a resilient societal environment, but ensuring access to decent housing, effective public transportation, respectful management of green public spaces, and fostering a participatory and inclusive urban planning and management.

Although we already explained in detail the Environmental Sustainability challenge in Sect. 2.6, we should add that in the global context of awareness about climate change and respect for the environment, cities face the challenge of finding the right balance between economic development and environmental sustainability.

Today, nothing can be thought, built or developed anymore without taking into account its present and future impact on the ecosystem. There are many dimensions to consider when designing for environmentally sustainable urban planning, such as preserving heritage, using non-polluting or aggressive technologies, ensuring the social impact of these plans, promoting urban mobility without impacting the environment and the environmental relationship with the exterior and other communities (Goi, 2017).

The study made by The Economist Intelligence Unit (EIU) in 2012, called "The Green City Index" (Economist Intelligence Unit and Siemens, 2012), included the multiple components we must consider when analyzing how sustainable a city is for the environment. It analyzes $CO_2$ Emissions, Energy use, Building's energy efficiency, Transport (green and reduction of private), Waste and land use (Circular City), Water use, Air Quality and Environmental Governance (Planning, Management, Participation) with 3–4 main parameters each.

The EU stresses this topic in its principles for a city that respects the environment and nature. Those principles set that city authorities should have the responsibility to manage energy resources in a coherent and rational way, prevent pollution, protect nature and green spaces and understand that the respect for nature is a determining factor in the sense of community and pride in its development (European Urban Charter II, 2008b).

A final reflection: the concept of ecology and environmental sustainability becomes one of the three fundamental pillars in the discourse on SmartCities with the horizon set out in the 2030 goals. The ideas presented cover the entire spectrum. On the one hand, an absolutely *organic* city where everything that is not natural, sustainable, circular, with zero environmental impact is despised as dirty and bad. What are the implications of a strictly ecological city where economic development takes a back seat, thus compromising financing for the main objective..?

At the other extreme, we find a *survival* city, where achieving a minimum quality of life overcomes thinking about the future of the environmental impact that is being caused. It is thought that ecology is a *rich-people* thing without realizing that neglecting the city environment will make it uninhabitable, unhealthy and will drive away talent and investment, turning it into a huge and uncontrolled dump. It's like shooting yourself in the foot. . .

As in most things in life, virtue is in the middle ground, in setting a goal of a livable city, which combines the objectives of environmental sustainability with those already discussed of social and economic sustainability.

**How to Measure It?**

There are many indicators on cities' use of energy, water, green spaces, clean transport, etc. As we saw, the EUI Green Cities Index includes a fairly complete study of the components of environmental sustainability, but the details by city is only available for some European cities, and it has not been updated since 2012, so we cannot use it.

We will base the analysis on two important, comprehensive and highly regarded studies: the IESE Cities in Motion and the ARCADIS Sustainable Cities Index.

The IESE Cities in Motion's chapter on Environmental Indicators (Berrone & Ricart, 2019a) analyzes this area by using several aggregated indicators about $CO_2$ and methane emissions and other air quality gases conditions, Environmental performance Index (EPI), Water access and resources, waste management and city future global warming impact assessment.

We want to highlight this study because apart from the necessary technical measurements, it addresses the current city's ecosystem status with the Yale University Environmental Performance Index study (EPI). It is relevant because we may be taking important measures, but if our ecosystem is already very degraded, we must also regenerate it. It is not just about buying electric buses, cleaning the city and hiding all what we do not want anyone to see in the surroundings; we must evaluate how our ecosystem is doing as a whole. It is also important to add the future impact that climate change will have on the city.

The 2018 Arcadis Sustainable Cities Index studies the sustainability in its three dimensions: Social (they label it People); Economic (they label it Profit); and Environmental (they label it Planet). We will take this latest, Environmental or *Planet* Sustainability as another comprehensive approach to our topic.

The Arcadis Index (Arcadis, 2018) incorporates 11 areas, giving greater weight to the five fundamental ones (energy, air pollution, greenhouse gas emissions, waste and water management). It is relevant to highlight the analysis made of the use of electric vehicles and bicycles, very appropriate in this term. The actions and facilities for carbon capture and storage are also studied, something very novel when most cities are still considering how to reduce emissions. In other words, they look at the objective of carbon-negative when most look at the objective of carbon-neutral. The characteristics of exposure to natural disasters and their monitoring are also added, although with little weight. We believe that this characteristic is inherent to the city due to its geographic location, although its monitoring, prevention and resilience are also important public environmental services.

Both studies (Sustainable City Index by ARCADIS and Environment Ranking by IESE Cities in Motion) are very relevant and comprehensive. We are surprised by finding some main differences in some cities from both approaches, so, to avoid biases and to aggregate all available knowledge, the best approach is to give them the same weight.

(See Appendix VII for City Profitability. Services. Environmental Sustainability Ranking)

## 6.2.7   City Services' Performance: Culture/Tourism

### Why Is This Proxy Relevant?

The concept of Culture is very present in all of this analysis because it is included in many facets and is intimately linked with the city's human activity. We already studied in Chap. 5 the contribution of Culture to City Magnetism from its history, cultural events, museums, etc. We also studied the education services that the city provides to generate, retain and attract talent. We are now going to study culture as a semi-permanent service that the city offers its citizens. It is not a static offer derived from the existence of important cultural elements like UNESCO heritage places (we have already studied this in the City Identity), but rather from the city's dedication to arts, entertainment and recreation. These activities have, in many cities, a strong association to service tourism. Furthermore, the tourism received by most of the studied major cities is fundamentally cultural tourism; that is, they are not cities to go for a beach or resort vacation, but cities to discover, walk around and find cultural attractions. Therefore, the organization of a cultural proposal for the city's inhabitants is also a touristic attraction for its visitors. So, we merge both concepts in this section.

We need to understand that creative talent is also artistic, and all those artists should ask themselves whether that city is a good destination to help them to fully develop their genius because the city recognizes, appreciates and invests in culture. It's easy to find in the biography of the most well-known artists many city movements, just because they were looking for the best city to work in and express their creativity. Many artistic and cultural movements are associated with the city which led them like Bolognese School, Paris Academia, Athens, Florence, Venice schools, Amsterdam Impressionism, Düsseldorf School, Hague School, Heidelberg School, Lyon School, Norwich School, Vienna Secession, Berliner Sezession, Camden Town Group, Gothenburg Colorists, Neue Künstlervereinigung München, Ecole de Paris, Scuola Romana, Chicago Imagists and many more.

We sincerely believe that the robotization brought about by the Fourth Industrial Revolution will mean a special appreciation for everything that is intrinsically human, including artistic creations. We believe that we will experience a cultural renaissance again. We must be dreamers though, because data shows employment in the arts, entertainment and the recreation sector is falling in Europe. The 2008 economic crisis brought bad consequences for professionals in the cultural area, where unemployment increased to 22.4% (Startup Europe Awards, 2020).

We should also say that the cultural proposal has neither the appropriate digital format nor the speed of exposure that the digital age has accustomed us to. No millennial will gladly face the reading of Homer's Iliad, studying certain concepts of Greek to understand its musicality and beauty; it is simply too much effort and time for the expected aesthetic emotion. However, many would like to watch a summary of no more than an hour, or a movie (that is, something like the Troy (Petersen, 2004) movie, but this time true to the original text). Therefore, we are not insensitive to beauty, passion, feeling, love or human suffering, the only problem is that we have become accustomed to a different format, the digital one, where emotions run fast.

The *EU Urban Manifesto for New Urbanity* (EU Urban Charter II, 2008c) again explains the principles for Culture in towns, highlighting that city must ensure all citizens the right to access culture. Culture is a strong economic and social development contributor. Culture also promotes exchange and respect for all different communities and foreign people inside our city. Culture diversity encourages innovation. Finally, cultural tourism has a positive impact on the local economy.

**How to Measure It?**

To measure cultural services, we could find a long list of indicators such as the number of theaters, museums, festivals, exhibition halls, art shops, activities of all kinds, etc. We have found one that serves to unify and value the city's appreciation for culture and its offer of cultural services. The study is from the World Cities Cultural Forum. Global leadership on culture in cities provides us with more than 70 cultural city indicators. We will use the percentage of professionals dedicated to cultural activities in the categories of arts, entertainment and recreation (World Cities Cultural Forum, 2020). That way, the greater the percentage of professionals dedicated to culture, the higher appreciation and official attention it deserves, making the city more attractive from the Cultural Services' and cultural jobs' points of view.

To analyze the city's tourist services or the attractions for cultural tourism, we must understand how many tourists they attract. It is not easy to distinguish which visitors are tourists and which are simply business travelers. A good approach will be the number of international visitors. Thus, we use the Top 100 City Destinations 2019 Edition by Euromonitor. This study includes some 400 cities and evaluates arrivals in thousands/ year (Yasmeen, 2019).

As we only want to evaluate cultural tourism, we assume the excess in the data from international business travelers could be compensated by internal cultural tourism not captured. In any case, the intention is more to compare, than to achieve an 100% data accuracy, so any error, if any, will be same for all.

Then, we take these two indicators: Culture Creative Jobs % and City Destination 000s International visitors/year. No evidence on which should be more relevant, so we equally weigh them.

(See Appendix VII for City Profitability. Services. Culture-Tourism Ranking)

## 6.2.8   City Services' Performance: Urban Mobility

**Why Is This Proxy Relevant?**

We dedicated the full Sect. 2.5 to explaining the superior relevance of urban mobility as a city service, for many the most relevant city service for their daily lives.

Let us add here the *EU Urban Manifesto for New Urbanity* (EU Urban Charter II, 2008d) Principles for Urban Mobility, highlighting that the city must provide an affordable and efficient way to move across the city, while trying to reduce the amount of vehicles, especially private cars, allowing the coexistence of different forms of transportation: public, private, shared, rented, with or without driver or even autonomous, giving special preference to the non-polluting ones such as electric vehicles and bicycles. The street must be recovered as a public social space, like the former Greek agora or market. Finally, special training must be conducted to make the citizens aware of the new alternatives and their benefits for them and for the city.

**How to Measure It?**

In order to evaluate urban mobility, we are going to tackle the three fundamental axes of the problem: on the one hand, traffic, with its negative consequences in loss of time, risk of accidents and pollution; on the other hand, we will comprehensively study mobility including all means of transport and vehicles; and finally, we will dedicate two special analytics to new technologies that provide us with effective parking spaces' management and car-sharing alternatives as the most outstanding, innovative trend nowadays.

We will start with these new technologies.

To study smart parkings in SmartCities, we turned to the "EasyParkGroup SmartCity Index 2019" (Easypark Group, 2019) study. This Smart Parking indicator includes two components: Availability of parking apps in the city and real usage (Source: Apps stores like Google-Android, Apple IOS); and availability and amount of parking slots downtown (/km$^2$) (Source: OpenStreetMaps).

To analyze Car Sharing's new market impact, the EasyPark study reports two components as well: one is simply the number of car sharing services available in the city, and the other the size of car-sharing total fleets/inhabitant (Sources: some local reports, plus all available car sharing companies sites like Autolib, Bluemove, car2Go, Communauto, DriveNow, Enjoy, Flinkster, GoCar, GoGet, GreenMobility, LetsGo, Mobility Carsharing, Moia, Sunfleet, XXImo, Zipcar. City population data from web.)

After these two small, but relevant reports due to the use of advanced technologies' services, let's study the main urban mobility problem: traffic. There are different studies, but the best is the "INRIX, 2019 Global Traffic Scorecard". The INRIX (INRIX, 2019) platform is permanently monitoring traffic in around 1000 cities in the world, from around 45 countries. The best indicator about traffic conditions' quality is congestion. INRIX measures the number of lost hours during rush-hour times in every city. This index takes the estimated 240 working days per year, then applies the average number of hours spent in traffic during peak hours. Peak hours are traditionally 6–9 am and 4–7 pm, although this varies and should be adapted to every city's local culture and commuting patterns/business hours. We like this indicator a lot because it is based on real data, avoiding surveys or estimations, and clearly spots the main issue about traffic in cities.

Finally, to study the whole city transportation system including traffic ((index, inefficiencies, time commuting), bikes, metro performance, flights, high-speed train, vehicles load, and the overall multimodal commuting, we'll take the IESE 2019 Cities in Motion report, using the Urban Mobility (Berrone & Ricart, 2019b) set of indicators.

As we have explained, we have two main components: An in-depth traffic analysis from INRIX, (the main issue) and an overall all-mobility means study from IESE Cities in Motion, so we'll give them the main weight shares (40% each). The other two elements (Smart Parking and Car Sharing Services) are relevant, but still small, modern, advanced solutions for the main traffic problem, so we'll assign them 20% to split between them.

(See Appendix VII for City Profitability. Services. Urban Mobility ranking)

### 6.2.9   City Services' Performance: Urban Planning

**Why Is This Proxy Relevant?**

We have studied how much urbanism marks the city identity and life, how it impacts the lifestyle and even the happiness of its inhabitants. We have studied that our cities must be rebuilt from the current concept of cities built for cars (as more than 40% of the city's space is dedicated to cars, their movement, operation and parking) (Peters, 2020) to the concept of cities built for humans, recovering spaces and making the city walkable again. We saw that the ideal *happy* city is the one where 95% of everything you need is within a 15 min walk or microEV riding. We saw the excellent work in urban transformation that cities like Bilbao or Copenhagen have undertaken and that have meant a human revolution for them. We studied the opposite: the Koolhaas' generic city, the inhuman, sad, cold, repetitive city, annihilating creativity and human encounter. We studied how all this composes the city's identity and its magnetism. Now, we are going to study Urban Planning-as-a-service. The city has, or should urgently have a team of architects and urban planners who must plan the city's urban future in a 5, 10 or even 25/30 years' plan, laying out very clear strategies, marking a clear path, deciding what to achieve, and defining a strategic plan and an annual practical-implementation plan. In short, the city provides us with a service in the form of urban development, sorting out the city's shape and spaces. For a talented citizen, it is very important to know whether that city has a plan, has a team of experts which leads its development, or on the contrary, permit the city to grow amorphously, amoeboid, spreading tentacles where there is private investment fresh money, without counting on the citizens, in a chaotic development, as a metastasis.

Urban planning provides us with constructive services such as urban planning, the different physical networks like sewage, water, energy, communications. Thinking of our cities today, they are building bicycle lanes, recovering spaces from cars and converting them into areas of human relationship such as boulevards and promenades. We must study what our city canvas is like, in height or width- are there enough spaces for humans? What are our buildings and houses like? Are there decent homes for everyone, or is there overcrowded housing? Is there control, and a strategy in place for the balanced and sustainable construction of skyscrapers?

The EU stresses this topic within its principles for a city that respects the citizens, while designing a sorted-out urban strategy. Those principles set by the city should account for citizens' input on all major urbanistic developments, explaining what's going to be built, the purpose, potential, resources and benefits. Urban and regional planning must be conducted by professionals avoiding opportunistic, chaotic growth. Ideas, suggestions and co-creation, especially from those younger should be encouraged (EU Urban Chapter II, 2008e).

296   6 City Profitability (Yield)

**How to Measure It?**

It is very difficult to measure urban planning-as-a-service, since it depends on each city's characteristics, its climate, and its lifestyle, but there are things that everyone assumes are good or bad, and that can be measured.

The best approach to this concept has been made (again) by the IESE Cities in Motion study, in the Urban Planning chapter (Berrone & Ricart, 2019c). This way, the study analyzes the use of spaces for city bicycles, adequate sanitation (this is highly-relevant in some emerging world cities), and the city's housing strategy (very relevant for most cities; for large, attractive cities because they need to accommodate a massive amount of immigrants, and for the least attractive because they need to avoid slums and house overcrowding). Then the indicator evaluates the excessive number of skyscrapers and the real-estate status (we studied its correlation with city attractiveness in the JLL report in Chap. 3)

(See Appendix VII for City Profitability. Services. Urban Planning Ranking)

## 6.2.10   City Services' Performance: Safety

**Why Is This Proxy Relevant?**

City safety is one of the fundamental decision criteria when choosing a city in which to live. We think it is the first criterion and works by a process of elimination. Just as we saw in the selection criteria of our 140 analyzed cities, we eliminated those that did not meet a minimum of 50 in The Economist Liveable Cities ranking, since they are cities where living entails a risk to physical integrity (see Chap. 4). Well, once we understand that our potential-candidate city has acceptable conditions, studying its security is a very important decision component. We discussed the challenge of security for the city in Sect. 2.7, and explained the risks in both physical and virtual or digital security (cybersecurity).

The European Union highlights safety in its list of fundamental urban principles. Pursuing and preventing crime is a city task, in permanent collaboration with its citizens and with other supra-local administrations such as the state, country or even international governance level. At the local level, the persecution of organized gangs, especially drug gangs, is of particular importance. Priority should be given to caring for victims and reintegrating the convicted, as well as providing security forces with the necessary financial resources (EU Urban Chapter II, 2008f).

**How to Measure It?**

If we think about security from the perspective of the talent that explores cities in which to settle down, it is clear that the main priority is personal security. For this reason, we will dedicate a specific section to it.

In addition to physical personal security, a Safe City must be considered as a wider concept that integrates other facets of life such as virtual, digital or cybersecurity; health security (although this section has already been included in the health and social services); and the physical city's infrastructure security and its resilience.

To study Personal Safety, we will take the already-known "INSEAD Global Talent Competitiveness Index" (Lanvin & Monteiro, 2020f). This Global analysis includes a special study for cities, and Personal Safety is measured in homicide rate/100,000 inhabitants. Data is provided by the UN Office on Drugs and Crime, UN-Habitat, Eurostat, and the FBI.

"The Economist's Safe Cities Index" 2019 report (Sahgal & Sharma, 2019) ranks more than 60 cities with 57 indicators. It covers four angles: Digital Security (including privacy, cyberthreats, identity), Health Security (already studied in other indicators, but can't be excluded here), Infrastructure Security (interesting approach to study the infrastructures resilience, transport, natural disasters), and Personal Security as a physical reinforcement of the previous indicator (mainly focused on police, crime, gun regulations, political stability and effective justice).

The Safe Cities Index makes an integrated analysis on all the potential threats a citizen can suffer from in a city. We have added the Personal Safety specific data from INSEAD because of its capital relevance here, and to keep the main focus on it. That way, we don't lose the integrated picture nor the specific priority. Both indicators take same 50% weight, so we make them impactful.

(See Appendix VII for City Profitability. Services. Safety ranking)

### 6.2.11   City Services Performance: All Data Sources Integration

It's very important to notice that we are not assigning any weight to these 10 main areas. App users will do. They will provide their inputs. In other words, we are giving the users (citizens, cities) the freedom to tune the tool to match their preferences, to choose the City Services that best match their needs or their scale of values according to their particular situation in life, and according to their dependencies from children or elder relatives at their charge.

Thus, we will ask the user to assign some weights (which will be normalized to total 100) for each of those ten areas. The questions to ask would be:

Evaluate and assign weights to each of these City Service/Performance groups according to your preferences.

- DIGITAL GOVERNMENT: Democratic, efficient, transparent, participatory, digitalized city government. Digital government-as-a-Service.
- EDUCATION . Lifelong Training: Quality Business Schools, Training and Development on the job.
- EMPLOYABILITY: Talent Demand. Local demand matching offer.
- CONNECTIVITY: Internet infrastructure. 4G/5G Deployment. Wi-Fi.

- HEALTHCARE/SOCIAL SERVICES.
- ENVIRONMENTAL SUSTAINABILITY: Water, Energy efficiency. Air quality. Carbon emissions reduction, Carbon-Neutral Plans. Circular City.
- CULTURE-TOURISM: Culture-as-a-City-Service, not as customs/traditions; again, not emotions, but valuable services.
- URBAN MOBILITY: Traffic. Public Transportation. Mobility as a Service.
- URBAN PLANNING: Urbanism-as-a-City-Service. Design and functionality.
- SAFETY: Physical and Virtual Safety. Personal and City Resiliency.

Then, we can draw the complete City Profitability–Services' Area with these indicators/descriptors: (W=Weight) (See Table 6.2)

(See Appendix VII for City Profitability. Services. Summary)

## 6.3   City Cost of Living. Net Purchasing Power

In our citizenship contract, we have already studied what the city provides to us based on public services. We will now try to understand the other side: what we *pay* for living in that city in comparison with another. This component is essential when making decisions about our future. The economic question is not the only element to evaluate, and we daresay it is not the most important either. For many millennials and talented young people, money is less important than for previous generations. Cities are located in different economies, with different working conditions, and offer on-average very different labor compensations. Not everything is about the salary, we must take into account the city's tax burden and understand how much money we have available for our purchases, from the most basic to personal preferences in culture, leisure, etc. Also, with the same money we will buy different amounts of the same things in one city or another. In the end, this analysis will try to understand the social justice that each city grants me; that is, the things that I can buy or do at month end by doing the same kind of work in different cities. Imagine that we have the same work function and living standards in two different cities. At the end of the month, we will make a different net salary to buy what we want. That is the price we pay to live in one city compared to others. We can also look at the issue with the opposite approach: think about the opportunity cost, or how much we are losing today by not immediately moving to a better place with better opportunities with which to develop our full potential. In other words, doing the same type of work, paying all the required taxes and after buying my necessary things according to my lifestyle, such as food, housing, education, health, mobility, utilities, public services, how much money will be left in my pocket at month's end? It is important to note that some cities offer higher wages, but also higher taxes or higher costs of living. The ideal would be a city with high wages and quality of life, but low taxes and an affordable cost of living. Does it exist? Let's explore the alternatives.

**Table 6.2**  City Profitability-Services model

| W | Class | W | Indicator | Sub indicator | Entity |
|---|-------|---|-----------|---------------|--------|
| User Input | Digital Government | 25 | Online Service Index | | United Nations |
| | | 50 | eParticipation Index | | United Nations |
| | | 25 | Digitalization of Government | | Easy Park Group |
| User Input | Education. Life-Long Training | 33,3 | Quality of Management Schools | | INSEAD – GTCI |
| | | 33,3 | Prevalence of Training in firms | | INSEAD – GTCI |
| | | 33,3 | Employee Development | | INSEAD – GTCI |
| User Input | Employability | 50 | LinkedIn Talent Hiring Demand | | LinkedIN |
| | | 50 | Employability | | INSEAD – GTCI |
| User Input | Connected City | 20 | 4G LTE | | Easy Park Group |
| | | 20 | Internet Speed | | INSEAD – GTCI |
| | | 20 | Wifi Hotspots | | Easy Park Group |
| | | 40 | ICT Infraestructure | | INSEAD – GTCI |
| User Input | Health/Social SVS | 40 | Social Expenditure (% GDP) | | OECD |
| | | 20 | Life Expectancy at age 60 | | United Nations |
| | | 20 | Physicians (per 1k) | | INSEAD – GTCI |
| | | 20 | Public Health Expenditure (%GDP) | | World Health Organization |
| User Input | Environmental Sustainability | 50 | Sustainable City Index | Planet | Arcadis |
| | | 50 | Environment | | IESE Cities Motion |
| User Input | Culture-Tourism | 50 | Culture Creative Jobs % | | World Cities Culture Forum |
| | | 50 | City Destination. | | Euromonitor International |
| User Input | Urban Mobility | 10 | Smart Parking | | Easy Park Group |
| | | 10 | Car Sharing Services | | Easy Park Group |
| | | 40 | Traffic INRIX Congestion | | INRIX |
| | | 40 | Mobility and Transportation | | IESE Cities Motion |
| User Input | Urban Planning | 100 | Urban Planning | | IESE Cities Motion |
| User Input | Safety | 50 | Safe Cities Index | | The Economist |
| | | 50 | Personal Safety | | INSEAD – GCTCI |

## 6.3.1    Cost of Living: Net Real Income

**Why Is This Proxy Relevant?**
The idea is to analyze how much money (Net real Income) is left in my pocket after receiving my professional activity's compensation and paying all my obligations (taxes). A good approach will be based on AVERAGE WAGE – (DIRECT TAXES + SOCIAL CONTRIBUTIONS) = AFTER TAXES INCOME. With this money, at the moment of purchasing anything, we'll pay the INDIRECT TAXES (basically sales taxes or VAT). The remaining is the NET REAL INCOME that we can spend.

**How to Measure It?**
First, we need to analyze the average wage per city in constant USD. There are many different sources and financial analysts from which to choose, but all use UN information as a base reference. Let's take that one. In fact, we'll use the United Nations Economic Commission for Europe (UNECE, 2015). UNECE Statistical Database >> Economy >> Labor Force & Wages >> Gross Average Monthly Wages by Country and Year in Constant USD. As complementary information for some difficult cities and to take alternative sources of information, we go to the basics again, now to the International Labor Organization Statistics (ILOSTAT) (International Labor Organization, 2020). Although our total compensation includes many components such as grants, insurances, and many other benefits, ILOSTAT tries to assess pure gross remuneration, before any deduction like taxes, social security, social contributions, pension plans, unions or other obligations. As an additional source of information, we'll use the OECD Statistics database (OECD, 2020b).

Starting with a given salary, we have to immediately pay direct taxes and social contributions. This concept also varies very much, not only country-to-country, but also, within same country, it depends on the specific personal situation (single or married, number of children, and many other specific details). There are large books and reports annually published by experts like PwC (PwC, 2020) or KPMG (KPMG, 2020) on a specific country's taxation model. Our intention here is to compare cities, so, let's take the basic idea of a single person with no children, and find the average total taxes (direct + social contributions) for our 140 cities. We then reference again the OECD Statistics' information (OECD Stats, 2020c).

Once we get the after-taxes income, we will deduct the sales tax applicable to every city. We will take the standard VAT (value-added tax) or GST (Goods & Sales Tax) or sales tax, as there are different taxes depending on the goods, basic, standard or even luxury goods. There are also different state or city taxes, so we'll take the average applicable to a standard purchase in every studied city. We again use the OECD information (OECD STATS, 2020c). Then, we'll obtain the desired Net Real Money or the After Taxes and VAT Average Income for a Single, No Children.

We are using USD Constant dollar 2018. The formula is quite simple:

AVG Wage × (1–(Direct Tax + Social Contribution)) × (1 – Indirect tax) = Net
   Real Income
(See Appendix VIII for City Profitability. Cost of Living. Net Real Income Ranking)

### 6.3.2   Cost of Living: Cost of Life. Net Purchasing Power

**Why Is This Proxy Relevant?**
Ok, then with this pocket money, we go to the market to buy all kind of goods. Those
things have different prices in every city. This is not new, and it's very well studied
by many famous indicators like the BigMac Index (The Economist, 2020). Proposed
by The Economist magazine in 1986, the Big Mac Index compares the prices of a
very popular hamburger in each of the studied cities in the world (that have this
restaurant chain). As it is exactly the same type of food and requires basically the
same staff and effort to produce it, the Big Mac is considered a good, uniform and
simplified economic indicator of a country's individual purchasing power.

For our study we will use the PPP (Purchasing Power Parity) instead, because it is far
more comprehensive and standard. PPP compares purchasing power in different
cities in buying a different set of things (*basket of goods*). The aim is to inform the
consumer (in our case, the new citizen) of what is the cost of life in that city
compared to another. New York City is used as a unit (NYC = 1). This means,
for example, that a city with PPP = 0.8 is on average 20% less expensive than NYC.
We could then say that the BigMac Index is like a PPP where there is only one item
in the basket of goods,

There are other good calculators of different cities' cost of life. In those, you can
specify your personal situation, activity, locations, etc., and they will help you
compare the economic terms for those two different cities. Here, we mention
*"SalaryExplorer"* (Salary Explorer, 2020) and "Cost of living Reports" (Cost of
Living Reports, 2020) with detailed information by country.

**How to Measure It?**
The best and largest prices' database per city is Numbeo (Numbeo, 2020). This
incredibly large database includes (as of April 2020) around six million price items
from 9520 cities. We'll take the standard PPP including housing rent. We do that not
to forget the cost of accommodation or housing, very relevant in most cities. Then,
we'll take the Cost of Living plus Rent Index 2020, with New York City as reference
= 1.

So, our final Net Purchasing Power will be calculated as previous Net Real
Income divided by this PPP, i.e.: if we had $1000 as Net Real Income and
PPP-RentIncluded for our studied city is 0.5 (50% less expensive than NYC) then
the final Net Purchasing Power will be 1000/0.5 = $2000.

**Table 6.3**  City Profitability-Net Purchase Power model

| Subarea | W. | Class | W. | Indicator | Subindicator | Entity |
|---|---|---|---|---|---|---|
| Cost of Living. Net Purchase Power | 50 | Net Real Income | 100 | Avg Wages/month | SINGLE, No CHILD | UNECE, ILOSTAT |
| | | | 100 | Direct Tax + Social Contributions | | OECD |
| | | | 100 | Indirect Tax | | OECD |
| | 50 | Cost Of Life | 100 | Purchase Power Parity Plus Rent (NY=1) | | Numbeo |

## 6.3.3  Cost of Living: Integration of All Data Sources

In the Table 6.3, we can see the full description of items used to calculate our Net Purchasing Power per studied city.

(See Appendix VIII for City Profitability. Summary Cost of Living. Net Purchase Power Ranking)

## References

Akande, A., et al. (2019). The Lisbon ranking for smart sustainable cities in Europe. *Sustainable Cities and Society, 44*, 476.

Arcadis. (2018). Sustainable cities index. Planet pillar. *Chamber of Commerce Amsterdam*, the Netherlands p. 29 https://www.arcadis.com/media/1/D/5/%7B1D5AE7E2-A348-4B6E-B1D7-6D94FA7D7567%7DSustainable_Cities_Index_2018_Arcadis.pdf and https://www.arcadis.com/en/global/our-perspectives/sustainable-cities-index-2018/citizen-centric-cities/#ranking. Accessed 5 Jan 2020.

Augustine. (1958). Cfr. *La ciudad de Dios*, BAC, Salvador Cuesta, De la teoría Del Estado según San Agustín, Pensamiento, 1945 pp. 63–70.

Berg, V. d., et al. (1999). The attractive city: Catalyst of sustainable urban development. In *European Institute for Comparative Urban Research (EURICUR)* (p. 489). Erasmus Universiteit Rotterdam.

Berrone, P., & Ricart, J. E. (2019a). IESE cities in motion 2019, *IESE*. p. 18 https://media.iese.edu/research/pdfs/ST-0509.pdf. Accessed 2 Jan 2020.

Berrone, P., & Ricart, J. E. (2019b). IESE cities in motion 2019, *IESE*. p. 19. https://media.iese.edu/research/pdfs/ST-0509.pdf. Accessed 2 Jan 2020.

Berrone, P., & Ricart, J. E. (2019c). IESE cities in motion 2019, *IESE*. p. 20. https://media.iese.edu/research/pdfs/ST-0509.pdf. Accessed 2 Jan 2020.

Bibri, S. E., & Krogstie, J. (2017). Smart sustainable cities of the future: An extensive interdisciplinary literature review. *Sustainable Cities and Society, 31*, 183–212. p. 185. https://www.sciencedirect.com/science/article/abs/pii/S2210670716304073?via%3Dihub. Accessed 15 Jan 2020

Bloom Consulting. (2017). *Digital city rank*. Bloom Consulting. https://www.digitalcityindex.com/city-index-results. Accessed 8 Jan 2020.

Braun, E. (2008). City marketing: Towards to an integrated approach. *Erasmus School of Economics*, pp. 55-60 Erasmus University Rotterdam.

CEPE. (2015). Key performance indicators for sustainable smart cities to assess achievement of sustainable development goals, *CEPE*, 1603 ITU-T L.1603. International Telecommunication Union (ITU) p.4.

Citizenlab. (2019). *The beginners guide to Digital Participation* (p. 10). CitizenLab.

Cost of Living Reports. (2020). https://costoflivingreports.com/. Accessed 4 Jan 2020.

Creighton, J. L. (2017). *La participación ciudadana en la era digital* (p. 23). CIVICITI OpenSeneca.

Easy Park Group. (2019). *EasyPark Group SmartCity Index 2019*. https://www.easyparkgroup.com/smart-cities-index/. Accessed 28 Jan 2020.

EU Urban Charter II. (2008a). *Manifesto for new urbanity*. p. 55. https://rm.coe.int/urban-charter-ii-manifesto-for-a-new-urbanity-publication-a5-58-pages-/168095e1d5. Accessed Jan 2020.

EU Urban Charter II. (2008b). *Manifesto for new urbanity*. p. 51. https://rm.coe.int/urban-charter-ii-manifesto-for-a-new-urbanity-publication-a5-58-pages-/168095e1d5. Accessed Jan 2020.

EU Urban Charter II. (2008c). *Manifesto for new urbanity*. p. 54. https://rm.coe.int/urban-charter-ii-manifesto-for-a-new-urbanity-publication-a5-58-pages-/168095e1d5. Accessed Jan 2020.

EU Urban Charter II. (2008d). *Manifesto for new urbanity*. p. 52. https://rm.coe.int/urban-charter-ii-manifesto-for-a-new-urbanity-publication-a5-58-pages-/168095e1d5. Accessed Jan 2020.

EU Urban Charter II. (2008e). *Manifesto for new urbanity*. p. 56. https://rm.coe.int/urban-charter-ii-manifesto-for-a-new-urbanity-publication-a5-58-pages-/168095e1d5. Accessed Jan 2020.

EU Urban Charter II. (2008f). *Manifesto for new urbanity*. p. 53. https://rm.coe.int/urban-charter-ii-manifesto-for-a-new-urbanity-publication-a5-58-pages-/168095e1d5. Accessed Jan 2020.

Eurostat. (2018). https://ec.europa.eu/eurostat/. Also from Iniciativa de Acciones Innovadoras Urbanas. 16/09/2019 – 12/12/2019 UIA. Urban Innovative Actions. EU. pp. 20–21. Also https://www.uia-initiative.eu/sites/default/files/2019-09/ToR_Call%205_UIA_16_09_2019_ES.pdf. Accessed 21 Jan 2020.

Goi, C. (2017) The impact of technological innovation on building a sustainable city. *International Journal of Quality Innovation* 3, 6. p. 1. Also at https://doi.org/10.1186/s40887-017-0014-9. Accessed 12 Jan 2020.

Habermas, J. (2006). *The splintered West* (pp. 128–129). Trotta.

Hobbes, T. (1651). *Leviathan* (Vol. XVIII). Andrew Crooke.

INRIX. (2019). *INRIX 2019 global traffic scorecard*. https://inrix.com/scorecard/. Accessed 10 Jan 2020.

International Labor Organization. (2020). Earnings and Labor cost. https://ilostat.ilo.org/resources/methods/description-earnings-and-labour-cost/. Accessed 12 Jan 2020.

International Telecommunication Union. (2017). ICT Development Index 2017. Measuring the Information Society Report 2017, also at http://www.itu.int/en/ITU-D/Statistics/Pages/publications/mis2017.aspx. Accessed 20 Jan 2020.

KPMG. (2020). *Global withholding taxes*. https://tax.kpmg.us/articles/2020/global-withholding-taxes-guide.html. Accessed 5 Jan 2020.

Lanvin, B., & Monteiro, F. (2020a). INSEAD Global Talent Competitiveness index (GTCI), Global Talent in the Age of Artificial Intelligence, p. 355, Fontainebleau, INSEAD. https://www.insead.edu/sites/default/files/assets/dept/globalindices/docs/GTCI-2020-report.pdf. Accessed 3 Feb 2020.

Lanvin, B., & Monteiro, F. (2020b). INSEAD Global Talent Competitiveness index (GTCI), Global Talent in the Age of Artificial Intelligence, pp. 326–329, Fontainebleau, INSEAD. https://www.insead.edu/sites/default/files/assets/dept/globalindices/docs/GTCI-2020-report.pdf. Accessed 3 Feb 2020.

Lanvin, B., & Monteiro, F. (2020c). INSEAD Global Talent Competitiveness index (GTCI), Global Talent in the Age of Artificial Intelligence, p. 113, Fontainebleau, INSEAD. https://www.insead.edu/sites/default/files/assets/dept/globalindices/docs/GTCI-2020-report.pdf. Accessed 3 Feb 2020.

Lanvin, B., & Monteiro, F. (2020d). INSEAD Global Talent Competitiveness index (GTCI), Global Talent in the Age of Artificial Intelligence, p. 352, Fontainebleau, INSEAD. https://www.

insead.edu/sites/default/files/assets/dept/globalindices/docs/GTCI-2020-report.pdf. Accessed
    3 Feb 2020.
Lanvin, B., & Monteiro, F. (2020e). INSEAD Global Talent Competitiveness index (GTCI), Global
    Talent in the Age of Artificial Intelligence, p. 357, Fontainebleau, INSEAD. https://www.
    insead.edu/sites/default/files/assets/dept/globalindices/docs/GTCI-2020-report.pdf. Accessed
    3 Feb 2020.
Lanvin, B., & Monteiro, F. (2020f). INSEAD Global Talent Competitiveness index (GTCI), Global
    Talent in the Age of Artificial Intelligence, p. 114, Fontainebleau, INSEAD. https://www.
    insead.edu/sites/default/files/assets/dept/globalindices/docs/GTCI-2020-report.pdf. Accessed
    3 Feb 2020.
LinkedIN. (2020). Talent pool report. *LinkedIN*. https://www.linkedin.com/insights/report/create.
    Live tool last consulted by 8 April 2020.
Manyika, J. (2020). The social contract in the 21st century. p.36 *McKinsey*. also at https://www.
    mckinsey.com/industries/social-sector/our-insights/the-social-contract-in-the-21st-century.
    Accessed 2 Feb 2020.
Mirete, J. L. (1998). Cfr. *Pacto social en Santo Tomás de Aquino*. Anales de Derecho,
    16, pp.155–160 Murcia:Univ. Murcia.
Numbeo. (2020). Cost of living index by city 2020. https://www.numbeo.com/cost-of-living/
    rankings.jsp. Accessed 28 Jan 2020.
OECD. (2020a). Social spending (indicator) doi:10.1787/7497563b-en. https://data.oecd.org/
    socialexp/social-spending.htm. Accessed 12 Apr 2020.
OECD. (2020b). Total gross earnings before taxes. https://stats.oecd.org/Index.aspx?
    QueryId=57321 Accessed 17 Jan 2020.
OECD. (2020c). Consumption tax trends 2018. VAT/GST and excise rates, trends and policy
    issues. OECD http://www.oecd.org/tax/consumption/consumption-tax-trends-19990979.htm
    Accessed 12 Jan 2020.
OECD STATS. (2020). Table I.6. All-in average personal income tax rates at average wage by
    family type. https://stats.oecd.org/index.aspx?DataSetCode=TABLE_I6. Accessed 13 Jan
    2020.
Peters, A. (2020). Here's how much space U.S. cities waste on parking. FAST Company. https://
    www.fastcompany.com/90202222/heres-how-much-space-u-s-cities-waste-on-parking.
    Accessed 12 Jan 2020.
Petersen, W. (2004). *Troy*.
Plato. *Rep*. 2.358e.
Plato. *Crito*. pp.51b.
PwC. (2020). *Worldwide tax summaries*. https://www.pwc.com/gx/en/services/tax/worldwide-tax-
    summaries.html. Accessed 2 Jan 2020.
Rawls, J. (1971). Cfr. *A Theory of Justice*. Belknap Press
Rousseau, J.-J. (1762). *On the social contract*, published in Amsterdam
Sahgal V., & Sharma N. D. (2019). Safe Cities Index. The Economist Intelligence Unit (EIU). p.11.
    https://safecities.economist.com/safe-cities-index-2019/? Accessed 12 Jan 2020.
Salary Explorer. (2020). Cost of living calculator. Compare your monthly spending to that of other
    people. http://www.salaryexplorer.com/cost-of-living-calculator.php. Accessed 22 Jan 2020.
Sinkene, J., & Kromalcas, S. (2010). *Concept, direction and practice of city attractiveness
    improvement*. p. 151. Kaunas University of Technology, Kaunas.
Solarte, R. (2006). Ciudadanía, contrato social y proyecto alternativo. *THEOLOGICA
    XAVERIANA, 158*, 325.
Startup Europe Awards. (2020). https://startupeuropeawards.eu/project-view/creative/. Accessed
    11 Jan 2020.
The Economist. (2020). Big Mac Index. https://www.economist.com/news/2020/01/15/the-big-
    mac-index. Accessed 4 Jan 2020.

The Economist Intelligence Unit (EIU) and SIEMENS. (2012). The Green City Index—a summary of the Green City Index research series. https://www.siemens.com/entry/cc/features/greencityindex_international/all/en/pdf/gci_report_summary.pdf. Accessed 20 Oct 2018.

UN. (1987). UN's world commission on environment and development. p. 4. https://sustainabledevelopment.un.org/content/documents/5987our-common-future.pdf. Accessed 20 Jan 2020.

UN DATA. (2012). World Health Organization. http://data.un.org/Data.aspx?q=life+expectancy&d=WHO&f=MEASURE_CODE%3AWHOSIS_000015. Accessed 20 Oct 2018.

UNDP. (2020). Goal 11: Sustainable cities and communities. UNDP (United Nations Development Programme). https://www.undp.org/content/undp/en/home/sustainable-development-goals/goal-11-sustainable-cities-and-communities.html. Accessed 30 Jan 2020.

UNECE. (2015). *Gross average monthly wages by country and year*. UNECE Statistical Database. https://w3.unece.org/PXWeb2015/pxweb/en/STAT/STAT__20-ME__3-MELF/60_en_MECCWagesY_r.px/. Accessed 22 Jan 2020.

United Nations. (2018a) United Nations E-Government Survey 2018, *Department of Economic and Social Affairs*, UN, New York, p. 96, also at https://publicadministration.un.org/en/research/un-e-government-surveys. Accessed 22 Jan 2020.

United Nations. (2018b) United Nations E-Government Survey 2018, *Department of Economic and Social Affairs*, UN, New York, p. 211, also at https://publicadministration.un.org/en/research/un-e-government-surveys. Accessed 22 Jan 2020

World Bank. (2020a). Business Surveys. www.enterprisesurveys.org. Accessed 7 Jan 2020.

World Bank. (2020b). World Development indicators World Bank. https://datacatalog.worldbank.org/dataset/world-development-indicators. Accessed 15 Jan 2020.

World Cities Cultural Forum. (2020). *Global leadership on culture in cities*. BOP. http://www.worldcitiescultureforum.com/data/creative-industries-employment. Accessed 15 Jan 2020.

World Economic Forum. (2018). Executive opinion survey. https://reports.weforum.org/global-competitiveness-report-2018/appendix-b-the-executive-opinion-survey-the-voice-of-the-business-community/. Accessed 20 Feb 2020.

World Health Organization. (1998). Health promotion glossary, p.13. *World Health Organization*, Geneva  https://www.who.int/healthpromotion/about/HPR%20Glossary%201998.pdf?ua=1. Accessed 20 Oct 2018.

World Health Organization. (2017). Global health expenditure database. https://apps.who.int/nha/database/Select/Indicators/en. Accessed 20 Jan 2020.

World Health Organization. (2020). Healthy city checklist. World Health Organization. Regional Office for Europe. http://www.euro.who.int/en/health-topics/environment-and-health/urban-health/who-european-healthy-cities-network/what-is-a-healthy-city/healthy-city-checklist. Accessed 10 Jan 2020.

Yasmeen, R. (2019). Top 100 City Destinations 2019 Edition. Euromonitor International. https://go.euromonitor.com/white-paper-travel-2019-100-cities.html. Accessed 12 Jan 2020.

# Chapter 7
# City Attractiveness. Research. Key Findings. Conclusions

## 7.1 City Attractiveness Model

To summarize, the full Model for City Attractiveness includes 67 indicators for City Magnetism and 33 for City Profitability, plus three for PreConditions (Main Religion, Main Language, Landscape) for a total of 103 Indicators. The number of sub-indicators within them is very large, as some include more than 100 components.

In parallel, our City Attractiveness Index is calculated by multiplying City Magnetism × City Profitability, so each has a 50% weight. Inside City Magnetism, the user will provide the weights for its three components (City Identity, City Dynamism and City Strategy). Inside City Profitability, we have City Services Performance with 10 main areas that the user must weigh as well. This City Services Performance is multiplied by Net Purchasing Power to calculate City Profitability. So, the user must provide 3 + 10 weights or preferences, plus some preconditions (if any) about Religion, Language and Landscape for the desired cities.

Find at Table 7.1 a full description for City Attractiveness: (W=Weight) Magnetism and profitability are 50% weighted

### 7.1.1 Methodology to Combine/Rationalize Data Indicators

All variables are rationalized to 0–10 interval (direct classic standardization)
Then, the following standardization approach is used:

$$\text{Score } x_i = \left( 10 \times \frac{a_i - a_{min}}{a_{MAX} - a_{min}} \right)$$

J. A. Ondiviela, *Beyond Smart Cities*, https://doi.org/10.1007/978-3-030-83371-8_7

**Table 7.1** Full description for city attractiveness

| Area | W. | Sub area | W | Class | W | Indicator | W | Entity |
|---|---|---|---|---|---|---|---|---|
| Magnetism | User Input | Identity | 20 | History. Culture | 20 | Age | 70 | Own Work |
| | | | | | | UNESCO | 20 | UNESCO |
| | | | | | | Top Museums | 10 | Wikipedia |
| | | | | Government Basics | 10 | Democracy Index | 50 | The Economist |
| | | | | | | Safe City Index | 50 | The Economist |
| | | | | Reputation | 10 | Reputation | 100 | Reputation Institute |
| | | | | Space. Density | 10 | % Natural Space | 50 | Own Work |
| | | | | | | Density (inh/km2) | 50 | Demographia |
| | | | | Climate | 15 | Avge. Temperature Desviation | 33,3 | Climatemps |
| | | | | | | Avge. Precipitation Desviation | 33,3 | Climatemps |
| | | | | | | Avge. Daily Sunshine | 33,3 | Climatemps |
| | | | | Geo Risk | 5 | Natural Disaster Risk | 100 | World RiskReport |
| | | | | Geo Economics | 10 | GDP Proximity | 100 | Own Work |
| | | | | Gastronomy | 5 | RK Food Index | 50 | OXFAM |
| | | | | | | Michelin Guide | 50 | Via Michelin |
| | | | | Branding. External Image | 15 | Movies | 25 | Own Work |
| | | | | | | Sports | 50 | Football DatabaseNBATopendsports |
| | | | | | | Main Events | 25 | Olympics org |
| | | | | | | | | Wikipedia |
| | | | | | | | | Day Zero Project |
| | User Input | Dynamism | 25 | Compe titiveness | 25 | Creativity Index | 25 | Martin Prosperity |
| | | | | | | Global Competitivenes | 25 | World Economic Forum |
| | | | | | | Cities In Motion | 25 | IESE |

| Dimension | Weight | Category | Subcategory | Subcat. weight | Indicator | Weight | Source |
|---|---|---|---|---|---|---|---|
| Profitability | 50 | User Input | | 25 | Global Talent Competitiveness | 25 | INSEAD-GTCI |
| | | | Expat Social Experience | 25 | Life Style – Quality | 33,3 | HSBC Expat Explorer |
| | | | | | People Around | 33,3 | HSBC Expat Explorer |
| | | | | | Relationship – Social Life | 33,3 | HSBC Expat Explorer |
| | | | Ethics. Well-being | 25 | Happiness | 40 | Happiness Report |
| | | | | | World Giving Score | 20 | Charities Aid Foundation |
| | | | | | Civic Engagement | 20 | OECD |
| | | | | | Work-Life Balance | 20 | OECD |
| | | | Equality | 25 | GINI Index | 25 | WorldBank |
| | | | | | Gender | 25 | INSEAD-GTCI |
| | | | | | Tolerance | 25 | INSEAD-GTCI |
| | | | | | Poverty | 25 | IndexMundi |
| | | Strategy | Human Capital | 20 | Population Age Average Per Country | 20 | Own Work |
| | | | | | Ranking Human Capital | 80 | IESE Cities Motion |
| | | | Smart Cities Plan | 50 | Plan Smart Cities | 100 | Own Work |
| | | | Innovation | 30 | R&D (% GDP) | 25 | INSEAD – GTCI |
| | | | | | Global Innovation Index | 25 | Cornell INSEAD WIPO |
| | | | | | Innovation Cities | 50 | 2ThinkNow |
| | | Services | Digital Government | User Input | Online Service Index | 25 | United Nations |
| | | | | | eParticipation Index | 50 | United Nations |
| | | | | | Digitalization of Government | 25 | Easy Park Group |
| | | | Education. LifeLong Training | User Input | Quality of Management Schools | 33,3 | INSEAD – GTCI |
| | | | | | Prevalence of Training in firms | 33,3 | INSEAD – GTCI |

(continued)

**Table 7.1** (continued)

| Area | W. | Sub area | W | Class | W | Indicator | W | Entity |
|---|---|---|---|---|---|---|---|---|
| | | | | | 33,3 | Employee Development | | INSEAD – GTCI |
| | | | User Input | Employ ability | 50 | LinkedIn Talent Hiring Demand | | LinkedIN |
| | | | | | 50 | Employability | | INSEAD – GTCI |
| | | | User Input | Connected City | 20 | 4G LTE | | Easy Park Group |
| | | | | | 20 | Internet Speed | | INSEAD – GTCI |
| | | | | | 20 | Wifi Hotspots | | Easy Park Group |
| | | | | | 40 | ICT Infraestructure | | INSEAD – GTCI |
| | | | User Input | Health/ Social SVS | 40 | Social Expenditure (% GDP) | | OECD |
| | | | | | 20 | Life Expectancy at age 60 | | United Nations |
| | | | | | 20 | Physicians (per 1k) | | INSEAD-GTCI |
| | | | | | 20 | Public Health Expenditure (%GDP) | | World Health Organization |
| | | | User Input | Environ mental Sustain ability | 50 | Sustainable City Index | | Arcadis |
| | | | | | 50 | Environment | | IESE Cities Motion |
| | | | User Input | Culture-Tourism | 50 | Culture Creative Jobs % | | World Cities Culture Forum |
| | | | | | 50 | City Destination. | | Euromonitor International |
| | | | User Input | Urban Mobility | 10 | Smart Parking | | Easy Park Group |
| | | | | | 10 | Car Sharing Services | | Easy Park Group |
| | | | | | 40 | Traffic INRIX Congestion | | INRIX |
| | | | | | 40 | Mobility and Transportation | | IESE Cities Motion |
| | | | User Input | Urban Planning | 100 | Urban Planning | | IESE Cities Motion |
| | | | User Input | Safety | 50 | Safe Cities Index | | The Economist |
| | | | | | 50 | Personal Safety | | INSEAD – GCTCI |
| | 50 | | 50 | Net Real Income | 100 | Avg Wages/month | | UNECE, ILOSTAT |

| Cost of Living. Net Purchase Power | 50 | Cost Of Life | 100 | Direct Tax + Social Contributions | OECD |
| | | | 100 | Indirect Tax | OECD |
| | | | 100 | Purchase Power Parity Plus Rent (NY=1) | Numbeo |
| | ADDITIONAL PRE-CONDITIONS: | | | Landscapes | Own Work |
| | | | | Language | Wikipedia |
| | | | | Religion | Wikipedia |

When we consolidate into the three main City Magnetism areas: City Identity, City Dynamism and City Strategy, or the 10 City Profitability Service areas, we are rationalizing 1–10, as we don't want to multiply any of these areas' inputs by less than 1, so the standardization approach is slightly different:

$$Score\ x_i = \left( 9 \times \frac{a_i - a_{min}}{a_{MAX} - a_{min}} \right) + 1$$

We had for City Profitability = City Services Performance x Net Purchasing Power. These two items weigh equally, or 50%.

(See Appendix IX for City Profitability. Summary ranking using the City Services Performance provided by the SmartCityExpo attendee survey (will be explained later)).

### 7.1.2  Honest/Fair Analysis Disclaimer

The obtained results are a true reflection of user input and the data obtained from the aforementioned studies. Only on very few occasions where some data from a city is missing, then an attempt is been made to extrapolate from other well-known data from nearby or similar cities. There has never been any favoritism towards any city, or towards achieving a striking, curious or beautiful model. The results are what they are. A model is always a simplified representation of a very complex reality. This is the best model/approach to the concept of Attractive City. It will need an annual evolution and adaptation as our society changes and as new disruptive technologies appear. In our presentations/discussions to multiple cities, some have given slight pushback over one indicator that they did not like or that did not reflect their city's merits in their opinion. We mainly agree, and we showed them the information sources and suggested that they can explain their arguments to those sources. We have neither had the time nor the resources to do a comprehensive, from-scratch study, without counting on the numerous sets of studies already published in most of studied some areas. Feedback is always welcome.

## 7.2  City Attractiveness. Field Work

*We especially need imagination in science. Not everything is mathematics and not every-thing is simple logic, it is also a bit of beauty and poetry* María Montessori (Montessori, 1912).

That is one of the principles of this research: to analyze a study on the city combining the technological, urbanistic and above all, humanistic perspectives. We have built a model for Attractive Cities. Let's test it. Let's add some statistics to our human model.

We are conducting a meta-analysis investigation, choosing the best available reports/studies for all the analyzed city dimensions, as proxies to model the sought concept: City Attractiveness. In addition, as a way to reduce bias and offer the best information for each and every citizen, we are allowing them to enter their preference weights in all variable items (economic terms are fixed, so, it's out of the question). To test the model, we'll expose it directly to many different cities and will run two surveys among clearly talented citizens and city experts.

We established that we were not going to publish another cities' ranking. We are going to allow readers, all of them talented citizens, a good degree of freedom to decide which city style (Magnetism) they like best, and which city services they most appreciate at this point in their lives. Unfortunately, they can't decide on cost of life, as this is a clear city characteristic/fixed term. That's the price you have to pay for your bet on an attractive city.

To prove that the model works and that all its components are relevant, we are going to carry out two surveys as a test. If any element is not minimally valuable, it should not be there. We will also take into consideration that the model is understood in a short period of time and that the weight assessment for each element can be answered in a few minutes, if not seconds.

We ran two surveys in two SmartCities events, so our audience will include a two-fold advantage: They will be quite familiar with the SmartCity concept, and we can nominate them all as talented citizens.

We used the same questions for both surveys, slightly adapting them to match each event's main theme. So, we are basically creating a custom sorting of the three City Magnetism Components and then the 10 City Performance Services. In addition, some control information was requested such as sex, age and some relevant personal circumstances that will impact those prioritizations, like Dependency for Children or Dependency for elderly people at your charge. It seems obvious that depending on these conditions, one will differently weigh the city services, because we mainly live within families and our decision to move to one particular city will have a greater or lesser impact on them.

## 7.2.1   Survey at NordicEdge Event

We ran our first survey at the NordicEdge (Nordicedge, 2018) event in Stavanger (Norway) in September 2018. This annual event is the largest SmartCity event in the Nordics. The 2018 edition attracted around 4500 visitors, mainly from Norway and all other Nordic countries like Finland, Sweden, and Denmark. Solution-provider companies brought professionals from many other countries, but mainly from Europe and China, and they held some specific activities at this event.

**Table 7.2** City services
ranking from SmartCity Expo
2018 survey

| City services – Scale of values | RK |
|---|---|
| Urban mobility/Transportation | 1 |
| SOCservices/Health | 2 |
| Env. sustainability | 3 |
| Safety (physical/virtual) | 4 |
| Education | 5 |
| Employability | 6 |
| Urban planning | 7 |
| Governance | 8 |
| Connected city | 9 |
| Cultural SVS/Tourism | 10 |

Source: Author

(The specific questionnaire can be found in Appendix X)

To follow the event's suggestion, we used same main theme *"Smart with a Heart,"* and we asked about City Performance/Services by asking about *Smart*, while we asked about Magnetism by asking attendees to answer, *with the Heart*.

The survey ran live for just two days, as we had the opportunity to briefly explain the concept the second day of the event, and it ended the following day.

We received 264 answers, which for a population (using attendees) of N=4500 means a valid and informative test, with Confidence=90% and Error=5% (Surveymonkey Calculator, 2018).

We can confidently say that the sample target is a good representation of talented, IT-related, cities-related, Nordic professionals in 2018. Let's analyze the results. (See results Data Summary at Appendix XI)

Our target had an average age of 41 years, most of them with children (62%) and with no elderly people at their charge (only 20%). There was a balance in gender, (48–52%) which is very good for a sector (Information Technologies) where professionals are mainly in STEM, (Sciences, Technology, Engineering, Math) currently composed mostly of men.

Magnetism: All three components are very similarly weighted, (Identity 33%, Dynamism 36% and Strategy 31%) which means that these three areas are very telling about the topic. Nordic cities are not very strong on branding and projected identity, so it's not a surprise that Dynamism was the most appreciated topic, then Identity, then Strategy. Strategy is important, but it is perceived as something unknown, (the future's main problem is that it's unknown...) so we consider this as something we can fix or easily improve, while the past is the consequence of our acts and experiences, and it takes longer to change (we stated that a city needs at least 50 years to define a new City Identity). Younger people prefer Strategy over Identity. It's a good indicator that Identity is more and more appreciated as people get older, improving from the least-valued item for younger people, to the best for people over 50. Men and women agree on Magnetism, which means they have the same preferences, aesthetics, same education and customs.

Overall Ranking for City Services shows (see Table 7.2):

**Table 7.3**  Top10 attractive cities for NordicEdge attendees

| City | Country | Magnetism | Profitability | Attractiveness | Attractiveness index |
|------|---------|-----------|---------------|----------------|----------------------|
| Melbourne | Australia | 9,31 | 9,18 | 85,40 | 1 |
| Adelaide | Australia | 8,38 | 10,00 | 83,84 | 2 |
| Stockholm | Sweden | 9,69 | 8,46 | 81,98 | 3 |
| Zurich | Switzerland | 8,26 | 9,60 | 79,32 | 4 |
| Berlin | Germany | 9,00 | 8,70 | 78,28 | 5 |
| Sydney | Australia | 9,46 | 8,10 | 76,66 | 6 |
| Bern | Switzerland | 7,39 | 9,99 | 73,89 | 7 |
| Montreal | Canada | 8,22 | 8,98 | 73,77 | 8 |
| Oslo | Norway | 8,99 | 8,00 | 72,00 | 9 |
| Gothenburg | Sweden | 8,07 | 8,75 | 70,68 | 10 |

Source: Author

We can identify three zones: top positions, (1, 2, 3, 4) then mid, (5, 6) then low (7, 8, 9, 10). We can appreciate changes along the different studied age ranges but also within these groups, which are very well identified.

The first good impression is that all 10 studied areas are relevant, as all take an 8–12% score, so none is well over the rest, and the differences are not peaking. It's not a surprise to see Environmental Sustainability as a top score in the Nordics, who are leading this topic, and especially in this event, which has a clear motivation to invest in and highlight the importance of this concept. Then Health/SocialSVS, Urban Mobility and Safety take top positions along the range of ages. Environmental issues are more relevant for younger people, and Urban Mobility for those over 50, meaning that Environmental Sustainability is a relatively new concept, and younger people have this fresher from their education, while older people know of the problems associated with poor mobility, or the advantages of a good system. Younger people were born with decent mobility, so they can't appreciate the benefit. By gender, there is almost the same rankings, with the only differences in the low range. Those with children give a greater priority to Education, those without value especially mobility (more freedom to move?, the desire to experience new places?, quickly and efficiently move around the city?) People with elderly at their charge place Health/Social Services at the top as expected, those without placed employ-ability first (they think more about themselves, as they don't have to take care of others). Finally, it's sad to see that the least-appreciated City Services are in Culture/Tourism. Although it's not far from the others, this is clearly a main pending subject for more of our cities: to serve as a permanent *citizen university*, while constantly offering, incentivizing and promoting cultural services. A more-skilled society is always a more prosperous one, and the opposite is also true.

If we assign these scores (three Magnetism and 10 City Services) to our model, we find at Table 7.3 that four main Nordic cities are among the top 10 positions, (not a surprise as well), only surpassed by some Australian and Swiss cities because of their excellent Profitability and Net Purchasing power, with high wages, moderated taxes and cost of life.

## 7.2.2  Survey at SmartCityExpo WW Congress Event

We ran our second, but largest and most significant exploration at the largest SmartCity event in the world, the SmartCityExpo WW Congress (Smartcity Expo, 2018) that Barcelona holds every November. At the 2018 event, we had the chance to include our survey in the post-event feedback, reaching more than 21,000 attendees.

Attendees come mainly from Western Europe (around half of them, mainly from Spain) and the other half from the rest of the world, (mainly the U.S. and Asia) which means there are people from 146 countries. Attendees' profiles are again SmartCity-familiar people, from demand to offer, with good technical skills. There are also decision makers from cities, well-balanced with salespeople from exhibitors, and government officials from the many participating cities across the globe. Tthe specific questionnaire can be found in Appendix XI)

To follow the event's suggestion, we used same main theme of *Cities to Live IN,* and we asked attendees to think about City Performance/Services and Cities Magnetism from Attractive cities they could consider to *Live IN.*

The survey ran live for one week after the event, since attendees received a communication asking for feedback and to complete the survey. We had the opportunity to briefly explain the concept the second day of the event to a limited audience (around 200 people), so the whole concept was absolutely new for most people who answered. We got 1550 answers, which for a population (total attendees) of N=21,334 means a solid, valid and very informative test, with Confidence=95% and Error=2% (Surveymonkey Calculator, 2018).

We can confidently confirm that the sample target is a good representation of the whole SmartCity Industry and world cities' officials; including urban technology experts, talented IT-related people, Cities-related people, and mainly European professionals in 2018. Let's analyze the results. (See results Data Summary at Appendix XII).

The results are not very different than those from NordicEdge, although the confidence provided by the large number of answers provides a greater model reliability. Our target had an average age of 42 years old, half of them with children (51%) and no elderly people at their charge (only 25% had). It was an unbalanced gender sample, with 67% males, which is consistent with a very male-driven technological market.

Magnetism: Again, Dynamism rules, then Identity them Strategy. Identity and Dynamism are significantly larger than Strategy, confirming the trend that Future and potential is less valued than present facts or gained experience and Identity. This result can easily be associated to a Southern Europe Latin lifestyle, more interested in the present, loving the past, and not very forward-looking, but differences are not so large to consider Strategy as irrelevant (the survey received a worldwide participation). Identity is more and more appreciated as people get older, improving to becoming the most valued for people over 50. Again, men and women agree on Magnetism, which means same preferences, aesthetics, same education and customs.

**Table 7.4**  City Performance/Services Ranking for SmartCityExpo Attendees

| City services – Scale of values | RK | 1-10 | Over 100 | INPUT 1..5 |
|---|---|---|---|---|
| Urban mobility/Transportation | 1 | 10,00 | 13,54 | 4,44 |
| Social services/Health | 2 | 9,04 | 12,66 | 4,35 |
| Env. Sustainability | 3 | 8,95 | 12,57 | 4,34 |
| Safety (physical/virtual) | 4 | 8,37 | 12,04 | 4,28 |
| Education | 5 | 7,67 | 11,40 | 4,21 |
| Employability | 6 | 7,11 | 10,87 | 4,16 |
| Urban planning | 7 | 4,78 | 8,72 | 3,93 |
| Governance | 8 | 2,85 | 6,95 | 3,74 |
| Connected city | 9 | 1,83 | 6,01 | 3,64 |
| Cultural services/Tourism | 10 | 1,00 | 5,24 | 3,56 |

Source: Author

Overall Ranking for City Services shows (see Table 7.4):

Again, we can very clearly identify three zones top positions, (1, 2, 3, 4) scoring more than 8,30, then mid, (5,6) (Education and Employability) then low (7, 8, 9, 10). We can appreciate changes along the different studied age ranges, but always within these groups, which are very well identified.

All 10 studied areas are relevant, as all get a minimum of 3,5 out of 5 on average, so we can say that none is irrelevant, and none is leading by a great distance compared to the rest. The main top area is Urban Mobility, as everybody recognizes that this city service is crucial to keeping a city alive; as we have named it, the *city's bloodstream*. It's not strange to consider it as such if we define a city as a point in space/time where people meet/encounter each other; then the service that is making that possible, moving people around, should be the most appreciated. Then Health/SocSVS, Environmental, Safety are following, grouped at a short distance. Safety is number one for those over 60. Then the Education and Employability group. We were surprised by finding these in positions five and six, and not higher. It must be that our attendees are so talented that they face no challenges in these areas. In any case, Education jumps to position three for younger people, which seems reasonable. Employability falls to the bottom position (10) for those over 60, unsurprising as they are about to retire. Urban Planning, Governance, Connected City, and CulturalSVS take the lowest positions across all segments. We were expecting more from Connected City; maybe the audience didn't understand the concept and the disruptive implications that 5G will bring, or maybe they consider this as a static, obvious service like water or energy, and see no difference in it implemented within cities. Governance and Urban Planning are not perceived as star city services, but as business as usual; regular tasks that must be provided, but not brilliant vocal services citizens perceive as new, innovative or disruptive. They have been there since the city's foundation. By gender, there are almost the same rankings, with few differences among top choices, as women position Health/SocSVS as number one and men promote EnvSustainability to the top two. Those with children give greater consideration to EnvSustainability (thinking about the planet we leave for them?), and those without exactly follow the average. People with elderly at their charge place Health/Social Svs at the top as expected, while those without improve the score of EnvSustainability. Finally, again it's sad to see that least-appreciated City Service is the Culture/Tourism one as mentioned before.

If we assign these scores (three Magnetism and 10 City Services) to our model, then we find top positions for Australian and Swiss cities, plus some Nordic ones, Berlin, Austria, Amsterdam, Phoenix (AZ). Extraordinary Profitability with good wages and reasonable taxes push them to those positions. The best in Magnetism like Stockholm, Vienna, and Amsterdam compete from the other angle.

We can perceive a balanced summary of results with no surprises on which cities take leadership (in the SmartCityExpo leaders' opinion). Given the large amount of answers and small margin for error, we can conclude that the model works, it is easy to understand, and it correctly reflects the complex reality (Attractive City) it describes. We'll study this in greater detail in the next chapter.

## 7.3    Main Overall Analysis

Once again, if we take the inputs from the attendees of the SmartCityExpo 2018, then we can observe the cities' score and balance Magnetism vs Profitability contributions. Later in the following chapters, we will analyze Magnetism components and Profitability components.

(See the full list of 140 Cities Attractiveness Score with SmartCityExpo attendees' input in Appendix XIV)

Looking at the worldwide selected top 140 cities' list, we can group them into four areas:

Advanced: From position 1 to 70, we find the advanced Western Civilization. Australian cities lead, with their four cities studied among the top 13 positions, with Melbourne (1); then trying to learn and approach them is New Zealand starting from Wellington (25). Then, we find all Western Europe, starting from the Swedish Stockholm (3) and the rest of the Nordic countries, to the Swiss Zurich (4). Then Vienna (12) leading the German, and the Dutch world Amsterdam (15), then the UK led by London (21). Just after it, the South follows, with France Paris (47), Spain with Barcelona (40), Madrid (50), Dublin (51), Belgium Antwerp (61) and we ended up in Italy with Milan (69) and Rome (70). In parallel to the UK, North America begins, in Canada with Montreal (8) and Toronto (20) ahead of the U.S., which is led by Phoenix (14) and NYC (27). From Asia, only the main tigers compete to enter this leading squad, such as Seoul (34), Japan with Tokyo (49) while the rest of Japan is around (65), Singapore (60) and Hong Kong (73).

Competition in this leading group is fierce. Climbing a few positions means strong investments, solid, well-ordered and executed plans and dedicated teams with a strong budget and international influence. Southern European cities may fall into the next group if they don't accelerate smart investments soon. Their magnetism and quality of life are very significant, but they won't be in that group much longer without a strong innovation component as well. We especially see Italy on this border.

Someone might question why we dedicate 50% of the studied cities to this advanced segment. The answer is within the question. Precisely because it is the most interesting segment for talented citizens exploring the world of cities, we must add more granularity and detail to it, and that is why we have included half of the cities. Also, if we remember the criteria for selecting cities from Chap. 4, we find this same photo from the original source of potential cities to study. We have included the five continents and all cultures, but the indicators evaluate and select the best into this group.

**Challengers** In this area we group cities from positions 70 to 90 which progress rapidly, competing to join the leading group, following the example of the Asian tigers. We are talking about the Middle East, led by Israel Tel-Aviv (71), Eastern Europe Prague (76), Emirates Dubai (82) and the Gulf. Any of these cities can join the main group as soon as they gain prestige and consolidate their interesting advances made in recent years.

**Emerging** Positions 91–122. We find in this group Buenos Aires (91) leading Latin America, then Mexico (100), Montevideo (102), Brazil with Rio de Janeiro (103) and now with Brasilia (112), to Colombia with Bogotá (117) and Medellín (121). All of China is led by Shanghai (95) to Shenzhen (116). Turkey with Istanbul (99), and Russia with Moscow (96). It is like a BRIC group, but without India, which needs strong urban transformation (they already have an ambitious 100 SmartCities plan). Malaysia has Kuala Lumpur (107) although with obvious different dimensions. The cities in this group have plans, recognize this global competition, and are making rapid progress.

**Starters** Positions 123–140. South Africa with CapeTown (123), India starting from Delhi (124), Maghreb starting from Tunis (135), Southeast Asia with Bangkok (122), Manila (131), Vietnam with Hanoi (134), and we finished with Cairo (139). These cities begin to plan their position in the competition for talent world although they continue to be burdened with solving basic social and economic issues.

If we look at Table 7.5, we can study the average positions of the studied cities by geographic area. It is curious to see the head-to-head competition between North America and Western Europe, with the same average position (38). Western Europe enjoys more Magnetism, history, culture, human values, but it pays a high price in taxes to maintain that societal well-being and its Profitability worsens.

North America does the opposite: it makes up for a lack of history, cultural and human flavor, but they compete strongly and win all economic and competitive issues, with high profitability, high wages, moderate taxes and a good cost of living.

In APAC (Asia-Pacific) we find the best and the worst, with Australia leading the concept of City Attractiveness (its only problem is far distances), and with New Zealand, South Korea, Japan and Singapore pushing very hard, and with very good results in citizen services, but with Southeast Asia as a whole ranked in

**Table 7.5**  Average positions. Attractive cities by geographic area

| Area | n | Magnetism | Profitability | Attractiveness |
|------|------|-----------|---------------|----------------|
| Africa | 5 | 122 | 133 | 129 |
| Asia-Pacific | 17 | 69 | 64 | 66 |
| CE Europe | 17 | 90 | 96 | 92 |
| China Ext | 9 | 102 | 101 | 103 |
| India | 3 | 131 | 125 | 128 |
| LatinAmerica | 17 | 110 | 112 | 112 |
| Middle East | 10 | 108 | 84 | 98 |
| NorthAmerica | 18 | 43 | 34 | 38 |
| WesternEurope | 44 | 34 | 41 | 38 |
|  | 140 |  |  |  |

Source: Author

very low positions. Some initiatives are seen in Kuala Lumpur, Bangkok and Jakarta, but Vietnam is among the last positions in almost all indicators.

In Eastern Europe, we observe central positions, from Prague (76) to Kiev (118). It is a segment with a good Identity, following in the wake of Western Europe, with some good initiatives in innovation such as Tallinn and Moscow, but with great problems in creativity, competitiveness and mainly social sustainability, so its Magnetism is not what we expected. In Profitability, low wages mean that while taxes are low, the bottom line is not attractive as many desired products carry *German* price standards.

In the Middle East, we find promising cities in middle positions such as Israel and the Emirates/Gulf region. Among them, there is Kuwait with a zero-tax wage system that strives to be attractive. Yet, it is not just an economic issue, and they can improve a lot if they develop innovation, citizen services and private competitiveness (not only with public money). Turkey has a good Identity and an acceptable cost of living, but it fails in everything else. The negative surprise is in Saudi Arabia, that has the same approach as Kuwait in economic attractiveness, but is very poor in the other indicators. Closing the group there is Cairo, with everything to improve and fix. In general, the Arab world must progress a lot in social sustainability, especially when the oil-based economic impulse is being strongly counteracted by environmental sustainability issues, and prices will continuously drop.

Let's look at extended China, including Hong Kong and Taiwan (Taipei). These two cities show the Attractive city road to the rest of Chinese cities. Strengthening Identity and Strategy, and the ability to offer advanced services put these two cities in intermediate positions, with the capacity to attract foreign talent. This is not the case with Chinese cities despite strong state-directed investments, because there are still insurmountable barriers for foreign talent. Internal talent sees good opportunities and development, but we live in a global world, and when Chinese companies are going to compete abroad they must take into account their ability to recruit and attract talent. They are paying more to compensate for the lack of appeal that social, ethical and reputational issues bring, weighing down on China'ss global position.

Latin America has huge potential in the emerging group, due to its human capital and resources. We started with Santiago (80) with parameters close to Europe, but with a problem of distances and seismic risks. Then Argentina, Buenos Aires (91) with more plans than execution; Montevideo (102) with a new, local talent surge and development; Mexico with problems of services, especially social, although with enormous academic potential; Brazil, where the main problems are strategy and the social balance; Colombia, which is falling back into inaction after important advances; finally, we find populism where technology does not exist in places like Bolivia and Paraguay.

Indian cities range from Delhi (124), Mumbai (129) to Bangalore, (130) where a massive, central-government managed SmartCity program is activated, but is far from competing in the global race for talent due to poor social conditions.

The same situation exists in the studied areas from Africa, North – Maghreb region with Tunis (135) and Casablanca, (136) which have some directed projects from central governments, as does South Africa (123–127).

To summarize, we found no surprises where economic and social problems are a main priority, a very active middle zone trying to achieve a relevant role in the global context, and a wide zone of leading cities in North America and Western Europe that are investing heavily to stand out over the others, in a tremendous fight for talent that also further expands the Western appeal.

Graphically, using the weights provided by the SmartCity Expo survey, we obtain the following honors' board per indicator. See Table 7.6.

## 7.4  City Magnetism Findings

First, and as a precondition, we shouldn't forget that Landscape, Language, Religion are also positive/negative Magnets. We are talking about personal preferences, so landscape implies a strong consideration most times; the seashore or mountains' proximity means happiness, or the opposite, for many. Man is the best animal on Earth able to adapt to all ecosystems, true, but we personally prefer some places over others. There are also some healthcare conditions impacted by this. Language is also very fundamental, as it impacts our ability to socialize/communicate with others. So, use of English as an alternative global language is a must for all top-city candidates. Spanish and Chinese are also globally spoken, but not so clearly accepted. Finally, Religion, our personal choice on connecting with the divine. There are tolerant or intrusive religions to different degrees, depending on the geographic areas and civilizations. This component is also very relevant to Ethics, and affects the way followers treat women, immigrants, non-believers, etc., so it's preferable to study those candidate cities' religion first, and avoid being surprised later.

The cities with the highest Magnetism are London, Stockholm, Amsterdam, Paris, NYC, Sydney, Vienna, Barcelona, Melbourne …no surprises here. (look at full City Magnetism Ranking at Appendix VI). There is a combination of strong Identity, branding, and reputation in geographical conditions that push the city's

**Table 7.6** Attractive Cities Rankings Honors board by Indicator using SmartCityExpo Survey inputs

| Honor Ranking (TOP 1) | | | | | | |
|---|---|---|---|---|---|---|
| Attractiveness | | Melbourne | | | | |
| Magnetism | London | | | | | |
| | Identity | London | Dynamism | Toronto | Strategy | Copenhagen |
| | History/Culture | Rome | Competitiveness | New York City | Human Capital | London |
| | Government basics | Oslo | Expat Social Experience | Madrid | Smart city | Copenhagen |
| | Reputation | Tokyo | Ethics. well-being | Amsterdam | Innovation | New York City |
| | Space/Density | Hong Kong | Equality | Helsinki | | |
| | Climate | Jerusalem | | | | |
| | Georisk | Doha | | | | |
| | Geoeconomics | Prague | | | | |
| | Gastronomy | Bern | | | | |
| | Branding. Ext. image | London | | | | |
| Profitability | Bern | Bern | | | | |
| Performance | Amsterdam | Cost of Living. Net purchase power | Kuwait City | | | |
| Digital government | Copenhagen | Avg wages/month | Zurich | | | |
| Education. Lifelong Training | Zurich | After DIR taxes income | Zurich | | | |
| Employability | San Francisco | Net real income | Zurich | | | |
| Connected city | Singapore | Cost of life | Córdoba (ARG) | | | |
| Health/Social SVS | Paris | | | | | |
| Environmental sustainability | Stockholm | | | | | |

| | London | Amsterdam | Toronto | Tokyo |
|---|---|---|---|---|
| Culture-tourism | | | | |
| Urban mobility | | | | |
| Urban planning | | | | |
| Safety | | | | |

Source: Author

development; together with current conditions of a vibrant, creative, suggestive economy, in a friendly social environment, with equity and justice and with respect and equality; and with a strategy, a strong investment in innovation and in generation of human capital. All these components build the city of our dreams. It is the perfect city to live in, with the perfect environmental, cultural, social and innovation conditions for creativity, development and progress. We just need the numbers to be adequate too, in terms of received services and cost of living. Thus, we see cities with an important gap between Attractiveness and Magnetism, cities with enormous Magnetism that is being wasted by their leaders, since the conditions of services and cost of living do not help at all. They are cities with a lot of flavor, but with little future if they do not react and ride the wave of innovation and improve the economy. The city with the largest gap in this regard is Lisbon, along with several Italian ones. It is unfortunate to observe how the historical effort of its inhabitants is not leveraged now to make top, attractive cities. We can say that the reality of low wages, or high taxes, kills Magnetism and turns it into nostalgia, and we neither live nor prosper from that.

Of the two surveys, Talented Citizens prefer City Dynamism (Vibrant, Competitive, Friendly, Equity, Equality) because we live in the present. The Identity (past) is also very important (short distance) since we need past references to plan the future, so the (future) Strategy is considered the least relevant (the future can be arranged. . .) Also, because many citizens live daily, without preparing for the future, or attributing to it less importance, thinking that they will have time for it, when what is really scarce in our ephemeral life is just that, time. We have therefore found, in the Magnetism study, the most brilliant and prosperous cities in the world. We could have concluded the City Attractiveness study here, but the Profitability aspect makes us stand firm, and also attend to the reality of our *citizenship contract* terms and conditions: the city's benefits/services and its economic terms.

EUR (European) cities have a great advantage due to their strong Identity. They enjoy it from many years of branding, but the main cities of the U.S./CAN/AUS are also in the first positions due to Dynamism and Strategy.

- Identity (Past): Balance the use of the city's assets in history, climate, and reputation, while constantly building branding. It is a continual construction process that is eroded by competition with other cities.

The top 30 are fundamentally traditional European cities led by London (with the exceptions of Seoul (8), NYC (12), and Tokyo (19)). Apart from the historical component, which is also present in other civilizations such as China, the rest of Asia, etc., European cities have built a strong Identity as the cradle of Western civilization, and contribute to branding this image. The enormous concentration of people in a small space has favored human density and cultural development for centuries.

As for History, obviously Rome and Athens are in the lead, with the rest of Europe behind, but matching Seoul and the Chinese cities. This component is a handicap for the U.S. and AUS, although they compensate it with other topics. History is always the benchmark, although too much could turn into a drag on the spirit of entrepreneurship, exploring the unknown, which is so strong in these new world countries. On the other hand, the sense of belonging, or citizenship is stronger in cities with a longer historical culture. The feeling of *I'm proud to live here* runs deeper in old cities than new, *planned* ones, with almost no clear Identity yet created. The sense of community is also stronger in smaller cities, because long distances imply less contact, sharing, density and less sense of community. So, small and historical cities enjoy a stronger sense of Identity.

The governance marks the acceptable basics of democracy and security to develop our public and political facet. In this respect, Oslo, CAN, Nordics, AUS, EUR take the lead. CHN, RUS and the Middle East have severe problems in this regard.

A reputation takes decades to be built, and only a few days to be destroyed. Leading this aspect is Tokyo, Nordics, AUS, CAN, while CHN, Colombia and the Arab countries have severe problems in this fundamental concept. Recent riots for independence have partially destroyed the long-cultivated reputation of Barcelona.

Green spaces/Density. We are looking for the perfect city that combines large green areas for recreation (and incidentally, millions of trees to contribute to Carbon-neutral objectives) with very-high human density, for the development of social creativity and competitiveness. With this definition, Hong Kong takes the lead, with 40% of green space but with a density of more than 26,000 inhabitants/km$^2$, then Singapore, but also Oslo, and CHN with its new, large, green and highly populated cities. Here, the U.S. has problems with the excessive space dedicated to cars, as does the UAE, that has a lot of sand and few trees.

Climate. We look for the city with the perfect climate. Although global warming will have an important impact, making arid areas that were formerly very rich and sensitive, destroying coastal cities, forcing now-desert countries to live underground, protected from the sun, and improving conditions in places today that are extremely cold such as the Nordic countries, Canada, etc.; it's clear we are going to have to study the known climate. We are looking for a city in the middle: mild, temperate, neither humid nor dry, without significant variations, without downpours or droughts, and with many hours of real sun so that citizens can get out of their houses and do big things together: develop the city. The leading city with average temper-ature, rain, without great peaks and with a lot of sun is Jerusalem. Then follow Johannesburg, Montevideo, San Francisco, Lisbon, Madrid, Nice, Washington D.C. On the contrary, the cities with the most infernal climate of those studied are the Indies, and those of Southeast Asia, with Mumbai (too hot, too many monsoons, and too little sun).

Geolocation. A good Geolocation is a huge advantage. As for risk due to geographical location, the most stable and least-risky city is Doha, then the rest of the Middle East, the Nordic countries, CH (Switzerland) and Europe in general. The Netherlands (situated below sea level), Chile and Manila suffer from this condition due to high seismic and tsunami risk. The geographical location also helps economic relations and foreign trade, as well as the ability to do same-day business travel (understood as distances requiring less than 2.5-hour flights). Prague (CZR), EUR, and CHN surprisingly lead in this regard. The U.S., AUS, Latam, and the Middle East do suffer the distances' problem.

Gastronomy. Although OXFAM's analysis on quality and quantity of healthy food includes that it must be affordable, the study in general takes little account of the price of food. EUR, CH lead, followed by the rest of the West. My favorite city in this sense, Bilbao (Spain) is in 14th place, although it has an incredible number of excellent restaurants. The analysis shows poorer gastronomy is available in India and Southeast Asia.

Branding: It is the area that we cannot neglect, and how the city Identity is expressed abroad. The abundance of international events, sports, activities of global importance, etc., position the most brilliant cities as leaders: LON, NYC, PAR, BCN, LA, Melbourne. . . .it is an individual competition. This is where cities play alone, without their countries in the background, in competition with all others. The same countries' *number two* cities greatly suffer in the shadow of these special cities, with which they compete for this international relevance. Thus, many European cities fight against their capitals. As an example, Linz is a long way from Vienna in this respect.

- Dynamism (present): We try to measure the city's present and dynamic attractiveness. It is a balance between a competitive, creative and vibrant society, combined with a friendly treatment of immigrants and excellent social sustainability (equity, happiness, equality, tolerance). It is not easy to achieve, and it is the most observed topic because it reflects the conditions with which talent will be faced as soon as it arrives. Toronto leads, and the rest of CAN, then NZ, AUS, and Western Europe. The U.S. is very competitive, but suffers from social imbalance. Among the worst positions, we find China (good competitiveness, but with very poor Ethics and Equality), India (that treats expatriates very well, but has poor social sustainability).

  Competitiveness. The U.S. leads, followed by the most prosperous cities such as Singapore, LON, AMS, PAR, Copenhagen, Sydney. Thus, in Creativity, AUS, and the U.S. lead, then NZ, CAN, and the Nordics. In the specific Competitiveness index, the top positions are occupied by Singapore, the U.S., Hong Kong, NED, and CH. The Cities in Motion and GTCI (Global Talent Competitiveness) Indexes are closely aligned and place LON, NYC, AMS, PAR in front. We see this section is closely related to economic prosperity.

  Expatriate experience. Here, we are going to try to understand what the arrival will be like, the newcomer's social immersion experience, or in another way, how friendly and welcoming the city is from a social point of view. It is a very important point because it connects with the very essence of the city. Here we see Madrid leading, then the rest of Spain, Portugal, NZ, CAN, Singapore, MEX, Colombia, France, AUS, India. On the other extreme, tough, difficult, almost hostile cities for foreigners would be the Arabian ones, CHN, Belgium, Eastern Europe, UK, CH. This is a very relevant point to consider for explorers, and thus, we have included it here.

Ethics. As for social sustainability, or social Ethics, NED, AUS, lead, then CAN, and NZ. We start with happiness. Although the Happiness Index is, in my opinion, mainly a well-being and comfort index, and assigns a large weight to the city's economic success, leaving the rest to a matter of perceptions and opinions, forgetting relevant questions like number of suicides, let's take it as the best approach. It scores Helsinki, NZ, CH, Nordics, NED, CAN as the happiest cities. Someone might wonder why many citizens from these cities escape to the South to seek sun to avoid falling into depression once again, but we will not question any report until another more accurate one appears.

Giving. The concept of Giving is interesting, very strong in the U.S., NZ, AUS, IRE, CAN, UK; that is, very rooted in Commonwealth and something that other countries should learn in school: donate part of their achieved success.

Civic Engagement. AUS, NED, lead, then KOR, BEL, NZ, UK, the U.S., being an excellent sign of freedom, social participation and of a mature and advanced society.

Work/life balance is mainly a European concept, with NED, ITA, Western Europe, being one of the most important European social achievements in the last century. The absence of labor rights for the sake of competitiveness destroys the family and mentally drains workers' creativity.

Finally, Equality. Here Helsinki, the Nordics, CAN, AUS, NED, NZ, and CH rule. The GINI index, which measures inequality and imbalance in the wealth distribution, is very important, as we already anticipated. The leadership of NED, Nordics and Europe in general is not surprising, making these cities places with good social balance and sustainability. Imbalanced societies such as South Africa (already well-known and divided), UAE, BRA, Hong Kong, and Colombia score very poorly. The U.S. obtains bad results, as we have already studied the tremendous imbalance in wealth distribution.

Gender equality. Eastern Europe (Baltic countries) leads, then Nordics, then the U.S. The advanced position that the Nordic countries have achieved in this regard is very relevant and definitely leads the world.

Tolerance. It is key to open the city gates with tolerance so that talent can enter. Dublin leads as a paradigm of a Western technological city open to talent, then POR, FIN, CAN, Nordics, AUS. It is surprising to see the severe reluctance and barriers that are still placed on talent, even in cities with low human capital, and therefore, with a great need to attract it.

Poverty. There are different criteria depending on the country and cluster, and it is surprising to see advanced countries with impossible numbers and countries with serious problems with very good ones. In any case, this is the official report, and it allows us to compare the four groups that we have found in the results.

• Strategy (Future): As we studied, this is a very granular issue, as it depends a lot on the city managers' leadership and their ability to attract investment. We are not talking about having a correct and efficient governance; it is about looking to the future and being able to think and dream about what city we want to achieve and where we want to go. We find in the first positions the leading cities in innovation and SmartCity plans those like Copenhagen, Seoul, San Francisco, Stockholm, and NYC.

In Human Capital, we combine young cities like those Emerging, with the creation of human capital from that large number of young people. Jakarta, and the U.S., lead, then UK, Moscow, LON, and Western Europe. It is good to see that there is a universal *sowing* of raw talent, giving everyone a chance to use it, nurture it to prosper or simply lose it.

In the SmartCity Plan, we see the real implementation of this strategy and where the city points its priorities. Western Europe and AUS lead, then some star cities such as Tel-Aviv, Taipei, Doha, San Francisco, Seoul, Hong Kong. It is extremely important to see how many cities use this SmartCity plan to compensate for a lack of City Identity or social issues in City Dynamism. Some cities, like the Swiss ones, are at the beginning of their SmartCities plans, basically because they were attractive enough per se, without having to pay attention to this. Fortunately, they are realizing the importance of the concept and reacting.

Innovation: We are going to look for the money to invest in innovation, and we find this fresh money betting on the city's future in the U.S., KOR, JAP, GER, ISR, and in Western Europe.

## 7.5  City Profitability Findings

• Best Combined Profitability (Services x NetPurchasePower) at Swiss Cities, led by Bern, then AUS, the Nordics, Germany, then the U.S. It is about combining excellent citizen services with high wages, moderate taxes and a cost of living that does not ruin final net purchasing power.
• Best in Services are in Western Europe, led by AMS, STO, BER, LON, OSL, then NYC, Tokyo, Gothenburg, Vienna, Frankfurt, Copenhagen, Zurich. We can say that with certain exceptions, the best cities public services among all its 10 groups are enjoyed in Western Europe.

By Service, in Digital Government, Copenhagen leads, then the Nordics, the U. S., UK, with surprisingly low scores in BEL, AT, CH, because of the low use of technologies to connect to citizens online. In India, Brazil, and Latam they are showing good improvements and scorings.

In Education or Long-life Training, we have no surprises with CH, the U.S., SGP, NED, the Nordics, UK, BEL, CAN leading. SPA, and mainly ITA could do better.

In Employability, the U.S. leads, then NED, Dublin, Germany, CH. Malaysia and Philippines are doing well.

Best Connectivity is enjoyed in SGP, then Vienna, Budapest, Seoul, NZ, and some specific cities with good operators' investment like Antwerp, Montreal, Sydney, Eindhoven, Madrid. The Gulf is doing well here, while in ITA this area is weak. The best Asian cities have an advantage in Connectivity, and as soon as 5G is available, this leadership will grow larger.

In Health/Social Services, at the top is France, SWE, AT, NOR, ITA, DK, BEL, GER, FIN, SPA, so Western Europe excels in Social Services and quality of Healthcare. They are not so good in NED, CH, and Eastern Europe possibly because they depend too much on private intervention?

Stockholm leads Environmental Sustainability, with surprisingly, Montevideo right after, NZ, the Nordics, AT, with Paraguay, Panama, and La Paz doing a good job. Poor job from Kiev, and the U.S. in general, although here, cities, grouped in C40 and other associations are facing inaction from the Federal Government.

London tops Culture/Tourism, with Hong-Kong, Paris, Tokyo, Seoul, Bangkok, Los Angeles, Rome, Amsterdam following the lead. The number of visitors gives an extra boost to Asian cities competing with the paramount Western cultural ones.

Urban Mobility. Amsterdam, Germany, Vienna, Spain, and NED are in the best positions, paying attention to public transportation and the traffic problem. Japan, London, the U.S., CAN, AUS are suffering with this, and this score is pushing them down the overall services' performance.

Urban Planning sets Toronto at the top, CAN, the U.S., and surprisingly Taiwan and Hong-Kong; AUS, London, Amsterdam, Rotterdam are the first European ones in 9th, 11th, and 16th positions. Good surprise from Latam. Worst ones in India, and South Africa.

Safety is ruled by Tokyo, SGP, Japan, South Korea, NED, the Nordics, AUS, CAN. Poor score from most of the U.S., closing with Latam and SouthAfrica. The right to own guns definitely acts as a brake in U.S. cities' attractiveness.

- Best NetPurchasePower (NPP) is enjoyed in Kuwait, AUS, CH, and then U.S. cities cover the top 15 positions. The U.S. has a predominant position is this context because of good wages, and moderated or low taxes. Cost of living (especially in NYC, and San Francisco) is high, but not enough to ruin the deal. Kuwait takes that position after applying a moderated wage, a very-low direct tax (5%) and zero indirect ones (VAT).
- Best Gross Wages found at CH, LUX, the Nordics, Germany, the U.S., AUS...
- Best Final Net Income is enjoyed in CH, Kuwait, the US, AUS, the Nordics. CH has moderated taxes for single people with no children (that's the studied case). Even at this low-level step of the progressive taxes' ladder, the worst taxes are suffered in Western Europe, with many countries paying more than 30% direct and more than 20% indirect like BEL, GER, DK, AT, ITA, NED, FR.
- Most Expensive Cost of Living is found in CH, the Nordics, some parts of the U. S., JPN cities. With NYC as Cost of life = 1 as the reference (including housing), we can only find one more expensive place, San Francisco, with 1.02. Other expensive areas are CH with Zurich at 0.96. This Cost of life is helping some cities to improve the total Net Purchasing Power because of their low one, like in Santiago, with a 0.29 that is raising the city to position 59 in Net Final income. So cheap cities are perfect, but wages are the most important component of the economic equation. You can ruin a good wage with high taxes (like in Western

Europe), or improve a moderate one with low taxes (Santiago); but if your wage is very small, then there is no way to add more money on top of it.

There is significant opportunity for mid-size/non-capital cities because they can offer similar, high-quality services as in the main capitals, but the better cost of life (not so expensive) will eventually raise the net purchasing power. This is the case of Phoenix (U.S.) making it to the 4th position in Net Purchasing Power, or Gothenburg scoring better than Stockholm, or Cologne better than Berlin, Rotterdam vs Amsterdam and so on. To ensure that we have chosen a good wine, we can pay a lot of money. We can do the same, paying a high price and cost of living over choosing an expensive city, but also with high-quality benefits/services. This is easy but expensive. It will be difficult to find a very good wine for an affordable price. Here we have again the same concern: it is advisable to look for *second* cities, where you are not going to pay the extra that the capital status implies, while you enjoy the same, or even better quality of services.

There are cities with good quality of services that take average positions in Profitability due to their mid wages and high taxes (ITA, POR, Eastern Europe, ISR). Also, cities failing to reach top positions in Performance/Services because of taxes, like Paris, or the opposite: good salary, low-tax cities, poorly-balanced by low-quality city services like Saudi Arabia, Qatar or Kuwait.

There is an opportunity for Emerging Latam cities (fix the basics and enroll in the global game!), like ARG, BRA, MEX.

Special guest stars: Apart from above best. . .Gulf countries, Asian Tigers (KOR, SGP, TWN, HNK) that have good services and moderately high wages, can challenge the top leaders.

## 7.6  Balancing City Magnetism with City Profitability

The Indian Government's "Smart Cities Mission" is a massive development program for 100 smart cities, and postulates that there is no single SmartCity model, neither globally, nor locally in India. The concept varies from site to site, depending on many factors such as the initial level of development, commitment, resources and aspirations of the inhabitants. Depending on each city's economic and socio-cultural situation, digital modernization will create different cities with different social and cultural benefits (India Government, 2020).

We are, therefore, impacting the fixed terms that make up the city Identity with the development of better services to make them evolve, transforming the city, while improving general living conditions (social and economic). It is a balance between transforming the essence of the city, (its physical and virtual shape) while improving its benefits and services. One thing feeds the other. The essence of the city determines how the services provided will improve, while the new services' impact transforms the essence of the city in a virtuous cycle.

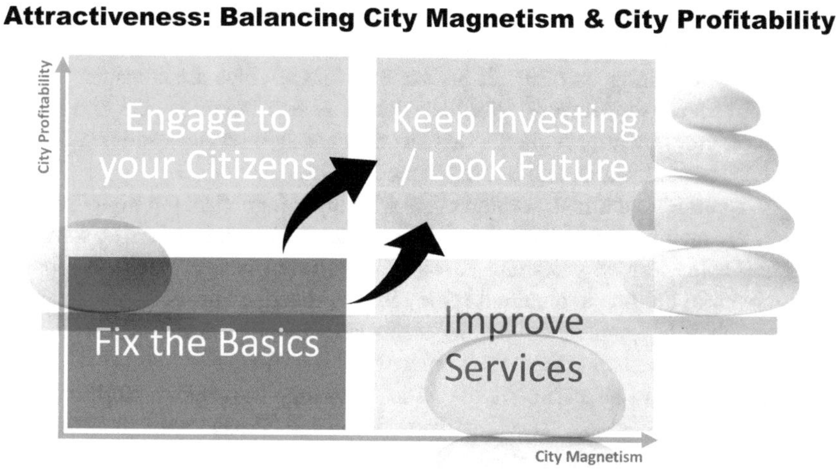

## Attractiveness: Balancing City Magnetism & City Profitability

**Fig. 7.1**  Balancing City Magnetism and City Profitability. (Source: Author)

Investing in creating an Attractive city contributes to well-being, prosperity and sustainable development. The transition to an information and knowledge economy represents a revolution due to its new acceleration and speed, but also a challenge when balancing the concept of an Attractive and accessible city with social and environmental progress (Van Den Berg, 2006).

Therefore, we must look for cities that inspire us, that motivate us, and that humanly enrich us, magnetic cities where living has meaning, a flavor, a destiny and a mission; cities that compensate us for our daily effort, that help us with good services and benefits, that provide us with good living conditions and where the end-of-the-month numbers are enough to pay for the development of our aspirations. If we are just looking for a beautiful and suggestive city, then we may find it very difficult for us to develop our potential due to lack of benefits or financial compensation. If we are just looking for a perfect city as a good deal or transaction, we can find ourselves living in a generic, horrible, boring city that psychologically destabilizes us, and where displaying our human face is almost impossible. We must therefore find full sustainable development, social and human, economic and labor, and environmental and urban planning. We return to the three intertwined facets: technology, urban planning and humanism.

We can study our 140 cities according to this balance. We found four quadrants that suggest where they are and where they should move to. The magic quadrant is the upper right, (see Fig. 7.1) where we find cities with high Magnetism and Profitability. These are mainly Advanced & Challenger cities. These cities compete hard day-by-day to stay there, gain positions little by little, with a lot of economic effort and talent. The message for them is clear: keep investing, keep progressing, anything else is failing; it's falling, and the recovery is even more difficult because the competition is fierce and they will neither forgive nor stop investing.

In the lower left quadrant, we see cities with low Magnetism and Profitability. These are Emerging and mainly Starter cities, as we have called them before. (See Sect. 7.3). Our message is clear: *fix the basics*. If these cities are considered in this study, it is because they have possibilities, potential, size and relevance, and because they can progress by improving the two facets in parallel: services and benefits, and citizen engagement, social and human attractiveness.

In the upper left quadrant, we find cities with low Magnetism but high Profitability. They are mainly some non-magnetic ones in the U.S., Japanese cities, some very Industrial, cold German cities and Kuwait. They have the opportunity to improve and evolve into the magic quadrant if they invest in achieving social sustainability, improving their Dynamism, cultivating their scarce Identity, designing an attractive future plan and connecting with their citizens.

In the lower right quadrant, we find cities with high Magnetism but little Profitability. They are cities with great Identity, tradition and human values, but our talents also seek compensation and professional and personal success. They must improve the provision of citizen services and the economic equation, or they run the risk of going back to the basic group. This is the case for the Italian and Portuguese cities with high Magnetism and flavor, but poor Profitability. Hong-Kong also has high Magnetism, but declining Profitability with China's integration process.

(See at Appendix XV.- Attractive Cities. City Magnetism vs City Profitability Quadrants. All studied cities are positioned according to their scores and named according to their UNLOCODE three letters nomination, so you can easily position any of them.) The correlation factor $R^2 = 0.6053$ is high and means that both magnitudes are highly related. In this way, we see that most cities obtain approximate results in both Magnetism and Profitability. This suggests that, in general, cities that take care of their image, that have achieved a strong Identity and have good social and economic sustainability, also offer advanced services and a reasonable cost of living. On the contrary, neglected cities, or those with social sustainability problems, a lack of strategy, identity and reputation, are offering us poor services and a low net purchasing power. But the city is a living entity, and it evolves. We know that today's prosperity helps, but does not guarantee the future. We can find many examples of past, brilliant cities that are now mediocre or even very unattractive. Relying just on history, none can live in the present, nor is the future already built. On the other hand, City Magnetism due to social sustainability is impossible without economic sustainability. In other words, Magnetism requires constant investment and good economic terms to shine. When the economy fails, social development tremble. Good salaries and high net incomes make life easier and improve well-being; remember that the City Happiness indicator has GDP/Capita as the first and main non surveys'-based component. When we say that emerging or starter cities should fix the basics, we mainly mean that they should fix or improve their economies.

Let's study those unbalanced cities as well (i.e.: cities with more than three net points (out of 10), or 30% of maximum potential score difference between Magnetism and Profitability, or with poor correlation). (See Table 7.7)

**Table 7.7** Unbalanced cities according to the city attractiveness model

| City | Country | Magnetism | Profitability | Attractiveness | Attractiveness index | Unbal |
|---|---|---|---|---|---|---|
| Kuwait City | Kuwait | 1,84 | 6,41 | 11,81 | **97** | 4,57 |
| Paris | France | 9,49 | 5,33 | 50,57 | **47** | 4,16 |
| Milan | Italy | 8,25 | 4,20 | 34,63 | **69** | 4,05 |
| London | United Kingdom | 10,00 | 6,07 | 60,65 | **21** | 3,93 |
| Rome | Italy | 7,79 | 3,95 | 30,78 | **70** | 3,84 |
| Lisbon | Portugal | 7,32 | 3,50 | 25,63 | **77** | 3,82 |
| Shanghai | China | 5,90 | 2,23 | 13,13 | **95** | 3,67 |
| Barcelona | Spain | 9,30 | 5,79 | 53,83 | **40** | 3,52 |
| Florence | Italy | 7,36 | 3,87 | 28,49 | **74** | 3,50 |
| Porto | Portugal | 7,26 | 3,78 | 27,43 | **75** | 3,48 |
| Moscow | Russia | 5,67 | 2,25 | 12,74 | **96** | 3,42 |
| New York City | United States | 9,48 | 6,07 | 57,49 | **27** | 3,41 |
| Hong Kong | Hong Kong | 7,28 | 4,04 | 29,46 | **73** | 3,24 |
| Rio de Janeiro | Brazil | 5,20 | 2,02 | 10,47 | **103** | 3,18 |
| San Francisco | United States | 8,59 | 5,51 | 47,34 | **56** | 3,08 |
| Cape Town | South Africa | 4,15 | 1,15 | 4,77 | **123** | 3,00 |

Source: Author

On one hand we find Kuwait, with good profitability, mainly due to close-to-zero taxes. Good deal? Yes, but Magnetism is really poor. Short history, questionable government basics, low reputation, little space, extreme weather, far from other economies, basic gastronomy, and no international image making for a poor Identity score. Poor creativity and competitiveness, poor expat experience, basic Ethics, and a long room for improvement in Equality make Dynamism poor as well; finally, low human capital, a short SmartCity plan, and little innovation sets a low score for Strategy.

To counter this, we find cities with a significant gap between an acceptable or very-good Magnetism score, and a very poor one in Profitability. These cities are very Magnetic, but very expensive as well (so, low Profitability) like Paris, Milano, London, Barcelona, NYC, San Francisco; or they are Magnetic, but offer low wages, so final income is low (Profitability) like in Portuguese cities, Rome, Florence, and Hong-Kong; finally, cities with mid-range Magnetism but with very low wages, (so having a significant gap as well) include those like Shanghai, Moscow, and Cape Town.

These cities have great potential and a chance to improve Attractiveness if they fix the lowest term. Those very-high tax cities should maximize services (if they can't reduce taxes). Those with low wages will have to pay extra if they want to retain and attract talent.

## 7.7   City Attractiveness vs Population vs GDP

We study the possible correlation of City Attractiveness with city population (Metropolitan Area). In Fig. 7.2, we can see the 140 studied cities, distributed horizontally according to their size, and vertically according to their score in the

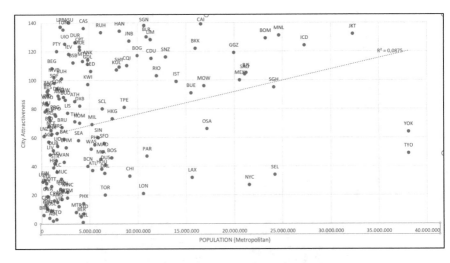

**Fig. 7.2**   City Attractiveness ranking vs Population (Metropolitan Area). (Source: Author)

model. There are megacities in high and low positions, as well as medium-sized cities. In the chapter dedicated to Magnetism, we rated high-density as positive, as an enabler of personal communication and development of activity. We also commented that despite the possible dispersion in small towns brought by the new communication and Internet technologies, citizens continue to prefer living in medium and large cities over living in isolated small towns. We should not confuse small cities close in commuting time to other large cities: as we have already explained, they must be associated to that main city. For humans, they are psychologically the same city, same metropolis.

From the observation and the correlation coefficient $R^2 = 0.0875$ we conclude that there is NO correlation between City Attractiveness and city size. Furthermore, we see that largest cities are strongly attractive due to Magnetism, although they are usually more expensive, and therefore with less Profitability, but that the second/third ranked cities in each country are more affordable, maintaining very good performance standards and high Profitability, although they are less Magnetic, so both things are offset in both city sizes. Perhaps we could say that we find megacities with more problems and handicaps to be leaders in Attractiveness, but they provide a bonus when it comes to Magnetism that is important to value.

In Fig. 7.3, we can compare City Attractiveness with GDP/Capita. Here $R^2 = 0.7294$, indicating a strong correlation between these two magnitudes. No surprises: larger budgets with which to invest improves city branding, the external image, events, cultural activities, competitiveness and obviously the city services and Net purchasing power, because of higher wages. The opposite is also true: as we studied, low budgets with which to invest lead to poorer city development, urbanism, quality of live and services and lower wages, so all main items are severely impacted. Again,

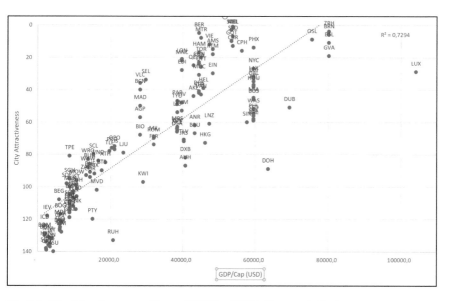

**Fig. 7.3**  City Attractiveness ranking vs GDP/Cap (USD). (Source: Author)

we cannot conclude that City Attractiveness is a just a matter of rich cities. That's not true, as we can see in vertical (same GDP) all the U.S. cities ranging from 20 to 60 positions, but obviously city wealth and capacity to invest strongly contributes to City Attractiveness.

## 7.8    Attractive Cities vs SmartCities

We are going to study the impact of investments in SmartCities on making the city more Attractive. We found that for many cities, investments in their SmartCity plan are the main axis of their strategy to improve their Attractiveness. These investments directly improve performance in city services, and therefore their City Profitability. In addition, they improve their investment in the future, their strategy, also their image of modernity and their reputation, and therefore, their Magnetism. For many cities, it is an important question of prestige (Chinese cities). However, we see many cities that pay little attention to a consolidated SmartCities plan, (even if they offer very good services) because they do not consider that they should improve their external image because they think they do not need it, since they are already very attractive... We place the Swiss cities here.

Let's study Fig. 7.4. The horizontal line at zero: Over that line. cities more Attractive than Smart; under that line, they are more Smart than Attractive.

On the vertical axis, the orange line marks rank 70, or the midpoint in Attractiveness, so to the left are the cities classified as Advanced; to the right the Challenging, then Emerging, then Starters.

To the left, above the top arrow we find the Swiss cities, much more attractive than smart, with poor smart city plans, but they don't need them either! However, they are reacting and realizing that they need to invest in technology to maintain that leadership. Just below that arrow and to the right we find many German cities, with

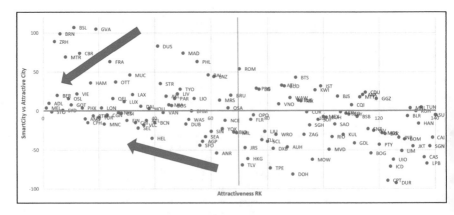

**Fig. 7.4**  City Attractiveness ranking vs gap (SmartCity vs AttractiveCity). (Source: Author)

very good attractiveness, but that should improve their SmartCity plan. Next, we find American and European cities such as Madrid with SmartCity plans that can be improved. We then reach the orange line that marks Rome, on the border with the challenging cities. On this same left side, at the bottom, we find the leading cities in SmartCity, those investing heavily to improve positions in Attractiveness (Copenhagen, Amsterdam, Helsinki, Barcelona...) Here is where the main battle for Attractiveness is fought nowadays, with large investments in Sustainability, citizen services, etc.

From the vertical orange line to the right, we see that most cities are at under the horizontal line: they are the Challengers, investing heavily in SmartCity plans to get promoted to the advanced group (Tel-Aviv, Hong Kong, Doha, Taipei and many from Eastern Europe...) If we advance to the right, then we enter the Emerging group first and the Starters at the right end. We see that they all obtain better positions in SmartCity than in Attractiveness (most under the horizontal line), which indicates that they all use investments in SmartCity to improve their services for citizens, their image of modernity and their Attractiveness in general.

Therefore, as a general guideline, the SmartCities' Plan fulfills its mission of improving citizen services (Profitability), while helping in strategy, reputation, modernity (Magnetism) and becoming the most powerful and short-mid-term tool to improve in Attractiveness. Little can be done about fixed issues like geolocation. Investments in changing or improving Identity are slow and always in the medium-long term. It is difficult to quickly improve economic conditions and net purchasing power. Therefore, the obvious lever, with more short-term results (even in a four-year legislature) is to invest heavily in a solid SmartCities plan. The cities that fail in this, have either fallen asleep in the leadership glory, (and are now waking up, like the Swiss) or are losing positions and do not take advantage of excellent Magnetism to improve positions (Southern Europe). On the other hand, cities with handicaps in Magnetism, either due to a lack of history (U.S.), weather conditions (Nordics) or long distances (AUS) compensate with attractive plans that improve their attractiveness to leadership positions.

Finally, at Appendix XVI.- Attractive Cities vs SmartCities by GDP we can see that investing in SmartCities is quite independent from GDP, so all cities can invest resources on creating and executing a compelling SmartCity Plan. This will improve Attractiveness, and if investment is done rationally, progress can be very significant with a moderate cost (we have seen great progress in Latam Cities with very reasonable budgets, but wise investments). On the other hand, Attractiveness is more directly dependent on GDP, so everything that could contribute to improving it counts and is welcome (including the improvement in talent and investors' investment because of an increase in awareness due to a brilliant SmartCity plan). So, we are circling around same concept. As a conclusion, all areas are intertwined, and a balanced plan will touch the most-effective levers.

## 7.9   Cities Attractiveness Analytics' Deliverables

### 7.9.1   City Radiography

With this model and its more than 100 indicators, we can make a complete radiography of a city, and evaluate its SmartCity plans, all in comparison with the rest of the world or only with its cluster of nearby cities, as we have seen.

Let's look at an example of a city radiography in Fig. 7.5.

In the city radiography we observe which elements add and which subtract from the city's total result. This is very easy, just comparing the city ranking on them with the aggregated ranking. (See areas in green – those which contribute, yellow, neutral, or red are those that push the result down)

There are components which are impossible to change due to their fixed nature, like climate or geographical conditions. They are elements that will help (and therefore we can take advantage of them and use them as a city flag or benefit) like mild climate in Jerusalem or those that represent a handicap (and therefore must have their impact mitigated or minimized) like seismic risk in Santiago de Chile.

There are other components that can be changed such as taxes, macroeconomic or sociological elements (educational, health system, etc.) that do not depend directly on the city management, but on the state or the country. In any case, the city can modify them to some extent, reinforcing those that are short on local services or policies, for example, reinforcing social services or healthcare services, or postgraduate training or non-regulated education or languages skills.

Where the city can make a great impact is on everything that depends on its management, its inherent public services, its governance, its branding, its SmartCity

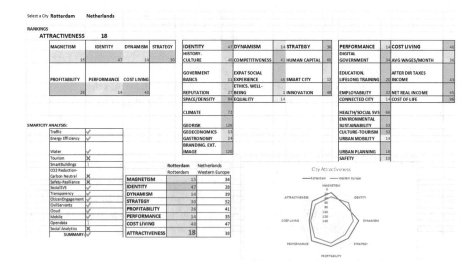

**Fig. 7.5** Example of city radiography using the Attractive cities model. City of Rotterdam (The Netherlands). (Source: Author)

Plan. These are the elements to study more in depth; and once they have been compared to others, cities need to determine priorities, design a strategy and implement it.

We can also compare the city with its nearby cluster and discover its advantages and the areas in which it should improve. This is very important in the last term decision; that is, let's imagine that a Syrian-by-origin talented citizen is very well deciding for The Netherlands, then the last term decision will be where within the Netherlands, and then this nearby, mini-competition between Dutch cities is established.

## 7.9.2 Cities' Real Testing

Many cities have checked the model so far. For 18 months (1 Sept 2018 – 31 March 2020) the model has been directly explained to main city officials, the results analyzed, and feedback obtained from these cities (M stands for direct Mayor conversation):

Spain: Madrid (M), Barcelona, Bilbao, Santander (M), Pamplona-Navarra, Sevilla, Zaragoza (M), Málaga, Cartagena, Murcia, Santiago de Compostela // Italy: Rome, Milano, Firenze // Austria: Vienna // Switzerland: Basel // Ireland: Dublin (M) // UK: Belfast, London // Germany: Cologne // Belgium: Brussels, Antwerp, Ghent, Mechelen // The Netherlands: Amsterdam, Rotterdam, Eindhoven, Alkmaar (M), Haarlemmermeer // Luxembourg // Denmark: Esbjerg, Frederiksberg // Sweden; Stockholm, Gothenburg, Helsingborg, Umea, Jönköpings, Lunds, Örebro, Nacka // Portugal: Lisbon, Braga // Finland; Helsinki, Oulu, Turku // Norway: Stavanger, Bergen, Oslo, Bodø, Sandnes // Japan: Tokyo // U.S.: Atlanta // Panama // Colombia: Medellín.

All of them understood it, found their cities very well represented in the facts, and very few challenged the data (they wanted to drill down on the contributing data indicators to challenge sources). It is not our intention to challenge data sources; we simply took the best data available that match our selection criteria, as explained. All exposed cities took good note of areas to improve and thankfully said they were going to, or were already planning on prioritizing those red areas.

## 7.9.3 Conferences. Congresses

For the same time (1 Sept 2018 – 15 Apr 2020), the model has been shared directly with more than 12,000 people in many different events and congresses like NordicEdge (Stavanger, Norway), Mobile World Congress (Barcelona, Spain), SmartSuisse (Basel, Switzerland), Technopolis EU Innovation (Brussels, Belgium), Trilateral Commission Meeting (Paris, France), European Week of Regions and Cities (Brussels, Belgium), SmartCityExpo WW Congress (Barcelona, Spain) and

Netexplo/UNESCO, to mention the most relevant. In addition, delivered in Alcobendas-Madrid (Spain) in Feb 2019, my TEDx Speech was based on Cities Attractiveness (Author, 2019). You can watch it in Spanish or English.

### *7.9.4   Smartphone Apps*

As we want end users to use the model to find the best city according to their preferences, we released the AttractiveCities App in Nov 2019 in most popular smartphones' stores:

Android (Google) (Android Store, 2020), and IOS (Apple) (IOS Store, 2020) (See also AttractiveCities App downloading QR Codes & App Screenshots at Appendix XVII)

When using the tool, you enter your input (weights) on City Magnetism (Identity, Dynamism and Strategy), and 10 City Services – Profitability. There are also pre-conditions such as Religion, Language and Landscape which can be selected. The tool returns your best top 15 cities, matching your preferences.

### *7.9.5   Other Future Deliverables*

We are developing a WW Observatory on Attractive Cities, together with university and relevant companies. Annually updated, the plan is to release a new version for all the indicators used here, updated or replaced by other better ones to describe any relative topic. This WW Observatory will be shown at SmartCityExpo & WW Congress event (www.smartcityexpo.com) and at Universidad Francisco de Vitoria (www.ufv.es) websites. Interested reader should point their browser there for updates.

This action provides a continuation in time for this research objectives: help Millennials and talented citizens choose the best city for their preferences and make well-informed decisions, as well as helping City managers to properly prepare their cities to compete for talent. Additionally, the plan is to use this observatory as a reference site for documents, training, solutions and consultancy about creating Attractive cities, including the SmartCities plans.

## 7.10 Conclusions. Recommendations to Create a More Attractive City

### 7.10.1 Placing the Citizen Back at the Center of Cities' Priorities

We already studied in depth in Sect. 2.3 the Citizen at the Center, and Sect. 3.6 Humanizing SmartCities, with the importance of designing and implementing our city strategies WITH citizens and FOR citizens. The best actions will always be those that promote a sense of community, that serve all and that take advantage of the city's mission: deploying social synergy, where the collective is much more powerful than the sum of the parts. It is the humanistic concept of the city, but it must be complemented by urbanism, creating the appropriate spaces and distances to make that human encountering easy and possible; and technology always present to help us connect, communicate, monitor and manage our city, achieving higher levels of well-being and developing the brain of the city, as a network where we are all connected and in which we all contribute, like the Avatar neural tree. In this development process, fostering transparent collaborations, having a democratic use of data, and finding the creative ways of communication, engagement with citizens and social marketing are keys to success. This is the most difficult part of a good strategy in SmartCities: the citizen buy-in. It is much more difficult than finding financing, choosing the best technology and implementing it. None of that makes sense if citizens do not appreciate it, use it or find improvements in their lives because of this new urban benefit. Many times, simpler and more direct solutions are more impactful than others that are often more complex, expensive and sophisticated. You have to ask first, do pre-tests, work with the trial-error method, and above all, get to know your citizens.

The SmartCity plan should not be interpreted as the technology that some experts propose to help citizens. It must go much further, and it must think about how citizens shape and transform their city through technology's capabilities. It is about citizens being empowered enough, through the use of technology, to contribute to urban change and achieve their professional and social ambitions. Thus, the SmartCity simply provides the conditions and resources to make that possible: as we have said many times, technology is the great enabler. SmartCity is a huge urban laboratory, like an ecosystem (with many stakeholders) of innovation, an agent of change, a catalyzer, an engine of transformation driven and directed by citizens, aimed at helping them solve their problems. Thus, the city develops its collective intelligence; it becomes smart.

It is a tool for citizens, but as we have said, it must be a process WITH citizens, a human process. Therefore, it must address the moral aspects like ethics and privacy. It must understand the motivations and needs of citizens and engage with smart services (Gothenburg Smartcity, 2020). And it must operate in a decentralized way so that everyone is heard, and all initiatives are taken into account.

We often make four fundamental mistakes which turn our SmartCity plan into something that is not as human as it should be, and it becomes just a sum of technologies that supposedly offer functionality and benefit, but without the expected human orientation (Privacy International, 2017).

1. We don't think about our citizens' human rights when we implement technologies. We are blinded by technical possibilities and do not value that the real final users are our citizens, that we often use their data, and that we should not manipulate them with information or physically handle them as herds. We must always keep clear the rights to non-discrimination (solutions must be able to be used by all), so as to not affect the basic rights of freedom of movement and expression, essential in a city, and with the utmost respect for privacy and virtual identity.

2. We make many decisions in the SmartCity plan without having all the agents that must contribute to it. It is good that it is managed by technology experts, but you also have to listen to citizens individually or organized, to the private sector, in academia, etc. We must always seek equity and equality, paying special interest to marginalized people or people with various disabilities, making an inclusive city. The strategy must be open from the beginning to allow for transparency and the flow of contributions and experiences.

3. In order to seek synergies, save on costs and simplify processes, we often adopt *one size fits all* technologies. This impedes the services' personalization and adaptation, shortens transparency and security, and finally, impacts efficiency, questioning their transparency, security, openness and effectiveness. We must, and as technology enables us, we also can offer personalized services that understand each citizen's specific needs.

4. Security, privacy and respect for each citizen's sensitive and personal information must be new design conditions by default. When using citizen data, we must comply with data protection regulations such as GDPR. Specifically, we must observe the principles of collection limitation in quantity and quality; data must be specific, and only the necessary data should be used; preserve security in your treatment; openness and transparency to know why they are used and their purpose; and finally, always act with responsibility and strict compliance with the laws.[1]

---

[1] Main are in Europe: EU Council of Europe Convention for the Protection of Individuals with regard to Automatic Processing of Personal Data (No. 108), 1981 and the Organization for Economic Co-operation and Development revised Guidelines on the Protection of Privacy and Transborder Flows of Personal Data (2013), and 2018 EU General Data Protection Regulation.

## 7.10.2 Cities of the Future. How Might They Look? Talent Race. Zero City

Just as there is no ideal person to serve as a model for all others, but there are virtues and goodness that are an example for all of us, it happens that there is no ideal city. Each city is different and by knowing its virtues (where it offers better benefits or what characteristics make it unique) and its defects or areas to improve, it defines its strategy and marks its future path.

We can summarize the main cities' future strategies in two parallel lines that converge in the future: On the one hand the competition for talent, and on the other, the *Zero* objective in many fundamental city parameters.

The race to retain and attract talent.

As we have already studied, we are at the beginning of the Fourth Industrial Revolution, and the most disruptive general technology here is Artificial Intelligence. Artificial Intelligence powers robotics, autonomous cars, city intelligence, and we can find it in all the advanced applications we use today, such as this word processor, our smartphone, our new car or our conference call tool. This Industrial Revolution does not have a clearly highlighted city or area that serves as a beacon or lighthouse for talent attraction. For this reason, all advanced cities want and are striving to become international Artificial Intelligence centers, cultivating their own talent in innovation centers with local universities, and attracting the best external talent with relevant city investments and innovative companies. To achieve this, cities prepare, improve their Magnetism, their image, their branding and also their skilling and professional development offer around Artificial Intelligence (Lanvin & Monteiro, 2020). Proper working conditions in terms of innovation, wages, ethics, diversity, time schedules and respect for work/life balance will pave the way to welcome talent.

Given its importance, Artificial Intelligence becomes the city services' transformation and improvement plan's fundamental engine. In this way, the city becomes a huge test bench for Artificial Intelligence technologies, introducing them by default in the innovation design for all its services (security, traffic, social services/health, water management, energy, citizen engagement and information analysis.) If a city stands out due to its use of Artificial Intelligence in its citizen services, then it is positioned as a SmartCities leader, and therefore, in Attractiveness for talent.

Cities of the Future. The *Zero* City

*Zero* is Cities' magic score. McKinsey (Frem et al., 2018) mentions around six, but we could figure out around 36 *Zeroes*. The best cities of the future will score zero in most of these relevant indicators:

- Zero traffic congestion.
- Zero traffic fatalities, as states by the Zero Vision (Swedish parliament)
- Zero impact of planet future. (Environmentally sustainable in buildings and operations). Self-sufficient in energy, water.

- Zero Pollution. Clean air.
- Zero noise pollution.
- Zero wasted space for cars, unused space. All possible space dedicated to a chain of interconnected green areas, parks, gardens. reduce current cars space dedication from 40% to 25%.
- Zero net carbon emissions. Carbon Neutral first, then Carbon negative, then Carbon free.
- Zero fossil fuel energy consumption. All from renewable energy (solar, wind mainly, then hydro-powered, other)
- Zero private owned cars. Large walkable and bikeable areas and public spaces. Cars-as-a-service, ride sharing, public transportation as default. Transforming a city made for cars into a city made for humans. Mobility-as-a-Service as urban mobility standard.
- Zero wastage water supply chain. All water from natural and sustainable resources or from green powered desalination and purification.
- Zero untreated grey water. Energy production, purification before return to nature or city cycle.
- Zero non-recycled matter. Aim to reach *fabcity* concept (a city self-sufficient in matter)
- Zero poverty. Zero hunger. Guaranteed access to food in quantity and quality. Zero homeless people.
- Zero physical or virtual crime.
- Zero damage. Resilient City against human-made or natural hazards.
- Zero Generic Cities. Inspiring landscapes and human urbanism public spaces design, incenting a strong sense of belonging, community, and emotional affection.
- Zero healthcare inefficiencies. Zero uncontrolled pandemics. Zero elder people with undesired loneliness. Zero unattended vulnerable citizens.
- Zero bureaucracy. Zero non-digital administration. Zero citizen abstention (full participation).
- Zero discrimination. Zero inequity. Zero inequality. Zero gender violence, ethnic discrimination. Zero human rights/liberties repression.
- Zero excessive working hours patterns. (perfect work/life balance). Respect for leisure, entertainment, culture, arts, sports or divine.
- Zero cash. All transactional, traceable, and taxable trading's. Cashless Cities.
- Zero illiteracy, Zero digital gap.
- Zero unemployment.

## 7.10.3  Cities of the Future. The Real-Time City

New technologies allow us to create a *continuum* City. Just as we are continuously sensing, and we immediately react to external inputs, new technologies like (bottom-up order) the massive amount of sensors and citizens' smartphones, 5G connectivity and fiber infrastructure, edge computing, cooperative intelligent transportation systems, short-term processing (also known as *fog* cloud with very short latency), multiformat (structured, unstructured data) massive analytics in Datalakes, IoT Platforms, Digital twins, Advanced Artificial Intelligence Algorithms equip the city with the tools to achieve a real-time live-response organization. That way, traffic can be dynamically adapted and changed to prioritize specific paths, the mayor can take the pulse on citizens' opinions and their feedback every few hours (as soon as they react), remote care allow to permanently monitor health constants and alerts from vulnerable people at home, a digital twin can offer us a real-time vision of what's happening in the city, first responders' forces (police, healthcare, civil protection, firemen) can react and face any challenge in real-time. All those examples are almost automatic, in the already-explained concept of the *Senseable* city, only pending for humans to make decisions applying our common sense and ethics.

Interaction and engagement with citizens must also be universal, permanent and immediate, like our brain is connected to our members or a large tree is connected to all its thousands of leaves. Apps, tools, alerts, must be in place, engaging and incentivizing citizens to use them, providing them with clear justification and benefits, encouraging them to provide some private information to better serve them, always ensuring maximum protection and regulations' compliance. This is critical to multiply the city management, create a crowdsourcing for information, alerts, safety, donations, contributions of any kind. Imagine that I am the real-time witness of an accident or a crime, I can take video and stream it to police. Some famous arrests would have never happened without this kind of real-time cooperation. It's the same if I see a broken waste basket or a pothole in the pavement, or a dried tree, or I have an idea to improve the efficiency of that cross, or I want to receive invitations for all cultural events around symphonic rock bands. . .

Real-time translation for tourists or newcomers, opening our city up to them. Real-time, location-dependent information around what you are discovering in front of you (augmented reality). This is very relevant for visitors, and also for visually impaired citizens, making an inclusive city.

Real-time environment, energy, water consumption monitoring, minimizing use and maximizing production and use of renewables. Real-time waste, disposal, matter cycle management.

We have explained the Predictive City. The City must know what's very likely going to happen tomorrow, next week, next month, next season, next festivals or relevant events, plan next year, and design strategy for the next 10 or even 25 years. Take that massive amount of unused historical and real-time data, and place it all in a Datalake Artificial Intelligence-fueled cloud and start understanding your citizens and your city behavior!

Cities can't improvise, can't be surprised even by a natural disaster; they must be resilient, must be prepared for the next hit, and for next opportunity.

## 7.10.4   City of the Future. Balancing Distances and Commuting

The ideal city should provide 95% of all you might need within a 15 min walking/ microEV riding distance radius, including your job. Short distances mean short times, less energy consumption, no need for large vehicles (micro electric vehicles like eScooters are rocking). For anything else, public transportation should make commuting affordable in terms of cost and time.

We have explained that the city dimension is permanently growing as urban mobility efficiency improves, and all reachable places in less than 90 min commuting time is psychologically associated to same metropolis, the same City.

True, the perfect plan is the association of a large number of micro communities, where you enjoy the balance between both short-distance, mid-distance terms, with most things you need at hand, but all other wonderful things you need in your life like an Opera house, a theater, your favorite football team stadium, your preferred museum or library, your university or confessional place are also reachable in acceptable and efficient terms. Urban Mobility is the cities' bloodstream, as we stated in this research, and let's remember that SmartCityExpo survey responders placed it as most important urban service (over safety, healthcare, environment or employment), so it requires special attention. It marks city Dynamism, it makes all other services work, it tells a lot of information and characteristics about the city and its dwellers, and it is the first impression visitors have of the city. You won't take a second chance to make a wonderful first impression. . .

## 7.10.5   Transforming Your City Magnetism

We studied that City Magnetism is a status that is reached after many years of construction and evolution. The city Identity and shape cannot be changed overnight; it requires a transformation process that may need a minimum of 15 years. We are talking about how changing or generating a new City Identity from scratch could take us 50 years. This is a long time for the speed we are accustomed to in the digital age, but it is the physical city pace of change. This slow, but constant evolution should not discourage us from its transformation. Before beginning the development and implementation of a strategy for transforming the City Identity/Magnetism, we must analyze very well where we start from and precisely know our city. We must recognize our existing advantages, assets, our values, identity, heritage, culture, and use them to build on it, lean on them to thrive. There are things that we cannot change such as the geographical location, landscape, the climate, the geological and natural risk, some customs. The main language, main religion/ethics can change, but very slowly. Yet, there are many other things that we can change and impact upon, such as large areas for urban planning, cultural activities and places, the city promotion and international projection in sporting, cultural and arts events and activities. We must understand in which sociocultural areas we are strong and maximize them, and also where we are unattractive to implement a plan to fix it. We must think of our city as a house that we want to sell; or rather, that we want to rent to talented citizens. We must include in that house the most appreciated elements so that this talent can live, achieve maximum well-being and develop its potential, and all this with a reasonable income or price (citizenship contract). Magnetism is the continent (the house itself), Profitability will be the content (services available in the house) and rent (price) for that house.

We must balance past and future, preserving our identity, history and culture, with a strong investment in the future, in innovation, in external image.

Let us have exquisite care with reputation; we must avoid populisms, manipulations, or otherwise our city image will suffer.

A city with low Magnetism like those secondary or tertiary cities in a country with a recognized, and strong leading capital can transform and stand out globally if the right political decisions are made and all citizens contribute to that regeneration. The transformational plan must be the result of debate and consensus among all political leaders and interest groups (Sinkien & Kromalcas, 2005) and must be a long-term plan (we seriously doubt the actual implementation of any city plan that does not last more than five years; anything more shorter-term than that seems to be populist to us; opportunistic and associated to little impact). This plan must be reflected in a city vision for 10 or more years, and there must be an agreement to develop it even if the ruling political party changes. There must also be strong popular support and consensus, and the conditions we described in Chap. 3 on change management.

We are talking about large numbers: macro projects, never specific actions that improve a specific service. A combination of the three fundamental axes is needed: Urbanism, Humanism and Technology, with urbanism leading and the others supporting and complementing.

We can tackle a fundamentally urban transformation like the one Bilbao (Spain) did in the 90s, changing the city center, from a declining industrial environment, with high unemployment, in the midst of a strong social conflict aggravated by the natural disaster of an intense flood; for a new environment, various new buildings, each by a famous architect, and a new subway system and a brand-new museum (Guggenheim) built by Frank Gehry. Bilbao is studied as a model for transforming the city shape, but this was also made possible by the strong and resilient spirit of its citizens, the ambition for improvement and solidarity. Today, Bilbao is a very Attractive city with very high well-being and quality of life standards. (See KPMG (Haynes, 2014), "Magnet Cities" study)

We can, therefore, consider a strong urban action, develop a new neighborhood, transform and regenerate an area, build a new sports stadium, reconvert an industrial area, clean up a devastated natural area, recover a river walk, build a famous museum, design a huge park etc. We remember some urbanism plans that said, *let's invest something worth 500 million euros in this area to revamp it and bring tourism there.*

In parallel, we should invest on the city image/branding. Let's recall how Barcelona invested for being part of a Woody Allen's film cover. We must realize the impact that sporting events like Real Madrid have in Madrid, or the Nobel prizes in Stockholm, or the film festival in Nice-Cannes or the F1 race in Monaco. There are many cities that should seriously consider appearing in the eyes of the world with one of these shocking activities. It is an investment on projected image, on branding. This investment in human perception must be complemented by a high reputation and minimum standards of social and economic sustainability. Otherwise, it seems like an unnecessary superfluous expense in a city or country that should first fix its basic problems.

Finally, the technological part, from investment in innovation, the focus on human capital and the proposal of an ambitious SmartCity plan. That is future.

Thus, fundamentally with urbanism we transform the past, the body of the city built for a long time; with humanism we change the social and economic present; with technology we look to the future, and design our dreams.

Finally, a reflection from Mr. Luca Bergamo (Bergamo, 2020), Vice Mayor for culture of Rome (Italy). In a recent online meeting, he said that *"Culture is missing in the SDGs. If we don't have the cultural tools to think and live in a sustainable way – there is no way we can behave sustainably and therefore achieve the SDGs. In this sense, the city has also based the city strategy on article 27 of the charter of human rights that put participation and culture at the center."*

Where is Culture in all this process? In all this City Attractiveness model? Same role as technology, it is everywhere from fixed City Identity, to changing Dynamism, and planned Strategy to Culture as a City Service or benefit. So, changing the City Magnetism is always a cultural change, and citizens must participate in the entire process, from beginning to end, due to the required social adaptation to the new city reality.

Then, let's hire an architect or urbanists to design the big transformation, a sociologist or phycologists to ensure citizens are always central, and finally a Chief Technology Officer (CTO) to put technology and strategic SmartCity Plan over it all.

### 7.10.6    Improving Your City Profitability (Citizenship Contract)

It is difficult to change the City Net Purchasing Power because its salary conditions, taxes and cost of living (prices) depend mostly on decisions or fixed terms at the state or country level. You can improve the cost of living by influencing the price of various things like housing and some others, but this is a long-term, complex strategy. In any case, as we have studied, when a city is Attractive to talent, a vicious cycle may occur in rising wages, then purchasing power, then again rising prices, increased cost of living,...then it stops being Attractive for all (the case of Seattle area), and intervention is needed in the housing market, urbanization and social areas. So, this attraction process should be monitored. Progress is never uniform, and sometimes creates inequalities, but those inequalities help create incentives to overcome them and serve as lessons to others (Deaton, 2013). The opposite is also true: as jobs disappear in a certain area, the falling value of houses traps people in certain neighborhoods, because sometimes the value of their pending mortgage principal is higher than the real house price, and if they stop paying and move, then they lose the house and everything they have already paid.

Undoubtedly, the area where we can most clearly impact is the provision of City Services. We have studied 10 groups of City services/benefits. The SmartCity plan, as we explained in Chap. 3, should make an evaluation of where we are in each of those services compared to the leaders; define priorities (there are always many possibilities to impact); design a strategy and implement it.

You need to balance the concept of doing everything well with excelling at something. We think it is not about being the best in one thing, but being very good in many, so that talent appreciates a holistic city, with a solid strategy, without ups and downs, without fissures, without large problems to solve. In other words, a city that may not be the best in traffic, urban mobility, social services, security, environmental sustainability, employability, but that does not have a serious deficiency in any of them and is progressing in all of them in parallel. Here we can think of plans of four or less years, impacting on priority areas. But it is also a continuous process, because we must recognize that everyone progresses and competes with each other, and a good position in one area can become mediocre next year. It is, therefore, a continuous plan for innovation, adding new technologies as they appear, leveraging their advantages and improving services to citizens together with the city's general attractiveness. It is a circular process around getting current data/ status, analyzing it, comparing, evaluating and prioritizing, then making decisions, implementing new technologies, impacting the citizens, then get data again, and start over. It is a constant and unstoppable process, led by technology, with urban planning as a follower, and as always, with the citizen as co-creator, implementer and user. It's very important to note that we must start moving, without thinking too much, avoiding paralysis by analysis. Action is what matters, as it is a process of constant learning and feedback: we think, execute, implement, adjust, learn and readjust, or we may have to throw away what we have done so far and start again, always looking at what other cities do, and the availability of the latest technologies in the market.

You have to play and bet big, accepting to be wrong sometimes, but to win strong and establish distances. This may seem crazy, but please remember that this is mainly a technology-driven process, and we know how accelerated the pace of technology is, and its ability to quickly create advantages.

There are model cities, which have been doing certain things very well for years, such as Barcelona in branding, or Tokyo and NYC in security, or Amsterdam in Circular City or Rotterdam in sustainability, or Copenhagen in Carbon Neutral, or Helsinki in activating the data to understand its citizens, or Tel-Aviv in citizen participation. They are examples for the others, although, as we said before, each city is unique, different, and must create its own path by walking it.

## 7.11    Final Reflection: Technology as an Enabler

*Medellin was an isolated city, cut-off from the evolution of the world and lagging behind, so we invested 2.4% of its GDP in technological innovations, four times Colombia's national average* (Cathelat, 2019). Elkin Echeveria, Medellin city pilot

### 7.11.1    Technology as an Omnipresent Enabler and Catalyzer

We live in a world of idols (success, recognition, money, information). We have also put technology in the idol position. We have deified it and we think that there is a kind of magic that makes our smartphone work, and that technology is the solution to all our problems. Advances in Artificial Intelligence and science fiction movies fuel this belief about the quasi-divine quality of technology. Technology enjoys choice, omniscience, taste, ethics, and even personality. Serious mistake. Personally, as a technologist, I am fed up with all that undocumented criticism of technology as the root cause for our current dehumanization. Without technology, we would be dead from the cold, and behave like starved animals in our cavern, exposed to the elements and vermin. We live in the best moment of our human history, yes, human, thanks to technology. The problem is that we have turned it into a God, assuming that it is capable of explaining everything and answering everything, including our existential questions. Watch technology idolatry at this master Polish movie (Kieslowski, 1988). Serious mistake once again. Technology helps us do an unbelievable and massive amount of simple tasks in a very short time period, but it only does (and should continue to do if we use Artificial Intelligence with responsibility and following ethical principles) exclusively those tasks that humans who create and code it specifically order it to do. That's it; no magic, no surprises. Attributing other human virtues to it is simply pretentious and false. And turning it into real dogma is more than risky, it is very dangerous, as we have seen in so many dystopian movies. It must be said that technology never fails if the information is correct, technically speaking. Error is human, and comes from attributing to technology a transcendent, almost divine dimension. Technology is a human creation, and we should never forget it. Nor should it be demonized, it must be understood and used for the purpose it was designed, nothing more, nothing less.

With this is mind, we should trust technology, trust Artificial Intelligence, because it works for good. The next human prosperity and well-being aspiration is only achievable with intense use of Artificial Intelligence, and as we stated, Artificial Intelligence needs three confluent components: Data, Cloud Computing power and Human algorithms. So, we need data about our city and everything inside it, all things, all humans, all behavioral information, all aspirations and dreams. But it's not just about data, not about creating a *Datapolis*. We need data in SmartCity 2.0, but we need to turn all that data into insights, into knowledge to serve the citizens, our core center, our mission. Then, we need massive computing power and analytics, and we need it at an affordable cost, and have it always on, always ready to serve us, always secure and compliant, and respecting environmental sustainability. The only technical solution for those requirements is public Cloud systems, because they provide the availability, scalability, computing power, portfolio of tools and solutions, environmental efficiency, security, and affordable cost. Without Cloud computing, a city should hire a legion of engineers to code, maintain security, scale and adapt power when needed. Also, it will need to purchase an oversized supercomputer, which will become obsolete before it starts serving its purpose, to be occasionally used, at less than 10% of its capacity, and that is environmentally inefficient, a luxury, an unaffordable solution. Cloud allows to use and pay for technology as it is needed, providing the flexibility required to respond to a dynamic city's demand.

Finally, we need talent to code and design the neural city system, the Artificial Intelligence solutions, the main objective for City Attractiveness.

Good luck to Talented Citizens when exploring the world and choose the best city to develop your personal and professional potential. May this research orient and help you. Don't be blinded by shine; look for human values and explore second-tier cities as well.

Good luck to City Managers and mayors when preparing the city to become the most Attractive possible to retain and attract talent, the only way to thrive and create a better city in a better world. May this research also help you. Compete hard, but fair, and please, never forget about your citizens. This is about humans first, and then technology and urbanism.

# 7.12  Extra Content: SmartCities in COVID-19 Times

I was in Madrid, stretching my working days to spend time writing this research after dinner and weekends, when the COVID-19 pandemic surprised us and forced me to a long confinement that has allowed me to finish this earlier than expected. I don't want to thank the virus for anything. On the contrary, this pandemic is the worst thing that has happened to mankind since WWII and deeply attacks the essence and the social base of the city. Nothing will be the same, everything will change, and I hope we learn the lesson and leverage this to progress as a community. I am going to detail some reflections on the new role that many basic aspects of our daily life will take after this pandemic.

* New role of technology.

   The use of technology has been strongly highlighted, valued and understood. Imagine this pandemic without advanced communications, without teleworking, without smartphones, without Internet. The world would have stopped, the economy would not have slowed down sharply, it would simply have collapsed. Imagine the impact on education without remote classes, the impact of a stopped supply chain, the impact of the pandemic without data analysis, without the massive communication and information sharing between different health systems. The impact would have been devastating. And that, as Bill Gates anticipated in his 2015 TedTalk (Gates, 2015), we were not prepared for. It seems incredible to me that the communication lines have solidly supported the exponential increase in demand. Without massive Cloud Computing systems, the impact would have been tremendous; without teleworking, without the ability to remotely provision computing capacity when the supply of computers and resources are so limited and everything must happen with the utmost urgency, because people are dying. We thought about the vertigo that the accelerated speed of technology imposed on us...thank God it is so fast, and that it has helped us respond in a reasonable time, or we would have had figures similar to the 1918 Spanish flu (25% of the world infected, 50 million deaths). We have also understood that technology helps, but humans manage, and they must get down to work. No time for long discussions, we need to trust the data and evidence from technology and then make fast decisions and agile governance. We all dream of the vaccine, and we trust that technology will help us get it as soon as possible, but we have all understood that it takes a lot of human effort to get things done, that technology is a wonderful enabler, but it is human-made like us, it is not divine.

- New role of nature. Despite the continuous mobilizations and contributions from experts and scientists, we were completely ignoring the process of climate change, maintaining an unsustainable pace of urbanization and fossil fuel consumption. The relationship of this climate deterioration situation to the spread of the virus is not yet clear, but several fundamental issues have been demonstrated. On the one hand, we must listen to the experts about natural outbreaks and risks, and react by changing our habits, even if it has an economic impact. One the other, we live on a single planet, and we breathe a single, common atmosphere that requires the entire human race to collectively care, otherwise all without exception will suffer the consequences, as this pandemic has taught us by a slap to our face. We have learned how low human activity while in confinement has caused our planet to recover clear skies, and slightly improve from unsustainable levels of greenhouse gases. It also seems that the hole in the ozone layer has shown improvement. It's like Gaia (mother Earth) was showing us the way to react and that we can recover the planet, that not all is lost, if we learn the lesson. We have learnt in the city about new Spring colors, new smells, new fresh air, new noises (birds, air flows...) Animals like rabbits, deer, bears, wild boars have returned to empty streets.
- New role of time. Now we have time to empty to zero our inbox, write this research and reflect. We realize the enormous amount of time wasted going to work, on trips with no strong justification for making them. We should recognize that same-day traveling to see one single client makes little sense, unless there is a strong business reason. We will travel, but for several days, and we will travel much less.
- New form of events/meetings. Entertainment has moved from large-scale events such as soccer, basketball, etc to smaller, family or neighbor performances. We have discovered that we have artistic neighbors or simply ones with certain musical culture. Events and large gatherings are things of the past. An event is

no longer conceived without a strong online component, if not 100%. All this needs, once again, technology to make it happen. Education will no longer be mainly in-person; online will be the preferred type, with high touch when needed, but mostly small groups or 1:1's. Technology arena as well.

- New role of Ethics. We were living without ethical values, in complete relativism (all is ok, no need to think). With this crisis, we all have gained renewed respect for ethics and human rights. We have seen healthcare staff having to decide who was given access to a ventilator and who was not, and left to die. We have seen politicians despise the lives of our elders, who fought so hard for us. We have seen enormous lessons of humanity, of healthcare personnel facing the virus almost without protection (and falling sick and dying, because they are also human). We have seen the altruistic organization of volunteer teams. We have seen humans again living in the cities. Dutch philosopher Rutger Bregman indicates that though the virus is contagious, so is our solidarity (Bregman, 2020). It's true that the virus is impacting both our human health as well as our human conscience, our dignity (Slijkhuis, 2020). We have had to learn civic behavior in a few hours to stay in confinement for many days. We have seen the value from many anonymous people making things work, not only in health and safety, but for logistics, utilities, farmers, etc.; all low-valued jobs, assuming their role and responsibility and taking the minimum, but unavoidable risk. We have had time to reflect on what really matters: family, friends. Who still thinks of soccer? We can live without it, who would have said it a month ago? Can we live without many other vanities like jewelry, luxuries? How long has it been since we put on a suit and tie? As the only way to stop the virus' spread is social tracing, citizens will need to cooperate. They will have to consent to a decrease in their freedom and give up some privacy for the city to implement a movement tracking system, to know where an infected person has moved around and who has been close to him/her, so that everyone takes the proper measures for testing or confinement.

- New role of Public Civil Servants/Governments. The worst countries handling the pandemic are not those with the worst technology or health systems, but those with poorly qualified and unprepared politicians. Should we trust the skilled managers more than the very vocal and propaganda producing, populist politicians? We have learnt the power of information mismanagement and manipulation. We have learned the value of many professionals and public officials. Before this, we thought that we had way too many civil servants and that we had to limit their wages. Now we appreciate their professionalism, especially those who have been at the forefront of the battle against the virus, such as nurses, doctors, health personnel, and also the security forces, who have gained prestige and our trust. To combat the pandemic, we have had to confine ourselves for a long time, and that is only maintained with respect for our security forces.

- New Economics and business activities. The impact on the economy and business is massive, especially those small businesses, services' companies, tourism, airlines. We have learned how vital our critical infrastructure is, such as utilities (energy, water, gas), goods' transportation and logistics, telcos and digital communications and financials. Social distancing will also impact all the services' business one way or another. Companies have learned how to telework, have discovered many new technological abilities. Many will question the required offices space. Will 50% keep teleworking? The offices' real-estate crisis is served. Another more to the long list. Forget about cash. . .who has touched that bill or coin? We were going to a cashless city, now at an accelerated rate, towards all-digital transactions.

- New role of Cities. Social distancing is here to stay. Even after the gradual reopening, people will fear about socializing, especially in crowded spaces. This is terrible as the City essence is about creating social conditions, spaces. So, cities will have to learn how to readapt/rebuild spaces. Should all those unused cars on streets be moved away to external parking? We have lived for more than two months without cars; do we still need all of them? Urban mobility must be reconsidered as well, as needed distances and capacities will change. It's time to allow bikes and eScooters massively. People will prefer to go out within walking distance or using mono-user small vehicles versus taking public transportation to reach the city's other end, even if the available restaurant is not so trendy. The concept of proximity will be very much appreciated. Cities must prepare for the next wave, (as the vaccination will still take its time and virus will be present for years) becoming more resilient and better equipped with a strong, first responder plan and resources and, again, technology. Cities have a unique opportunity to engage with citizens with new communication tools, offering official, accurate information about city services and protecting them from the common enemy spread. We were talking about how difficult citizen engagement and co-creation is. Now, we see citizens contributing, creating new communication pathways, opening their windows at 8pm to applaud caregivers in general (health and safety). We have many collective tasks to accomplish together, like economic recovery, which will require extra solidarity and crowdsourcing. Most impacted cities will see a decrease in reputation and Attractiveness which will take time to be forgotten.

I open the window from my confinement, and I do not see a city, but thousands of people trapped in their flats, in their own cages, as we do with animals (another message from Gaia?) This is the anti-city, the anti-social, anti-human. Lesson learned, please stop; may the vaccine do its job, and we take care about future threats.

# References

Android Store. (2020). *AttractiveCities.* https://play.google.com/store/apps/details?id=com. barrabes.attractivecities. Accessed 12 Dec 2020.
Author. (2019). Attractive cities: Contest for talent *TEDx Alcobendas.* Youtube in Spanish: https://www.youtube.com/watch?v=vu7pmcVrUAM and https://www.ted.com/talks/jose_antonio_

ondiviela_attractive_smartcities_contest_for_talent and doubled into English: https://www.youtube.com/watch?v=DAABkQRIcM8. Accessed 20 Apr 2019.

Bergamo, L. (2020). How are local governments co-creating local actions for Agenda 2030. p. 5 Online session Diana Lopez, *UN-Habitat*.

Bregman, R. (2020). The virus is contagious, and so is our behavior. *DW*. Made for minds. https://www.dw.com/en/rutger-bregman-the-virus-is-contagious-and-so-is-our-behavior/a-52924554. Accessed 12 Apr 2020.

Cathelat, B. (2019). *Smartcities shaping the society of 2030* (p. 154). UNESCO and NETEXPLO.

Deaton, A. (2013). *Cf. The Great Escape: Health, Wealth, and the Origins of Inequality*. Princeton University Press.

Frem, et al. (2018). *Thriving amid turbulence: Imagining the cities of the future*. McKinsey. https://www.mckinsey.com/industries/public-sector/our-insights/thriving-amid-turbulence-imagining-the-cities-of-the-future. Accessed 17 Feb 2020

Gates, B. (2015). The next outbreak? We are not ready. *TEDTalk* https://www.ted.com/talks/bill_gates_the_next_outbreak_we_re_not_ready. Accessed 10 Apr 2020.

Gothenburg SmartCity. (2020). https://www.thisisgothenburg.com/smart-city. Accessed 12 Jan 2020.

Haynes, C. (2014). *Magnet cities. Decline | Fightback | Victory* (pp. 4–32). KPMG.

India Government. (2020). *Smart Cities Mission*. http://smartcities.gov.in/content/. Accessed 20 Jan 2020.

IOS Store. (2020). *AttractiveCities*. https://apps.apple.com/es/app/attractive-cities/id1487782051. Accessed 12 Dec 2020.

Kieslowski, K. (1988). *Dekalog, jeden – Dekalog 1*, translated as *Decalogue I: You shall love God above all thing, or you shall have no other gods before me*.

Lanvin, B., & Monteiro, F. (2020). *INSEAD Global Talent Competitiveness index (GTCI) Key findings*. INSEAD. https://gtcistudy.com/key-findings/ Accessed 10 Feb 2020

Montessori, M. (1912). *The Montessori method* (p. 198) (Anne Everett George, Trans.). Frederick A. Stokes Company.

NordicEdge. (2018). *Stavanger*. https://www.nordicedgexpo.org/. Accessed 12 Oct 2018.

Privacy International. (2017). *Smart cities: Utopian vision, Dystopian reality* (pp. 22–23) www.privacyinternational.org. Accessed 14 Jan 2020.

Sinkien, J., & Kromalcas, S. (2005). *Concept, directions and practice of city attractiveness improvement* (p. 152). In International symposium enhancing City attractiveness for the future. Nagoya Congress Centre, Japan.

Slijkhuis, M. (2020). COVID-19 rethinking future. *LinkedIN*. https://www.linkedin.com/pulse/covid-19-rethinking-future-martin-slijkhuis/. Accessed 12 Apr 2020.

SmartCity Expo & WW Congress. (2018). www.smartcityexpo.com. Accessed Dec 2018.

SurveyMonkey Calculator. (2018). https://www.surveymonkey.com/mp/margin-of-error-calculator/. Accessed Oct 2018.

Van den Berg, L. (2006). *The attractive city: Catalyst of sustainable urban development* (p. 489). Erasmus University. San Sebastián: Eusko Ikaskuntza.

# Appendix

## I.- Wittgenstein's Vienna. Main Actors in the Same Place and Play

© The Author(s), under exclusive license to Springer Nature Switzerland AG 2021
J. A. Ondiviela, *Beyond Smart Cities*, https://doi.org/10.1007/978-3-030-83371-8

## WITTGENSTEIN'S VIENNA (1890-1914)

| SURNAME | NAME | S | PHILOSOPHER | ARCHITECT | POET | WRITER | JOURNALIST | MUSICIAN | PAINTER | MEDICINE | MATHS | PHYSICS · ENGINEER | DRAMATIST | POLITICIAN | Comments |
|---|---|---|---|---|---|---|---|---|---|---|---|---|---|---|---|
| ADLER | VIKTOR | | | | | X | | | | | | | | X | |
| ALTENBERG | PETER | | | | X | X | | | | | | | | | MODERNISM |
| ANDREAS-SALOME | LOU | | | | | X | X | | X | | | | | | PSYCHOANALYSIS |
| ANDRIAN (von) | LEOPOLD | | | | | X | | | | | | | X | | |
| AUERNHEIMER | RAOUL | | | | | X | | | | | | | | X | |
| BAHR | HERMANN | | | | | X | | | | | | | X | | |
| BEER-HOFMANN | RICHARD | | | | X | X | | | | | | | X | | |
| BERNATZIK | WILHELM | | | | | | | | X | | | | | | |
| BILLROTH | THEODOR | | | | | | | | | X | | | | | |
| BOLTZMANN | LUDWIG | | X | X | | | | | | | X | X | | | THERMODYNAMICS |
| BRAHMS | JOHANNES | | | | | | | X | | | | | | | |
| BRENTANO | FRANZ | | X | | | | | | | | | | | | |
| BREUER | JOSEPH | | | | | | | | X | | | | | | PSYCHOANALYSIS |
| BROCH | HERMANN | | | | | X | | | | | | | | | MODERNISM |
| BRUCKNER | ANTON | | | | | | | X | | | | | | | ROMANTICISM |
| BUBER | MARTIN | | X | | | X | | | | | | | | | DIALOGUE |
| BÜHLER | KARL | | | | | | | | X | | | | | | PSYCOLOGY |
| CARNAP | RUDOLF | | X | | | | | | | | | | | | POSITIVISM |
| CHAMBERLAIN | HOUSTON STEWART | | X | | | X | X | | | | | | | | ANTISEMITISM |
| DEHMEL | RICHARD | | | | X | X | X | | | | | | | | |
| DÖRMANN | FELIX | | | | | X | | | | | | | | | FILMPRODUCER |
| EBNER | FERDINAND | | X | | | | | | | | | | | | DIALOGUE |
| ENGELMANN | PAUL | | | X | | | | | | | | | | | |
| FICKER (VON) | HEINRICH | | | | | | | | | | | X | | | METEOROLOGIST |
| FREGE | GOTTLOB | | X | | | | | | | | X | | | | ANALYTIC |
| FREUD | SIGMUND | | | | | | | | X | | | | | | PSYCHOANALYSIS |
| FRIEDELL | EGON | | X | X | | X | X | | | | | | X | | |
| GOLDMANN | PAUL | | | | | X | X | | | | | | X | | |
| GROPIUS | WALTER | | | X | | | | | | | | | | | |
| HANSLICK | EDUARD | | | | | X | | X | | | | | | | |
| HAUER | JOSEF MATTHIAS | | | | | | | X | | | | | | | CHROMATIC STYLE |
| HEBRA | FERDINAND | | | | | | | | X | | | | | | DERMATOLOGIST |
| HERTZ | HEINRICH | | | | | | | | | | X | | | | ELECTROMAGNETISM |
| HERZL | THEODOR | | | | X | X | | | | | | | X | | ZIONIST |
| HOFFMANN | JOSEF | | | X | | | | | | | | | | | |
| HOFMANNSTHAL (VON) | HUGO | | | | X | X | X | | | | | | X | | |
| HUSSERL | EDMUND | | X | | | | | | | | | | | | |
| DAVID | JAKOB JULIUS | | | | X | X | | | | | | | | | |
| KAFKA | FRANZ | | | | X | X | | | | | | | | | |
| KELSEN | HANS | | X | | | X | | | | | | | | X | LEGAL POSITIVISM |
| KLIMT | GUSTAV | | | | | | | | X | | | | | | EXPRESSIONISM |
| KOKOSCHKA | OSKAR | | | | | | | | X | | | | | | EXPRESSIONISM |
| KRAFFT-EBING | RICHARD | | | | | | | | X | | | | | | PSYCHIATRIST |
| KRAUS | KARL | | | | | X | X | | | | | | X | | |
| KÜMBERGER | OTTO | | | | | X | | | | | | | | | PULP WRITER |
| KURZWEIL | MAX | | | | | | | | X | | | | | | |
| LASKER-SCHÜLER | ELSE | | | | X | X | X | | | | | | | | |
| LAZARSFELD | PAUL | | | | | X | | | | | | | X | | SOCIOLOGIST |
| LEHÁR | FRANZ | | | | | | X | | | | | | | | OPERETTAS |
| LIEBKNECHT | WILHELM | | | | X | X | | | | | | | X | | |
| LINDNER | ANTON | | | | X | X | X | | | | | | | | |
| LOOS | ADOLF | | | X | | X | X | | | | | | | | |
| MACH | ERNST | | X | | | | | | | X | X | | | | PSYCHOLOGY |
| MAHLER | GUSTAV | | X | | | | | X | | | | | | | ROMANTICISM |
| MAKART | HANS | | | | | | | X | | | | | | | |
| MANN | HEINRICH | | | | | X | X | | | | | | X | | |
| MAUTHNER | FRITZ | | X | | | X | X | | | X | | | X | | PSYCHOLOGY |
| MEYNERT | THEODOR | | | | | | | | X | | | | | | PSYCHIATRIST |
| MOSER | KOLOMAN | | | | | | | X | | | | | | | ARTIST |
| MUSIL | ROBERT | | | | X | X | | | | | | | | | |
| NAGEL | ERNEST | | X | | | | | | | | | | | | SCIENCE |
| NESTROY | JOHANN | | | | | | | | | | | | X | | |
| NIETZCHE | FRIEDRICH | | X | | X | X | | X | | | | | X | | |
| OFFENBACH | JACQUES | | | | | | | X | | | | | | | OPERETTAS |
| OLBRICH | JOSEPH-MARIA | | | X | | | | | | | | | | | |
| OTHENIO | ABEL | | | | | | | | | | | X | | | PALEONTOLOGIST |
| RAIMUND | FERDINAND | | | | | | | | | | | | X | | |
| RAMSEY | FRANK | | X | | | | | | | | X | | | | ECONOMIST |
| REDL | ALFRED | | X | | | | | | | | | | | X | |
| REE | PAUL | | X | | | X | | | | | | | | | |
| REINHARDT | MAX | | | | | | | | | | | | X | | |
| RILKE | RAINER MARIA | | | | X | X | | | | | | | | | |
| SALTEN | FELIX | | | | | X | | | | | | | | | |
| SCHIELE | EGON | | | | | | | | X | | | | | | EXPRESSIONISM |
| SCHLICK | MORITZ | | X | | | | | | | X | X | | | | VIENNA CIRCLE |
| SCHNITZLER | ARTHUR | | | | X | X | | | X | | | | | | HIPNOTISM, MODERNISM |
| SCHÖNBERG | ARNOLD | | | | X | X | X | X | X | | | | | | DODECAPHONICS |
| SCHOPENHAUER | ARTHUR | | X | | | | | | | | | | | | |
| SEMMELWEIS | IGNAZ | | | | | | | | X | | | | | | ANTISEPTICS |
| ŠKODA | JOSEPH | | | | | | | | X | | | | | | DERMATOLOGY |
| SPECHT | RICHARD | | | | | X | X | | | | | | X | | |
| SPENGLER | OSWALD | | X | | | X | | | | | | X | X | | |
| SPITZER | LEO | | | | | X | | | | | | | | | PULP WRITER |
| SRAFFA | PIERO | | | | | X | | | | | | | | | ECONOMIST |
| STEINTHAL | HEYMANN | | X | | | | | | | X | | | | | PSYCHOLOGY |
| STRAUSS | RICHARD | | | | | | X | | | | | | | | OPERA |
| STRINDBERG | AUGUST | | | | X | X | X | X | | | | | | | |
| STRINDBERG | FRIDA | | | | | X | | | | | | | | | |
| TRAKL | GEORG | | | | X | | | | | | | | | | |
| VAN DER NÜLL | EDUARD | | X | | X | | | | | | | | | | OPERA ARCHITECT |
| VON LILIENCRON | DETLEV | | | | X | X | X | | | | | | | | |
| VON UCHATIUS | FRANZ BARON | | X | | | | | | | | | X | | | HEAVY WEAPONS |
| WAGNER | RICHARD | | | | | X | | X | | | | | X | | OPERA |
| WAGNER | OTTO | | | X | | | | | | | | | | | |
| WAISMANN | FRIEDRICH | | X | | | | | | | X | X | | | | |
| WALTER | BRUNO | | | | | | | X | | | | | | | DIR ORCHESTRA |
| WASSERMANN | JAKOB | | | | | X | | | | | | | | | |
| WEDEKIND | FRANK | | | | | X | X | | | | | | X | | |
| WEININGER | OTTO | | X | X | | X | | | | | | | | | |
| WERFEL | FRANZ | | | | X | X | X | | | X | | | | | |
| WITTGENSTEIN | LUDWIG | | X | X | | X | | | | X | X | | | | |
| WOLF | HUGO | | | | | X | X | X | | | | | | | ROMANTICISM |
| WOLTER | CHARLOTTE | | | | | | | | | | | | X | | ACTRESS |
| ZWEIG | STEFAN | | | | X | X | | | | | | | | | |
| 104 | | 7 | 25 | 9 | 14 | 51 | 22 | 14 | 9 | 14 | 7 | 10 | 13 | 11 | |

| | |
|---|---|
| Wiener Werkstätte | ARCHITECTURE — BAUHAUS |
| Vienna Circle | PHYLOSOPHY – WRITER - SCIENCES |
| Secession | PAINTER-DECORATION |
| Young Vienna | WRITER |
| | LOU ANDREAS-SALOMÉ LOVERS |
| | WITTGENSTEIN's MAIN INFLUENCER |

**Fig. A.I**  Wittgenstein's Vienna. Main Actors in the same place and play. Author

# II.- Cities Selection. Top140 from 2018 Mercer Quality of Live Index & IESE Cities in Motion Index

**Table A.1** Cities selection. Top140 from 2018 Mercer Quality of live index & IESE cities in motion index

| City | Country | Mercer QoL RK | IESE CiM RK | Avg | Combined ranking |
|---|---|---|---|---|---|
| Zurich | Switzerland | 2 | 13 | 7,5 | 1 |
| Vienna | Austria | 1 | 15 | 8,0 | 2 |
| Berlin | Germany | 13 | 9 | 11,0 | 3 |
| Amsterdam | Netherlands | 12 | 10 | 11,0 | 4 |
| Munich | Germany | 4 | 19 | 11,5 | 5 |
| Geneva | Switzerland | 8 | 17 | 12,5 | 6 |
| Vancouver | Canada | 5 | 21 | 13,0 | 7 |
| Dusseldorf | Germany | 6 | 20 | 13,0 | 8 |
| Sydney | Australia | 11 | 16 | 13,5 | 9 |
| Toronto | Canada | 17 | 11 | 14,0 | 10 |
| Melbourne | Australia | 16 | 14 | 15,0 | 11 |
| Bern | Switzerland | 14 | 20 | 17,0 | 12 |
| San Francisco | United States | 30 | 5 | 17,5 | 13 |
| Copenhagen | Denmark | 9 | 27 | 18,0 | 14 |
| Boston | United States | 35 | 4 | 19,5 | 15 |
| Paris | France | 38 | 3 | 20,5 | 16 |
| Ottawa | Canada | 18 | 24 | 21,0 | 17 |
| London | United Kingdom | 40 | 2 | 21,0 | 18 |
| Frankfurt | Germany | 7 | 36 | 21,5 | 19 |
| Stockholm | Sweden | 20 | 25 | 22,5 | 20 |
| New York City | United States | 44 | 1 | 22,5 | 21 |
| Auckland | New Zealand | 3 | 44 | 23,5 | 22 |
| Singapore | Singapore | 25 | 22 | 23,5 | 23 |
| Adelaide | Australia | 28 | 20 | 24,0 | 24 |
| Canberra | Australia | 29 | 20 | 24,5 | 25 |
| Hamburg | Germany | 19 | 34 | 26,5 | 26 |
| Montreal | Canada | 23 | 31 | 27,0 | 27 |
| Washington, D.C. | United States | 49 | 6 | 27,5 | 28 |
| Tokyo | Japan | 48 | 8 | 28,0 | 29 |
| Basel | Switzerland | 10 | 47 | 28,5 | 30 |
| Oslo | Norway | 32 | 26 | 29,0 | 31 |
| Wellington | New Zealand | 15 | 44 | 29,5 | 32 |
| Chicago | United States | 47 | 12 | 29,5 | 33 |
| Helsinki | Finland | 31 | 29 | 30,0 | 34 |
| Luxembourg | Luxembourg | 21 | 40 | 30,5 | 35 |
| Seattle | United States | 46 | 15 | 30,5 | 36 |

(continued)

**Table A.1** (continued)

| City | Country | Mercer QoL RK | IESE CiM RK | Avg | Combined ranking |
|------|---------|---------------|-------------|-----|------------------|
| Brussels | Belgium | 27 | 40 | 33,5 | 37 |
| Dublin | Ireland | 34 | 33 | 33,5 | 38 |
| Stuttgart | Germany | 26 | 45 | 35,5 | 39 |
| Barcelona | Spain | 42 | 35 | 38,5 | 40 |
| Los Angeles | United States | 59 | 18 | 38,5 | 41 |
| Milan | Italy | 41 | 38 | 39,5 | 42 |
| Madrid | Spain | 51 | 28 | 39,5 | 43 |
| Baltimore | United States | 60 | 20 | 40,0 | 44 |
| Seoul | South Korea | 77 | 7 | 42,0 | 45 |
| Philadelphia | United States | 56 | 30 | 43,0 | 46 |
| Dallas | United States | 64 | 23 | 43,5 | 47 |
| Lyon | France | 39 | 50 | 44,5 | 48 |
| Edinburgh | United Kingdom | 45 | 45 | 45,0 | 49 |
| Linz | Austria | 46 | 46 | 46,0 | 50 |
| Lisbon | Portugal | 43 | 52 | 47,5 | 51 |
| Phoenix | United States | 60 | 37 | 48,5 | 52 |
| Houston | United States | 67 | 32 | 49,5 | 53 |
| Rome | Italy | 57 | 43 | 50,0 | 54 |
| Yokohama | Japan | 52 | 52 | 52,0 | 55 |
| Cologne | Germany | 45 | 60 | 52,5 | 56 |
| Florence | Italy | 60 | 49 | 54,5 | 57 |
| Prague | Czech Republic | 69 | 41 | 55,0 | 58 |
| Málaga | Spain | 60 | 51 | 55,5 | 59 |
| Hong Kong | Hong Kong | 72 | 42 | 57,0 | 60 |
| Birmingham | United Kingdom | 53 | 62 | 57,5 | 61 |
| Liverpool | United Kingdom | 60 | 55 | 57,5 | 62 |
| Atlanta | United States | 65 | 50 | 57,5 | 63 |
| Miami | United States | 68 | 48 | 58,0 | 64 |
| Eindhoven | Netherlands | 60 | 58 | 59,0 | 65 |
| Rotterdam | Netherlands | 60 | 59 | 59,5 | 66 |
| Manchester | United Kingdom | 65 | 57 | 61,0 | 67 |
| Marseille | France | 50 | 73 | 61,5 | 68 |
| Nice | France | 50 | 74 | 62,0 | 69 |
| Osaka | Japan | 60 | 72 | 66,0 | 70 |
| Valencia | Spain | 70 | 63 | 66,5 | 71 |
| Antwerp | Belgium | 70 | 65 | 67,5 | 72 |
| Warsaw | Poland | 82 | 54 | 68,0 | 73 |
| Dubai | United Arab Emirates | 74 | 66 | 70,0 | 74 |
| Taipei | Taiwan | 85 | 56 | 70,5 | 75 |
| Tallinn | Estonia | 90 | 53 | 71,5 | 76 |
| Abu Dhabi | United Arab Emirates | 79 | 64 | 71,5 | 77 |

(continued)

**Table A.1** (continued)

| City | Country | Mercer QoL RK | IESE CiM RK | Avg | Combined ranking |
|---|---|---|---|---|---|
| Budapest | Hungary | 78 | 67 | 72,5 | 78 |
| Ljubljana | Slovenia | 76 | 70 | 73,0 | 79 |
| Vilnius | Lithuania | 81 | 71 | 76,0 | 80 |
| Bilbao | Spain | 80 | 75 | 77,5 | 81 |
| Bratislava | Slovakia | 83 | 77 | 80,0 | 82 |
| Gothenburg | Sweden | 80 | 88 | 84,0 | 83 |
| Riga | Latvia | 91 | 82 | 86,5 | 84 |
| Buenos Aires | Argentina | 93 | 83 | 88,0 | 85 |
| Kuala Lumpur | Malaysia | 86 | 92 | 89,0 | 86 |
| Montevideo | Uruguay | 80 | 99 | 89,5 | 87 |
| Santiago | Chile | 95 | 85 | 90,0 | 88 |
| Athens | Greece | 87 | 94 | 90,5 | 89 |
| Shanghai | China | 102 | 80 | 91,0 | 90 |
| Zagreb | Croatia | 99 | 84 | 91,5 | 91 |
| Porto | Portugal | 87 | 98 | 92,5 | 92 |
| Panama City | Panama | 97 | 97 | 97,0 | 93 |
| Wroclaw | Poland | 100 | 95 | 97,5 | 94 |
| Medellín | Colombia | 105 | 96 | 100,5 | 95 |
| Sofia | Bulgaria | 116 | 91 | 103,5 | 96 |
| Beijing | China | 120 | 90 | 105,0 | 97 |
| Tel Aviv | Israel | 105 | 106 | 105,5 | 98 |
| Mexico City | Mexico | 128 | 87 | 107,5 | 99 |
| Bucharest | Romania | 107 | 109 | 108,0 | 100 |
| Córdoba | Argentina | 110 | 107 | 108,5 | 101 |
| Bangkok | Thailand | 131 | 86 | 108,5 | 102 |
| Brasilia | Brazil | 109 | 109 | 109,0 | 103 |
| Jerusalem | Israel | 110 | 108 | 109,0 | 104 |
| Monterrey | Mexico | 110 | 111 | 110,5 | 105 |
| Guangzhou | China | 121 | 102 | 111,5 | 106 |
| Sao Paulo | Brazil | 123 | 101 | 112,0 | 107 |
| Cape Town | South Africa | 94 | 133 | 113,5 | 108 |
| Asuncion | Paraguay | 115 | 115 | 115,0 | 109 |
| Rio de Janeiro | Brazil | 118 | 114 | 116,0 | 110 |
| Istanbul | Turkey | 133 | 104 | 118,5 | 111 |
| Lima | Peru | 124 | 116 | 120,0 | 112 |
| Doha | Qatar | 108 | 132 | 120,0 | 113 |
| Bogota | Colombia | 129 | 113 | 121,0 | 114 |
| Durban | South Africa | 88 | 158 | 123,0 | 115 |
| Guadalajara | Mexico | 130 | 121 | 125,5 | 116 |
| Johannesburg | South Africa | 96 | 155 | 125,5 | 117 |
| Tunis | Tunisia | 114 | 137 | 125,5 | 118 |

(continued)

**Table A.1**  (continued)

| City | Country | Mercer QoL RK | IESE CiM RK | Avg | Combined ranking |
|------|---------|------|------|------|------|
| Quito | Ecuador | 122 | 130 | 126,0 | 119 |
| Shenzhen | China | 136 | 118 | 127,0 | 120 |
| Kuwait City | Kuwait | 126 | 128 | 127,0 | 121 |
| Moscow | Russia | 168 | 89 | 128,5 | 122 |
| Belgrade | Serbia | 138 | 124 | 131,0 | 123 |
| Chengdu | China | 137 | 137 | 137,0 | 124 |
| St Petersburg | Russia | 176 | 103 | 139,5 | 125 |
| Manila | Philippines | 135 | 148 | 141,5 | 126 |
| Kiev | Ukraine | 174 | 119 | 146,5 | 127 |
| Casablanca | Morocco | 125 | 171 | 148,0 | 128 |
| Ho Chi Minh City | Vietnam | 152 | 146 | 149,0 | 129 |
| Jakarta | Indonesia | 143 | 156 | 149,5 | 130 |
| Chongqing | China | 147 | 157 | 152,0 | 131 |
| Riyadh | Saudi Arabia | 167 | 138 | 152,5 | 132 |
| Ankara | Turkey | 160 | 147 | 153,5 | 133 |
| Hanoi | Vietnam | 156 | 156 | 156,0 | 134 |
| Mumbai | India | 154 | 159 | 156,5 | 135 |
| Shenyang | China | 158 | 162 | 160,0 | 136 |
| Bangalore | India | 146 | 174 | 160,0 | 137 |
| New Delhi | India | 161 | 161 | 161,0 | 138 |
| La Paz | Bolivia | 157 | 170 | 163,5 | 139 |
| Cairo | Egypt | 165 | 163 | 164,0 | 140 |

**Table A.2** III.- City Magnetism. Identity. Summary

| City | Country | History | Government | Reputation | Space/Density | Climate | Georisk | Geoeconomics | Gastronomy | Branding | Identity summary |
|---|---|---|---|---|---|---|---|---|---|---|---|
| London | United Kingdom | 3 | 34 | 31 | 18 | 101 | 45 | 32 | 22 | 1 | 1 |
| Rome | Italy | 1 | 73 | 18 | 16 | 13 | 87 | 25 | 36 | 8 | 2 |
| Madrid | Spain | 14 | 60 | 32 | 19 | 8 | 54 | 46 | 37 | 9 | 3 |
| Paris | France | 3 | 56 | 41 | 118 | 51 | 15 | 28 | 11 | 3 | 4 |
| Barcelona | Spain | 14 | 63 | 30 | 75 | 16 | 54 | 46 | 35 | 4 | 5 |
| Vienna | Austria | 14 | 41 | 12 | 6 | 65 | 31 | 4 | 18 | 34 | 6 |
| Milan | Italy | 3 | 72 | 26 | 37 | 61 | 87 | 25 | 29 | 7 | 7 |
| Seoul | South Korea | 3 | 40 | 72 | 12 | 58 | 41 | 3 | 83 | 19 | 8 |
| Marseille | France | 27 | 56 | 62 | 44 | 9 | 15 | 28 | 27 | 35 | 9 |
| Zurich | Switzerland | 14 | 23 | 6 | 13 | 95 | 6 | 18 | 2 | 87 | 10 |
| Florence | Italy | 3 | 73 | 38 | 82 | 11 | 87 | 25 | 16 | 92 | 11 |
| New York City | United States | 61 | 44 | 38 | 47 | 18 | 65 | 88 | 38 | 2 | 12 |
| Nice | France | 27 | 56 | 62 | 47 | 7 | 15 | 28 | 5 | 76 | 13 |
| Valencia | Spain | 14 | 63 | 42 | 68 | 38 | 54 | 46 | 32 | 45 | 14 |
| Dublin | Ireland | 27 | 17 | 32 | 36 | 80 | 81 | 51 | 20 | 26 | 15 |
| Manchester | United Kingdom | 14 | 34 | 50 | 41 | 79 | 45 | 32 | 51 | 40 | 16 |
| Lyon | France | 14 | 56 | 62 | 75 | 52 | 15 | 28 | 12 | 71 | 17 |
| Stockholm | Sweden | 61 | 7 | 2 | 13 | 119 | 10 | 16 | 21 | 29 | 18 |
| Tokyo | Japan | 46 | 18 | 1 | 113 | 61 | 132 | 8 | 52 | 17 | 19 |
| Bilbao | Spain | 46 | 60 | 42 | 21 | 57 | 54 | 46 | 14 | 37 | 20 |
| Athens | Greece | 1 | 85 | 57 | 50 | 39 | 125 | 93 | 64 | 22 | 21 |
| Amsterdam | Netherlands | 46 | 11 | 27 | 98 | 78 | 126 | 13 | 7 | 32 | 22 |

(continued)

**Table A.2** (continued)

| City | Country | History | Government | Reputation | Space/Density | Climate | Georisk | Geoeconomics | Gastronomy | Branding | Identity summary |
|---|---|---|---|---|---|---|---|---|---|---|---|
| Edinburgh | United Kingdom | 27 | 34 | 34 | 57 | 104 | 45 | 32 | 19 | 46 | 23 |
| Lisbon | Portugal | 46 | 66 | 54 | 57 | 5 | 52 | 68 | 44 | 38 | 23 |
| Oslo | Norway | 78 | 1 | 10 | 2 | 124 | 13 | 24 | 30 | 44 | 25 |
| Berlin | Germany | 46 | 27 | 50 | 92 | 100 | 19 | 39 | 39 | 14 | 26 |
| Brussels | Belgium | 27 | 70 | 48 | 77 | 76 | 29 | 22 | 9 | 56 | 27 |
| Porto | Portugal | 27 | 66 | 54 | 109 | 12 | 52 | 68 | 42 | 49 | 27 |
| Geneva | Switzerland | 46 | 23 | 6 | 82 | 55 | 6 | 18 | 3 | 132 | 29 |
| Bern | Switzerland | 46 | 23 | 6 | 24 | 103 | 6 | 18 | 1 | 120 | 30 |
| Munich | Germany | 78 | 28 | 23 | 69 | 89 | 19 | 39 | 26 | 12 | 31 |
| Linz | Austria | 27 | 41 | 36 | 56 | 63 | 31 | 4 | 34 | 137 | 31 |
| Málaga | Spain | 27 | 63 | 42 | 64 | 21 | 54 | 46 | 49 | 132 | 33 |
| Sydney | Australia | 78 | 10 | 5 | 10 | 31 | 82 | 114 | 45 | 13 | 34 |
| Hamburg | Germany | 27 | 28 | 67 | 74 | 105 | 19 | 39 | 25 | 68 | 35 |
| Shanghai | China | 14 | 126 | 75 | 50 | 47 | 103 | 2 | 102 | 18 | 36 |
| Basel | Switzerland | 61 | 23 | 6 | 94 | 86 | 6 | 18 | 4 | 99 | 37 |
| Frankfurt | Germany | 61 | 28 | 37 | 31 | 92 | 19 | 39 | 28 | 64 | 38 |
| Budapest | Hungary | 14 | 91 | 61 | 96 | 69 | 96 | 4 | 61 | 50 | 38 |
| Hong Kong | Hong Kong | 14 | 75 | 59 | 1 | 137 | 103 | 57 | 75 | 72 | 40 |
| Prague | Czech Republic | 27 | 81 | 40 | 38 | 108 | 36 | 1 | 50 | 89 | 41 |
| Liverpool | United Kingdom | 46 | 34 | 50 | 86 | 94 | 45 | 32 | 48 | 47 | 42 |
| Cologne | Germany | 46 | 28 | 67 | 43 | 84 | 19 | 39 | 31 | 75 | 43 |
| Los Angeles | United States | 103 | 44 | 60 | 27 | 14 | 65 | 76 | 82 | 5 | 44 |

| | | | | | | | | | | | |
|---|---|---|---|---|---|---|---|---|---|---|---|
| Jerusalem | Israel | 3 | 77 | 81 | 82 | 1 | 43 | 126 | 63 | 90 | 45 |
| Luxembourg | Luxembourg | 27 | 39 | 46 | 116 | 109 | 14 | 37 | 8 | 128 | 46 |
| Rotterdam | Netherlands | 46 | 11 | 27 | 94 | 72 | 126 | 13 | 24 | 120 | 47 |
| Melbourne | Australia | 95 | 14 | 15 | 132 | 34 | 82 | 114 | 56 | 6 | 48 |
| Copenhagen | Denmark | 78 | 7 | 11 | 81 | 111 | 27 | 38 | 13 | 94 | 49 |
| Eindhoven | Netherlands | 78 | 11 | 27 | 30 | 98 | 126 | 13 | 6 | 99 | 50 |
| Sofia | Bulgaria | 14 | 87 | 83 | 34 | 70 | 80 | 53 | 99 | 83 | 51 |
| Antwerp | Belgium | 61 | 70 | 48 | 116 | 73 | 29 | 22 | 10 | 113 | 52 |
| San Francisco | United States | 103 | 43 | 34 | 121 | 4 | 65 | 76 | 40 | 31 | 53 |
| Montreal | Canada | 78 | 2 | 18 | 96 | 121 | 37 | 88 | 73 | 10 | 54 |
| Belgrade | Serbia | 27 | 96 | 83 | 98 | 41 | 99 | 52 | 93 | 65 | 55 |
| Istanbul | Turkey | 3 | 123 | 100 | 65 | 19 | 97 | 86 | 135 | 28 | 56 |
| Washington, D.C. | United States | 103 | 44 | 65 | 105 | 6 | 65 | 82 | 47 | 19 | 57 |
| Stuttgart | Germany | 61 | 28 | 67 | 91 | 102 | 19 | 39 | 23 | 120 | 58 |
| Birmingham | United Kingdom | 61 | 34 | 50 | 88 | 110 | 45 | 32 | 59 | 114 | 59 |
| Gothenburg | Sweden | 103 | 7 | 2 | 70 | 88 | 10 | 16 | 17 | 126 | 60 |
| Wroclaw | Poland | 27 | 91 | 94 | 66 | 114 | 34 | 11 | 66 | 94 | 61 |
| Dusseldorf | Germany | 78 | 28 | 67 | 105 | 81 | 19 | 39 | 55 | 120 | 62 |
| Bratislava | Slovakia | 61 | 86 | 76 | 62 | 68 | 42 | 4 | 69 | 114 | 63 |
| Boston | United States | 95 | 44 | 56 | 134 | 35 | 65 | 88 | 67 | 25 | 64 |
| Chicago | United States | 103 | 44 | 73 | 135 | 43 | 65 | 78 | 46 | 11 | 64 |
| Toronto | Canada | 103 | 2 | 18 | 109 | 92 | 37 | 88 | 72 | 15 | 66 |
| Helsinki | Finland | 103 | 6 | 4 | 23 | 128 | 4 | 71 | 41 | 52 | 66 |
| Ljubljana | Slovenia | 14 | 82 | 76 | 133 | 113 | 51 | 63 | 91 | 108 | 68 |
| Beijing | China | 27 | 126 | 129 | 108 | 33 | 103 | 55 | 115 | 23 | 69 |

(continued)

**Table A.2** (continued)

| City | Country | History | Government | Reputation | Space/Density | Climate | Georisk | Geoeconomics | Gastronomy | Branding | Identity summary |
|---|---|---|---|---|---|---|---|---|---|---|---|
| Adelaide | Australia | 103 | 14 | 15 | 78 | 28 | 82 | 114 | 33 | 57 | 70 |
| Osaka | Japan | 129 | 21 | 24 | 54 | 50 | 132 | 8 | 42 | 58 | 71 |
| Wellington | New Zealand | 95 | 19 | 13 | 29 | 43 | 90 | 137 | 54 | 83 | 72 |
| Philadelphia | United States | 78 | 44 | 104 | 129 | 15 | 65 | 88 | 87 | 41 | 73 |
| Chengdu | China | 3 | 126 | 129 | 7 | 67 | 103 | 63 | 120 | 120 | 74 |
| Warsaw | Poland | 61 | 91 | 94 | 66 | 115 | 34 | 11 | 58 | 94 | 75 |
| Zagreb | Croatia | 78 | 94 | 83 | 53 | 59 | 79 | 54 | 60 | 79 | 76 |
| Mexico City | Mexico | 46 | 109 | 121 | 70 | 26 | 112 | 98 | 108 | 16 | 77 |
| Vancouver | Canada | 129 | 2 | 18 | 45 | 71 | 37 | 84 | 65 | 33 | 78 |
| Rio de Janeiro | Brazil | 61 | 98 | 87 | 21 | 75 | 92 | 97 | 76 | 30 | 79 |
| Buenos Aires | Argentina | 61 | 89 | 88 | 103 | 24 | 61 | 122 | 95 | 39 | 80 |
| Tunis | Tunisia | 3 | 119 | 137 | 125 | 26 | 101 | 81 | 114 | 106 | 81 |
| Tallinn | Estonia | 46 | 79 | 79 | 111 | 123 | 5 | 72 | 78 | 82 | 82 |
| Yokohama | Japan | 129 | 21 | 24 | 70 | 59 | 132 | 8 | 52 | 111 | 83 |
| Auckland | New Zealand | 95 | 19 | 13 | 114 | 35 | 90 | 137 | 76 | 114 | 84 |
| Singapore | Singapore | 95 | 69 | 42 | 3 | 135 | 26 | 106 | 57 | 43 | 85 |
| Atlanta | United States | 129 | 44 | 74 | 128 | 30 | 65 | 70 | 86 | 27 | 85 |
| Vilnius | Lithuania | 61 | 82 | 79 | 11 | 127 | 12 | 67 | 103 | 102 | 85 |
| Chongqing | China | 3 | 126 | 129 | 49 | 95 | 103 | 63 | 118 | 110 | 88 |
| Seattle | United States | 129 | 44 | 47 | 119 | 45 | 65 | 84 | 70 | 36 | 89 |
| Córdoba | Argentina | 78 | 89 | 88 | 62 | 17 | 61 | 122 | 90 | 73 | 90 |
| Ottawa | Canada | 103 | 2 | 18 | 59 | 117 | 37 | 96 | 68 | 98 | 91 |
| Miami | United States | 121 | 44 | 58 | 130 | 91 | 65 | 87 | 61 | 24 | 92 |
| Riga | Latvia | 46 | 84 | 83 | 101 | 126 | 33 | 72 | 89 | 126 | 93 |

| City | Country | | | | | | | | | | |
| --- | --- | --- | --- | --- | --- | --- | --- | --- | --- | --- | --- |
| Shenyang | China | 3 | 126 | 129 | 122 | 84 | 103 | 55 | 126 | 137 | 93 |
| Bucharest | Romania | 61 | 95 | 128 | 38 | 55 | 100 | 66 | 104 | 108 | 95 |
| Canberra | Australia | 129 | 14 | 15 | 73 | 29 | 82 | 114 | 15 | 132 | 96 |
| Baltimore | United States | 121 | 44 | 104 | 137 | 21 | 65 | 82 | 81 | 77 | 97 |
| Moscow | Russia | 27 | 133 | 126 | 79 | 136 | 59 | 78 | 106 | 21 | 97 |
| Tel Aviv | Israel | 103 | 77 | 120 | 35 | 21 | 43 | 109 | 85 | 69 | 99 |
| Casablanca | Morocco | 27 | 136 | 137 | 19 | 20 | 102 | 111 | 129 | 128 | 100 |
| Cairo | Egypt | 14 | 140 | 124 | 79 | 42 | 3 | 100 | 136 | 118 | 101 |
| Sao Paulo | Brazil | 78 | 98 | 102 | 26 | 81 | 92 | 108 | 80 | 52 | 102 |
| Kiev | Ukraine | 27 | 104 | 140 | 119 | 120 | 28 | 74 | 97 | 93 | 103 |
| Phoenix | United States | 129 | 44 | 104 | 127 | 48 | 65 | 75 | 84 | 65 | 104 |
| Cape Town | South Africa | 78 | 101 | 117 | 32 | 10 | 115 | 132 | 119 | 117 | 105 |
| Dallas | United States | 129 | 62 | 104 | 135 | 24 | 65 | 94 | 92 | 52 | 106 |
| Houston | United States | 129 | 44 | 104 | 124 | 53 | 65 | 94 | 79 | 42 | 107 |
| Johannesburg | South Africa | 103 | 101 | 117 | 42 | 2 | 115 | 132 | 125 | 59 | 108 |
| Dubai | United Arab Emirates | 78 | 113 | 66 | 140 | 87 | 63 | 120 | 100 | 61 | 109 |
| Ankara | Turkey | 27 | 123 | 127 | 87 | 49 | 97 | 125 | 133 | 130 | 110 |
| Taipei | Taiwan | 103 | 68 | 81 | 90 | 132 | 103 | 57 | 116 | 78 | 111 |
| Brasilia | Brazil | 95 | 98 | 102 | 17 | 77 | 92 | 110 | 71 | 120 | 111 |
| Bogota | Colombia | 78 | 115 | 135 | 9 | 45 | 119 | 129 | 113 | 80 | 113 |
| Quito | Ecuador | 61 | 120 | 96 | 104 | 37 | 131 | 128 | 121 | 104 | 113 |
| Guangzhou | China | 46 | 126 | 129 | 50 | 129 | 103 | 57 | 123 | 118 | 115 |
| Hanoi | Vietnam | 27 | 137 | 114 | 54 | 133 | 135 | 62 | 134 | 83 | 116 |
| Montevideo | Uruguay | 121 | 76 | 96 | 102 | 3 | 139 | 101 | 98 | 106 | 117 |
| Manila | Philippines | 46 | 108 | 116 | 28 | 139 | 140 | 57 | 131 | 102 | 118 |
| Lima | Peru | 61 | 112 | 91 | 25 | 116 | 121 | 132 | 122 | 97 | 119 |
| Monterrey | Mexico | 78 | 109 | 122 | 98 | 99 | 112 | 98 | 110 | 50 | 120 |

(continued)

**Table A.2** (continued)

| City | Country | History | Government | Reputation | Space/Density | Climate | Georisk | Geoeconomics | Gastronomy | Branding | Identity summary |
|---|---|---|---|---|---|---|---|---|---|---|---|
| St Petersburg | Russia | 78 | 133 | 71 | 114 | 134 | 59 | 78 | 105 | 62 | 121 |
| Santiago | Chile | 103 | 80 | 88 | 85 | 32 | 138 | 124 | 107 | 91 | 122 |
| Panama City | Panama | 95 | 88 | 91 | 59 | 95 | 130 | 129 | 87 | 104 | 123 |
| Guadalajara | Mexico | 78 | 109 | 122 | 123 | 40 | 112 | 119 | 111 | 137 | 124 |
| Jakarta | Indonesia | 61 | 120 | 101 | 33 | 106 | 137 | 112 | 138 | 73 | 125 |
| Mumbai | India | 61 | 106 | 109 | 4 | 140 | 122 | 103 | 139 | 55 | 126 |
| Asuncion | Paraguay | 103 | 122 | 96 | 107 | 65 | 50 | 102 | 127 | 70 | 127 |
| Bangalore | India | 103 | 106 | 109 | 38 | 63 | 122 | 103 | 137 | 67 | 128 |
| Shenzhen | China | 95 | 126 | 129 | 5 | 130 | 103 | 57 | 124 | 130 | 129 |
| Abu Dhabi | United Arab Emirates | 121 | 113 | 113 | 139 | 89 | 63 | 120 | 74 | 87 | 130 |
| Bangkok | Thailand | 121 | 118 | 78 | 111 | 122 | 118 | 118 | 101 | 48 | 130 |
| La Paz | Bolivia | 103 | 135 | 96 | 59 | 74 | 95 | 136 | 128 | 101 | 132 |
| Medellín | Colombia | 103 | 115 | 135 | 15 | 112 | 119 | 129 | 109 | 80 | 133 |
| New Delhi | India | 129 | 117 | 109 | 8 | 83 | 122 | 103 | 140 | 63 | 133 |
| Durban | South Africa | 129 | 101 | 117 | 88 | 53 | 115 | 132 | 117 | 59 | 135 |
| Kuwait City | Kuwait | 103 | 125 | 112 | 45 | 117 | 82 | 140 | 93 | 137 | 136 |
| Doha | Qatar | 121 | 105 | 125 | 126 | 107 | 1 | 139 | 96 | 135 | 137 |
| Kuala Lumpur | Malaysia | 129 | 97 | 93 | 138 | 137 | 129 | 106 | 112 | 135 | 138 |
| Riyadh | Saudi Arabia | 121 | 139 | 139 | 131 | 124 | 2 | 127 | 130 | 111 | 139 |
| Ho Chi Minh City | Vietnam | 121 | 137 | 114 | 92 | 131 | 135 | 113 | 131 | 83 | 140 |

**Table A.3** IV.- City Magnetism. Dynamism. Summary

| City | Country | Competitiveness | Expat social experience | Ethics well-being | Equality | Dynamism summary |
|---|---|---|---|---|---|---|
| Toronto | Canada | 16 | 10 | 10 | 5 | 1 |
| Montreal | Canada | 32 | 10 | 11 | 5 | 2 |
| Vancouver | Canada | 38 | 10 | 11 | 5 | 3 |
| Ottawa | Canada | 42 | 10 | 11 | 5 | 4 |
| Wellington | New Zealand | 50 | 8 | 5 | 17 | 5 |
| Auckland | New Zealand | 54 | 8 | 14 | 17 | 6 |
| Sydney | Australia | 12 | 24 | 7 | 9 | 7 |
| Amsterdam | Netherlands | 8 | 45 | 1 | 15 | 8 |
| Melbourne | Australia | 18 | 24 | 4 | 9 | 9 |
| Oslo | Norway | 35 | 42 | 22 | 2 | 10 |
| Adelaide | Australia | 25 | 24 | 7 | 9 | 11 |
| Canberra | Australia | 25 | 24 | 7 | 9 | 11 |
| Helsinki | Finland | 28 | 67 | 24 | 1 | 13 |
| Rotterdam | Netherlands | 41 | 45 | 1 | 14 | 14 |
| Eindhoven | Netherlands | 45 | 45 | 1 | 15 | 15 |
| Stockholm | Sweden | 13 | 67 | 27 | 3 | 16 |
| Copenhagen | Denmark | 9 | 67 | 6 | 13 | 17 |
| Gothenburg | Sweden | 37 | 67 | 38 | 3 | 18 |
| Madrid | Spain | 48 | 1 | 64 | 80 | 19 |
| Munich | Germany | 21 | 34 | 44 | 36 | 20 |
| Singapore | Singapore | 3 | 14 | 95 | 35 | 21 |
| Berlin | Germany | 29 | 34 | 44 | 36 | 22 |
| Paris | France | 10 | 20 | 60 | 63 | 23 |
| New York City | United States | 1 | 84 | 25 | 44 | 24 |
| Barcelona | Spain | 53 | 7 | 68 | 80 | 25 |

(continued)

**Table A.3** (continued)

| City | Country | | | | | |
|---|---|---|---|---|---|---|
| Vienna | Austria | 46 | 48 | 54 | 21 | 26 |
| Luxembourg | Luxembourg | 65 | 34 | 32 | 29 | 27 |
| Hamburg | Germany | 40 | 34 | 44 | 36 | 28 |
| Dusseldorf | Germany | 43 | 34 | 44 | 36 | 29 |
| Frankfurt | Germany | 47 | 34 | 44 | 36 | 30 |
| Cologne | Germany | 55 | 34 | 44 | 36 | 31 |
| Stuttgart | Germany | 56 | 34 | 44 | 36 | 32 |
| San Francisco | United States | 4 | 84 | 28 | 44 | 33 |
| Boston | United States | 5 | 84 | 18 | 44 | 34 |
| Dublin | Ireland | 44 | 76 | 43 | 20 | 35 |
| Valencia | Spain | 70 | 6 | 65 | 80 | 36 |
| Málaga | Spain | 71 | 5 | 65 | 80 | 37 |
| Los Angeles | United States | 6 | 84 | 26 | 44 | 38 |
| Chicago | United States | 7 | 84 | 19 | 44 | 39 |
| London | United Kingdom | 2 | 102 | 33 | 58 | 40 |
| Bilbao | Spain | 73 | 4 | 65 | 80 | 41 |
| Linz | Austria | 63 | 48 | 54 | 21 | 42 |
| Washington, D.C. | United States | 11 | 84 | 15 | 44 | 43 |
| Lisbon | Portugal | 72 | 2 | 99 | 27 | 44 |
| Zurich | Switzerland | 23 | 98 | 39 | 23 | 45 |
| Dallas | United States | 22 | 84 | 16 | 44 | 46 |
| Lyon | France | 61 | 20 | 60 | 63 | 47 |
| Houston | United States | 24 | 84 | 17 | 44 | 48 |
| Miami | United States | 20 | 84 | 21 | 44 | 49 |
| Phoenix | United States | 17 | 84 | 28 | 44 | 50 |
| Porto | Portugal | 80 | 2 | 99 | 27 | 51 |
| Seattle | United States | 19 | 84 | 28 | 44 | 52 |

| Atlanta | United States | 27 | 84 | 20 | 44 | 53 |
|---|---|---|---|---|---|---|
| Basel | Switzerland | 33 | 98 | 39 | 23 | 54 |
| Bern | Switzerland | 34 | 98 | 39 | 23 | 55 |
| Geneva | Switzerland | 36 | 98 | 39 | 23 | 56 |
| Philadelphia | United States | 31 | 84 | 23 | 44 | 57 |
| Baltimore | United States | 30 | 84 | 28 | 44 | 58 |
| Nice | France | 64 | 20 | 60 | 63 | 59 |
| Marseille | France | 69 | 20 | 60 | 63 | 60 |
| Edinburgh | United Kingdom | 39 | 102 | 33 | 58 | 61 |
| Manchester | United Kingdom | 52 | 102 | 33 | 58 | 62 |
| Liverpool | United Kingdom | 57 | 102 | 33 | 58 | 63 |
| Birmingham | United Kingdom | 58 | 102 | 33 | 58 | 64 |
| Brussels | Belgium | 59 | 121 | 51 | 31 | 65 |
| Tokyo | Japan | 14 | 51 | 112 | 67 | 66 |
| Prague | Czech Republic | 79 | 54 | 76 | 33 | 67 |
| Antwerp | Belgium | 62 | 121 | 51 | 43 | 68 |
| Milan | Italy | 68 | 55 | 56 | 112 | 69 |
| Seoul | South Korea | 51 | 72 | 74 | 90 | 70 |
| Rome | Italy | 77 | 55 | 56 | 112 | 71 |
| Yokohama | Japan | 49 | 51 | 115 | 67 | 72 |
| Florence | Italy | 82 | 55 | 56 | 112 | 73 |
| Ljubljana | Slovenia | 76 | 109 | 73 | 32 | 74 |
| Osaka | Japan | 60 | 51 | 115 | 67 | 75 |
| Taipei | Taiwan | 66 | 43 | 117 | 75 | 76 |
| Tel Aviv | Israel | 74 | 55 | 53 | 124 | 77 |
| Dubai | United Arab Emirates | 67 | 61 | 77 | 107 | 78 |
| Abu Dhabi | United Arab Emirates | 75 | 61 | 75 | 107 | 79 |

(continued)

372

**Table A.3** (continued)

| Santiago | Chile | 85 | 63 | 82 | 85 | 80 |
|---|---|---|---|---|---|---|
| Jerusalem | Israel | 83 | 55 | 59 | 128 | 81 |
| Warsaw | Poland | 86 | 109 | 79 | 72 | 82 |
| Sao Paulo | Brazil | 101 | 73 | 70 | 102 | 83 |
| Bangkok | Thailand | 100 | 50 | 103 | 87 | 84 |
| Hong Kong | Hong Kong | 15 | 44 | 124 | 133 | 85 |
| Wroclaw | Poland | 90 | 109 | 79 | 72 | 86 |
| Tallinn | Estonia | 84 | 109 | 78 | 79 | 87 |
| Bratislava | Slovakia | 95 | 109 | 69 | 88 | 88 |
| Buenos Aires | Argentina | 96 | 63 | 98 | 77 | 89 |
| Rio de Janeiro | Brazil | 110 | 73 | 71 | 102 | 90 |
| Vilnius | Lithuania | 91 | 109 | 83 | 74 | 91 |
| Brasilia | Brazil | 112 | 73 | 71 | 102 | 92 |
| Moscow | Russia | 88 | 81 | 91 | 98 | 93 |
| Budapest | Hungary | 89 | 109 | 94 | 89 | 94 |
| Córdoba | Argentina | 108 | 63 | 105 | 77 | 95 |
| Kuala Lumpur | Malaysia | 87 | 71 | 125 | 86 | 96 |
| Bogota | Colombia | 119 | 15 | 101 | 126 | 97 |
| St Petersburg | Russia | 102 | 81 | 92 | 98 | 98 |
| Riga | Latvia | 94 | 109 | 84 | 106 | 99 |
| Kiev | Ukraine | 121 | 81 | 114 | 34 | 100 |
| Doha | Qatar | 105 | 126 | 89 | 30 | 101 |
| Mexico City | Mexico | 111 | 15 | 81 | 138 | 102 |
| Manila | Philippines | 123 | 33 | 119 | 105 | 103 |
| Medellín | Colombia | 128 | 15 | 113 | 126 | 104 |
| Montevideo | Uruguay | 107 | 127 | 106 | 19 | 105 |
| Panama City | Panama | 118 | 63 | 88 | 115 | 106 |

| | | | | | | |
|---|---|---|---|---|---|---|
| Monterrey | Mexico | 115 | 15 | 85 | 138 | 107 |
| Guadalajara | Mexico | 116 | 15 | 85 | 138 | 108 |
| Athens | Greece | 106 | 55 | 111 | 119 | 109 |
| Belgrade | Serbia | 113 | 109 | 96 | 76 | 110 |
| Bucharest | Romania | 103 | 109 | 97 | 110 | 111 |
| Zagreb | Croatia | 109 | 109 | 104 | 100 | 112 |
| Istanbul | Turkey | 114 | 31 | 118 | 134 | 113 |
| Sofia | Bulgaria | 104 | 109 | 107 | 111 | 114 |
| Jakarta | Indonesia | 133 | 80 | 110 | 109 | 115 |
| Cape Town | South Africa | 122 | 77 | 93 | 121 | 116 |
| Johannesburg | South Africa | 127 | 77 | 90 | 121 | 117 |
| Ankara | Turkey | 130 | 31 | 109 | 134 | 118 |
| Durban | South Africa | 125 | 77 | 102 | 121 | 119 |
| Ho Chi Minh City | Vietnam | 120 | 107 | 127 | 70 | 120 |
| Shanghai | China | 78 | 132 | 128 | 91 | 121 |
| Hanoi | Vietnam | 134 | 107 | 126 | 71 | 122 |
| Beijing | China | 81 | 132 | 131 | 91 | 123 |
| Guangzhou | China | 93 | 132 | 130 | 91 | 124 |
| Shenzhen | China | 92 | 132 | 132 | 91 | 125 |
| Chengdu | China | 97 | 132 | 132 | 91 | 126 |
| Chongqing | China | 98 | 132 | 132 | 91 | 127 |
| Shenyang | China | 99 | 132 | 132 | 91 | 128 |
| Mumbai | India | 129 | 28 | 139 | 130 | 129 |
| Bangalore | India | 131 | 28 | 139 | 130 | 130 |
| New Delhi | India | 135 | 28 | 137 | 130 | 131 |
| Kuwait City | Kuwait | 126 | 140 | 87 | 116 | 132 |
| Lima | Peru | 124 | 127 | 120 | 120 | 133 |

(continued)

**Table A.3** (continued)

| Quito | Ecuador | 132 | 127 | 122 | 118 | 134 |
|---|---|---|---|---|---|---|
| Riyadh | Saudi Arabia | 117 | 139 | 108 | 125 | 135 |
| Asuncion | Paraguay | 138 | 127 | 123 | 117 | 136 |
| Tunis | Tunisia | 139 | 123 | 136 | 101 | 137 |
| La Paz | Bolivia | 136 | 127 | 121 | 137 | 138 |
| Casablanca | Morocco | 137 | 123 | 129 | 136 | 139 |
| Cairo | Egypt | 140 | 123 | 138 | 129 | 140 |

# V.- City Magnetism. Strategy. Summary

**Table A.4** V.- City Magnetism. Strategy. Summary

| City | Country | Human capital | Smartcity | Innovation | Strategy summary |
|---|---|---|---|---|---|
| Copenhagen | Denmark | 26 | 1 | 30 | 1 |
| Seoul | South Korea | 15 | 12 | 2 | 2 |
| San Francisco | United States | 12 | 12 | 5 | 3 |
| Stockholm | Sweden | 56 | 2 | 16 | 4 |
| New York City | United States | 3 | 25 | 1 | 5 |
| Chicago | United States | 11 | 18 | 5 | 6 |
| Melbourne | Australia | 30 | 5 | 25 | 7 |
| Manchester | United Kingdom | 20 | 5 | 46 | 8 |
| London | United Kingdom | 1 | 25 | 10 | 9 |
| Amsterdam | Netherlands | 35 | 5 | 27 | 10 |
| Sydney | Australia | 27 | 8 | 32 | 11 |
| Helsinki | Finland | 53 | 4 | 34 | 12 |
| Tel Aviv | Israel | 109 | 2 | 15 | 13 |
| Taipei | Taiwan | 21 | 8 | 45 | 14 |
| Berlin | Germany | 5 | 25 | 11 | 15 |
| Phoenix | United States | 14 | 18 | 27 | 16 |
| Toronto | Canada | 28 | 12 | 24 | 17 |
| Los Angeles | United States | 2 | 53 | 4 | 18 |
| Atlanta | United States | 38 | 25 | 12 | 19 |
| Boston | United States | 4 | 53 | 5 | 20 |
| Hong Kong | Hong Kong | 18 | 12 | 47 | 21 |
| Dallas | United States | 13 | 41 | 8 | 22 |
| Washington, D.C. | United States | 8 | 41 | 12 | 23 |
| Seattle | United States | 50 | 25 | 8 | 24 |
| Singapore | Singapore | 43 | 34 | 16 | 25 |
| Vienna | Austria | 23 | 34 | 23 | 26 |
| Miami | United States | 19 | 53 | 18 | 27 |
| Houston | United States | 38 | 41 | 12 | 28 |
| Adelaide | Australia | 30 | 12 | 73 | 29 |
| Rotterdam | Netherlands | 60 | 12 | 48 | 30 |
| Edinburgh | United Kingdom | 24 | 25 | 57 | 31 |
| Paris | France | 6 | 63 | 20 | 32 |
| Cologne | Germany | 59 | 18 | 44 | 33 |
| Gothenburg | Sweden | 74 | 18 | 42 | 34 |
| Tokyo | Japan | 9 | 77 | 3 | 35 |
| Moscow | Russia | 7 | 34 | 75 | 36 |
| Barcelona | Spain | 45 | 25 | 56 | 37 |
| Yokohama | Japan | 9 | 41 | 54 | 38 |
| Oslo | Norway | 69 | 25 | 51 | 39 |

(continued)

**Table A.4**  (continued)

| City | Country | Human capital | Smartcity | Innovation | Strategy summary |
|------|---------|---------------|-----------|------------|------------------|
| Hamburg | Germany | 29 | 53 | 31 | 40 |
| Eindhoven | Netherlands | 80 | 18 | 58 | 41 |
| Milan | Italy | 33 | 41 | 60 | 42 |
| Antwerp | Belgium | 95 | 8 | 72 | 43 |
| Birmingham | United Kingdom | 36 | 53 | 60 | 44 |
| Jerusalem | Israel | 117 | 25 | 37 | 45 |
| Shanghai | China | 25 | 77 | 37 | 46 |
| Vancouver | Canada | 81 | 41 | 52 | 47 |
| Dublin | Ireland | 92 | 34 | 63 | 48 |
| Tallinn | Estonia | 46 | 41 | 91 | 49 |
| Zurich | Switzerland | 34 | 93 | 21 | 50 |
| Wellington | New Zealand | 67 | 41 | 79 | 51 |
| Philadelphia | United States | 17 | 118 | 19 | 52 |
| Ottawa | Canada | 42 | 63 | 70 | 53 |
| Valencia | Spain | 96 | 18 | 84 | 54 |
| Munich | Germany | 61 | 77 | 22 | 55 |
| Montreal | Canada | 49 | 77 | 43 | 56 |
| Lyon | France | 51 | 70 | 55 | 57 |
| Luxembourg | Luxembourg | 71 | 41 | 81 | 58 |
| Málaga | Spain | 89 | 18 | 96 | 59 |
| Nice | France | 71 | 53 | 68 | 60 |
| Frankfurt | Germany | 44 | 87 | 36 | 61 |
| Liverpool | United Kingdom | 63 | 70 | 60 | 62 |
| Osaka | Japan | 70 | 70 | 50 | 63 |
| Stuttgart | Germany | 68 | 77 | 39 | 64 |
| Dubai | United Arab Emirates | 126 | 34 | 69 | 65 |
| Canberra | Australia | 30 | 87 | 73 | 66 |
| Baltimore | United States | 54 | 105 | 27 | 67 |
| Florence | Italy | 57 | 63 | 88 | 68 |
| Santiago | Chile | 85 | 41 | 106 | 69 |
| Auckland | New Zealand | 87 | 63 | 79 | 70 |
| Jakarta | Indonesia | 16 | 87 | 113 | 71 |
| Bilbao | Spain | 102 | 41 | 87 | 72 |
| Doha | Qatar | 139 | 8 | 123 | 73 |
| Basel | Switzerland | 52 | 118 | 33 | 74 |
| Bern | Switzerland | 66 | 105 | 41 | 75 |
| Marseille | France | 86 | 77 | 65 | 76 |
| Wroclaw | Poland | 84 | 53 | 105 | 77 |
| Ljubljana | Slovenia | 88 | 53 | 99 | 78 |
| Abu Dhabi | United Arab Emirates | 134 | 41 | 89 | 79 |
| Beijing | China | 62 | 124 | 35 | 80 |
| Prague | Czech Republic | 55 | 105 | 64 | 81 |
| Cape Town | South Africa | 122 | 34 | 121 | 82 |

(continued)

**Table A.4** (continued)

| City | Country | Human capital | Smartcity | Innovation | Strategy summary |
|---|---|---|---|---|---|
| Kuala Lumpur | Malaysia | 101 | 77 | 78 | 83 |
| Brussels | Belgium | 98 | 87 | 53 | 84 |
| Mexico City | Mexico | 58 | 93 | 100 | 85 |
| Madrid | Spain | 40 | 124 | 59 | 86 |
| Vilnius | Lithuania | 22 | 93 | 111 | 87 |
| Bogota | Colombia | 93 | 63 | 117 | 88 |
| Rio de Janeiro | Brazil | 100 | 70 | 101 | 89 |
| St Petersburg | Russia | 37 | 105 | 97 | 90 |
| Geneva | Switzerland | 82 | 124 | 26 | 91 |
| Budapest | Hungary | 41 | 118 | 76 | 92 |
| Durban | South Africa | 122 | 34 | 133 | 93 |
| New Delhi | India | 135 | 53 | 103 | 94 |
| Linz | Austria | 79 | 105 | 67 | 95 |
| Rome | Italy | 47 | 124 | 66 | 96 |
| Porto | Portugal | 108 | 70 | 91 | 97 |
| Shenzhen | China | 118 | 93 | 49 | 98 |
| Buenos Aires | Argentina | 64 | 105 | 102 | 99 |
| Lisbon | Portugal | 76 | 105 | 82 | 100 |
| Dusseldorf | Germany | 83 | 124 | 39 | 101 |
| Sofia | Bulgaria | 75 | 87 | 107 | 102 |
| Zagreb | Croatia | 97 | 63 | 124 | 103 |
| Sao Paulo | Brazil | 111 | 87 | 94 | 104 |
| Warsaw | Poland | 78 | 105 | 95 | 105 |
| Guadalajara | Mexico | 104 | 70 | 128 | 105 |
| Montevideo | Uruguay | 113 | 53 | 134 | 107 |
| Athens | Greece | 77 | 118 | 90 | 108 |
| Lima | Peru | 106 | 77 | 129 | 109 |
| Riga | Latvia | 73 | 105 | 110 | 110 |
| Bangkok | Thailand | 115 | 93 | 93 | 111 |
| Quito | Ecuador | 112 | 63 | 137 | 112 |
| Bucharest | Romania | 90 | 93 | 108 | 113 |
| Shenyang | China | 118 | 105 | 83 | 114 |
| Chongqing | China | 118 | 118 | 71 | 115 |
| Medellín | Colombia | 114 | 93 | 112 | 116 |
| Monterrey | Mexico | 64 | 131 | 114 | 117 |
| Mumbai | India | 137 | 93 | 98 | 118 |
| Kiev | Ukraine | 91 | 93 | 126 | 119 |
| Istanbul | Turkey | 107 | 131 | 85 | 120 |
| Córdoba | Argentina | 104 | 93 | 132 | 121 |
| Panama City | Panama | 127 | 77 | 136 | 122 |
| Belgrade | Serbia | 94 | 105 | 120 | 123 |
| Johannesburg | South Africa | 124 | 93 | 125 | 124 |
| Bratislava | Slovakia | 48 | 133 | 118 | 125 |

(continued)

Table A.4 (continued)

| City | Country | Human capital | Smartcity | Innovation | Strategy summary |
|------|---------|---------------|-----------|------------|------------------|
| Ho Chi Minh City | Vietnam | 131 | 93 | 122 | 126 |
| Casablanca | Morocco | 138 | 77 | 135 | 127 |
| Bangalore | India | 116 | 124 | 104 | 128 |
| La Paz | Bolivia | 133 | 70 | 139 | 129 |
| Cairo | Egypt | 125 | 105 | 130 | 130 |
| Brasilia | Brazil | 129 | 105 | 114 | 131 |
| Guangzhou | China | 110 | 135 | 86 | 132 |
| Hanoi | Vietnam | 131 | 118 | 127 | 133 |
| Ankara | Turkey | 99 | 135 | 109 | 134 |
| Chengdu | China | 118 | 139 | 77 | 135 |
| Kuwait City | Kuwait | 136 | 124 | 131 | 136 |
| Manila | Philippines | 128 | 135 | 118 | 137 |
| Riyadh | Saudi Arabia | 140 | 133 | 114 | 138 |
| Asuncion | Paraguay | 103 | 135 | 140 | 139 |
| Tunis | Tunisia | 130 | 140 | 138 | 140 |

# VI.- City Magnetism. Summary

Table A.5 VI.- City Magnetism. Summary

| City | Country | Identity | Dynamism | Strategy | Magnetism |
|------|---------|----------|----------|----------|-----------|
| London | United Kingdom | 1 | 40 | 9 | 1 |
| Stockholm | Sweden | 18 | 16 | 4 | 2 |
| Amsterdam | Netherlands | 22 | 8 | 10 | 3 |
| Paris | France | 4 | 23 | 32 | 4 |
| New York City | United States | 12 | 24 | 5 | 5 |
| Sydney | Australia | 34 | 7 | 11 | 6 |
| Vienna | Austria | 6 | 26 | 26 | 7 |
| Barcelona | Spain | 5 | 25 | 37 | 8 |
| Melbourne | Australia | 48 | 9 | 7 | 9 |
| Copenhagen | Denmark | 49 | 17 | 1 | 10 |
| Oslo | Norway | 25 | 10 | 39 | 11 |
| Berlin | Germany | 26 | 22 | 15 | 12 |
| Seoul | South Korea | 8 | 70 | 2 | 13 |
| Toronto | Canada | 66 | 1 | 17 | 14 |
| Rotterdam | Netherlands | 47 | 14 | 30 | 15 |
| Manchester | United Kingdom | 16 | 62 | 8 | 16 |
| Helsinki | Finland | 66 | 13 | 12 | 17 |

(continued)

Appendix 379

**Table A.5** (continued)

| City | Country | Identity | Dynamism | Strategy | Magnetism |
|---|---|---|---|---|---|
| San Francisco | United States | 53 | 33 | 3 | 18 |
| Madrid | Spain | 3 | 19 | 86 | 19 |
| Los Angeles | United States | 44 | 38 | 18 | 20 |
| Eindhoven | Netherlands | 50 | 15 | 41 | 21 |
| Adelaide | Australia | 70 | 11 | 29 | 22 |
| Zurich | Switzerland | 10 | 45 | 50 | 23 |
| Montreal | Canada | 54 | 2 | 56 | 24 |
| Milan | Italy | 7 | 69 | 42 | 25 |
| Dublin | Ireland | 15 | 35 | 48 | 26 |
| Cologne | Germany | 43 | 31 | 33 | 27 |
| Valencia | Spain | 14 | 36 | 54 | 28 |
| Chicago | United States | 64 | 39 | 6 | 29 |
| Hamburg | Germany | 35 | 28 | 40 | 30 |
| Edinburgh | United Kingdom | 23 | 61 | 31 | 31 |
| Munich | Germany | 31 | 20 | 55 | 32 |
| Washington, D.C. | United States | 57 | 43 | 23 | 33 |
| Nice | France | 13 | 59 | 60 | 34 |
| Gothenburg | Sweden | 60 | 18 | 34 | 35 |
| Lyon | France | 17 | 47 | 57 | 36 |
| Boston | United States | 64 | 34 | 20 | 37 |
| Tokyo | Japan | 19 | 66 | 35 | 38 |
| Wellington | New Zealand | 72 | 5 | 51 | 39 |
| Vancouver | Canada | 78 | 3 | 47 | 40 |
| Málaga | Spain | 33 | 37 | 59 | 41 |
| Marseille | France | 9 | 60 | 76 | 42 |
| Rome | Italy | 2 | 71 | 96 | 43 |
| Frankfurt | Germany | 38 | 30 | 61 | 44 |
| Luxembourg | Luxembourg | 46 | 27 | 58 | 45 |
| Bilbao | Spain | 20 | 41 | 72 | 46 |
| Singapore | Singapore | 85 | 21 | 25 | 47 |
| Ottawa | Canada | 91 | 4 | 53 | 48 |
| Atlanta | United States | 85 | 53 | 19 | 49 |
| Bern | Switzerland | 30 | 55 | 75 | 50 |
| Seattle | United States | 89 | 52 | 24 | 51 |
| Florence | Italy | 11 | 73 | 68 | 52 |
| Auckland | New Zealand | 84 | 6 | 70 | 53 |
| Basel | Switzerland | 37 | 54 | 74 | 54 |
| Lisbon | Portugal | 23 | 44 | 100 | 55 |
| Linz | Austria | 31 | 42 | 95 | 56 |
| Geneva | Switzerland | 29 | 56 | 91 | 57 |
| Hong Kong | Hong Kong | 40 | 85 | 21 | 58 |
| Stuttgart | Germany | 58 | 32 | 64 | 59 |

(continued)

**Table A.5**  (continued)

| City | Country | Identity | Dynamism | Strategy | Magnetism |
|------|---------|----------|----------|----------|-----------|
| Porto | Portugal | 27 | 51 | 97 | 60 |
| Liverpool | United Kingdom | 42 | 63 | 62 | 61 |
| Miami | United States | 92 | 49 | 27 | 62 |
| Canberra | Australia | 96 | 11 | 66 | 63 |
| Antwerp | Belgium | 52 | 68 | 43 | 64 |
| Phoenix | United States | 104 | 50 | 16 | 65 |
| Birmingham | United Kingdom | 59 | 64 | 44 | 66 |
| Brussels | Belgium | 27 | 65 | 84 | 67 |
| Dallas | United States | 106 | 46 | 22 | 68 |
| Philadelphia | United States | 73 | 57 | 52 | 69 |
| Houston | United States | 107 | 48 | 28 | 70 |
| Jerusalem | Israel | 45 | 81 | 45 | 71 |
| Prague | Czech Republic | 41 | 67 | 81 | 72 |
| Dusseldorf | Germany | 62 | 29 | 101 | 73 |
| Tel Aviv | Israel | 99 | 77 | 13 | 74 |
| Yokohama | Japan | 83 | 72 | 38 | 75 |
| Taipei | Taiwan | 111 | 76 | 14 | 76 |
| Baltimore | United States | 97 | 58 | 67 | 77 |
| Osaka | Japan | 71 | 75 | 63 | 78 |
| Ljubljana | Slovenia | 68 | 74 | 78 | 79 |
| Shanghai | China | 36 | 121 | 46 | 80 |
| Budapest | Hungary | 38 | 94 | 92 | 81 |
| Tallinn | Estonia | 82 | 87 | 49 | 82 |
| Wroclaw | Poland | 61 | 86 | 77 | 83 |
| Moscow | Russia | 97 | 93 | 36 | 84 |
| Athens | Greece | 21 | 109 | 108 | 85 |
| Dubai | United Arab Emirates | 109 | 78 | 65 | 86 |
| Rio de Janeiro | Brazil | 79 | 90 | 89 | 87 |
| Warsaw | Poland | 75 | 82 | 105 | 88 |
| Vilnius | Lithuania | 85 | 91 | 87 | 89 |
| Buenos Aires | Argentina | 80 | 89 | 99 | 90 |
| Mexico City | Mexico | 77 | 102 | 85 | 91 |
| Sofia | Bulgaria | 51 | 114 | 102 | 92 |
| Bratislava | Slovakia | 63 | 88 | 125 | 93 |
| Santiago | Chile | 122 | 80 | 69 | 94 |
| Belgrade | Serbia | 55 | 110 | 123 | 95 |
| Sao Paulo | Brazil | 102 | 83 | 104 | 96 |
| Zagreb | Croatia | 76 | 112 | 103 | 97 |
| Istanbul | Turkey | 56 | 113 | 120 | 98 |
| Beijing | China | 69 | 123 | 80 | 99 |
| Abu Dhabi | United Arab Emirates | 130 | 79 | 79 | 100 |
| Riga | Latvia | 93 | 99 | 110 | 101 |
| Córdoba | Argentina | 90 | 95 | 121 | 102 |

(continued)

**Table A.5** (continued)

| City | Country | Identity | Dynamism | Strategy | Magnetism |
|---|---|---|---|---|---|
| Bogota | Colombia | 113 | 97 | 88 | 103 |
| St Petersburg | Russia | 121 | 98 | 90 | 104 |
| Bucharest | Romania | 95 | 111 | 113 | 105 |
| Cape Town | South Africa | 105 | 116 | 82 | 106 |
| Kiev | Ukraine | 103 | 100 | 119 | 107 |
| Jakarta | Indonesia | 125 | 115 | 71 | 108 |
| Montevideo | Uruguay | 117 | 105 | 107 | 109 |
| Brasilia | Brazil | 111 | 92 | 131 | 110 |
| Guadalajara | Mexico | 124 | 108 | 105 | 111 |
| Doha | Qatar | 137 | 101 | 73 | 112 |
| Bangkok | Thailand | 130 | 84 | 111 | 113 |
| Monterrey | Mexico | 120 | 107 | 117 | 114 |
| Chongqing | China | 88 | 127 | 115 | 115 |
| Panama City | Panama | 123 | 106 | 122 | 116 |
| Johannesburg | South Africa | 108 | 117 | 124 | 117 |
| Shenyang | China | 93 | 128 | 114 | 118 |
| Chengdu | China | 74 | 126 | 135 | 119 |
| Kuala Lumpur | Malaysia | 138 | 96 | 83 | 120 |
| Medellín | Colombia | 133 | 104 | 116 | 121 |
| Durban | South Africa | 135 | 119 | 93 | 122 |
| Manila | Philippines | 118 | 103 | 137 | 123 |
| Ankara | Turkey | 110 | 118 | 134 | 124 |
| Shenzhen | China | 129 | 125 | 98 | 125 |
| Quito | Ecuador | 113 | 134 | 112 | 126 |
| Lima | Peru | 119 | 133 | 109 | 127 |
| Hanoi | Vietnam | 116 | 122 | 133 | 128 |
| New Delhi | India | 133 | 131 | 94 | 129 |
| Guangzhou | China | 115 | 124 | 132 | 130 |
| Mumbai | India | 126 | 129 | 118 | 131 |
| Bangalore | India | 128 | 130 | 128 | 132 |
| Casablanca | Morocco | 100 | 139 | 127 | 133 |
| Tunis | Tunisia | 81 | 137 | 140 | 134 |
| Cairo | Egypt | 101 | 140 | 130 | 135 |
| Ho Chi Minh City | Vietnam | 140 | 120 | 126 | 136 |
| Kuwait City | Kuwait | 136 | 132 | 136 | 137 |
| La Paz | Bolivia | 132 | 138 | 129 | 138 |
| Asuncion | Paraguay | 127 | 136 | 139 | 139 |
| Riyadh | Saudi Arabia | 139 | 135 | 138 | 140 |

# VII.- City Profitability. Services. Summary

**Table A.6** VII.- City Profitability. Services. Summary

| City | Country | Government digital | Education life long | Employ ability | Connectivity | Health / Social SVS | Env. sustain ability | Culture / Tourism | Urban Mobility | Urban planning | Safety | Services summary |
|---|---|---|---|---|---|---|---|---|---|---|---|---|
| Amsterdam | Netherlands | 4 | 20 | 10 | 13 | 66 | 20 | 9 | 1 | 11 | 29 | 1 |
| Stockholm | Sweden | 7 | 24 | 28 | 35 | 5 | 1 | 47 | 8 | 49 | 12 | 2 |
| Berlin | Germany | 57 | 40 | 12 | 29 | 16 | 22 | 17 | 3 | 42 | 45 | 3 |
| London | United Kingdom | 53 | 27 | 24 | 16 | 35 | 23 | 1 | 39 | 9 | 32 | 4 |
| Oslo | Norway | 14 | 55 | 39 | 11 | 9 | 8 | 99 | 12 | 56 | 5 | 5 |
| New York City | United States | 6 | 5 | 1 | 36 | 42 | 58 | 15 | 41 | 2 | 62 | 6 |
| Tokyo | Japan | 21 | 65 | 29 | 41 | 24 | 54 | 4 | 22 | 25 | 1 | 7 |
| Gothenburg | Sweden | 8 | 24 | 38 | 37 | 5 | 5 | 90 | 11 | 79 | 28 | 8 |
| Vienna | Austria | 107 | 57 | 68 | 2 | 7 | 7 | 14 | 5 | 46 | 21 | 9 |
| Frankfurt | Germany | 73 | 40 | 33 | 26 | 16 | 28 | 65 | 7 | 26 | 25 | 10 |
| Copenhagen | Denmark | 1 | 26 | 61 | 62 | 13 | 4 | 42 | 21 | 74 | 8 | 11 |
| Zurich | Switzerland | 81 | 1 | 19 | 38 | 69 | 10 | 24 | 32 | 69 | 36 | 12 |
| Paris | France | 5 | 51 | 42 | 24 | 1 | 47 | 3 | 52 | 51 | 54 | 12 |
| Rotterdam | Netherlands | 34 | 20 | 32 | 14 | 66 | 53 | 32 | 14 | 16 | 10 | 14 |
| Hamburg | Germany | 60 | 40 | 33 | 59 | 16 | 24 | 69 | 2 | 58 | 26 | 15 |
| Helsinki | Finland | 2 | 23 | 49 | 60 | 23 | 6 | 138 | 27 | 66 | 14 | 16 |
| Munich | Germany | 63 | 40 | 12 | 55 | 16 | 38 | 39 | 26 | 61 | 22 | 17 |
| Singapore | Singapore | 37 | 19 | 30 | 1 | 106 | 31 | 20 | 34 | 33 | 2 | 18 |
| Osaka | Japan | 19 | 65 | 44 | 72 | 24 | 14 | 13 | 37 | 87 | 4 | 19 |
| Yokohama | Japan | 22 | 65 | 53 | 73 | 24 | 51 | 28 | 20 | 26 | 3 | 20 |
| Madrid | Spain | 26 | 75 | 59 | 10 | 28 | 38 | 18 | 13 | 34 | 49 | 21 |

| City | Country | | | | | | | | | | | |
|---|---|---|---|---|---|---|---|---|---|---|---|---|
| Antwerp | Belgium | 120 | 32 | 23 | 6 | 14 | 48 | 54 | 23 | 44 | 53 | 22 |
| Dusseldorf | Germany | 79 | 40 | 27 | 45 | 16 | 16 | 84 | 18 | 113 | 23 | 23 |
| Toronto | Canada | 74 | 34 | 40 | 17 | 60 | 35 | 27 | 84 | 1 | 18 | 23 |
| Montreal | Canada | 56 | 34 | 40 | 7 | 60 | 42 | 37 | 85 | 7 | 10 | 25 |
| San Francisco | United States | 11 | 5 | 1 | 52 | 42 | 87 | 40 | 68 | 13 | 66 | 26 |
| Basel | Switzerland | 101 | 1 | 19 | 47 | 69 | 18 | 52 | 6 | 117 | 38 | 26 |
| Eindhoven | Netherlands | 33 | 20 | 10 | 9 | 66 | 91 | 36 | 28 | 70 | 7 | 28 |
| Barcelona | Spain | 38 | 75 | 66 | 89 | 28 | 44 | 12 | 17 | 31 | 50 | 29 |
| Canberra | Australia | 39 | 47 | 22 | 79 | 56 | 72 | 110 | 33 | 19 | 14 | 30 |
| Auckland | New Zealand | 40 | 59 | 87 | 4 | 40 | 3 | 45 | 69 | 55 | 33 | 31 |
| Luxembourg | Luxembourg | 54 | 38 | 37 | 53 | 64 | 32 | 114 | 35 | 51 | 44 | 31 |
| Sydney | Australia | 35 | 47 | 45 | 8 | 56 | 40 | 41 | 102 | 24 | 9 | 33 |
| Valencia | Spain | 30 | 75 | 88 | 33 | 28 | 20 | 98 | 10 | 53 | 42 | 33 |
| Vancouver | Canada | 51 | 34 | 62 | 42 | 60 | 52 | 55 | 59 | 3 | 24 | 35 |
| Stuttgart | Germany | 76 | 40 | 33 | 78 | 16 | 49 | 104 | 19 | 92 | 29 | 35 |
| Ottawa | Canada | 58 | 34 | 62 | 39 | 60 | 40 | 68 | 77 | 6 | 18 | 37 |
| Seoul | South Korea | 20 | 82 | 85 | 5 | 87 | 36 | 5 | 31 | 29 | 6 | 37 |
| Bern | Switzerland | 101 | 1 | 31 | 47 | 69 | 61 | 58 | 16 | 97 | 38 | 39 |
| Wellington | New Zealand | 22 | 59 | 70 | 18 | 40 | 27 | 83 | 58 | 43 | 33 | 40 |
| Edinburgh | United Kingdom | 12 | 27 | 24 | 66 | 35 | 56 | 49 | 43 | 104 | 20 | 41 |
| Geneva | Switzerland | 89 | 1 | 19 | 54 | 69 | 37 | 58 | 29 | 120 | 38 | 42 |
| Melbourne | Australia | 28 | 47 | 45 | 51 | 56 | 71 | 57 | 73 | 15 | 14 | 42 |
| Brussels | Belgium | 121 | 32 | 47 | 23 | 14 | 49 | 31 | 62 | 50 | 64 | 44 |
| Lyon | France | 24 | 51 | 77 | 12 | 1 | 62 | 82 | 57 | 73 | 46 | 45 |
| Phoenix | United States | 9 | 5 | 15 | 21 | 42 | 98 | 23 | 25 | 62 | 102 | 46 |
| Los Angeles | United States | 29 | 5 | 15 | 15 | 42 | 105 | 7 | 104 | 14 | 79 | 47 |

(continued)

**Table A.6** (continued)

| City | Country | Government digital | Education life long | Employ ability | Connectivity | Health / Social SVS | Env. sustain ability | Culture / Tourism | Urban Mobility | Urban planning | Safety | Services summary |
|---|---|---|---|---|---|---|---|---|---|---|---|---|
| Adelaide | Australia | 41 | 47 | 65 | 70 | 56 | 78 | 110 | 30 | 19 | 14 | 48 |
| Hong Kong | Hong Kong | 75 | 80 | 52 | 88 | 96 | 43 | 2 | 51 | 8 | 35 | 49 |
| Linz | Austria | 109 | 57 | 68 | 43 | 7 | 19 | 92 | 15 | 123 | 13 | 50 |
| Manchester | United Kingdom | 16 | 27 | 24 | 66 | 35 | 68 | 58 | 63 | 95 | 27 | 51 |
| Boston | United States | 17 | 5 | 1 | 46 | 42 | 83 | 93 | 114 | 22 | 88 | 52 |
| Chicago | United States | 25 | 5 | 1 | 28 | 42 | 94 | 93 | 75 | 5 | 116 | 52 |
| Milan | Italy | 59 | 84 | 79 | 71 | 10 | 64 | 10 | 36 | 59 | 63 | 52 |
| Cologne | Germany | 71 | 40 | 55 | 44 | 16 | 82 | 52 | 4 | 115 | 29 | 52 |
| Seattle | United States | 9 | 5 | 1 | 30 | 42 | 89 | 93 | 92 | 77 | 69 | 56 |
| Washington, D.C. | United States | 3 | 5 | 1 | 57 | 42 | 96 | 93 | 86 | 10 | 121 | 57 |
| Birmingham | United Kingdom | 52 | 27 | 82 | 74 | 35 | 60 | 64 | 54 | 71 | 41 | 58 |
| Dublin | Ireland | 88 | 39 | 14 | 64 | 83 | 33 | 44 | 100 | 88 | 51 | 59 |
| Miami | United States | 18 | 5 | 43 | 30 | 42 | 100 | 46 | 64 | 38 | 93 | 60 |
| Dallas | United States | 42 | 5 | 1 | 21 | 42 | 103 | 112 | 71 | 72 | 101 | 61 |
| Houston | United States | 42 | 5 | 15 | 20 | 42 | 104 | 119 | 88 | 17 | 106 | 62 |
| Málaga | Spain | 32 | 75 | 93 | 33 | 28 | 75 | 87 | 9 | 103 | 42 | 63 |
| Nice | France | 36 | 51 | 64 | 58 | 1 | 72 | 78 | 87 | 107 | 60 | 64 |
| Bilbao | Spain | 31 | 75 | 93 | 19 | 28 | 80 | 106 | 24 | 85 | 37 | 64 |
| Marseille | France | 55 | 51 | 77 | 49 | 1 | 89 | 88 | 60 | 76 | 70 | 66 |
| Baltimore | United States | 27 | 5 | 1 | 30 | 42 | 99 | 116 | 82 | 48 | 129 | 67 |

| City | Country | | | | | | | | | | | |
|---|---|---|---|---|---|---|---|---|---|---|---|---|
| Liverpool | United Kingdom | 47 | 27 | 48 | 66 | 35 | 92 | 63 | 70 | 96 | 47 | 68 |
| Porto | Portugal | 65 | 88 | 58 | 86 | 33 | 11 | 79 | 79 | 119 | 56 | 69 |
| Lisbon | Portugal | 66 | 88 | 71 | 94 | 33 | 34 | 50 | 99 | 75 | 56 | 70 |
| Tallinn | Estonia | 45 | 91 | 86 | 65 | 79 | 12 | 56 | 98 | 64 | 67 | 71 |
| Atlanta | United States | 42 | 5 | 1 | 25 | 42 | 111 | 121 | 91 | 63 | 125 | 72 |
| Philadelphia | United States | 13 | 5 | 15 | 40 | 42 | 95 | 113 | 109 | 45 | 129 | 73 |
| Prague | Czech Republic | 134 | 90 | 67 | 61 | 73 | 56 | 11 | 40 | 78 | 52 | 74 |
| Tel Aviv | Israel | 85 | 92 | 36 | 96 | 74 | 25 | 75 | 117 | 35 | 97 | 75 |
| Rome | Italy | 62 | 84 | 90 | 87 | 10 | 84 | 8 | 97 | 121 | 65 | 76 |
| Taipei | Taiwan | 86 | 80 | 80 | 82 | 115 | 108 | 38 | 49 | 12 | 48 | 77 |
| Warsaw | Poland | 93 | 118 | 50 | 92 | 80 | 93 | 115 | 67 | 19 | 68 | 78 |
| Florence | Italy | 15 | 84 | 120 | 104 | 10 | 102 | 30 | 50 | 127 | 61 | 79 |
| Vilnius | Lithuania | 92 | 102 | 113 | 85 | 86 | 13 | 107 | 74 | 60 | 89 | 79 |
| Ljubljana | Slovenia | 114 | 98 | 116 | 56 | 65 | 29 | 107 | 76 | 89 | 71 | 81 |
| Budapest | Hungary | 125 | 134 | 60 | 3 | 84 | 59 | 35 | 55 | 80 | 77 | 82 |
| Wroclaw | Poland | 95 | 118 | 50 | 93 | 80 | 85 | 120 | 80 | 47 | 72 | 83 |
| Riga | Latvia | 119 | 113 | 99 | 90 | 88 | 15 | 107 | 72 | 28 | 91 | 84 |
| Santiago | Chile | 115 | 87 | 112 | 101 | 90 | 67 | 72 | 65 | 30 | 92 | 85 |
| Dubai | United Arab Emirates | 50 | 61 | 75 | 27 | 131 | 131 | 21 | 56 | 86 | 59 | 86 |
| Bratislava | Slovakia | 113 | 109 | 117 | 76 | 85 | 17 | 105 | 95 | 68 | 87 | 87 |
| Shanghai | China | 94 | 68 | 81 | 106 | 120 | 112 | 67 | 53 | 39 | 78 | 88 |
| Jerusalem | Israel | 108 | 92 | 57 | 95 | 74 | 45 | 19 | 120 | 128 | 97 | 89 |
| Kuala Lumpur | Malaysia | 87 | 56 | 54 | 98 | 133 | 106 | 25 | 66 | 90 | 103 | 90 |
| Athens | Greece | 112 | 130 | 122 | 84 | 27 | 81 | 16 | 93 | 116 | 74 | 91 |

(continued)

386                                                                                              Appendix

**Table A.6** (continued)

| City | Country | Government digital | Education life long | Employ ability | Connectivity | Health / Social SVS | Env. sustain ability | Culture / Tourism | Urban Mobility | Urban planning | Safety | Services summary |
|---|---|---|---|---|---|---|---|---|---|---|---|---|
| Abu Dhabi | United Arab Emirates | 46 | 61 | 75 | 63 | 131 | 138 | 103 | 38 | 108 | 55 | 92 |
| Montevideo | Uruguay | 83 | 103 | 100 | 103 | 76 | 2 | 90 | 119 | 81 | 128 | 92 |
| Zagreb | Croatia | 124 | 127 | 121 | 69 | 82 | 30 | 100 | 103 | 82 | 86 | 94 |
| Beijing | China | 91 | 68 | 91 | 99 | 120 | 125 | 102 | 48 | 65 | 76 | 95 |
| Shenzhen | China | 96 | 68 | 105 | 110 | 120 | 107 | 33 | 44 | 94 | 80 | 96 |
| Buenos Aires | Argentina | 131 | 107 | 111 | 102 | 77 | 69 | 22 | 125 | 18 | 96 | 97 |
| Guangzhou | China | 96 | 68 | 105 | 110 | 120 | 109 | 62 | 42 | 98 | 80 | 98 |
| Belgrade | Serbia | 116 | 120 | 92 | 91 | 91 | 46 | 125 | 110 | 109 | 85 | 99 |
| Sofia | Bulgaria | 110 | 128 | 83 | 80 | 89 | 78 | 61 | 90 | 129 | 73 | 100 |
| Moscow | Russia | 48 | 111 | 118 | 83 | 104 | 117 | 70 | 81 | 23 | 109 | 100 |
| Chengdu | China | 96 | 68 | 105 | 110 | 120 | 132 | 127 | 44 | 98 | 80 | 102 |
| Chongqing | China | 96 | 68 | 105 | 110 | 120 | 132 | 127 | 44 | 98 | 80 | 102 |
| Shenyang | China | 96 | 68 | 105 | 110 | 120 | 132 | 127 | 44 | 98 | 80 | 102 |
| Doha | Qatar | 118 | 63 | 95 | 50 | 119 | 136 | 71 | 111 | 114 | 56 | 105 |
| Córdoba | Argentina | 133 | 107 | 130 | 105 | 77 | 65 | 130 | 112 | 111 | 95 | 106 |
| Bucharest | Romania | 127 | 132 | 110 | 77 | 97 | 88 | 124 | 115 | 84 | 75 | 107 |
| Kiev | Ukraine | 136 | 126 | 89 | 100 | 114 | 100 | 136 | 108 | 4 | 100 | 108 |
| St Petersburg | Russia | 72 | 111 | 118 | 81 | 104 | 126 | 66 | 118 | 54 | 110 | 109 |
| Brasilia | Brazil | 69 | 121 | 137 | 107 | 101 | 74 | 122 | 94 | 102 | 119 | 110 |
| Sao Paulo | Brazil | 68 | 121 | 125 | 108 | 101 | 76 | 89 | 129 | 41 | 122 | 111 |
| Kuwait City | Kuwait | 123 | 101 | 98 | 75 | 98 | 119 | 131 | 78 | 138 | 90 | 112 |
| Mexico City | Mexico | 49 | 104 | 103 | 118 | 107 | 115 | 81 | 121 | 37 | 131 | 113 |
| Monterrey | Mexico | 64 | 104 | 127 | 116 | 107 | 120 | 123 | 61 | 35 | 136 | 114 |

| Ho Chi Minh City | | | | | | | | | | | |
|---|---|---|---|---|---|---|---|---|---|---|---|
| Medellín | Colombia | 77 | 99 | 123 | 119 | 93 | 97 | 85 | 105 | 83 | 140 | 117 |
| Bangkok | Thailand | 135 | 124 | 96 | 124 | 127 | 118 | 6 | 126 | 32 | 112 | 118 |
| Ankara | Turkey | 104 | 137 | 131 | 121 | 99 | 114 | 132 | 83 | 91 | 99 | 119 |
| Panama City | Panama | 128 | 139 | 136 | 115 | 92 | 26 | 134 | 122 | 93 | 120 | 120 |
| Istanbul | Turkey | 104 | 137 | 131 | 117 | 99 | 116 | 29 | 123 | 67 | 94 | 121 |
| Rio de Janeiro | Brazil | 67 | 121 | 140 | 109 | 101 | 86 | 80 | 135 | 40 | 134 | 122 |
| Guadalajara | Mexico | 78 | 104 | 103 | 120 | 107 | 137 | 136 | 101 | 56 | 137 | 122 |
| Quito | Ecuador | 132 | 97 | 128 | 136 | 95 | 70 | 135 | 128 | 110 | 127 | 124 |
| New Delhi | India | 80 | 94 | 72 | 130 | 136 | 130 | 26 | 113 | 140 | 117 | 125 |
| Bogota | Colombia | 82 | 99 | 123 | 123 | 93 | 77 | 85 | 137 | 105 | 135 | 126 |
| Durban | South Africa | 103 | 114 | 126 | 125 | 128 | 109 | 76 | 89 | 124 | 133 | 127 |
| Mumbai | India | 61 | 94 | 72 | 129 | 136 | 129 | 34 | 131 | 134 | 104 | 128 |
| Tunis | Tunisia | 117 | 125 | 129 | 134 | 112 | 66 | 133 | 133 | 135 | 113 | 129 |
| Manila | Philippines | 84 | 64 | 56 | 133 | 139 | 123 | 117 | 139 | 137 | 118 | 130 |
| Bangalore | India | 70 | 94 | 72 | 128 | 136 | 124 | 101 | 132 | 133 | 114 | 131 |
| Johannesburg | South Africa | 106 | 114 | 101 | 125 | 128 | 112 | 43 | 116 | 130 | 138 | 132 |
| Asuncion | Paraguay | 139 | 133 | 138 | 140 | 116 | 9 | 139 | 127 | 136 | 132 | 133 |
| Hanoi | Vietnam | 129 | 135 | 114 | 138 | 117 | 140 | 74 | 107 | 118 | 104 | 133 |
| La Paz | Bolivia | 138 | 131 | 135 | 139 | 110 | 55 | 126 | 130 | 124 | 124 | 135 |
| Cape Town | South Africa | 90 | 114 | 101 | 125 | 128 | 122 | 117 | 124 | 126 | 139 | 136 |
| Lima | Peru | 111 | 110 | 133 | 135 | 113 | 128 | 97 | 134 | 122 | 126 | 137 |
| Jakarta | Indonesia | 137 | 117 | 97 | 137 | 140 | 121 | 77 | 140 | 131 | 111 | 138 |
| Casablanca | Morocco | 126 | 129 | 134 | 122 | 134 | 127 | 140 | 136 | 132 | 115 | 139 |
| Cairo | Egypt | 140 | 140 | 139 | 132 | 135 | 132 | 48 | 138 | 112 | 123 | 140 |

# VIII.- City Profitability. Cost of Living. Net Purchase Power

**Table A.7** VIII.- City Profitability. Cost of living. Net purchase power

| City | Country | Monthly wages avg | Net real income | Cost of life | Net purchase power |
|------|---------|-------------------|-----------------|--------------|--------------------|
| Kuwait City | Kuwait | 43 | 5 | 62 | 1 |
| Adelaide | Australia | 29 | 18 | 70 | 2 |
| Bern | Switzerland | 1 | 1 | 133 | 3 |
| Phoenix | United States | 15 | 7 | 93 | 4 |
| Melbourne | Australia | 29 | 18 | 91 | 5 |
| Canberra | Australia | 29 | 18 | 92 | 6 |
| Basel | Switzerland | 1 | 1 | 136 | 7 |
| Geneva | Switzerland | 1 | 1 | 137 | 8 |
| Zurich | Switzerland | 1 | 1 | 138 | 9 |
| Houston | United States | 15 | 14 | 105 | 10 |
| Montreal | Canada | 39 | 31 | 68 | 11 |
| Dallas | United States | 15 | 14 | 107 | 12 |
| Baltimore | United States | 15 | 8 | 112 | 13 |
| Atlanta | United States | 15 | 6 | 115 | 14 |
| Philadelphia | United States | 15 | 8 | 117 | 15 |
| Liverpool | United Kingdom | 46 | 48 | 66 | 16 |
| Sydney | Australia | 29 | 18 | 116 | 17 |
| Gothenburg | Sweden | 33 | 28 | 81 | 18 |
| Ottawa | Canada | 39 | 31 | 82 | 19 |
| Dusseldorf | Germany | 8 | 37 | 72 | 20 |
| Cologne | Germany | 8 | 37 | 73 | 21 |
| Miami | United States | 15 | 8 | 124 | 22 |
| Doha | Qatar | 67 | 26 | 106 | 23 |
| Wellington | New Zealand | 54 | 35 | 88 | 24 |
| Berlin | Germany | 8 | 37 | 78 | 25 |
| Birmingham | United Kingdom | 46 | 48 | 74 | 26 |
| Riyadh | Saudi Arabia | 80 | 76 | 47 | 27 |
| Stuttgart | Germany | 8 | 37 | 83 | 28 |
| Luxembourg | Luxembourg | 5 | 13 | 126 | 29 |
| Manchester | United Kingdom | 46 | 48 | 76 | 30 |
| Stockholm | Sweden | 33 | 28 | 103 | 31 |
| Hamburg | Germany | 8 | 37 | 89 | 32 |
| Auckland | New Zealand | 54 | 35 | 98 | 33 |
| Oslo | Norway | 6 | 25 | 119 | 34 |
| Chicago | United States | 15 | 24 | 127 | 35 |
| Edinburgh | United Kingdom | 46 | 48 | 85 | 36 |
| Frankfurt | Germany | 8 | 37 | 94 | 37 |
| Los Angeles | United States | 15 | 22 | 130 | 38 |
| Vancouver | Canada | 39 | 31 | 113 | 39 |

(continued)

**Table A.7** (continued)

| City | Country | Monthly wages avg | Net real income | Cost of life | Net purchase power |
|------|---------|-------------------|-----------------|--------------|--------------------|
| Rotterdam | Netherlands | 36 | 45 | 96 | 40 |
| Seattle | United States | 15 | 23 | 131 | 41 |
| Boston | United States | 15 | 12 | 134 | 42 |
| Eindhoven | Netherlands | 36 | 45 | 99 | 43 |
| Toronto | Canada | 39 | 31 | 114 | 44 |
| Málaga | Spain | 71 | 71 | 54 | 45 |
| Valencia | Spain | 71 | 71 | 55 | 46 |
| Vienna | Austria | 51 | 59 | 75 | 47 |
| Washington, D.C. | United States | 15 | 8 | 135 | 48 |
| Dublin | Ireland | 35 | 27 | 125 | 49 |
| Munich | Germany | 8 | 37 | 109 | 50 |
| Linz | Austria | 51 | 59 | 84 | 51 |
| Copenhagen | Denmark | 7 | 30 | 121 | 52 |
| Osaka | Japan | 62 | 53 | 104 | 53 |
| Seoul | South Korea | 61 | 56 | 102 | 54 |
| Jerusalem | Israel | 65 | 57 | 101 | 55 |
| Marseille | France | 56 | 62 | 79 | 56 |
| Lyon | France | 56 | 62 | 80 | 57 |
| Yokohama | Japan | 62 | 53 | 108 | 58 |
| Santiago | Chile | 86 | 80 | 40 | 59 |
| Antwerp | Belgium | 44 | 68 | 77 | 60 |
| Brussels | Belgium | 44 | 68 | 87 | 61 |
| Helsinki | Finland | 53 | 61 | 100 | 62 |
| Nice | France | 56 | 62 | 95 | 63 |
| Tokyo | Japan | 62 | 53 | 117 | 64 |
| Barcelona | Spain | 71 | 71 | 67 | 65 |
| Amsterdam | Netherlands | 36 | 45 | 123 | 66 |
| Bilbao | Spain | 71 | 71 | 69 | 67 |
| Abu Dhabi | United Arab Emirates | 77 | 66 | 97 | 68 |
| Madrid | Spain | 71 | 71 | 71 | 69 |
| Tel Aviv | Israel | 65 | 57 | 120 | 70 |
| Singapore | Singapore | 60 | 44 | 128 | 71 |
| New York City | United States | 15 | 17 | 139 | 72 |
| San Francisco | United States | 15 | 16 | 140 | 73 |
| London | United Kingdom | 46 | 48 | 129 | 74 |
| Dubai | United Arab Emirates | 77 | 66 | 111 | 75 |
| Ankara | Turkey | 97 | 96 | 7 | 76 |
| Córdoba | Argentina | 99 | 111 | 1 | 77 |
| Paris | France | 56 | 62 | 122 | 78 |
| Tallinn | Estonia | 83 | 83 | 52 | 79 |
| Florence | Italy | 68 | 77 | 86 | 80 |
| Ljubljana | Slovenia | 76 | 81 | 58 | 81 |
| Rome | Italy | 68 | 77 | 90 | 82 |

(continued)

**Table A.7** (continued)

| City | Country | Monthly wages avg | Net real income | Cost of life | Net purchase power |
|------|---------|------------------|-----------------|--------------|--------------------|
| Istanbul | Turkey | 97 | 96 | 14 | 83 |
| Prague | Czech Republic | 82 | 84 | 53 | 84 |
| Wroclaw | Poland | 90 | 92 | 33 | 85 |
| Guadalajara | Mexico | 111 | 108 | 8 | 86 |
| Bucharest | Romania | 94 | 95 | 30 | 87 |
| Vilnius | Lithuania | 95 | 91 | 41 | 88 |
| Athens | Greece | 81 | 85 | 56 | 89 |
| Taipei | Taiwan | 87 | 82 | 64 | 90 |
| Bratislava | Slovakia | 89 | 86 | 51 | 91 |
| Milan | Italy | 68 | 77 | 110 | 92 |
| Zagreb | Croatia | 88 | 89 | 48 | 93 |
| Riga | Latvia | 93 | 90 | 46 | 94 |
| Buenos Aires | Argentina | 99 | 111 | 11 | 95 |
| Monterrey | Mexico | 111 | 108 | 14 | 96 |
| Warsaw | Poland | 90 | 92 | 44 | 97 |
| Porto | Portugal | 84 | 87 | 56 | 98 |
| Hong Kong | Hong Kong | 79 | 70 | 132 | 99 |
| Lisbon | Portugal | 84 | 87 | 61 | 100 |
| Shenyang | China | 102 | 101 | 21 | 101 |
| Mexico City | Mexico | 111 | 108 | 22 | 102 |
| Kuala Lumpur | Malaysia | 109 | 100 | 32 | 103 |
| Budapest | Hungary | 92 | 98 | 39 | 104 |
| Rio de Janeiro | Brazil | 114 | 116 | 16 | 105 |
| Chengdu | China | 102 | 101 | 28 | 106 |
| Chongqing | China | 102 | 101 | 28 | 106 |
| Brasilia | Brazil | 114 | 116 | 17 | 108 |
| St Petersburg | Russia | 117 | 113 | 27 | 109 |
| Montevideo | Uruguay | 96 | 99 | 42 | 110 |
| Sao Paulo | Brazil | 114 | 116 | 23 | 111 |
| Guangzhou | China | 102 | 101 | 38 | 112 |
| La Paz | Bolivia | 123 | 123 | 3 | 113 |
| Sofia | Bulgaria | 119 | 119 | 31 | 114 |
| Panama City | Panama | 101 | 94 | 63 | 115 |
| Lima | Peru | 110 | 115 | 43 | 116 |
| Bangalore | India | 126 | 127 | 2 | 117 |
| Shenzhen | China | 102 | 101 | 50 | 118 |
| Moscow | Russia | 117 | 113 | 49 | 119 |
| Medellín | Colombia | 124 | 125 | 6 | 120 |
| New Delhi | India | 126 | 127 | 4 | 121 |
| Cairo | Egypt | 129 | 124 | 10 | 122 |
| Casablanca | Morocco | 120 | 122 | 19 | 123 |
| Bogota | Colombia | 124 | 125 | 9 | 124 |
| Beijing | China | 102 | 101 | 59 | 125 |

(continued)

**Table A.7** (continued)

| City | Country | Monthly wages avg | Net real income | Cost of life | Net purchase power |
|---|---|---|---|---|---|
| Tunis | Tunisia | 131 | 132 | 5 | 126 |
| Quito | Ecuador | 121 | 120 | 37 | 127 |
| Shanghai | China | 102 | 101 | 65 | 128 |
| Mumbai | India | 126 | 127 | 17 | 129 |
| Belgrade | Serbia | 130 | 130 | 25 | 130 |
| Kiev | Ukraine | 132 | 131 | 20 | 131 |
| Bangkok | Thailand | 122 | 121 | 60 | 132 |
| Durban | South Africa | 133 | 136 | 13 | 133 |
| Hanoi | Vietnam | 136 | 134 | 26 | 134 |
| Johannesburg | South Africa | 133 | 136 | 24 | 135 |
| Asuncion | Paraguay | 139 | 139 | 12 | 136 |
| Ho Chi Minh City | Vietnam | 136 | 134 | 35 | 137 |
| Cape Town | South Africa | 133 | 136 | 34 | 138 |
| Manila | Philippines | 136 | 133 | 45 | 139 |
| Jakarta | Indonesia | 140 | 140 | 36 | 140 |

# IX.- City Profitability. Summary

**Table A.8** IX.- City Profitability. Summary

| City | Country | Services | Net purchase power | Profitability summary |
|---|---|---|---|---|
| Bern | Switzerland | 39 | 3 | 1 |
| Adelaide | Australia | 48 | 2 | 2 |
| Zurich | Switzerland | 12 | 9 | 3 |
| Basel | Switzerland | 26 | 7 | 4 |
| Canberra | Australia | 30 | 6 | 5 |
| Phoenix | United States | 46 | 4 | 6 |
| Melbourne | Australia | 42 | 5 | 7 |
| Montreal | Canada | 25 | 11 | 8 |
| Gothenburg | Sweden | 8 | 18 | 9 |
| Geneva | Switzerland | 42 | 8 | 10 |
| Berlin | Germany | 3 | 25 | 11 |
| Stockholm | Sweden | 2 | 31 | 12 |
| Oslo | Norway | 5 | 34 | 13 |
| Dusseldorf | Germany | 23 | 20 | 14 |
| Sydney | Australia | 33 | 17 | 15 |
| Houston | United States | 62 | 10 | 16 |
| Ottawa | Canada | 37 | 19 | 17 |
| Hamburg | Germany | 15 | 32 | 18 |

(continued)

**Table A.8** (continued)

| City | Country | Services | Net purchase power | Profitability summary |
|------|---------|----------|--------------------|-----------------------|
| Dallas | United States | 61 | 12 | 19 |
| Frankfurt | Germany | 10 | 37 | 20 |
| Baltimore | United States | 67 | 13 | 21 |
| Wellington | New Zealand | 40 | 24 | 22 |
| Luxembourg | Luxembourg | 31 | 29 | 23 |
| Stuttgart | Germany | 35 | 28 | 24 |
| Cologne | Germany | 52 | 21 | 25 |
| Rotterdam | Netherlands | 14 | 40 | 26 |
| Vienna | Austria | 9 | 47 | 27 |
| Atlanta | United States | 72 | 14 | 28 |
| Auckland | New Zealand | 31 | 33 | 29 |
| Miami | United States | 60 | 22 | 30 |
| Liverpool | United Kingdom | 68 | 16 | 31 |
| Edinburgh | United Kingdom | 41 | 36 | 32 |
| Munich | Germany | 17 | 50 | 33 |
| Manchester | United Kingdom | 51 | 30 | 34 |
| Copenhagen | Denmark | 11 | 52 | 35 |
| Toronto | Canada | 23 | 44 | 36 |
| Birmingham | United Kingdom | 58 | 26 | 37 |
| Philadelphia | United States | 73 | 15 | 38 |
| Chicago | United States | 52 | 35 | 39 |
| Eindhoven | Netherlands | 28 | 43 | 40 |
| Vancouver | Canada | 35 | 39 | 41 |
| Amsterdam | Netherlands | 1 | 66 | 42 |
| Osaka | Japan | 19 | 53 | 43 |
| Los Angeles | United States | 47 | 38 | 44 |
| Valencia | Spain | 33 | 46 | 45 |
| Yokohama | Japan | 20 | 58 | 46 |
| Kuwait City | Kuwait | 112 | 1 | 47 |
| Tokyo | Japan | 7 | 64 | 48 |
| Boston | United States | 52 | 42 | 49 |
| Seattle | United States | 56 | 41 | 50 |
| Antwerp | Belgium | 22 | 60 | 51 |
| Helsinki | Finland | 16 | 62 | 52 |
| Seoul | South Korea | 37 | 54 | 53 |
| Linz | Austria | 50 | 51 | 54 |
| Washington, D.C. | United States | 57 | 48 | 55 |
| New York City | United States | 6 | 72 | 56 |
| London | United Kingdom | 4 | 74 | 57 |
| Dublin | Ireland | 59 | 49 | 58 |
| Málaga | Spain | 63 | 45 | 59 |
| Lyon | France | 45 | 57 | 60 |

(continued)

**Table A.8**  (continued)

| City | Country | Services | Net purchase power | Profitability summary |
|------|---------|----------|--------------------|------------------------|
| Singapore | Singapore | 18 | 71 | 61 |
| Madrid | Spain | 21 | 69 | 62 |
| Barcelona | Spain | 29 | 65 | 63 |
| Brussels | Belgium | 44 | 61 | 64 |
| Marseille | France | 66 | 56 | 65 |
| San Francisco | United States | 26 | 73 | 66 |
| Paris | France | 12 | 78 | 67 |
| Nice | France | 64 | 63 | 68 |
| Bilbao | Spain | 64 | 67 | 69 |
| Tel Aviv | Israel | 75 | 70 | 70 |
| Santiago | Chile | 85 | 59 | 71 |
| Doha | Qatar | 105 | 23 | 72 |
| Jerusalem | Israel | 89 | 55 | 73 |
| Tallinn | Estonia | 71 | 79 | 74 |
| Milan | Italy | 52 | 92 | 75 |
| Hong Kong | Hong Kong | 49 | 99 | 76 |
| Abu Dhabi | United Arab Emirates | 92 | 68 | 77 |
| Dubai | United Arab Emirates | 86 | 75 | 78 |
| Rome | Italy | 76 | 82 | 79 |
| Prague | Czech Republic | 74 | 84 | 80 |
| Florence | Italy | 79 | 80 | 81 |
| Riyadh | Saudi Arabia | 115 | 27 | 82 |
| Ljubljana | Slovenia | 81 | 81 | 83 |
| Porto | Portugal | 69 | 98 | 84 |
| Wroclaw | Poland | 83 | 85 | 85 |
| Vilnius | Lithuania | 79 | 88 | 86 |
| Taipei | Taiwan | 77 | 90 | 87 |
| Lisbon | Portugal | 70 | 100 | 88 |
| Warsaw | Poland | 78 | 97 | 89 |
| Riga | Latvia | 84 | 94 | 90 |
| Bratislava | Slovakia | 87 | 91 | 91 |
| Athens | Greece | 91 | 89 | 92 |
| Zagreb | Croatia | 94 | 93 | 93 |
| Córdoba | Argentina | 106 | 77 | 94 |
| Budapest | Hungary | 82 | 104 | 95 |
| Buenos Aires | Argentina | 97 | 95 | 96 |
| Kuala Lumpur | Malaysia | 90 | 103 | 97 |
| Ankara | Turkey | 119 | 76 | 98 |
| Bucharest | Romania | 107 | 87 | 99 |
| Montevideo | Uruguay | 92 | 110 | 100 |
| Shenyang | China | 102 | 101 | 101 |
| Chengdu | China | 102 | 106 | 102 |
| Chongqing | China | 102 | 106 | 102 |

(continued)

**Table A.8** (continued)

| City | Country | Services | Net purchase power | Profitability summary |
|---|---|---|---|---|
| Guangzhou | China | 98 | 112 | 104 |
| Istanbul | Turkey | 121 | 83 | 105 |
| Monterrey | Mexico | 114 | 96 | 106 |
| Shenzhen | China | 96 | 118 | 107 |
| Sofia | Bulgaria | 100 | 114 | 108 |
| Guadalajara | Mexico | 122 | 86 | 109 |
| Brasilia | Brazil | 110 | 108 | 110 |
| St Petersburg | Russia | 109 | 109 | 111 |
| Mexico City | Mexico | 113 | 102 | 112 |
| Moscow | Russia | 100 | 119 | 113 |
| Shanghai | China | 88 | 128 | 114 |
| Beijing | China | 95 | 125 | 115 |
| Sao Paulo | Brazil | 111 | 111 | 116 |
| Rio de Janeiro | Brazil | 122 | 105 | 117 |
| Belgrade | Serbia | 99 | 130 | 118 |
| Panama City | Panama | 120 | 115 | 119 |
| Medellín | Colombia | 117 | 120 | 120 |
| Kiev | Ukraine | 108 | 131 | 121 |
| New Delhi | India | 125 | 121 | 122 |
| Bogota | Colombia | 126 | 124 | 123 |
| Bangalore | India | 131 | 117 | 124 |
| Quito | Ecuador | 124 | 127 | 125 |
| La Paz | Bolivia | 135 | 113 | 126 |
| Tunis | Tunisia | 129 | 126 | 127 |
| Bangkok | Thailand | 118 | 132 | 128 |
| Mumbai | India | 128 | 129 | 129 |
| Lima | Peru | 137 | 116 | 130 |
| Ho Chi Minh City | Vietnam | 116 | 137 | 131 |
| Durban | South Africa | 127 | 133 | 132 |
| Manila | Philippines | 130 | 139 | 133 |
| Casablanca | Morocco | 139 | 123 | 134 |
| Johannesburg | South Africa | 132 | 135 | 135 |
| Hanoi | Vietnam | 133 | 134 | 136 |
| Asuncion | Paraguay | 133 | 136 | 137 |
| Cape Town | South Africa | 136 | 138 | 138 |
| Cairo | Egypt | 140 | 122 | 139 |
| Jakarta | Indonesia | 138 | 140 | 140 |

## X.- NordicEdge Event Survey Questionnaire

**NORDIC EDGE**
# Smart with a Heart
# Research: What makes a City
# Attractive?

Nordic Edge Expo is pleased to introduce a research study, in cooperation with Jose A. Ondiviela from Microsoft, to better understand what our attendees consider an irresistible city to live in.
The study is part of a wider PhD research by Mr. Ondiviela based on citizen involvement from people living in 140 Smart Cities worldwide. The research will give insights into citizens' preferences and help authorities develop even more attractive cities, which people wish to live in.
------------------
Please feel free to complete this short survey. It only takes 30 seconds. Participation is anonymous. If you wish to receive a copy of the results we ask that you submit your e-mail address. This will not be used for any other purposes. The results are expected towards the end of 2018.

THANK YOU VERY MUCH FOR YOUR TIME AND HELP.

1. SMART: City Services: If you were to move to another city, what services would be decisive? Please answer according to your values and at this time in your life. Rate the questions on a scale from 0 to 5. 0=Irrelevant – 5=Most Significant. All answers are valid, but try to assign differences to highs and lows. 10 Areas. No answer means 0. *

|  | 0 | 1 | 2 | 3 | 4 | 5 |
|---|---|---|---|---|---|---|
| Governance | ○ | ○ | ○ | ○ | ○ | ○ |
| Education | ○ | ○ | ○ | ○ | ○ | ○ |
| Employability | ○ | ○ | ○ | ○ | ○ | ○ |
| Connected City (IoT - Citizens) | ○ | ○ | ○ | ○ | ○ | ○ |
| Social Services / Health | ○ | ○ | ○ | ○ | ○ | ○ |
| Sustainability / Environment | ○ | ○ | ○ | ○ | ○ | ○ |
| Cultural Services / Tourism | ○ | ○ | ○ | ○ | ○ | ○ |
| Urban Mobility / Transportation | ○ | ○ | ○ | ○ | ○ | ○ |
| Urban Planning | ○ | ○ | ○ | ○ | ○ | ○ |
| Safety (Physical/Virtual) | ○ | ○ | ○ | ○ | ○ | ○ |

**Fig. A.2** X.- NordicEdge Event Survey Questionnaire

# XI.- NordicEdge Event Survey Results

Table A.9  XI.- NordicEdge Event Survey Results

## DATA AVERAGES

| CITY SERVICES - SCALE OF V | RK | 1-10 | Over 100 | INPUT | CHILDREN | | ELDER | | AGE | | | | | | GENDER | |
|---|---|---|---|---|---|---|---|---|---|---|---|---|---|---|---|---|
| | | | | | Yes | No | Yes | No | 18-29 | 30-39 | 40-49 | 50-59 | 60-65 | 65+ | Female | Male |
| GOVERNANCE | 9 | 1,30 | 9% | 3,21 | 3,24 | 3,16 | 2,85 | 3,29 | 3,45 | 3,12 | 3,17 | 3,00 | 3,50 | 5,00 | 3,16 | 3,26 |
| EDUCATION | 5 | 6,06 | 10% | 3,92 | 4,12 | 3,60 | 3,69 | 3,96 | 3,55 | 4,12 | 4,26 | 3,25 | 4,00 | 5,00 | 4,06 | 3,79 |
| EMPLOYABILITY | 6 | 4,74 | 10% | 3,73 | 3,76 | 3,68 | 3,92 | 4,65 | 3,64 | 3,59 | 3,61 | 3,92 | 5,00 | 5,00 | 3,84 | 3,62 |
| CONNECTED CITY | 8 | 1,51 | 9% | 3,24 | 3,02 | 3,60 | 3,08 | 3,27 | 3,91 | 2,59 | 3,17 | 3,25 | 5,00 | 5,00 | 2,97 | 3,50 |
| SOCSERVICES / HEALTH | 2 | 8,99 | 12% | 4,36 | 4,46 | 4,20 | 4,31 | 4,37 | 4,64 | 4,53 | 4,26 | 3,92 | 5,00 | 5,00 | 4,47 | 4,26 |
| ENV. SUSTAINABILITY | 1 | 10,00 | 12% | 4,52 | 4,46 | 4,60 | 4,00 | 3,63 | 4,73 | 4,47 | 4,52 | 4,42 | 5,00 | 5,00 | 4,75 | 4,29 |
| CULTURAL SVS / TOURISM | 10 | 1,00 | 8% | 3,17 | 2,98 | 3,48 | 3,38 | 3,37 | 3,73 | 2,59 | 3,09 | 3,17 | 5,00 | 5,00 | 3,16 | 3,18 |
| URBAN MOBILITY / TRANSPOR | 3 | 7,47 | 11% | 4,14 | 3,88 | 4,56 | 4,31 | 4,08 | 4,45 | 3,94 | 3,87 | 4,42 | 5,00 | 5,00 | 4,22 | 4,06 |
| URBAN PLANNING | 7 | 2,31 | 9% | 3,36 | 3,24 | 3,56 | 2,92 | 3,25 | 3,64 | 3,47 | 3,13 | 3,17 | 4,00 | 5,00 | 3,38 | 3,35 |
| SAFETY (PHYSICAL/VIRTUAL) | 4 | 6,46 | 11% | 3,98 | 4,05 | 3,88 | 4,08 | 3,96 | 4,09 | 4,06 | 4,13 | 3,33 | 5,00 | 4,00 | 4,09 | 3,88 |

| MAGNETISM PREFERENCES | RK | 1-10 | Over 100 | INPUT | CHILDREN | | ELDER | | AGE | | | | | | GENDER | |
|---|---|---|---|---|---|---|---|---|---|---|---|---|---|---|---|---|
| | | | | | Yes | No | Yes | No | 18-29 | 30-39 | 40-49 | 50-59 | 60-65 | 65+ | Female | Male |
| IDENTITY | 2 | 4,72 | 33% | 3,71 | 3,63 | 3,84 | 4,00 | 3,64 | 3,18 | 3,88 | 3,39 | 4,33 | 4,50 | 5,00 | 3,63 | 3,79 |
| DYNAMISM | 1 | 10 | 36% | 4,00 | 3,93 | 4,12 | 4,23 | 3,94 | 4,09 | 4,00 | 3,78 | 4,17 | 4,50 | 5,00 | 3,88 | 4,12 |
| STRATEGY | 3 | 1 | 31% | 3,45 | 3,34 | 3,64 | 3,69 | 3,40 | 3,73 | 3,47 | 3,30 | 3,17 | 4,50 | 5,00 | 3,47 | 3,44 |

## RANKINGS

| CITY SERVICES - SCALE OF V | RK | 1-10 | Over 100 | INPUT | CHILDREN | | ELDER | | AGE | | | | | | GENDER | |
|---|---|---|---|---|---|---|---|---|---|---|---|---|---|---|---|---|
| | | | | | Yes | No | Yes | No | 18-29 | 30-39 | 40-49 | 50-59 | 60-65 | 65+ | Female | Male |
| GOVERNANCE | 9 | 1,30 | 9% | 9 | 7 | 10 | 10 | 8 | 10 | 8 | 7 | 10 | 10 | 1 | 8 | 9 |
| EDUCATION | 5 | 6,06 | 10% | 5 | 3 | 6 | 6 | 4 | 9 | 3 | 2 | 6 | 7 | 1 | 5 | 5 |
| EMPLOYABILITY | 6 | 4,74 | 10% | 6 | 6 | 5 | 5 | 1 | 7 | 6 | 6 | 3 | 1 | 1 | 6 | 6 |
| CONNECTED CITY | 8 | 1,51 | 9% | 8 | 9 | 6 | 8 | 9 | 5 | 9 | 7 | 6 | 1 | 1 | 10 | 7 |
| SOCSERVICES / HEALTH | 2 | 8,99 | 12% | 2 | 1 | 3 | 1 | 2 | 2 | 1 | 2 | 3 | 7 | 1 | 2 | 2 |
| ENV. SUSTAINABILITY | 1 | 10,00 | 12% | 1 | 1 | 1 | 4 | 6 | 1 | 2 | 1 | 1 | 1 | 1 | 1 | 1 |
| CULTURAL SVS / TOURISM | 10 | 1,00 | 8% | 10 | 10 | 9 | 7 | 7 | 6 | 9 | 10 | 8 | 1 | 1 | 8 | 10 |
| URBAN MOBILITY / TRANSPOR | 3 | 7,47 | 11% | 3 | 5 | 2 | 1 | 3 | 3 | 5 | 5 | 1 | 7 | 1 | 3 | 3 |
| URBAN PLANNING | 7 | 2,31 | 9% | 7 | 7 | 8 | 9 | 10 | 7 | 7 | 9 | 8 | 1 | 1 | 7 | 8 |
| SAFETY (PHYSICAL/VIRTUAL) | 4 | 6,46 | 11% | 4 | 4 | 4 | 3 | 4 | 4 | 4 | 4 | 5 | 1 | 10 | 4 | 4 |
| n | | | | | 41 | 25 | 13 | 53 | 11 | 17 | 23 | 12 | 2 | 1 | 32 | 34 |
| | | | | | 62% | 38% | 20% | 80% | 17% | 26% | 35% | 18% | 3% | 2% | 48% | 52% |
| | | | | | | | | | 24 | 35 | 45 | 55 | 62 | 67 | | |

AVG AGE: 41,6

# XII.- SmartCityExpo WW Congress Event Survey Questionnaire

# SMARTCITY
## EXPO WORLD CONGRESS

# Research: What's making a City Attractive to LIVE IN?

SmartCityExpo & WW Congress is very pleased to introduce a research study, in cooperation with Jose A. Ondiviela from Microsoft, to better understand what our attendees consider an irresistible city to live in. The study is part of a wider PhD research by Mr. Ondiviela based on citizen involvement from people living in 140 Smart Cities worldwide. The research will give insights into citizens' preferences and help authorities develop even more attractive cities, which people wish to live in.
------------------
Please feel free to complete this short survey. It only takes 40 seconds. Participation is anonymous. If you wish to receive a copy of the results we ask that you submit your e-mail address. This will not be used for any other purposes. The results are expected towards the end of 2018.

THANK YOU VERY MUCH FOR YOUR TIME AND HELP.

1. CITIES TO LIVE IN: (What do they offer to me? What's the deal?: According to your scale of values, and in this moment in your life, what are the most important SERVICES a City should offer you to consider that city a potential next home? (0=Irrelevant; 5: The most Important. All answers are valid, but try to be crisp, assigning significant differences to highs and lows. 10 Areas. No answer = 0. *

| | 0 | 1 | 2 | 3 | 4 | 5 |
|---|---|---|---|---|---|---|
| Governance | ○ | ○ | ○ | ○ | ○ | ○ |
| Education | ○ | ○ | ○ | ○ | ○ | ○ |
| Employability | ○ | ○ | ○ | ○ | ○ | ○ |
| Connected City (IoT - Citizens) | ○ | ○ | ○ | ○ | ○ | ○ |
| Social Services / Health | ○ | ○ | ○ | ○ | ○ | ○ |
| Sustainability / Environment | ○ | ○ | ○ | ○ | ○ | ○ |
| Cultural Services / Tourism | ○ | ○ | ○ | ○ | ○ | ○ |
| Urban Mobility / Transportation | ○ | ○ | ○ | ○ | ○ | ○ |
| Urban Planning | ○ | ○ | ○ | ○ | ○ | ○ |
| Safety (Physical/Virtual) | ○ | ○ | ○ | ○ | ○ | ○ |

**Fig. A.3** XII.- SmartCityExpo WW Congress Event Survey Questionnaire

# XIII.- SmartCityExpo WW Congress Survey Results

Table A.10  XIII.- SmartCityExpo WW Congress survey results

## DATA AVERAGES

| CITY SERVICES - SCALE OF V | RK | 1-10 | Over 100 | INPUT | CHILDREN Yes | No | ELDER Yes | No | 18-29 | 30-39 | 40-49 | 50-59 | 60-65 | 65+ | Female | Male | N.A. |
|---|---|---|---|---|---|---|---|---|---|---|---|---|---|---|---|---|---|
| GOVERNANCE | 8 | 2,85 | 6,95 | 3,74 | 3,71 | 3,77 | 3,76 | 3,73 | 3,67 | 3,84 | 3,71 | 3,70 | 3,72 | 4,11 | 3,80 | 3,71 | 3,92 |
| EDUCATION | 5 | 7,67 | 11,40 | 4,21 | 4,24 | 4,19 | 4,15 | 4,23 | 4,30 | 4,37 | 4,19 | 4,03 | 3,96 | 4,22 | 4,32 | 4,17 | 4,19 |
| EMPLOYABILITY | 6 | 7,11 | 10,87 | 4,16 | 4,10 | 4,22 | 4,07 | 4,19 | 4,23 | 4,31 | 4,10 | 4,11 | 3,60 | 4,00 | 4,32 | 4,08 | 4,12 |
| CONNECTED CITY | 9 | 1,83 | 6,01 | 3,64 | 3,63 | 3,65 | 3,68 | 3,63 | 3,66 | 3,55 | 3,61 | 3,76 | 3,81 | 3,72 | 3,61 | 3,66 | 3,42 |
| SOCSERVICES / HEALTH | 2 | 9,04 | 12,66 | 4,35 | 4,31 | 4,38 | 4,38 | 4,34 | 4,33 | 4,40 | 4,27 | 4,42 | 4,19 | 4,72 | 4,49 | 4,28 | 4,35 |
| ENV. SUSTAINABILITY | 3 | 8,95 | 12,57 | 4,34 | 4,32 | 4,35 | 4,33 | 4,34 | 4,38 | 4,32 | 4,35 | 4,33 | 4,26 | 4,44 | 4,40 | 4,32 | 4,00 |
| CULTURAL SVS / TOURISM | 10 | 1,00 | 5,24 | 3,56 | 3,53 | 3,58 | 3,60 | 3,54 | 3,42 | 3,56 | 3,55 | 3,64 | 3,61 | 3,78 | 3,60 | 3,54 | 3,42 |
| URBAN MOBILITY / TRANSPOR | 1 | 10,00 | 13,54 | 4,44 | 4,39 | 4,49 | 4,37 | 4,46 | 4,44 | 4,47 | 4,42 | 4,46 | 4,26 | 4,50 | 4,48 | 4,43 | 4,50 |
| URBAN PLANNING | 7 | 4,78 | 8,72 | 3,93 | 3,88 | 3,98 | 3,94 | 3,93 | 3,96 | 3,99 | 3,85 | 3,94 | 3,89 | 4,11 | 3,98 | 3,91 | 4,00 |
| SAFETY (PHYSICAL/VIRTUAL) | 4 | 8,37 | 12,04 | 4,28 | 4,29 | 4,28 | 4,36 | 4,26 | 4,23 | 4,21 | 4,28 | 4,40 | 4,30 | 4,44 | 4,35 | 4,26 | 3,81 |

| MAGNETISM PREFERENCES | RK | 1-10 | Over 100 | INPUT | CHILDREN Yes | No | ELDER Yes | No | 18-29 | 30-39 | 40-49 | 50-59 | 60-65 | 65+ | Female | Male | N.A. |
|---|---|---|---|---|---|---|---|---|---|---|---|---|---|---|---|---|---|
| IDENTITY | 2 | 8,43 | 35,33 | 4,14 | 4,12 | 4,15 | 4,12 | 4,14 | 4,08 | 4,08 | 4,14 | 4,23 | 4,07 | 4,44 | 4,18 | 4,12 | 3,96 |
| DYNAMISM | 1 | 10 | 36,93 | 4,19 | 4,18 | 4,19 | 4,19 | 4,19 | 4,13 | 4,27 | 4,17 | 4,16 | 4,02 | 4,44 | 4,21 | 4,18 | 4,23 |
| STRATEGY | 3 | 1 | 27,74 | 3,89 | 3,90 | 3,88 | 4,03 | 3,85 | 3,81 | 3,90 | 3,88 | 3,90 | 4,04 | 4,28 | 3,84 | 3,93 | 3,42 |

## RANKINGS

| CITY SERVICES - SCALE OF V | RK | 1-10 | Over 100 | INPUT | CHILDREN Yes | No | ELDER Yes | No | 18-29 | 30-39 | 40-49 | 50-59 | 60-65 | 65+ | Female | Male | N.A. |
|---|---|---|---|---|---|---|---|---|---|---|---|---|---|---|---|---|---|
| GOVERNANCE | 8 | 2,85 | 6,95 | 3,74 | 8 | 8 | 8 | 8 | 9 | 8 | 8 | 9 | 8 | 6 | 8 | 8 | 7 |
| EDUCATION | 5 | 7,67 | 11,40 | 4,21 | 5 | 6 | 5 | 5 | 4 | 3 | 5 | 6 | 5 | 5 | 6 | 5 | 3 |
| EMPLOYABILITY | 6 | 7,11 | 10,87 | 4,16 | 6 | 5 | 6 | 6 | 6 | 5 | 6 | 5 | 10 | 8 | 5 | 6 | 4 |
| CONNECTED CITY | 9 | 1,83 | 6,01 | 3,64 | 9 | 9 | 9 | 9 | 9 | 10 | 9 | 8 | 7 | 10 | 9 | 9 | 9 |
| SOCSERVICES / HEALTH | 2 | 9,04 | 12,66 | 4,35 | 3 | 2 | 1 | 2 | 2 | 2 | 4 | 4 | 4 | 1 | 1 | 3 | 2 |
| ENV. SUSTAINABILITY | 3 | 8,95 | 12,57 | 4,34 | 2 | 3 | 3 | 3 | 2 | 4 | 2 | 2 | 2 | 3 | 3 | 2 | 5 |
| CULTURAL SVS / TOURISM | 10 | 1,00 | 5,24 | 3,56 | 10 | 10 | 10 | 10 | 10 | 9 | 10 | 10 | 9 | 9 | 10 | 10 | 9 |
| URBAN MOBILITY / TRANSPOR | 1 | 10,00 | 13,54 | 4,44 | 1 | 1 | 2 | 1 | 1 | 1 | 1 | 1 | 2 | 2 | 2 | 1 | 1 |
| URBAN PLANNING | 7 | 4,78 | 8,72 | 3,93 | 7 | 7 | 7 | 7 | 7 | 6 | 7 | 6 | 6 | 6 | 7 | 7 | 5 |
| SAFETY (PHYSICAL/VIRTUAL) | 4 | 8,37 | 12,04 | 4,28 | 4 | 4 | 4 | 4 | 5 | 4 | 3 | 3 | 1 | 3 | 4 | 4 | 8 |
| n | | | | | 786 | 764 | 383 | 1,167 | 230 | 424 | 496 | 325 | 57 | 18 | 482 | 1,040 | 26 |
| | | | | | 51% | 49% | 25% | 75% | 15% | 27% | 32% | 21% | 4% | 1% | 31% | 67% | 2% |
| AVG AGE: | | | | | | | | | 24 | 35 | 45 | 55 | 62 | 67 | | | |

AVG AGE: 42,1

Table Appendix.10 XIII.- SmartCityExpo WW Congress Survey Results

**Table A.11** XIV.- City Attractiveness Ranking (as per SmartCityExpo attendees input weights)

| City | Country | Magnetism | Identity | Dynamism | Strategy | Profitability | Performance | Cost living | Attractiveness |
|---|---|---|---|---|---|---|---|---|---|
| Melbourne | Australia | 9 | 48 | 9 | 7 | 7 | 42 | 5 | 1 |
| Adelaide | Australia | 22 | 70 | 11 | 29 | 2 | 48 | 2 | 2 |
| Stockholm | Sweden | 2 | 18 | 16 | 4 | 12 | 2 | 31 | 3 |
| Zurich | Switzerland | 23 | 10 | 45 | 50 | 3 | 12 | 9 | 4 |
| Berlin | Germany | 12 | 26 | 22 | 15 | 11 | 3 | 25 | 5 |
| Bern | Switzerland | 50 | 30 | 55 | 75 | 1 | 39 | 3 | 6 |
| Sydney | Australia | 6 | 34 | 7 | 11 | 15 | 33 | 17 | 7 |
| Montreal | Canada | 24 | 54 | 2 | 56 | 8 | 25 | 11 | 8 |
| Oslo | Norway | 11 | 25 | 10 | 39 | 13 | 5 | 34 | 9 |
| Gothenburg | Sweden | 35 | 60 | 18 | 34 | 9 | 8 | 18 | 10 |
| Basel | Switzerland | 54 | 37 | 54 | 74 | 4 | 26 | 7 | 11 |
| Vienna | Austria | 7 | 6 | 26 | 26 | 27 | 9 | 47 | 12 |
| Canberra | Australia | 63 | 96 | 11 | 66 | 5 | 30 | 6 | 13 |
| Phoenix | United States | 65 | 104 | 50 | 16 | 6 | 46 | 4 | 14 |
| Amsterdam | Netherlands | 3 | 22 | 8 | 10 | 42 | 1 | 66 | 15 |
| Copenhagen | Denmark | 10 | 49 | 17 | 1 | 35 | 11 | 52 | 16 |
| Hamburg | Germany | 30 | 35 | 28 | 40 | 18 | 15 | 32 | 17 |
| Rotterdam | Netherlands | 15 | 47 | 14 | 30 | 26 | 14 | 40 | 18 |
| Geneva | Switzerland | 57 | 29 | 56 | 91 | 10 | 42 | 8 | 19 |
| Toronto | Canada | 14 | 66 | 1 | 17 | 36 | 23 | 44 | 20 |
| London | United Kingdom | 1 | 1 | 40 | 9 | 57 | 4 | 74 | 21 |
| Manchester | United Kingdom | 16 | 16 | 62 | 8 | 34 | 51 | 30 | 22 |
| Cologne | Germany | 27 | 43 | 31 | 33 | 25 | 52 | 21 | 23 |
| Frankfurt | Germany | 44 | 38 | 30 | 61 | 20 | 10 | 37 | 24 |
| Wellington | New Zealand | 39 | 72 | 5 | 51 | 22 | 40 | 24 | 25 |

(continued)

**Table A.11** (continued)

| City | Country | Magnetism | Identity | Dynamism | Strategy | Profitability | Performance | Cost living | Attractiveness |
|---|---|---|---|---|---|---|---|---|---|
| Ottawa | Canada | 48 | 91 | 4 | 53 | 17 | 37 | 19 | **26** |
| New York City | United States | 5 | 12 | 24 | 5 | 56 | 6 | 72 | **27** |
| Edinburgh | United Kingdom | 31 | 23 | 61 | 31 | 32 | 41 | 36 | **28** |
| Luxembourg | Luxembourg | 45 | 46 | 27 | 58 | 23 | 31 | 29 | **29** |
| Eindhoven | Netherlands | 21 | 50 | 15 | 41 | 40 | 28 | 43 | **30** |
| Munich | Germany | 32 | 31 | 20 | 55 | 33 | 17 | 50 | **31** |
| Los Angeles | United States | 20 | 44 | 38 | 18 | 44 | 47 | 38 | **32** |
| Chicago | United States | 29 | 64 | 39 | 6 | 39 | 52 | 35 | **33** |
| Seoul | South Korea | 13 | 8 | 70 | 2 | 53 | 37 | 54 | **34** |
| Dallas | United States | 68 | 106 | 46 | 22 | 19 | 61 | 12 | **35** |
| Valencia | Spain | 28 | 14 | 36 | 54 | 45 | 33 | 46 | **36** |
| Atlanta | United States | 49 | 85 | 53 | 19 | 28 | 72 | 14 | **37** |
| Houston | United States | 70 | 107 | 48 | 28 | 16 | 62 | 10 | **38** |
| Helsinki | Finland | 17 | 66 | 13 | 12 | 52 | 16 | 62 | **39** |
| Barcelona | Spain | 8 | 5 | 25 | 37 | 63 | 29 | 65 | **40** |
| Dusseldorf | Germany | 73 | 62 | 29 | 101 | 14 | 23 | 20 | **41** |
| Stuttgart | Germany | 59 | 58 | 32 | 64 | 24 | 35 | 28 | **42** |
| Vancouver | Canada | 40 | 78 | 3 | 47 | 41 | 35 | 39 | **43** |
| Auckland | New Zealand | 53 | 84 | 6 | 70 | 29 | 31 | 33 | **44** |
| Miami | United States | 62 | 92 | 49 | 27 | 30 | 60 | 22 | **45** |
| Boston | United States | 37 | 64 | 34 | 20 | 49 | 52 | 42 | **46** |
| Paris | France | 4 | 4 | 23 | 32 | 67 | 12 | 78 | **47** |
| Liverpool | United Kingdom | 61 | 42 | 63 | 62 | 31 | 68 | 16 | **48** |
| Tokyo | Japan | 38 | 19 | 66 | 35 | 48 | 7 | 64 | **49** |
| Madrid | Spain | 19 | 3 | 19 | 86 | 62 | 21 | 69 | **50** |

| City | Country | | | | | | | | # |
|---|---|---|---|---|---|---|---|---|---|
| Dublin | Ireland | 26 | 15 | 35 | 48 | 58 | 59 | 49 | **51** |
| Washington, D.C. | United States | 33 | 57 | 43 | 23 | 55 | 57 | 48 | **52** |
| Birmingham | United Kingdom | 66 | 59 | 64 | 44 | 37 | 58 | 26 | **53** |
| Lyon | France | 36 | 17 | 47 | 57 | 60 | 45 | 57 | **54** |
| Philadelphia | United States | 69 | 73 | 57 | 52 | 38 | 73 | 15 | **55** |
| San Francisco | United States | 18 | 53 | 33 | 3 | 66 | 26 | 73 | **56** |
| Málaga | Spain | 41 | 33 | 37 | 59 | 59 | 63 | 45 | **57** |
| Seattle | United States | 51 | 89 | 52 | 24 | 50 | 56 | 41 | **58** |
| Baltimore | United States | 77 | 97 | 58 | 67 | 21 | 67 | 13 | **59** |
| Singapore | Singapore | 47 | 85 | 21 | 25 | 61 | 18 | 71 | **60** |
| Linz | Austria | 56 | 31 | 42 | 95 | 54 | 50 | 51 | **61** |
| Antwerp | Belgium | 64 | 52 | 68 | 43 | 51 | 22 | 60 | **62** |
| Marseille | France | 42 | 9 | 60 | 76 | 65 | 66 | 56 | **63** |
| Yokohama | Japan | 75 | 83 | 72 | 38 | 46 | 20 | 58 | **64** |
| Nice | France | 34 | 13 | 59 | 60 | 68 | 64 | 63 | **65** |
| Osaka | Japan | 78 | 71 | 75 | 63 | 43 | 19 | 53 | **66** |
| Brussels | Belgium | 67 | 27 | 65 | 84 | 64 | 44 | 61 | **67** |
| Bilbao | Spain | 46 | 20 | 41 | 72 | 69 | 64 | 67 | **68** |
| Milan | Italy | 25 | 7 | 69 | 42 | 75 | 52 | 92 | **69** |
| Rome | Italy | 43 | 2 | 71 | 96 | 79 | 76 | 82 | **70** |
| Tel Aviv | Israel | 74 | 99 | 77 | 13 | 70 | 75 | 70 | **71** |
| Jerusalem | Israel | 71 | 45 | 81 | 45 | 73 | 89 | 55 | **72** |
| Hong Kong | Hong Kong | 58 | 40 | 85 | 21 | 76 | 49 | 99 | **73** |
| Florence | Italy | 52 | 11 | 73 | 68 | 81 | 79 | 80 | **74** |
| Porto | Portugal | 60 | 27 | 51 | 97 | 84 | 69 | 98 | **75** |
| Prague | Czech Republic | 72 | 41 | 67 | 81 | 80 | 74 | 84 | **76** |
| Lisbon | Portugal | 55 | 23 | 44 | 100 | 88 | 70 | 100 | **77** |

(continued)

**Table A.11** (continued)

| City | Country | Magnetism | Identity | Dynamism | Strategy | Profitability | Performance | Cost living | Attractiveness |
|---|---|---|---|---|---|---|---|---|---|
| Tallinn | Estonia | 82 | 82 | 87 | 49 | 74 | 71 | 79 | **78** |
| Ljubljana | Slovenia | 79 | 68 | 74 | 78 | 83 | 81 | 81 | **79** |
| Santiago | Chile | 94 | 122 | 80 | 69 | 71 | 85 | 59 | **80** |
| Taipei | Taiwan | 76 | 111 | 76 | 14 | 87 | 77 | 90 | **81** |
| Dubai | United Arab Emirates | 86 | 109 | 78 | 65 | 78 | 86 | 75 | **82** |
| Wroclaw | Poland | 83 | 61 | 86 | 77 | 85 | 83 | 85 | **83** |
| Vilnius | Lithuania | 89 | 85 | 91 | 87 | 86 | 79 | 88 | **84** |
| Athens | Greece | 85 | 21 | 109 | 108 | 92 | 91 | 89 | **85** |
| Budapest | Hungary | 81 | 38 | 94 | 92 | 95 | 82 | 104 | **86** |
| Abu Dhabi | United Arab Emirates | 100 | 130 | 79 | 79 | 77 | 92 | 68 | **87** |
| Warsaw | Poland | 88 | 75 | 82 | 105 | 89 | 78 | 97 | **88** |
| Doha | Qatar | 112 | 137 | 101 | 73 | 72 | 105 | 23 | **89** |
| Bratislava | Slovakia | 93 | 63 | 88 | 125 | 91 | 87 | 91 | **90** |
| Buenos Aires | Argentina | 90 | 80 | 89 | 99 | 96 | 97 | 95 | **91** |
| Riga | Latvia | 101 | 93 | 99 | 110 | 90 | 84 | 94 | **92** |
| Zagreb | Croatia | 97 | 76 | 112 | 103 | 93 | 94 | 93 | **93** |
| Córdoba | Argentina | 102 | 90 | 95 | 121 | 94 | 106 | 77 | **94** |
| Shanghai | China | 80 | 36 | 121 | 46 | 114 | 88 | 128 | **95** |
| Moscow | Russia | 84 | 97 | 93 | 36 | 113 | 100 | 119 | **96** |
| Kuwait City | Kuwait | 137 | 136 | 132 | 136 | 47 | 112 | 1 | **97** |
| Sofia | Bulgaria | 92 | 51 | 114 | 102 | 108 | 100 | 114 | **98** |
| Istanbul | Turkey | 98 | 56 | 113 | 120 | 105 | 121 | 83 | **99** |
| Mexico City | Mexico | 91 | 77 | 102 | 85 | 112 | 113 | 102 | **100** |
| Bucharest | Romania | 105 | 95 | 111 | 113 | 99 | 107 | 87 | **101** |
| Montevideo | Uruguay | 109 | 117 | 105 | 107 | 100 | 92 | 110 | **102** |

| | | | | | | | | | |
|---|---|---|---|---|---|---|---|---|---|
| Rio de Janeiro | Brazil | 87 | 79 | 90 | 89 | 117 | 122 | 105 | 103 |
| Sao Paulo | Brazil | 96 | 102 | 83 | 104 | 116 | 111 | 111 | 104 |
| Beijing | China | 99 | 69 | 123 | 80 | 115 | 95 | 125 | 105 |
| St Petersburg | Russia | 104 | 121 | 98 | 90 | 111 | 109 | 109 | 106 |
| Kuala Lumpur | Malaysia | 120 | 138 | 96 | 83 | 97 | 90 | 103 | 107 |
| Belgrade | Serbia | 95 | 55 | 110 | 123 | 118 | 99 | 130 | 108 |
| Shenyang | China | 118 | 93 | 128 | 114 | 101 | 102 | 101 | 109 |
| Chongqing | China | 115 | 88 | 127 | 115 | 102 | 102 | 106 | 110 |
| Guadalajara | Mexico | 111 | 124 | 108 | 105 | 109 | 122 | 86 | 111 |
| Brasilia | Brazil | 110 | 111 | 92 | 131 | 110 | 110 | 108 | 112 |
| Monterrey | Mexico | 114 | 120 | 107 | 117 | 106 | 114 | 96 | 113 |
| Ankara | Turkey | 124 | 110 | 118 | 134 | 98 | 119 | 76 | 114 |
| Chengdu | China | 119 | 74 | 126 | 135 | 102 | 102 | 106 | 115 |
| Shenzhen | China | 125 | 129 | 125 | 98 | 107 | 96 | 118 | 116 |
| Bogota | Colombia | 103 | 113 | 97 | 88 | 123 | 126 | 124 | 117 |
| Kiev | Ukraine | 107 | 103 | 100 | 119 | 121 | 108 | 131 | 118 |
| Guangzhou | China | 130 | 115 | 124 | 132 | 104 | 98 | 112 | 119 |
| Panama City | Panama | 116 | 123 | 106 | 122 | 119 | 120 | 115 | 120 |
| Medellin | Colombia | 121 | 133 | 104 | 116 | 120 | 117 | 120 | 121 |
| Bangkok | Thailand | 113 | 130 | 84 | 111 | 128 | 118 | 132 | 122 |
| Cape Town | South Africa | 106 | 105 | 116 | 82 | 138 | 136 | 138 | 123 |
| New Delhi | India | 129 | 133 | 131 | 94 | 122 | 125 | 121 | 124 |
| Quito | Ecuador | 126 | 113 | 134 | 112 | 125 | 124 | 127 | 125 |
| Durban | South Africa | 122 | 135 | 119 | 93 | 132 | 127 | 133 | 126 |
| Johannesburg | South Africa | 117 | 108 | 117 | 124 | 135 | 132 | 135 | 127 |
| Lima | Peru | 127 | 119 | 133 | 109 | 130 | 137 | 116 | 128 |
| Mumbai | India | 131 | 126 | 129 | 118 | 129 | 128 | 129 | 129 |

(continued)

**Table A.11** (continued)

| City | Country | Magnetism | Identity | Dynamism | Strategy | Profitability | Performance | Cost living | Attractiveness |
|------|---------|-----------|----------|----------|----------|---------------|-------------|-------------|----------------|
| Bangalore | India | 132 | 128 | 130 | 128 | 124 | 131 | 117 | **130** |
| Manila | Philippines | 123 | 118 | 103 | 137 | 133 | 130 | 139 | **131** |
| Jakarta | Indonesia | 108 | 125 | 115 | 71 | 140 | 138 | 140 | **132** |
| Riyadh | Saudi Arabia | 140 | 139 | 135 | 138 | 82 | 115 | 27 | **133** |
| Hanoi | Vietnam | 128 | 116 | 122 | 133 | 136 | 133 | 134 | **134** |
| Tunis | Tunisia | 134 | 81 | 137 | 140 | 127 | 129 | 126 | **135** |
| Casablanca | Morocco | 133 | 100 | 139 | 127 | 134 | 139 | 123 | **136** |
| La Paz | Bolivia | 138 | 132 | 138 | 129 | 126 | 135 | 113 | **137** |
| Ho Chi Minh City | Vietnam | 136 | 140 | 120 | 126 | 131 | 116 | 137 | **138** |
| Cairo | Egypt | 135 | 101 | 140 | 130 | 139 | 140 | 122 | **139** |
| Asuncion | Paraguay | 139 | 127 | 136 | 139 | 137 | 133 | 136 | **140** |

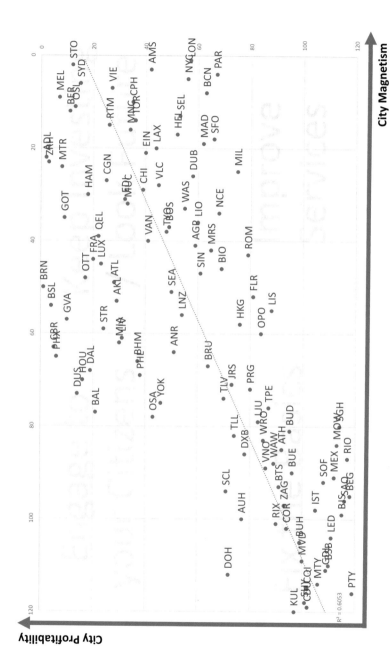

**Fig. A.4** XV.- Attractive Cities. City Magnetism vs City Profitability quadrants

# XVI.- Attractive Cities vs SmartCities by GDP

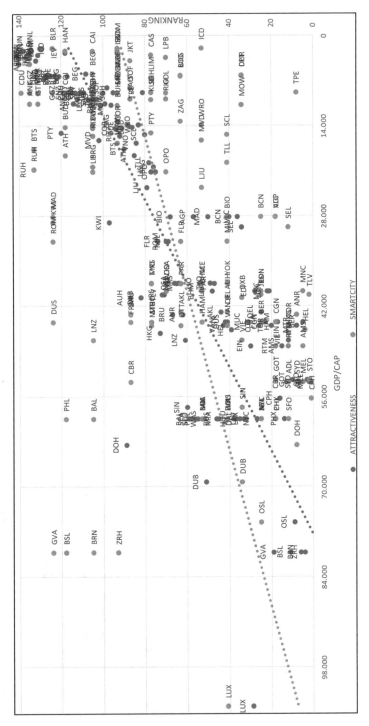

**Fig. A.5** XVI.- Attractive Cities vs SmartCities by GDP

# XVII.- AttractiveCities App Downloading QR Codes & App Screenshots

# Attractive Cities, wanna try?
Get list of top 15 WW Cities better matching your preferences

https://play.google.com/sto
re/apps/details?id=com.barr
abes.attractivecities

https://apps.apple.com/e
s/app/attractive-
cities/id1487782051

**Fig. A.6**   XVII.- AttractiveCities App downloading QR codes & App screenshots

Printed in the United States
by Baker & Taylor Publisher Services